THE SURGE:
A MILITARY HISTORY

The Surge:
A Military History

KIMBERLY KAGAN

ENCOUNTER BOOKS

New York and London

First American edition published in 2009 by Encounter Books, an activity of
Encounter for Culture and Education, Inc., a nonprofit, tax exempt corporation.
Encounter Books website address: www.encounterbooks.com

Book design and composition by Wesley B. Tanner/Passim Editions, Ann Arbor.
Manufactured in the United States and printed on acid-free paper.
∞ The paper used in this publication meets
the minimum requirements of ANSI/NISO Z39.48–1992 (R 1997) (Permanence of Paper).

FIRST AMERICAN EDITION

Library of Congress Cataloging-in-Publication Data

Kagan, Kimberly, 1972–
    The surge : a military history / by Kimberly Kagan. — 1st American ed.
        p. cm.
    Includes bibliographical references and index.
    ISBN-13: 978-1-59403-249-3 (hardcover : alk. paper)
    ISBN-10: 1-59403-249-1 (hardcover : alk. paper) 1. Iraq War, 2003—Campaigns. I. Title.
    DS79.76.K33 2008
    956.7044'342—dc22

                                                            2008032354

■ ■ ■ *Acknowledgments*

I wholeheartedly thank those who have supported my analysis, research, and writing about Iraq. In late January 2007, Joel Armstrong and Dan Dwyer encouraged me to write about the newsworthy events. They and others had helped educate me about counter-insurgency operations, enemy groups, and military planning. I began writing in February. My good friends H. R. McMaster and Joel Rayburn read my first essays and encouraged me to keep writing them.

So, too, did Bill Kristol. Accordingly, I published some of these early essays as Iraq Reports, a joint venture between my nascent Institute for the Study of War and the *Weekly Standard*. The staff of the *Standard* supported the effort, and I could list the entire masthead here. Richard Starr and Michael Goldfarb at the *Standard* patiently read and edited each Iraq Report and posted it online. Catherine Lowe graciously publicized the effort. Philip Chalk drew maps, chose photos, and designed the issues—late at night, and on deadline. Others here in Washington, D.C., expressed their interest and offered their support. I extend special thanks to Jack Keane, Cliff May, and Dany Pletka. Beyond the beltway, Dennis Showalter has been an exemplary mentor, as has Steve Rosen, at Harvard's Olin Institute for Strategic Studies.

I could not have comprehended the ongoing operations or written about them without the talented staff at the Institute for the Study of War. Marisa Cochrane, ISW's Research Coordinator, brilliantly kept a fingertip feel of Baghdad throughout 2007 from publicly available sources. She tirelessly researched Special Groups, Corps offensives, and at times, some of the provinces. She also coordinated ISW's staff and interns, ensuring that we published timely, top-quality analysis while never losing sight of ongoing military or political developments. She edited our work. Readers can find the fruits of ISW's research, including many color maps depicting the campaigns described in this book, as well as analysis of ongoing events, at ISW's website, www.understandingwar.org.

Eric Hamilton and Farook Ahmed, the other members of ISW's research staff, have enriched my ability both to synthesize and analyze events throughout the theater and put them in historical perspective. So, too, have Patrick Gaughen, William Waddell, Nathaniel Rabkin, Wesley Morgan, Ed Stein, Leah Gould, Jonathan Bronitsky, Adrian Myers, Cassiah Rasmussen, and Eric Sayers. I extend my thanks also to James Danly, Bonnie Fautua, and Adriel Domenech, who have helped manage programs at ISW this year. Last, but certainly not least, Andrea So helped ISW from her first days as a Master's Student at Georgetown's Security Studies Program. Andrea invigorated our research with her scholarly insight and her sharp wit.

Thanks also go to many in Iraq. General David Petraeus invited me to visit Iraq in May 2007 and circulate through the battlefield, and he and his staff have welcomed me several times since. Multi-National Force-Iraq supported my research unfailingly through these visits to Iraq and through their public affairs efforts, honoring ISW's frequent requests for interviews and information. Likewise, I thank Lieutenant General Odierno's III Corps/MNC-I staff, who also facilitated my travel and research. H. R. McMaster and Joel Rayburn were magnificent guides and educators during my first battlefield circulation. J. R. Martin and Ylber Bajraktari guided me through a strikingly changed theater in July 2007. Joel Rayburn took me through Iraq again in February 2008, and we stood peacefully with U.S. forces and Iraqi civilians in neighborhoods that were impassable in May 2007.

The talented commanders whom I met during my circulations surprised me not only with their skills, but also with their warm reception. Division and brigade commanders and their staffs briefed me for hours. They and their soldiers drove me through their battlespace. They and their battalion commanders walked me through main streets, side streets, markets, and villages throughout Iraq. Many participated in follow up interviews and answered ISW's persistent queries. It has been a pleasure to host some of them at the Institute for the Study of War in Washington, D.C.

My father and brother, Kal and Eric Kessler, have been great supporters and avid readers of my essays, if a little perplexed by my determination to carry a map of Iraq around with me at all times. Don and Myrna Kagan have been similarly thoughtful readers, while Bob, Toria, Leni, and David have engaged me in long conversations about Iraq with patience and enthusiasm. Fred has been a true comrade in arms throughout this fight.

I began writing as the Baghdad Security Plan began in February 2007. I wished to understand unfolding military operations. Enemy and friendly interactions became exponentially more dynamic and complex as additional U.S. forces arrived. I had written military history, but I had never studied a military operation with so many moving pieces. And I had always known the outcome of events before I began writing. This time, I had no inkling of what the results would be.

Many of my friends, former colleagues, and former students were on the ground in Iraq when I started researching and writing this book. I read their names in news stories or press releases. I corresponded with several throughout the fall of 2006. Some of them had deployed to areas in Baghdad that U.S. and Iraqi forces had cleared in Operations Together Forward. Others were in remote locations north or south of the capital. They were all combat veterans before they arrived. In October 2006, they thought the violence horrible. In November, they thought it worse.

I have dedicated this book to my students. The first class I taught at West Point graduated into a peacetime army on a rainy day in 2001. My last class of former plebes graduated in 2007, having volunteered to serve in an army at war. I have had the privilege of seeing many of them in the field commanding companies, leading platoons, serving on staffs, or advising Iraqi Security Forces. I could be neither prouder nor more humbled. My students and their families have carried the burden of America's wars with grace, dignity, and indescribable courage, worthy of themselves and their country.

■ ■ ■ *Contents*

■ ■ ■ *Introduction*

It is never an easy thing to make sense of war, much less so an ongoing and increasingly complex conflict like the one in Iraq. Too many Americans perceive the war in Iraq as a cauldron of random and utterly senseless violence. With every new piece of bad news, the big picture grows more and more blurry, a collection of distressing but seemingly meaningless statistics. The average American does not connect a spike or drop in violence with particular engagements and operations. He does not see a car-bomb in a crowded marketplace as part of a deliberate plan by a specific enemy group with very particular local goals—and larger objectives—in mind. Even the idea that the Coalition interacts with these enemies on the battlefield, rather than suffering their predations at random while preoccupied with "nonkinetic" (that is, non-combat) reconstruction efforts, seems to have been lost on many.

But it is important to grasp that Coalition Forces are not dealing with a shadowy enemy committing violence for its own sake, nor are they "sitting ducks" at the mercy of the next sniper bullet or IED. In fact they have a very clear understanding of where the violence in Iraq is coming from and what it is meant to achieve. I hasten to emphasize that if the general public is largely ignorant of these particulars—if it believes that violence in Iraq is chaos—some responsibility for their misconceptions lies with the military, the media, and the Bush Administration.

The first problem was the military's excessive focus on the nonkinetic elements of counterinsurgency that characterized its strategy from 2003 to 2006. Although American soldiers and Marines were fighting and being attacked every day, our military leaders spoke as though these fights were distractions, if not diversions, from the main effort of repairing the Iraqi political system, economy, and civil society—the key aim of nation-building and thus of counterinsurgency. The emphasis on these nonkinetic activities was sound. But it left open the question: What was the purpose of American military operations? Whom were we fighting, and why?

The usual answer—that we were preparing the Iraqi Security Forces to take responsibility for their country—did not offer a useful framework for understanding why any particular American unit was fighting any particular group of Iraqi insurgents. It might as well have been a matter of chance, that they happened to be in the same place at the same time. Coalition operations before the middle of 2006 seemed reactive and incoherent, reinforcing the sense of chaotic and random violence suggested by news reports.

As for the flaws in the media's coverage, they stemmed neither from political bias nor from Bush Administration spin. (The Administration and the military rightly decided not to report the numbers of enemy killed, but their other metrics for progress—areas transferred to "Iraqi control," for instance, or the number of Iraqi military units "in the lead"—were no more instructive to the general public about the direction of American or enemy strategy.) The media's shortcomings came first from the fact that understanding and explaining the role of combat in a counterinsurgency is inherently very difficult. Major media outlets generally reported explosions and terror attacks in the passive voice, declining to assign any agent to the violence, let alone any purpose. And since they could not effectively explain the aims of this so-called "random violence," neither could they help the public to see the rhyme and reason in our military response to it.

The second problem is the media's practice of extrapolating from an individual story to capture larger trends and developments. This *Saving Private Ryan* approach to reporting is ill-suited to the complexities of the present conflict, which the U.S. Army's counterinsurgency manual calls a "mosaic war."[1] The brave journalists and photographers who have accompanied small units into action, who have interviewed soldiers, Marines, civilians, and even insurgents, certainly have produced some magnificent and indelible impressions of the war. They have told the American public of the trials, sacrifices, and inner struggles of American soldiers and Iraqis. But these reports can only go so far. The platoon fight in Fallujah in 2004 is not representative of the struggle in Najaf that same year. The Sunni interviewed about Shiite death squads in one Baghdad neighborhood tell us nothing about the feelings of their co-sectarians in Baqubah or Ramadi, let alone of the Shia in the next neighborhood over or the Kurds to the north.

In other words, there is no shortage of compelling individual stories, but the glut of such stories often obfuscates more than it clarifies. Even if reporters and camera crews flooded Iraq and their reports flooded our televisions and newspapers—and even if many Americans spent their days devouring such coverage—it would not be possible to make sense of events simply by piecing together all of the individual stories.[2] The snippets and anecdotes read and watched by most Americans, however emotionally powerful those stories may be, are far more likely to obscure the overarching picture of events than to illuminate it.

So what ought to be reported? A good example of a genuinely illuminating story is the discovery made by American soldiers on December 19, 2006. It was minor enough: a map of Baghdad captured while patrolling just north of the capital. It was a rough, hand-drawn sketch of the capital, and the handwriting was little better than a scribble. Its meaning, however, was perfectly clear: al Qaeda in the Land of the Two Rivers, the Iraqi franchise of the global al Qaeda movement, had divided Baghdad and environs into sectors, each with its own commander, as part of its terrorist campaign.

The discovery of this map crystallized the dawning understanding by American military commanders that security in Baghdad required clearing the safe havens and holding the transit routes used by al Qaeda in Iraq (AQI) to sustain its operations within the city. That realization, in turn, led to the development of a series of sophisticated military operations in Baghdad and throughout central Iraq that led within fifteen months to the disruption of AQI and the restoration of a degree of peace and normalcy unknown in that area since 2004. Those operations, along with political, economic, and diplomatic efforts, transformed the war in Iraq and created a possibility for the American effort to succeed.

The AQI map—and revelations from captured al Qaeda and Shia militia leaders over the course of 2007—shows clearly that the enemy groups knew what they were doing. They did not kill at random, on the whole—much killing was in fact carefully targeted. They did not aim simply to create chaos or generate headlines. The enemy groups on both sides saw the conflict with American and Iraqi forces as a war in which organization, training, equipment, holding terrain, denying terrain to the enemy (us or each other), leadership, doctrine, tactics, and strategy were all very important.

The reality presented by this map should have been explained to the American public at every possible opportunity. In the past, that public had capably followed the movement of its armies on maps of Europe, Korea, and, in 1991, the Persian Gulf. That the current conflict has been presented largely through disjointed horror stories is a very real problem, the result of which is that citizens with only the vaguest conception of ongoing operations feel qualified to pronounce their own country's defeat.

Understanding war requires, above all else, understanding what the leadership on each side is trying to do. Violence, even terrorist violence, is rarely "pointless." Soldiers, insurgents, and terrorists use violence in pursuit of political aims. The al Qaeda map, the Jaysh al Mahdi's response to Moqtada al Sadr's "cease-fire" orders, and the establishment and elaboration of the Iranian-backed Special Groups are all indications of the planning and organization that went into creating enemy violence in Iraq. The Coalition operations of 2007 and 2008 are proof that a well-designed military campaign executed with a comprehensive political and economic effort can defeat enemy groups and bring violence under control.

This work aims to provide a point of departure for the development of the American military's thinking about insurgency and unconventional war in general. What is the role of kinetic operations in unconventional war? Speaking more technically, what is the operational level of war in an insurgency?[3] Numerous discussions with friends and colleagues at West Point and throughout the Army today, as well as the perusal of current doctrine and much military writing, have persuaded me that there is no consensus about these important questions, no serious current theory about how to plan and conduct combat operations at higher levels of command in support of counterinsurgency efforts.

These are gaps in our thinking that will continue to hinder the planning and conduct of future unconventional conflicts. I believe that I can see in the shape of the successive Corps offensives planned and conducted from January 2007 through spring 2008 the outlines of an operational level of counterinsurgency—and the foundations on which one could construct at least part of a theory and doctrine for the use of combat operations in this type of war. Others may disagree. A narrative of the operations in 2007 is the prerequisite for the discussions of counterinsurgency doctrine, its implementation, and the implications for future conflicts of the campaign for Iraq in 2007.

The intention of this book is to provide such a narrative in terms clear and simple enough for any civilian to make sense of. It is essential for not only the military but also the American people to think seriously about the role of combat in the Iraq war. In a democracy, war cannot be a technical problem beyond the comprehension of the ordinary citizen, nor can it be reduced to heartbreaking photographs or gripping vignettes that manipulate the emotions without informing the intellect. Americans have always been able to understand even complex wars when presented with the information, analysis, and context they need. This volume is an effort to provide such a framework for understanding not only where we have been and how we got to where we are now, but also what happens as we move forward.

For my students

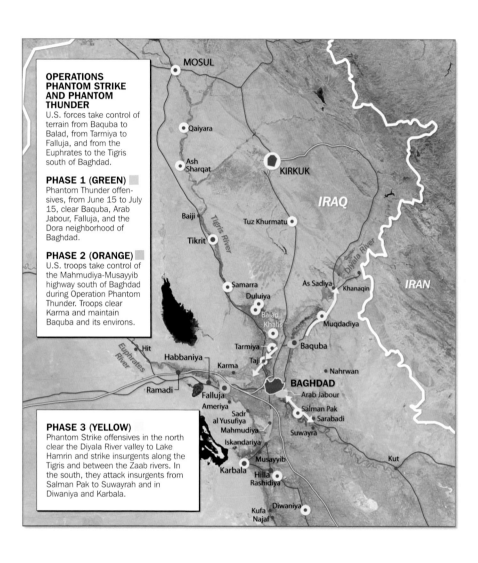

OPERATIONS PHANTOM STRIKE AND PHANTOM THUNDER
U.S. forces take control of terrain from Baquba to Balad, from Tarmiya to Falluja, and from the Euphrates to the Tigris south of Baghdad.

PHASE 1 (GREEN)
Phantom Thunder offensives, from June 15 to July 15, clear Baquba, Arab Jabour, Falluja, and the Dora neighborhood of Baghdad.

PHASE 2 (ORANGE)
U.S. troops take control of the Mahmudiya-Musayyib highway south of Baghdad during Operation Phantom Thunder. Troops clear Karma and maintain Baquba and its environs.

PHASE 3 (YELLOW)
Phantom Strike offensives in the north clear the Diyala River valley to Lake Hamrin and strike insurgents along the Tigris and between the Zaab rivers. In the south, they attack insurgents from Salman Pak to Suwayrah and in Diwaniya and Karbala.

MOSUL
Qaiyara
Ash Sharqat
KIRKUK
IRAQ
Baiji
Tuz Khurmatu
Tikrit
Tigris River
Diyala River
IRAN
Samarra
Duluiya
As Sadiya
Khanaqin
Balad
Khalis
Muqdadiya
Hit
Euphrates River
Tarmiya
Baquba
Habbaniya
Karma
Taji
Nahrwan
Ramadi
BAGHDAD
Falluja
Arab Jabour
Ameriya
Salman Pak
Sadr al Yusufiya
Sarabadi
Mahmudiya
Suwayra
Iskandariya
Musayyib
Kut
Karbala
Hilla
Rashidiya
Diwaniya
Kufa
Najaf

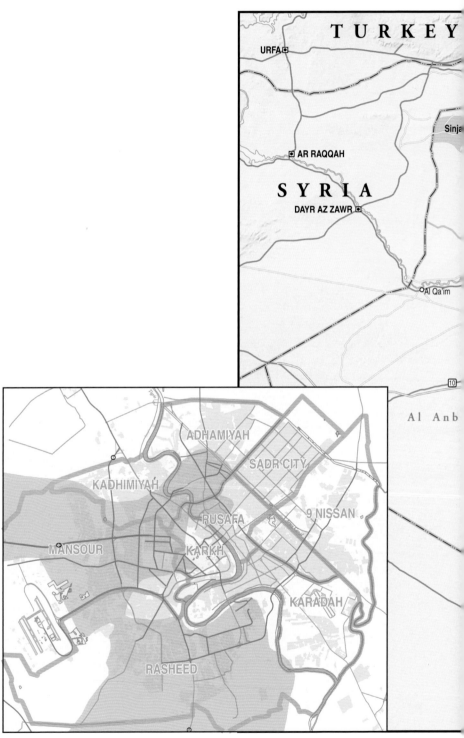

Al Qaeda in Iraq, December 2006

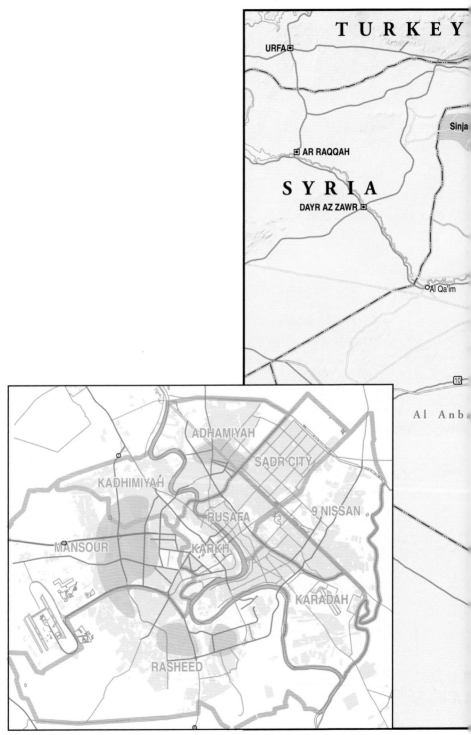

Al Qaeda in Iraq, December 2007

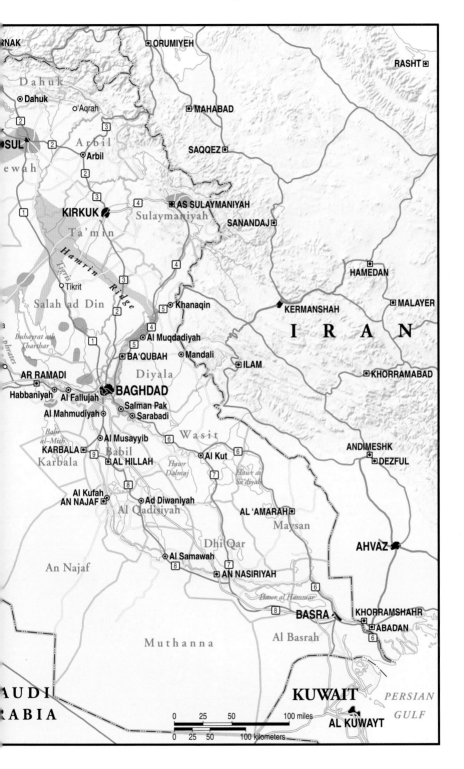

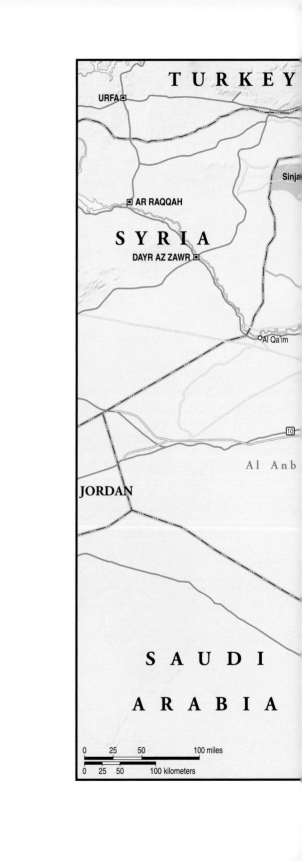

NAK

ORUMIYEH

RASHT

Dahuk

Dahuk

o'Aqrah

MAHABAD

Arbil

SUL

Arbil

SAQQEZ

Ta'min

KIRKUK

AS SULAYMANIYAH

Sulaymaniyah

SANANDAJ

ewah

HAMEDAN

Hamrin Ridge

Tigris

Tikrit

Salah ad Din

MALAYER

KERMANSHAH

I R A N

Khanaqin

Buhayrat ath Tharthar

Al Muqdadiyah

KHORRAMABAD

BA'QUBAH

Mandali

AR RAMADI

Diyala

ILAM

Habbaniyah

Al Fallujah

BAGHDAD

Al Mahmudiyah

Salman Pak

Sarabadi

Bahr al-Milh

Al Musayyib

W a s i t

KARBALA

Babil

AL HILLAH

Karbala

Hawr Dalmaj

Al Kut

ANDIMESHK

DEZFUL

Hawr as Sa'diyah

Al Kufah

AN NAJAF

Al Qadisiyah

Ad Diwaniyah

AL 'AMARAH

An Najaf

Dhi Qar

Maysan

Al Samawah

AN NASIRIYAH

AHVAZ

Hawr al Hammar

BASRA

KHORRAMSHAHR

ABADAN

Muthanna

Al Basrah

KUWAIT

AL KUWAYT

PERSIAN GULF

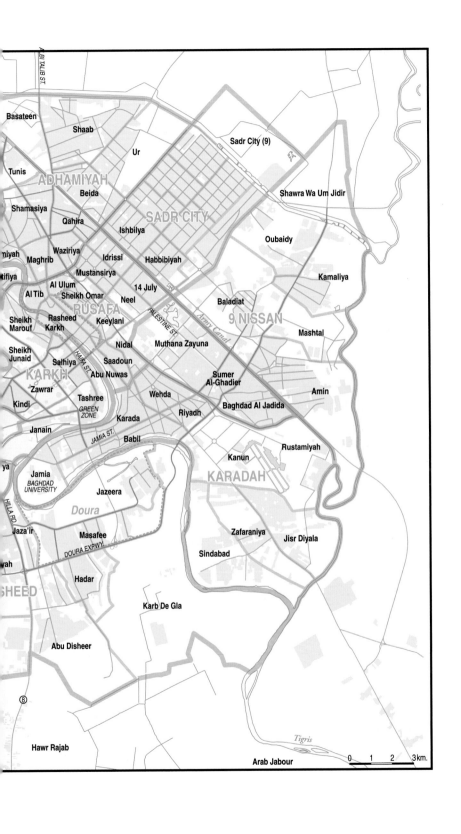

Basateen

Shaab

Ur

Sadr City (9)

ADHAMIYAH

Tunis

Beida

Shawra Wa Um Jidir

Shamasiya

Qahira

Ishbilya

SADR CITY

Oubaidy

miyah Waziriya

Maghrib Idrissi Habbibiyah

Kamaliya

tifiya

Mustansirya

Al Ulum 14 July

Al Tib Sheikh Omar Neel Baladiat

9 NISSAN

RUSAFA

Sheikh Rasheed Keeylani Mashtal
Marouf Karkh

PALESTINE ST.

Army Canal

Sheikh Nidal Muthana Zayuna
Junaid Salhiya Saadoun

KARKH Abu Nuwas Sumer Amin
Al-Ghadier

Zawrar Wehda

Kindi Tashree Baghdad Al Jadida
GREEN Karada Riyadh
ZONE

Janain Babil

JAMIA ST.

Rustamiyah

Jamia Kanun
BAGHDAD
UNIVERSITY KARADAH

Jazeera

HILLA RD.

Doura

Jaza'ir Masafee Zafaraniya Jisr Diyala

DOURA EXPWY. Sindabad

wah

Hadar

HEED

Karb De Gla

Abu Disheer

⑧

Tigris

Hawr Rajab

Arab Jabour

0   1   2   3km.

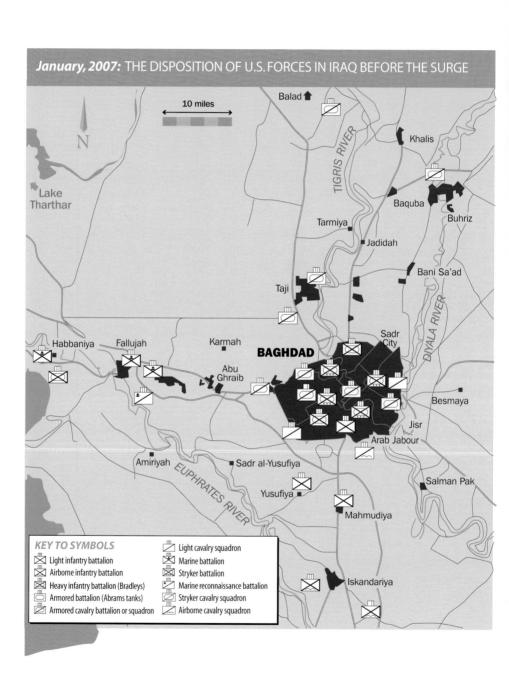

January, 2007: THE DISPOSITION OF U.S. FORCES IN IRAQ BEFORE THE SURGE

N

10 miles

Balad

Khalis

TIGRIS RIVER

Baquba

Buhriz

Lake
Tharthar

Tarmiya

Jadidah

Bani Sa'ad

DIYALA RIVER

Taji

Sadr
City

Habbaniya

Fallujah

Karmah

BAGHDAD

Abu
Ghraib

Besmaya

Jisr

Arab Jabour

Amiriyah

Sadr al-Yusufiya

Salman Pak

EUPHRATES RIVER

Yusufiya

Mahmudiya

Iskandariya

KEY TO SYMBOLS

- Light infantry battalion
- Airborne infantry battalion
- Heavy infantry battalion (Bradleys)
- Armored battalion (Abrams tanks)
- Armored cavalry battalion or squadron

- Light cavalry squadron
- Marine battalion
- Stryker battalion
- Marine reconnaissance battalion
- Stryker cavalry squadron
- Airborne cavalry squadron

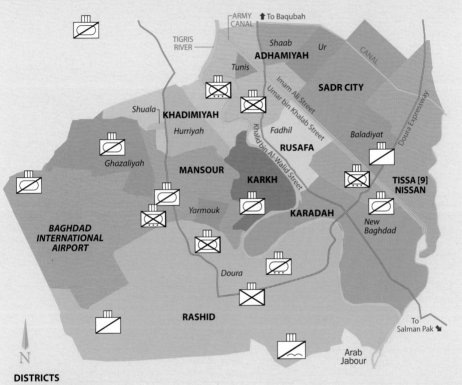

January, 2007: U.S. FORCES IN BAGHDAD BEFORE THE SURGE.

To Baqubah
ARMY CANAL
TIGRIS RIVER
CANAL
Shaab
Ur
ADHAMIYAH
Tunis
SADR CITY
Imam Ali Street
Umar bin Khalab Street
Shuala
KHADIMIYAH
Hurriyah
Fadhil
Khalid bin Al-Walid Street
Baladiyat
Doura Expressway
RUSAFA
Ghazaliyah
MANSOUR
KARKH
TISSA [9] NISSAN
Yarmouk
New Baghdad
BAGHDAD INTERNATIONAL AIRPORT
KARADAH
Doura
To Salman Pak
RASHID
Arab Jabour
N

DISTRICTS
Important Neighborhoods
Major Roads
WATERWAYS

KEY TO SYMBOLS

 Armored cavalry battalion or squadron
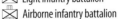 Light cavalry squadron

☒ Light infantry battalion
☒ Airborne infantry battalion
☒ Heavy infantry battalion (Bradleys)
▭ Armored battalion (Abrams tanks)

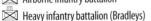 Stryker battalion
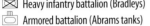 Stryker cavalry squadron
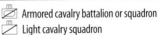 Airborne cavalry squadron

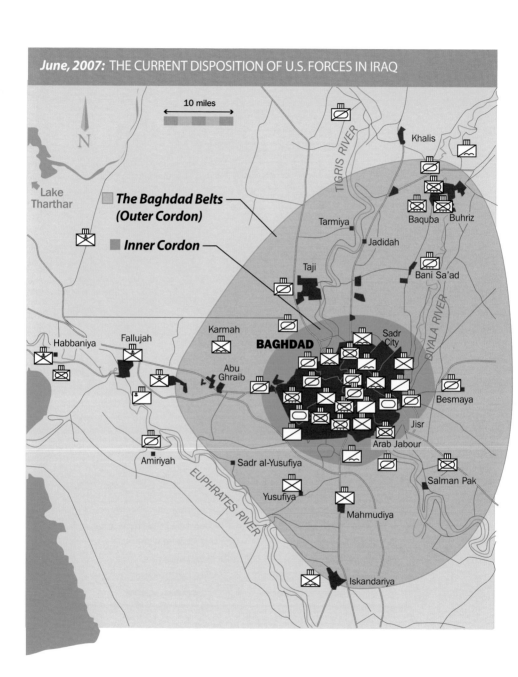

June, 2007: THE CURRENT DISPOSITION OF U.S. FORCES IN IRAQ

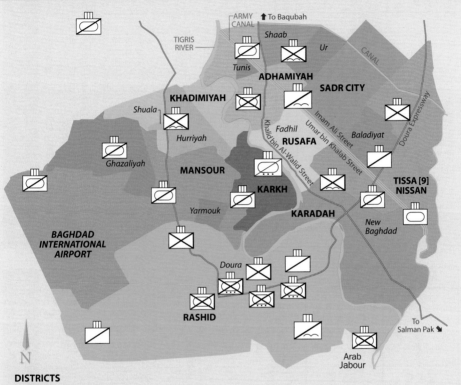

June, 2007: CURRENT U.S. FORCES IN BAGHDAD

To Baqubah

ARMY CANAL

TIGRIS RIVER

Shaab

Ur

CANAL

Tunis

ADHAMIYAH

SADR CITY

KHADIMIYAH

Shuala

Imam Ali Street

Doura Expressway

Hurriyah

Fadhil

Umar bin Khalab Street

Baladiyat

Khalid bin Al-Walid Street

RUSAFA

Ghazaliyah

MANSOUR

KARKH

TISSA [9] NISSAN

Yarmouk

KARADAH

New Baghdad

BAGHDAD INTERNATIONAL AIRPORT

Doura

To Salman Pak

RASHID

Arab Jabour

N

DISTRICTS
Important Neighborhoods
Major Roads
WATERWAYS

KEY TO SYMBOLS

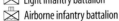 Light infantry battalion

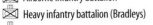 Airborne infantry battalion

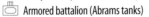 Heavy infantry battalion (Bradleys)

Armored battalion (Abrams tanks)

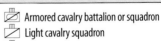 Armored cavalry battalion or squadron

 Light cavalry squadron

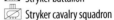 Stryker battalion

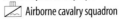 Stryker cavalry squadron

Airborne cavalry squadron

Operation Phantom Strike: August 13–Present

	Khalis Corridor	Baqubah	Diyala River Valley	Kana'an and east
Operation Lightning Hammer launched August 13				
August	Enemy groups compete for control in Khalis Hebheb corridor.	Security operations continued to destroy AQI support zones near Baqubah.	U.S. and Iraqi forces pushed northeast along the Diyala River during Operation Greywolf Hammer I.	Clearing operations against AQI conducted in the Wajihiyah-Kana'an corridor.
		U.S. and Iraqi forces work to reestablish essential services in Baqubah.	Reconciliation meeting with more than 100 tribal leaders on August 19 in the Wajihiyah-Kana'an corridor.	
Operation Lightning Hammer II launched September 5				
September	U.S. and Iraqi forces target Special Groups.	U.S. and Iraqi forces continue work to reestablish essential services in Baqubah.	Muqdadiyah and Lake Hamrin areas cleared during Operation Greywolf Hammer II.	U.S. and Iraqi forces targeted Special Groups and other Shia extremists; they also targeted AQI elements south of Balad Ruz in the Turki Area
October	Reconciliation meeting with local, elected officials and tribal sheiks held in Khalis on October 24.		Reconciliation meeting with Diyala Government and tribal sheiks in Muqdadiyah area on October 24.	

Operation Phantom Thunder: June 15–August 12

	Khalis Corridor	Baqubah	Diyala River Valley	Kana'an and east
May		U.S. Forces began shaping operations and established presence in eastern Baqubah, known as Old Baqubah.		
Operation Arrowhead Ripper launched on June 19.				
June	Supporting operations conducted in Khalis during Arrowhead Ripper; AQI attempts to disrupt Coalition progress.	Western Baqubah cleared during Operation Arrowhead Ripper.	Operation Ithaca and Olympus drive AQI from Haimer, Abu Nasim, Jamil and Anbakia	Supporting operations conducted during Arrowhead Ripper in Khan Bani Sa'ad to dislodge enemy groups.
July	Khalis tribal reconciliation meeting on June 23.	Second phase of Arrowhead Ripper began on July 17 with clearing of Old Baqubah.		
August	despite sectarian violence in Khalis.	Reconciliation agreement signed by 18 paramount sheiks on August 2 in Baqubah.		

THE SURGE:
A MILITARY HISTORY

Chapter 1
■ ■ ■ The Battle for Baghdad in 2006

The widespread violence that characterized Baghdad in late 2006 was generated by a battle between organized extremist groups deliberately fighting to control terrain in the city. Al Qaeda and Shia extremists used sectarian cleansing as a way to gain physical control over neighborhoods, to intimidate the population into compliance, and to obtain their desired political outcomes. Ordinary Baghdad residents mobilized into vigilante groups to defend their neighborhoods as the violence escalated. By December, the population of Baghdad had mobilized to fight the sectarian conflict. Enemy groups contested neighborhoods of Baghdad, creating a mosaic of conflicts. Iraq was on the brink of a civil war.

The counterinsurgency strategy of 2007, made possible by the troop increase, leadership changes, and new mission, reduced violence within Baghdad dramatically. Explaining the military operations that made success possible requires understanding the conflict in late 2006, when sectarian violence peaked. This, in turn, requires a quick review of the goals, methods, and evolution of the enemy groups that perpetrated most of this violence.

Violence in Baghdad in 2006 did not emerge from the antipathy between Sunni and Shia neighbors, or from a cataclysmic terrorist act, but rather from an armed political competition between extremist groups. Al Qaeda's bombing of the al Askariyah mosque in Samarra is conventionally, but incorrectly, seen as the moment when Iraq's retributive sectarian violence began. In fact, sectarian cleansing and retributive violence predated the Samarra mosque bombing.

Enemy groups resisted the establishment of a new government in 2004 and 2005, the year of Iraq's elections.[4] Al Qaeda in Iraq established its fearsome reputation and presence in the Sunni community with televised kidnappings, beheadings, hangings, and other executions. The U.S. Marines besieged and cleared Fallujah in November 2004 to expel al Qaeda from this city before the first elections in January 2005. Al Qaeda in Iraq leaders, under the command of Abu Musab al Zarqawi, consequently fled their main urban stronghold in eastern Anbar, though many remained in that province and ultimately returned to the city; others migrated elsewhere in Iraq. U.S. forces in 2004 likewise fought Moqtada al Sadr and his militia, the Jaysh al Mahdi (JAM), in Sadr City in 2004. They pursued and defeated the Jaysh al Mahdi in the Shia holy city of Najaf. JAM could not match U.S. forces in direct combat, and the remnants of this militia negotiated their safe passage from the Imam Ali Shrine in Najaf, along with Moqtada al Sadr himself.[5]

Both al Qaeda and the Jaysh al Mahdi groups failed to achieve their aims in 2004. The first Iraqi elections occurred in January 2005, within months of the U.S. military victories in Fallujah and Najaf. At the beginning of 2005, therefore, the Jaysh al Mahdi and al Qaeda had to reconstitute themselves—both in new physical terrain and in new political circumstances. They were adaptive enemies.

Shia Extremist Organizations in 2005 and 2006

Hezbollah and the Iranian Revolutionary Guards Corps-Qods Force rebuilt the Jaysh al Mahdi after the battle of Najaf. They trained some of its members in Iran in 2005 and then returned them to Iraq; these became known as Special Groups or Secret Cells. It is not clear whether those who trained in Iran after the defeat at Najaf left Iraq at the behest of Moqtada al Sadr, or whether his former colleague Qais Khazali was organizing this retraining initiative. The two were old acquaintances, but hostile at this time. Moqtada al Sadr ostensibly expelled Qais Khazali from the Jaysh al Mahdi after the latter gave an "unauthorized order" during the battle of Najaf. These Special Groups developed their own organizational hierarchy in Iran and gained new military capabilities (such as the training to use explosively-formed penetrators). Members of Special Groups returned to Iraq to fight Coalition Forces, Iraqi Security Forces, and the nascent government. By May 2006, Qais Khazali was the head of Special Groups in Iraq and answered to authorities in Iran.[6] Moqtada al Sadr established a political party that was highly successful in the parliamentary elections, but he lost—or was deprived of—control over those members of his militia who trained in Iran.

Al Qaeda and the Sunni Insurgency in 2005 and 2006

As al Qaeda dispersed from Fallujah, its activity rose elsewhere in Iraq—not just in Anbar, but also in Ninewah, Baghdad, and the Euphrates River Valley to its southwest. Al Qaeda in Iraq was not new to Baghdad in 2005. Zarqawi had assigned the mission of establishing AQI in Baghdad to Abu Ayyub al Masri, who had trained with Zarqawi in Afghanistan and moved to Iraq as a founding member of AQI. Abu Ayyub al Masri had established the original AQI cell in Baghdad in 2003. He closely assisted Zarqawi's subordinates in Fallujah in 2004. Al Masri had great expertise in explosives, and particularly vehicle-borne improvised explosive devices (VBIEDs), which became AQI's signature weapon. He distributed VBIEDs and suicide bombers throughout Iraq.[7]

In some respects, the story of al Qaeda in Iraq in 2005 is the story of its dispersion from Fallujah and its reestablishment elsewhere in Iraq, under the same leadership, with greater ties to the former Baathist elements. In addition to designing AQI's hallmark VBIED campaign, Abu Ayyub al Masri helped merge other terrorist and insurgent groups into the Zarqawi network.[8] Baghdad became the focus of their operations.

Al Qaeda and other Sunni groups attempted to derail the elections by deterring the population from voting and by attacking the U.S. forces that would make such elections possible. Just as the VBIED was AQI's primary weapon, the improvised explosive device (IED) was the signature weapon of Sunni insurgents, who deployed them along roadways to prevent Coalition forces from transversing them. Sunni insurgents fought hard prior to the elections. Accordingly, the number of daily improvised explosive device (IED) attacks spiked to the high levels seen in Ramadan in 2004 levels just prior to the voting in January, May, and October 2005. The Sunni insurgents used other techniques to intimidate potential voters. "Shortly before the elections in January 2005, Sunni groups, perhaps al Qaeda, distributed flyers in Saydiyah, as well as in the Sunni areas of Jihad and Ameriyah, warning residents to stay away from polling centers and security forces in the neighborhood. While there were no attacks in Saydiyah itself, these information operations were accompanied by attacks on polling places elsewhere in the city, including the use of a mentally-retarded man as a suicide bomber at a polling center in the west Baghdad neighborhood of Iskan."[9] AQI and the Sunni insurgents persuaded most of the Sunni community to abstain from the elections in order to delegitimize the electoral process and, thereby, the government it produced. The history of the Sunni insurgency and al Qaeda in Iraq falls beyond the scope of this essay, but it is not possible to understand the patterns of violence in 2006 without providing this essential background.

Shia Militias and Death Squads

The transitional Iraqi government and its security forces in 2005 developed in the context of AQI's violent opposition to elections, especially in western Baghdad neighborhoods such as Saydiyah, Jihad, Ameriyah, and Iskan, where AQI had begun to establish strongholds. In response to AQI's pre- and post-election violence, Shia death squads began deliberate sectarian cleansing campaigns in the capital. Shia death squads operated in the West Rashid district of Baghdad, which includes Saydiyah and Jihad, as early as March 2005.[10] Interior Ministry forces deliberately executed Sunni residents of Iskan, in west-central Baghdad, in July and August 2005.[11]

The death squads emerged shortly after Bayan Jabr became the transitional government's Interior Minister—a position which made him responsible for commanding police forces—in February 2005. Bayan Jabr was a partisan of the Supreme Council of the Islamic Revolution in Iraq (SCIRI), which had developed in Iran long prior to the invasion. That organization had a militia, the Badr Corps, more developed than the Jaysh al Mahdi. In spring 2005, the Iraqi Security Forces incorporated Badr Corps into its ranks, giving militia elements the opportunity to become part of the legitimate security forces of the state at best, and at worst to operate under official cover inside the capital. The interim Iraqi government also launched a campaign to secure Baghdad that spring.

Badr's Wolf Brigade, which became the Second Brigade of the First Iraqi National Police Division, was one of the earliest, most persistent, and most effective engines of executions of Sunni in Baghdad. The Wolf Brigade conducted targeted raids against Sunni in west Baghdad throughout the second half of 2005.[12] It was sufficiently complicit in cleansing that it was banned from entering the southeastern Baghdad neighborhood of Dora without U.S. escorts by the end of April 2006. By May 2006, the Wolf Brigade had arrested more than 1400 Iraqis, crammed them into a single facility, and beaten or tortured many of them. The unit continued to perpetrate death squad activities in Saydiyah in summer 2007.[13]

The Sunni population of Baghdad was terrorized by the death squad activities of the official Iraqi Security Forces throughout 2005. Sunni complained of indiscriminate arrests and shot back at patrols. Iraqi police had imprisoned and abused Sunni males in an underground facility, discovered in November of 2005.[14] Al Qaeda and insurgent groups responded in kind with vehicle bomb and other attacks. They also developed their own death squads. In summer of 2005, Sunni death squads conducted kidnappings and executions in the Saydiyah neighborhood, in southwest Baghdad, targeting Shia members of the transitional government with residences in this neighborhood.[15]

The Samarra Mosque Bombing

The sectarian violence, reprisals, and death squad activities, therefore, preceded the Samarra mosque bombing in February 2006. Lieutenant General Pete Chiarelli, the Corps commander in Iraq in 2006, described the differences that he perceived between the pre- and post- Samarra violence: "[W]e viewed sectarian violence with totally different lenses prior to the bombing in Samarra in February of last year than we do today. And the definition of that is very, very difficult . . . . AQI has been conducting large-signature attacks throughout Iraq prior to the bombing in Samarra and after the bombing in Samarra. They are in fact spectacular attacks designed to kill a large number of people. And in the post-Samarra bombing period, they have stated point-blank that they conduct those attacks to incite sectarian violence. When a VBI[E]D, or vehicle-borne improvised [explosive] device, goes off in the center of Sadr City or anywhere where there's a large Shia population, what we have seen in the post-Samarra period is a reaction—a reaction from death squads, death squads who may move to Sunni neighborhoods, [and] Sunnis who move—[if] the attack takes place in a Sunni neighborhood to Shi'a neighborhoods. And what we see in this instance is executions, executions of individuals, individuals that are picked off the street, sometimes from lists, taken to a location and tortured, some not even taken to a location and tortured and just executed. To me, that is the difference that I've seen in that period from post-February and the thing that we've got to get a handle on and we're working so hard to get a handle on, to not allow AQI to use these spectacular attacks to create the conditions with—which allow a spiral of sectarian violence throughout Iraq."[16]

Yet the bombing of the Samarra mosque did not immediately bring Sunni and Shia residents, or Shia militias and al Qaeda, into direct conflict throughout Baghdad. Civilian casualties from all sources—murders, executions, mortar attacks, IEDs—rose only 3 percent from March to April 2006.[17] The exponential increase in violence occurred later in the year. The number of civilian casualties was 39 percent higher in May 2006 than in March and 73 percent higher in July 2006 than in March.[18]

The dramatic rise in violence coincided with the formation of the Maliki government, which also occurred in May 2006. Special Groups, reorganized in spring 2006, launched a campaign of assassinations and kidnappings aimed at government officials, generating chaos as the government formed.[19] Al Qaeda in Iraq and other Sunni insurgent groups conducted a campaign to increase attacks and control territory around Baghdad in an effort to undermine the Maliki government.[20] In late June, as Sunni and Shia extremists engaged one another in gunfights in the capital, the Maliki government declared a state of emergency in Baghdad.[21]

The leadership changes in al Qaeda in Iraq also accelerated this violence. U.S. Forces killed Zarqawi in June 2006. His death provided opportunities to kill and capture mid-level leaders of the terrorist organization in Baqubah, Baghdad, and the Euphrates River Valley. Zarqawi's death, however, also produced competition among potential successors to prove their effectiveness in the organization. Zarqawi's colleague, the vehicle bomb mastermind Abu Ayyub al Masri, earned this recognition partly through the series of car bombings he organized in June 2006. Osama bin Laden released a tape on July 1 of that year recognizing al Masri, also known as Sheikh Abu Hamza al Muhajer, as the new leader of al Qaeda in Iraq. In the tape, he also encouraged al Masri to transform Iraq into the center of a larger Islamic caliphate.[22] As if to signal the advent of new leadership, al Qaeda in Iraq detonated a car bomb in a Sadr City market on July 2, killing sixty-two and wounding 120, the deadliest of its attacks since the seating of the Iraqi government in May.[23] A spate of car bombs followed over the next week.[24]

The spiraling retributive violence emerged at this time. On July 9, in the late morning, Shia death squads affiliated with the Jaysh al Mahdi attacked the predominantly Sunni neighborhood of Jihad, on the west side of Baghdad. They pulled Sunni from their homes, executing some immediately by shooting them in the head, torturing others with drills, hanging still others, opening fire on groups of people whom they had rounded up, and dumping bodies onto streets.[25] The massacre killed between thirty and forty people.[26] Hours later, a car bomb exploded near a Shia mosque in Khadra, a neighborhood to the north of Jihad, apparently in retribution. Jaysh al Mahdi members on the east side of Baghdad established checkpoints to guard their neighborhoods against attack.[27] U.S. forces imposed a curfew in Baghdad on the night of July 9, for the purpose of containing the violence.[28]

There are several reasons why Shia extremists might have perpetrated the Jihad massacre. The cleansing of Jihad might have been a response to al Qaeda's increasingly lethal explosions against Shia civilians, such as the July 2 Sadr City bombing. The cleansing might also have been a consequence of a conflict between U.S.-backed Iraqi Security Forces and a Secret Cell of the Jaysh al Mahdi. The day before the Jihad cleansing, U.S. and Iraqi forces raided a cell's stronghold in Sadr City, eliminated thirty or forty members, and captured the leader.[29] The massacre might also have been the byproduct of a week's worth of smaller-scale but escalating reprisal attacks in Jihad and Furat, the neighborhood just to its west: a militia group kidnapped and executed approximately fifteen people; an insurgent group attacked a mosque and destroyed a National Police vehicle responding to the violence; insurgents coordinated an attack against an Iraqi Security Forces checkpoint; a vehicle bomb exploded at a Sunni mosque perhaps as a reprisal for the previous events; a vehicle bomb exploded at a Shia mosque, also perhaps as a reprisal.[30] The death squad marauding occurred just after this series of attacks.

Regardless of the proximate cause, the attack on Jihad produced violent and dramatic reprisals in the neighborhoods of Baghdad where al Qaeda and Sunni extremists had established strongholds earlier in the year. Days later, for example, gunmen attacked a busload of Shia mourners in Dora, in the southern portion of Baghdad; another group beheaded a family from that same neighborhood.[31] Iraqi Security Forces locked down Sunni neighborhoods on the west side of the river, particularly Jihad, Ghazaliyah, Ameriyah, and Dora, where they fanned out into

checkpoints. Militia groups flooded these areas and established illegiti-
mate checkpoints, targeting Sunnis for execution.

Within ten days, Sunni residents of these western Baghdad neighborhoods had organized vigilante groups to defend against attacks. Many
residents left their homes for Jordan or Syria; airlines had increased their
flights from Baghdad International Airport to these destinations. Other
residents left their homes stealthily, heading for refugee camps in the
capital.[32]

Most of the murders in June and July were concentrated in a few
neighborhoods of Baghdad: Dora, Aamel, Ameriyah, and Shula on the
west side; Adhamiyah, Shaab and Ur, and Sadr City on the east side.[33]
By late July 2006, Dora's inhabitants could not recover corpses of victims executed in the neighborhood for burial; the risk of sniper fire was
too high to walk the streets.[34] Nevertheless, organized groups of Jaysh al
Mahdi and Sunni extremists engaged in reciprocal revenge killings in
other locations in the country.[35]

Failing to Secure Baghdad in 2006:
Operation Together Forward I and II

On July 13, 2006, the new government, caught in Baghdad's rising violence, announced a joint Iraqi and Coalition plan to secure the capital.
Operation Together Forward I (OTF I), as it was called, sought to restore
security in Baghdad by enforcing a curfew, banning the use of weapons by those outside of the Iraqi Security Forces, placing Iraqi Security
Forces in checkpoints throughout the city to search vehicles, patrolling hotspots in Baghdad, and improving basic services.[36] The combined
Coalition and Iraqi Army foot patrols focused on neighborhoods which
had been particularly violent in June, such as Saydiyah, Bayaa, Ghazaliyah,
and Adhamiyah.[37] Security forces were, however, distributed throughout
the capital.[38]

OTF I was an Iraqi-led operation. According to Prime Minister Maliki,
the Iraqi National Police, under the direction of the Ministry of Interior,

were charged with leading the security initiative; Iraqi Army and Coalition Forces functioned in support roles. In all, forty-eight battalions were committed to OTF: thirteen Iraqi Army battalions, twenty-five Iraqi National Police battalions, and ten Coalition battalions. Altogether, nearly 50,000 Iraqi and Coalition troops were involved in the operation—21,000 Iraqi Police, 13,000 Iraqi National Police, 8,500 Iraqi Army soldiers, and roughly 7,200 Coalition Forces.[39]

By August 6, 2006, when OTF I concluded, 411 individuals associated with death squads had been either killed or captured; 32,382 combat patrols had been conducted; and over forty-three weapons caches had been seized.[40] Most of the operations were reactive, responding to crises as they arose throughout the city.[41]

In late July, as sectarian violence increased, President Bush and Prime Minister Maliki met in Washington, D.C., and discussed a new security plan for Baghdad.[42] General John Abizaid, commander of U.S. Central Command, announced that he would send more U.S. troops to the capital.[43] He committed the remainder of the theater reserve in Kuwait, and battalions from other sectors in Iraq moved to Baghdad.[44] In addition, Secretary of Defense Donald Rumsfeld and General George Casey extended the tours of about 4,000 soldiers beyond the one-year mark, so that commanders could use the 172nd Stryker Brigade in the Baghdad fight. That brigade had been based in Mosul prior to July.[45] Its intended replacement, the 3rd Brigade of the 2nd Infantry Division, maintained security in Mosul while the 172nd carried out the new Baghdad operation.[46] The total number of American troops in Iraq rose above 130,000.[47]

Operation Together Forward II (OTF II), which began on August 7, 2006, was the second phase of the Iraqi-led operation aimed at increasing security and reducing sectarian violence in Baghdad.[48] Like OTF I, OTF II involved the Iraqi National Police, the Iraqi Army, and the Iraqi Police. U.S. soldiers from Multi-National Division-Baghdad (MND-B) again worked alongside the Iraqi forces. Approximately 6,000 Iraqi Security Forces and 5,500 U.S. troops were also sent to Baghdad to provide further support during OTF II.[49]

Prime Minister Maliki directed Iraqi and Coalition Forces to secure Baghdad's most violent locales, namely Khadimiyah, Mansour, Dora, and Adhamiyah. These were predominantly Sunni neighborhoods in which al Qaeda had established strongholds.[50] Iraqi Security Forces were to clear them of extremist elements and to hold them securely while the government, with Coalition assistance, built up essential services and infrastructure.

The plan failed. U.S. forces cleared the focus areas, but Iraqi Security Forces could not hold the neighborhoods. There were not enough Iraqi soldiers, and the National Police were insufficiently trained to handle the situation. They had also been infiltrated by militia loyalists who increased sectarian violence. In the process, they delegitimized the Iraqi Security Forces in the eyes of the Sunni population. Extremist groups tried to re-enter the focus areas during the clearing operations, and sectarian violence actually rose in some focus areas. For example, U.S. and Iraqi Forces cleared Dora three times during the Together Forward series, a sign of the repeated struggle for control over that neighborhood.[51] Sectarian violence not only increased in some focus areas, but also spread throughout the city.[52] In October, a military spokesman noted, "In Baghdad alone, we've seen a 22 percent increase in attacks during the first three weeks of Ramadan, as compared to the three weeks preceding Ramadan. In Baghdad, Operation Together Forward has made a difference in the focus areas but has not met our overall expectations of sustaining a reduction in the levels of violence."[53]

As Operations Together Forward I and II progressed, the nature of the sectarian murders changed. Earlier violence included kidnapping for the purpose of ransoming the victims, or kidnapping and torturing victims in remote locations. A military spokesman reported that "with the increased presence of the Iraqi security forces and Coalition Forces in the city, it has shifted more to murders that were generally conducted on the spot because of the increased Coalition and Iraqi security force presence out there" and the death squads' consequent "inability to move freely throughout the city."[54]

U.S. commanders and the Iraqi government stopped Operation Together Forward in mid-October 2006, as the operation had become counterproductive. Having failed to reduce the violence after two major operations, U.S. forces and the Iraqi government conducted reviews both in Baghdad and in Washington, D.C., to determine the proper course of action: "We're taking a lot of time to go back and look at the whole Baghdad security plan. We're asking ourselves if the conditions under which it was first devised and planned still exist today or have the conditions changed and therefore a modification to that plan needs to be made."[55] The details of those reviews are beyond the scope of this book, but the situation in Baghdad and the trends in violence that prompted the review are critical to understanding the chosen course.

The operational concept that American and Iraqi leaders tried to implement in 2006 was fundamentally flawed. Coalition and Iraqi Security Forces did not aim to secure the population from AQI and Shia death squads, and could not do so given the low force levels and the disposition of troops concentrated on large Forward Operating Bases (FOBs) that were separated from the population.[56]

There were insufficient troops to carry out the plan. Generals John Abizaid and George Casey designated still more reinforcements to support the ongoing operations in Baghdad in September 2006. They committed the 2nd Brigade Combat Team, 1st Infantry Division, which was initially designated as the CENTCOM theater-wide reserve, to Baghdad.[57] The Dagger Brigade assumed responsibility for Northwest Baghdad in early November, 2006, joining the three other brigade headquarters in the capital. Their reinforcement in the fall, just as in July, was an incremental increase in troops in the face of an exponential rise in violence.

In addition, the surprising resilience of al Qaeda undermined the assumption that the violence in Baghdad could be ended by directing attention to Sunni neighborhoods where the terrorist organization had established safe havens. "We've seen a tremendous pushback by some Sunni extremist elements, some al Qaeda elements recently in some of the areas we're operating, where we've probably taken more of our casualties than in other areas," a spokesman reported in October 2006.[58] Targeting particular Sunni neighborhoods, as though the tumor of al Qaeda could simply be removed, was an ineffective way to defeat the enemy: Al Qaeda had bases outside of Baghdad from which it regenerated within the capital. The OTF series was predicated on assumptions about the causes of violence that did not fully account for the enemy's campaign design and objectives, which eluded analysts in the summer of 2006.

The Enemy's Objectives and Campaign Design

JAM/Special Groups and AQI fought for terrain in Baghdad throughout 2005 and 2006, because controlling the capital was the prerequisite for defeating one another and gaining power and influence within the newly forming state. The enemy groups designed campaigns thoughtfully and focused on military objectives that would lead to their political success. Consequently, some of the violence in 2006 did not result from reprisal attacks spreading from neighborhood to neighborhood, as if a contagion. Nor was the violence dispersed randomly throughout the city. Rather, JAM and AQI fought one another and the Coalition wherever they needed to control terrain, roads, or entry points to Baghdad necessary for taking control of the capital.

JAM and Special Groups had established their strongest base of operations in Baghdad itself, inside Sadr City. They conducted operations within Baghdad and its immediate environs. They needed first and foremost to maintain the lines of communication (the supply routes, roads, and rivers) along which they conveyed weapons, money, and trainers from Iran. They could not fight well against the government, the Coalition, and Sunni extremists without receiving these resources. Secondly, these Shia extremist groups aimed to "create a buffer zone between the Sunni population concentrations" by expanding the territory they controlled within Baghdad and pushing into important areas outside the city. Shia expansion emanated from three general areas of Baghdad:

East Baghdad, including Sadr City; west Rashid, particularly Bayaa and Aamel; and Khadimiyah. JAM aimed to prevent AQI operatives in mixed Sunni and Shia neighborhoods from reinforcing one another by moving easily among sympathetic residents. Thirdly, Shia extremists aimed to push the Sunni population out of small cities, such as Mahmudiyah, that effectively controlled the routes to Karbala and Najaf, the Shia holy cities south of Baghdad. These cities sat astride major supply lines and pilgrimage routes, making the movement of supplies difficult for Special Groups and making the transient Shia population vulnerable to attack by Sunni extremists and AQI residing there.[59]

JAM and Special Groups conducted multiple, simultaneous and successive operations to control Baghdad throughout 2006, involving combat (kinetic operations, the neologism that U.S. forces would use) and a wide array of economic, social, and religious (non-kinetic) instruments. Their first priority was controlling east Baghdad through kinetic and non-kinetic means. They consolidated their control over east Baghdad over the second half of 2006. At the same time, they placed their main effort on expansion in west Baghdad. The enemy conducted shaping operations north and south of the city in order to influence the main effort. Their operations were very effective. Shia extremist expansion placed pressure on Sunni-populated areas in the center of Baghdad: Mansour and Karkh, Rusafa, and Adhamiyah.[60]

As JAM expanded in the summer of 2006, Sunni insurgents and AQI converged upon Baghdad from the provinces in order to establish and retain strongholds in the capital. Sunni insurgents thereby attempted to set the conditions to restore themselves to political power, and AQI to gain such power in the first place.

Sunni insurgents and AQI, like their Shia opponents, needed to keep their own lines of communication open. They relied heavily upon supply routes from the northern Tigris River Valley and Anbar province. AQI transferred accelerants to violence—car bombs, suicide bombers, and other necessary personnel and supplies—into Baghdad along the Fallujah-Abu Ghraib highway that entered Baghdad proper at Ghazaliyah, in the northwest quadrant; along Highway 8, which runs into Rashid in the southwestern quadrant; and from Taji and Khan Bani Saad, just to the north. By encircling Baghdad, AQI could move accelerants freely in and out of the capital from these predominantly Sunni support zones immediately around the city.

Abu Musab al Zarqawi and Abu Ayyub al Masri had developed a sophisticated concept of operations for controlling Baghdad by means of safe havens outside of it. In mid-December 2006, Coalition Forces captured an AQI map depicting the battle for Baghdad. The map showed how AQI had divided the areas around the capital into regions, identified Baghdad as the center of the fight, and carried the fight south of Baghdad toward areas primarily inhabited by Shia. AQI divided Baghdad and its belts, the terrain and lines of communication surrounding the capital, into regions corresponding with the avenues of approach they used to transfer accelerants from their safe havens outside it. AQI assigned responsibilities for these sectors to different commanders.

In this regard, AQI's encirclement of Baghdad resembled Saddam Hussein's plan to defend the city. Saddam had established concentric defensive rings defense around the city. The Hammurabi zone began to the west of the capital; the al Nida zone to the north and east; the Adnan zone immediately south of the city; and the Medina zone lay further south and east along the roads from Kuwait. The divisions assigned to these sectors protected the outer ring of Baghdad's defense; others protected two concentric rings inside the city, supported by the Saddam Fedayeen. The convergence between AQI's plan to encircle the city and Saddam's defense of the city might have arisen because the terrorist organization modeled their approach on his or because AQI's planners intuitively grasped the advantages of this disposition for controlling the city.[61]

Al Qaeda in Iraq fought to cut the lines of communication between Baghdad and Iran that allowed JAM and Special Groups to maintain their expansion and cleansing campaign within the city, as their ability to destroy those groups' capacity to fight was otherwise limited. The contest to cut supply routes was especially vigorous just north of the capital, where JAM was expanding from Husseiniyah, and just south, in the Mahmudiyah area. JAM expansion within the city further hampered AQI's ability to move freely within Baghdad itself. AQI therefore fought Shia extremists and the Coalition in order to retain their ability to stage spectacular attacks. In the summer and fall of 2006, AQI's primary bases of operation in Baghdad were Mansour, Adhamiyah, Rusafa, and Dora. As Shia extremists expanded from the bordering neighborhoods, these AQI strongholds became the most violent areas in the city—attacked by JAM and defended by AQI—and remained extremely violent even as Coalition and Iraqi operations began.[62]

Violence Spikes During the Operational Pause

Ironically, U.S. and Iraqi operations to secure Baghdad in 2006 had the contrary effect. They made the city more violent, allowed al Qaeda to establish itself more firmly, and accelerated Shia expansion. The clearing operations in Together Forward concentrated very heavily on Sunni areas, such as Mansour, Ghazaliyah, Ameriyah, Dora, and Adhamiyah, from which al Qaeda in Iraq attacks emanated. Shia militia groups pressed hard on these neighborhoods and engaged in the execution of Sunni community members. Many Sunnis in Baghdad distrusted the legitimate Iraqi Security Forces (ISF) because Shia militias infiltrated their ranks and attacked their neighborhoods. The residents in the focus areas turned to AQI for further protection against the death squads that threatened their survival.

When the offensive operations undertaken by U.S. and Iraqi Security Forces ceased in late October 2006, the conflict between Shia militia groups and al Qaeda in Iraq quickly resumed on an even larger scale.

Masafee, in Dora, was al Qaeda's strongest safe haven in Baghdad in 2007. That same neighborhood was the epicenter of sectarian violence in 2006 and the focal point of Operations Together Forward. Dora was emblematic of the accelerating violence of November and December

2006. The area once housed a robust mixture of Sunni, Shia, and Christian families in its large homes, making it a prime target for sectarian cleansing by militias—and for reciprocal bombings and vigilante attacks by Sunni inhabitants. Its location on Baghdad's main highways made it easy for death squads to move in and out, and controlled access to southern supply lines. Only a single U.S. battalion remained in Dora after the "clear" phase of Operation Together Forward II.

As Iraqi Security Forces backfilled U.S. troops in the "hold" phase, sectarian violence and vigilantism increased in the neighborhood. Sunni vigilante groups in Dora rearmed and reorganized, as Solomon Moore described in the *Los Angeles Times* last November: "'We have zero trust in the Iraqi army and minus-zero trust in the police,' said Ahmed Suheil Juburi, 33, a Sunni Arab who has thrown in his lot with a group of former military officers in Saddam Hussein's Baathist regime patrolling the Baghdad neighborhood of Dora."[63] The Juburis have enormous clout in Dora, and were long associated with Baathist insurgents. They also had connections with other Sunni groups—such as al Qaeda in Iraq—which ultimately moved into a few sub-districts of the neighborhood, established a radical religious and political program, and fortified a defensive position there with IEDs, deep-buried IEDs, and other explosives.

In November 2006, as Americans celebrated Thanksgiving weekend, al Qaeda-linked terrorists detonated a huge vehicle bomb in Sadr City, killing 215 people. Militias retaliated throughout Baghdad, instigating a string of executions, mortar attacks, and drive-by shootings in Sunni neighborhoods. Three days of reciprocal violence left several hundred Baghdadis dead and injured.

November 2006 is when Dora, already troublesome because of militia-infiltrated police units and sparse U.S. presence, went from bad to dramatically worse. By December, a third of all killings in Baghdad had occurred in Dora.

It is difficult to identify the most dangerous place within a neighborhood like Dora, but the Dora market certainly deserved consideration for that grim distinction in December 2006. The large marketplace was a safe haven for al Qaeda terrorists. They used its facilities as a dumping ground for corpses. For several weeks in December, U.S. soldiers with the 2-12 Infantry Battalion reconnoitered the Dora market. They encountered twenty IEDs and fifteen corpses in that brief time.

Two days before Christmas, the 2-12 Infantry cleared the Dora market. They proceeded building by building; it might take a company several hours to clear a block. The operation took twelve hours. They then occupied the site 24-7.

In January, CBS's Lara Logan, embedded with the 2-12, reported: "Since U.S. forces took the market back just before Christmas, Sergeant Maddi says they haven't found a single body here. That's helped breathe a little life back into the place with the return of simple pleasures, shoppers seeking some semblance of normal life, as a small number of stores begin to open their doors once again. The market is the lifeblood of this community. So any improvement resonates. But 90 percent of the businesses remain closed. Their owners have seen U.S. efforts fail twice here in the last six months. Three marks on every door, evidence of the number of times American soldiers have cleared these very streets."[64]

Shia Groups Move West

In October, November, and December 2006, Shia militia groups—a combination of Special Groups, Jaysh al Mahdi, and Badr Corps—expanded their control of areas in west Baghdad through a campaign of intimidation and sectarian cleansing.[65] In addition to various sanctuaries on the east side of the Tigris, the Kadhimiyah shrine and its environs provided an important safe haven on the west side of Baghdad for Shia extremists, as did the neighborhood of Shula.

In October 2006, militia groups cleansed Sunni from Washash, in northwest Baghdad.[66] They displaced the Sunni population from the neighborhood of Hurriyah in the northwest Kadhimiyah district, and from Adl, a small neighborhood immediately to its south.[67] At the same time, Shia expanded from Shurta northward toward Route Irish, driving the Sunni of West Rasheed into two small pockets, one a corridor astride the roadway in Ameriyah and Hateen, the other in Saydiyah.[68] Because extremist militia groups had infiltrated the Iraqi Army, Iraqi Police, and National Police, the dispersion of Iraqi Security Forces throughout West Baghdad created a network through which Shia extremists could move people, funds, and weapons. The main roads linking Kadhimiyah and Mansour became the lines of communication by which Shia extremists pressed southward toward Rashid.[69] By intimidating Shia families and displacing Sunni families from mixed neighborhoods, militias gained new footholds in west Baghdad from which to extend their power.

Al Qaeda responded to the Shia militia campaign by targeting Jaysh al Mahdi operatives, leaders, and strongholds in important Baghdad terrain; defending its safe havens; and fighting to cut JAM's lines of communication. Violence skyrocketed in Baghdad and across Iraq. In the month of December 2006 alone, roughly 3,000 Iraqi civilians were killed.[70] The total number of attacks in December hovered at approximately 5,500; this included over 1,500 IED attacks.[71]

The Battle for Haifa Street

The fighting spread toward the center of the city, as JAM effectively expanded its control over formerly Sunni and mixed areas. Haifa Street, in the Karkh neighborhood, became emblematic of the contest between al Qaeda and Jaysh al Mahdi for control of terrain in Baghdad. Haifa Street is premier real estate along the west bank of the Tigris River. High-rise apartments, often given by Saddam Hussein to government employees or loyal Sunnis, line the street.[72] These modern apartments have a view of the water and overlook both west and east Baghdad, defining the limits of wealth and poverty at the river boundary. Because of their central location, height, commanding view of Baghdad, and proximity to the Green Zone, the high-rise buildings on Haifa Street are dominant urban terrain, and easy to defend.[73]

The strategic and symbolic importance of Haifa Street was not lost on either al Qaeda in Iraq nor the Jaysh al Mahdi, who had fought to control this street previously. By the beginning of 2005, insurgents were using Haifa Street as a safe haven. In spring 2005, the 1-9 Cavalry Regiment (assigned to the 4th BCT of the 1st Cavalry Division) cleared the neighborhood, conducted presence-patrols along with Iraqi forces, and repaired damage that they had caused to the roads during combat. They departed, and left Iraqi forces in charge.[74]

Thereafter, some Shia fleeing Khadimiyah, to the north of Karkh, moved into residences on Haifa Street. They were "protected" by a leading member of the Jaysh al Mahdi who operated in the vicinity of Haifa Street until he was arrested. Sunni insurgents, including AQI foreign fighters, then returned to the Haifa Street area from other neighborhoods and victimized the Shiite refugees inhabiting the buildings.[75] As JAM expanded into west Baghdad from areas on the east side of the river, AQI defended against the expansion from the highrises. U.S. forces patrolled the area in mid-October 2006. Snipers shot at U.S. forces from rooftops and threw grenades at them from the high-rises during these patrols.[76]

AQI intimidated residents of Haifa Street and the Iraqi Security Forces responsible for the sector. On Saturday, January 6, 2007, Iraqi troops on patrol discovered a fake checkpoint in the neighborhood, manned by insurgents. The Iraqi forces killed thirty insurgents on that day.[77] That night, the insurgents dumped approximately twenty-seven corpses of Shiites whom they had executed.[78] On Sunday, January 7, a sniper killed two Iraqi security guards manning a neighborhood mosque where he was hiding. The following day, "gunmen roamed the streets, distributing leaflets threatening to kill anyone who might enter the area."[79] When the Iraqi unit attempted to oust the insurgents from their stronghold later that day, two of their soldiers were killed. The unit then called in American forces to help them clear out the insurgents' safe haven.[80]

American reinforcements came from nearby neighborhoods of Baghdad. The 1st Battalion, 23rd Infantry Regiment (part of the 3rd Brigade of the 2nd Infantry Division, equipped with Stryker light armored vehicles), had been operating as a strike force in early January, going to hotspots and temporarily improving local force ratios. Elements of that unit had been conducting Operation Arrowhead Strike III, in and around the Hurriyah neighborhood of the Khadimiyah district in northwestern Baghdad before they were sent to Haifa Street. (Militia and terrorist activity had increased in Hurriyah after the large displacement of Sunni families in October 2006. Arrowhead Strike III attempted to disrupt those enemy activities and allow coalition and Iraqi forces to control the area.)[81]

The 1-23rd Infantry Battalion, nicknamed the Tomahawks, responded to the deteriorating situation on Haifa Street, moving out of its assembly area at 3:30 a.m. on Tuesday, January 9. Two hours later, it had joined with the Iraqi forces around Tala'al Square, on the north end of Haifa Street and in the center of the neighborhood, occupying buildings and rounding up suspects.[82] Approximately 1,000 U.S. and Iraqi troops were in the area.[83] At 7:00 a.m., the insurgents began firing on U.S. and Iraqi troops and their vehicles from sniper positions on the roofs and in the doorways of buildings. Their mortar fire suggested a high degree of training and coordination. They also continued to fight, rather than running away from American forces (as the enemy typically had done), which surprised American forces.

U.S. and Iraqi forces had not cordoned off the area before or during the fight. The insurgents occupied positions in successive buildings, moving effectively from building to building as the American and Iraqi forces went from one to the next.[84] The Tomahawks called for close air support from Apache helicopters and F-18s, which targeted the snipers on the building roofs until approximately noon.[85] On the ground, the Tomahawks remained engaged for eleven hours.[86] They patrolled the area after dark with their heavy vehicles, and Iraqi soldiers took positions on the rooftops.[87] No U.S. troops were killed in action. They killed fifty-one insurgents and captured twenty-one, including several foreign fighters.[88]

The Iraqi unit remained in the neighborhood, but the Stryker battalion had left the area by January 16, 2007. The First Cavalry Division took responsibility for patrolling Haifa Street.[89] Insurgents had reinfiltrated it by January 23, just two weeks after the Tomahawks first confronted them, according to intelligence reports cited by a spokesman for Prime Minister Maliki.[90]

The Tomahawks returned to clear the area once more.[91] Operation Tomahawk Strike 11, as it was called, began when that battalion entered the area from the south at 2:00 a.m. on January 24. They were ultimately joined by Iraqi forces and by elements of the Dagger Brigade, the 2nd BCT of the 1st Cavalry Division.[92] Their mission, according to officials, was "aimed at rapidly isolating insurgents and gaining control of this key central Baghdad location . . . . Reducing sectarian violence is vital in transferring security responsibilities to the Iraqi security forces and provides a safer living environment for Iraqi residents."[93] Together, the units brought infantry, Strykers, and Bradleys (fighting vehicles more heavily armed than Strykers, with tracks rather than wheels) into the fight. Americans moved from building to building. An enemy in a Shiite neighborhood on the east side of the Tigris River shelled them with mortars, and snipers opposed them from covered positions on street level and from the windows of buildings.[94] They identified a major weapons cache at Karkh High School, cordoned off the area, and allowed only pedestrian traffic on Haifa Street.[95]

The engagement on January 24 was not part of the Baghdad Security Plan (BSP), according to Iraqi officials. Rather, it was meant to "prepare the way for a more concerted effort to clear out and hold troubled neighborhoods."[96] Like the operations in the Baghdad suburbs, the fight for Haifa Street was an effort to create the preconditions for the success of the BSP by denying the insurgents bases and safe havens from which to disrupt that operation when it began.

By February 1, 2007, the Tomahawks had left Haifa Street again, and elements of the 6th Iraqi Army Division were patrolling that sector.[97]

The battles on Haifa Street illustrate a pattern of U.S. and Iraqi Army engagements in Baghdad. U.S. forces cleared the area of insurgents in 2005, and then turned the area over to Iraqi troops. The year of sectarian violence destabilized the area, allowing Shiite militiamen to gain some control over the neighborhood. The Iraqi soldiers were able to patrol the area, though obviously not without challenge, in late 2006. Then Sunni militants moved in, took over the stronghold, and tried to gain control of the area. The Iraqi unit responded first in the emergency, but it did not think that it had the capability to clear the area without American assistance. (Given the difficulty that American forces encountered, the Iraqis' assessment was correct.) The Iraqis received American help within twenty-four hours.

U.S. forces did not remain in sufficient numbers to retain the area. It was the Iraqi troops who stayed behind, and it took less than two weeks for insurgents to reoccupy the area. When U.S. forces had flowed elsewhere, the insurgents reentered the neighborhood.

The Stryker Brigade, which has different vehicles and capabilities from other U.S. units, did not have a bounded area of operations (AO) in Baghdad.[98] Rather, in this time period, it served as a Quick Reaction Force, responding to problems throughout the Baghdad AO whenever it was needed. A battalion of the Stryker Brigade had the ability to clear a small but thorny area. It did not remain to control and retain areas, nor did other American forces. Rather, it left Iraqis behind, exposing the neighborhood to insurgents after it withdrew.

The second battle of Haifa Street fits two patterns. It was a reaction to the failure of U.S. forces to hold the neighborhood after January 9, 2007. It was also a high-profile preliminary operation that set the conditions for the Baghdad Security Plan in February 2007. Haifa Street is emblematic of the reactive posture that U.S. forces adopted throughout the theater in December 2006 and early January 2007. When intelligence—whether Iraqi or U.S. or Coalition—pinpointed a major insurgent stronghold, U.S. forces raided it to capture insurgents and deny them a safe haven. Such activities did not create general security by themselves, even when combined with a broader raiding program. They did, however, weaken enemy forces in preparation for significant clear-and-retain operations. It is unclear whether this was the objective of American operations on

Haifa Street in January 2007, but the operations set the conditions for the Blackjack Brigade, 2nd Brigade of the 1st Cavalry Division, under the command of Colonel Bryan Roberts, to secure the area as soon as the new Baghdad Security Plan began.

Chapter 2
■ ■ ■ The New Way Forward

In November and December 2006, the strategic direction of the Iraq war was fluid. Commanders in Baghdad had recognized the failure of their efforts to contain sectarian violence after Operation Together Forward II. They were considering their options. The American people saw that failure for themselves and put great pressure on the Bush Administration, through the November 2006 Congressional elections, to find a new way forward. Immediately after the elections, President Bush accepted Secretary of Defense Donald Rumsfeld's resignation and nominated former CIA Director Robert Gates to replace him. The administration had already launched several strategic reviews, including the Iraq Study Group, established in March 2006, and a military planning effort set up by Chairman of the Joint Chiefs of Staff, General Peter Pace, in September 2006.[99] The results of those reviews and Baghdad-based planning efforts were presented to the president in December, along with an independent report and proposal by the American Enterprise Institute. The President met with the Chiefs at the Pentagon on Wednesday, December 13, 2006, to choose among the policy options which were being proposed.[100]

The options under review differed enormously. Commanders in Iraq presented diverging views. Lieutenant General Ray Odierno, who replaced Lieutenant General Pete Chiarelli as the Corps commander on December 14, 2006, argued that a troop increase of five to ten brigades could transform the situations in Baghdad and Anbar, especially if the troops focused on securing the population.[101] Generals Casey and Abizaid did not advocate a troop increase, however, arguing that its impact would be temporary because of the infighting among Iraqi political leaders.[102] The recommendations of the Joint Chiefs' review were not publicly released.[103] In December, Lieutenant General David Petraeus, then commander of the Combined Arms Center at Fort Leavenworth, Kansas, formally published a new version of the Army's counterinsurgency field manual that emphasized securing the population as the necessary prerequisite to defeating insurgencies. The Iraq Study Group in Washington, D.C., had proposed accelerating the strategy that Generals Casey and Abizaid were already pursuing—training Iraqi forces, transitioning responsibility to them, and withdrawing U.S. forces first from combat roles, then from Iraq, as rapidly as possible. The report of the American Enterprise Institute, championed by retired Army Vice Chief of Staff General Jack Keane, advocated sending five additional Army brigades and two Marine Corps regiments to support a new strategy that prioritized securing the Iraqi population.[104]

The formulation of the new Iraq policy, an intricate and dynamic process, falls outside the scope of this book. The outline of events must suffice. After the meeting with the Chiefs, President Bush leaned toward some sort of troop increase. He requested additional information from the Office of Management and Budget about the cost of sending reinforcements to Iraq, as well as an assessment from the Joint Staff about which additional brigades might be available.[105] President Bush met with his War Cabinet at Crawford, Texas on December 28, 2006 to consider this additional information, consult with his advisors (including the new Secretary of Defense), and make a decision about Iraq strategy.[106]

In the boldest stroke of his presidency, Bush changed the mission, strategy, force size, and entire leadership team of the American war effort in Iraq. He changed the mission of U.S. forces from transitioning responsibility to Iraqi Security Forces to securing the population of Baghdad from sectarian violence. American forces would aim "to help Iraqis clear and secure neighborhoods, to help them protect the local population, and to help ensure that the Iraqi forces left behind are capable of providing the security that Baghdad needs."[107] The new mission statement pursued the recommendations in General Petraeus' counterinsurgency doctrine. President Bush nominated General Petraeus to replace General Casey as the commander of Coalition Forces in Iraq.[108] In addition, Admiral William "Fox" Fallon would replace General John Abizaid at CENTCOM, and Ambassador Ryan Crocker would replace Ambassador Zalmay Khalilzad in Baghdad. The President ordered the deployment of an additional five Army brigades and two Marine battalions to support this strategy, and reinforced them with the aviation, engineering, and other assets that enabled them to perform their specific tasks. President Bush thus gave General Odierno most of the additional forces that he had requested as the commander of combat forces in Iraq. President Bush's sweeping decisions, publicly announced on January 10, 2007, changed the course of the war.

The Coalition's Objectives and Operational Concept: Baghdad and Its Belts

The new mission marked a major shift in U.S. policy. As late as December 2006, America pursued the objective of , turning the responsibility for security over to Iraqi forces as quickly as possible. General Casey encapsulated the mission in MNF-I's year-end statement: "Since the inauguration of the Iraqi government, MNF-I forces remain in Iraq at the behest of its leaders. Coalition Forces are committed to supplementing Iraqi Security Forces in ongoing operations—and striking at al Qaeda in Iraq in particular—but increasingly are focused on helping build and train the ISF with the eventual goal of leaving Iraq able to secure its streets, its borders and its citizenry without Coalition help."[109]

As a result of the President's decision to change the mission, establishing security in Baghdad became the primary military objective in 2007. General Odierno explained his mission as follows: military operations in Iraq aimed "to create stability and security to protect the Iraqi people, first and foremost in Baghdad. The population and the government of Iraq are the center of gravity. Creating a stable environment in

Baghdad should provide time and space for the Iraqi government to continue to mature as a government and continue to build its capacity."[110] The maturation of the Iraqi government was envisioned as a step toward America's strategic goal: a stable, secure Iraq with a legitimately elected government, at peace with its neighbors, and an ally of the United States in the war on terror.

In order to execute President Bush's new mission, the generals in Iraq had to determine the best way to secure Baghdad. Generals Petraeus and Odierno considered two methods of securing the capital with military forces: "[D]o we cut [the enemy] off outside of Baghdad, or do we provide more security inside?"[111] In other words, should U.S. forces attempt to establish security by clearing and patrolling the city's neighborhoods? Or should they secure the capital by eliminating the enemy from safe havens just outside Baghdad? General Petraeus's new counterinsurgency doctrine recommended using combat forces to protect the population in major cities and to clear insurgent safe havens. Providing security within Baghdad would directly support the mission of protecting its population from sectarian violence. Consequently, as one element of the new plan, Generals Petraeus and Odierno dispersed U.S. and Iraqi forces throughout Baghdad in order to establish, expand, and maintain safe areas within the capital.

The generals deemed this solution necessary but insufficient. General Odierno explained: "The areas surrounding Baghdad, which we refer to as the 'Baghdad belts,' are also key to its security."[112] AQI's car bombs, weapons, and fighters often originated outside of Baghdad, in its "belts," rather than in the city itself. The Baghdad belts are residential, agricultural, and industrial areas that encircle the city, and networks of roadways, rivers, and other lines of communication that lie within a twenty- or thirty-mile radius of Baghdad. In order to encircle and thereby control Baghdad, AQI had established bases in the belts outside of the capital. AQI used these suburban safe havens in Baghdad's "belts" as part of a complex system for moving weapons into the city. The previous chapter described AQI's campaign design, its division of Baghdad's belts into sectors, and its convergence upon the capital in the second half of 2006.

U.S. forces had contested the enemy's occupation of the belts minimally in 2006, focusing primarily on the sector southwest of Baghdad. Consequently, the enemies of the Coalition and the Iraqi government were able to control the terrain around Baghdad, to use it to project forces and funnel supplies into the capital, and to move freely around the city into the provinces, explaining AQI's regenerative capacity in the wake of OTF I and II, operations which focused on AQI's safe-havens inside Baghdad but largely ignored the ones outside the city.

U.S. plans to secure Baghdad developed from the Corps staff's understanding of AQI's operational concept, and the importance of the belts to AQI's control of Baghdad. As General Odierno explained, "Attacks occurring in Baghdad often originate in these outerlying regions. Sectarian lines begin to blur in these belts, creating a flashpoint for extremists looking to assert their control over Baghdad. Al Qaeda in Iraq and Shia extremists want to control these areas."[113] Generals Petraeus and Odierno therefore decided that securing Baghdad required large-scale offensive combat operations outside the city, in addition to operations inside the capital aimed at protecting the population.

Generals Petraeus and Odierno developed a plan to improve Baghdad's security in both the belts and the city using all of the forces available to them.[114] The new brigades that President Bush had authorized arrived at the rate of one each month from February to June 2007. In addition, a Marine Expeditionary Unit (MEU) arrived in June. Corps plan 07-01 established the way that the existing and new brigades would be incorporated into the fight for the capital. Odierno incorporated each new brigade—and the MEU—into operations as it arrived. He deployed two of the new brigades to Baghdad and three to the belts around the city. He thereby carefully set the conditions for a summer offensive against AQI in the belts, while implementing a plan to protect Baghdad's population beginning in February.

The Baghdad Security Plan: Operation Fardh al Qanoon

The Baghdad Security Plan, known as Operation Fardh al Qanoon (Arabic for "Enforcing the Law"), began on February 14, 2007. Major General Joseph Fil, who as the division commander coordinated the U.S. brigades in Baghdad, described the operation's goal: " . . . [T] he government of Iraq is seeking to show the Iraqi people and the international community that it is able to protect all its citizens, regardless of sect or ethnicity. An improved security situation will provide the government of Iraq with a breathing space to reach out to the country's different groups, through a process of national reconciliation, to ensure them all a stake in the future of Iraq."[115]

General Odierno added two new brigade headquarters (and twelve battalions, rather than the six that would normally make up two brigades) to increase the troop density in Baghdad sufficiently to protect the population.[116] He also generated combat forces for Baghdad by changing the deployment and tasks of the U.S. forces that had been situated on Forward Operating Bases since fall 2006. He dispersed the pre-Surge troops away from the isolated FOBs to Joint Security Stations (JSSs) and Combat Outposts (COPs—later known as Coalition Outposts under the same acronym) located in Baghdad's neighborhoods, better enabling Coalition Forces to protect local Iraqis. MNF-I and the Government of Iraq conducted their first operations in Baghdad in locations where commanders thought they would reduce violence most effectively.[117] The contested, high-violence neighborhoods in northeastern and northwestern Baghdad received the most additional attention in the first months of the Baghdad Security Plan.

In 2006, the overwhelming majority of American combat forces had been concentrated on FOBs, from which they reinforced Iraqi Security Forces and conducted patrols in violent areas. U.S. military operations tended to be reactive rather than proactive, episodic rather than sustained. The insufficiently trained and equipped Iraqi Security Forces had been pushed prematurely into the fight. Rather than conducting counterinsurgency operations they often relied on ineffective checkpoints. As a result, security ebbed and flowed through neighborhoods and towns but was rarely lasting, and the presence of Coalition Forces provided little sense of security for Iraqi civilians.

After President Bush announced the troop increase for Baghdad in mid-January, many U.S. forces stationed in Baghdad prepared to move from their FOBs into the neighborhoods. Major General William Caldwell, the spokesman for MNF-I, explained, "[W]e have realized, to protect the population . . . we the coalition force . . . can't be living on some big operating base. We need to move our forces off those big operating bases down into the city and be co-located with our Iraqi counterparts, both the Iraqi army and the Iraqi police, so that we have a better feel for what's going on in that neighborhood."[118]

U.S. forces constructed smaller, fortified positions off the Forward Operating Bases to distribute small units through the neighborhoods. They moved off the FOBs in Baghdad in January 2006. Dagger Brigade, responsible for security in northwest Baghdad, constructed two Combat Outposts in Ghazaliyah COP Casino, housing a company of U.S. soldiers and some Iraqi Army units, was the first of its kind and was planned before the troop increase began; nearby COP Wildcard was completed by January 23, 2006.[119] Paratroopers constructed and occupied COP Callahan in Adhamiyah in eastern Baghdad.[120] The 2nd Battalion of the 82nd Airborne Division's 319th Airborne Infantry Regiment built COP War Eagle in Adhamiyah on the Tigris.[121]

The concept of Combat Outposts was not new. U.S. forces occupied company-level Combat Outposts in Baghdad after the invasion in 2003, but U.S. commanders withdrew them to FOBs, consistent with the prevailing view that U.S. forces were an irritant that inflamed the insurgency.[122] U.S. forces also used Combat Outposts, rather than FOBs, to project troops inside Ramadi in 2006, in an effort that ultimately secured Anbar's capital.[123]

U.S. forces built and manned Joint Security Stations in Baghdad's neighborhoods, along with Iraqi Army, Iraqi Police, and National Police troops. The concept of the Joint Security Station arose in part to accommodate the command arrangements that General Casey had negotiated with the Maliki government, which established an Iraqi chain of command for the Baghdad operations that would be separate from U.S. forces. American units followed the orders of American commanders; Iraqi units received separate orders from Iraqi commanders.

Maliki chose Lieutenant General Aboud Qanbar to head the newly-created Baghdad Operations Command with responsibility for all Iraqi Security Forces in the capital. This was the first time that the Iraqi Government had designated a single official responsible for operations and assets in Baghdad. General Aboud established the Karkh and Rusafa Area Commands, each commanded by an Iraqi major general, to coordinate Iraqi activities on each side of the Tigris. He initially divided Baghdad into ten security districts and allocated one Iraqi brigade to each of them.[124]

Joint Security Stations transformed the ability of U.S. brigades to secure Baghdad's districts. They also made it possible for U.S. forces to train Iraqis by including them in the planning and execution of combat operations. The Iraqi Security Forces learned new tactics, techniques, and procedures by operating alongside American troops daily. Americans and Iraqis resided together so that they could share their mission, operational concepts, and information, despite their separate chains of command. Partnership at echelon—the pairing of U.S. soldiers and officers with their Iraqi counterparts—supplemented and magnified the effectiveness of the small, officer-intensive Military Advisory Training Teams (MiTTs) that had characterized the transition effort in 2006.

By February 6, 2007, U.S. forces had built and occupied two Joint Security Stations in western Baghdad, accompanied by Iraqi soldiers and police.[125] Two days later, U.S. forces had built ten new Joint Security Stations and began to reside in them jointly with Iraqi police, Iraqi National Police, and Iraqi Army units.[126] As soon as the first "Surge" brigade, the

2nd BCT of the 82nd Airborne Division arrived, some of its units immediately constructed the Joint Security Station in Hurriyah, a formerly
Sunni neighborhood in western Baghdad, which Jaysh al Mahdi had
contested.[127] COP Casino quickly became a full Joint Security Station
in Ghazaliyah.[128] U.S. forces quickly moved off the FOBs. By February 21,
there were fourteen JSSs.[129] Most of these had been built in about a two-
week period.

Battalions then radiated further into Baghdad from the larger hubs
of the Joint Security Stations to additional Combat Outposts and Patrol
Bases, creating a net of small units in the city. Brigades also created additional Joint Security Stations in the capital in order to shift forces from
areas that they had secured to areas where forces were badly needed.

General Fil described the operational design of the Baghdad Security Plan: "This new plan involves three basic parts: clear, control and
retain. The first objective within each of the security districts in the
Iraqi capital is to clear out extremist elements neighborhood by neighborhood in an effort to protect the population. And after an area is
cleared, we're moving to what we call the control operation. Together
with our Iraqi counterparts, we'll maintain a full-time presence on the
streets, and we'll do this by building and maintaining joint security
stations throughout the city. This effort to re-establish the joint security stations is well under way. The number of stations in each district
will be determined by the commanders on the ground who control
that area. An area moves into the retain phase when the Iraqi security
forces are fully responsible for the day-to-day security mission. At this
point, Coalition Forces begin to move out of the neighborhood and
into locations where they can respond to requests for assistance as
needed. During these three phrases, efforts will be ongoing to stimu-
late local economies by creating employment opportunities, initiat-
ing reconstruction projects and improving the infrastructure. These
efforts will be spearheaded by neighborhood advisory councils, district advisory councils and the government of Iraq."[130]

General Fil explained that the "hold" and "build" phases of

Operations Together Forward I and II (the operations in Baghdad in summer and fall of 2006) did not involve the application of military forces or the extensive use of U.S. soldiers because of the way they were defined and designed. The "control" phase and even the "retain" phase of the new Baghdad Security Plan involved the application of military forces to ensure that the security of the people of Baghdad is solidly established and sustained. In other words, General Fil believed that combat troops would be present and operating even after they cleared the neighborhoods, and that they would not withdraw rapidly from the neighborhoods.

The five brigades in the city of Baghdad proper increased their ability to maneuver in the first four months of Operation Enforcing the Law by establishing Combat Outposts and reconnoitering routes, tracking the enemy, and destroying weapons caches. Discrete operations to secure neighborhoods accompanied the ink-like spread of troops into Baghdad. From February through June, the five brigades in the capital fortified markets with concrete barricades, protected residential areas, and established safe neighborhoods as models. The Stryker brigade reinforced each brigade during its most intensive phase of clearing operations.

In doctrinal terms, the Baghdad Security Plan aimed to establish area security.[131] American and Iraqi commanders approached this task in a number of different ways, of which military clear-and-control operations were only a part. In 2006 most of Baghdad's large markets had been open to vehicular traffic, making them particularly vulnerable to vehicle bombs. As Operation Fardh al Qanoon began, commanders turned some markets into pedestrian-only zones, allowing vehicles to deliver their goods before the market opened and then leave the area.[132] In this way, they reduced opportunities for insurgents to conduct mass-casualty attacks. Commanders also changed the traffic pattern in Baghdad to alter the routes usually employed by terrorists and insurgents. They built barriers along major highways and exits to prevent insurgents from moving easily into neighborhoods.[133]

The Disposition of Forces in Baghdad

Lieutenant General Odierno and Major General Joseph Fil, the commander of Multi-National Division-Baghdad, divided the capital into five sectors and assigned each one to a U.S. brigade headquarters. The Dagger Brigade, under the command of Colonel J. B. Burton, oversaw northwest Baghdad (Mansour and Kadhimiyah); the Dragon Brigade under Colonel Ricky Gibbs oversaw southwest Baghdad (East and West Rashid); Blackjack Brigade under Colonel Bryan Roberts oversaw central Baghdad (Karkh); the Falcon Brigade under Colonel B. D. Ferris oversaw northeast Baghdad (Adhamiyah, Rusafa, and Sadr City); and the Strike Brigade under Colonel Jeffrey Bannister oversaw southeast Baghdad (9 Nissan and Karadah).

The Arrowhead Brigade (3rd Stryker Brigade Combat Team, 2nd Infantry Division), under the command of Colonel Steve Townsend, served as the strike-force for Multi-National Division-Baghdad. Colonel Townsend contrasted the function of the strike-force with the role of the five "landowning" brigades: "In this role, we do not own battlespace, but we are a mobile and offensively oriented force that disrupts insurgent activity and clears areas of Baghdad where the insurgents are operating in strength. We also deal with time-sensitive targets and other rapidly emerging threats here in Baghdad."[134] Arrowhead Brigade also served as the operational reserve for Multi-National Corps-Iraq.[135]

The re-positioning of forces within Baghdad began before the "Surge" brigades arrived. Dagger's headquarters took command of several units already stationed in that area when it arrived in November 2006, reconsolidated its task force, and prepared to move off the FOB.[136] Its first Joint Security Stations and Combat Outposts were in Ghazaliyah, a neighborhood in the Mansour district of western Baghdad. To improve Dagger Brigade's capacity, General Odierno reinforced the Dagger Brigade with battalions from the "Surge" brigades (before March 15).[137] As the JSSs and COPs were ready, Dagger's subordinate battalions then formally assumed responsibility for areas within the brigade's sector.[138] Dagger Brigade moved from west to east, disrupting al Qaeda's movement along Route Irish, the highway connecting Baghdad International Airport with the city center. (Route Irish was a major conduit for vehicle bombs from Fallujah and Abu Ghraib at that time.) Dagger Brigade cleared Ghazaliyah, just north of Route Irish. The brigade then moved from the residential neighborhoods north and east of Ghazaliyah.

Falcon (2nd Brigade of the 82nd Airborne Division) was the first fresh brigade to enter Baghdad as part of the troop increase, taking responsibility for the capital's Adhamiyah district. There, it patrolled the Sha'ab, Ur, and Baida neighborhoods on the northwestern borders of Sadr City. By the first week of March, 2/82nd ABN had established a Joint Security Station just inside Sadr City.[139] The arrival of the Falcon Brigade added between 2,700 and 3,000 troops to Baghdad, which, along with the Iraqi Army and police units, brought the total U.S. forces in the city above 35,000, and the total with Iraqi forces to between 90,000 and 112,000.[140]

The Dragon Brigade (4th Brigade Combat Team, First Infantry Division), arrived next, beginning operations in Iraq on March 1, 2007.[141] General Odierno and Major General Joseph Fil, commander of Multi-National Division-Baghdad, assigned the brigade to Baghdad's West and East Rashid Security Districts. Rashid has a population of about 700,000 and occupies an area the size of San Francisco. It contains Sunni neighborhoods, Shia neighborhoods, and a small neighborhood of Christians; the area was a focal point of the sectarian conflict in fall 2006.[142] By adding the Dragon Brigade, General Odierno effectively doubled the number of troops in Rashid between March and May.[143] The 4th Brigade of the 1st ID incorporated elements of seven different battalions, some of which were already stationed in Baghdad when it arrived, into Task Force Dragon, a formation of roughly 4,000 soldiers.[144]

Prime Minister Maliki ordered the deployment of three additional Iraqi Army brigades to Baghdad to support the operation. The Iraqi government drew units into Baghdad from the northern and western part of the country, rather than from the south (where only two Iraqi Army divisions were responsible for nine provinces), for the beginning of the Baghdad Security Plan. These forces supplemented the brigades of the 6th Iraqi Army division that had long been stationed in Baghdad.

During Operations Together Forward I and II in 2006, the three Iraqi brigades requested did not arrive in Baghdad. MNF-I examined the reasons for this failure and corrected many of them. Iraqi Army units successfully deployed to Baghdad for Operation Enforcing the Law in part because of increased capacities of the Iraqi government and improved deployment procedures. Iraqi soldiers received two weeks of training before they deployed, two weeks of training in Baghdad, combat pay, hazardous duty pay, and a fixed six-month term and end-date for their deployment. In previous operations, Iraqi soldiers had been offered none of these basic incentives or preparations. In addition, the Joint Security Stations provided them with proper housing facilities in Baghdad—something else that was lacking in the previous effort.[145]

Units from the Iraqi Army began to arrive in Baghdad from other parts of the country before Operation Enforcing the Law began. They included the 3rd Battalion, 1st Brigade of the 3rd Division from Al Kasik (outside the northern city of Mosul); the 4th Battalion, 1st Brigade of the 4th Division from Tikrit (north of Baghdad in Salah ad-Din province); and the 4th Brigade of the 1st Division from Habbaniyah (west of Baghdad in al Anbar province), all of which arrived with about 70 percent of their soldiers. Battalions from the 3rd Brigade, 4th Division from Suleimaniyah and Kirkuk (Kurdish units from northern Iraq) also arrived, the first at only 56 percent strength. The Iraqi Army also sent the 1st Brigade of the 2nd Division from Irbil (also a Kurdish unit).[146]

Operations against Shia Militias during the Baghdad Security Plan

The first moves of the Baghdad Security Plan aimed to reduce the capacity of Jaysh al Mahdi and Special Groups to perpetrate the sectarian cleansing and Shia expansion that characterized late 2006, without provoking a direct confrontation between U.S. forces and JAM.

U.S. operations in late 2006 had not targeted the Jaysh al Mahdi in its strongholds because the Iraqi government had declared Sadr City off-limits and instead had focused on fighting Sunni extremists in Sunni neighborhoods. The power relationships among Iraq's political leaders constrained the government's willingness to act. Prime Minister Nouri al Maliki had handled Moqtada al Sadr warily since coming into office in May 2006. Parliamentary politics caused some of Maliki's hesitations. Moqtada al Sadr and Abdul Aziz al Hakim, both leaders of important parliamentary blocs, helped to place the Prime Minister in power at the head of the United Iraqi Alliance, a Shiite bloc and the largest single grouping in the Iraqi parliament. The relative military strength of Sadr's Jaysh al Mahdi and Hakim's Badr Corps militias also constrained Maliki, whose Dawa Party did not have an armed wing. Both Sadr's and Hakim's militias could operate independently of Iraqi Army structures, and in a complicated interconnected manner with the Iraqi National Police, which they had heavily infiltrated. In addition, Sadrist ministers controlled several important service ministries, including Health, Agriculture, and Transportation, and used their patronage over these resources to support their party rather than the government.

The Surge empowered Maliki to oppose armed militias. On January 11, after President Bush announced the Surge but before the Baghdad Security Plan officially began, Prime Minister Maliki ordered leaders of the Shiite militias to disarm or face attack.[147] Maliki soon announced, "When military operations start in Baghdad, all other tracks will stop.... We gave the political side a great chance, and we have now to use the authority of the state to impose the law and tackle or confront people who break it."[148]

As early as January 14, some leaders of the Jaysh al Mahdi successfully ordered militia members not to wear their black uniforms, including face masks, or to carry their weapons.[149] They withdrew their checkpoints from certain neighborhoods, including Talbiyah (just outside Sadr City) and Hurriyah, where the Jaysh al Mahdi recently had displaced Sunni residents. Some people in civilian clothes nevertheless guided traffic.[150] Moqtada al Sadr ordered the Jaysh al Mahdi not to fight the Iraqi government or U.S. forces during the Islamic holy month of Muharram, establishing the first cease-fire agreement between his militia and the government.[151]

U.S. and Iraqi forces systematically removed "rogue" leaders of the Jaysh al Mahdi who did not respond to Sadr's orders not to fight, or who had engaged in criminality—such as leading kidnapping and execution rings—through their official positions. A spokesman for Prime Minister Maliki emphasized that Iraqi Security Forces could arrest any person who committed illegal acts, but that the government did not wish to fight the Jaysh al Mahdi.[152]

U.S. and Iraqi forces had killed or captured five Jaysh al Mahdi leaders by January 19, in a series of special operations aimed at the circle closest to Moqtada al Sadr. After midnight on Tuesday, January 16, U.S. and Iraqi forces killed or captured a high-level Jaysh al Mahdi figure in Sadr City.[153] At two o'clock in the morning on January 19, U.S. and Iraqi forces conducted a raid on a Shiite holy site in Baladiyat, on the east side of the Tigris. They captured and arrested Sheikh Abdul-Hadi al Darraji, Sadr's media chief in Baghdad, and a few of his associates.[154] Darraji allegedly had assassinated members of the Iraqi Security Forces and coordinated cells perpetrating sectarian violence against civilians.[155] On February 8, U.S. and Iraqi forces raided the Ministry of Health and arrested Hakim al Zamili, the Deputy Health Minister, a Sadrist and a Special Groups leader. He allegedly had diverted government funds to militias and provided the use of hospital facilities to perpetrate sectarian violence.[156] A few days earlier, U.S. and Iraqi forces killed the director of Moqtada al Sadr's political office in Baqubah, in Diyala Province, where al Qaeda and Jaysh al Mahdi had been conducting reprisal attacks against one another by terrorizing civilians.[157]

These precise military operations immediately changed the political dynamics within the Iraqi government. As operations targeted rogue JAM and Special Groups leaders, the Sadrist politicians responded by ending a boycott on attending parliament that they had begun in November 2006, when Prime Minister Maliki met with President Bush in Amman, Jordan. Without the thirty Sadrist members, Iraq's parliament had difficulty achieving the quorum of members necessary to meet and legislate.[158] Furthermore, the leader of Sadr City's neighborhood council promised that he and residents would cooperate with the Iraqi government's security plan.[159] Militia members in other Shiite neighborhoods of Baghdad, such as Shula, also reported that they had been ordered to put down all arms, hide them, and avoid confrontation.[160]

Some leading Sadrists, apparently fearing for their safety, left their homes. Some went from Baghdad to Najaf, and others headed for Syria and Iran, Prime Minister Maliki's office reported on January 31.[161] By the end of January, Moqtada al Sadr himself had left Iraq for Iran, either to ensure his safety, to seek assistance, or both.[162]

Any Jaysh al Mahdi member who continued to fight U.S. and Iraqi forces, contravening Moqtada al Sadr's orders not to do so, was considered a rogue member of the militia and was subject to arrest. Both Sadr and Hakim reiterated their support for the Baghdad Security Plan and their orders to their followers not to attack Sunnis or to resist Coalition Forces. This public support from the heads of the three major Shiite parties was a marked difference between Fardh al Qanoon and Operations Together Forward in 2006.

Operation Enforcing the Law Reaches Sadr City

Following the raids aimed at rogue Jaysh al Mahdi leaders and members of Special Groups, U.S. and Iraqi forces conducted a coordinated series of operations to reach Sadr City. These operations began in the first week of February and continued into March 2007. U.S. and Iraqi forces in Adhamiyah prepared the groundwork for entering Sadr City by securing the bordering neighborhoods of Shaab and Ur.[163]

Raids in the week preceding the announcement of the Baghdad Security Plan aimed to remove illegal weapons from Shaab and Ur and to detain suspected insurgents found there. Troops from the 5th Battalion, 20th Infantry Regiment (from the 2nd Infantry Division's 3rd Stryker Brigade Combat Team) conducted highly-focused raids on specific sites in Shaab where insurgents operated. They began by striking the homes of known insurgents. Troops then searched a nearby lot filled with abandoned cars. They discovered body armor and uniforms used by militia members to impersonate legitimate Iraqi Security Forces. They went on to a compound containing a factory and warehouses, to search for bomb-making materials. Finally, they went to a school nearby to gather additional information about the insurgents. Tips from local Iraqis had helped U.S. troops target these insurgents.[164]

A few days later, the Iraqi Police began to replace uniformed militiamen at the checkpoints in and out of Sadr City. The Iraqi Army also arrived in force on Sadr City's fringes.[165] Some U.S. and Iraqi troops began operating inside of Sadr City around this time.[166]

The Strykers of the 5th Battalion, 20th Infantry Regiment opened the way for broader operations by the newly arrived paratroopers from the Falcon brigade. During the first days of Fardh al Qanoon, paratroopers and Iraqi forces from COP Callahan met the residents of their area by going from door to door, introducing themselves, learning names, drinking tea with inhabitants, collecting business cards, and asking questions about the neighborhood.[167] A week later, these troops knocked on the doors of residents in Shaab and Ur and searched their homes.[168]

The U.S. and Iraqi Forces patrolling the neighborhoods thereby began to develop intelligence about locally-based insurgents. In Adhamiyah, forces captured an insurgent (linked to a vehicle bomb ring, so possibly associated with Sunni Islamic extremists) who had based himself in a hospital during the "knock-and-search" operations to avoid interrogation.[169]

While the house-to-house operations continued, U.S. and Iraqi forces also interdicted the flow of fighters and supplies through those neighborhoods into Sadr City. They managed vehicle checkpoints, for example, and searched cars passing through. Paratroopers at a new checkpoint in Shaab detained men driving through that neighborhood with the corpses of four executed victims in the trunk of their car.[170] Jaysh al Mahdi fighters in 2006 often buried their victims in pre-dug burial pits outside of Sadr City.[171]

Coalition and Iraqi forces then targeted Special Groups and rogue Jaysh al Mahdi in other Baghdad neighborhoods. For example, they secured the perimeter of the Barantha Mosque in Kadhimiyah, and Iraqi forces entered it and captured a large weapons cache used by militia groups.[172] Likewise, they captured rogue Jaysh al Mahdi leaders in the Karadah peninsula.[173]

During the last days of February and the first days of March, U.S. and Iraqi forces targeted important individuals who remained in Sadr City, arresting sixteen suspects, leaders and members of a rogue Jaysh al Mahdi cell or Special Group, whom they alleged organized sectarian kidnapping and execution.[174]

U.S. and Iraqi presence spread further into Sadr City from Forward Operating Base Loyalty on its eastern edge. The sector received two additional U.S. battalions and a new Iraqi Army unit, the 1-4-1 Infantry Battalion, which rotated into Baghdad from Fallujah. These Iraqi forces arrested a suspect who tried to pass through a joint U.S. and Iraqi checkpoint on the Zafaraniyah Freeway in Sadr City without inspection, by claiming that he was a member of the Jaysh al Mahdi, as, indeed, he apparently was.[175]

On March 4, 600 U.S. and 550 Iraqi forces, with armored vehicles, began to go house-to-house in the Jamil neighborhood in Sadr City, knocking on doors and speaking with residents. The soldiers came from several different brigades: elements of Falcon and Arrowhead Brigades, from the United States Army, and on the Iraqi side, the 8th Brigade, 2nd Iraqi National Police Division and the 3rd Battalion, 2nd Brigade, 10th Iraqi Army Division.[176] The initial clearing operations took several days, at the end of which U.S. and Iraqi forces established their fifteenth JSS, in Sadr City.[177]

The Maliki government's decision to press Shia militias combined with Sadr's first cease-fire order allowed the Coalition to make unprecedented progress against key accelerants of violence that had previously been off-limits. Operations in northeast Baghdad introduced U.S. forces into terrain which had been controlled by Shia militias in 2006.

Changing the Mission West of the Tigris

In northwest Baghdad, the change of mission to securing the population required commanders to undertake operations against both Shia and Sunni extremists. The push against militia groups there began almost immediately after the launch of Fardh al Qanoon.

Colonel J. B. Burton, the commander of Dagger Brigade, reconceived the brigade's mission: "When we came in, the mission statement that we were handed focused on the defeat of al Qaeda and associated movements. But when I was looking at the problem set with my staff, it became very apparent . . . that we had to stop the cycle of violence that was going on inside of northwest Baghdad. In order to do that, we had to stop the expansion of Shia extremism into the largely Sunni areas of the Mansour Beladiyah, and that includes Ghazaliyah, Khadra, Jamiya, Adl . . . . We had to stop Jaysh al Mahdi and their surrogates and the extremists that were operating under the banner of Jaysh al Mahdi and deny them access to the communities. Meanwhile, we had to defeat al Qaeda wholesale, across the board, we had to deny them freedom of action throughout the zone, to deny them access to the International Zone, the seat of government for the Government of Iraq, and we had to get them out of our town."[178]

Dagger Brigade began by clearing Ghazaliyah, significant terrain within Baghdad because it extends from the western border of the city, near Abu Ghraib, into the city center. The road through Ghazaliyah to Abu Ghraib, known as Alternate Supply Route Sword, runs to Fallujah, then an insurgent hotspot. Insurgents flowed along this route into Baghdad, making it an important Sunni insurgent support zone in Baghdad. In 2006, Sunni residents in Ghazaliyah, threatened by JAM expansion, turned to AQI for protection. Hence, by the winter of 2006-2007, Ghazaliyah was a major al Qaeda stronghold in western Baghdad. In January 2007, it became the site of the first COPs and JSSs in Baghdad.

As Dagger Brigade radiated into the neighborhood, U.S. forces discussed their objectives with the residents of Ghazaliyah to see how they could stop the spread of violence.[179] As a result of this dialogue, soldiers from the Dagger Brigade began constructing barrier walls along the northern edge of the neighborhood to stop the expansion of Shia extremists from Khadimiyah into Ghazaliyah.[180] The effects of the wall were immediate; the very next week, murders in Ghazaliyah were down 50 percent.[181] Moreover, residents began informing U.S. and Iraqi forces at the Joint Security Station in Ghazaliyah about large weapons caches in their neighborhood, which were subsequently secured. The neighborhood's high crime rate dropped significantly after the JSS became operational.[182]

Troops from the Dagger Brigade also conducted Operation Virginia Creeper, establishing more concrete barriers along ASR Sword on the southern edge of Ghazaliyah. According to J. B. Burton, "Those double barriers were designed to prevent al Qaeda and their surrogates from getting off the highway and driving back into the neighborhoods and rearming and refitting their associates so they could continue their campaign of violence against Coalition [Forces], ISF, and local nationals."[183]

In mid-March 2007, U.S. forces completed construction of JSS Thrasher in southern Ghazaliyah. Because Coalition Forces now had a foothold in Ghazaliyah, they launched operations to clear the neighborhood of al Qaeda elements in March 2007.[184] Troops from Arrowhead and Dagger Brigades worked together during Operation Arrowhead Strike 9, as the clearing operation was called, targeting AQI elements in Ghazaliyah and other neighborhoods of the Mansour security district. By May 1, 2007, Arrowhead Strike 9 was completed. In all, U.S. forces reduced 3,200 roadside bombs, captured 161 insurgents, forty-two of whom were placed in long-term detention, and seized "enough weapons and explosives to outfit an enemy infantry battalion."[185]

The operation to clear Mansour was the first in Baghdad to take advantage of the synergy between a U.S. brigade fully established in its Joint Security Stations, its partner unit in the Iraqi Army, and the clearing capabilities of the Stryker Brigade. Arrowhead Strike 9 became the model for subsequent clearing operations in urban terrain.

"[T]he battlespace owners and the landowning brigades . . . were an integral part of this operation; in fact, my clearing operations supported their efforts," reported Colonel Steve Townsend, commander of the Arrowhead Brigade.

"I provided them some additional . . . manpower to do some of these tasks that they find it difficult to do in large scale, so they have the forces they need to control the area. So my job is to help reduce the enemy activity in the area so they can then control it with their Iraqi security partners . . . . [W]hile we were doing our operations, the Dagger Brigade was doing things like clearing adjacent sectors and manning their checkpoints, running routine patrols, talking with the people, instituting civic action projects, building safe neighborhoods and markets, cleaning the streets . . . and working with their Iraqi partners. . . .

"[Arrowhead Strike 9] was successful primarily because of the superb integration with . . . our sister brigade, the Dagger Brigade. They were veterans in their area of operations. Previously, on some of these operations, we did clearance operations that were designed to introduce new forces into their zone—arriving forces that are part of the Surge, both Iraqi and U.S. So they . . . were less able to assist us because they were new to the area themselves. The Dagger Brigade are a bunch of veteran soldiers that have been operating in Mansour for a while, so they were very familiar with the ground. They helped us about as much as we helped them. This synergy, I think, helped make it much more successful.

"Additionally, the Iraqi security forces are much more prepared for this. They've got adequate forces in this sector now, and they were commanded by a very capable Iraqi army general named Major General Abdul Amir. He is the Karkh Area Command deputy commanding general, and he was the tactical commander for this operation. Both the Dagger Brigade commander and myself worked for General Abdul Amir, and he ran the operation, and we supported him throughout with his forces as well operating alongside of us."[186]

Colonel Burton described the enemy reaction to the changes in Dagger's area of operations: "While we were putting the JSSs in, I truly believe that our adversaries were in a reconnaissance mode. They're trying to figure out what we were doing....They didn't want to approach... in a frontal fight because they couldn't win that fight. But they needed to understand what we were doing, what our patterns were, and how they would get after us. And so in April and May after we completed the combined operations called Arrowhead Strike IX, I believe that al Qaeda and extremists Jaysh al Mahdi felt that that was the time that they could then take the fight to the Coalition. And they did. And they came after us hard in the principally Sunni areas of Ameriyah, south Ghazaliyah, Khadra, and Jamiya." These four neighborhoods were especially vulnerable to al Qaeda and to militias because they lacked standing police forces.

Violence spiked in May, as enemy groups targeted U.S. and Iraqi forces throughout the neighborhoods with improvised explosive devices. Indirect fire attacks also rose. At the same time, murders dropped precipitously because the spread of troops into the neighborhoods had dampened sectarian violence.[187]

Ameriyah became the site where the most intense fighting occurred, because the Islamic State of Iraq claimed it as a future headquarters. "[I]t got pretty ugly in there," remarked Colonel J. B. Burton. "We were having 750-pound bombs that were attacking our soldiers, deep-buried into the streets, very violent activity, a very hard-won fight, and the local nationals were passively supporting al Qaeda and their surrogates inside that neighborhood. The neighborhood was not closed off, the neighborhood had some gates and barriers around it, but you could still walk in and out whenever you wanted to. We went into an effort to isolate the entire community. A kidnapping took place against one of the leaders of Ameriyah's families, and that leader of Ameriyah said, 'That is enough. We have gone too far.'"[188]

A group of residents associated with the Islamic Army, a national-
ist insurgent group run by supporters of the former regime, contacted
Lieutenant Colonel Kuehl, the commander of the 1-5 Cavalry, the unit
responsible for southern Mansour Security District.[189] They informed
Colonel Kuehl that they would be fighting al Qaeda in Ameriyah, and
refused initial offers of U.S. assistance.[190] On Tuesday May 29, 2007, the
group publicly criticized al Qaeda's murder of innocent Sunni civilians at
a local mosque.[191] The next day, they posted another message condemn-
ing AQI on the wall of building and buried an improvised explosive
device (IED) nearby.[192] When AQI insurgents were dispatched to erase
the message, they were struck by the IED. This event sparked a days-long
battle between al Qaeda insurgents and the Islamic Army; during the
course of the week, members of the 1920s Revolution Brigade joined in
the fight against al Qaeda.[193]

As the battle continued, the residents of Ameriyah appealed again to
U.S. forces for weapons, ammunition, and medical aid. The U.S. forces,
in turn, approached an Iraqi Army commander, Brigadier General Ghas-
san, for authorization from the Iraqi Ministry of Defense to reinforce
the movement.[194] The Iraqi Security Forces provided ammunition for the
Baghdad Patriots, as the Ameriyah residents were initially called. They
continued the fight against AQI in coordination with U.S. and Iraqi
forces. According to Colonel J. B. Burton, "the Baghdad Patriots then
established a joint command and control center in southeast Ameriyah,
where Coalition Forces, [Iraqi Security Forces], and the volunteers came
together inside the walls of a mosque to coordinate actions against al
Qaeda [across] all of Ameriyah."[195] In the weeks that followed, U.S. forces
made an agreement with the residents that formalized the partnership and created rules that would require full partnership on all operations. The Forsan Al Rafidain, or Knights of the Two Rivers, as the group
became known, continued the fight against AQI in Ameriyah over the
next two months. Abu Abed, the leader of the Knights of Ameriyah and
a former officer in Saddam's Army, met daily with U.S. forces from the 1-5
Cavalry, coordinating all operations with them.[196]

Shaping Operations in Rasheed

Rasheed was one of the most violent areas in the capital, primarily due to its location in Baghdad, the sectarian composition of its population, and the complexity of the enemy systems in the district. The districts in northern Baghdad remained the main effort for clearing operations in spring 2007, and the limited number of U.S. troops in Rasheed diminished the efficacy of their efforts to roll up the enemy networks in southern Baghdad. Establishing U.S. forces in Rasheed, and then clearing the district, required months of preparation.

The Rasheed district, in southern Baghdad, lies east of the Baghdad International Airport and west of the Tigris River. It has a population of roughly 1.2 million and an area of about sixty square miles, making it Baghdad's largest district.[197]

The military units within Rasheed divided their battlespace into eastern and western sections, separated by Highway 8/Hillah Road (known as Route Jackson to U.S. troops). The division between West and East Rasheed generally corresponded with the disposition of enemy groups. Shia militia groups were deeply embedded in West Rasheed, particularly in Aamel and Bayaa, and Sunni extremists had strongholds in East Rasheed, particularly in Masafee, a sub-neighborhood of Dora. These groups competed for control of terrain in the district.

In January 2007, violence raged across Rasheed. Yet at that time, only three battalions were deployed in southern Baghdad. The 2-12 Infantry had just deployed to the troubled Aamel and Bayaa neighborhoods of West Rasheed. The 1-18 Mechanized Infantry was responsible for security in Saydiyah. The 1-14 Stryker Cavalry was responsible for all of East Rasheed, including Dora.

In East Rasheed, U.S. forces continued their efforts not only to target AQI insurgents in Dora, but also to disrupt their supply lines from the south. On February 23, 2007, the week following the launch of Operation Fardh al Qanoon in Baghdad, Coalition Forces engaged gunmen attempting to smuggle weapons by boat across the Tigris in southeastern Baghdad.[198] It is likely that these insurgents were carrying munitions and supplies from Arab Jabour, intended for Dora. Further south, in Hawr Rajab, soldiers from the 1-40 CAV and 5-4-6 IA conducted Operation Lion's Roar on February 27 to stem sectarian violence south of Baghdad.[199] During the operation, troops raided a number of buildings in the village and detained several insurgents.[200]

Given the paucity of forces and the precarious security situation in the district, Rasheed became one of the first priorities for the deployment of additional troops. On February 28, the 4th Brigade Combat Team (BCT), 1st Infantry Division (ID), led by Colonel Ricky Gibbs, arrived in Rasheed. The introduction of the Task Force Dragon brigade headquarters gave the district the increase in U.S. forces necessary to conduct the large-scale clearing operations called for under Fardh al Qanoon. By March, the 1-28 Infantry replaced the 2-12 Infantry in northwestern Rasheed; the 2-12 moved into Dora, along with the 1-4 Cavalry (RSTA), joining the 1-14 Stryker Cavalry already operating in the area. The 1-18 Mechanized Infantry remained responsible for Saydiyah. In addition, elements from the Iraqi National Police also operated in the battle space.[201]

Setting the Conditions for Clearing Rasheed

Despite all this, it took months for the Corps and Multi-National Division-Baghdad to concentrate enough combat power in Rasheed to begin clearing operations. Task Force Dragon had to establish its Joint Security Stations throughout the large district, which took time. During the month of March, Coalition Forces began to fan out into the neighborhoods of Rasheed, beginning construction on Joint Security Stations (JSSs) and Combat Outposts (COPs) throughout the district.[202] By March 22nd, soldiers from the 4th BCT, 1st ID had built four JSSs and five COPs across Rasheed, and planned four more COPs.[203] In an effort to secure and revive the Dora market, Coalition Forces also constructed hardened blast walls around the perimeter.[204] These barriers restricted traffic in and out, preventing extremist elements from infiltrating the area to conduct spectacular attacks on civilians. By March 31, when General David Petraeus visited the market, there were signs of improvement, as 141 of the 700 stores were open for business.[205]

In addition, the enemy groups had established themselves so thoroughly in Rasheed in 2006 that they could maintain intense attacks against U.S. and Iraqi forces spreading throughout the district. Some incidents in March help to characterize the intensity of the violence. On March 7, a car bomb detonated at a checkpoint, killing twelve NPs and ten civilians in the district, one day after a car bomb elsewhere in the district killed three.[206] An IED struck a combat patrol in Dora on March 13, killing one soldier with the 2-12 Infantry.[207] One week later, in northwestern Rasheed, another IED hit a combat patrol, killing two soldiers with the 1-28 Infantry. On March 24, a car bomb detonated at an Iraqi Police (IP) compound in Dora's Jazeera neighborhood, killing thirty-three IPs and wounding dozens more.[208] Days later, two car bombs detonated in the neighborhoods of Jihad and Bayaa, killing four IPs.[209] Still, Coalition and Iraqi Forces continued to target extremist elements in Rasheed, recovering eight large weapons caches and detaining numbers of suspected insurgents.[210]

In April, U.S. forces continued their push into the neighborhoods of Rasheed and their construction of COPs. They also increased the number of combat patrols. Again, in doing so, they made more frequent contact with the enemy. During April, ten Multi-National Division-Baghdad (MND-B) soldiers died in the Rasheed district alone, roughly one tenth of all U.S. casualties in Iraq during that month.[211] Most of these casualties occurred in Dora, where U.S. forces were preparing for a major clearing operation.

Violence in Rasheed also increased as Arrowhead Strike 9 unfolded in Mansour. The operations in northwest Baghdad pushed both Shia and Sunni enemy elements south into Rasheed. Sectarian violence increased. On April 15, two car bombs detonated in the district's Aeros market.[212] Days later in Bayaa, U.S. forces received small arms fire from

Shia extremists in a nearby mosque.[213] Aviation support was called in and two insurgents were killed as the firefight escalated.[214] Following the incident, a weapons cache was discovered in a house near the mosque.[215] On April 24, a bomb exploded at the Khudir al Janabi Sunni mosque in Bayaa, heavily damaging the building.[216] This attack was probably executed by Shia extremists, and in the weeks that followed, AQI stepped up its retaliatory attacks.[217]

In early May, after three months of shaping operations, U.S. forces began clearing operations in Rasheed, in what was to be the main effort for MND-B over the summer months. Operation Dragon Fire West/Arrowhead Strike 10, the first phase of these clearing operations, began on May 2, 2007. The 1-38 and 2-23 Stryker Infantry Battalions moved into East Rashid to reinforce Task Force Dragon during these operations, increasing troop density in Dora.[218] The operations netted some high value individuals and weapons. Early in the month, Iraqi Special Operations Forces, with Coalition advisers, captured five insurgents in the Aamel neighborhood, who were involved in death squad activity and VBIED construction.[219] From May 4 to May 9, Coalition Forces discovered three VBIEDs, including a large tanker truck bomb, an explosively-formed penetrator (EFP) construction site, and a cache containing EFP parts.[220] On May 16, another VBIED was discovered in the Bayaa neighborhood, following a suspicious vehicle report.[221] By the end of the month, Coalition Forces had cleared twenty-one mahallas, or small neighborhoods (similar to postal ZIP Code areas in U.S. cities), throughout West Rasheed.[222]

In late May, Operation Dragon Fire East expanded the aggressive clearing operations into East Rasheed. The operation's focus was Masafee, where al Qaeda had entrenched itself, fortifying its positions with deep-buried IEDs. Roughly 2,000 U.S. soldiers took part in Dragon Fire East, along with Iraqi forces from the 7th Brigade, 2nd National Police Division.[223] Coalition Forces actively targeted AQI networks across Dora. On May 23 and 24, U.S. and Iraqi soldiers discovered eighteen IEDs in the area, due in large part to tips from residents.[224] By June 1, over 170 weapons caches had been recovered and more than 100 individuals had been detained.[225]

By the end of May, murders and sectarian violence in Rasheed were declining, although violence against Coalition Forces had increased because of the density of U.S. forces in Rasheed and their mission to clear some of the worst neighborhoods in the capital.[226] In May, eighteen U.S. soldiers were killed clearing enemy strongholds across the Rasheed district, and many more were injured.[227]

Although violence between Shia and Sunni extremists was declining, these enemy groups continued their efforts to incite sectarian violence. Shia militias targeted on a number of Sunni mosques in West Rasheed during the month of May; on May 30, they destroyed the Omar al Farooq mosque in Risalah, probably in retaliation for an AQI car bomb that detonated the day before at a Shia mosque in Aamel.[228] The Omar al Farooq mosque was one of the last Sunni mosques in West Rasheed; its destruction had the practical consequence of rendering the district less habitable for Sunni.[229]

Jaysh al Mahdi Fractures

The operations at the beginning of Fardh al Qanoon harmed al Qaeda in Iraq, but its position in the belts enabled the organization to maintain and reinforce its car bomb campaign. The effect of the operations on Jaysh al Mahdi was more immediate and profound.

Moqtada al Sadr's decision in early 2007 not to oppose the Baghdad Security Plan, and to declare a truce between the Jaysh al Mahdi and the Iraqi Security Forces, meant that those rogue militia groups that continued to fight were not protected by the aegis of al Sadr. For the first time in the various operations to secure Baghdad, including the failed Operations Together Forward I and II, Iraqi Security Forces had the full support of the Iraqi government to remove violent Shia actors that continued to operate outside of the legitimate Iraqi Security Forces. As the loyal elements of Moqtada al Sadr's army put down their arms, these rogue elements became more vulnerable to targeting by Coalition and Iraqi Security Forces.

The decision by Moqtada al Sadr to leave for Iran at the start of the Baghdad Security Plan was controversial, as Shia militia groups had to determine how to respond to Sadr's absence and what goals to pursue. Tensions existed not only between the Jaysh al Mahdi and the Iraqi Security Forces, but also within the Jaysh al Mahdi itself, between those affiliated with Special Groups and those who were not. Moqtada al Sadr's departure and the variations in funding, supply, and training created fractures within the Jaysh al Mahdi organization.

Those Special Groups that received funding, training, supply, and backing from the Iranian Revolutionary Guards Corps-Qods Force maintained their campaign against U.S. forces and against the Government of Iraq. They did so through the use of explosively-formed penetrators (EFPs) and indirect fire attacks on government and Coalition sites. From April to June 2007, the number of indirect mortar and rocket attacks—tactics used by these groups—increased.

The ability of Jaysh al Mahdi to function as a cohesive organization in Baghdad decreased dramatically by May 2007. Between February and May, JAM fractured into multiple groups. Some elements of JAM concentrated efforts on gaining control of the Shia provinces south of Baghdad, a fight that would ultimately have important ramifications within the capital.

The move south was in part a matter of timing. Moqtada al Sadr's truce coincided not only with the start Baghdad Security Plan but also with the Shia holy month that extends from Ashura to Arbaeen. During this forty-day period, which in 2007 ran from the end of January to March, it is customary for Iraqi Shia to make pilgrimages to Shia holy sites, particularly in Karbala. As Sadr announced his truce and the Baghdad Security Plan began, many Shia were leaving Baghdad for Karbala or the homes of their relatives in the southern Iraq for the solemn holiday celebration. In addition, some Shia militia groups within Baghdad left the city because of the increased presence of U.S. forces, moving south to regroup and return later in 2007.

Individuals and groups reestablished their network of connections in the five-city area to the south of Baghdad. These five cities—Najaf, Karbala, Hillah, Diwaniyah, and Al Kut—are situated roughly halfway between Baghdad and the southernmost provinces of Iraq. The 8th Iraqi Army Division, commanded in 2007 by General Oothman, was stationed in Diwaniyah and had responsibility for the entire five-city area. Very few U.S. forces were present in this area either before or during the 2007 Surge.

As the Jaysh al Mahdi and Special Groups migrated southward during the Arbaeen period, violence increased, particularly in Diwaniyah. The violence that erupted in Diwaniyah in March and April 2007 was not sectarian, as the area is overwhelming Shia. Rather, it was a political contest for control of the city and, indeed, the entire province. The main actors in the struggle were the Jaysh al Mahdi and the 8th Iraqi Army Division.

The Jaysh al Mahdi did not have a large presence in Qadisiyah Province. Its political wing, the Office of the Martyr Sadr, had a headquarters in the city. The leading JAM commander in Diwaniyah was Kifah al Qureity, who arranged high-profile attacks in the city in August 2006. He was detained by U.S. and Iraqi forces in October of that year, but subsequently released; he was evidently a driving force behind JAM's campaign to control the city center, beginning in that time period.[230] During that time, Jaysh al Mahdi militia groups in Diwaniyah conducted violent attacks against the population in order to establish safe havens. In a city of some 400,000 people, this presented a serious security challenge for the 8th Iraqi Army Division, as well as a political challenge to the Government of Iraq in Baghdad and the provincial government in Qadisiyah.

The political fight was further complicated by the fact that the governor of Qadisiyah Province was a member of the Islamic Supreme Council in Iraq (ISCI), the main Shia rival of the Sadrists. ISCI is the political party that makes up the other large portion of the United Iraqi Alliance, the main Shia bloc within parliament. The leader of ISCI was Abdul Aziz al Hakim, and the political leader of ISCI was Adel Mehdi. Hence, Qadisiyah Province was politically aligned with the ISCI party and not with the Jaysh al Mahdi. The campaign of the Jaysh al Mahdi in the five-cities area was also driven by the fact that some of the soldiers within the 8th Iraqi Army Division were associated with the Badr Corps, the militia of ISCI. These Badr Corps units had been incorporated into the legitimate Iraqi Security Forces as part of the effort to disarm illegal militias and set up an Iraqi Security Force that was responsive to the central government. While the commanders of the 8th Iraqi Army Division showed strength, professionalism, and a connection to Baghdad, the soldiers who were members of the Badr Corps intensified the violence against Jaysh al Mahdi in retaliation for their aggressive campaign to expand into Diwaniyah.

One reporter described the situation in Diwaniyah as the Baghdad Security Plan began. "In the city of Ad Diwaniyah, 80 miles south of Baghdad, a fragile truce had held between Badr and Mahdi fighters since last August, when heavy clashes left dozens dead. Then in March, militiamen from the capital began to join up with a local Mahdi commander named Kifah al Qureity. Emboldened, Qureity turned his guns on the local government, run by SCIRI officials, and on Coalition Forces. (Locals in Ad Diwaniyah say he rallied his new forces, some 400 strong, while wearing a suicide vest.)"[231]

The battle that erupted is best characterized as a fight between rogue elements of JAM and the legitimate Iraqi government forces in Diwaniyah. The 8th Iraqi Army Division, commanded by General Oothman Ali Farhood, contested the attempt of rogue Jaysh al Mahdi to control the city. He modeled his campaign against Jaysh al Mahdi insurgents within Diwaniyah on operations underway during Fardh al Qanoon, which was unfolding from February to April 2007. In order to undertake operations against the Jaysh al Mahdi in Diwaniyah, General Oothman requested and received additional support from Coalition Forces. The 1-14 Stryker Cavalry Battalion, which acted as the theater-wide reserve and had previously worked to clear northeast Baghdad, deployed to Diwaniyah to assist in the fight. In response to these operations, Jaysh al Mahdi launched indirect fire attacks against the 8th Iraqi Army Division Headquarters and also against their Coalition counterparts, the Polish division which operated in Multi-National Division-Center South. Mortars were most commonly used in these attacks. The Jaysh al Mahdi also attempted to establish positions within the city during this time.

General Oothman launched Operation Black Eagle on April 6, 2007, supported by the 4th Brigade Combat Team, 25th Infantry Division.[232] He aimed to clear and hold a portion of the city during this multi-week counteroffensive. He launched the next phase of Black Eagle on June 4, while troops from the Polish Division conducted a supporting operation in Kut.[233] During this operation, the 8th Iraqi Army Division raided a market in search of two individuals known to be militia leaders and wanted by Coalition Forces. His efforts yielded the capture of one as well as the successful identification of weapons caches.[234]

Black Eagle was only a partial success. There were insufficient numbers of Iraqi and Coalition Forces to hold more than a few neighborhoods of Diwaniyah against the Jaysh al Mahdi, which consequently maintained a presence in Diwaniyah and escalated its political fight with the ISCI groups for control of the five-city area.[235]

The effects of JAM's fracture and the fight in Diwaniyah rippled into the fight in northwest Baghdad that transpired from April to June 2007. In April and May, Najaf-based elements of the Jaysh al Mahdi also returned to Baghdad, calling themselves the "Golden Mahdi Army" and establishing themselves as a counterweight to units of rogue JAM present in the area. This movement from Najaf into Baghdad seemed to be an attempt by the Najaf portion of the organization to purge the movement of leaders and members who were not responsive to Moqtada al Sadr.[236] Violence between local elements of Jaysh al Mahdi and the elements of JAM arriving from Najaf increased. This friction was particularly evident in northwest Baghdad, where different factions of Jaysh al Mahdi battled for control of terrain. There, a pragmatic group calling themselves the "noble" faction worked to reduce violence and to collaborate with U.S. troops. Special Groups also contested northwest because they sought to establish a perimeter around the Kadhimiyah shrine.[237] Control of the shrine was desirable. It was the holiest Shia shrine in Baghdad and an important source of revenue for whoever controlled it. The area around the Kadhimiyah shrine was affluent and considered valuable real estate for the Shia community; this created social, financial, and religious incentives for these different factions to insert their power and their influence.

The dispersal of militia members from Baghdad and Diwaniyah, and the attempt to regain control of Baghdad from Najaf, demonstrated the fracture within the Jaysh al Mahdi created by Moqtada al Sadr's cease-fire. The legitimate Iraqi Security Forces fought the Jaysh al Mahdi. Rivalries between the Jaysh al Mahdi and Special Groups intensified. Away in Iran and lacking firm control of his militias, Moqtada al Sadr lost his ability to participate forcefully in Iraqi politics.

Chapter 3
■ ■ ■ Anbar Awakens

For Americans, the war's most important events from August to December 2006 occurred in Baghdad. For al Qaeda and other Sunni Islamic extremist enemies in Iraq, equally important events in that period occurred in Ramadi, the capital city of Anbar Province. Al Qaeda terrorism provoked many of Anbar's sheikhs actively to cooperate with U.S. Forces, oppose all terrorists in the province, support the Iraqi Police and Army, form an effective city government, and strengthen the provincial council. The sheikhs called their movement "the Awakening." The hostility of the local population changed Ramadi from an al Qaeda stronghold into an area effectively contested by U.S. and Iraqi forces.

The presence of U.S. forces conducting counterinsurgency missions to secure the population made the local rejection of al Qaeda possible and effective. The leadership and example of the sheikhs of Ramadi inspired sheikhs in neighboring cities to cooperate with U.S. and Iraqi forces. As a result of their efforts, especially in late 2006 and early 2007, al Qaeda no longer controlled Ramadi or Fallujah. By February 2007, U.S. and Iraqi forces were pushing the enemy from other cities in the province. U.S. forces conducted deliberate counterinsurgency operations to secure the population from terrorism. Together with the Iraqi Security Forces, they cleared, controlled, and retained cities in the Euphrates River Valley. U.S. forces exploited opportunities created by the enemy and by the local population.

Cooperation among U.S. forces, Iraqi Security Forces, and many of Anbar's sheikhs deprived the terrorist organization of its most secure base in Iraq. As U.S. and Iraqi efforts to clear, control, and retain Baghdad and the cities of Anbar progressed, al Qaeda faced the choices available to any hard-pressed enemy, conventional or unconventional: surrender, counterattack, or move operations elsewhere. Al Qaeda pursued two policies in February and March 2007: counterattacking in Baghdad and Ramadi, and shifting and moving its bases elsewhere in theater. Al Qaeda lashed out at specific targets in Ramadi and Fallujah in order to attempt to win back their bases in the western part of Anbar Province.

Al Qaeda's attacks, including suicide bombs and car bombs, did not aim at random targets. Often these spectacular attacks occurred against very specific targets and conveyed very specific messages. Al Qaeda was trying to disrupt U.S. and Iraqi preparations for decisive operations in Baghdad, and to escalate the conflict by inciting sectarian violence in and around the capital. The organization also attempted to dissuade the population of the Euphrates River Valley from participating in the Awakening. Al Qaeda used bases in western Baghdad in order to foment violence against Shiite and mixed neighborhoods, and in order to link the violence in Fallujah with that in Baghdad. Some al Qaeda and Sunni extremists regrouped in Tarmiyah just north of Baghdad and in neighboring Diyala Province. From there, the enemy launched attacks to incite sectarian violence and undermine the ongoing security plan.

Anbar: From Decisive Operations to Shaping Operations

Military doctrine distinguishes between decisive operations and shaping operations. Decisive operations directly accomplish the objectives set by a headquarters.[238] Securing Baghdad was the decisive operation planned in 2007. At the same time, extensive shaping operations occurred in Anbar and Diyala provinces in the first quarter of 2007. Shaping operations "create and preserve conditions for the success of the decisive operation . . . . They support the decisive operation by affecting enemy capabilities and forces, or by influencing enemy decisions . . . . They may occur before, concurrently with, or after the start of the decisive operation."[239]

Many decisive U.S. operations had taken place in Anbar Province, to the west of Baghdad. In 2004, U.S. forces conducted decisive operations in Fallujah, where the Sunni Arab insurgency had emerged in summer of 2003. U.S. Marines besieged the city for six weeks from March to May 2004. At that time, U.S. forces turned control of Fallujah over to its local leaders, who used the opportunity to develop a broader-based insurgency in the city. They colluded with Abu Musab al Zarqawi, then the leader of al Qaeda in Iraq, who established his headquarters in Fallujah and used the city as a base for exporting violence to other areas of Iraq. In November and December 2004, U.S. Marines again attacked the city, clearing it of insurgents.[240]

Zarqawi and the core al Qaeda leadership escaped from Fallujah before the November 2004 attack, organized the Samarra Mosque bombing in February 2006, and provoked the sectarian violence that escalated afterwards. Ultimately, some of that leadership, including Zarqawi, based itself near Baqubah, in Diyala Province, to the north of Baghdad and northeast of Fallujah. Other al Qaeda leaders and operatives relocated themselves locally in Anbar Province, across the Euphrates River in the city of Ramadi, to the west of Fallujah. Many local leaders supported al Qaeda elements, and the insurgency in Anbar province resumed forcefully in the spring of 2006.

As the violence in Baghdad increased in 2006, U.S. forces shifted decisive operations from the provinces to the capital. By summer 2006, Anbar was no longer the main effort. Rather, U.S. units in Anbar conducted shaping operations to support the main effort in Baghdad.[241]

Operations in Anbar province in late 2006 and 2007 shaped events throughout the theater. Ramadi turned increasingly hostile to al Qaeda and its post-Zarqawi offshoot, the Islamic State of Iraq. The Anbar Awakening created the precedent for American forces engaging with tribal leaders in order to clear and control terrain throughout central Iraq.

Terrain and Communications in Anbar Province

Anbar Province stretches west of Baghdad to Iraq's borders with Syria and Jordan. Foreign fighters flowed from those borders toward Baghdad prior to 2007. The lush Euphrates River Valley constitutes the province's main line of communication. Numerous cities and settlements line the river, which flows across the province through the cities of Al Qaim, Rawah, Haditha, Hit, Ramadi, Habbaniyah, and Fallujah.

Some of these cities are hubs for the road network in Anbar, which foreign fighters used to traverse Iraq in 2006 and earlier. Roads from Syria, running along the south bank of the Euphrates, converge in the town of Al Qaim, about twenty-five miles east of the border. Haditha is the next major town along the route for foreign fighters, who then then followed roads through Hit and Ramadi, the next choke-point along the road network. From Ramadi, they could continue to Fallujah, from which roads lead east to Baghdad, or travel southeast to Amiriyah, Yusifiyah, and Mahmudiyah on the southern outskirts of the capital.

Foreign fighters could bypass the Euphrates routes by crossing the sparsely inhabited Syrian Desert south of the river, following a few main roads that ultimately lead to the vicinity of Baghdad. Major roads from the Jordanian and Syrian borders converge at the desert town of Rutbah (about 250 miles west of the capital). Fighters and facilitators could also bypass towns like Rutbah, Hit, Haditha, and Al Qaim by taking the numerous desert roads that defy effective blockade.

These desert lines of communication linked the major towns of the western Euphrates with the cities of northern Iraq in which former Baathist regime elements and al Qaeda operated. Former Baathists, including the sons of Saddam Hussein, based out of Mosul in 2003; Saddam Hussein was captured near his hometown of Tikrit; Tall Afar became an al Qaeda safe haven in late 2004 and was cleared of insurgents in 2005-2006; al Qaeda manipulated the oil supply at Bayji refinery to finance the insurgency.

The river valley was well-supplied with weapons. During Saddam Hussein's regime, Habbaniyah Airfield and the former Republican Guard compound east of Fallujah, which lie more or less on the Euphrates River, were stocked with munitions. One can only speculate about how much explosive material was stolen from these facilities before the Coalition brought them under its control.

Al Qaeda in Iraq relied on the extensive infrastructure that the organization had developed along the Euphrates. Foreign fighters crossed the border unarmed, evading arrest. They then proceeded along the cities of the Euphrates to rural training camps or staging areas, such as those near As Zaidon (southeast of Fallujah), Karmah (toward Lake Tharthar),[242] or Wadi Sakron (near Barwanah in the Haditha Triad).[243] Insurgents supplied trained fighters from large weapons caches in the Euphrates River Valley. For example, in December 2006, U.S. Marines discovered two huge caches near the Euphrates containing a wide variety of munitions and command-and-control devices, including a surface-to-air missile and launcher, radios, grenade fuses, cell phones and chargers, thousands of link rounds, binoculars, and mortar sights.[244] Such caches served as warehouses from which insurgents drew weapons, bringing them to smaller bases and hiding them in local caches to carry out attacks.

Fallujah was still a staging area for attacks on Baghdad in March 2007, when U.S. forces captured or killed al Qaeda operatives in Abu Ghraib, the last stop on the road between Anbar and the capital.

The Significance of Ramadi for al Qaeda

Ramadi (population approximately 400,000) is the capital city of Anbar Province, housing its provincial government offices and two-thirds of the province's population.[245] Ramadi is a predominantly Sunni city in a predominantly Sunni province. Members of one major tribe, the Dulaimi, account for most of the population. (The Dulaimi tribe also extends in an arc from Anbar to Salah ad-Din .) Locals belong to different subtribes of the Dulaimi. Ramadi and Anbar province escaped much of the sectarian violence that characterized Baghdad and Baqubah in 2006.

Nevertheless, Ramadi was violent. From June 2006 to March 2007, one U.S. BCT controlled not only Ramadi but also a large area beyond the city extending "along the western shores of the three large lakes to the west to the capital . . . about a hundred miles north to south, about 85 miles east to west."[246]

Several enemy groups operated in Ramadi in summer 2006. Foreign fighters in Ramadi represented a small but important segment of the enemy, including nearly all of its suicide bombers. "Local AQ sympathizers" were "relatively small in number . . . but . . . a very lethal part of the insurgency." Most enemies rejected the government in Baghdad and aided the insurgency for that reason; others opportunistically engaged in criminal activities that lack of government permitted.[247] Locals harmed by al Qaeda organized retaliatory attacks against the enemy.[248]

By summer 2006, al Qaeda and other insurgents prevented government from functioning in Ramadi. Colonel Sean MacFarland, commander of the 1st BCT, 1st Armored Division, stationed there, remarked in July 2006, "About a dozen buildings around the government center have become really little more than shells of buildings and don't serve any purpose other than to hide snipers and IED triggermen."[249] Government workers did not come to work regularly. Insurgents maintained sniper fire at the government compound, despite its fortifications and U.S. Marine guard. By August 2006, the province's governor, Maamoun Sami Rashid al Awani, had evaded thirty attempts on his life. Insurgents had killed four members of the Anbar Provincial Council over the summer. Colonel MacFarland referred to al Awani as "a government of one."[250] When Al Qaeda moved into Ramadi, it disrupted the local population and increased residents' antipathy for government. "They intimidated, through murder and other acts of violence, the people of Ramadi and forced them into their homes, away from their places of employment, and really have turned Ramadi into a battleground."[251]

Mission: Clearing Ramadi in 2006

The 1st Brigade, 1AD and other units conducted successful counterinsurgency operations in Ramadi from June 2006 to February 2007.
According to Col. MacFarland, the brigade commander, the mission of
the 1st BCT, 1st Armored Division when it arrived on June 11, 2006 was "to
partner with the Iraqi security forces and to conduct combined counterinsurgency operations to neutralize the enemy and to set the conditions for the transfer of security operations to the Iraqi security forces,
and also to support the transfer of governance to provincial control . . .
in Al Anbar, Ramadi being the capital of the province." To do so, he identified four key tasks: 1) form the BCT into a coherent team; 2) "set the
conditions for victory, first by isolating Ramadi from enemy resupply
and reinforcements" and second by preparing "the Iraqi security forces
for the challenges ahead"; 3) "fight the enemy"; 4) "consolidate . . . gains,"
especially by building the Iraqi Army and Police.[252]

The operational concept behind the counterinsurgency effort in
Ramadi became the model for Operation Fardh al Qanoon, a modified
"inkblot" approach to clearing, controlling, and retaining a hostile city. In
June 2006, U.S. forces established control over the entry points along the
roads into the city and "five new . . . Combat Outposts (COPs) and patrol
bases in and around the city." They moved from their Forward Operating
Base (FOB) into the COPs, clearing and holding neighborhoods as they
went.[253] Controlling access was important not only to prevent insurgents
from moving through Ramadi, but also because insurgents based themselves in the suburbs of Ramadi, from which they orchestrated attacks
into the city.[254] Al Qaeda facilitators in Ramadi also helped operatives
stage attacks in nearby cities. One such terrorist provided money, weapons, and propaganda to organize and publicize an October 2006 suicide
car-bombing in Habbaniyah.[255]

Four weeks into the operation, Colonel MacFarland reported,
"These [COPs] have had a very disruptive effect on the enemy. Most

importantly, though, it's given us the opportunity to engage the people of Ramadi . . . . And we've established real relationships with the people in parts of the city that we hadn't been able to in the past." He noted that progress was slow, and that the population's feeling toward "these Combat Outposts has been changing from hostile to neutral and neutral to good, but in some places it's moving faster than others. It's a process, and it's going in the right direction, but we still have a way to go."[256]

Residents helped Coalition and Iraqi forces develop intelligence about the enemy: "Once people . . . near these new Combat Outposts and patrol bases understand that the Iraqi security forces are there to stay and they're not just sweeping through the neighborhoods, they begin to open up a little bit more and provide us . . . with intelligence, and they start to talk to us about their concerns, their needs and their desires that we can then address" during the build phase.[257]

The transition to provincial control presupposed the existence of Iraqi Security Forces to maintain security in the area once it was achieved. Few Anbaris, however, joined the Iraqi Police and Iraqi Army in the first half of 2006, deterred largely by al Qaeda's destruction of every police station in Ramadi on the same day early in that year.[258] Monthly recruiting consequently slowed to a trickle. March 2006 saw no new recruits; twenty or thirty volunteered in each of the summer months.[259] In August, Ramadi had only 300 policemen of the 3,000 that the Iraqi government authorized.[260] After months of violence and counterinsurgency operations in Ramadi, a major effort throughout the Euphrates River Valley produced 950 new recruits in August. They began their training on August 21, 2006.[261]

The Turning Point

On that same day, al Qaeda operatives assassinated Sheikh Abu Ali Jassim, who had encouraged many of his tribesmen to join the police forces. They further angered local tribesmen and sheikhs by hiding the body in a field, rather than returning the corpse for swift burial as prescribed.[262] Al Qaeda had committed a serious error. In retrospect, U.S. commanders recognized the assassination as a turning point leading to the organization of an "Awakening" in Ramadi. By early October, eleven sheikhs participated in the movement.[263]

In late September, tribal leaders demanded that Prime Minister Maliki recognize Iraq as an Arab state, fairly distribute oil revenues, and release political prisoners.[264] They also demanded that the U.S. withdraw its forces. The government of Iraq offered, instead, to consider ways for Sunni Baathists who had not engaged in terrorism to return to government posts, which their past allegiances legally prevented them from holding.[265]

U.S. forces, local civilians, and al Qaeda each responded to the others' actions and pursued their own objectives. The situation in Ramadi changed gradually at first. At the end of October, insurgents led a demonstration in Ramadi proclaiming the Islamic State of Iraq and aiming to recreate the Islamic caliphate.[266] The Islamic State of Iraq emerged from al Qaeda elements after the death of Zarqawi. The group established councils to impose its extreme interpretation of Shariah, or Islamic law, on the local population, and used terrorist tactics to compel the local population to obey. The determination of the Islamic State of Iraq to enforce a radical interpretation of Islamic law, and to use terrorist tactics to enforce compliance, induced more sheikhs to oppose the insurgency and to join the Awakening.[267]

As the sheikhs organized themselves and their populations in the fall, U.S. and Iraqi forces conducted a variety of counterinsurgency operations to oust insurgents from Ramadi. First, they conducted targeted raids against high-value targets. The Tamin neighborhood, in the west of Ramadi, posed particularly grave challenges. U.S. forces killed a significant facilitator and, in October, captured members of a terrorist ring responsible for the production of car bombs.[268] In subsequent operations, a precision airstrike killed an emir (military commander) in eastern Ramadi,[269] and Coalition Forces raided an al Qaeda meeting place and captured forty-eight suspects.[270] At the end of October, U.S. and Iraqi forces established a Security Station in central Ramadi, bringing the total number of new fortified positions in the city to eight.[271]

The establishment of this security station apparently enabled U.S. forces to achieve an objective planned since July, namely, demolishing damaged buildings, many of which harbored terrorists, around the government center. The goal was "accelerating the urban renewal and rejuvenation of Ramadi."[272] Destroying and rebuilding the government center was a necessary prerequisite for establishing provincial government, by making it safe for employees to work downtown in the provincial capital.

Coalition Forces fought to clear the government center for at least three months. In early October, terrorists still controlled the center of Ramadi and prevented employees from coming to work.[273] By November, U.S. forces controlled the area to their satisfaction. They demolished the wrecked buildings and hauled away millions of tons of rubble, leaving room for a new common area for Ramadi's citizens.[274] Reconstruction of the area began on November 18, 2006, when Anbar's deputy governor and a Coalition Civil Affairs Team began to repair a broken water pump that had caused flooding. Every day, Iraqi Army units searched and secured the repair workers and their equipment.[275]

In November, December, and January, sheikhs in Ramadi urged their own tribesmen to join the Iraqi Police, and four hundred did so in November.[276] A thousand recruits joined in December[277] and approximately 800 in January. A subsequent recruiting drive in Anbar generated 2,000 volunteers.[278] Recruits received their training at a police academy in Jordan.[279] U.S. forces enhanced their recruiting and retention of Iraqi Security Forces in Anbar by providing them with pay and supplies, which they did not receive from the central government. Though the government provided far less funding than needed, al Qaeda diverted much of the money that Baghdad did disperse.[280]

Retaining the recruits posed special challenges. A basic literacy requirement rendered only 50 percent of applicants qualified for the job.[281] U.S. and Iraqi forces set up a literacy program in Ramadi in spring 2007 to educate recruits who initially had been rejected.[282] Recruits also needed to meet certain medical standards.[283] They were vetted to ensure that they had not participated in recent insurgent activity or retained ties to the Baath Party.[284]

The Iraqi Army, meanwhile, worked alongside U.S. forces and gradually took on greater responsibilities in the city.[285] Together, they took a census in Ramadi, one neighborhood at a time.[286] The census was critical to the counterinsurgency effort because it enabled U.S. and Iraqi forces to issue identification cards that would distinguish between residents of Ramadi and the transient population.

Coalition Forces worked creatively to spread legitimate government authority in Anbar, and to connect cities with neighboring towns and villages. For example, the danger of traversing roads from villages to Ramadi prevented some nearby towns from supplying recruits for local police forces. Consequently, these towns did not have police forces. In January, U.S. Marines transported forty applicants along the Euphrates River so that they could join the police. Recruits trained for six weeks, and then returned to their home town for duty, increasing security in and around Ramadi.[287]

Enemy Reaction to the Awakening and Counterinsurgency Operations

As U.S. and Iraqi forces moved into Ramadi's government center in November, al Qaeda tenaciously defended its territory in the city's northern and northeastern sectors, including Tamin, Sofia, and Hamaniyah. As counterinsurgency operations continued, the enemy also vigorously counterattacked, targeting Iraqi Security Forces, Coalition Forces, and Ramadi's civilians.

Al Qaeda launched a campaign targeting the Iraqi Police in Ramadi, in order to deter further recruiting efforts, as well as the Iraqi Security Forces as they took responsibility for new missions. The enemy engaged in coordinated and repeated attempts to attack one tribe, which were repelled at a checkpoint first by Iraqi, then by U.S. forces.[288] To hurt recruitment efforts, they kidnapped and murdered policemen,[289] attacked police stations,[290] and, in northern Ramadi, murdered a policeman and killed or wounded members of his family in their home.[291]

U.S. and Iraqi Forces Continue to Clear and Retain Ramadi

U.S. and Iraqi forces nevertheless continued to sweep neighborhoods in north-central Ramadi. Operations throughout December cleared weapons caches from central Ramadi and from terrain to its north and east.[292] Four new tribes joined the Awakening after this clearing operation.[293] U.S. and Iraqi Forces also secured government buildings once occupied by terrorists, and constructed police stations from which they could routinely patrol the city.[294]

By early January, they had moved into the violent Tameem neighborhood and established a police station.[295] By the middle of the month, Iraqi forces manned fourteen police stations through Ramadi, and eight more were planned so that the newly trained recruits could work in the city.[296] Next, they constructed a station in Ramadi's Sofia district, which U.S. forces had cleared in December.[297] Beginning in January 2007, the Mayor of Ramadi, police chiefs, and U.S. forces met routinely to coordinate the large police force and to plan future security operations.[298]

The dramatically expanded Iraqi Police Force discovered numerous weapons caches in January and February, citizens' tips and foot patrols having provided them with intelligence about the locations. The average number of discovered caches rose to two each day, instead of two each week. One large cache in eastern Ramadi, containing 300 mortar rounds, represented approximately six months' supply of that ammunition at the enemy's average pace of one to two rounds per day. The Iraqi Police discovered 300 more rounds that month in various caches.[299] In January, police recruits finished their training at the

Phoenix Academy in Camp Ramadi. Construction began in March for a large police training facility in Habbaniyah, which became operational in summer 2007.

Exploiting Success in Ramadi: U.S. and Iraqi Forces Expand Operations in the Euphrates Valley

While some U.S. forces cleared Ramadi, others interdicted insurgents in the areas north and west of the city. In December, U.S. and Iraqi Security Forces began also to roust al Qaeda from the Haditha Triad (consisting of three adjoining cities, Haditha, Barwanah, and Haqlaniyah).[300] Most importantly, U.S. and Iraqi forces took control of the Euphrates River itself. They trained Iraqi Police to patrol the river by boat, denying the enemy freedom of movement along that major line of communication.

Enemy Reaction to the Anbar Awakening: The First Chlorine Gas Attacks

In the first months of 2007, al Qaeda attempted to use chemical weapons against Iraqi civilians. The first known attempt to detonate a vehicle bomb with chlorine gas occurred in Ramadi on January 28. The explosion killed sixteen people, though the chlorine gas apparently did not cause any of the casualties.[301] The first attempted chlorine bomb attack apparently aimed to kill and terrorize police and recruits, consistent with al Qaeda's wider campaign against Ramadi's police. The bomber drove the dump truck of explosives into the post housing the police quick-reaction force in Ramadi.[302]

The Baghdad Security Plan Begins

When Operation Enforcing the Law began on February 14, 2007, Major General Gaskin was the commander of Multi-National Forces-West (Anbar province) and the II Marine Expeditionary Force (Forward). His mission was to interdict foreign insurgents who "are coming into the country, mainly using the Euphrates River Valley," and to support the Baghdad Security Plan by preventing insurgents from traveling between Anbar and Baghdad. Maj. Gen. Gaskin and his forces secured the Euphrates River and six major cities in Anbar province, and interdicted foreign fighters traveling into and out of Baghdad.[303]

The number of troops in Anbar Province rose even before the Surge began. Some units in Anbar had their tours extended when the BSP was announced. The number of U.S. troops in Ramadi rose slightly in December, January, and February, after the mid-tour leave program ended.[304] On February 19, Colonel MacFarland and the 1BCT of the 1st Armored Division relinquished command of Ramadi to Colonel John Charlton and the 1BCT, 3rd Infantry Division, and a full, pre-leave complement of soldiers.[305] The Iraqis provided many additional forces. By February, the Ramadi sheikhs' recruitment drive had also produced 4,500 new policemen, where previously there had been only 300.[306] Major General Gaskin noted that the increased troop levels enabled him to expand operations in Anbar while also supporting efforts in Baghdad. The operations in Anbar built upon those in Ramadi, and worked synergistically with the Baghdad Security Plan. The combination helped to interdict and disrupt terrorist movements and supplies through the province into Baghdad.[307]

Enemy Movements Between Anbar, Diyala, and Baghdad

Al Qaeda launched a series of car, truck, and suicide bomb attacks in and around Baghdad shortly after the BSP commenced. Some of these targeted Shiite civilians and, apparently, aimed to incite sectarian violence by inviting reprisal attacks. The Jaysh al Mahdi did not respond to these provocations as a coherent organization, nor did the Shiite population of Baghdad. Al Qaeda also attempted to terrorize civilians through its chlorine bomb campaign.

Al Qaeda detonated its next chlorine gas suicide bomb in Ramadi on February 19.[308] Another bomber detonated a chlorine tanker truck in Taji, a large city and major U.S. base north of Baghdad, just a few days later.[309] A third followed in a mixed neighborhood in Baghdad on the next day, on the road linking Baghdad International Airport (BIAP) with the western part of the city.[310] Shortly thereafter, U.S. forces found a large quantity of chlorine and other chemicals in Karmah, a location near Fallujah where al Qaeda terrorists also staged and constructed vehicle bombs.[311] The Karmah staging area was a convenient location for attacks against Anbar, Baghdad, and Taji, as the western highways lead from Fallujah east to BIAP (along the most direct route) or east to Taji (along a northerly route). U.S. forces later discovered another chlorine vehicle-bomb-making operation just north of Taji.[312]

The chlorine bomb attacks in Taji were part of a wider offensive by al Qaeda in Iraq in February and March. The Islamic State of Iraq, having been pushed from some of its key bases such as Ramadi and Ghazaliyah, attempted to hold terrain between Anbar, Diyala, and Salah ad-Din so that they could retain staging areas for counterattacks. The Awakening in Anbar drove fighters north into Tarmiyah and Diyala, west into Baghdad, and into the northeastern fringes of Diyala Province. Maj. Gen. Mixon, the commander of MND-North and Maj Gen. Gaskin, the commander of MND-West, each made this speculation on different occasions.[313]

Anbar and the Central Government

Counterinsurgency operations in Iraq in 2007 aimed to promote ties between central, provincial, and local government. The ties between the central government in Baghdad, the ministries, and the provincial government in Anbar were exceptionally weak in 2006. De-Baathification laws and policies prevented many Sunni from participating in government and military service. Because Sunni leaders boycotted the 2005 elections, they did not obtain strong political representation in parliament. As sectarian violence spiraled, some ministries in Baghdad ignored the province's needs further, and could not deliver funds or services.

On March 13, 2007, Prime Minister Maliki made his first personal, official visit to Ramadi. He had last traveled to Anbar Province in 1976, when he worked there as a teacher before fleeing Saddam Hussein's regime.[314] Sheikhs and other leaders came from all parts of Anbar to meet with him. The Anbar provincial governor and other officials met him on the tarmac.[315] The meetings were civil, but argumentative and voluble.[316]

"At a news conference," it was reported, "Mr. Maliki praised the tenaciousness of the province's residents and thanked those tribal leaders who opposed the creeping influence of al Qaeda. He assured them that the central government would not ignore their demands for improved public services, development aid and support for the security forces here. He promised to open factories, deliver food to the needy and hold provincial elections as soon as possible."[317]

Abdul Sattar Buzaigh al Rishawi, one of the leaders of the Awakening, explained that the sheikhs had asked Prime Minister Maliki to reward the Anbaris for their support by meeting these demands.[318]

Al Qaeda Escalates Its Attacks Against Anbaris

Al Qaeda increased its intense attacks against Anbaris shortly after Prime Minister Maliki's visit, attempting to use chemical weapons several times a week in the latter half of March. Insurgents tried to coordinate three chlorine bomb attacks against residents of Ramadi, Fallujah, and Amariyah on March 18. One aimed at a tribal sheikh who supported the Awakening and the people of his tribe who came to visit him. That bomb detonated at its target in the Albu Issa tribal area, three miles south of Fallujah.[319] The other two bombs exploded at security checkpoints outside of Amariyah, a city on the Euphrates between Fallujah and Yusifiyah, and another northeast of Ramadi. Although these explosions all inflicted casualties, none harmed their intended target.[320]

Next, al Qaeda launched coordinated conventional attacks on Iraqi police stations in the tribal areas supporting the Awakening. On March 20, for example, insurgents attacked a police station in Amariyah with mortars for an hour. Iraqi police engaged the insurgents in a firefight for several hours, and U.S. forces terminated the engagement by bombing and strafing the insurgents' position.[321] On March 23, Ramadi police apprehended a potential suicide bomber driving a truck of chlorine toward a new Iraqi police station. The bomb did not detonate.[322] And on March 30, insurgents in three separate trucks rigged with explosives and chlorine attempted to penetrate the fortified perimeter of Fallujah's government center, partially rebuilt since the Marines fought through the city in spring 2004. As in Amariyah and Ramadi, the Iraqi Security Forces in Fallujah prevented the trucks from entering the compound, and detonated the explosives safely.[323]

Coalition and Iraqi Security Forces Continue Counterinsurgency Operations

Coalition and Iraqi Security Forces nevertheless worked aggressively to clear the remainder of Ramadi. From late February to April 2007, Coalition Forces and their Iraqi counterparts fanned throughout the Ramadi, "clearing the city, street by street, house by house," under the new counterinsurgency strategy.[324] Coalition Forces established over forty Joint Security Stations and Combat Outposts in the city and worked alongside members of the Iraqi Security Forces to protect the neighborhoods.[325] The Iraqis assisted with the offensive clearing operations. Brig. Gen. Khalil Ibrahim Hamadi, the police chief in Ramadi, led 500 Iraqi policemen during a ten-hour operation to clear an area of central Ramadi on March 20, 2007.[326] Days later, Coalition and Iraqi Forces began a separate, major clearing operation to establish security in western Ramadi.[327]

By April, many al Qaeda insurgents had fled Ramadi and reconstituted in pockets on the outskirts of the city. Coalition and Iraqi Security Forces maintained their offensive by conducting operations targeting the remaining hotspots in their area of operations.[328] A number of the insurgents fleeing Ramadi went to Albu Bali, an area located fifteen kilometers northeast of the city on the northern bank of the Euphrates River. Coalition Forces, recognizing the increasing insurgent activity in the area, launched Operation Forsythe Park to clear Albu Bali in April.[329] During the five-day operation, Coalition and Iraqi troops constructed a Joint Security Station to establish a permanent Iraqi Security Force presence in Albu Bali.[330] They also found numerous weapons caches, including twenty-eight IEDs, three anti-aircraft guns, mortars, and thousands of pounds of explosive materials.[331] Coalition and Iraqi Forces pursued al Qaeda in the surrounding areas.

In order to maintain security, U.S. troops also recruited local Iraqis to participate in the security efforts. As of late April, they had constructed twenty-three police stations in the city of Ramadi and its surrounding areas.[332] According to Colonel John Charlton, "We knew that we had to establish Iraqi police presence in these neighborhoods after we cleared them . . . . So we had to go and recruit locally to get those forces to man these police stations [because we] didn't have enough police to hold the areas we just cleared."[333] The support of the tribal leaders in the area helped these efforts. At the behest of their tribal sheikhs, many Iraqi men turned out to join the police force.[334]

Because of the lengthy process of joining the Iraqi Security Forces, Coalition Forces initially employed many of the locals as security volunteers known as Concerned Local Citizens (CLC) or Sons of Iraq. Some CLC members volunteered without pay, while many others were paid by Coalition commanders through contracts. These groups maintained the security of their neighborhoods, and Coalition Forces worked hard over the following months to get their volunteers integrated into the regular Iraqi Security Forces. The efforts paid off in the late summer when they "were able to get all 4,000 on the [Ministry of Interior] payroll."[335]

Coalition Forces had completed the majority of clearing operations by the end of April 2007. They sought to solidify and build on the security gains by devoting more time to the tasks of reconstruction, political reconciliation, and economic development.[336] On April 11,

tribal sheikhs and Ramadi city officials met for the first time in years
to "start laying the groundwork for rebuilding the damaged infrastructure in Ramadi." This meeting was especially important because
it marked a new "cooperation between all the security elements in
the city and all the councils," which was vital to moving forward on
any major reconstruction projects.[337] Reconstruction remained the
primary focus in Ramadi throughout the months that followed. By
late 2007, Ramadi had transformed "from a war zone into a thriving
community."[338]

Although al Qaeda in Iraq had been defeated in Ramadi, operatives still sought to reinfiltrate and regain control of the city because
of its symbolic and strategic importance as the "stated capital of the
Islamic State of Iraq."[339] During May and June, al Qaeda prepared a
large insurgent force south of Ramadi to retake the city. During a routine patrol on June 30, 2007, U.S. forces came upon as many as seventy
heavily-armed AQI fighters preparing an attempt to retake the city and
kill their primary target, Anbar Awakening leader Sheikh Sattar Abu
Risha.[340] A heavy firefight ensued, lasting throughout the night. During
the fight, the AQI fighters displayed "unsettling determination" and
"tactics that the Americans said mirrored their own."[341] In all, two U.S.
Marines were killed and eleven U.S. troops were wounded during the
Battle of Donkey Island, as it was subsequently named; about thirty-
two insurgents were killed.[342] Coalition and Iraqi Forces maintained
security in the area, rendering al Qaeda's attempt unsuccessful.

Al Qaeda in Iraq maintained no operational cells in the city of
Ramadi or surrounding areas.[343] Moreover, there had not been an attack
in the city of Ramadi since March 31, 2007.[344] The non-kinetic aspects of
the counterinsurgency strategy also worked to revive the city's economy and government. Coalition and Iraqi efforts had jump-started
political and economic development by early August 2007. By the time
Colonel Charlton redeployed in March 2008, Ramadi had become one
of the safest areas of Iraq.[345]

Conclusions

There is a common myth that the "Awakening" movement in Anbar occurred independently of—even in spite of—the Coalition military operations in 2007. The truth is that it began emerging in 2006 thanks to the hard and skillful fighting and negotiating of Army Colonel Sean MacFarland and a number of Marine officers and their subordinates. General Odierno met with Sheikh Sattar Abu Risha in December 2006 and encouraged U.S. soldiers in Anbar to continue fighting and negotiating in support of Abu Risha's efforts.

As other groups emerged in and around Baghdad, Odierno and Petraeus seized on opportunities to make friends of former enemies. This was no easy decision. Americans had been dying at the hands of Sunni Arab resistance groups since 2003. Many of the CLCs were themselves former members of the insurgency. There was some grumbling among U.S. troops about cooperating with former enemies, not to mention concern that the "transformation" of these insurgents into partners would be temporary at best.

Petraeus and Odierno, however, saw it as an opportunity. Contrary to popular misconception, they refused requests to provide weapons to the CLCs, who almost invariably had their own weapons anyway. They insisted that all CLCs provide detailed biometric data, including fingerprints and retinal scans, the serial numbers of their weapons, their home addresses, and details of their family relationships. Counterinsurgency experts have often wryly remarked that it would be easy to end an insurgency if the enemy would only wear uniforms. By collecting all of this information about the CLCs, Odierno and Petraeus were in essence forcing them to wear uniforms. Any CLC who turned against the Coalition or Iraqi forces could be readily identified if he, or his weapon, was captured—and Coalition troops would know immediately where he and his family lived. There have been very few reports to date of CLC members taking such a risk.

Petraeus and Odierno transformed the tribal movement in Anbar into a national phenomenon supportive of government institutions. U.S. commanders fostered grassroots movements throughout Iraq, methodically negotiating security agreements with local officials, tribes, and former insurgent leaders. They thus achieved one of the major objectives of the counterinsurgency strategy by reconciling much of the Sunni population with the government.

The Awakening begun in 2006 turned out to be more than just a product of revulsion against violence and terror. It has evolved, at least in some areas, into political movements responding to Iraqis fed up with the gridlock in the central government in Baghdad.

The Anbar Awakening continues to combat AQI efforts to reinfiltrate the province. It has also generated a complex set of political parties and factions that seriously challenge the Iraqi Islamic party—the party nominally representing most of Iraq's Sunni Arabs in the Council of Representatives after the 2005 elections.

Chapter 4
■ ■ ■ Preliminary Operations in Diyala

Defeating al Qaeda in Diyala was especially important because the province had political as well as military significance for al Qaeda. It was there that the organization attempted to establish the capital of its Islamic state in 2006, and its activities in the province increased as the Anbar Awakening spread.

The task of defeating violent enemies in Diyala and establishing a political process was exceptionally difficult. The enemy controlled Baqubah, the capital of Diyala, so thoroughly that it had fortified defensive positions within the city. The enemy also controlled the rural terrain along the province's roads and rivers. The ethnic and sectarian diversity of Diyala's population amplified the opportunities for al Qaeda's violence and its effects, including reprisal violence by Shia militias, security forces, and neighboring villages. Re-establishing security in Diyala required more than six months of preparatory operations before June 2007, followed by a series of offensive operations over months, all aimed at controlling urban areas, rural terrain, and lines of communication such as roads and rivers.

The Enemy in Diyala

According to Colonel David Sutherland, the commander of the 3rd Brigade Combat Team, 1st Cavalry Division (known as Greywolf), which operated in Diyala from October 2006 through the end of November 2007: "Our problem set is extremely different and extremely complex for a province in Iraq. Basically all the issues and conflicts that exist through all of Iraq ... exist here." Al Qaeda was the main security threat in Diyala in 2007, and its objective was to create lawlessness and sectarian conflict in order to establish a Wahhabist state. Sunni rejectionists aided al Qaeda in order to reassert their power and influence. Shia militias, including the Jaysh al Mahdi and Badr Corps, also operated in the province to cleanse areas of Sunni and establish the Shia domination of Diyala. The Iranians established secret cells in Diyala in order to support those in Baghdad, undermine the Maliki government, and trap U.S. forces in Iraq. The Iranians also had special concern about the Mujahedeen E-Khalq (MEK), a terrorist group that opposed Iran during the Iran-Iraq War. The MEK was confined by Coalition Forces to an area in Diyala in 2007, but the organization attempted to obstruct Iranian influence through intelligence networks and proxies.[346]

Al Qaeda in Baqubah and the Diyala River Valley

Al Qaeda was the most destabilizing threat to Diyala in 2006. The province had special significance for al Qaeda: Abu Musab Zarqawi had designated it the capital of the caliphate that he aimed to establish in Iraq when he was head of al Qaeda in the country.[347] In April 2006, Zarqawi located his headquarters at Hebheb, a village northwest of Baqubah along the Baghdad-Kirkuk road. In the same month, Colonel Sutherland explained, "specifically on Saddam Hussein's birthday, al Qaeda conducted seven coordinated attacks inside the province. They attacked Udaim, on the northwestern side of the province; they attacked into Muqdadiyah; they attacked Balad Ruz, Kana'an, Khalis, Khan Bani Sa'ad, and Baqubah." These attacks constituted al Qaeda's first major offensive into Diyala.

Even after U.S. Special Forces killed Zarqawi on June 8, 2006, al Qaeda continued to use Diyala as a staging ground and potential capital. Al Qaeda terrorists lived in rural areas, but concentrated in safe houses inside Baqubah. They discredited the Iraqi Security Forces through numerous attacks, and the Iraqi government by threatening employees with death if they showed up for work. The organization used the canalized terrain east and southeast of that city, the former hunting grounds of Saddam Hussein stretching from Balad Ruz to Turki Village, as a major supply base for its Diyala and Baghdad operations.

Al Qaeda also based itself in villages in the Diyala River Valley, northeast of Baqubah. They fought to control Muqdadiyah, which established a line of communication to Lake Hamrin. From there, al Qaeda maintained communications along roads into Iran via Khanaqin and into the Kurdish provinces via Kirkuk. Finally, it established itself in the Khan Bani Sa'ad tribal area south of Baqubah, all the way down to Salman Pak, south and east of Baghdad. These areas were under al Qaeda control— whether through physical presence or psychological intimidation—by November 2006.[348]

The Iraqi Security Forces Respond to al Qaeda

The Iraqi Security Forces attempted to halt al Qaeda's campaign to control Diyala. Colonel Sutherland explained, "[I]n August/September . . . of 2006 Iraqi Security Forces, specifically the Iraqi Army, conducted an operation in Baqubah and detained about 500 individuals. They did wide-cast wide-sweep operations inside the city of Baqubah detaining every military-age male . . . creating a perception of the Iraqi Security Forces as being sectarian. It was further compounded in Baqubah when during Holy Ramadan of 2006 the Iraqi Army and Iraqi Police conducted another operation and detained about 400 other military-aged men. There was no intelligence driving these operations. There was no evidence. They . . . detained close to, in total, 900 individuals. . . . [A]ll but two were Sunni, so it gave the perception of the Iraqi Security Forces as a sectarian organization. In reality the Iraqi Security Forces were conducting operations based on the training that they had received under Saddam. Saddam's method was to go in, conduct these wide-sweep, wide-cast operations, detain as many people as possible, and then investigate them."[349]

Further, Sutherland said, "The Iraqi Police at that time during our arrival were recruited, not from the neighborhoods, but from outside the neighborhoods. In fact the police chief at the time, Gassan al Bawi, the provincial director of police, was recruiting from Baghdad. He had recruited about 300 individuals from the Wolf Brigade, which was a National Police organization, very Shia organization, and he recruited them to assume roles as policemen inside Baqubah, again further fueling that perception of sectarianism."[350] By recruiting from the Wolf Brigade, Gassan al Bawi ensured that the Iraqi Police in Diyala had little connection with residents, and substantial connections with the National Police (which were mainly stationed in Baghdad). The Iraqi Police in Diyala supported an agenda consistent with extreme members of the Supreme Council for the Islamic Revolution in Iraq (SCIRI), one of the parties in the parliamentary bloc supporting Prime Minister Nouri al Maliki. Former Minister of the Interior Bayan Jabr incorporated the Wolf Brigade, a Badr Corps organization, into the National Police in 2005, before he became Minister of Finance. The Wolf Brigade had a reputation for sectarian cleansing.

These ISF operations in Diyala did not ensure Shia dominance in Diyala. The Iraqi Security Forces not only failed in their attempts to stop al Qaeda, but they also damaged their own reputation with the population. The actions of the Iraqi Security Forces fueled Sunni support for al Qaeda. "[I]t created a perception of sectarian bias," Sutherland said. "So you had Sunnis turning to other organizations for security against the Iraqi Security Forces."[351]

Al Qaeda Ascendant in Diyala

Al Qaeda's efforts to undermine the credibility of the Iraqi government and security forces succeeded. The government simply could not function in Diyala. The distribution of food to Diyala's population stopped in September 2006, and the distribution of fuel in October. The Diyala provincial government ceased meeting in October 2006. By March

2007, the provincial government had spent only two percent of its 2006 budget. The Iraqi Security Forces were the only sign of Iraqi government in the province, but they could not control it. The Iraqi Police withdrew from Buhriz, the area just south of Baqubah, in November and December 2006; terrorists had bombed their former police station. By the end of 2006, al Qaeda—not the government of Iraq—controlled the city of Baqubah and much of Diyala Province. Al Qaeda and other organizations began to impose their religious and political agendas.

As the sectarian violence in Iraq spread in fall 2006, extremist elements of different ethno-sectarian groups contested the area. Shia militias and Iraqi Security Forces moved into the area from Baghdad to contest the presence of Sunni terrorists, arresting and killing hundreds upon hundreds of Sunni civilians. Kurds migrated southward toward Khanaqin, on the province's northeastern fringe, bordering on Iran. Some of the Kurds in Khanaqin were Shiite; Sunni Kurds also lived nearby.[352]

As the Awakening displaced al Qaeda and Islamic State of Iraq from Ramadi in autumn 2006, the organization regrouped in Diyala and nearby Tarmiyah, increasing violence in these areas. AQI established a safe haven south of Balad Ruz in November 2006, complete with training areas and weapons caches, one of the first manifestations of al Qaeda's migration from Anbar to Diyala.

The Battle for Balad Ruz and Turki Village

A large Wahhabist terrorist group with links to al Qaeda operated in the southern outskirts of Balad Ruz, a town of roughly 80,000 in Diyala Province located about an hour's drive north of Baghdad and thirty-five miles east of Baqubah. Balad Ruz sits upon the secondary roads that link Muqdadiyah with Baqubah and southeastern Baghdad. Terrorists were able to circumvent U.S. forces stationed in Muqdadiyah and Baqubah by using this road to avoid the main routes that led northeast from Baqubah to Muqdadiyah and southwest of Baqubah into Baghdad.

Also, Balad Ruz is located midway on the route from Baqubah to

Mandali, a town on the secondary road that follows the mountains dividing Iran and Iraq. Mandali is not an official border crossing, but rather an important node on a smuggling route from the Iran-Iraq border. The legitimate border crossing is forty-eight miles north of Mandali at Khanaqin.

The Wahhabists in this area incited sectarian violence in Balad Ruz and Baqubah. The Council, as they called themselves, issued judgments (a common practice of Sunni Islamist groups when they controlled an area, and one of the first means they use to assert the supremacy of Shariah law as they interpret it), and they were tied to al Qaeda and Zarqawi.[353] In November, they kidnapped several families from local Shiite tribes, and killed all the men—thirty-nine civilians.[354] They also perpetrated attacks almost daily on the people of Balad Ruz, Iraqi forces, and Coalition Forces. They frightened the local residents in the town and outlying lands where they established their safe havens. Many left the area, while the remainder complied with the terrorists' demands out of sympathy or fear.[355] Consequently, the terrorists turned the tiny villages south of Balad Ruz, once predominantly Shiite, into almost exclusively Sunni habitations.[356] As the terrorists perpetrated violence, merchants closed their shops.[357]

When the 5th Squadron of the 73rd Cavalry Regiment (3rd BCT, 1st Cavalry Division) conducted reconnaissance operations just south of Balad Ruz on November 12, 2006, they discovered a weapons cache in thick date palm groves and irrigation canals.[358] At that time, well-trained enemies defended the stockpiles, and the U.S. forces took four days to defeat them. Then U.S. forces returned to their base to develop intelligence about this enemy, unusual because it did not behave like other insurgent groups, which often detonate weapons remotely, flee when U.S. forces make contact, and return only when forces have departed.[359]

The 3rd BCT, 1st Cavalry Division conducted deliberate, small-scale raids and air assaults (the movement of infantry soldiers into combat by helicopter) during the next six weeks in order to establish and identify patterns of enemy behavior. The enemy became predictable by moving south whenever it was attacked from the north. These raids also drove the enemy into what it thought was a safe haven or good defensive position.[360] The terrorists massed their forces in sparsely populated agricultural areas, rather than in the population center in Balad Ruz.

The enemy was well organized and well prepared to fight. Because the terrain was criss-crossed with irrigation canals and ditches,[361] they developed a complex system of signals, fortified irrigation ditches and dug spider holes in them, used motorcycles to move through the canals, and fought in squads (small formations of nine to eleven soldiers operating together—the squad is the smallest unit in most armies).[362] These enemy fighters also separated themselves from the population, making it possible to conduct major combat operations without harming civilians. U.S. forces nevertheless informed the villagers that they would soon be arriving in force, to ensure that the civilian population knew that military forces were coming and what their intentions were.[363]

On January 4, 2007, the 3rd BCT, 1st Cavalry Division launched Operation Turki Bowl (named after Turki Village, the southernmost objective), partnering with the 5th Iraqi Army Division. Air assault operations closed off the southern escape routes, while maneuver forces began to clear the agricultural villages from the north.[364] The enemy destroyed bridges and placed obstacles on the roads in order to slow forward movement and divert vehicles toward explosives. Enemy forward elements sent up a smoke signal to indicate that U.S. and Iraqi forces had arrived. And U.S. and Iraqi forces did not find any military-age men in the villages it cleared on the first day of operations.[365] Likewise, they found few young or middle-aged men in their house-to-house searches on subsequent days.[366] According to one detained witness, insurgents fled into the irrigation canals on motorcycles as soon as they heard U.S. helicopters.[367]

During operations, U.S. forces spotted some bands of men on motorcycles driving through the canals, and called in artillery or close air support.[368] Masked men had also used the vehicles regularly to inform inhabitants about which roads the group had mined, and, indeed, the insurgents continued to mine return routes after American vehicles passed through in their forward sweep.[369] U.S. and Iraqi forces ultimately found concealed motorcycles, in addition to arms caches.[370] During the operation, other villagers informed the ground forces about weapons caches, escape routes, and safe havens.[371]

After several days, some of the men returned home to the villages. Troops discovered and questioned a group of seven and another of nine on two farms—suggesting that a few insurgent squads or their remnants had returned. U.S. soldiers found no evidence against them. They also detained a group of fifteen men in Turki Village for illegal possession of heavy weapons, including an Iranian-made machine gun.[372]

The operation concluded on January 13, 2007. U.S. and Iraqi forces killed 100 insurgents and detained fifty others during Operation Turki Bowl, although the enemy had not fought as intensely as it had in November of the previous year. Coalition troops discovered twenty-five weapons caches, which contained armaments that would sustain a large terrorist network: 1,172 Katyusha rockets, 1,039 rocket-propelled grenades, 171 TOW anti-tank missiles, machine guns, and anti-tank mines.[373] The insurgents were clearly prepared to defend their position against infantry and vehicle assaults. They apparently were perpetrating violence and supplying weapons as far west as Baqubah.[374]

Following combat operations, the U.S. and Iraqi forces built a combat outpost where they each stationed a company permanently to patrol the area as part of their mission to provide security for the area and to prevent insurgent reinfiltration.[375] In subsequent patrols, Iraqi and U.S. companies discovered another substantial weapons cache.[376]

In the months that followed, shopkeepers in Balad Ruz reopened their businesses. The mayor allocated attention and local resources to the area, which had not been governed effectively by the town. The governor of Diyala also visited Balad Ruz, and worked with the mayor to create a plan to get the money from Baghdad necessary for reconstruction and economic growth.[377] These efforts were all made in the hopes that former residents would be able to return.

The network did not regroup locally, but it did manage to carry out subsequent attacks. Suicide bombers attacked processions during the Ashura holiday in Balad Ruz and Mandali. Another attacker placed a bomb in a garbage can in downtown Khanaqin, where Shiite Kurdish residents and perhaps pilgrims gathered for the procession.[378] He killed twenty and wounded sixty people in this attack, designed to kill and inspire fear in local Shiites, undermining their confidence in the otherwise improving security situation.[379] Still, on February 1, 2007, the day after the attacks, local civic leaders and tribal sheikhs nevertheless met with the governor of Diyala Province and the commanders of the Iraqi Army and Police in the region to discuss the security situation and reconstruction. Locals also attended the meeting.[380]

U.S. and Iraqi forces operated in Baqubah and Muqdadiyah to follow up on their successes in Balad Ruz. On February 21, 2007, Iraqi border police found a large cache of weapons east of Balad Ruz in Mandali. It contained anti-personnel mines, mortar rounds, ammunition, and a rocket-propelled grenade.[381] The weapons might have come through the border crossing Khanaqin or along the trail that reaches Mandali. Coalition Forces had raided an alleged foreign fighter facilitator site near Khanaqin in early December 2006, and killed one terrorist who opened small-arms fire on a U.S. aircraft returning from the mission.[382] Together, this evidence suggests that Sunni foreign fighters had a network that operated between Iran and the towns of Khanaqin, Mandali, Balad Ruz, and Baqubah.

Operation Turki Bowl highlighted the relationship between AQI and sectarian violence in Iraq. Sunni and Shiite families were living together in rural villages outside of Balad Ruz without sectarian violence. The Council moved into the desolate rural area because it was not governed effectively from Balad Ruz, nor patrolled by U.S. or Iraqi forces, and because it offered excellent cover and concealment. The insurgents sparked a Shiite exodus from the area by kidnapping Shiite families and executing their young men. This terrorist act not only conveyed the horrible symbolic message of sectarian violence, but also deprived Shiite families of men to defend them from further violence.

The local Sunni population collaborated with the terrorists largely out of fear. When U.S. and Iraqi forces arrived in the tiny villages and searched from house to house, the locals provided information about weapons caches and insurgent activity. In Balad Ruz, sectarian violence and collaboration occurred because terrorists were physically present. When Coalition Forces removed the terrorists, the violence stopped, refugees began to return, and political and economic processes began anew.

After Operation Turki Bowl, Coalition Forces from the 3rd Brigade Combat Team, 1st Cavalry Division established a combat outpost between Balad Ruz and Turki Village. U.S. and Iraqi forces worked with the government and leaders of Balad Ruz and surrounding areas to establish municipal control over rural terrain, link the villages with the provincial government, and to establish a connection between the provincial and central governments, akin to the process underway in Ramadi at the same time.

U.S. and Iraqi forces, meanwhile, exploited intelligence given by residents and gleaned from their operations around Turki Village. Because U.S. forces controlled the rural terrain around Balad Ruz after the operation, they were able to move more freely into nearby areas where al Qaeda and the Islamic State of Iraq operated: toward Baqubah, Buhriz (a village to its south), and Muqdadiyah. Al Qaeda and affiliated Sunni extremists concentrated their forces in the Diyala River Valley (particularly, villages such as Zaganiyah and Qubbah); Buhriz (which similar enemies terrorized); and the terrain north and south of Lake Hamrin (the vicinity of Muqdadiyah).[383]

Reinforcing Diyala

In early 2007, Major General Benjamin Mixon, the commander of Multi-National Division-North for much of the year, requested additional troops for Diyala Province to assist forces already stationed there with securing its cities and roads. Lt. Gen. Odierno reinforced Diyala with the 5th Battalion, 20th Infantry Regiment, a Stryker Battalion from

Taji.[384] They had previously operated in Mosul and Baghdad. The Strykers arrived in Diyala on March 13, 2007.[385] The reinforcements increased troop density and mobility in the province. Prior to their arrival, only "a few dozen foot soldiers and a few tanks from Company B of the 1-12 Battalion" patrolled "the area from eastern Baqubah to Zaganiya—an insurgent-dominated region of hundreds of thousands of people" in the Diyala River Valley.[386]

Colonel Sutherland explained that as the reinforcements arrived in Diyala, "attacks against Coalition Forces and Iraqi security forces [increased]. These attacks are in part due to the Iraqi army—their growing capabilities and effectiveness. However, due to our increased operations, partnered with the Iraqi army and Iraqi police, the enemy is increasing[ly] relying on surface-laid, hastily emplaced IEDs . . . . [W]e have also seen a drop in the overall sectarian violence in the province. Attacks against the local population are becoming more spectacular to induce fear with the people. This is the enemy we are facing right now, an enemy that targets innocent civilians, that destroys their homes and even their mosques. Even though they have changed their names to the Islamic State of Iraq to portray themselves as an Iraqi resistance group, this is the same foreign-led group dedicated to death and destruction. The deployment of the 5th Battalion, 20th Infantry Regiment Strykers will support our current counterinsurgency strategy. They will be used to build upon recent successes in the area of Buhriz, Tahrir, Mufrek, and in the Baqubah area."[387]

Col. Sutherland assigned the new Stryker battalion to the area around Buhriz, just south of Baqubah. The date palm groves around Buhriz, and the underbrush beneath them, had provided good cover for insurgents. Within forty-eight hours of beginning offensive operations, the Stryker battalion found and destroyed a large weapons cache, including 300 blasting caps (used to make IEDs) and terrorist documents.[388] Members of Sunni Islamic extremist groups responded with an attempted suicide bombing. On March 16, 2007, Iraqi forces killed a suicide bomber as he attempted to assassinate the police chief of Balad Ruz and local civilians while the official visited the Balad Ruz Hospital.

The combat patrols near Buhriz preceded a major, multi-week clearing operation that lasted from March 24 to April 8, 2007. This operation targeted "an Islamic State of Iraq power base at the Diyala River Valley," in Zaganiyah and Qubbah, villages halfway between Baqubah and Muqdadiyah along the Tigris (rather than the main road).[389]

During these operations, elements of the 5th Iraqi Army Division and U.S. Army 5th Squadron, 73rd Cavalry Regiment, attached to the 3rd BCT, 1st Cavalry Division captured and killed terrorists and discovered eight weapons caches.[390] On March 29, these same units discovered a fortified defensive position and al Qaeda training camp in the palm groves at Zaganiyah.[391] They subsequently discovered seven more large weapons caches, for a total of fifteen, killed thirty terrorists, and detained twenty-eight suspects.[392] So approximately sixty al Qaeda terrorists, with over 17,000 rounds of small-arms ammunition, 130 mortar rounds, 175 rocket propelled grenades, eighty grenades, twenty IEDs, and IED-making material, had been operating from these bases, training camps, and fortified positions.[393] The enemy in Zaganiyah, like the enemy in Turki Village, was well-trained, well-organized, well-supplied, and capable of conducting complex attacks and defenses.

The following day, and perhaps in response, al Qaeda detonated three suicide car and truck bombs in Khalis, to the west of Zaganiyah on the far side of the Tigris. The first two bombs targeted civilians, and a subsequent bomb targeted first-responders from the Iraqi Security Forces.[394] Unlike the previous suicide bombings in Diyala, which individuals conducted, this attack used vehicles and required more sophisticated timing and coordination. (The next spectacular vehicle-borne bombs in Diyala detonated nearly three weeks later, on April 23 and 24, in Baqubah and As Sadah, immediately to its north, respectively.) In March, U.S. and Iraqi forces arrested Khalis's police chief for inciting sectarian violence, indicating that rogue Shiite militias operated in the city.[395] So the al Qaeda attack on Khalis presumably targeted that city because of the presence of Shiite militias.

U.S. forces thus encircled Baqubah and attempted to cut the insurgents' supply lines into the city. They then moved into the city itself.[396] They cleared Old Baqubah and Buhriz (south of Baqubah), shortly after completing the major operation to push the Islamic State of Iraq and al Qaeda from Zaganiyah. The Baqubah City Council advised the U.S. and Iraqi forces that they wished to reopen the Old Baqubah market to safe commerce. Elements of the 5th Stryker Battalion, 20th Infantry Regiment, cleared the market of Old Baqubah during a multi-day operation that began on April 2. That unit maintained a twenty-four-hour presence in the area, hunted for terrorists, identified weapons caches, and established checkpoints to search vehicles moving into the area.[397] They "hardened" the neighborhood, emplacing concrete barriers throughout it to prevent vehicle bombs and to protect the Iraqi Security Forces there.

Subsequently, the Stryker Battalion, along with several Iraqi Army and Police units, entered Buhriz.[398] They conducted house-to-house searches for terrorists and weapons on April 10.[399] On April 12, they discovered five weapons caches and one vehicle bomb. These were sufficiently important that terrorists had set up an observation post to guard at least one of them.[400] Many of the terrorists left Buhriz before the Strykers arrived.[401] The U.S. and Iraqi forces planned to open an Iraqi Police station in the city.

By April 15, 2007, U.S. soldiers had established seven Combat Outposts in and around Baqubah, and residents were returning to Buhriz. Tribal leaders from Buhriz met in the government center and distributed food to their people. Some insurgents—mounted on the scooters typical of Sunni extremist groups—fought in the vicinity of these Combat Outposts.[402] A week later, U.S. forces reported that residents of Zaganiyah were volunteering information about the location of weapons caches.[403] Sunni tribal leaders in As Sadah, just north of Baqubah along the road to Muqdadiyah, and Had Maskar, near Zaganiyah (north of Baqubah along the Diyala), began to cooperate with residents, Iraqi Security Forces, and U.S. forces after they had cleared al Qaeda from the area.[404]

Al Qaeda responded with a coordinated attack on one of the seven new U.S. Combat Outposts—the one in As Sadah, which had been open since March. The vehicle-borne explosives did not detonate at the combat outpost; rather, the shockwave of the blast toppled a wall of the building and several homes and a mosque nearby. Al Qaeda achieved this effect by coordinating small arms and two vehicle bombs.[405] Al Qaeda sought to destroy the As Sadah outpost because it controlled communications between Khalis and Lake Hamrin, and because the local Sunni tribal leaders, following the pattern observed in Anbar province, had cooperated with Americans.

Yet even as al Qaeda targeted the local Sunni population, provincial government in Diyala resumed with the assistance of U.S. forces and Iraqi officials. The fuel shortage in Diyala was one of the province's most urgent problems. On March 18, 2007, the governor met with the Director General of Diyala's oil ministry to attempt to restore fuel services to the area. The Director General agreed to relocate from Khanaqin, on the Iranian border, to offices in Baqubah. Border enforcement officials were also present at that meeting.[406] The governor and the Diyala Provincial Council met on April 23 to discuss the province's budget.[407] A vehicle-borne bomb exploded at a checkpoint outside near the council's headquarters, through which a Coalition convoy previously had passed safely—indicating that the local government, rather than Coalition Forces, was the target of the attack.[408]

As the Coalition presence spread in Diyala, U.S. commanders helped tribal leaders negotiate disputes in order to reduce violence. There were twenty-five major tribes and almost 100 sub-tribes in Diyala in 2007, some of them crossing sectarian lines. The terms of inter-tribal agreements established in 2007 reveal the nature of the internecine violence that had occurred prior to then: "freeing previous kidnapped victims and stopping all kidnapping and killing operations; stopping indirect-fire attacks; providing the Iraqi police any members of their tribes which may be linked to insurgent groups; supporting the Iraqi army and police against terrorists; and resolving farming issues among the tribes."[409]

Colonel Sutherland began working with the tribes in December 2006, and more fruitfully in February 2007 after clearing Turki Village.[410] "In

February," he said, "I met with a group of individuals that are now leading the concerned local citizens in Baqubah, but this was facilitated .
. . in Diyala . . . by Sheikh Ahmed al Tamimi, who was the head of the
Shia Endowment Foundation inside Diyala . . . . [H]e facilitated this get-
together with . . . Sunni and Shia leaders. We also started reconciliation
efforts in earnest, specifically with . . . four of the paramount sheikhs."[411]
The two paramount sheikhs nearest Balad Ruz and Turki Village were the
first to sign and swear a peace agreement. (One represented al Kharki, a
Sunni tribe, and the other al Shammeri, a mixed Sunni/Shia tribe.) Their
negotiations began after the Turki Village operations and concluded formally three months later, on April 30, 2007.[412] This inter-tribal agreement
paved the way for others.

U.S. forces fostered connections between tribal leaders and government officials in order to integrate these two competing lines of
authority. Diyala's provincial governor, its director of police, and the
commanding general of the 5th Iraqi Army Division addressed a meeting of forty-five sheikhs from Diyala on May 23, 2007, laying out their
plans for the province. The government reported to the sheikhs on its
activities. The sheikhs raised issues important to them: "the failure of the
central government to focus on the problems of Diyala, the failure of the
Provincial Council to effectively represent the people and the common
goal of ridding the tribal lands of terrorists and foreign fighters."[413]

Influential Iraqis encouraged the sheikhs to support the Iraqi government: "Sheikh Ahmed Azziz, [Grand Ayatollah] Sistani's representative in
Diyala, continued to challenge the leaders to settle their differences and
work with the legitimate government; while [Governor] Ra'ad committed to continue meeting with different *nahias* [municipalities] throughout Diyala in an effort to create reconciliation at the lowest levels where
it can be most easily enforced."[414] Colonel Sutherland and Brigadier General Mick Bednarek, the Deputy Commanding General (Operations) for
MND-North, also attended the meeting.

Members of Parliament concerned about the province formed
the Diyala Support Committee and met on June 6, 2007. U.S. and Iraqi

commanders joined provincial leaders to address the group. By receiving regular briefings about security and essential services, the members of the committee aimed to increase the funding and attention given to Diyala by central government ministries.[415]

While these initial operations and negotiations did not solve Diyala's problems, they prepared the way for clearing Baqubah in June 2007, and for holding the city after combat operations. They also established the framework for restoring government to Diyala.

Chapter 5
■ ■ ■ The Real Surge: The Offensive in Baghdad's Belts

AQI Reacts to the Baghdad Security Plan

In the first half of 2007, as Generals Petraeus and Odierno conducted shaping operations and positioned the Surge forces in and around Baghdad, al Qaeda in Iraq attacked the capital and provinces with vehicle bombs. AQI thereby attempted to undermine the credibility of Coalition and Iraqi Security Forces, incite further sectarian violence, and break the will of the Iraqi government, the U.S. government, and its allies. As long as it maintained its support zones in the belts, AQI was able to continue to conduct its lethal car bomb campaign.

AQI's car bomb campaign was well organized and targeted specific locations. AQI conducted spectacular attacks in west Baghdad. In the Mansour district in February, they conducted a "possible assassination attempt" inside the Ministry of Public Works.[416] The most devastating attack occurred in the neighborhood of Iskan where a van exploded, killing sixteen people, and wounding forty others.[417] These types of attacks persisted in March, when a suicide car bomb hit the Mutanabi Street book market, killing twenty people and wounding more than sixty-five.[418] In the turbulent neighborhoods of Dora in east Rasheed, insurgents likewise used car bombs to target Coalition and Iraqi Security Forces, as well as Iraqi civilians.

Rusafa served as the primary safehaven for AQI's car bomb network inside of Baghdad, facilitating its targeting of East Baghdad. A string of vehicle and suicide bombs in January and February 2007 targeted the

Rusafa district's main markets and intersections, killing roughly 250 and wounding over 500.[419] In February and March, as part of Operation Safe Market and the Baghdad Security Plan, temporary barriers were erected around an area of the Shorja market to control vehicular traffic, reduce the likelihood of car bombings, and revive the flagging economy.[420] While improvised explosive device (IED) attacks continued throughout March, they were less deadly than the attacks of the previous two months. Moreover, on March 21, 2007, Coalition Forces rolled up the Rusafa car bomb network, capturing its leader and three other key members.[421]

AQI insurgents, unable to penetrate market protective barriers, focused their attacks elsewhere. On April 12, 2007, AQI detonated a truck bomb that destroyed the Sarafiyah Bridge, killing ten as vehicles fell into the Tigris.[422] The Sarafiyah Bridge connected western and eastern Baghdad, symbolically and physically. Shia death squads running from Sadr City to western Baghdad used the bridge as one of their crossings. Six days later, a car bomb detonated in a parking lot near the Sadriya market; while nearby concrete barriers remained intact, the VBIED still managed to kill a staggering 115 and to wound 137 more.[423]

In eastern Baghdad, AQI's car bomb attacks were not limited to the Rusafa district. Indeed, from its safe havens in the neighborhoods of Adhamiyah and Fadhil, AQI conducted a car bomb campaign elsewhere in the Adhamiyah and Sadr City districts, where Shia extremist groups operated. AQI detonated a bomb in the Shalal market in the Shaab-Ur area, killing scores of Shiite civilians, on March 29.[424]

In order to stem the violence, Coalition and Iraqi Forces stepped up efforts to destroy AQI's networks in Adhamiyah. In late March and early April, Coalition Forces captured several leaders of a car bomb cell in that neighborhood.[425] Iraqi Army troops also captured ten individuals allegedly involved in an Adhamiyah terrorist cell.[426] In April, Coalition and Iraqi forces conducted cordon and search operations, particularly in Rusafa's turbulent Fadhil neighborhood.

The construction of a concrete barrier wall around the Adhamiyah neighborhood in April and May 2007 contributed enormously to the security of East Baghdad. Coalition Forces erected these temporary barriers as a part of the Baghdad Security Plan's "Safe Neighborhood" project in order to protect the local population from sectarian attacks, while at the same time preventing insurgents within Adhamiyah from carrying out violent attacks elsewhere.[427] According to U.S. military officials, "Murders [were] down 61 percent in Adhamiyah between the beginning of April, when construction began, and May 28," when the project concluded.[428]

In March and April AQI also attempted to perpetrate bomb attacks in Sadr City, aimed at its large Shia population. In early March, Iraqi Army soldiers foiled an attempted car bomb attack in Sadr City, as the vehicle tried to avoid a checkpoint.[429] At the end of the month, a car bomb detonated near a hospital in Sadr City killing five and wounding fifteen.[430] Days later, in early April, another car bomb exploded at the Sadr City Joint Security Station; no one, however, was injured or killed in the attack.[431] As Coalition and Iraqi Forces rolled up the AQI networks in Adhamiyah and Rusafa, and constructed barriers around the Adhamiyah neighborhood, attacks in Sadr City declined.

Reconnoitering Insurgent Routes Through Baghdad's Belts

Securing Baghdad from AQI's car bombs required simultaneous offensive clearing operations across the Baghdad belts and in the capital, in order to fragment the entire AQI network in central Iraq. Al Qaeda's capabilities in Iraq, and particularly in Baghdad, depended on its ability to move around the capital, as well as through it. Al Qaeda's sustained campaign of vehicle bombing relied on an extensive support system outside the city to supply stolen and stripped vehicles and run vehicle-bomb-making factories. Strong links around the city made it possible for al Qaeda to transport weapons and fighters, finance their activities, and move the vehicle bombs from factory to detonation site. Disrupting al Qaeda's operations in Baghdad required disrupting the enemy's freedom to move through the belts around Baghdad, rather than expelling them from any one safe haven inside or outside of the city.

The operations in Baghdad from February to June did not squeeze al Qaeda terrorists into the belts, the networks of roadways, rivers, and other lines of communication within a thirty-mile radius of the capital. Al Qaeda terrorists were already well established there, and U.S. and Iraqi forces began to whittle the organization away as the Surge began.[432] Al Qaeda's strongholds and sanctuaries were in Salman Pak, Arab Jabour, Fallujah, Abu Ghraib, Karmah, Tarmiyah, and Baqubah. In early 2006, al Qaeda also moved fighters along the Euphrates River Valley between Anbar Province and North Babil. U.S. and Iraqi Security Forces were especially sparse in these rural areas.

A description of al Qaeda's operating areas illustrates the scope of that organization's movements and infrastructure in the spring of 2007.

Al Qaeda operated almost freely in a pendulum-like arc south of Baghdad, swinging from the Euphrates to the Tigris.[433] They traveled southeast along the Euphrates River, often by boat, from Fallujah to Sadr al Yusifiyah.[434] They followed the roads that link Sadr al Yusifiyah, Yusifiyah, and Mahmudiyah. Consequently, U.S. forces gradually reconnoitered and secured the area between Yusifiyah and Mahmudiyah, due south of Baghdad. They cleared Mahmudiyah over the winter of 2006-2007, but al Qaeda and Jaysh al Mahdi continued to compete with one another for control of the city.

Terrorists were captured north of Mahmudiyah on April 7, 2007.[435] Soldiers of the 2-15 Field Artillery, 10th Mountain Division, discovered a stockpile of new Iranian weapons in Mahmudiyah on April 22.[436] A few days later, their Iraqi partner-unit discovered a vehicle bomb emplaced on a highway in northern Mahmudiyah.[437] On June 9, an al Qaeda vehicle bomb destroyed part of a highway overpass just east of Mahmudiyah.[438] The most spectacular al Qaeda attack in Mahmudiyah was the kidnapping of three U.S. soldiers in May.[439] In addition, al Qaeda launched attacks on mixed sectarian areas of northern Babil province from its sanctuaries near Mahmudiyah. They also traveled from Mahmudiyah to Baghdad.[440]

The arc by which al Qaeda circumnavigated Baghdad also extended through the highly canalized farmlands stretching from Mahmudiyah toward Salman Pak, a town on the east bank of the Tigris. Arab Jabour was the most important al Qaeda sanctuary in that section of rural terrain. The dense date palm groves in Arab Jabour easily concealed weapons caches, fighter routes, safe houses, and training camps. An extensive canal system runs through the area, so waterways disrupt the terrain and drove both enemy and friendly forces onto specific roads and bridges.[441] Neither Iraqi nor U.S. forces were present in Arab Jabour in large numbers in early 2007, making it possible for al Qaeda terrorists to establish their organization there.[442]

The Tigris River separates Arab Jabour from Salman Pak, fifteen miles south of Baghdad. No U.S. forces were stationed in Salman Pak for three years before the Surge brigades arrived. Consequently, this former Baathist resort town on the east bank of the Tigris became an important al Qaeda stronghold.[443] The terrorist network used that town to control and cross the river. General Odierno called Salman Pak "an area known for producing car and truck bombs that are sent north into Baghdad."[444] U.S. forces targeted car bomb factories there between January and May, 2007,[445] and then the Third Infantry Division conducted reconnaissance operations there when its subordinate units arrived.[446]

The road network linked Salman Pak to active al Qaeda locations on the east side of Baghdad. A highway runs from Salman Pak to Baghdad's Rusafa neighborhood, where U.S. forces worked methodically to destroy a car bomb factory and network between February and April.[447] Another smaller road network runs from Salman Pak to the disused canal that borders the east side of Sadr City. These routes sugges the paths that AQI used to funnel car bombs, operatives, and weapons from Salman Pak to Sadr City, a frequent target of al Qaeda's spectacular attacks.

Weapons Flow Along the Tigris to Baghdad

In addition to vehicle bombs, a supply of arms flowed to Salman Pak, and then to Arab Jabour, where they were stored in large quantities.[448] From there, al Qaeda transported the munitions to Baghdad.[449] The Tigris River was their primary supply route from Baghdad's environs into the city.[450]

Fighters and weapons moved from Arab Jabour into the capital's Rashid district in particular. Arab Jabour is an easy commute to al Qaeda-held areas of Rashid, such as Dora, suggesting a connection between them. Colonel Ricky Gibbs, the commander of the Dragon Brigade (4th Brigade Combat Team, 1st Infantry Division) in Rashid reported in late May that some enemy fighters in his area came into the district from outside of Baghdad, and indeed, from other areas of Iraq.[451] More importantly, Colonel Gibbs estimated that fifteen or twenty percent of the IEDs his troops encountered were EFPs, although he did not indicate whether they were highly refined Iranian weapons or indigenously constructed copycats. He stated that the EFPs were being used in terrain controlled by al Qaeda, not by Shia militias. It is possible that the EFPs were flowing into Dora from Arab Jabour and other points south along the Tigris.

Al Qaeda West and Northwest of Baghdad

Karmah, a village twelve miles northeast of Fallujah, was likewise already a well-established al Qaeda safe haven when Operation Enforcing the Law began on February 14. On February 20, a U.S. battalion identified a fully established car bomb factory there, which had a welding shop, an area for converting cars into car bombs, car bombs in various states of preparation, and chemicals such as fertilizer and chlorine.[452]

A single al Qaeda security emir oversaw military operations in Eastern Anbar province in the first months of 2007. U.S. intelligence indicated that he personally operated in Karmah and Amiriyah, the town south of Fallujah (distinct from the Ameriyah neighborhood of Baghdad). He ran the vehicle bomb network that had attempted to enhance its weapons with chlorine, a substance with which al Qaeda had experimented in February, March, and April in operations northwest of Baghdad, in Baghdad, and in Anbar Province. U.S. forces killed the emir on

April 20, 2007, northwest of Baghdad.[453] They also exploited this discovery in subsequent operations. They captured foreign fighter facilitators and terrorists involved with making or distributing chlorine VBIEDs north of Karmah on May 2 or May 3.[454]

In April and May, al Qaeda operated in the terrain north of the Ramadi-Fallujah-Karmah roadline. The rural area, hardly crisscrossed by any highways or roads, extends north toward Lake Tharthar and along its eastern shore toward Salah ad-Din province. General Odierno identified the terrain south of Lake Tharthar, between Karmah and Tarmiyah, as "a known al Qaeda transit route."[455] Subsequent operations revealed the extent of al Qaeda activity in that terrain. Marines discovered and destroyed a truck bomb near Karmah on April 26.[456] U.S. forces captured an anti-aircraft training cell northeast of Karmah on May 8,[457] detained suspected foreign fighter facilitators there on May 14,[458] and killed financiers and detained their associates on May 15.[459]

Subsequent raids there targeted al Qaeda senior leaders.[460] U.S. forces discovered hostages in a torture house, and an extensive kidnapping and execution ring, in Karmah just a week later.[461] These Special Operations raids continued into June.[462] A few conventional operations supported these special strikes. U.S. troops, for example, established a Joint Security Station fifteen kilometers northeast of Ramadi, in the rural village of Albu Bali on May 2, after noticing an increase in enemy activity there beginning in mid-April.[463]

The southern and northern belts were connected. Some of the same al Qaeda operatives or couriers moved in each of the belts and through Baghdad. In Samarra, north of Baghdad, U.S. forces found the identification cards of two of those soldiers kidnapped near Mahmudiyah, in the southern belt.[464]

Setting Conditions for the Battle for the Belts

As has been noted, discussions of the Surge often mistake preparatory operations (aimed at setting the conditions for a decisive campaign against the enemy) for the decisive operations themselves. The flow of troops into Baghdad in February and March; the fight for Diyala province, the southern belt, and eastern Anbar, and the continued clearing operations in Baghdad in April and May, were preliminary operations to set the conditions for multiple Corps offensives in the second half of 2007. The Corps (Multi-National Corps-Iraq) is the largest military unit that fights in Iraq, and General Odierno commanded it in 2007. It consists of multiple divisions of U.S. and allied forces. A Corps offensive is a set of coordinated military operations by all the forces that fight in the theater. It requires months of planning and preparations because so many troops are involved, conditions must be set, the mission is complex, and different divisions must coordinate their plans and operations.

Planning and preparations for a Corps-wide decisive operation began in December, before President Bush announced the "surge" of troops into Iraq. Generals Petraeus and Odierno had determined before the launch of Fardh al Qanoon that securing Baghdad would require a major campaign to dislodge al Qaeda from the belts around Baghdad. The battle for the belts was a Corps-level mission not only because of its great significance, but also because it required coordination across multiple division areas of operation: the Multi-National Divisions in North, Center, and Baghdad, and the combined Marine and Army force in West.

Commanders "set the conditions" for decisive operations by deploying their forces to the theater, establishing bases for the forces, supplying them, organizing command structures, reconnoitering the terrain, developing intelligence about the enemy, and creating maneuver corridors. These tasks often involve units in combat. Forces moving into enemy-controlled areas often must fight to establish their new bases. When scouts reconnoiter new areas, they may make contact with the enemy and fight skirmishes. In each case, the purpose of operations is not to fight and eliminate the enemy from an area, but rather to create the preconditions for successful *decisive* operations to follow. These preliminary operations aim to reconnoiter terrain, map enemy behavior, prepare friendly forces, seize key positions, establish a relationship of basic trust with the population, and weaken the enemy wherever possible.

From January to June 2007, General Odierno used military forces to set the conditions for decisive operations in Baghdad and the belts. General Petraeus described this process: "We have been doing what we might call shaping operations in a lot of these different areas. We've been feeling their edges, if you will, doing intelligence gathering, putting in some special operators, going in but then coming out. And now for the first time we're really going into a couple of the really key areas in the belt from which, again, al Qaeda has sallied forth with car bombs, additional fighters and so forth. . . . [S]o we think we can build on what has been done—if you will, the foundation of intelligence and base structure and all the rest that has been put in place over the last several months."[465]

Before Operation Enforcing the Law began in February, General Odierno used American troops to disrupt al Qaeda strongholds in and around Baghdad. U.S. forces fought to enter violent terrain that the enemy had firmly controlled in 2006, such as Haifa Street (Baghdad), Balad Ruz (Diyala), and Yusifiyah (southwest of Baghdad).

General Odierno and his Iraqi counterparts then began Operation Enforcing the Law. He moved U.S. forces from their Forward Operating Bases near the capital to more dispersed Joint Security Stations in Baghdad. As the new brigades arrived, he sent some to Baghdad. U.S. forces within Baghdad reconnoitered their areas from their Joint Security Stations and cleared the enemy from key positions that U.S. units needed to occupy or transverse in order to continue counterinsurgency operations. By conducting regular neighborhood patrols, they laid the groundwork for future counterinsurgency operations.

From February through June, U.S. brigades continued to fight within the city to expand their territorial control. General Odierno re-concentrated and re-positioned troops in western and southern

Baghdad in April to counter the enemy and to prepare for further clearing operations. Extensive clearing operations in southern Baghdad, where al Qaeda established strong defensive positions in 2006, began in mid-May.

While operations in Baghdad continued, General Odierno deployed additional troops into the belts around Baghdad. He reinforced Diyala province, northeast of Baghdad, in March and in May. In April, he deployed a new Surge brigade in Besmaya, east of Sadr City. These new U.S. forces began to maneuver in the eastern and southeastern belts of the capital in May. Additional troops reinforced the southwestern belt that runs from Sadr al Yusifiyah to Mahmudiyah. The new Marine Expeditionary Unit began operating northeast of Fallujah and northwest of Baghdad, along the southern shore of Lake Tharthar. Finally, General Odierno re-positioned U.S. forces north and west of Baghdad so that they operated as seamlessly as possible within that terrain.

By the beginning of June, General Odierno had encircled Baghdad with Coalition Forces—not literally, with an unbroken chain, but rather by placing brigades on every main road to and from the city. On June 15, 2007, General Odierno launched multiple, simultaneous offensives around Baghdad in order to disrupt enemies surrounding the city. This Corps offensive was called Operation Phantom Thunder, and it aimed to eliminate the enemy from the belts, disrupt their ability to coordinate and reinforce across the theater, and prevent them from reestablishing themselves in or near the city.

General Odierno's placement of the additional brigades secured the particular area in which each was located. More importantly, he deployed each brigade in a discernable pattern, with an eye to securing Baghdad as a whole. He concentrated U.S. forces in two rings around Baghdad, one fifteen to thirty miles outside the city, and the other along the city's circumference. The outer ring ran from Taji (north of Baghdad between the eleven and twelve o'clock position), clockwise to Tarmiyah (one), Buhriz (two), Besmaya (three), Salman Pak (five), Mahmudiyah (six), Sadr al Yusifiyah (eight), Fallujah (nine) and Karmah (ten). An inner ring took shape along the border of Baghdad itself, as troops moved off the FOBs surrounding the city: Adhamiyah (one-two), Rashid (four-seven), western Mansour (nine-eleven). In addition, troops have fanned out into the central areas of Baghdad, particularly into Karkh. Finally, they operated on the southeastern fringes of the city, such as Kamiliyah.

General Odierno's deployment constituted a deep encirclement of Baghdad, which aimed to prevent the enemy from moving from sector to sector during Phantom Thunder. General Odierno's disposition of forces also concentrated troops in volatile, densely populated areas, which lay along sectarian fault lines.

Generals Petraeus and Odierno made other preparations for the Corps offensive between January and June: For example, U.S. forces captured and killed al Qaeda leaders and operatives, especially in Baghdad's belts, Karmah, Balad, and the northern city of Mosul. They likewise killed and captured rogue militia leaders and arms smugglers in Baghdad and in southern Iraq. The Iraqi Security Forces planned and conducted a counterinsurgency campaign to quell militia violence in the southern city of Diwaniyah. U.S. forces also assisted in the growth of provincial government and the Iraqi Security Forces during this same period.

Preparing the Inner Cordon and Net: Reinforcing Baghdad During the Deployment of Surge Brigades

This encirclement of the city by U.S. forces was the most complex and significant military development of the first six months of the Surge. General Odierno added two new "Surge" brigades to Baghdad for Operation Fardh al Qanoon.[466] The five brigades in Baghdad proper increased their ability to maneuver in the first four months of Fardh al Qanoon. They established Combat Outposts, reconnoitered routes, tracked the enemy, and destroyed weapons caches. Discrete operations to secure neighborhoods accompanied the creeping spread of troops into Baghdad. From February through June, the five brigades in the capital hardened markets, protected residential areas, and established safe neighborhoods as models.

Spreading the Net, Tightening the Inner Cordon, and Preparing the Belts

Phantom Thunder, the campaign to control the belts, began after U.S. forces within Baghdad achieved a certain level of security in parts of the capital and disrupted the enemy's movements in the city. General Odierno gave a general disposition of troops and situation report on Baghdad as Operation Phantom Thunder began: "In Multi-National Division-Baghdad, we have five brigade combat teams operating inside Baghdad proper, and a sixth brigade combat team operating in Taji north of the city. Some parts of Baghdad are doing well and seeing progress while others still have high levels of violence. Our current focus is clearing and controlling the security districts of Adhamiyah in northeast, Rashid in the south, and portions of Mansour in the northwest. These are the areas where we're seeing the majority of violence inside of Baghdad. These are areas where sectarian fault lines exist, [a] convergence of AQI and Shia extremists."[467]

U.S. forces deliberately attacked some of the largest concentrations of al Qaeda in the city, particularly in Ghazaliyah and Rashid, before and during Operation Phantom Thunder.

The brigades in western Baghdad moved toward one another during reinforcing and clearing operations, creating a cordon in Baghdad's interior sometime in May. The clearing in Ghazaliyah drove fighters from that area—perhaps to southern Baghdad—while preventing enemy reinforcements from arriving from the west. The clearing in Rashid killed, captured, and pushed fighters into a tighter area in Dora, a collection of mahallas in that southern district.

The operations in Rashid laid the groundwork for the clearing of the southern belt by limiting the movement of al Qaeda into and out of the southern section of the capital. As U.S. troops squeezed al Qaeda in Ghazaliyah, southern Karkh, and western Rashid, the fighters in Dora could not easily move north or west. At least as importantly, the campaign in the belts prevented al Qaeda from escaping from Dora to Arab Jabour, or from reinforcing Dora from the south.

General Fil stated at the end of June that all Surge forces that would reinforce Baghdad had arrived. As a result, he said, he was "now able to really touch all parts of the city with Coalition Forces."[468] It is thus possible to speak of a "net" of U.S. and Iraqi forces within Baghdad's inner cordon.

Preparing Baghdad's Outer Cordon

General Odierno placed units in the belts in late December and early January. They began reconnoitering the Euphrates River and Arab Jabour in January with the aid of the 1-40 Cavalry Squadron already in theater. In addition, the 2 BCT/10th Mountain operated in Yusifiyah and elements of the 4BCT/25th Infantry in Iskandariyah. This relatively small force was technically responsible for large sections of terrain, but they by no means operated throughout the large area that encircled the city.

General Odierno deployed the next three arriving brigades to the belts around the capital. By placing three fresh brigades around the city, he prepared to contest the enemy's occupation of the Baghdad belts. Operations around Baghdad in February, March, April, and May aimed to "interdict accelerants" into Baghdad. In other words, Coalition Forces tried to prevent the flow of weapons and people who were supplying weapons, money, fighters, car or truck bombs, or otherwise enabling armed groups to fight one another and terrorize the population of Baghdad.[469]

As U.S. troops moved into Baghdad in force, some of the enemy predictably tried to take refuge in safe havens in the belts, as they had in the past.[470] General Petraeus noted in April: "[W]e expected, frankly, that as the pressure was exerted in Baghdad on al Qaeda in particular, but also

[on] some of the extremist militia elements, that they would migrate north and south respectively, and that has been the case."[471]

General Odierno's consistent deployment of forces into the Baghdad belts since January, however, put pressure on al Qaeda's safe havens. General Petraeus explained, "We have chased them in some cases. As you may know, we deployed a Stryker battalion from Baghdad to Diyala Province just north of Baghdad—northeast Baqubah, which is a city in the so-called fault line areas between both sects and ethnic groups. We have reinforced with some special operations elements the areas in Mosul and Nineveh Province. So we do believe … that we are keeping the pressure on, in fact, in those areas as those elements, in a sense, squirt or move out of Baghdad, and we are also going after them in the Baghdad belts. In fact, as these additional forces come in, they are not just going to the interior of Baghdad. In some cases they're going to the so-called belts around Baghdad—so-called throat of Baghdad—that have often been battle zones in which we have generally not dominated in the past but do need to dominate if we're to provide improved security in Baghdad proper."[472]

General Odierno's troop disposition thus encircled or pinched many insurgents who operated between the belts and Baghdad. In order to disrupt the flow of fighters back into Baghdad, Generals Petraeus and Odierno planned a Corps-level offensive consisting of many operations conducted simultaneously around the ring.

A New Division Headquarters:
Development of Multi-National Division-Center

General Odierno created a new division headquarters in order to conduct the fight in the belts, evidence of the priority and complexity of the operation he foresaw there. Multi-National Division-Baghdad, commanded by General Joseph Fil, controlled eight brigades, stretching from Tarmiyah (twenty miles north of Baghdad) through Iskandariyah (twenty-five miles south of Baghdad) until April 1.[473] The number of brigades assigned to the division, the complexity of the mission inside Baghdad, and the vast terrain the units covered presented a span-of-control challenge for the Baghdad Division commander.[474]

As Generals Petraeus and Odierno developed the campaign plan for the southern belt and added forces south and east of the city, they requested a new division headquarters to command that sector. Third Infantry Division, commanded by Major General Rick Lynch, oversaw the new Multi-National Division-Center, established on April 1, 2007, and operational soon thereafter.[475]

Generals Petraeus and Odierno had considered the Baghdad belts a priority—indeed, an integral part of the Baghdad Security Plan—since Operation Enforcing the Law began on February 14, 2007. General Fil spoke about the plans to add a division headquarters as early as February 16. He indicated at that time that General Odierno would use the division headquarters to manage the fight in the belts. The new division headquarters would oversee an outer cordon, allowing MND-Baghdad to focus exclusively on the capital city.[476] Generals Petraeus and Odierno, therefore, had judged in February that the fight for the Baghdad belts would require such extensive reinforcements that they would probably need to add a new division headquarters before operations began.[477] The development of MND-Center in April permitted more extensive operations south and east of Baghdad, in terrain that extended into Babil, Wasit, Baghdad, and Diyala provinces.[478]

The Final Pieces of the Surge

On May 31, General Odierno stated: "Units that are part of our surge into the theater began deploying in January, about the middle of January. However, the full impact of that surge is yet to be felt. . . . [T]he final pieces of the surge will soon be in place. In the coming weeks, about the next two weeks, 8,000 troops will begin to move into their assigned areas of responsibility. Second Brigade, 3rd Infantry Division; the 13th Marine Expeditionary Unit, as well as the 3rd Combat Aviation Brigade, will fill out the combat portion of the Surge. And that should occur here as they take up positions in the next couple weeks."[479] On June 16, Secretary of Defense Robert Gates remarked, "We began the process of building up our forces some months ago, but the fifth brigade as part of the Surge really only entered the fight within the last few days."[480]

General Petraeus indicated that some of the last units to arrive as part of the force increase were among the most critical. They included the Combat Aviation Brigade (CAB) for MND-C, which arrived in late May. The aviation brigade added important capabilities, including attack helicopters and Kiowa helicopters (for advanced reconnaissance missions).[481] The arrival of these air assets allowed paratroopers from MND-C to conduct sophisticated reconnaissance and air assaults—that is, the insertion of infantrymen by helicopter, often in order to move behind enemy positions.[482]

General Odierno positioned the 13th Marine Expeditionary Unit northwest of Baghdad to operate south of Lake Tharthar. He placed other Marines west of Baghdad, to occupy the portion of Anbar province between Fallujah and Abu Ghraib: "Just to the west of Baghdad, elements of the 6th Regimental Combat Team began operations against enemy safe havens near Kharma, while continuing to secure Fallujah. The 6th Regimental Combat Team is well into the process of establishing Iraqi police precincts in Fallujah, where violence has significantly decreased over the past few months."[483]

In late May and early June, General Petraeus and General Odierno closed the gaps in the belt west and northwest of Baghdad (with the Marines), and east and southeast of Baghdad (with the maneuver elements of the 3rd Infantry Division and its aviation assets). These holes—unprotected rural spaces, river crossings, and cities—had allowed enemies to transport and distribute weapons and maneuver fighters on roads and rivers without regularly encountering U.S. troops. Coalition partners provided the last supporting units in the summer of 2007, when a Georgian brigade arrived to secure Wasit Province, the capital city of which is al Kut, near the Iranian border.

General Odierno stated that the troop increase and the new disposition of forces gave him three new capabilities: to conduct "simultaneous and sustained operations," "to maintain pressure across the entire
theater on extremists," and "to operate in areas where we have not been
in a long time."[484]

The Real Surge Begins

General Odierno began Operation Phantom Thunder, a coordinated
offensive against insurgent strongholds in the belts, on June 15, 2007. Brigades from the Multi-National Division-North and (MND-N), Multi-
National Division-Center (MND-C), and Multi-National Division-West
(MND-W) began simultaneous clearing operations northeast, east,
southeast, and west of Baghdad. General Petraeus explained the next day
that "literally in the last twenty-four hours we have launched a number of different offensive operations, in the Baghdad belts in particular,
and we're continuing a number of operations that have been ongoing
in Baghdad itself." As a result, General Odierno noted, U.S. troops "can
maintain security forces inside of Baghdad while we're simultaneously
conducting operations in Baqubah, Arab Jabour, Fallujah. So that allows
us to keep pressure on [the enemy]."[485]

He went on to explain the operation more completely:

> Operation Phantom Thunder is a corps-level offensive operation that
> began on 15 June to defeat al Qaeda insurgents and extremists, deny
> enemy safe havens, interdict movement, logistics and communica-
> tions. It is an open-ended operation that will extend through the sum-
> mer and will be done in conjunction with civil-military operations to
> support political and economic efforts.
>
> It consists of carefully synchronized simultaneous operations at
> division and brigade level to clear al Qaeda, Sunni insurgents and Shi'a
> extremists in, near and around Baghdad. It also includes aggressive
> shaping op ions by our Special Operations Forces focused on al Qaeda
> in Iraq and other Special Groups.

These operations are intended to eliminate accelerants to Baghdad violence from enemy support zones in the belts that ring the city. In some cases this means we're operating in areas where—[we had not been. When we went] earlier this week into an area we have not operated in in a while, local Iraqis asked Coalition Forces, "Where have you been?" And, "Can our children go back to school now?"

The intent of Phantom Thunder is to protect the Iraqi population and render irreconcilable groups ineffective, while employing political and economic initiatives to buy time and space for the government of Iraq to move towards political accommodation.[486]

These component operations of Phantom Thunder included Arrowhead Ripper (Baqubah) and Marne Torch (Arab Jabour), along with other efforts to support them. Each of these individual operations aimed not only to clear of enemy forces the particular area in which U.S. forces are operating, but also to prevent movement around the Baghdad belts.

Conclusions

Operation Phantom Thunder was the first coordinated, offensive campaign against the insurgency in Iraq. The campaign is hitting insurgent strongholds throughout central Iraq simultaneously. Troops drove the enemy from the belts while continuing to clear Baghdad itself. The surge of additional troops allowed Generals Petraeus and Odierno to undertake this large-scale operation without drawing down forces in many other areas of the country or leaving major insurgent strongholds uncovered. Al Qaeda and other insurgent leaders who fled from individual operations were hard-pressed to find well-established safe havens near Baghdad.

Phantom Thunder took the initiative from the enemy at the operational, and strategic, level. Enemy cells continued to conduct suicide bombings or to plant IEDs, but Coalition Forces deliberately drove them to and trapped them in narrowing areas that could be cleared.

Phantom Thunder increased local support for Coalition operations. Commanders across the theater reported significant growth in the number and utility of tips about the location of enemy fighters, IEDs, caches, and traps.

Military operations in Iraq in the summer of 2007 disrupted al Qaeda's operations throughout the country. By mid-July U.S. forces had pushed al Qaeda out of its urban sanctuaries and broken up its operations in the belts, driving the enemy successively further from the capital. By August, the enemy occupied small, dispersed pockets, many of which were not mutually reinforcing.

Phantom Thunder was unusual in the annals of counterinsurgency for its scale and its combination of multiple, complex movements over a large area, all of which focused on essential tasks of counterinsurgency. Coalition Forces moved deliberately in clearing operations in order to minimize their own casualties as well as collateral damage and the loss of civilian life. They also engaged the population in the counterinsurgency effort. The operation was designed to avoid the pitfalls of previous approaches, denigrated by some critics as a "whack-a-mole" strategy that allowed defeated insurgents to flee to remote safe havens and reconstitute. The Coalition commanders accepted some risk in Salah ad-Din, Kirkuk, and Ninewah provinces, which were lightly held by Coalition Forces, in order to focus on Anbar, Baghdad, and the Baghdad belts. The focus of Phantom Thunder accorded with the original intention of the new strategy, which aimed to secure Baghdad.

A war this large and complex does not end with a single battle or campaign. The art of military command in such conflicts lies in tying multiple, simultaneous, and successive operations together over time in order to improve the situation on the ground.

Chapter 6
■ ■ ■ Phantom Thunder and Phantom Strike in Diyala

Operation Arrowhead Ripper, the Multi-National Division-North component of Phantom Thunder, cleared Baqubah. After this operation, the continued presence of U.S. troops, partnered with Iraqis and "concerned local citizens," prevented the organization from re-establishing itself there. The clearing of Baqubah was a turning point in the campaign because AQI control of the city in the first half of 2006 prevented U.S. forces from securing Baghdad and its belts.

The Diyala component of Phantom Thunder, and its follow-up offensive, called Phantom Strike, illustrate the complex relationship between combat and other lines of operation, such as political and economic development. As commanders interpreted counterinsurgency doctrine in Diyala, positive synergies developed between combat operations, governance, and the policy of tribal engagement that, together, made central Iraq more secure.

As U.S. and Iraqi forces eliminated enemy safe havens in Diyala, they encouraged some tribes and villages to turn against enemy groups. They also increased their operations against extremist militia groups which tried to establish control as al Qaeda's presence receded in the province. Commanders attempted to eliminate the insurgency more permanently in Diyala by linking tribal movements to national, provincial, and local government institutions.

Clearing and Holding Baqubah
During Operation Arrowhead Ripper

In May and June, U.S. forces conducted preliminary, or "shaping," oper-ations in order to set the conditions for Arrowhead Ripper.[487] Principally, they established a presence in the eastern portion of the city, known as Old Baqubah, and in Buhriz, a district to the south of Baqubah.

Nevertheless, between 300 and 500 insurgents remained in the west-ern neighborhoods of Baqubah (Khatoon, Mufredk, and Mujema).[488] Insurgents occupied residents' homes by force in order to establish strong military positions from which to attack U.S. and Iraqi troops. Insurgents also hoarded food and fuel in the city which the Iraqi govern-ment intended for distribution to residents.[489] The religious extremists terrorized Baqubah's residents by operating their own justice system to enforce their interpretation of Islamic law. U.S. troops in Baqubah ulti-mately discovered a courthouse and documents, a torture house com-plete with saws and blood-stained walls, a prison, and a grave containing five bodies.[490] One embedded reporter interviewed Baqubah's residents about al Qaeda's campaign of intimidation in the would-be capital of the Islamic state of Iraq in 2006 and 2007:

> Residents said the militants gradually began taking over last year, parad-ing through the streets in trucks, brandishing Kalashnikov assault rifles and using bullhorns to inform residents that they were now part of the Islamic State of Iraq. They banned smoking, closed down barbershops and coffeehouses, and required women to cover themselves in black robes with only a slit for their eyes. Iraqis working for the Baghdad gov-ernment or for U.S. forces were hunted down and killed, residents said. Even a trip to Baghdad was grounds for suspicion . . . . Scores of Shiite Muslim families were forced from their homes, which the insurgents used as temporary hide-outs or converted to house the institutions of their rule.

U.S. soldiers discovered a courthouse containing marriage certificates, records of civil disputes and a log of suicide bombers, including details about volunteers and where they could be found.

Residents said the gunmen stole food and collected government ration packs from the Shiites they displaced. Three storehouses were found containing bags of rice, corn flour, cooking oil and stacks of blankets.[491]

This religious extremism, in part, fractured the Sunni insurgent movement in Baqubah. Former Baathists in the 1920s Revolution Brigades, largely based in the eastern part of Baqubah, chose to assist U.S. forces in the fight against al Qaeda by providing them with intelligence about the latter group's precise positions in the city.[492] Special Forces targeted al Qaeda in Mufrek and Khatoon in the first weeks of June, preparing for the conventional operations ahead.[493]

At the beginning of Phantom Thunder, the Corps concentrated nearly 10,000 U.S. and Iraqi troops in Diyala to liberate the city and interdict any insurgents who tried to escape. U.S. forces planned operations in and around Baqubah that aimed to prevent insurgents from escaping during the fight. "Rather than let the problem export to some other place and then have to fight them again, my goal is to isolate this thing and cordon it off," said Col. Steve Townsend, the commander of the Third Stryker Brigade Combat Team, Second Infantry Division,[494] tasked with clearing the city. The Greywolf Brigade (3-1 Cavalry) supported the effort in Baqubah by conducting operations in the Diyala River Valley, to which al Qaeda might attempt to escape or from which they might derive support. Accordingly, the plan involved cutting the major lines of communication out of the city.

Arrowhead Ripper began on June 19, 2007: "In the first hours of the American military assault, after midnight early Monday, helicopters flew two teams of American troops and a platoon of Iraqi scouts so they could block the southern escape routes from the city. Stryker armored vehicles moved along the western outskirts of Baqubah and then down a main north-south route that cuts through the center of the city. By the time dawn broke on Tuesday, the insurgent sanctuary in western Baqubah had been cordoned off. Then, the American forces established footholds on the periphery of the section and slowly pressed in."[495] Rather than projecting force *from* established positions in eastern Baqubah and Buhriz, U.S. forces attempted to surprise the enemy by moving *toward* them.

Insurgents defended western Baqubah by pre-positioning explosives along major routes: "About 30 improvised explosive devices, or IEDs, were planted on Route Coyote, the U.S. code name for a main Baqubah thoroughfare."[496] Insurgents attempted "to use deep-buried bombs under the road and small-arms fire to force the soldiers to take refuge in the houses adjoining the route."[497] They rigged houses for detonation to destroy any troops taking refuge inside. "Col. Steve Townsend . . . said the network of house bombs here was the most extensive he had seen in Iraq. He said that in the first seven days of the attack, the brigade destroyed 21 house bombs."[498]

The careful reconnaissance of Baqubah, including the scouting and intelligence provided by the 1920s Brigades, enabled U.S. forces to destroy many of the deep-buried IEDs and houses rigged with explosives before they patrolled each city block on foot.[499] As clearing operations continued, soldiers erected concrete barriers around Baqubah's western neighborhoods to prevent insurgents from attacking or re-infiltrating their former safe havens.[500] Soldiers brought humanitarian aid, such as rice and water, to the residents of western Baqubah within ninety-six hours of commencing combat operations.[501]

Securing Baqubah required multiple kinds of activities: combat operations in the city; combat operations in Diyala province; aid for the population; and tribal reconciliation.

Emergency supplies and aid promptly followed clearing operations. By mid-July, convoys of trucks delivering medical supplies, fuel, and food had reached even the outer corners of Diyala Province.[502] By July 29, Diyala residents had received 284,000 kilograms of rice and 285,000 kilograms of flour, distributed with the assistance of the Iraqi Army and U.S. forces.[503]

The Iraqi Army also participated in reconstruction efforts. The 5th Iraqi Army Division's civil affairs officer visited west Baqubah's neighborhoods on July 31 to assess ongoing engineering projects and humanitarian aid.[504] Two days later, Baqubah's mayor and neighborhood leaders met to discuss the city's problems.[505]

Reconciliation efforts proceeded as soon as Arrowhead Ripper had cleared western Baqubah. The city's mayor met with nine tribal sheikhs and the head of the Diyala Operations Center (the overarching Iraqi military command in the province). Colonel Sutherland explained the need for locally recruited Iraqi police, and for a Concerned Citizens' Movement that might produce police candidates.[506] The meeting apparently produced an agreement that applied to the inhabitants of several Baqubah neighborhoods, including Buhriz, Tahrir, Mufrek, and Khatoon.[507]

U.S. forces conducted reactive operations in Baqubah against insurgents who took arms again in early July, as the first phase of combat operations subsided.[508] U.S. forces began a second phase of Arrowhead Ripper on July 17. The 3-2 Stryker Brigade, supported by elements of the 3-1 Cavalry, surrounded Old Baqubah, one of Baqubah's eastern neighborhoods. They cleared the area in a multi-day operation through house to house searches.[509]

The clearing of Old Baqubah made it possible and necessary for U.S. commanders and former insurgent groups to negotiate a longer-term relationship. Accordingly, in late July, Colonel Townsend "met with local citizens interested in contributing to the future security plan" in the city. After that meeting, locals formed the Baqubah Guardians.[510] The organization's members wear uniforms, are tracked in a U.S. Army database, and swear to cooperate with U.S and Iraqi forces in the effort to oust al Qaeda. The Baqubah Guardians were founded not as an alternative to the Iraqi Security Forces, but rather as a group that provided an extra layer of security for the provincial capital. Initially, they provided intelligence about al Qaeda weapons caches and reinfiltration into Baqubah.[511] They also served as first-responders in emergencies and assisted the Iraqi Security Forces. For example, al Qaeda attempted to reestablish itself in the Buhriz section of southern Baqubah, in mid-August. The Baqubah Guardians caught the first wave of insurgents, gunning down seven; they notified and fought alongside Iraqi Security Forces to hold that portion of the city.[512]

Security operations in early August continued to destroy zones that al Qaeda used to support its violent activities in the Baqubah area. U.S. forces conducted an air assault operation in an area south of Baqubah from which al Qaeda had launched mortar attacks, and they discovered weapons caches and vehicles the enemy intended to use as VBIEDs.[513] They cleared the village of Abu Tinah, northeast of Baqubah, from which al Qaeda threatened nearby villages.[514]

The Battle for Khalis

Arrowhead Ripper liberated Baqubah from terrorist control. U.S. forces killed or captured roughly 150 insurgents, including about 80 percent of ordinary al Qaeda fighters. But approximately 80 percent of the al Qaeda leaders in Baqubah escaped from the city before the combat operations began.[515]

The enemy that fled Baqubah in June dispersed into traditional safe havens outside the provincial capital. By June 26, Colonel Townsend had intelligence reports identifying al Qaeda's concentration points as Samarra, Khalis, and Khan Bani Sa'ad, reflecting recent activity in these areas.[516]

The city of Khalis, about ten miles northwest of Baqubah, sits between the Tigris and the Diyala Rivers on the highway that runs north from Baqubah to Kirkuk. The highways and back roads connect Khalis with important al Qaeda sanctuaries along the Tigris River Valley. The Khalis corridor was already a significant battleground for al Qaeda and Shia extremist militias before the former were chased from Baqubah. Al Qaeda and Shia militias fought to control that road, as well as the east-west routes through Khalis and the city itself.

Militia-affiliated local officials in Khalis, a primarily Shia city, aided some sectarian actors in charge of Diyala's security forces in 2006. Khalis contained a headquarters of a battalion of the Fifth Iraqi Army Division, a detention center, a city Emergency Response Force, and a major hospital.[517] The commander of the Fifth Iraqi Army Division in 2006 was General Shakir Hussain, who was placed in command before August 4, 2006 and relieved of command in mid-May 2007 by the Iraqi government because of his sectarian behavior.[518]

The Provincial Director of Police in 2006 was Gassan al Bawi, who had recruited Wolf Brigade members to police Baqubah on a sectarian basis, and who was also arrested.[519] Other sectarian actors arose, however, as new branches of the security service emerged. At the Khalis sheikhs meeting in July, Sunni sheikhs accused their Shia colleagues of supporting militants, and they accused the Iraqi Security Forces of acting on behalf of the Jaysh al Mahdi. The Sunni sheikhs voiced particular concerns about the Emergency Response Force commander, whom, they said, acted in a sectarian manner.[520] Indeed, Coalition Forces arrested "an extremist company commander" in Khalis on October 6, 2007.[521]

The Khalis corridor also served as a main supply route and safe haven for Iranian-backed Special Groups. U.S. forces found a huge cache in al Jadidah on February 25, 2007, which contained 130 copper disks for the fabrication of EFPs, a hallmark of Iranian-backed groups.[522] In late July, U.S. and Iraqi forces pursued Special Groups members through the Khalis and Qasarin areas.[523] Coalition Forces engaged in a firefight with twenty-five men while attempting to apprehend a Special Groups leader west of Baqubah on October 5. That leader facilitated the transportation of weapons from Iran into Iraq. That particular group was sufficiently organized and trained that it remained in its defensive positions as U.S. forces arrived, then began to maneuver from them into an attack, supported by anti-aircraft weapons which were used to engage Coalition air support.[524] Special Groups interacted with criminal networks in Khalis and Qasarin.[525] East of the Diyala River, individuals with close ties to the Iranian Revolutionary Guards Corps-Qods Force facilitated the movement of weapons in Kharnabat, just north of Baqubah, in July.[526] U.S. forces also found several large EFP caches south of Baqubah in October and November.[527] Between February and October, Special Groups might regularly transported weapons from Iran and stored them in depots along the banks of the Tigris and Diyala Rivers. Alternatively, Special Groups emplaced weapons there in February, and reactivated the supply lines and headquarters through southern Diyala as Arrowhead Ripper and its successors dislodged al Qaeda from the area.

The Special Groups and al Qaeda fought with one another for the control of Diyala's lines of communication throughout 2007. Al Qaeda attempted to cut the supply routes used by extremist militias and Iranian-backed secret cells in Diyala. They had based themselves at Hebheb, five miles south of Khalis, since 2006. Al Qaeda regularly launched spectacular attacks targeting government institutions in Khalis at one-month intervals (beginning in December 2006; attacks followed in January, February, the end of March, and the end of April 2007).[528] Al Qaeda in Iraq also attempted to cut access to the roads to and from Khalis by laying IEDs. For example, in early May, two IEDs targeted concrete carriers in Abu Shuwka, five kilometers south of Khalis. Al Qaeda frequently attacked these vehicles because they carried concrete for building police stations and facilities for the Iraqi Army and U.S. forces.[529]

Extremists—whose sectarian affiliation has not been identified—accelerated violence among villages in the vicinity of Khalis through mortar attacks.[530] Inter-village conflict erupted in mixed areas west of Hebheb in early May 2007.[531] An assassination campaign targeted key figures in Khalis: a judge and prosecutor on the appeal court (January); a Daini tribal leader (April); a Sunni local council member from the Jumaili tribe (May); civil servants (May). And extremists began a series of mass kidnappings in early June.[532]

Khalis During Arrowhead Ripper

Greywolf and Iraqi Security Forces, therefore, conducted supporting operations during the clearing of Baqubah in order to drive al Qaeda from Khalis, block escape through the Khalis corridor, and prevent the organization from regrouping there or dispersing across the Tigris.

They undertook preparatory operations in Khalis before Arrowhead Ripper. On June 5, attack aircraft and ground troops killed nineteen terrorists and wounded one in Koubat village, just north of Khalis, evidently an enemy stronghold. This set the conditions for securing Khalis during Arrowhead Ripper and blocking the enemy from using Khalis as an escape or reinforcement route during the battle of Baqubah.

As Arrowhead Ripper proceeded in Baqubah, so did the operations in and around Khalis. The 1st Battalion, 2nd Brigade, 5th Iraqi Army held checkpoints near the city, while Greywolf and the Iraqi Police conducted security operations around it.[533] Iraqi soldiers secured the main road into and out of Khalis, while others conducted patrols on nearby villages such as Salam.[534]

Organized al Qaeda units of fifteen to twenty fighters staged complex attacks to disrupt the progress of Coalition Forces in Khalis. On June 20, just one day into Arrowhead Ripper, al Qaeda conducted a complex attack on an Iraqi Army checkpoint near Khalis. Fifteen al Qaeda gunmen dismounted from four vans and fired on the checkpoint. The Iraqis fended off the attack, killing eleven of the fifteen enemy gunmen. The remaining four returned to their vehicles and fled toward a nearby village. The vehicles dispersed; a Coalition attack helicopter team followed one that seemed more important to Jamil nearby. The vehicle entered a compound in the village, and the pursued gunmen dismounted and ran into a house. The aviation assets killed the gunmen and destroyed the house, causing a series of secondary explosions—indicating the presence of a large weapons cache.

Meanwhile, al Qaeda attempted to ambush the reinforcements sent to the attacked Khalis checkpoint by emplacing false IEDs along the route. When the reinforcements stopped to secure the IED site, al Qaeda gunmen attacked them. The Iraqi soldiers and their American advisors killed two gunmen. They were reinforced by an attack helicopter, which killed a third.

Al Qaeda organized another counterattack a few days later. On June

22, Iraqi Police attempted to secure a village southwest of Khalis. Seventeen al Qaeda gunmen tried "to circumvent the IPs and infiltrate the village."[535] Coalition attack helicopters from the 25th Combat Aviation Brigade and ground forces from 3rd Brigade Combat Team, 1st Cavalry Division, spotted the enemy movement. The attack helicopters engaged, killing the gunmen and protecting the village.[536]

In addition to the battle between Coalition Forces, Iraqi forces, and al Qaeda groups, inter-village fighting erupted in the Khalis area a few days after the clearing operations. Villagers from Tohoyla, about ten kilometers north of Khalis, attacked residents of nearby al Koubat village. (Coalition Forces had begun the preparatory operations in Khalis by attacking terrorist positions in Koubat, three weeks earlier.) Citizens called the Provincial Joint Coordination Center and requested help. Iraqi Security Forces intervened to stop the gun fight, but four villagers were killed and nineteen wounded before they arrived.[537]

Arrowhead Ripper in Khan Bani Sa'ad

Coalition Forces conducted operations in Khalis simultaneously with others in Khan Bani Saad, south of Baqubah on the road to Baghdad (via the southeastern district, 9 Nissan). Khan Bani Saad city, the highway through it, and the tribal areas located nearby all also provided access to the Salman Pak area southeast of the capital. During a series of raids in Khan Bani Saad from June 20 to 22, "Coalition Forces discovered a terrorist safe house, containing weapons, handcuffs, ammunition, stretchers, black masks and homemade explosives . . . several weapons caches containing mortars, rockets, chemicals used for making explosives . . . a stolen fire department vehicle . . . [and] a vehicle in a palm grove rigged as a vehicle-borne improvised explosive device. All the weapons and explosives were safely destroyed on site."[538]

The simultaneous operations in Baqubah, Khalis, and Khan Bani Saad dislodged enemy groups from Diyala's capital and neighboring cities, and prevented them from moving from one city to another.

Pursuing the Enemy in the Diyala River Valley and the Khalis Corridor

U.S. and Iraqi forces did not stop their combat operations when they had cleared the urban areas. A series of follow-on operations pursued al Qaeda and prevented it from regrouping near the cities. Commanders had prepared for this chase before the Baqubah fight. "[T]he brigade commander put our unit up in this region to deny them [the enemy] the ability to exfil[trate] into this area," from Baqubah, Khalis, or Khan Bani Sa'ad, Lieutenant Colonel Andrew Poppas, a squadron commander in the Diyala River Valley, explained.[539] Poppas's squadron (5th Squadron, 73rd Cavalry Regiment, 82nd Airborne, attached to Greywolf) had conducted shaping operations on the east bank of the Diyala River Valley in April. Before Arrowhead Ripper, the unit operated from patrol bases in Zaganiyah and As Sadah. After the first phase of Arrowhead Ripper, 5-73 and its Iraqi partners reconnoitered positions along the Diyala River Valley where al Qaeda terrorists might establish themselves in the wake of Baqubah's clearing.[540]

Arrowhead Ripper thus extended from Baqubah through the Diyala River Valley. First, U.S. and Iraqi forces conducted a reconnaissance in force to detect al Qaeda positions. As U.S. forces cleared Baqubah, Khalis, and Khan Bani Sa'ad, 5-73 did not attempt to block movement through all of the battlespace assigned to it. Rather, Poppas noted, the squadron "put sensors out there, because it is a large expanse," in order to determine the enemy's positions. "[I]ndividual soldiers, through patrols and engagements," are the primary sensors, supplemented by other systems, in the counterinsurgency fight.

Routine patrols in the reconnaissance phase revealed a number of enemy positions. The squadron first found al Qaeda operatives during its patrols along the east bank of the Diyala. An organized group of approximately twenty-five terrorists had established itself with a weapons cache in a palm grove near Mukhisa. Three al Qaeda gunmen attacked U.S.

troops on patrol in the vicinity, from across the river (the west bank). U.S. forces returned fire, maneuvered against the position, and called in air support from a fixed-wing aircraft. They destroyed the enemy and weapons. "Throughout the firefight, a nearby mosque was broadcasting chants for local residents to 'rise up against' the Coalition Forces; the chants were later replaced by a voice that seemed to be giving orders."[541] Another combined U.S. and Iraqi patrol operating in the area discovered and destroyed a factory in the village of Mukhisa that produced home-made explosives, complete with protective chemical suits.[542] They did not clear Mukhisa at this time, but rather destroyed the enemy positions that they found.

To the west of the Diyala River, the intertwined fight between the villages, the extremists in the Security Forces, and al Qaeda accelerated in Khalis in early July. Arrowhead Ripper displaced al Qaeda from its positions near the city, allowing Shia extremists to pursue their sectarian agenda vigorously. On July 5, an Iraqi called the local Iraqi Army battalion commander and informed him "that a mob, backed by a local paramilitary group, had descended on the homes of the Albu-Abali Sunni family. The group was about to loot and set the properties on fire, the caller said."[543]

When the battalion arrived, it found the allegedly sectarian Khalis Emergency Response Force guarding the deserted streets, having searched the home of a Sunni leader there whom they suspected of working for al Qaeda. The following day, the same "six homes were looted and set on fire."[544] This was one incident in a series of retributive attacks on villages in the vicinity of Khalis, to the east of which Shia homes were burnt several days before.[545] On July 7 and 8, an extremist company commander from Khalis allegedly forced Sunnis out of their homes in Arab Danan, and then burned the homes and farms. This same commander, along with companions, allegedly ambushed and murdered a Sunni man on July 2.[546] U.S. and Iraqi Special Forces detained the extremist commander in early October 2007, as noted above.[547]

Supplemental intelligence suggested that some al Qaeda was moving into the area west of the Diyala, north and east of Baqubah and east of Khalis. The 5-73 consequently reconnoitered the area and observed a "large mass movement" into Anbakia, a village between the Diyala and the Khalis-Kirkuk highway.[548] "When we went in there, it was a predominantly Shia village . . . .We engaged with the mukhtar and the sheikh and then the locals, and we fanned out. [A]nd just through . . . questioning, we found out that most of them had been forced out of . . . villages to the south," namely, Haimer, Abu Nasim, and Jamil. (These villages are about twenty kilometers north of Baqubah.)

By engaging with the residents, the 5-73 gained specific intelligence on al Qaeda's positions in the villages. The displaced residents "drew handwritten maps of where their houses were. Others . . . told us" where the enemy "had started to sandbag" in order to create defensive positions, where "they were putting in strongpoints," and "where they'd put caches in the local palm groves." Unmanned aerial vehicles confirmed the locals' information.[549]

Operation Ithaca, a component of Arrowhead Ripper, drove al Qaeda from positions in Haimer, Abu Nasim, and Jamil.[550] Al Qaeda used these areas as support zones for its activities in the Diyala River Valley. A troop of 5-73 conducted an air assault into the villages (in an air assault, helicopters insert U.S. forces at multiple landing zones, often to get ground troops within or to the rear of an enemy position). Fixed-wing aircraft and attack helicopters fired on designated targets.[551] They killed twenty-nine al Qaeda gunmen and detained twenty-three others. They also discovered and released eight hostages whom the terrorists were set to execute. They discovered two weapons caches, destroyed a safe house, and eliminated the extortion ring that al Qaeda had used to force the local population to comply with its wishes.[552]

The squadron sent its Civil-Military Operations (CMO) Team toward Anbakia. Enemy groups had blocked the highway that ran north of Baqubah. The CMO team "conducted route clearance, removing improvised explosive devices, barriers, and illegal check points in order to allow Iraqis to use the main road to travel between Baqubah and Khalis."[553]

The squadron conducted combat operations together with civil-military operations, as part of Operation Olympus, ten days after the Ithaca fight. The American paratroopers conducted another air assault into two villages held by the enemy, while Iraqi forces supported them from ground positions. They destroyed the enemy positions in the villages. In nearby Anbakia, the CMO team provided food and medical support, protecting the refugees and villagers.[554]

The 5-73 deliberately assisted Anbakia because "'the town had been friendly to Coalition Forces,'" according to an officer working with the CMO team. "'They help us, so we help them,' he said. 'We will continue to work with them and not just abandon them.'" Poppas added, "Our deliberate destruction of anti-Iraqi forces throughout the entire region has set conditions for the repatriation of these dislodged individuals."[555]

Security and Tribal Reconciliation in Diyala

Negotiations with tribal leaders facilitated clearing operations in the Diyala River Valley. On July 10, before Operation Ithaca, two feuding tribes in the Khalis region north of Baqubah, the Anbakia and the Obeidi, signed a peace agreement.[556] This was the second small-scale reconciliation agreement in Diyala. According to Colonel Sutherland, it was significant because it catalyzed the concerned local citizens movement in Diyala.[557] The sheikhs in Dojima, some of whom were from the Obeidi tribe, formed a Concerned Local Citizens group at this time—almost concurrently with the clearing of Mukhisa, and just before the operations west of the Diyala, effectively denying al Qaeda its safe haven there.[558]

The Anbakia-Obeidi agreement also paved the way for the Obeidis to work with the government, an essential part of the reconciliation effort. There was an "individual on the provincial council who did not want the Obeidis to participate" in provincial government, said Sutherland, but the agreement helped the Obeidis become involved in the process.[559] The participation of the Obeidis quickly advanced tribal and civic negotiations in the Khalis district.

Provincial, municipal, and tribal leaders attended the first reconciliation meeting in Khalis on July 23, 2007, after the formation of the Dojima CLCs and between Operation Ithaca and Operation Olympus. Because Khalis was a focal point of Shia militia and al Qaeda violence in 2007, the meeting was highly contentious. Some Sunni sheikhs charged that many government actors were malign, and wished to hold these people accountable for illegal activity by bringing charges against them. Some Shia sheikhs accused Sunnis of facilitating the emplacement of IEDs by al Qaeda in order to cut off the city of Khalis. They named, in particular, Sheikh Majeed al Bayati. Some of the Obeidi from Dojima confirmed the accusation to the Coalition.[560] The sheikhs' comments illustrate sectarian and local antipathies, but also demonstrate their attempts to make the local and provincial government responsive to the needs and complaints of the population, such as the need for drinking water and irrigation.[561]

The tribal movements and local reconciliation initiatives in Baqubah city and Khalis county paved the way, in turn, for a broader reconciliation meeting in Diyala. Eighteen paramount sheikhs swore and signed a reconciliation agreement in Baqubah on August 2.[562] On August 19, more than 100 tribal leaders from the Diyala River Valley met and swore to "cooperate and support each other in fighting terrorism in our tribes." They also agreed to achieve the following objectives:

- End kidnapping and murdering, release all hostages, and cease rocket and mortar attacks on other tribes.

- Pass all information to ISF regarding expelled members who try to cause riot and sedition between tribes.

- Fight al Qaeda, JAM, Al Shura Council, foreign fighters, and all other illegal armed groups; try to limit the use of weapons to government forces only.

- Work on and cooperate with ISF to eradicate the corrupted members that work in these forces.

- Remove all IEDs that we find placed in our lands.

- Abide by law and support ISF in their fight against terrorism.

- Solve all problems existing between the tribes through dialogue.
- Bring all displaced families back to their homes.[563]

Nineteen of twenty-five paramount sheikhs in Diyala swore to and signed the agreement. The remaining six, from remote tribal areas in the north and east corners of the province, did not participate in the discussions. Colonel Sutherland attributed their absence to their relative distance from Diyala's most violent areas.[564]

The governor of Diyala province pursued this large meeting with a smaller gathering that aimed to assist with reconciliation among competing local villages in the Diyala River Valley.[565] Colonel Sutherland explained a situation that required special attention: "When we had a suicide VBIED go into a market, in a town called Abu Saydah, which is predominantly a Shia town, the people instantly believed that VBIED came from . . . villages known as Mukeisha abu Garmah and Qubbah, which are predominantly Sunni. And so that fueled more sectarian violence, and . . . Abu Saydah cut itself off from Mukeisha abu Garmah. And so there, they turned to al Qaeda as well, but that was because we could not get the word out through the lack of local media, what the real situation was."[566] The governor's engagement in these villages established relations between them, and also established the provincial government as an arbitrator between local groups.

The tribal reconciliation movements made it easier for U.S. forces to hold terrain against insurgents. Al Qaeda had chased the Iraqi Police out of the Diyala River Valley, so U.S. forces worked with the Iraqis to reestablish the police force.[567]

The Concerned Local Citizens groups thickened the Iraqi Security Forces where they were present, and protected villages from which ISF troops were absent. Leaders had positive incentives to ensure that their people acted against insurgents, including personal honor, influence with Iraqi and American leaders, and patronage for their community. U.S. and Iraqi leaders did not provide such benefits to sheikhs who failed to comply with their obligations.

Enemy Groups and Reconciliation Efforts Compete in Khalis

The wave of reconciliation movements in Diyala improved security and governance in the province, but it did not eliminate the hard-core insurgents who escaped from Baqubah into rural safe havens. Militias, Iranian groups, and al Qaeda—all of which had safe havens in Diyala north and east of Baqubah—fought actively to thwart the reconciliation efforts.

Khalis, once again, was a focal point for conflicting groups. On August 18, terrorists launched sixteen mortar rounds on the Shia Sharqiya neighborhood in that city, killing three and wounded twenty-two in the market.[568] Five hundred locals, concerned about the attack and frustrated with the city's government, conducted a large, multi-day demonstration that began on August 19 at the mayor's house and then expanded to block the main roads into and out of Khalis. Iraqi Security Forces secured the area, and Diyala government officials met with protesters on August 20 to hear their demands. When a convoy of Coalition Forces arrived, unidentified gunmen in the crowd fired at the Strykers. U.S. forces fired warning shots, but did not engage. The incident prompted another meeting among protesters, government officials, Iraqi Security Forces, and American brigade commanders. The residents complained about "irrigation, water, medical supplies, security and specific checkpoints." The crowd agreed to let the convoy through if the existing leaders in Diyala and Khalis worked to solve the problems within a few days.[569]

Subsequent events suggest that insurgents had cut off the water supply into the city. On August 27, Coalition Forces and the Fifth Iraqi Army Division launched Operation Church. They conducted an air assault into Gobia village in order to re-open a spillway that insurgents had blocked in order to cut off the water supply into Khalis (ten miles to the west). A large number of insurgents defended the village, demonstrating their intention to keep the spillway blocked. Coalition and Iraqi forces killed thirteen of them during the air assault and twenty more during firefights throughout the day. They also found large weapons caches containing homemade explosives, rocket-propelled grenades, and a ZSU-23 anti-aircraft machine gun with 2,000 rounds of ammunition.[570]

Colonel Sutherland reported a consistent problem with rogue militias (which often have drawn support from Special Groups). "Jaysh al Mahdi is a title. It's the rogue militia—those elements that will go in and clear [an area] or fill the vacuum after we've cleared an area—that we're concerned about. So we continue to attack them as well. But, again, they've lost support because they take away those services and the capabilities that, that quite honestly . . . the people want."[571]

This pattern emerged most severely in the Khalis-Hebheb corridor. Reports of extremist militia activity in the vicinity of Hebheb increased dramatically in September.[572] Subsequent military operations indicate that Special Groups were active in September and October, especially in the Khalis corridor.

Militia violence increased the number of retaliatory attacks by al Qaeda, including kidnappings, mortar attacks, and the bombing of a significant bridge connecting Khalis and its villages to Baqubah, aimed, evidently, at cutting extremists' movements.[573] Gunmen, whose affiliation is not specified, also increased attacks and established unauthorized checkpoints along the Khalis-Hebheb-Baghdad road.[574] Local government and tribal leaders intervened to quell the violence in late September and mid-October.[575]

As U.S. and Iraqi forces pushed northeastward along the Diyala River in September, others targeted the Special Groups and other Shia extremists in the southern portion of the province. In late September, U.S. forces arrested the Special Groups leader linked to the large cache found in Khan Bani Sa'ad in February. The suspect was responsible for the smuggling network north of Baghdad, including facilitating foreign fighters and training militants in bomb production.[576] They arrested Special Groups members in Qasarin who had smuggled weapons and aided rogue elements of the Jaysh al Mahdi, including a facilitator who made multiple trips to Iran.[577] A large firefight erupted between U.S. forces and a Special Groups cell west of Baqubah, terrain which lies in the Khalis corridor.[578] The arrest of extremist militia members and Special Groups members throughout October also mitigated the tensions.

These operations in Diyala resulted in a dramatic diminution of violence in the Khalis area by the middle of September.[579] Sutherland attributed most of the decline to local reconciliation efforts. "Reconciliation initiatives resulted in a forty-six (46) percent drop in violent acts in the Diyala River Valley and a seventy-one (71) percent drop in Khalis Qada. These agreements have also embedded or enabled the return of displaced families to a number of areas throughout the province. Approximately three thousand three hundred (3,300) displaced individuals have returned to their homes. An example is seventy-one (71) families from the Khalis area near Al Khalis."[580]

Pursuing the Enemy: Phantom Strike

Prior U.S. operations, such as those in Fallujah in 2004 and Tal Afar in 2005, cleared some of Iraq's cities of insurgents. The Corps did not, however, conduct simultaneous or follow-on operations to prevent the enemy from regrouping elsewhere. As has been noted, some critics of U.S. strategy in Iraq before 2007 characterized it as "whack-a-mole." Though U.S. brigade commanders had hoped to strangle al Qaeda fighters in Baqubah, the Corps planners designed Phantom Thunder differently. Corps planners resolved the problem of "whack-a-mole" not by tactical means (cordoning off cities and their exit routes), but rather by operational means (simultaneous and successive operations throughout the division areas of operations).

The overarching objective of Phantom Thunder was to stop insurgents in the provinces from supporting violence in Baghdad. Controlling Baqubah, and indeed the cities in Baghdad's belts, advanced U.S. forces toward that objective. In order to prevent al Qaeda from regrouping, U.S. forces conducted follow-up missions throughout Iraq as part of a second Corps offensive, called Phantom Strike. This campaign aimed to degrade other al Qaeda sanctuaries before Ramadan began in mid-September, as it was a time during which al Qaeda had increased attacks in previous years.

General Odierno described the operational concept of Phantom Strike shortly after that Corps offensive began on August 13:

> This week, we launched Operation Phantom Strike, a series of targeted operations designed to intensify pursuit of extremist elements across Iraq. With the elimination of safe havens and support zones due to Phantom Thunder, al Qaeda and Shia extremists have been forced into ever-shrinking areas, and it is my intent to pursue and disrupt their operations . . . .Over the coming weeks, we plan to conduct quick strike raids against remaining extremist sanctuaries and staging areas, carry out precision targeting operations against extremist leadership and focus missions to counter the extremists' lethal accelerants of choice, the IED and the vehicle-borne IED. We will continue to hunt down their leadership, deny them safe haven, disrupt their supply lines and significantly reduce their capability to operate in Iraq . . . .[581]
>
> [W]e are not going to give up any ground that we have attained so far. We have been able to liberate the major population centers, provide more security, and what we will do now is conduct quick operational strikes all around the country to go after these remaining small pockets that are still remaining out there of al Qaeda and also Shia extremists."[582]

Phantom Strike in Diyala

U.S. forces planned a campaign called Operation Lightning Hammer to attack al Qaeda members who had survived or escaped during Arrowhead Ripper. Al Qaeda leaders from Diyala reconstituted in several areas in northern Iraq after Arrowhead Ripper cleared Baqubah, Khalis, and the western Diyala River Valley. Some took refuge along

the Hamrin Ridge, just north of the Diyala River Valley, on a secondary road toward Kirkuk. Others, perhaps supported by al Qaeda in the
Hamrin Ridge, worked actively in Muqdadiyah and the Diyala River
Valley northeast of Baqubah. Still others reconstituted in tribal areas
just south of Baqubah, and some elements remained in strongholds
along the Tigris River Valley, such as Tarmiyah, Balad, and Samarra, and
in safe havens south of Baghdad. Al Qaeda and Sunni insurgent command-and-control elements concentrated in the Za'ab Triangle, terrain
that lies primarily in Ninewah province toward Kirkuk. The headquarters of the Islamic State of Iraq remained in Mosul.

Multi-National Division-North launched Operation Lightning Hammer 1 on August 13, 2007, in order to "target al Qaeda elements that
fled from Baqouba into the outlying regions north of Diyala's capital
city" while there were still U.S. and Iraqi troops "concentrated . . . in
Diyala province."[583] Lightning Hammer consisted of multiple brigade-
and battalion-sized operations in Diyala, Salah ad-Din , and Ninewah
provinces. The subordinate operation, Greywolf Hammer 1, in Diyala
Province, was the division's main effort.

Colonel Sutherland explained, "Lightning Hammer 1 was an . . .
MND-N operation all across the four provinces of Multi-National
Division-North. We [Greywolf] were the main effort and we conducted an operation, what was called Operation Pericles, in the Diyala
River Valley, where we cleared about thirteen different villages from
the northern part of Baqubah up to and including little Abu Saydah.
Sunni [and] Shia areas dotted them. I mean, literally, one area is Shia,
[the] next area is Sunni, [the] next area Shia, [the] next area Sunni. And
we cleared those. [The] final operation was focused on an area known
as three villages, Mukisha, Abu Karmah, and Qubbah."[584] Mukhisa is a
small village on the east side of the Diyala, surrounded by dense palm
groves. The village occupies an important position, roughly halfway
between Baqubah and Muqdadiyah, the next large population center
in the Diyala River Valley.

"As one squadron was conducting those operations through air assaults, another squadron, 6-9 CAV, was clearing the Wajihiyah-Kana'an corridor, where they fought about a company-size element of al Qaeda in that area, that had taken over the corridor between these two major cities. During that operation, we reduced . . . eighteen IEDs, killed or captured over forty al Qaeda members . . . reduced three house-borne IEDs and six VBIEDs that were . . . targeted as suicide VBIEDS for the city of Baqubah, we believe. We destroyed one al Qaeda company-size element . . . sixty-six individuals, to include a command post, medical outpost for treatment, and [we] discovered and destroyed ten caches that were also being used to resupply insurgents in and around the area; and then detained another thirty-nine al Qaeda suspects."[585]

These operations expanded the regions near Baqubah controlled by security forces. The development of patrol bases allowed forces to protect those areas, in a classic inkspot-like fashion.

Al Qaeda's August and September counteroffensive in Diyala included a campaign of spectacular and complex attacks against the Concerned Local Citizens, and an effort to retake terrain in the Baqubah area. As many as 200 al Qaeda fighters attacked multiple positions in Kan'an, east of Baqubah, on August 23, in response to the Greywolf Hammer operations in the Wajihiyah-Kana'an area. An initial enemy attack drew concerned citizens into a fight just east of the village, which they defended successfully. After fifteen minutes—as soon as the concerned citizens and security services responded to the emergency on the east side of the town—al Qaeda fighters moved west of the village, focusing on the Iraqi Police checkpoint and attacking the family (and mosque) of Sheikh Younis, who had refused to support al Qaeda.[586]

Al Qaeda's ability to concentrate forces in Diyala diminished. A handful of spectacular attacks in September signaled the decreasing capacity of al Qaeda's conventional elements in Diyala, and the problems posed by the Concerned Local Citizens. The most devastating such attack in Diyala occurred on September 24, when a suicide bomber attacked a reconciliation meeting of 250 to 300 Sunni and Shia leaders, including Diyala's governor, in the Shifta mosque in Baqubah, killing twenty and wounding thirty-eight.[587]

The operations along the Diyala "took away all of [al Qaeda's] logistics," Sutherland explained. "[W]e didn't necessarily have to defeat al Qaeda in the Diyala River Valley; we took away any support and so their perceived safe havens went away . . . .Those that we didn't kill or capture [headed] . . . further north, into the Muqdadiyah area; and we began conducting operations inside Muqdadiyah."[588]

Greywolf Hammer II: Securing Muqdadiyah and Lake Hamrin

U.S. and Iraqi forces continued to clear terrain along the Diyala River Valley in September and October. After establishing security in the villages near Mukhisa, they cleared the city of Muqdadiyah and pushed past Lake Hamrin. Colonel Sutherland described the purpose of this successive operation: "Greywolf Hammer II was focused on clearing Muqdadiyah, a large city, very important to the province, but important to al Qaeda for its lines of communications. Also, [the operation's purpose was to] establish . . . security outposts in the Diyala River Valley, [as well as] conducting essential service synchronization inside . . . Baqubah. And then the final part of it was to clear al Qaeda elements south of Balad Ruz that had attempted to reinfiltrate back into the Turki area."[589]

U.S. forces cleared Muqdadiyah's market of al Qaeda in late October, by which time there were 675 residents who were participating in the Concerned Local Citizens group in Muqdadiyah. During and after the clearing operations, they assisted U.S. forces in identifying weapons caches in the city and in neighboring villages.[590] U.S. forces then pressed beyond Muqdadiyah, north and east of Lake Hamrin, where insurgent groups had established logistics bases. They engaged the population in the area, and discovered major caches in As Saydiyah.[591] "During this operation, which . . . really lasted about a week and a half, ten days, we were able to defeat al Qaeda cells in Muqdadiyah . . . .We detained or killed . . . about a two-company al Qaeda force that was in Diyala. And then we were able to reduce over 109 IEDs, six house-borne IEDs, and three VBIEDs. And one suicide vest we found actually weighed 75 pounds and had quarter-inch ball-bearings in it, and we suspect that it was being targeted for a reconciliation meeting."[592]

The Diyala government and important sheikhs sponsored a rec-onciliation meeting on October 24 at the Iraqi Army base in the Muqdadiyah area, attended by seventy leaders from that part of the province. The paramount sheikh of the Jabouri, a Sunni tribe located primarily west of Lake Hamrin, swore a pledge of peace with the para-mount sheikh of the Tamimi, a Shia tribe located in the Diyala River Valley and south of Lake Hamrin. They agreed actively to fight terror-ists in their communities, and not to tolerate corrupt individuals who harbor or help them. The meeting also promoted the advantages of tribal reconciliation movements.[593]

Greywolf Hammer 2 also re-established government and essential services in Muqdadiyah. The operation permitted the government of Diyala to "reestablish the public distribution system of food inside the Muqdadiyah qadaa [county], not just the city itself."[594] The hospi-tal received supplies, water treatment plants operated, and the city received twelve hours of public electricity daily.

By early November, U.S. and Iraqi forces had cleared the entire Diyala River Valley, from Baqubah to Lake Hamrin. Al Qaeda groups concentrated along the northern and eastern shores of Lake Hamrin, far from population centers and major roads.[595]

Concerned Local Citizens and Iraqi Security Forces in Diyala

U.S. and Iraqi Security forces have since June integrated the tribal and concerned citizen movements with local and provincial govern-ment. They have involved government officials in negotiations with tribal leaders, who often presented the problems of the population to the government and held officials accountable. They attempted to use the Concerned Local Citizens movements to create a new cadre of police recruits. Some local officials have capitalized on tribal structures to improve their ability to govern. For example, on September 24, local elected officials in Khalis summoned their own reconciliation meeting, independently of Coalition Forces, and consulted with fifty sheikhs and local citizens, both Sunni and Shia, in order to resolve emerging problems.[596] Finally, the sheikhs have stood as legal guarantors of locals released from prison by Coalition Forces and Iraqi Police after their cases were dismissed.[597]

Tensions between the security forces and concerned local citizens rose in September as central government officials moved slowly to incorporate citizens into Diyala's police force. The government of Iraq promised to add 6,000 new police to Diyala, bringing the force to 21,000. Colonel Sutherland explained, "The Prime Minister, the Deputy Prime Minister, other Iraqi leaders have stated publicly that the authorization . . . would be approved. We're still waiting for the Minister of Interior to sign that document and give it to the provincial director of police, General Ghanem."[598]

Concerned local citizens staged a large, peaceful protest in Baqubah's government center on September 17 to demonstrate their concerns about the hiring practices of the provincial police chief. They presented an eleven-point request to the Diyala provincial governor.[599] The pressure on the provincial governor, however, did not result in agreement from Ministry of Interior.[600] "It is not happening. There is some friction or some . . . difficulty on getting hiring instructions for these CLCs," Sutherland said.

The problem is at the ministerial level. "The provincial director of police wants to hire policemen from the concerned local citizens. He wants to hire policemen from the neighborhoods. The tribal leaders want their men to have jobs; they want to participate in the security process. The concerned local citizens are not paid to guard their neighborhoods. They want to be policemen. The province has an authorization of 6,000 additional policemen. They have been waiting for several weeks for the Ministry of the Interior to provide hiring instructions so the director of police for the province can hire these men to be policemen, give them jobs . . . pay them to secure their neighborhood and enforce rule of law and domestic order."[601]

U.S. forces were still working on determining the source of the problem and conflict between the Iraqi Police and the concerned local citizens. To mitigate tensions at the provincial level, U.S. forces involved provincial Iraqi Police leaders in the process of hiring concerned local citizens on security contracts and to plan defensive engagements with them.[602]

The participation of the former insurgents in securing Diyala fractured insurgent groups. A large battle between al Qaeda members and tribesmen erupted in Hebheb in mid-October. Rumor evidently conveyed that the tribesmen were members of the 1920s Brigades. Local leaders denied this rumor in the press, asserting that the defenders of Hebheb were members of the Diyala "Awakening." Their statement does not preclude the possibility that these were former members of the 1920s Brigades who had turned against al Qaeda.[603] American sources confirm this possibility generically, if not in this specific instance. According to General Odierno, "[T]here are groups that used to be part of the 1920s Revolutionary Brigade who have sworn allegiance to the government of Iraq who are working with Iraqi security forces and Coalition Forces both in Diyala. But there are still some elements [of the 1920s Brigade] that are not. . . . [W]e continue to conduct operations against them. In fact, in some of these groups there has been a split between the groups, where some have decided they want to reconcile with the government of Iraq and are working with us. There are some that are not. Those that are, we go through a vetting process with them. They pledge their allegiance to the government of Iraq. They have proven over time now that they want to work with us, and they've been very helpful. Those that do not . . . we continue to go after and treat as criminals."[604]

Restoring Government and Services in Diyala

In September, as clearing operations reached Muqdadiyah area, Colonel Sutherland reported that "[b]ecause of these operations, essential services, not security are now the main priority for the people of Diyala and the number one discussion point during, engagement." Diyala's provincial government, which had ceased to function in November 2006, is now providing services. Sutherland's mid-September assessment is worth reproducing in full:

> Currently the public distribution system which is the Iraqi subsidized food program is functional in all five qadaas and the province. Local mayors are coordinating delivery of PDS [the provincial food distribution system] with the Iraqi Security Forces, making the delivery a routine event. The local government and the Security Forces are continuously providing humanitarian assistance to the most remote areas where PDS might not have the ability to reach the population on a regular basis.
>
> Local businesses are beginning to open and jobs are now becoming available. One of these businesses, a flour mill south of Baqubah, is currently producing flour that is available throughout the province. A work program within the city of Baqubah is on the way and producing very significant results.
>
> Water facilities are now being assessed by the local government. Some are working, some are need of minor repairs and chemicals to purify the water and others are in need of major repairs that will take time. The District General of Water and Irrigation is working to address these issues. Diyala receives an average of twelve (12) hours of electricity throughout the day; however, the electricity problem is a nationwide issue, which will take some time to get fixed. At the provincial level, the government is assessing the local electric network and is working to fix that network through provincial means.

Diyala hospitals and clinics are functioning and supplies are reaching outlying areas. The Baqubah hospital has received millions of dollars in equipment and supplies, and the provinces received thirty-five (35) new ambulances at a cost of over one million (1,00,000) dollars. The DG of Health has coordinated a multiple lifts of the medical supplies from Baghdad to clinics throughout the provinces.

Fuel is now coming to the province, with multiple shipments of diesel, kerosene and benzene arriving every week. Its government is also focusing on canal systems throughout the province. This is an agricultural province and water is essential for their crops. Canals have been cleaned to allow the flow of water to land . . . farmland throughout Diyala.

The government has allocated over one hundred and fourteen (114) million dollars from the two thousand six (2006) budget and over one million six, one hundred and six (106) million dollars from the two thousand seven (2007) budget for reconstruction projects throughout Diyala. Additionally, the provincial council is meeting every week to review new projects.

Schools are being reassessed to identify their needs prior to the beginning of the school year. In the coming weeks eight (8) truckloads, full of text books are being delivered to Baqubah by the Ministry of Education. Additionally, the Education Department warehouse is full of school materials and equipment for the schools in the Diyala area.

These are all signs of progress; however, these improvements could not be achieved without the support of the local Iraqi citizens. The tribal leaders are the pillars of these communities. The government has made significant progress in its efforts to reconcile the Diyala tribes in order to maintain improvements currently taking place. The governor has conducted over fifteen (15) tribal engagement and negotiated four (4) major reconciliation agreements to reduce tribal violence and unite the people. Last month governor Ra'ad Al Tamimi hosted a meeting that included virtually every Paramount Sheikh or their senior representative in the province. These individuals signed a provincial-wide tribal reconciliation agreement promising to work together for better future for all Iraqis, regardless of tribe or sect. These Sheikhs are now offering their sons to join the Iraqi Security Forces to protect their people and fight al Qaeda. . . .

There are problems and issues that are still in need of special attention. Al Qaeda and other extremist groups remain a threat to Diyala, but they are quickly learning they have no safe haven here. Today, the situation in Diyala is better than it was four (4) to six (6) months ago and it will continue to improve.[605]

Counterinsurgency Lessons from the Diyala Case Study

The campaign to secure Diyala shows the distinctive features of the 2007 counterinsurgency campaign in Iraq.

Combat operations in Diyala in summer 2007 aimed mainly at controlling terrain so that the enemy could not operate, and secondarily on killing or capturing the enemy. Multi-National Division-North, therefore, first cleared the enemy from Baqubah, and then prevented the enemy from re-infiltrating the city or re-establishing itself elsewhere. Al Qaeda attempted to reconstitute multiple times in the province, and on occasions succeeded in conducting complex attacks. Yet as continuous operations fragmented the enemy into small groups, the enemy launched fewer complex attacks at longer intervals, with decreasing success.

General Petraeus's emphasis on securing the population and General Odierno's insistence on denying the enemy safe havens and rural support zones encouraged brigade commanders in Diyala to liberate terrain from enemy control and to maintain those areas. This practice contrasts sharply with some practices of 2006, when Iraqis were supposed to control terrain through checkpoints (which often had the effect of freezing forces in static positions from which they could not respond to threats except in their immediate area). Commanders in 2007 sought to achieve their goals through a more expansive use of firepower and maneuver.

General Petraeus's counterinsurgency doctrine, as implemented in

Iraq, encouraged commanders to seek enduring, systemic solutions to problems, while tailoring their solutions to local needs. The Corps' determination to conduct multiple simultaneous and successive operations also ensured that division and brigade commanders had the time to conceptualize and execute operations addressing the systematic problems in Diyala, rather than treating the symptoms of these problems. Successive operations allowed commanders to adjust their plans more readily to changing situations on the ground.

Combat operations (or "kinetic operations") were a necessary part of counterinsurgency in Diyala. They were not subordinate to non-combat ("non-kinetic") operations, nor were they a hindrance to them. Rather, combat operations enabled other lines of operation, such as economic and political development, to succeed in areas contested by enemy groups. The new counterinsurgency strategy accepted ongoing combat operations along with ongoing reconstruction as necessary tools for ending the insurgency and securing the population, instead of expecting combat operations to end and reconstruction to follow.

Many problems in Diyala—even in small villages—were not localized and could not be solved without also addressing systematic problems of enemy forces and provincial government. Within Diyala, the counterinsurgency effort varied locally to suit the specific problems facing the population. Securing Baqubah and Khalis differed from securing small villages of the Diyala River Valley.

In the wider framework of General Petraeus's campaign plan, Sutherland thus saw the combat operations as *the* prerequisite for revitalizing civic and government institutions. "In the Diyala River Valley, we determined it was first [necessary to conduct] kinetic operations—go in, clear those areas. As you clear them, simultaneously, the hold factor became the reconciliation effort J150

[D]epending [on] where it was . . . it may be village on village reconciliation, it may be tribe on tribe, it may be sect on sect, but [it was a] reconciliation [effort] specific to that area. The next [task] was the establishment of essential services, synchronization, food and water;

and once we did that we needed to figure out who would guard those essential services. So we either established Concerned Local Citizens' networks, the individuals we had checked backgrounds on, or we established a police force."[606]

MND-North and its brigades carried the combat operations to their logical ends—all the way through the cities and the Diyala River Valley. In this way, the campaign avoided problems that had bedeviled previous Coalition efforts. If MND-North had not followed up the clearing of Baqubah and of Khalis with additional operations throughout the Diyala River Valley and in the Hamrin Ridge, it would have left its gains in the cities vulnerable and allowed the enemy a chance to regroup. By aggressively pursuing the enemy, MND-North dealt as decisive a blow to al Qaeda as it is possible to deal to a networked insurgent group.

These operations were successful because they were designed from beginning to end with the goal of establishing stable security in the region, not of transitioning to Iraqi control. As operations progressed, commanders were attuned to opportunities not only to advance current clearing operations but also to lay the preconditions for long-term stability in the area. The kinetic operations themselves were designed and conducted with that ultimate goal in mind—separating the insurgents from the population, defending those members of the population willing to oppose the insurgents, and protecting the population against retaliation and efforts to re-infiltrate.

Ongoing operations also worked to solve important local social, political, and economic problems. Commanders fought and negotiated in order to bring the local people together around an agreement to abjure violence and those who perpetrate it. American forces served as a buffer and a broker between mutually suspicious local factions whose members could more easily trust U.S. soldiers. Americans forces were able to protect and reward individuals and communities that actively rejected violence. Every command echelon emphasized establishing a durable and long-term stability in which American forces would continue to play an important part, rather than creating the short-term conditions that might seem superficially to justify the desired rapid transition to "Iraqi control." The new American objective of security, as well as the new counterinsurgency strategy, made it possible to liberate Baqubah and secure Diyala in 2007.

Colonel Sutherland expressed the changed relationship of Americans and Iraqis in Diyala as he stressed why American forces needed to stay in the province in order to let the Iraqis take control of their own security. "The level of violence, the increase in services, the efforts to get employment and jobs working will be determined by the people of Diyala. What I do is enable them. Right now . . . there are still al Qaeda elements out there that want to re-infiltrate back in. I will destroy them, working with the Iraqi security forces. There are still rogue militia organizations that want to control areas, for advancement of either secular or economic interests. I will destroy them, working with Iraqi security forces. There is corruption . . . in elements of the government that has to be attacked, and we will attack that. The people will determine the outcome of this; I will be their enabler."[607]

Chapter 7
■ ■ ■ Rasheed and the Southern Belt during Phantom Thunder and Phantom Strike

Simultaneous operations in the belts in June stemmed the flow of al Qaeda fighters and weapons to and from Baghdad. U.S. forces cleared most of Rashid in May, and the northern sector of Arab Jabour in June. As Operation Phantom Thunder began, U.S. forces pinned an al Qaeda cell in a few Dora mahallas.[608] Whereas Al Qaeda had "previously been . . . elusive when we actually got into an area and started to clear it . . . they are standing and fighting"[609]

The Double Encirclement Pins an al Qaeda Cell in Dora

General Fil explained how the operations inside and outside Baghdad achieved the synergistic effects that General Odierno had hoped for. "[W]e believe that we are into an area here in east Rashid, in the Dura area, where we're seeing a very strong al Qaeda cell. And as we have gone through the city and concentrated in a lot of areas where they had free reign sometime before, those areas are now denied to them. And so their freedom of maneuver inside of the city, their own battle space, has been more and more restricted, and their support zones have been severely restricted, both inside the city and also in the belts around the city. And so they're running out of maneuver space and they are starting to fight very hard."[610]

Dora became "the division's main effort over here inside of Baghdad," according to General Fil. The al Qaeda cell in Masafee built an impressive defensive position, burying massive IEDs under roads that caused enormous and lethal explosions. Because U.S. forces surrounded this pocket of well-armed and well-prepared al Qaeda fighters, cutting off its supply lines, the combat in Dora became especially intense. In early July, Generals Odierno and Fil reinforced the 2-12 Infantry Battalion with a total of three Stryker battalions. This concentration of combat power surpassed what Major General Mixon used to clear Baqubah during Operation Arrowhead Ripper.[611]

AQI From Dora to Saydiyah

The major clearing operations in Dora expelled al Qaeda from Masafee, but the organization attempted to regroup in nearby mahallas, such as Jazeera and Saydiyah in southern Rasheed. In June, AQI focused on attacking into Saydiyah, just west of Route Jackson—the major demarcation between West Rasheed, where militia groups had generally dominated the population, and East Rasheed, which had formerly fallen into AQI's control.

The clearing of Masafee escalated the JAM/AQI contest in Saydiyah. Before the launch of Phantom Thunder, the 1-18th Infantry Regiment constructed a combat outpost in Saydiyah and began presence patrols in the area. The National Police assigned to Saydiyah, from the 2nd Brigade, 1st National Police Division (the Wolf Brigade), facilitated death squad activity, executing some Sunni residents and forcibly displacing families. AQI, in turn, conducted a sophisticated car bomb and IED campaign there, projecting force from Sunni mosques in Saydiyah and from locations in Jazeera, the neighboring mahalla.[612] This brutal battle for Saydiyah continued from June through August 2007.

AQI funneled weapons, funding, and fighters to Saydiyah from its sanctuaries in the southern belts via strongholds in West Rasheed. Operation Phantom Thunder and its follow-on, Operation Phantom Strike, severed the line of communications between Rasheed and the southern belts. A series of operations in West Rasheed defeated resurgent AQI groups trying to re-establish safe havens in Jazeera and Hadar.

Operation Marne Torch

Coalition Forces launched Operation Phantom Thunder on June 15, 2007 after the final Surge forces were in place. This troop increase enabled Multi-National Division-Center (MND-C) to conduct a large-scale offensive to deny al Qaeda sanctuary in the southern belts. On June 16, MND-C launched Operation Marne Torch I, their division-level component of Phantom Thunder in the Arab Jabour region. Marne Torch I sought to disrupt and deny AQI safe havens in Arab Jabour that were being used to transport men, weapons, funds, and car bombs into the capital.[613]

Arab Jabour was a critical insurgent support zone, where al Qaeda could assemble and stockpile VBIEDs, IEDs, and other munitions, which could then be transported easily into Dora.[614] According to Colonel Terry Ferrell, who commanded the U.S. brigade in the area, al Qaeda in Iraq was able to use Arab Jabour as a safe haven to place its weapons caches and build its bomb-making factories. The area was a critical hub that pushed weapons, bombs, and fighters into Baghdad.[615] AQI had a sophisticated command and control network in the area that was "on the scale of a conventional military force."[616] Lines of communication ran between cells in Arab Jabour west to Hawr Rajab and south along the Tigris River Valley to Sayafiyah.[617] AQI in the area had some direct—as well as indirect—action cells.

According to Colonel Ferrell, by mid-June of 2007, when the 2nd Brigade of the 3rd Infantry Division moved into Arab Jabour, AQI had approximately 300 fighters manning the network in this area. It did not have a foreign fighter presence in Arab Jabour; the group was made up of Iraqis who used the organization's name and tactics to intimidate local farmers.[618]

AQI gradually reinforced its hub in Arab Jabour by relying on a complex network of deep-buried IEDs, house-borne IEDs, and weapons caches that it arrayed in defensive belts in order to prevent Coalition or Iraqi Security Forces from encroaching on this vital location.[619] Beyond the defensive belts, Coalition efforts were hindered by the many canals that irrigate Arab Jabour; they created bottlenecks, making it easier for insurgents to anticipate patrol and assault routes and to defend those bottlenecks with IEDs. Furthermore, the terrain in Arab Jabour consists mainly of rural farmland, with a large supply of fertilizer components, which made it easy for locals to produce homemade explosives. The dense palm groves along the Tigris River also concealed weapons caches.

From mid-June to mid-July, Coalition Forces conducted a series of kinetic and non-kinetic operations that sought to clear AQI from the rural villages and farmland southeast of Baghdad along the Tigris River Valley. In addition to these raids, U.S. forces built a number of patrol bases in the villages of Arab Jabour and Hawr Rajab, from which they would conduct frequent presence patrols. After clearing deep-buried IEDs, Coalition Forces increasingly encountered less lethal—and more easily spotted—surface-laid anti-personnel IEDs.[620] Coalition planners relied on intelligence from locals as well as airpower to find and clear suspected IEDs while minimizing the risk to soldiers.[621] After clearing areas, Coalition Forces quickly moved to initiate a number of projects to revive the economy and improve governance.

During Operation Marne Torch, 2,000 Coalition soldiers, partnered with 1,000 members of the Iraqi Security Forces, cleared 1,152 buildings, killed eighty-three insurgents, captured 278 more, unearthed fifty-one weapons caches, and destroyed fifty-one boats.[622] In addition, Special Forces captured a high-level al Qaeda in Iraq cell leader who "reportedly targeted Coalition Forces, distributed mortars, organized and ordered vehicle-borne improvised explosive device attacks . . . [and operated] out of the Karkh district of Baghdad, along with Mahmudiyah and the Arab Jabour districts."[623] Another raid killed Emir al Jabouri, an AQI military emir who headed a VBIED cell responsible for attacks in and around Baghdad.[624]

From Phantom Thunder to Phantom Strike

Phantom Thunder was a success. By the end of June, U.S. and Iraqi forces had liberated western Baqubah. By the end of July, they also controlled eastern Baqubah, Dora, and Fallujah—the major urban strongholds of AQI. By mid-August, they had also cleared other al Qaeda and Shia extremist strongholds south of Baghdad, including a terrorist safe haven in Musayyib, on the road from Karbala to Baghdad. The Phantom Thunder offensive killed over 1,100 enemy fighters and detained over 6,700, including 382 major figures. It drove most remaining al Qaeda into rural areas, far from population centers. The displacement of al Qaeda leaders and fighters made it possible for Special Forces to track many of them down. Phantom Thunder also fractured the belts, compartmentalizing some al Qaeda operations around the capital so that the surviving portions of the network could not readily support one another.

In order to prevent al Qaeda and Shia extremist groups from reestablishing themselves in cities or rural support areas, Generals Petraeus and Odierno launched Phantom Strike, the second Iraq-wide offensive, in the middle of August. Operation Phantom Strike, which lasted through the end of 2007, consisted of quick-strike raids aimed at destroying terrorist staging areas and preventing insurgents from establishing new sanctuaries.

Marne Husky

Follow-on operations were necessary in the southern belt. After the major clearing operation in Arab Jabour, enemy fighters moved southward along the Tigris just beyond the reach of U.S. forces. Thus, the opening campaign of Phantom Strike in August 2007 targeted insurgents and extremists trying to reconstitute further south along the Tigris River Valley. Though the population in areas immediately south of Baghdad is overwhelmingly Sunni, Iraqis further south in Babil and Wasit province are predominantly Shia. These populations limited al Qaeda's ability to reconstitute itself in safe havens much farther south of Baghdad than Mahmudiyah and Suwayrah. Consequently, most Sunni insurgents fleeing from Arab Jabour were forced to move from east to west, following the arc of roads and highways from the Tigris River Valley to Mahmudiyah.

MND-C launched Operation Marne Husky in the Tigris River Valley on August 15, 2007. It was a series of targeted raids and strikes further south in the Baghdad belts, designed to keep off balance those insurgents who had fled the previous offensive in Arab Jabour.[625] These operations were intelligence-driven and resulted in eighty insurgents captured and forty-three killed.[626]

The Division's Combat Aviation Brigade (CAB) led Marne Husky because U.S. forces, dispersed among numerous patrol bases after Marne Torch I, were too thinly spread to clear and hold the territory into which the enemy had moved. Coalition commanders, therefore, coupled the CAB with a battalion of ground troops to conduct eight different air assaults over forty-five days.[627] By contrast, the operations running concurrently in the Diyala River Valley were conducted by a heavy brigade of division cavalry. The air assaults south of Baghdad eliminated enemy positions, such as safehouses and weapons caches, in the arc from Suwayra to Iskandariya.

The key city of Mahmudiyah lies on the border of Sunni and Shia zones. It also sits astride the north-south line of communications that extremist militias used to push northward from Karbala to Baghdad, and on the east-west route along which al Qaeda operatives traveled from the Euphrates to the Tigris. U.S. forces consistently worked to eliminate insurgents from Mahmudiyah during the major offensives, and they drove al Qaeda further south toward Karbala and Babil. Operations in Mahmudiyah targeting facilitation of foreign terrorists south of Baghdad thus led Coalition Forces to a major figure within AQI, Abu Usama al Tunisi, in the third week of September. This Tunisian-born terrorist oversaw the movement of foreign terrorists in Iraq. He was a close associate of and likely successor to Abu Ayyub al Masri, the leader of AQI. Coalition Forces killed him in an airstrike on September 25, near Musayyib, on the road from Mahmudiyah to the Shia holy cities.

Marne Torch II

During Marne Torch I, some AQI insurgents, including a number of foreign fighters, were displaced from Arab Jabour and fled to Hawr Rajab,[628] a predominantly Sunni village situated immediately south of Baghdad proper, east of Route Jackson.[629] Hawr Rajab is wedged between three important areas: the farmland closer to the Tigris that U.S. forces cleared in June; the Mahmudiyah-Baghdad highway; and Baghdad's southernmost neighborhood, Abu Disheer, which is primarily Shia and sits on the underbelly of Dora.

AQI's position within Hawr Rajab was less firmly established than within Arab Jabour. The AQI network in Hawr Rajab received support from Salman Pak, just across the Tigris River in the 3rd BCT, 3rd ID's area of operations. Marne Torch I prevented al Qaeda from using boats Tigris River to bring weapons into Baghdad along the Tigris, and limited the enemy to crossing back and forth between its hub in Arab Jabour and supporting zone in Salman Pak.[630] Coalition operations focused on stopping this movement to isolate the different AQ cells further.[631]

In mid-September, after the period of consolidation that Marne Husky permitted, the main effort in MND-C shifted to Hawr Rajab. The influx of AQI insurgents after Marne Torch I brought an even more radical strain of extremist ideology to those villages. By early July, residents of Hawr Rajab had grown tired of AQI's ruthless practices. That month, two sheikhs reached out to U.S. forces, hoping to form a security alliance that would expel al Qaeda from Hawr Rajab.[632] Throughout August, soldiers from the 1-30 and the newly-formed Concerned Local Citizens group fought together to wrest control of the area from al Qaeda's hands.[633] These were the first such groups to be recruited in the Baghdad belts.[634]

During Marne Torch II, launched in mid-September 2007, the 1-30 Infantry pushed further south in Arab Jabour along the west bank of the Tigris River. Coalition soldiers were able to kill or capture about 250 insurgents, three of whom were high-value individuals. Furthermore, Coalition Forces uncovered thirty IEDs, unearthed over forty caches, and destroyed twelve boats that were being used to coordinate insurgent activities across the Tigris River.[635] Marne Torch II was supported by tips from over 700 Concerned Local Citizens from the Arab Jabour area who independently found seventeen of the caches that the Coalition removed. Colonel Terry Ferrell stated that Sons of Iraq "were significant to the operation, working along beside us, giving us information."[636]

Furthermore, under Marne Torch II, the 1-30 Infantry successfully established Patrol Base Hawkes further south in Arab Jabour, permitting the Coalition to reach into former AQI sanctuaries further south and southeast. After establishing the patrol base, the Coalition controlled more of the terrain. U.S. forces increased the inhabitants' momentum against AQI in Arab Jabour, as more Iraqis felt secure enough to come forward and volunteer for the Sons of Iraq program.[637] According to Colonel Ferrell, Marne Torch II dealt a "significant blow" to al Qaeda and reduced its ability to form direct-action cells while also degrading the group's command and control and support cells. AQI was not destroyed, however.[638]

Sons of Iraq

Over time, Concerned Local Citizens groups increasingly used the name "Sons of Iraq," a phrase which translated more easily into Arabic. The Coalition only began forming its Sons of Iraq program in Colonel Ferrell's area of operations in September 2007. By December, five separate groups of 1,200 Sunni tribesmen turned against the insurgency. By January 2008, the Sons of Iraq program had a total of 3,200 members who were operating in eight groups.[639]

From the end of Marne Torch II in mid-October until mid-January,

Sons of Iraq served as auxiliary police forces and augmented Coalition and Iraqi Security Force efforts to hold and build those territories, bringing a dramatic reduction in violence in the northern parts of the area of operations. This enabled the Coalition to increase efforts to assist in economic reconstruction and political development. By December, the 2nd Brigade of the Third Infantry Division established a new patrol base in Hawr Rajab and attempted to turn that town into a "model community" with improved security and government.[640]

Impact of MND-C Operations in 2007 on Baghdad

Hawr Rajab borders the predominantly Shia enclave of Abu Disheer in Rashid. In 2005 and 2006, the Shia residents of Abu Disheer were frequently attacked by IEDs, mortars, and rocket fire from Sunni insurgents in Dora and Hawr Rajab.[641] In response to these attacks, JAM militias moved into Abu Disheer, ostensibly to protect the Shia population. By February 2007, JAM militias had firmly established control over Abu Disheer.[642] A fight between Shia and Sunni in Abu Disheer, Dora, Hawr Rajab, and Arab Jabour persisted into 2007.

Relations between the tribes of these areas improved as Sons of Iraq groups developed in Hawr Rajab and Arab Jabour and fought off al Qaeda.[643] These improved relations were evident in September 2007 when the residents of Abu Disheer welcomed Sunni families who had been targeted by AQI for their participation in Sons of Iraq groups.[644]

Coalition Forces expanded the Sons of Iraq into southern Baghdad in September 2007, roughly concurrently with the development of this movement in Arab Jabour and Hawr Rajab. The fight in Saydiyah abated after U.S. forces established themselves in the neighborhood, the government removed some elements of the Wolf Brigade from Saydiyah, and as the campaign for control of AQI's safe havens in the southern belt disrupted its quest for terrain west of Route Jackson. The creation of a Sons of Iraq movement over the course of August and September helped U.S. forces respond to some of the death squad violence.[645]

But the development of the CLCs in a contested mixed neighborhood in the capital generated wider political controversies within the government of Iraq and political parties: "Apparently the establishment of an Awakening group in a mixed area, especially a strategically important area, struck a nerve with Shia political groups. On September 23, 'thousands' of Saydiyah residents staged a protest, demanding the dissolution of the Awakening Battalion. While there is no direct evidence on this point, it is reasonable to assume that this demonstration was sponsored by the local representatives of one of the major Shia parties. Several days later, between 600 and 1000 residents demonstrated in favor of the Awakening Battalion, arguing that it had helped to secure the Sunni areas of the neighborhood. Shia political parties pressed the issue; Shiite MP Ali al Adib argued in early October that the Saydiyah Awakening was composed of Anbari tribesman, not locals, and that they are involved in the kidnapping of Shia citizens in the area. Prime Minister Nouri al Maliki's media advisor slammed the Saydiyah Awakening several days later, alleging that they have kidnapped, murdered, and blackmailed innocent civilians."[646]

Coalition and Iraqi Security Forces maintained their offensive momentum throughout this time by conducting a number of large-scale operations in both Rasheed and the southern belt. Following the clearing of AQI from northern Dora and Masafee in the spring, and Saydiyah in the summer, insurgents reconstituted in Hadar, making it one of the last remaining concentrations of AQI in all of Baghdad.[647] On September 16, 2007, U.S. soldiers from the 2nd Stryker Cavalry and 4th BCT, 1st ID launched Operation Dragon Talon II in Rasheed.[648] The areas of southeast Dora, in particular the Hadar neighborhood, were the brigade's main effort.[649] From September to December, U.S. and Iraqi forces conducted daily operations to capture or kill enemy elements, seize weapons, and clear Hadar.[650] Over the course of these months, over 100 IEDs were discovered and reduced in Hadar and more than fifty caches were seized.[651] Elsewhere in Rasheed, U.S. forces continued to target Shia extremists operating in southern Baghdad.

In the fall and winter of 2007, it became clear that the operations to dismantle the enemy system in Baghdad were having their desired effect. In fact, from September to December, the violence trends in southern Baghdad fell steadily. From November 2006 to December 2007, attacks against Iraqi civilians in Baghdad dropped 80 percent; murders were down 90 percent.[652] Violence by Shia militia elements declined on account of the U.S. campaign against Special Groups and Moqtada al Sadr's announcement of a JAM cease-fire.[653] The effectiveness of AQI in Dora was greatly diminished as its support networks in Hawr Rajab and Arab Jabour were eliminated. Indeed, the number of car bomb attacks in Baghdad in December was down 70 percent at the end of 2007, as compared to that time in the previous year.[654] Also, and perhaps most importantly, CLC movements were underway in many areas of southern Baghdad and its immediate environs.

Chapter 8
■ ■ ■ Iran's Proxy War in Iraq Before and During the Surge

Iran, and its Lebanese proxy Hezbollah, have actively supported Shia militias and encouraged sectarian violence in Iraq since the invasion of 2003—and Iranian planning and preparation for that effort began as early as 2002. The precise purpose of this support is unclear, and may have changed over time, but one thing is unmistakably clear: Iran has consistently supplied weapons, its own advisors, and Lebanese Hezbollah advisors to multiple resistance groups in Iraq, both Sunni and Shia, and has supported these groups as they have targeted Sunni Arabs, Coalition Forces, Iraqi Security Forces, and the Iraqi government itself. Their influence runs from Kurdistan to Basra, and Coalition sources reported that by August 2007, Iranian-backed violence accounted for roughly half the attacks on Coalition Forces, a dramatic change from previous periods when the overwhelming majority of attacks came from the Sunni Arab insurgency and from al Qaeda. The Iranians increased their support for violence in Iraq since the start of the Surge.

The Coalition increased its efforts to combat Iranian intervention in Iraq during the Surge. By late summer 2007, Coalition successes against al Qaeda in Iraq and the Sunni Arab insurgency permitted the re-allocation of resources and effort against a problem that plagued attempts to establish a stable government in Iraq from the outset. Iranian intervention in Iraq had been secondary in importance to the raging Sunni Arab insurgency and al Qaeda in Iraq's spectacular attacks. With those problems increasingly under control, the Coalition turned to the problem of Iranian intervention.

Background

The Iranian Revolutionary Guard Corps-Qods Force organized, trained, funded, and equipped Iraqis to fight against Coalition and Iraqi Security Forces. Lebanon's Hezbollah has assisted the Qods Force in its effort to train and organize Shia resistance groups since 2003. The Iranian government provided substantial financial and technical support to militias in the second half of 2006 and increased its support in 2007. Hezbollah served as the Qods Force's proxy in its advisory effort.

After the fall of Saddam Hussein's regime, the U.S. military catalogued large quantities of enemy weapons in Iraq that have imprints proving Iranian manufacture. In particular, highly-lethal explosively-formed penetrators (EFPs) were made from special copper disks manufactured with highly-calibrated machine tools. Hezbollah used them in Lebanon, with Iranian military assistance. Many EFPs found in Iraq have markings indicating that they were manufactured in Iran as recently as 2006.[655] EFPs accounted for an increasing numbers of U.S. casualties between October 2006 and September 2007. The Iranian government also exported rockets, sniper rifles, and mortars to enemy groups in Iraq, and provided them with trainers and advisors responsive to Qods Force commanders, making certain Shia militia groups more effective and lethal than they previously had been.

In spring 2007, U.S. and Iraqi forces launched special operations within Iraq to capture the leaders of the Iranian-funded movement. The campaign aimed to reduce the ability of Shia extremists to destabilize the government and security situation of Iraq. These special operations supplemented the counteroffensive against al Qaeda extremists in central Iraq. U.S. and Iraqi forces captured numerous suspects with links to Iran and evidence documenting the Iranian government's support for violence in Iraq. U.S. forces publicly released some of this material. Meanwhile, Coalition and Iraqi forces took further steps to reduce the destructive power of the secret cells within Iraq. At the beginning of August 2007, General Ray Odierno, commander of Coalition combat forces in Iraq, announced the beginning of a more aggressive campaign against Shia militias, as well as Special Groups, in Baghdad. The governments of the United States and Iraq also engaged in diplomatic negotiations with Iran. Trilateral talks between the United States, Iran, and Iraq occurred on May 28 and July 24, 2007.

The Qods Force and Hezbollah

The highest echelons of the Iranian government and of Hezbollah in Lebanon worked together to organize a violent Shia resistance movement in Iraq. The Iranian Revolutionary Guard Corps-Qods Force (IRGC-QF) established, organized, and funded this movement. Ayatollah Khomeini established the Qods Force in 1979 to protect Iran's Islamic Revolution and to export it beyond Iran's borders. Brigadier General Qassim Sulleimani served as its commander from 2005 to 2007.[656] Although the Qods Force commander held a seat on Iran's national security council, along with the elected President of Iran, Mahmoud Ahmedinijad, he did not report to the president. Rather, he answered directly to Iran's Supreme Leader, Ayatollah Ali Khameini. General David Petraeus, commander of all Coalition Forces in Iraq, stated that "the Qods Force [is] an Iranian special operations organization that answers directly to Iranian supreme leader Ayatollah Ali Khamenei."[657]

Lebanese Hezbollah is likely the most important group developed with the assistance of the Iranian Qods Force. It emerged in 1983 with the aim of expelling Israel from southern Lebanon. From its inception, Hezbollah has enjoyed significant financial and material aid from Iran and Syria. The Qods Force, in particular, played a critical role in Hezbollah's foundation, funding, and training. Since 1992 Hezbollah has participated in governing Lebanon and has developed as a political entity. It subsequently used its extensive social support network to expand its political base in southern Lebanon and parts of Beirut.[658] In summer 2007, Hezbollah held fourteen seats in the Lebanese parliament, a significant achievement given that Shias were only allocated twenty-seven seats in

Lebanon's 128-member parliament. Its success over the past two decades has led some to view the organization as a "model of resistance."[659]

The Iranian Qods Force and Lebanese Hezbollah worked together since 2003 to support Shia extremists in Iraq and to develop those groups into an organization modeled on Hezbollah. Shia groups accounted for about half of the violence in Iraq in July 2007.[660] U.S. military officials estimated that the Qods Force provides between $750,000 and $3 million worth of equipment and funding to the Special Groups every month.

The Origins of Iranian-Backed Special Groups in Iraq

Iran began preparing to combat American forces in Iraq even before the invasion of 2003. According to an August 2005 article by Michael Ware based on classified intelligence documents, the Iranian Supreme Leader Ayatollah Ali Khamenei convened a council of war in Tehran that concluded: "It is necessary to adopt an active policy in order to prevent long-term and short-term dangers to Iran." As a result, Iranian intelligence services organized the various Iraqi resistance groups that they had been sheltering under Brigadier General Qassim Sullaimani, the current head of the Qods Force.[661]

Immediately after the U.S. invasion, thousands of members of these resistance groups, primarily from the Badr Corps, moved into Iraq and attempted to seize control of various key locations in the Shia areas. Ware cited an IRGC intelligence report of April 10, 2003, that "logs U.S. troops backed by armor moving through the city of Kut. But, it asserts, 'we are in control of the city.' Another, with the same date . . . claims 'forces attached to us' had control of the city of Amarah."[662] Other reports confirm this view: "In a sermon on May 2 [2003], Ayatollah Ahmad Janati, secretary general of Iran's powerful Council of Guardians, called on Iraqis to stage suicide attacks to drive U.S.-led forces from [Iraq] . . . .Two months later . . . Coalition Forces uncovered a document describing a fatwa, or religious edict, that had reportedly been issued in Iran for its Shiite supporters in Iraq. The fatwa urged 'holy fighters' in Iraq to get close to the enemy—the U.S.-led troops. These fighters, the fatwa said, should 'maintain good relations with the Coalition Forces' but at the same time create 'a secret group that would conduct attacks against American troops.'"[663]

The Badr Corps and Iranian agents were not the only ones involved in training and arming an anti-American Iraqi resistance under Iranian auspices. Lebanese Hezbollah also sent agents into Iraq in 2003. By August 2005, Abu Mustafa al Sheibani had developed an extensive "network of insurgents created by the Iranian Revolutionary Guard Corps with the express purpose of committing violence against U.S. and Coalition Forces in Iraq." Sheibani's group introduced into Iraq "'shaped' explosive charges," based on a model used by Hezbollah against the Israelis, and its fighters trained in Lebanon as well as Sadr City and "another country," according to U.S. intelligence sources.[664] An American military official in Baghdad explained that "the U.S. believes that Iran has brokered a partnership between Iraqi Shiite militants and Hizballah and facilitated the import of sophisticated weapons that are killing and wounding U.S. and British troops." An American Special Operations Task Force report claimed "the Lebanese Hizballah leadership believes that the struggle in Iraq is the new battleground in the fight against the U.S."[665] Sheibani's group was estimated to include 280 fighters organized into seventeen bomb-making teams and death squads.[666]

Tehran had a natural Shia proxy in the Badr Corps and SCIRI, but it hedged its bets from the beginning by backing Moqtada al Sadr as well. Sadr visited Tehran in June 2003, and was apparently receiving funds from Iranian Grand Ayatollah Kazem al Haeri until October of that year when al Haeri started to cut his ties to Sadr.[667] Sadr and three advisors traveled by road from Najaf to Ilam "where Iranian authorities had a ten-seat private plane waiting for them." In Tehran, the group met with Supreme Leader Ayatollah Ali Khamenei, former president Ali Akbar Hashemi Rafsanjani, and Ayatollah Mahmoud Hashemi Shahroudi. The invitation to Sadr apparently angered Iraqi clerical leaders in Najaf: "The marjas [the holy city's highest leaders] found it offensive that Moqtada would be officially invited to Iran,' says Sheikh Ali al Rubai, spokesman for one of the holy city's four top clerics, Grand Ayatollah Ishaq Fayadh. 'When Khamenei's representative came to Najaf [in August 2003], the marjas spoke to him in a rough way and demanded to know why they invited Moqtada.' The lavish reception was a particular slap to Ayatollah Mohammad Baqir al Hakim, a major beneficiary of Iranian support for two decades. Hakim threatened to cut ties with Tehran in protest."[668]

Hezbollah also established a long-term relationship with Moqtada al Sadr. The group apparently tried to establish relations with Sadr in July 2003 and had succeeded by August. At the end of that month, according to a U.S. intelligence report, "Hezbollah had established 'a team of 30 to 40 operatives' in Najaf in support of Moqtada Sadr's Shia paramilitary group." The report added that "Hezbollah was recruiting and training members of Sadr's militia. A later report . . . said that Hezbollah was 'buying rocket-propelled grenades . . . antitank missiles' and other weapons for Sadr's militia." Unconfirmed reports suggested that Hezbollah's Secretary General, Hassan Nasrallah, had sent a senior advisor to deliver funds to Sadr in Najaf.[669] In October 2005, a British government official "alleged that Iran had supplied explosive devices to Sadr's Jaysh al Mahdi." Prime Minister Tony Blair subsequently supported that assertion and "attributed the shipments to 'Iranian elements' or Iran's ally, Lebanese Hizballah, acting on Iran's behalf."[670]

The covert nature of Iranian support for its proxies was clear and disturbing from the outset. Iranian intelligence services penetrated Iraq rapidly and thoroughly, and the thrust of their collection efforts was "finding out what weapons U.S. troops were carrying and what kind of body armor they were wearing. Iranian agents also sought information on the location of U.S. Army and intelligence bases; on the routes traveled by U.S. convoys; on the operations of the Special Forces' elite Delta Force; and on the plans of the U.S. military and intelligence inside Iraq."[671] The Iranians preferred not to be directly implicated in attacks on U.S. forces, instead offering bounties to Iraqis for killing Americans, shooting down U.S. helicopters, and destroying American tanks.[672] Iran's proxies in Iraq also undertook a campaign of targeted assassinations. Reports suggest that in fall 2003 "a senior Iranian cleric in Tehran set up a special 100-member army, known as al Saqar, which means eagle in Arabic, to assassinate [CPA Director L. Paul] Bremer and carry out other terrorist attacks." This "eagle army" apparently "had trained for 30 days at an Iranian terrorist camp."[673]

In August 2005 Michael Ware reported, "More sinister are signs of death squads charged with eliminating potential opponents and former Baathists. U.S. intelligence sources confirm that early targets included former members of the Iran section of Saddam's intelligence services. In southern cities, Thar-Allah (Vengeance of God) is one of a number of militant groups suspected of assassinations . . . .The chief of the Iraqi National Intelligence Service, General Mohammed Abdullah al Shahwani, has publicly accused Iranian-backed cells of hunting down and killing his officers."[674] One former Iraqi Army officer reported "that he was recruited by an Iranian intelligence agent in 2004 to compile the names and addresses of Ministry of Interior officials in close contact with American military officers and liaisons." The Iranians wanted to know "'who the Americans trusted and where they were,' and pestered [the former officer] to find out if [he], using his membership in the Iraqi National Accord political party, could get someone inside the office of then Prime Minister Iyad Allawi without being searched." The Iranian agent "also demanded information on U.S. troop concentrations in a particular area of Baghdad and details of U.S. weaponry, armor, routes, and reaction times."[675]

Lebanese Hezbollah Trains Iraqis in Iran

The number and quality of Special Groups increased in 2005, as the Iranian government allowed Lebanese Hezbollah to train Iraqi militias in Iran. The three small camps used for training Iraqi militias were, as of summer 2007, located near Tehran. Twenty to sixty Iraqis could be trained at once in these facilities, and the training courses lasted from four to six weeks.[676]

The recruits were generally members of militias, including but not exclusively Jaysh al Mahdi.[677] They crossed the border at Zurbatiyah-Mehran, usually unarmed and in pairs, sometimes in buses.[678] Arrests by Iraqi Army soldiers revealed one recruiting technique used by Special Groups in Najaf, the Shia holy city where the Office of the Martyr Sadr was best established. The director of a charity, the Amin Allah Cultural and Humanitarian Establishment, funneled funds designated for humanitarian use through the charity for the purpose of recruiting foreign fighters, training rogue JAM operatives in lethal tactics, and trafficking weapons from Iran.[679] Two employees at the charity took advantage of their positions to offer $500 to those who would emplace IEDs. These same recruiters also facilitated the training of Iraqis in Iran and received money and weapons from Iran.[680]

The Qods Force and Hezbollah trained Iraqis in groups of twenty to sixty so that they functioned as a unit—a "secret cell" or "special group." The Iraqis returned to Iraq after their training, maintaining their group's organization. Thus, each "special group" in Iraq consisted of twenty to sixty Iraqis who had trained together in Iran in how "to use EFPs, mortars, rockets, as well as intelligence, sniper and kidnapping operations."[681] These Special Groups could be combined into larger organizations. The director of the Amin Allah charity coordinated "more than 200 rogue JAM members" and "ordered them to conduct assassinations on local citizens and government officials who oppose the group's illegal activities."[682]

Lebanese Hezbollah oversaw the Special Groups training effort by sending one of its members, Yussef Hashim, to serve as the organization's Head of Special Operations in Iraq.[683] The trainer leading this effort in 2005 was a Lebanese Hezbollah operative named Ali Mussa Daqduq, who had an impressive military career in that organization. He joined Lebanese Hezbollah in 1983; went on to command a special operations unit; coordinated the personal security of Hassan Nasrallah, the leader of Hezbollah in Lebanon; and coordinated operations in large sectors of Lebanon before he came to Iran.[684]

The Qods Force Reorganizes the Special Groups Using Lebanese Hezbollah as a Proxy

Though the Hezbollah training of Special Groups in Iran began in 2005, the Iranian government decided in May 2006 to adjust the way these groups were organized. A joint Qods Force-Hezbollah effort to organize these trained opposition groups into a Hezbollah-style structure began in May 2006. The Iranian Qods Force leadership sponsored the reorganization effort by holding a meeting with two Lebanese Hezbollah leaders who traveled to Tehran for that purpose: Yussef Hashim, the Hezbollah Head of Special Operations in Iraq, and his subordinate Ali Mussa Daqduq. In Tehran, they met with Hajji Yusif, the Deputy Commander of the Qods Force who heads its Department of External Special Operations. They also met with the commander.[685]

The Qods Force instructed Ali Mussa Daqduq "to make trips in and out of Iraq and report on the training and operations of the Iraqi Special Groups. In the year prior to his capture, Ali Mussa Daqduq made four such trips to Iraq. He monitored and reported on the training and arming of Special Groups with mortars and rockets, manufacturing and employment of improvised explosive devices, and kidnapping operations. Most significantly, he was tasked to organize the Special Groups in ways that mirrored how Hezbollah was organized in Lebanon."[686]

The Qods Force sponsored, or at least accepted, another significant personnel change at the same time. In June 2006, just a month after the Tehran meeting, Qais Khazali became the head of Special Groups in Iraq (whereas Ali Mussa Daqduq remained the chief advisor).[687] Khazali, an Iraqi, had at one time supported the Sadrist movement. According to a Sadrist spokesman, Moqtada al Sadr expelled Khazali from his organization in 2004 for giving "unauthorized orders" during the battle for Najaf.[688] Khazali thus had a reputation for working with but also undercutting

Moqtada al Sadr. It is unclear from the open sources what relationship existed between Khazali and al Sadr during his tenure as head of Special Groups. Khazali's relationship to Iran was clear: He reported to Hajji Yusif, the deputy commander of the Qods Force, Department of External Special Operations, just as Ali Mussa Daqduq did.[689]

Some members of Iraqi Special Groups observed or participated in the Hezbollah-Lebanon-Israel war in July 2006, traveling from Iraq to Syria to Lebanon and working alongside Hezbollah in groups of twenty to forty fighters.[690]

Iranian Support for al Qaeda

Iran never confined its support of anti-American fighters to Shia groups. It also supported Ansar al Islam, a radical Sunni terrorist group with close ties to al Qaeda. U.S. and British intelligence reports in 2004 "concluded that Ansar al Islam was working closely with Iran, and also al Qaeda, in its terrorist attacks against Coalition Forces . . . . [O]ne British defense report noted pointedly: 'Some elements of [Ansar al Islam] remain in Iran. Intelligence indicates that elements' of Iran's Islamic Revolutionary Guard Corps 'are providing safe haven and basic training to Iran-based AI [Ansar al Islam] cadres.'" A report by the Iraq Survey Group noted that a source had reported "approximately 320 Ansar al Islam terrorists being trained in Iran . . . for various attack scenarios including suicide bombings, assassinations, and general subversion against U.S. forces in Iraq.'" Another British intelligence source "said that Iranian government agencies were also secretly helping Ansar al Islam members cross into Iraq from Iran, as part of a plan to mount sniper attacks against Coalition Forces." American sources confirmed this information, adding that "an Iranian was aiding Ansar al Islam 'on how to build and set up' improvised explosive devices, known as IEDs. An analyst for the U.S. Central Command offered this assessment: 'AI [Ansar al Islam] is actively attempting to improve IED effectiveness and sophistication.'"[691]

More recently, Iranian arms dealers have supplied new weapons to al Qaeda in Iraq. A supply of arms flowed from Iran into al Qaeda strongholds in Salman Pak and Arab Jabour, presumably from the Iranian border to the south and east. From there, al Qaeda transported the munitions to Baghdad.[692]

Iranian arms became an important part of al Qaeda's arsenal. In May 2007, both Major General Rick Lynch, commander of Multi-National Division-Center, and Colonel Ricky Gibbs, commander of the 4th Brigade Combat Team, 1st Infantry Division, briefed on the use of EFPs by Sunni extremists south of Baghdad.[693] Moreover, al Qaeda promoted an expert with knowledge of how to obtain and use EFPs in May, demonstrating the high value placed on that technology. (U.S. forces killed that individual on May 25.)[694]

In June and July 2007, U.S. forces conducted targeted raids on insurgent safe houses in Arab Jabour during Operation Marne Torch, discovering caches of new weapons bearing Iranian markings. The weapons had been imported recently, rather than buried and stockpiled.[695] Weapons were being stored in Arab Jabour, indicating that it was a way station of sorts.

From Arab Jabour, al Qaeda smuggled these new Iranian weapons, along with the fighters that would employ them, into Baghdad.[696] The Tigris River was their primary supply route.[697] General Lynch explained, "[A]s we engage with the local population, they tell us that the only people on the Tigris River are extremists, insurgents. So what we've chosen to do is to take out all boats."[698] Colonel Wayne Grigsby, Jr., commander of 3rd Brigade, 3rd Infantry Division, reported that his forces had targeted and destroyed twenty-one boats during the first ten days of Operation Marne Torch.[699] Bombing the boats often generated secondary explosions, indicating that the rivercraft were transporting munitions.[700]

Fighters and weapons moved from Arab Jabour into the capital's Rashid district. Arab Jabour is an easy commute to al Qaeda-held areas of Rashid, such as Dora, which suggests a connection between them. Colonel Ricky Gibbs, the commander of the 4th Brigade Combat Team,

1st Infantry Division, in Rashid reported in late May that some enemy fighters in his area had come from outside of Baghdad, and, indeed, from other areas of Iraq.[701] More importantly, Colonel Gibbs estimated that fifteen or twenty percent of the IEDs his troops encountered were explosively-formed penetrators. He stated that the EFPs were being used in terrain controlled by al Qaeda, not by Shia militias. It is logical to conclude that the EFPs were flowing into Dora from Arab Jabour and other points south along the Tigris. Al Qaeda in Iraq cells created EFPs in indigenous factories, including one in Samarra, in summer of 2007, though they were unlikely to have replicated the technology that produced the highly-lethal copper disks.[702]

In early October 2007, U.S. forces conducted an operation in Tamim province, targeting a suspected al Qaeda emir of foreign terrorists involved in EFPs attacks on Coalition Forces.[703] A few weeks prior to this operation, a Qods Force officer involved in weapons trafficking was detained in Sulaymaniyah. These incidents suggest that Iranian support was not limited to Special Groups in central and southern Iraq.

Possible Aims of the Iranian Revolutionary Guards Corps-Qods Force

Initially, the Qods Force might have intended to pin U.S. forces in Iraq, rather than to eject them. According to Ware, "Intelligence sources claim that Brigadier General Sullaimani ordained in a meeting of his militia proxies in the spring of last year [2004] that 'any move that would wear out the U.S. forces in Iraq should be done. Every possible means should be used to keep the U.S. forces engaged in Iraq.'"[704]

In 2005 and 2006, "The Qods Force goal was to develop the Iraqi Special Groups into a network similar to the Lebanese Hezbollah. Special groups would be unable to conduct their terrorist attacks in Iraq without Iranian-supplied weapons and other support," according to a U.S. military spokesman.[705] The purpose of the Qods force effort, then, was to create a lethal network that relied upon the Iranian government to survive, increasing Tehran's ability to control or at least influence operations in Iraq.

Iran and Hezbollah made these changes as the current Iraqi government was being established. Parliamentary factions selected Nouri al Maliki as Prime Minister on April 21, 2006.[706] His cabinet took power on May 20, 2006. The Qods Force's reorganization of the Special Groups into a Hezbollah-like structure might have been either a deliberate Iranian response to the creation of an Iraqi government or, more specifically, to Maliki's premiership. The Qods Force certainly took these steps as Maliki's government was forming.

The Qods Force might have aimed to reorganize the Iraqi secret cells into a Hezbollah-style organization because that military advising effort has succeeded well. Yet the IRGC-QF might also have aimed to achieve goals in Iraq similar to those that Hezbollah has pursued in Lebanon, where for years the organization attempted to expel Israeli forces occupying territory in southern Lebanon. By extension, it seems possible that Hezbollah and the IRGC-QF viewed the Special Groups as an organization well-suited to expel Coalition Forces from Iraq. That would represent a change from the IRGC-QF strategy of 2004, articulated by Brigadier General Qassim Sullaimani, presuming Ware reported it correctly.

The IRGC-QF and Lebanese Hezbollah might have reorganized their efforts in 2006 to achieve broader political aims in Iraq and to undermine the American policy of supporting a democratic government. Hezbollah in Lebanon exists despite the presence of an elected government. It uses existing government structures and personnel to accomplish some of its goals. By reorganizing Iraqi Special Groups into a Hezbollah-like model, the Qods Force might have intended that the Special Groups should operate under the umbrella of Iraqi government institutions in order to compete with (or, indeed, effectively replace) Iraq's elected government, as Hezbollah had done in parts of Lebanon.

Ryan Crocker, the U.S. Ambassador to Iraq, suggested that the Qods Force might have the goal of assuring that southern Iraq remains beyond the control of the central government of Iraq and Iraqi Security Forces.

In this scenario, the Qods Force might desire an end-state in which those who receive their funding, weapons, and military training from Special Groups provide security and services in southern Iraq and hold political offices there. Ambassador Crocker stated, "The fact that we have arrested the Lebanese Hezbollah trainer and have had many long conversations with the head of the secret cells, so called, of the Jaysh al Mahdi, who has gone on at length about Iranian connections, has to leave you with the issue out there, is Iran intending a Lebanization or a Hezbollahzation of parts of the south. So in addition to . . . criminally driven violence, you cannot rule out the possibility of an overlay of not just politically directed violence but politically directed violence with outside support."[707]

The Qods Force Advisors In Iraq

Most members of Special Groups were Iraqis, including Qais Khazali, the former head of Secret Cells. Nevertheless there were Iranian operatives tied to the IRGC-Qods Force assisting the Special Groups from locations within Iraq at the end of 2006 and the beginning of 2007. U.S. Special Forces detained Chizari, the third-ranking official in the Qods Force, at the Baghdad compound of Abdul Aziz al Hakim on December 29, 2006. He and his captured colleague "had detailed weapons lists, documents pertaining to shipments of weapons into Iraq, organizational charts, telephone records and maps, among other sensitive intelligence information. Officials were particularly concerned about the fact that the Iranians had information about importing modern, specially shaped explosive charges into Iraq, weapons that have been used in roadside bombs to target U.S. military armored vehicles."[708] These two men claimed they had diplomatic passports. U.S. officials argued that they did not have diplomatic immunity, as they had used aliases. The Iraqi government, disagreeing, decided to expel them.[709] On January 11, 2007, Coalition Forces detained five Iranians, without proper diplomatic credentials, with links to the IRGC-QF in Irbil, in the Kurdish region in northeastern Iraq.[710] The IRGC-QF had ties with Ansar al Islam terrorists in the Kurdish region before and after the fall of Saddam Hussein. IRGC-QF had other operatives within the Kurdish region, including one who was arrested in the Kurdish city of Suleimaniyah in autumn 2007.[711]

Iranian advisors within Iraq assisted Special Groups. Iraqis functioned as liaisons for Iranian intelligence officers in the cities of Amarah and Majjar al Kabir, known havens for weapons smugglers.[712] Major General Rick Lynch, the commander of Multi-National Forces-Center, estimated in August 2007 that he had about fifty high-value targets in MND-C related to the Special Groups. Roughly thirty of them are "IRGC surrogates, people that have been trained by the IRGC in Iran who've come back in Iraq to conduct acts of violence." In addition, he said, "I believe I got some members of the IRGC, some Iranians, who are working in our battlespace." He believed that there were about twenty Iranian IRGC advisors "either training Iraqis to conduct acts of violence or conducting those acts of violence themselves .... And what they do is they transit the battlespace. They don't come in and then stay, but they're going back and forth."[713] These Qods Force operatives filled an important advisory niche, perhaps in the wake of the capture of Ali Mussa Daqduq.

Undermining the Iraqi Government: Special Group Activities in 2006

The Special Groups' operations contributed directly to turmoil in Iraq's central and provincial governments in 2006 and 2007, as they actively undermined the Maliki government from its inception.

The Special Groups contributed vigorously to the sectarian violence plaguing Iraq in 2006. Leaders of secret cells organized death squad activities by militia groups or government employees; they arranged kidnappings of Iraqi government officials and workers from their ministries; and they diverted Iraqi government funds to support their operations. Many used their official positions within the government of Iraq to fund, organize, staff, and execute these "secret cell" operations.

These groups also caused some of the personnel turmoil within the Maliki government that prevented it from functioning during the second half of 2006. Some of the targeted kidnappings of Iraqi officials in spring and summer 2006 are directly linked to secret cell leaders whom U.S. forces have captured and interrogated in recent months. These kidnappings removed mid-level functionaries—often but not exclusively Sunni—from the central Iraqi government and from the provincial governments.

Hakim al Zamili, Special Groups, Deputy Minister of Health

In June 2006, Diyala's provincial director of health was the Sunni nominee for one of the deputy minister positions in the Maliki government.[714] He traveled to Baghdad that month for a meeting with the Minister of Health, at the ministry building, and was kidnapped while inside. His kidnapping was organized by Hakim al Zamili, the deputy minister of health, whom U.S. and Iraqi forces apprehended on February 9, 2007.[715] Allegations against the Ministry had provoked previous operations by U.S. and Iraqi forces. For example, they had attempted to locate kidnap victims in the Ministry of Health in August 2006, but failed to find their targets.[716]

In November 2006, officials in the Ministry of Health were targets of kidnappings and assassinations. Men in police uniforms abducted Ammar al Safir, another deputy minister of health, on November 19, 2006.[717] Two days later, roadside bombs in eastern Baghdad wounded two guards in the convoy for Minister of State Mohammed Abbas Auraibi. On that same day, gunmen fired on Hakim al Zamili's convoy in Baghdad, killing two of his security guards.[718] All three men were Shia officials in the Iraqi government. The U.S. military did not indicate whether Hakim al Zamili and his secret cell were complicit in the November kidnapping of his colleague. Nor have they indicated whether the assassination attempt against Hakim al Zamili was a reprisal attack against him for that or any other action.

Hakim al Zamili used the resources of the Ministry of Health, such as ambulances, to transport weapons, death squads, and their victims between Sadr City and other locations in Baghdad. Al Zamili allegedly included death squad members on the payroll of the Ministry of Health.[719]

As part of the parliamentary compromise that brought Maliki to power, the minister of Health was appointed by the Sadrist bloc. Many employees in that Ministry have ties to the Office of the Martyr Sadr or to its military wing, the Jaysh al Mahdi. It is not possible from the evidence presented to conclude firmly whether Sadr personally directed Hakim al Zamili's activities in 2006, or whether Zamili acted independently. Zamili was one of the first officials arrested after Sadr left Iraq in late January 2007. His arrest preceded Operation Fardh al Qanoon.

Zamili was held throughout 2007, while prosecutors and judges built their case; however, when the trial finally began in February 2008, it was compromised by intimidation of witnesses and judges.[720] Ultimately, the three-judge panel dropped the corruption, kidnapping, and murder charges against Zamili, citing a lack of evidence.[721] Many of those scheduled to testify against Zamili had failed to show at court amid widespread reports of death threats. Zamili's trial was an important test of Iraq's judicial system, and it highlighted important challenges or flaws in the rule of law and judicial process.

Mass Kidnappings in June and July 2006

It is not clear from open sources which organizations—government forces, militia groups, secret cells, or private citizens—organized and perpetrated the mass kidnappings that plagued Iraq in June and July 2006. Many of these attacks were conducted by men wearing the uniforms of Iraq's police forces, probably militia members working also in the Iraqi Security Forces—or indeed, by Special Groups. Many of these June and July kidnappings targeted government officials, rather than randomly selected civilians, and therefore deserve consideration as part of the destabilization of the Maliki government, regardless of Special Groups involvement. Gunmen in camouflage uniforms seized three busloads of factory workers on their way home from a government-owned industrial plant in Taji on June 22, 2006.[722] In early July, gunmen kidnapped individuals working for the Iraqi government, including the Minister of Electricity (who was released) and his bodyguards, a female Sunni legislator and her bodyguards, and a consular official who was on leave in Baghdad from his routine diplomatic assignment in the Iranian city of Kermanshah.[723] On July 16, gunmen in police uniforms used official vehicles to kidnap the head of Iraq's Olympic Committee and about thirty other sports officials while they attended a conference in the Karadah neighborhood of eastern Baghdad.[724]

Azhar Dulaimi, Special Groups, and the Kidnappings of Iraqi Officials and U.S. Soldiers

On November 15, 2006, a secret cell kidnapped numerous employees of the Iraqi Ministry of Higher Education from its headquarters in Karadah. This garnered major public attention because of its scale and its contribution to unrest within the Iraqi government, culminating in the withdrawal of Sadrist members from the Iraqi Council of Representatives on November 29, 2006. The secret cell operative Azhar Dulaimi, whom U.S. forces killed during a raid on May 20, 2007, coordinated this operation.

Differing reports suggest that between fifty and eighty gunmen, all in police uniforms, stormed past security guards within the Ministry compound. The gunmen separated male from female employees, locked the latter in a room, and loaded the former into roughly thirty trucks belonging to the Interior Ministry, but without license plates.[725] U.S. officials estimated that fifty-five people had been kidnapped; they believed that the abductors took their victims to the Belidiyat neighborhood on the southeastern fringe of Sadr City.[726] Approximately forty of the hostages were released by the kidnappers or rescued by the Iraqi Army within twenty-four hours.[727] Prime Minister Maliki also immediately ordered the arrest of several police officials in Karadah, presumably for complicity in the plot (or, alternatively, for incompetence).[728]

Azhar Dulaimi organized other high-profile kidnappings executed by members of Special Groups. He participated in the January kidnapping of U.S. soldiers from the Provincial Joint Coordination Center in Karbala, where a small U.S. team worked with Iraqi Security Forces. Operatives entered the Provincial Joint Coordination Center unopposed in a convoy of civilian vehicles, wearing components of American military uniforms, and stormed into rooms where the U.S. soldiers were working. They ultimately killed the five kidnapped American soldiers.[729]

U.S. Forces Capture Qais Khazali and Ali Mussa Daqduq

U.S. forces captured Qais Khazali, Laith Khazali, and Ali Mussa Daqduq in a single operation on March 20, 2007, in Basra, Iraq's southernmost city. (The three obviously had worked together on occasion.) U.S. forces also captured a computer, false identification cards, and diaries in the raid. From these documents and separate interviews, U.S. forces confirmed that Qais Khazali, Laith Khazali, and Ali Mussa Daqduq were leaders of a network deliberately developed by the Iranian government to foment violence in Iraq. The U.S. military spokesman in Baghdad released a file early in July reproducing some of these documents.[730]

Multi-National Force-Iraq reported: "When Qais [Khazali] was captured, we found an in-depth planning and lessons learned document. It was about the attack the Special Groups coordinated against the Karbala Provincial Joint Coordination Center on January 20. This 22-page document provides a unique window into the planning and execution of special group operations here in Iraq. . . . Ali Musa Daqduq and Qais Khazali state that senior leadership within the Qods Force knew of and supported planning for the eventual Karbala attack that killed five coalition soldiers. Ali Musa Daqduq contends that the Iraqi Special Groups could not have conducted this complex operation without the support and direction of the Qods Force. Daqduq and Khazali both confirm that Qais Khazali authorized the operation, and Azhar al Dulaimi, who we killed in an operation earlier this year, executed the operation.

"The document that we captured showed the following. It showed that the group that attacked the Provincial Joint Coordination Center in Karbala had conducted extensive preparation and drills prior to the attack. Qods Force had developed detailed information regarding our soldiers' activities, shift changes and fences, and this information was shared with the attackers. They had American-looking uniforms, vehicles and identification cards that enabled the attackers to more easily penetrate the Provincial Joint Coordination Center and achieve surprise. [It] reported that the captured soldiers were killed when the attackers' dispersal from the site was interrupted."[731]

U.S. forces exploited the intelligence gained in these documents and from interviews with the captives to identify significant secret cell leaders and members of the weapons-smtuggling network. The affiliated kills and captures included secret cell leader Abu Zaki; Azhar al Dulaimi, the executor of the Ministry of Health and Karbala attacks and Abu Tiba, one of his gang members;[732] al Hilfi, the head of secret cells in Baghdad;[733] Sheikh (Ahmed) Mohammad Hassan Sbahi Al Khafaji, who supplied weapons to Baghdad;[734] and many others.[735]

Arming the Secret Cells with EFPs and Other Weapons

A variety of Iranian weapons flowed into Iraq through direct purchases by Iran's government. Coalition Forces first noticed that enemy groups were using EFPs in Iraq in the middle of 2004. The number of EFPs used against Coalition and Iraqi forces rose "at a rate of 150 percent" between January 2006 and December 2006, and increased every month in November 2006 through January 2007.[736] Weapons were typically smuggled from Iran to Iraq, and the Qods Force played a role in that process.[737]

The training alliance between Hezbollah, Iran, and Shia militias was coterminous with the increased use of EFPs in Iraq. This timing most likely was not coincidental. Iran originally manufactured EFPs for Lebanese Hezbollah. Copper EFPs require a great deal of metallurgical and technological precision to manufacture. Consequently, they cannot be made without specific machinery, access to which the Iranians controlled. Abu Mustafa al Sheibani supplied EFPs to Iraq from 2005, if not earlier.[738] His relative, Abu Yasier al Sheibani, served as "the deputy, key logistician and financier for this group in Iraq."[739] That is to say, the Sheibani network smuggled EFPs into Iraq.

The Sheibanis relied on a network within Iraq to distribute EFPs to Special Groups and other extremists, concentrating on Baghdad. Some smugglers in these distribution networks had direct connections to the Qods Force.[740]

Other weapons smuggled from Iran to Iraq in 2007 included: 81-mm mortars (the remainder of the region uses 82-mm mortars); repainted 107-mm rockets imported into Iran from China and marked for sale in the open markets; RPG-7; 60-mm canisters filled with Iranian-manufactured mortar rounds; and 240-mm rockets.[741]

In addition, earlier in 2007, American troops discovered over 100 Austrian-made Steyr HS50 .50 caliber sniper rifles in Iraq.[742] These high-powered rifles, which fire Iranian rounds, "can pierce all body armour from up to a mile and penetrate armoured Humvee troop carriers."[743] The rifles were part of a larger shipment legally purchased from the Austrian manufacturer by Iran a year ago under the justification that they would be used by the Iranian police to combat drug smugglers.[744] Although eyebrows were raised in both Washington and London at the time, the sale went through and the weapons were shipped to Iran.[745] The presence of these weapons shows a high level of sophistication in the Iranian arms flow into Iraq, as the purchase was made officially by the Iranian government.

The Special Groups Network Transit Routes for EFPs and other Weapons from Iran

The network of Special Groups transports EFPs along the major highways to Baghdad from Iranian border crossings in Diyala and Wasit provinces. Most of these routes lacked Coalition Forces in 2006, and the mission of Coalition Forces in 2006 did not regularly include interdiction operations, instead focusing on training Iraqi Security Forces for these and other missions.

In Wasit province, EFPs, weapons, recruits for Special Groups, and smuggled goods flowed through the major border crossing between Mehran, Iran, and Zurbatiyah, Iraq.[746] Iranian trucks did not transport weapons into Iraq through Zurbatiyah; rather, goods and weapons were trans-loaded from Iranian to Iraqi trucks near the border.[747] Legitimate commercial traffic also crosses the border at Zurbatiyah, as do religious pilgrims and political figures with ties to Iran, such as Amar al Hakim, now head of the Islamic Supreme Council of Iraq, a major political party in the Maliki government.[748]

The city of Kut, just to the west along the highway, has strong ties with ISCI and its military wing, the Badr Corps.[749] Kut is also the hub of the road and smuggling network from the Iranian border to Baghdad.[750] The road from Mehran runs through Kut, as does the road from Amarah. U.S. forces conducted a series of operations this summer to interdict the smuggling of Iranian weapons from Amarah to Sadr City,[751] and Iraqi Security Forces with the help of Coalition troops conducted operations in Kut against rogue elements of the Jaysh al Mahdi.[752]

Basra was another point of entry for Iranian arms and weapons. Certainly, there is evidence for the trafficking of weapons along the roads out of Basra to Amarah and Nasiriyah. In mid-June, Nasiriyah was the site of a firefight between Iraqi forces and the Jaysh al Mahdi.[753] On June 27, Iraqi Special Forces destroyed a weapons cache belonging to rogue Jaysh al Mahdi militiamen.[754] Among the weapons destroyed were thirty 60-mm mortar rounds, and ammunition of Iranian origin.[755] A day later, Iraqi Special Forces captured "a rogue Jaysh al Mahdi insurgent leader during an operation in Nasiriyah."[756] The man, later identified as Sheikh (Ahmed) Mohammad Hassan Sbahi Al Khafaji, is suspected of having "provide[d] financial support to weapons trafficking networks which supply rogue Jaysh al Mahdi units in the Baghdad area."[757]

Cities like Majjar al Kabir and Amarah in Maysan province, places known to be "smuggling routes for Secret Cell terrorists who facilitate Iranian lethal aid" as well as safe havens for "liaisons for Iranian intelligence operatives into Iraq," were the target of disruption operations in mid-June 2007.[758] Weapons and aid entering these towns near the Iranian border must still travel through the heavily Shia central five-city region before reaching Baghdad, thus increasing the violence in the south.

Iranian weapons and trained terrorists enter Iraq at key border crossings. Although the exact mechanism of Iranian arms supply remains unclear, it seems weapons are moved via extensive networks and that the so-called secret cells are often responsible for facilitating their transfer.

The IRGC-QF in Diyala

The Qods Force responded to the Surge by escalating its support for Special Groups in central and southern Iraq. Ali Mussa Daqduq recorded information about attacks in Basra, Amarah, Karbala, the Rusafa neighborhood of Baghdad, and Diyala.[759] The Special Groups also increased attacks in other neighborhoods of Baghdad. As it is not possible to detail every such incident, Diyala province, north and east of Baghdad, is an interesting case study of the Special Groups' reaction to the American troop increase in February 2007. Diyala also illustrates the reactions of Special Groups to American successes in August 2007.

Jaysh al Mahdi operated in Diyala in 2006 because of the mixture of sectarian and ethnic groups there, the al Qaeda stronghold that emerged in Baqubah, and the region's proximity to Baghdad. Diyala suffered from sectarian cleansing and terrorism in 2006. The Baghdad Security Plan did not "squirt" Jaysh al Mahdi fighters into Diyala. Rather, the Special Groups actively targeted Coalition and Iraqi Forces in Diyala province in March, April, and May 2007, by reinforcing the area and supplying it with weapons.

The spring 2007 conflict in Diyala consisted of a struggle between the Jaysh al Mahdi, al Qaeda, and U.S. forces to control the lines of communication to Baghdad. Special groups and rogue Jaysh al Mahdi moved into areas of Diyala as al Qaeda receded from its stronghold in Turki Village and re-concentrated in Baqubah, Tarmiyah, and the Diyala River Valley.[760]

The Special Groups in Diyala received direct attention from Qods Force proxies in Iraq. Some time before March 20, Ali Mussa Daqduq, the Lebanese Hezbollah operative, met with leaders of Special Groups who conducted small-arms and IED attacks against troops in Diyala, presumably to review their activities.[761] His visit illustrated the importance of Diyala to the Special Groups.

The Iranians increased their supply of weapons by February 24, 2007, just ten days after Operation Enforcing the Law began in Baghdad. Smuggling networks placed a large cache consisting of a hundred copper disks and other supplies used to make EFPs in Mandali. Mandali, in Diyala, sits on the secondary road that follows the mountains dividing Iran and Iraq, and is an obvious point on a smuggling route from the legitimate border crossing to its north at Khanaqin. U.S. troops discovered this stockpile on February 24, 2007. U.S. forces subsequently stated that they suspected these EFPs were linked to Shia extremists.[762] Secret cell networks in Diyala were being reviewed by the Qods Force proxy before March. The Mandali EFP cache seems, therefore, to have been brought by the Special Groups network for its own use, in order to escalate the fight against Coalition Forces in Diyala or in Baghdad in February.

The Special Groups in Baghdad did rely on weapons stored in and distributed from Diyala province. Coalition Forces captured an important facilitator near Qasarin, on the Tigris River in Diyala, whose responsibilities included distributing EFPs and other "weapons to Special Groups throughout the Baghdad area." This weapons smuggler made "numerous" trips to Iran, where he apparently had "ties to the Iranian Revolutionary Guards Corps-Qods Force."[763] Special Groups leaders operated in Qasarin and Khalis through October 2007, in the wake of U.S. clearing operations in and around Baqubah.[764]

Special Groups in Baghdad: Mortaring the Green Zone

Special groups, trained and equipped by Iran, escalated the number of mortar and rocket attacks against targets in the International
Zone throughout the spring of 2007. The accuracy of this indirect fire
improved as a result of training received in Iran and the quality of weapons supplied. General Odierno reported in June, "We have found a few
people that were Shia extremists that . . . had some training in Iran—
those mostly being the mortar and rocket teams inside of Baghdad . . . .
[T]hey were trained in Iran and came in here to conduct attacks against
not only coalition and Iraqi security forces, but government of Iraq targets inside of the Green Zone."[765]

Major General Fil, commander of Coalition Forces in Baghdad,
elaborated on this, explaining that most of the rocket and mortar
attacks originate from Sadr City or its environs, and that most of the
rockets and mortars are recently-made Iranian weapons. According to
Fil, "[M]uch of the indirect fire that we receive, especially that which
is pointed at the International Zone, the Green Zone, is in fact Iranian.
And when we check the tail fins of the mortars, when we find the
rockets—and frequently we're able to find them preemptively, before
they actually launch . . . there's no doubt that they're coming out of
Iran. Most of them are made fairly recently, in the past several years,
and they have lot numbers that we can . . . trace later on. I'll also say
that most of these are coming from the eastern side of the river, by far
the majority, in and around the Sadr City area. And so we focused our
efforts very strongly into discovering where these areas are that they're
frequently shooting from and denying those" areas to the enemy.[766]

General Odierno said, "I do concern myself, over time, about the
Iranian influence on Shia extremist groups and what that means in
the future. And we cannot allow this rogue Iranian influence to continue to influence, in my mind, and in many ways attack, the government of Iraq. Many of these indirect fire attacks that these groups have

done are directly against the government of Iraq in the Green Zone. So they're clearly challenging the government . . . .We cannot allow that to continue."[767]

The Relationship Between the Secret Cells and the Jaysh al Mahdi in 2007

The secret cells function alongside the Jaysh al Mahdi and other militia groups in Iraq. They are not identical, but rather overlapping groups. According to Brigadier General Kevin Bergner, a U.S. military spokesman, "They come from militia groups, and they are generally the more extreme members of those militia groups. Some of them have come from Jaysh al Mahdi. Some have come from other militia groups as well."[768] Bergner stressed that "[w]hile some of these people may have come from or been affiliated with Jaysh al Mahdi at one point—and these Special Groups were an outgrowth, perhaps, of relationships with Jaysh al Mahdi—they have in fact broken away from Jaysh al Mahdi." Furthermore, "[T]hey are cellular in nature . . . .We believe that these [Special Groups] are operating outside [Moqtada al Sadr's] control and that he shares our . . . concern in the seriousness that they represent."[769]

The Jaysh al Mahdi fractured in spring 2007. Moqtada al Sadr publicly ordered his militias not to fight Iraqi Security Forces during Operation Fardh al Qanoon. As a result, the Maliki government declared that all militia groups that fought the Iraqi Security Forces were "rogue elements" and therefore were subject to military targeting. Clashes between Iraqi Security Forces and rogue militia elements occurred in Diwaniyah in March and Amarah in June.

Moqtada al Sadr left Iraq for Iran in late January, which further undermined the leadership structure of the militia. In May, the Golden Jaysh al Mahdi, a Najaf-based group that claimed to be dispatched by Sadr, attempted to cleanse the Jaysh al Mahdi of rogue elements not responsive to Najaf.[770] Local groups, calling themselves the Noble Jaysh al Mahdi, emerged in Hurriyah in Baghdad to rebuff the attempt of the Golden JAM.[771]

General Petraeus emphasized that secret cells are "different from JAM." Unlike the standard militiaman in the Jaysh al Mahdi, the secret cells "have had extra training and selection," the training being conducted by the Qods Force.[772] These "secret cells" function as enablers, facilitating Iranian support for the Jaysh al Mahdi and coordinating continued attacks. Sadr City is the support base for the secret cells, Jaysh al Mahdi, and many rogue JAM militias within Baghdad. These networks overlap extensively.

A militia commander seized in Najaf illustrates a common relationship between the Special Groups and the Jaysh al Mahdi organization. "The former commander's Jaysh al Mahdi cell is suspected of conducting aggressive insurgent attacks using EFPs throughout southern Iraq during late 2005 and early 2006. After leaving Jaysh al Mahdi, he allegedly formed an independent cell of more than 150 Shia extremists that is believed to have conducted attacks on Iraqi and Coalition Forces."[773] U.S. Forces captured another extremist in Sadr City who broke from Jaysh al Mahdi, ran his own cell, and had ties to weapons provided by Special Groups.[774]

The U.S. and Iraqi Response Within Iraq to Iranian Intervention

U.S. forces and diplomats in Iraq recognize the destabilizing effect that Iranian support for secret cells is having on the Iraqi government. They aim to "get the surrogates that are operating within Iraq, which tend to be Iraqis, to reject what Iran is doing," according to General Odierno. "There are Iraqi extremist leaders here that are supporting this effort. If we can get . . . Iraqis to reject Iranians' lethal support inside of their country, we can stop this threat."[775] The Coalition and the Iraqi government have taken a multi-pronged approach to reducing Iranian influence within Iraq. "We do that first by taking down their supply networks," General Odierno stated. The second approach is political and diplomatic: "We do that by continuing to talk [with] the Iraqis" about their "tensions" with Iran and the effects that Iranian influence might have "over your own country."[776] This coordinated diplomatic and military policy seeks "to have Iraqis reject Iran doing this," General Odierno remarked, "Once that occurs, I think we'll be able to eliminate this threat from inside of Iraq."[777]

The Diplomatic Response

Ambassador Ryan Crocker began engaging in direct discussions with Iran about security in Iraq in May 2007. On May 29, he met with Iran's ambassador to Iraq in a four-hour session hosted and chaired by Prime Minister Maliki. He made it clear that the discussion was confined to Iraq and avoided any of the other issues in conflict between Iran and the United States. He said, "We also made it clear, from the American point of view, that this is about actions, not just principles, and I laid out before the Iranians a number of our direct specific concerns about their behavior in Iraq, their support for militias that are fighting both the Iraqi Security Forces and Coalition Forces, the fact that a lot of the explosives and ammunition that are used by these groups are coming from Iran, that such activities, led by the IRGC Qods Force, needed to cease, and that we would be looking for results."

He continued, "The Iranians did not respond directly to that. They did, again, emphasize that their policy is support of the government [of Iraq]." About the specific concerns Crocker described, he said, "The Iranians did not go into any great detail. They made the assertion that the Coalition presence was an occupation and that the effort to train and equip Iraqi Security Forces had been inadequate to the challenges it faced." The Iranians then proposed a "trilateral mechanism to coordinate on security matters," which Crocker referred to Washington. Asked again about the Iranian response to the specific accusations he had made, Crocker repeated: "In terms of security specifics, we laid out a number of them. The Iranians did not offer any detailed response. They did say they rejected such allegations, but again, there was no detailed exchange."[778]

The prospects for follow-up meetings did not appear good in the weeks following this exchange. State Department Spokesman Sean McCormack repeated on several occasions in June and July that there had been no formal request from any party for an additional meeting, and said that the U.S. was more interested in what the Iranians were doing than in what they said at such meetings: "We said that we're not going to have another meeting just for the sake of having another meeting. We would like to see these—this mechanism actually result in some changes. I think at this point, it's safe to say we haven't seen any substantial change in terms of Iranian behavior." Asked what changes he was looking for, McCormack said, "Well, for starters, stop supplying money, technology, and training for people who are trying to kill our troops. . . . They can stop funding those individuals and groups who are trying to stoke sectarian tensions in Iraq."[779]

Nevertheless, Crocker met once again with the Iranian ambassador, the Iraqi foreign minister, and the Iraqi national security advisor, at the request of the Iraqi Government on July 24, 2007. Crocker repeated the concerns he had laid out in the May meeting about Iranian involvement in the violence in Iraq, noting that, in fact, "over the roughly two months since our last meeting we've actually seen militia related activity that can be attributed to Iranian support go up and not down. . . . [T]hus far what we've seen on the ground over the last couple of months has in many respects represented an escalation and not a de-escalation." He noted, "The Iranians, in their response, followed pretty much the same line as the Iranian foreign ministry spokesman . . . which is to say we have absolutely nothing to do with this." The Iranians nevertheless proposed establishing a security subcommittee "to discuss the problem of extremist militias."[780] Such a committee was apparently established, as McCormack noted that it met at the sub-ambassadorial level in early August "to talk about security issues related to Iraq."[781] McCormack also noted that representatives from MNF-I and the U.S. Embassy in Baghdad attended a meeting of Iraq's neighbors (as observers) in Damascus on August 8 to address "the issue of Iraq's borders and the flow of foreign fighters, the flow of the kind of technologies and money that are adding to the instability in Iraq." He concluded, "Thus far, our diplomatic engagement through the channel that Ambassador Crocker has set up hasn't yielded positive results . . . . As a matter of fact, you've seen, as General Odierno pointed out, an actual increase in the attacks from these EFP networks."

Both Crocker and McCormack repeatedly pointed out that Iran's publicly declared policy matched that of the United States and the government of Iraq, but that its actions did not match that policy, and that it denied any involvement in supporting violence within Iraq despite all evidence to the contrary. They stressed the conclusion that it was unlikely that further talks or additional diplomatic mechanisms would be productive until the Iranians adjusted their behavior to match their public and private statements. They also noted that between May and July, Iranian actions had moved even farther from Iranian statements as Iranian weapons and advisors flowed into Iraq in increasing numbers.

The Military Response

Although Coalition Forces in Iraq concentrated their offensive activities against al Qaeda during Operation Phantom Thunder, they also conducted operations targeting the Jaysh al Mahdi. MNF-I removed multiple leaders of Sadrist secret cells throughout the country almost daily in May and June, and their targets frequently include Sadrists in Sadr City itself. In May and June 2007, Coalition and Iraqi forces executed at least eighteen operations in Baghdad and its immediate surroundings, targeting secret cell activity. They have also conducted such raids against secret cell leaders and militias in Karbala, Amarah, Nasiriyah, and Basra.

The operations have resulted in the capture or elimination of key secret cell leaders, individuals responsible for EFP attacks against Coalition Forces, members of Shia death squads and kidnapping cells, as well as those responsible for the importation and use of Iranian arms.

Disrupting Networks and Interdicting Illegal Weapons East and South of Baghdad

General Odierno's first step, disruption of supply networks, required a redeployment of Coalition and Iraqi forces along key nodes in the lines of communication between Iran and Iraq. There were insufficient Coalition Forces to disrupt these supply lines in 2006, even with targeted raids.

The disposition of U.S. forces in 2006 left a dramatic hole east of Baghdad, allowing Iranian weapons, secret cell leaders, and militia groups to flow freely through this area. The troop increase brought the 3rd BCT/3rd Infantry Division (Sledgehammer, under the command of Colonel Wayne Grigsby) to this area, which had been without U.S. forces for years, in April 2007. Forward Operating Base Hammer is at Besmaya, about fifteen or twenty miles east of the city. Southern Diyala province abuts northern Wasit in the desolate terrain east of Baghdad, within Hammer Brigade's area of operations. Secondary roads through that terrain link Mandali, the major EFP cache site in Diyala, with the eastern border of Sadr City. Roads along the southeastern edge of Baghdad link the same terrain with the Tigris River Valley.

Secret cells valued this communications route east of Baghdad, which links Sadr City and its surrounding neighborhoods with Diyala Province. Coalition Forces actively targeted these weapons smugglers east and northeast of Baghdad. U.S. and Iraqi Forces detained a smuggler responsible for transporting EFPs and Katusha rockets from Iran to Iraq and distributing them to secret cells throughout Baghdad.[782] A few days later, U.S. forces detained two suspects with direct links to the IRGC on the Iranian border east of Baghdad.[783]

On July 11, insurgents launched Iranian rockets at FOB Hammer, killing one soldier and wounding fifteen others. On August 7, the 3rd Brigade Combat Team "conducted a raid on a militant house in the town of Nahrawan, which is about twenty miles east of Baghdad on the east side of the Tigris River. They arrested one of our division's most valued targets, high-value targets," according to Major General Rick Lynch, the 3rd ID commander. "[H]e acted as a link between Iran and the Jaysh al Mahdi militia. He was the main Shia conduit in that region for getting Iranian EFPs and rockets into Baghdad, and his capture was a big blow to that network."[784] Whatever the ultimate effect of that particular capture, the incident shows the importance of interdicting the supply lines east of Baghdad.

In 2006, Coalition Forces were also spread too thin to cover the lines of communication south of Baghdad. For example, only 200 soldiers from the Polish Division in Multi-National Division Central-South were stationed in Kut through spring 2007, detached from the bulk of their unit.[785] Thus, smugglers could bring Iranian weapons without expecting interdiction along open routes in 2006.

The Surge's increase in U.S. and Coalition Forces, including the addition of another Division Headquarters, made it possible to begin interdicting weapons flowing along the major highways and the Tigris River. Multi-National Force-Iraq reinforced Kut with 2,000 soldiers from the Republic of Georgia, who arrived in July and August 2007 for operations that will commence in September.[786] MND-C plans to use this brigade to search every truck coming along the highway through Kut.[787]

Coalition and Iraqi Special Forces and conventional forces targeted rogue Jaysh al Mahdi units and Special Groups in Diyala, Baghdad, and southern Iraq in June, July, and August. Some of these activities aimed at disrupting supply networks. At the end of August 2007, General Odierno reported, "We've had some success in taking down some of the leaders in the supply networks . . . within Diyala province, within Sadr City and within southern Iraq."

Capturing Secret Cell Leaders and
Rogue Jaysh al Mahdi Commanders

U.S. and Iraqi forces conducted a multi-phased campaign against secret cell supply networks. First, Special Forces captured or killed high-value targets, exploiting the intelligence gained from the capture of Ali Mussa Daqduq and the Khazali brothers. They focused particularly on Sadr City, the base of Special Groups in Baghdad, and southern Iraqi cities such as Amarah and Basra. As weapons trafficking networks linked Amarah and Baghdad, the operations in the south contributed directly to captures in the capital.[788]

A second wave of operations against secret cells occurred in July, presumably as Coalition and Iraqi forces gained intelligence in the wake of Phantom Thunder. The scope of these raids widened, and included Diyala province and cities in the south.[789]

After al Qaeda in Iraq was driven from Adhamiyah, Masafee, Jazeera, and Hadar, the remaining violence within Baghdad stemmed primarily from Shia extremist groups. The Special Groups orchestrated the majority of that violence. Accordingly, U.S. and Iraqi forces intensified their campaign against secret cell leaders in Baghdad in late July and August, frequently operating against rogue militias in western Baghdad as well as Sadr City. These operations dramatically decreased violence within Baghdad in the fall of 2007.

The weapons provided by the Qods Force and its agents made their way from Sadr City to rogue militias in the western half of the capital. The hotspots for EFP use in Baghdad and for secret cell arrests suggest a path from Sadr City to its northeastern outlying neighborhoods, Shaab and Ur, then to Adhamiyah and Hurriyah on the east bank of the Tigris, and from there to Khadimiya and Shula in northern Mansour, Yarmouk in southern Mansour, and Aamel and Bayaa in Rashid.

Khadimiya is the most significant Shia pilgrimage site in Baghdad. Different groups of the Jaysh al Mahdi, some from Baghdad and others from Najaf, have competed with one another for control of the

Khadimiya shrine in May 2007.[790] EFP activity near the Khadimiyah shrine indicated the presence of rogue Jaysh al Mahdi or secret cells.

A rogue JAM brigade commander, captured in mid-August, led a cell of 150 insurgents. They bought and sold weapons in Sadr City for use in Hurriyah. Their death squads targeted Iraqi government employees who opposed their activities. They set up illegal checkpoints in that neighborhood to kill Sunni civilians, conducted indirect fire attacks on Iraqis, and, finally, emplaced complex IEDs against Coalition and Iraqi Security Forces.[791]

Militia elements and al Qaeda likewise threatened the population of the nearby Sunni enclave in Mansour and mixed neighborhoods such as Shula. Accordingly, on July 31, 2007, U.S. forces conducted raids against weapons traffickers with links to the Qods Force in Shula.[792] U.S. and Iraqi Security Forces also captured members of an assassination cell in Shula on August 8.[793] Rogue militia attacked U.S. troops searching for a weapons cache in Shula, which, indeed, contained EFPs and other arms. Ground forces and their close air support killed the militiamen who opened fire.[794] In northwestern Baghdad, the 6th Iraqi Army Scout Platoon captured members of a cell that conducted extrajudicial killings in the Atafiyah neighborhood as well as IED attacks against Coalition Forces.[795]

The Rashid district of Baghdad also contained a major Sunni-Shia faultline and a great deal of militia activity. U.S. forces conducted major clearing operations in Rashid in May, and focused intensely on the al Qaeda stronghold in Dora and the JAM network in Bayaa in June and July 2007. Iraqi and Coalition Forces also targeted rogue Jaysh al Mahdi leaders in Baghdad and in the south, as well as JAM and special cell operatives in Rashid, just as they did in Shula: a death-squad leader on July 25;[796] an IED and EFP facilitator for Bayaa and Aamel on July 26;[797] a rouge JAM insurgent group that conducted attacks against Coalition Forces and Iraqi citizens on August 6;[798] a rogue JAM death squad leader and four of his cell members in East Rashid on August 8; a high-value Special Groups financier for Bayaa on August 13;[799] and a rogue JAM sniper on August 16.[800] In addition, they targeted a splinter JAM group that had conducted extra-judicial killings in southwestern Baghdad.[801]

Operation Phantom Strike, the Corps offensive that began on August 15, 2007, targeted secret cells and rogue Jaysh al Mahdi units that benefited from their support.

The Iraqi Army Fights Rogue Shia Militias

Prime Minister Maliki supported operations against the secret cells with Iraqi Security Forces, particularly Iraqi Special Operations Forces and some units of the Iraqi Army. General Odierno confirmed that "[the secret cells] are attacking the government of Iraq. The Iraqis understand this, and they've understood this because they have sent their own forces on operations against these elements. So it's clear that Prime Minister Maliki is very aware that they are conducting attacks against the government of Iraq, or [the Iraqis] wouldn't use their own security forces, along with our forces, to take down these elements."[802]

The 8th Iraqi Army Division is the best example of conventional Iraqi forces engaging rogue Jaysh al Mahdi militias. They conducted a series of operations against militias in Diwaniyah, the capital of Qadisiyah province, in 2007, including Operations Black Eagle and Lion's Pounce. Polish troops and some U.S. Special Forces support the Eighth Iraqi Army Division, as does an American Military Transition Team.

After the Black Eagle Operation in Diwaniyah, General Oothman continued his operations against militia groups in Diwaniyah, including a major fight in August against extremist militias. The Eighth Iraqi Army Division also vigorously pursued Special Groups operatives throughout its area, apprehending a recruiter for Special Groups in Najaf on July 15, another on August 4, and a third on August 12.[803] An independent militia commander who was formerly affiliated with the Jaysh al Mahdi participated in the August battle, along with his organization of 150 operatives. The 8th Iraqi Army Division detained him after a raid in eastern Najaf on August 14.[804]

These campaigns against secret cells led rogue militia and Iranian-backed elements to retaliate. An assassination campaign in August successfully targeted officeholders affiliated with the Supreme Iraqi Islamic Council (which, along with the two other leading Shia parties, Dawa and the Sadrist Trend, made up the political bloc that originally helped Prime Minister Nuri al Maliki to power). Another assassination campaign targeted Grand Ayatollah Ali Sistani's aides in southern provinces. The disturbances became more widespread.

On August 28, rogue militia elements or Special Groups disrupted the Shia pilgrimage in Karbala. They tried to shoot their way past mosque guards, but failed. The 8th Iraqi Army Division rapidly deployed to Karbala and helped to secure the shrine and evacuate the thousands of pilgrims in the city. Prime Minister Maliki traveled to Najaf on September 5 and met with the grand ayatollah. According to an official press release, Maliki and Sistani talked about "technocratic" government and about security in the holy cities.

The incident prompted Moqtada al Sadr to issue a statement once again requesting that militia members loyal to him lay down their arms. He already had called on loyal Jaysh al Mahdi members to put down their arms at the beginning of the Baghdad security plan. Those who disobeyed this second declaration would again be subject to the attempts of U.S. forces and Iraqi Security Forces to rid Iraq of violent militia extremists. U.S. and Iraqi forces continued to target rogue elements of the militia that did not respond to Sadr's request throughout September and October.

The combination of Moqtada's restatement of the cease-fire, Sistani's discussion with Maliki, and the dangers created by Special Groups' activities, induced regular Jaysh al Mahdi fighters who were not affiliated with Special Groups to lay down their arms in late August and early September.

The renewal of Sadr's cease-fire, and the vigorous campaign against Special Groups, reduced violence in Baghdad further in the weeks after

Ramadan. In northwestern Baghdad, "murders are down from a peak of over 161 reported murders per week a year ago to less than five per week now, and our continued efforts to defeat sectarian expansion continue to drive these numbers down," reported Colonel J. B. Burton, the sector's commander, in mid-October. "IED and small arms attacks are down from a peak of fifty per week in June to less than five per week since the end of August. And vehicle-borne IED attacks are down nearly 85 percent thanks to our combined efforts to defeat the Karkh VBIED and IED networks—which has had a tremendous impact on insurgents' ability to instruct and employ those types of weapons effectively."

The elimination of important secret cell leaders in western Baghdad dramatically reduced EFP attacks in northwestern Baghdad. According to Colonel Burton, "Very rarely do we find an effective EFP within our . . . former . . . EFP hot spots, given the increased participation of local nationals in helping us to find these weapons, the increased responsiveness of the Iraqi security forces to defeat these cells and the increased effectiveness of our targeting operations to defeat the entire network."

Coalition and ISF operations in 2007 disrupted the operations of Special Groups and contributed significantly to the fragmentation of the Jaysh al Mahdi. These successes led to a decrease in EFP attacks in late 2007, but the Special Groups reorganized and attacks rose again early in 2008. Shia militias, particularly the Special Groups, remain a significant threat both to the Iraqi government and to Coalition and Iraqi forces. Maintaining the pressure on JAM and Special Groups, their lines of communications, and their key leadership has been an essential component of the progress in 2007 made toward reducing overall violence in Iraq. It will likely continue to be an important challenge facing the Iraqi government and the U.S. forces assisting it for a long time.

■ ■ ■ *Conclusion*

Violence in Iraq decreased dramatically in the second half of 2007. The number of enemy attacks in Iraq fell to levels that last existed in mid-2005, and stabilized at that low level from October 2007 to March 2008.[805] Attack trends dropped by 60 percent throughout Baghdad in 2007, according to General Odierno. "In 2006, civilian deaths throughout Iraq were over 3,000 in the month of December. In less than a year, they had plummeted by 70 percent. In the Baghdad Security Districts specifically, ethno-sectarian attacks and deaths decreased by 90 percent over the course of 2007."[806]

General Odierno also noted that "[e]xplaining the reduction in violence and its strategic significance has been the subject of much debate. It's tempting for those of us personally connected to the events to exaggerate the effects of the Surge. By the same token, it's a gross oversimplification to say, as some commentators have, that the positive trends we're observing have come about because we paid off the Sunni insurgents or because Moqtada al Sadr simply decided to announce a cease-fire. These assertions ignore the key variable in the equation— the Coalition's change in strategy and our employment of the Surge forces."[807]

Security in Iraq improved from June through November 2007 because of three successive, large-scale military operations made possible by the new strategy and the increase in troops. The first was Fardh al Qanoon, or the Baghdad Security Plan, which dispersed U.S. and Iraqi troops throughout the capital in order to secure its inhabitants. The second was Phantom Thunder, the Corps offensive to clear al Qaeda sanctuaries in the belts around Baghdad. The third was Phantom Strike, the Corps offensive to pursue al Qaeda operatives and other enemies as they fled their former sanctuaries and attempted to regroup in smaller areas throughout Iraq.

These sweeping military operations drove al Qaeda in Iraq out of its sanctuaries around Baghdad: the Tigris and Euphrates River Valleys south of the capital; the Karmah-Taji corridor to its northwest; and Diyala province to its northeast. These areas had supported al Qaeda operations throughout 2006. Although a number of other factors, particularly the "Sunni Awakening," played key roles in making possible the tremendous success the Surge achieved, the change in American strategy early in 2007 was the critical variable that made any success possible.

Awakenings and Sons of Iraq

The population of Iraq generally rejected al Qaeda, Shia extremists, and other terrorist groups over the course of 2007, which is one reason why Iraq became safer. Much credit for improving security justifiably goes to the Iraqis who publicly opposed terrorist groups and mobilized their population behind them. But the tribal movement did not simply "grow" and "spread" organically from one area to the next, nor did security spread exclusively because of tribes' rejection of al Qaeda.

As has been noticed, it is not uncommon to find in the media and among the general public a belief that the "Awakening" in Anbar occurred independently of the Coalition's 2007 military operations. It really would not have been possible without the hard and skillful fighting and negotiating of Army Colonel Sean MacFarland and a number of Marine officers and their subordinates. And it was Odierno who leapt on it and further encouraged it not only in Anbar, but also throughout Iraq. He met with the originator of the Awakening movement, Sheikh Sattar Abu Risha, in December 2006 and encouraged U.S. soldiers in Anbar to continue fighting and negotiating in support of Abu Risha's efforts.

"Will you stay this time?" That was one of the first questions prospective CLCs asked of U.S. troops in 2007. Memories of intermittent security and of the brutal punishments meted out by the returning insurgents to individuals (and their families) who had collaborated with the Coalition made many Iraqis wary. But thanks to the change in strategy and operations inaugurated by Petraeus and Odierno, American soldiers could promise to stay. As more and more Iraqis came to believe in this promise, the movement blossomed, spreading rapidly to Baghdad, Diyala, Babil, and parts of Salah ad-Din province as it consolidated in Anbar. In December 2006, Iraqi society was mobilizing for a sectarian civil war; by December 2007, it was mobilizing to stop the violence.

The Awakening movement begun in 2006 has evolved, at least in some areas, into grassroots political movements. Much of the Sunni population turned emphatically against al Qaeda in Iraq. Some Baathist insurgent groups fractured, as former insurgents sought to assist the Coalition against al Qaeda and enter the political process. Tribal groups likewise sought to participate in the Government of Iraq by establishing new political parties. While the Anbar Awakening continues to combat AQI efforts to reinfiltrate the province, it is also forming a complex set of political parties and factions that pose a serious challenge to the Iraqi Islamic Party that nominally represents most of Iraq's Sunni Arabs in the Council of Representatives.

Of the belief that U.S. forces somehow bribed enemy groups to lay down their arms, General Odierno remarked, "It overlooks our significant offensive push in the last half of 2007 and our rise in casualties in May and June as we began to take back neighborhoods. It overlooks the salient point that many who reconciled with us did so from a position of weakness, rather than strength. The truth is that the improvement in security and stability is the result of a number of factors, and what Coalition Forces did throughout 2007 ranks among the most significant."[808]

Diyala Province, which has an extremely complex network of Sunni, Shia, and mixed tribes, illustrates the complementary relationship between improved security and new movements of Concerned Local Citizens. As U.S. forces reconnoitered Baqubah and its vicinity, some locals who once had fought the Americans as insurgents began cooperating with U.S. and Iraqi security forces against al Qaeda. These leaders helped U.S. forces clear enemy sanctuaries during the summer offensive by revealing enemy positions and weapons caches. For example, members of the 1920s Revolution Brigades—a Sunni insurgent group that operated alongside al Qaeda until May—in Baqubah identified the specific locations of rigged houses and deep-buried IEDs before the city was cleared in June. Reconciliation efforts proceeded as soon as U.S. and Iraqi forces had cleared western Baqubah, and rippled outward through the Diyala River Valley as U.S. forces eliminated the enemy there. Tribal leaders in Diyala recruited locals to guard their communities alongside U.S. and Iraqi forces. Citizens did so with the aim not only of preventing the return of terrorists, but also of joining the Iraqi Police and thus supporting their legitimate national government.

The summer offensive widened the scope of the population's movement against al Qaeda and other terrorists. Locals willing to cooperate with Americans and Iraqi security forces jump-started clearing efforts, as in Hawr Rajab, but few locals turned against al Qaeda before military operations cleared terrorist sanctuaries. Rather, Concerned Local Citizens movements generally spread after U.S. and Iraqi forces, partnered together, cleared an area.

For example, after removing al Qaeda leadership in Tarmiyah, U.S. conventional forces conducted a series of large, coordinated operations there in mid-September, to remove an illegal Shariah court and clear gigantic caches of explosives. These operations set the stage for the Concerned Local Citizens movement in Tarmiyah, which had proceeded fitfully in June, July, and August because of al Qaeda's presence in the city. In mid-September, over 1,200 men volunteered within two days to serve as volunteers for a new provisional security group known as the Critical Infrastructure Security Contract Force to help defend Tarmiyah, alongside U.S. and Iraqi security forces. As of November 1, 2007, approximately 60,000 Iraqis had volunteered to protect their communities as part of these carefully screened and monitored forces.

The results of this transformation in attitudes were tangible and reinforced American efforts to establish security. U.S. forces found and cleared

6,963 weapons caches in 2007, compared to the 2,960 in 2006—largely a result of tips from the population and CLC groups, combined with the challenges that increasing security now imposed on insurgents. In March 2008, approximately 91,000 Iraqis helped secure their neighborhoods as contracted members of a Sons of Iraq group. Nineteen percent of these Iraqis were Shia.[809] Local participation improved the ability of U.S forces to maintain security in cleared areas. The Iraqi Security Forces, partnered with U.S. forces throughout Baghdad, likewise improved their tactical capabilities and magnified their ability to clear and control neighborhoods. The dramatic turnaround in Iraq in 2007 can only be understood in the context of the important synergy between the change in American strategy and tactics and the shift in attitudes among the Iraqi people—a shift facilitated by that change.

Kinetic Operations and Campaign Design

Combat operations did not by themselves transform Iraq in 2007, but they were an essential part of the overarching strategy that did. The role of combat operations in counterinsurgency has not received remotely enough attention in recent years, and the campaign of 2007 can and must serve as a departure point for serious theoretical and practical thought about this important question.

As is well known, General Petraeus oversaw the writing of a new counterinsurgency doctrine before being sent to Iraq. The doctrine did not, however, provide a great deal of detail about how to plan and conduct such operations across a theater as large as Iraq. It was Odierno who creatively adapted sophisticated concepts from conventional fighting to the problems in Iraq, filling gaps in the counterinsurgency doctrine and making the overall effort a success. For all the sophistication of this integrated political-military and kinetic/non-kinetic approach to the conflict, Odierno is likely to be remembered in military history as the man who redefined the operational art of counterinsurgency with a series of offensives in 2007 and 2008.

"Operational art" is the theory of how to conduct campaigns, developed most comprehensively in the Cold War era—when doctrine called for multiple, simultaneous, and successive operations across a theater. A well-designed campaign consisted of multiple battles occurring at the same time to achieve a common goal (for instance, the landings on different Normandy beaches to dislodge the enemy from a defensive position on D-Day) followed by a rapid series of fights and maneuvers to pursue the enemy, drive him from his objectives, and prevent him from regrouping (Patton's relentless pursuit of German forces in France and Germany in 1944 and 1945). Before 2007 there had been considerable debate within the Army about whether there even was an "operational art" in counterinsurgency, never mind what it might be. Odierno demonstrated that there was indeed.

He explained that the Surge allowed for "simultaneous and sustained offensive operations, in partnership with the Iraqi Security Forces." In conjunction with Petraeus and his staff, Odierno planned and conducted three successive, large-scale military operations in 2007, and a fourth in early 2008. Operations Fardh al Qanoon, Phantom Thunder, and Phantom Strike are described above. Odierno's last major offensive was Operation Phantom Phoenix, launched just weeks before his departure, to pursue the enemy into Diyala and to set the conditions for the battle for Mosul—while providing essential services and jump-starting provincial government in less-contested areas.

The key to the success of these operations was the combination of breadth and continuity. All of them struck multiple enemy safe havens and lines of communication at the same time—in contrast with previous U.S. military operations that generally had attacked enemy concentrations one at a time. Enemy groups could no longer move easily from one safe area to another and those that tried to move suffered serious losses as they dispersed. The rapid movement from one operation to the next denied the enemy time to regroup. As scattered insurgent leaders and fighters attempted to reconsolidate in new areas, Coalition Forces hit them again and again.

AQI fighters driven from Anbar, Baghdad, and the suburban belts into Diyala found reinforced Coalition and Iraqi Security Forces there, waiting to fight them. Those that survived fled north along the Hamrin Ridge toward Mosul, where Coalition Forces pursued them and doggedly prevented them from establishing secure bases even in that remote and rugged terrain. As AQI attempted to reconstitute in and around Mosul, it once again encountered a growing U.S. and Iraqi presence attacking before it could fully dig in. The simultaneity of the attacks and the relentlessness of the pursuit shattered al Qaeda in Iraq, reducing it to ever smaller and more isolated pockets that increasingly lack the ability to coordinate the type of large-scale terror operations it conducted in 2006.

As a purely military operation, the series of MNC-I offensives easily bears comparison with Patton's race across France or the Soviet destruction of German forces in 1944 and 1945. That the Iraq operations occurred in the midst of a counterinsurgency and helped gain the support of the local populations is a testimony to the tactical skill and precision with which American forces fought, as well as to the brilliance of the political and diplomatic efforts of Petraeus and Crocker to set the non-kinetic conditions for success.

What should be the role of combat operations in counterinsurgencies? From the beginning of the post-conflict efforts in Iraq, a succession of American military commanders understood the importance of non-kinetic operations, of integrating military operations with political, economic, social, and other efforts, and of subordinating military operations to political goals at all times. The Petraeus Doctrine was innovative not so much in its emphasis on the role of non-kinetic operations, as in recognizing the essential synergy between the kinetic tasks of providing security to the population and the non-kinetic tasks that had already been receiving the attention of American commanders and civilian leaders.

Petraeus emphasized that establishing security—with all of the risks, losses, and damage to local populations and their infrastructure attendant on combat—was not a distraction from the "main effort" of the non-kinetic operations, but a key element that first made those operations possible and then helped them succeed.

One can debate the best way to apply the lessons of 2007 to 2008 or to any future war, but one thing is very clear: any counterinsurgent force must understand clearly how it intends to use its military power in support of its political objectives. Petraeus and Odierno developed a highly sophisticated method of applying combat power discriminately but in a highly coordinated fashion so that it accomplished its essential tasks with the least possible collateral damage. Other wars and even other phases of this war will require different approaches, but the planning and execution of combat operations will always be a core component of counterinsurgency, and the U.S. military must work hard to build an intellectual framework around the practical exercise it undertook in 2007 in order to be able to succeed in different circumstances in future conflicts.

The Military Campaign of 2008 Takes Shape

As this book goes to press, the main outlines of the military conflict in Iraq in 2008 seem clear. Coalition Forces continue to fight al Qaeda in and around Mosul. When that fight is complete, subsequent operations against remnant al Qaeda cells fleeing Mosul will probably be necessary, as well as additional operations against irreconcilable Sunni insurgents that still remain in the Tigris River Valley. Al Qaeda cells are working to regenerate throughout the country, and the reduction in American forces resulting from the end of the Surge will provide them with opportunities to reconstitute. Other fights of greater or lesser severity may emerge in northern Iraq, even in Baghdad, but we can confidently predict that large-scale efforts will be required in Mosul and its environs.

The Iraqi government's attack on illegal militias in Basra has turned into a meeting engagement, drawing in increasing portions of Jaysh al Mahdi and Special Groups throughout the country. Iraqi Security Forces have cleared many of the JAM-held neighborhoods in Basra, as well as taking and holding the ports there. Tribal movements have emerged in Nasiriyah and helped to stabilize Dhi Qar province. Iraqi Security Forces engaged with JAM fighters and Special Groups in Karbala and Hillah, and they seem to have driven the enemy mostly out of Najaf, Kut, and Diwaniyah. ISF troops, with some American support, cordoned off Sadr City and have pressed into its outer areas. They denied Special Groups the terrain on the west side of Sadr City from which they were launching rockets into the International Zone. ISF and American forces have most of the rest of Baghdad and its environs reasonably under control.

The Shia areas of Iraq are likely to consume a great deal of our attention in 2008, particularly Basra, Dhi Qar, and possibly Maysan Province and Sadr City, as well as Karbala and Hillah. It remains to be seen how much American or other Coalition Forces will be drawn into this struggle, but the Iraqi Security Forces are certain to be heavily engaged in these areas for some time to come.

The shifting nature of the conflict—mostly to our advantage—will continue to change the nature of the fighting. The general stabilization of central and western Iraq has allowed both U.S. and Iraqi leaders to focus on problem areas in the south and north that had been under-resourced for a long time. The destruction of most of the enemy's large urban sanctuaries probably means that the fighting will become even more complex, but at a lower level of intensity. The task of planning and conducting multiple simultaneous and successive kinetic operations in support of political and military objectives will be even more difficult when the enemy groups are smaller and more fragmented, and U.S. forces thinner on the ground. Consequently, the challenges of understanding the flow of such complex operations for journalists, historians, and interested Americans are likely to grow. But we will all have to rise to these military and intellectual challenges in order to make sound decisions about this critical war.

NOTES AND INDEX

■■■ Notes

1   Army FM 3-24, *Counterinsurgency*, December 2006: 1-37.

2   Kimberly Kagan, *The Eye of Command* (University of Michigan Press, 2006).

3   Military organizations must set and meet a hierarchical series of objectives that will accomplish the overall goal: tactical objectives, such as destroying a safe haven or holding a piece of terrain; operational objectives, such as securing a city; and strategic objectives, such as establishing a safe and democratic government. These objectives are hierarchical: the tactical objectives must contribute to the operational level objectives, and they in turn must lead to the strategic level objectives. It is not possible simply to focus on strategic objectives or on tactical objectives; one must accomplish tactical missions and operational missions to achieve strategic success.

4   Iraq already had an interim government before the elections took place. The first Iraqi elections, held in January 2005, established the Transitional National Assembly. This body, in turn, formed the transitional government of Iraq. Ibrahim al Jafaari took office as its president and Iyad Allawi as its prime minister on May 3, 2005. The transitional government drafted the Iraqi constitution, approved by a popular referendum on October 15, 2005. The Iraqi people voted for the current Council of Representatives in elections held on December 15, 2005.

5   John F. Burns, "Rebel Cleric in Najaf Sends Messages of Conciliation," *The New York Times*, August 19, 2004.

6   Kimberly Kagan, "Iran's Proxy War against the United States and the Iraqi Government," *Iraq Report 6*, August 29, 2007, p. 10.

7   Press Briefing by Major General William Caldwell, Spokesman for Multi-National Force-Iraq, Topic: Ongoing Investigations in Iraq, Location: Baghdad, Iraq, July 5, 2006.

8   Press Briefing by Major General William Caldwell, Spokesman for Multi-National Force-Iraq, Topic: Ongoing Investigations in Iraq, Location: Baghdad, Iraq, July 5, 2006.

9   Patrick Gaughen, "Baghdad Neighborhood Project: Saydiyah," Backgrounder #15, Institute for the Study of War, November 21, 2007, p. 4.

10   Patrick Gaughen, "Baghdad Neighborhood Project: Washash and Iskan," Backgrounder #13, Institute for the Study of War, September 25, 2007, p. 2-3.

11   Patrick Gaughen, "Baghdad Neighborhood Project: Washash and Iskan," Backgrounder #13, Institute for the Study of War, September 25, 2007, p. 2-3.

12   Michael Moss, "Iraq's Legal System Staggers Beneath the Weight of War," *The New York Times*, December 17, 2006; Lionel Beehner, "Shiite Militias and Iraq's Security Forces," Council on Foreign Relations, November 30, 2005.

13   "Riding Herd on the Iraqi Police's Dirty 'Wolf Brigade,'" National Public Radio, Morning Edition - Host: Steve Inskeep, Guest, Major Charles Miller, former National Police Advisor for 1-2-1 NP (Wolf Brigade) March 28th, 2007; Joshua Partlow, "'I Don't Think This Place Is Worth Another Soldier's Life': After 14 months in a Baghdad district torn by mounting sectarian violence, members of one U.S. unit are tired, bitter and skeptical," *The Washington Post*, October 27, 2007.

14   Sabrina Tavernise, "Baghdad Bolsters Security, but Firefights Still Crackle," *The New York Times*, June 15, 2006.

15   Patrick Gaughen, "Baghdad Neighborhood Project: Saydiyah," Backgrounder #15, Institute for the Study of War, November 21, 2007, p. 4-5.

16   Department of Defense News Briefing with Commander Multinational Corps Iraq, Lt. Gen. Peter Chiarelli, Location: Iraq, September 15, 2006.

17   Press Briefing by Major General William Caldwell, Spokesman for Multi-National Force-Iraq, Topic: Security Operations in Iraq, Location: The Combined Press Information Center, Baghdad, Iraq, September 6, 2006.

18   Press Briefing by Major General William Caldwell, Spokesman for Multi-National Force-Iraq, Topic: Security Operations in Iraq, Location: The Combined Press Information Center, Baghdad, Iraq, September 6, 2006.

19   Press Briefing by Multi-National Force-Iraq Deputy Chief of Staff for Strategic Effects Brigadier General Kevin Bergner, Topic: Security Operations in Iraq, Location: The Combined Press Information Center, Baghdad, Iraq, July 2, 2007.

20   Colonel David Sutherland, Commander, Greywolf Brigade Combat Team, Interview with the Institute for the Study of War, October 25, 2007.

21   Richard Sisk, "Lockdown in Baghdad," *Daily News (New York)*, June 24, 2006.

22   "Osama Backs His New Abu," *New York Post*, July 2, 2006.

23   Edward Wong, "Car Bomb Kills More Than 60 in Iraq Market," *The New York Times*, July 2, 2006.

24   Kirk Semple, "Baghdad Erupts in Mob Violence by Gun and Bomb," *The New York*

Times, July 10, 2006, Section A; Column 6.

25   Joshua Partlow and Saad al-Izzi, "Scores of Sunnis Killed in Baghdad; Neighborhood Residents Describe Signs of Torture," *The Washington Post*, July 10, 2006, A01.

26   Kirk Semple, "Baghdad Erupts in Mob Violence by Gun and Bomb," *The New York Times*, July 10, 2006, Section A; Column 6.

27   Kirk Semple, "Baghdad Erupts in Mob Violence by Gun and Bomb," *The New York Times*, July 10, 2006, Section A; Column 6.

28   Robert H. Reid, "Shiite-Sunni Violence Kills 58 in Baghdad," *Associated Press Online*, July 9, 2006.

29   Kirk Semple, "Joint Raid Captures 2 Linked to Rebel Shiite Leader," *The New York Times*, July 8, 2006, Section A, Column 3.

30   Press Briefing by Major General William Caldwell, Spokesman for Multi-National Force-Iraq, Topic: Iraq Operational Update Briefing, Location: Combined Press Information Center, Baghdad, Iraq, July 20, 2006, slide 49.

31   Kirk Semple, "Wave of Violence in Baghdad Puts 3-Day Death Toll Past 100," *The New York Times*, July 12, 2006, Section A, Column 5.

32   Joshua Partlow and Naseer Nouri, "'Neighbors Are Killing Neighbors'; Across Baghdad, Violence Leaves Residents Fleeing or Imprisoned at Home," *The Washington Post*, July 18, 2006, A16.

33   Press Briefing by Major General William Caldwell, Spokesman for Multi-National Force-Iraq, Topic: Iraq Operational Update Briefing, Location: Combined Press Information Center, Baghdad, Iraq, July 20, 2006, Slide 50.

34   Kimberly Kagan, "Potemkin Story: Understanding the Dora market," *National Review Online*, September 5, 2007; Sabrina Tavernise, "Baghdad oasis 'falling to terrorists," *The International Herald Tribune*, June 24, 2006.

35   Jonathan Finer and Bassam Sebti, "Sectarian Violence Kills Over 100 in Iraq, Shiite-Sunni Anger Flares Following Bombing of Shrine," *The Washington Post*, February 24, 2006, A01; "Insurgents kill 20 Iraqis in prison break," *Associated Press*, March 21, 2006.

36   "Iraqi TV reports security plans for Baghdad," BBC Monitoring Middle East - Political, June 13, 2006.

37   Sharon Behn, "Security crackdown begins in Baghdad," *The Washington Times*, June 15, 2006, A01.

38   Michael R. Gordon, "Battle for Baghdad Boils Down to Grabbing a Slice at a Time," *The New York Times*, July 26, 2006, Section A, Column 1.

39   Press Briefing by Major General William Caldwell, Spokesman for Multi-National Force-Iraq, Topic: Iraq Operational Update Briefing, Location: Combined Press Information Center, Baghdad, Iraq, July 20, 2006.

40   Multi-National Force-Iraq Press Release No. 20060808-05, "Phase II of Operation Together Forward kicks off in Baghdad," Multi-National Division - Baghdad PAO, August 8, 2006.

41   Press Briefing by Major General William Caldwell, Spokesman for Multi-National Force-Iraq, Topic: Iraq Operational Update Briefing, Location: Combined Press Information Center, Baghdad, Iraq, July 20, 2006.

42   Joseph Curl, "Bush, al-Maliki seek new plan for security; 6-week-old strategy for Baghdad dropped," *The Washington Times*, July 25, 2006, A04.

43   Michael R. Gordon, "More Troops to Be Deployed In Baghdad, General Says," *The New York Times*, July 22, 2006, Section A, Column 5.

44   Michael R. Gordon, "More Troops to Be Deployed in Baghdad, General Says," *The New York Times*, July 22, 2006, Section A, Column 5; Joseph Curl, "Bush, al-Maliki seek new plan for security; 6-week-old strategy for Baghdad dropped," *The Washington Times*, July 25, 2006, A04.

45   Edward Wong, "Pentagon Extends Tour for 4,000 Troops, Increasing Number in Iraq," *The New York Times*, July 30, 2006, Section 1, Column 1.

46   Josh White, "3,700 Troops' Stay In Iraq Is Extended," *The Washington Post*, July 28, 2006, A21.

47   Edward Wong, "Pentagon Extends Tour for 4,000 Troops, Increasing Number in Iraq," *The New York Times*, July 30, 2006, Section 1, Column 1.

48   "Phase 2 of Operation Together Forward Kicks Off in Baghdad," American Forces Press Service, Aug. 8, 2006.

49   "Phase 2 of Operation Together Forward Kicks Off in Baghdad," American Forces Press Service, Aug. 8, 2006.

50   Press Briefing by Major General William Caldwell, Spokesman for Multi-National Force-Iraq, Topic: Security Operations in Iraq, Location: The Combined Press Information Center, Baghdad, Iraq, September 6, 2006.

51   Press Briefing by Major General William Caldwell, Spokesman for Multi-National Force-Iraq, Topic: Iraq Operational Update Briefing, Location: The Combined Press Information Center, Baghdad, Iraq, October 19, 2006.

52   Press Briefing by Major General William Caldwell, Spokesman for Multi-National Force-Iraq, Topic: Iraq Operational Update Briefing, Location: The Combined Press Information Center, Baghdad, Iraq, October 19, 2006.

53   Press Briefing by Major General William Caldwell, Spokesman for Multi-National Force-Iraq, Topic: Iraq Operational Update Briefing, Location: The Combined Press Information Center, Baghdad, Iraq, October 19, 2006.

54   Press Briefing by Major General William Caldwell, Spokesman for Multi-National Force-Iraq, Topic: Iraq Operational Update Briefing, Location: The Combined Press Information Center, Baghdad, Iraq, October 12, 2006.

55   Press Briefing by Major General William Caldwell, Spokesman for Multi-National Force-Iraq, Topic: Iraq Operational Update Briefing, Location: The Combined Press Information Center, Baghdad, Iraq, October 19, 2006.

56   Frederick W. Kagan and Kimberly Kagan, "The Patton of Counterinsurgency: With a sequence of brilliant offensives, Raymond Odierno adapted the Petraeus doctrine into a successful operational art," *The Weekly Standard*, Volume 013, Issue 25, March 10, 2008.

57   Institute for the Study of War interview with Col. J. B. Burton, Commander, 2nd Brigade Combat Team, 1st Infantry Division, November 14, 2007.

58   Press Briefing by Major General William Caldwell, Spokesman for Multi-National Force-Iraq, Topic: Iraq Operational Update Briefing, Location: The Combined Press Information Center, Baghdad, Iraq, October 19, 2006.

59   Unclassified Briefing, III Corps After-Action Review Conference, San Antonio, Texas, April 9, 2008.

60   Unclassified Briefing, III Corps After-Action Review Conference, San Antonio, Texas, April 9, 2008.

61   Unclassified Briefing, III Corps After-Action Review Conference, San Antonio, Texas, April 9, 2008; for Saddam Hussein's defensive plan, see "Iraqi Plan Presented in Baghdad on 18 DEC 02 Obtained by HUMINT Source in FEB 03," in the map section of Michael R. Gordon and General Bernard E. Trainor, *Cobra II: The Inside Story of the Invasion and Occupation of Iraq*.

62   Unclassified Briefing, III Corps After-Action Review Conference, San Antonio, Texas, April 9, 2008.

63   Solomon Moore, "Rising violence swells ranks of Iraq's militias; Men with no previous affiliation are taking up arms, citing distrust of the security forces for the rush to self-defense," *Los Angeles Times*, November 28, 2006, Home Edition, Part A, p. 1.

64   Laura Logan, "US and Iraqi troops patrol 24/7 in Dora District," Transcript, CBS Evening News, January 22, 2007.

65   Institute for the Study of War interview with Col. J. B. Burton, Commander, 2nd Brigade Combat Team, 1st Infantry Division, November 14, 2007; Patrick

Gaughen, "Baghdad Neighborhood Project: Washash and Iskan," Backgrounder #13, Institute for the Study of War, September 25, 2007.

66   Institute for the Study of War interview with Col. J. B. Burton, Commander, 2nd Brigade Combat Team, 1st Infantry Division, November 14, 2007; Patrick Gaughen, "Baghdad Neighborhood Project: Washash and Iskan," Backgrounder #13, Institute for the Study of War, September 25, 2007.

67   Institute for the Study of War interview with Col. J. B. Burton, Commander, 2nd Brigade Combat Team, 1st Infantry Division, November 14, 2007.

68   Institute for the Study of War interview with Col. J. B. Burton, Commander, 2nd Brigade Combat Team, 1st Infantry Division, November 14, 2007.

69   Institute for the Study of War interview with Col. J. B. Burton, Commander, 2nd Brigade Combat Team, 1st Infantry Division, November 14, 2007.

70   Press Briefing by Lt. Gen. Ray Odierno, Multi-National Corps-Iraq Commander, Topic: Operational Update, Location: Baghdad, Iraq, October 31, 2007, slide 5.

71   Slides from Multi-National Forces Iraq, <http://understandingwar.org/files/Iraq%20Statistics%20Reference%20January%202008.pdf>.

72   Marc Santora, "The War in Iraq; 'A Show of Force,'" *The Houston Chronicle*, January 10, 2007, A9.

73   Louise Roug, "The Conflict in Iraq: Reconstruction Efforts: Battle in Baghdad; 1,000 Troops Strike Heart of Baghdad; American and Iraqi forces battle gunmen in a daylong fight; 51 Suspects Killed," *Los Angeles Times*, January 10, 2007, Home Edition, A1; Ernesto Londono and Joshua Partlow, "Troops Battle Insurgents in Central Baghdad; U.S. and Iraqi Forces are Attacked from High-Rises," *The Washington Post*, January 25, 2007, Final Edition, A20.

74   Louise Roug, "The Conflict in Iraq: Reconstruction Efforts: Battle in Baghdad; 1,000 Troops Strike Heart of Baghdad; American and Iraqi forces battle gunmen in a daylong fight; 51 Suspects Killed," *Los Angeles Times*, January 10, 2007, Home Edition, A1.

75   Marc Santora, John F. Burns, and Iraqi employees of the New York Times, "U.S. and Iraqis Hit Insurgents in All-Day Fight," *The New York Times*, January 10, 2007, A1.

76   "Knowing the enemy is difficult in Baghdad. NBC's Richard Engel is embedded with the 172nd Stryker Brigade Combat Team as it patrols a dangerous part of Baghdad," MS-NBC news (transcript), October 18, 2006.

77   Sudarsan Raghavan and Joshua Partlow, "U.S. Airstrikes Back Troops in Baghdad Clash; Insurgents Wage Fierce Battle in Mostly Sunni Arab Enclave," *The Washington Post*, January 10, 2007, A1.

78 Marc Santora, John F. Burns, and Iraqi employees of the New York Times, "U.S. and Iraqis Hit Insurgents in All-Day Fight," *The New York Times*, January 10, 2007, A1.

79 Louise Roug, "The Conflict in Iraq: Reconstruction Efforts: Battle in Baghdad; 1,000 Troops Strike Heart of Baghdad; American and Iraqi forces battle gunmen in a daylong fight; 51 Suspects Killed," *Los Angeles Times*, January 10, 2007, Home Edition, A1.

80 Sudarsan Raghavan and Joshua Partlow, "U.S. Airstrikes Back Troops in Baghdad Clash; Insurgents Wage Fierce Battle in Mostly Sunni Arab Enclave," *The Washington Post*, January 10, 2007, A1.

81 Together, they conducted twenty-two raids in two days, rounded up thirteen insurgents, and a small but serious weapons cache. "The road to Baghdad: Unit brings expertise with urban environment," Compiled from Multinational Forces releases, *The Northwest Guardian*, January 11th, 2007 (web). They were paired with 5th Battalion, 20th Infantry Regiment, and soldiers from a brigade of the Iraqi army and the Iraqi police. This operation apparently had concluded by January 9, when the 1st of the 23rd moved to Haifa Street. By January 11, elements of the 5th Battalion, 20th Infantry Regiment conducted operations in Dora, a difficult neighborhood south and west of the Tigris River, also supporting this deduction. It is not clear, however, whether the same companies were involved in both operations. See "Breaking through the underbrush: Soldiers trek through palm groves near Iraq capital in search of hideouts," Cpl. Alexis Harrison, 2nd BCT, 1st Cav. Div. Public Affairs, *Northwest Guardian*, February 8th, 2007 (web).

82 Sudarsan Raghavan and Joshua Partlow, "U.S. Airstrikes Back Troops in Baghdad Clash; Insurgents Wage Fierce Battle in Mostly Sunni Arab Enclave," *The Washington Post*, January 10, 2007, A1; Marc Santora, "The War in Iraq; 'A Show of Force,'" *The Houston Chronicle*, January 10, 2007, A9.

83 Sudarsan Raghavan and Joshua Partlow, "U.S. Airstrikes Back Troops in Baghdad Clash; Insurgents Wage Fierce Battle in Mostly Sunni Arab Enclave," *The Washington Post*, January 10, 2007, A1.

84 Sudarsan Raghavan and Joshua Partlow, "U.S. Airstrikes Back Troops in Baghdad Clash; Insurgents Wage Fierce Battle in Mostly Sunni Arab Enclave," *The Washington Post*, January 10, 2007, A1.

85 Marc Santora, "The War in Iraq; 'A Show of Force,'" The Houston Chronicle, January 10, 2007, A9.

86 Sudarsan Raghavan and Joshua Partlow, "U.S. Airstrikes Back Troops in Baghdad Clash; Insurgents Wage Fierce Battle in Mostly Sunni Arab Enclave," *The Washington Post*, January 10, 2007, A1.

87 Marc Santora, John F. Burns, and Iraqi employees of the New York Times, "U.S. and Iraqis Hit Insurgents in All-Day Fight," *The New York Times*, January 10, 2007, A1; Marc Santora, "The War in Iraq; 'A Show of Force,'" *The Houston Chronicle*, January 10, 2007, A9.

88 Louise Roug, "The Conflict in Iraq: Reconstruction Efforts: Battle in Baghdad; 1,000 Troops Strike Heart of Baghdad; American and Iraqi forces battle gunmen in a daylong fight; 51 Suspects Killed," *Los Angeles Times*, January 10, 2007, Home Edition, A1.

89 Nancy A. Youssef and Zaineb Obeid, McClatchy Newspapers, "View from Haifa Street: New plan isn't working," *The Seattle Times*, January 16, 2007, Fourth Edition, A8.

90 Ernesto Londono and Joshua Partlow, "Troops Battle Insurgents in Central Baghdad; U.S. and Iraqi Forces are Attacked from High-Rises," *The Washington Post*, January 25, 2007, Final Edition, A20.

91 Damien Cave and James Glanz, "In a New Join U.S.-Iraqi Patrol, the Americans Go First," *The New York Times*, January 25, 2007, Final Edition, A12. LTC Van Smiley, who commands the 1st Battalion, 23rd Infantry Regiment, Stryker Brigade, http://www.lewis.army.mil/123in/, accessed February 19, 2007, is named in this article as the commander of the attack on January 24, according to this article, which permits the identification of the battalion.

92 Alexandra Zavis, "The Conflict in Iraq: Military Offensive in Baghdad; U.S.-Iraqi forces strike 'Sniper Alley,'; The operation targets a Sunni insurgent enclave in a residential and commercial area near Baghdad's Green Zone," *Los Angeles Times*, January 25, 2007, Home Edition, A5. Soldiers from the 5th Battalion, 20th Infantry Regiment, attached to the 2nd Brigade Combat Team, 1st Cavalry Division, seem to be working together with the 1-23 Infantry much of the time: "The road to Baghdad: Unit brings expertise with urban environment," Compiled from Multinational Forces releases, *The Northwest Guardian*, January 11th, 2007.

93 Officials quoted in "Combined Operation Nets Insurgents, Weapons in Baghdad," American Forces Press Service, Washington, Jan. 24, 2007.

94 Damien Cave and James Glanz, "In a New Join U.S.-Iraqi Patrol, the Americans Go First," *The New York Times*, January 25, 2007, Final Edition, A12. LTC Van Smiley, who commands the 1st Battalion, 23rd Infantry Regiment, Stryker Brigade, http://www.lewis.army.mil/123in/, accessed February 19, 2007, is named in this article as the commander of the attack on January 24, according to this article, which permits the identification of the battalion.

95 Alexandra Zavis, "The Conflict in Iraq: Military Offensive in Baghdad; U.S.-Iraqi forces strike 'Sniper Alley,'; The operation targets a Sunni insurgent enclave in a

residential and commercial area near Baghdad's Green Zone," *Los Angeles Times*, January 25, 2007, Home Edition, A5.

96   Alexandra Zavis, "The Conflict in Iraq: Military Offensive in Baghdad; U.S.-Iraqi forces strike 'Sniper Alley,'; The operation targets a Sunni insurgent enclave in a residential and commercial area near Baghdad's Green Zone," *Los Angeles Times*, January 25, 2007, Home Edition, A5.

97   Master Sgt. Dave Larsen, 1st Cavalry Division Public Affairs, "Post troops clear, secure Iraqi hotbed of insurgency," *The Northwest Guardian*, February 1, 2007.

98   "Speed and force: Stryker readiness unit responds to threats across the battle-field in Iraq," by Spc. L. B. Edgar, 7th Mobile Public Affairs Detachment, *The Northwest Guardian*, January 25th, 2007. Two battalions of the 3-2 Stryker Brigade Combat Team have been in Baghdad since July and August, 2006; their remaining battalions and their headquarters remained in Mosul until December 11, 2007, according to "The road to Baghdad: Unit brings expertise with urban environment", Compiled from Multinational Forces releases, *The Northwest Guardian*, January 11, 2007.

99   "Pace Group to Put Forth Iraq Strategy Alternatives by Mid-December," *Inside the Pentagon*, Vol. 22 No. 45, November 9, 2006.

100   David E. Sanger and Michael R. Gordon, "Options Weighed for Surge in G.I.'s to Stabilize Iraq," *The New York Times*, December 16, 2006.

101   John F. Burns, "Military Considers Sending as Many as 35,000 More U.S. Troops to Iraq, McCain Says," *The New York Times*, December 15, 2006.

102   John F. Burns, "Military Considers Sending as Many as 35,000 More U.S. Troops to Iraq, McCain Says," *The New York Times*, December 15, 2006.

103   Thomas E. Ricks, "Pentagon May Suggest Short-Term Buildup Leading to Iraq Exit," *The Washington Post*, November 20, 2006, A01.

104   The author participated in the Iraq Planning Group exercise at the American Enterprise Institute in December 2006, which generated this report.

105   David E. Sanger and Michael R. Gordon, "Options Weighed for Surge in G.I.'s to Stabilize Iraq," *The New York Times*, December 16, 2006.

106   David S. Cloud and Jeff Zeleny, "Bush Considers Up to 20,000 More Troops for Iraq," *The New York Times*, December 29, 2006.

107   President George W. Bush, "President's Address to the Nation," January 10, 2007; http://www.whitehouse.gov/news/releases/2007/01/20070110-7.html accessed February 14, 2007.

108   Michael R. Gordon, "A New Commander, in Step with the White House on

Iraq," *The New York Times*, January 6, 2007.

109 See Kimberly Kagan, "From 'New Way Forward' to New Commander, January 10 – February 10, 2007," *Iraq Report*, March 1, 2007, p. 2.; Multi-National Force-Iraq, "2006 Year in Review: Iraq," available at http://www.mnf-iraq.com/images//2006_yir_24feb.pdf.

110 Department of Defense Press Briefing with Multi-National Corps-Iraq Commander Lieutenant General Ray Odierno, May 31, 2007. The mission statement has not changed since the Baghdad Security Plan began. See Department of Defense News Briefing with Multi-National Corps-Iraq Commander Lieutenant General Ray Odierno, February 22, 2007; Department of Defense News Briefing with Multi-National Corps-Iraq Commander Lieutenant General Ray Odierno, April 13, 2007. The "center of gravity" is a phrase used to describe the objective in a military operation that will lead to victory. In conventional operations, the "center of gravity" is often the enemy's army, the destruction of which renders an enemy willing to surrender or unable to fight. In counterinsurgency operations, the "center of gravity" is the population, for whose loyalty the legitimate government and the insurgents compete. When the population supports the government, the insurgents lack the physical support that they need to continue to fight and the sympathy that they need to win the conflict.

111 Department of Defense News Briefing with Multi-National Corps-Iraq Commander Lieutenant General Ray Odierno, April 13, 2007.

112 Department of Defense Press Briefing with Multi-National Corps-Iraq Commander Lieutenant General Ray Odierno, May 31, 2007.

113 Department of Defense Press Briefing with Multi-National Corps-Iraq Commander Lieutenant General Ray Odierno, May 31, 2007.

114 Multi-National Corps-Iraq (MNC-I) has command over all Coalition combat forces in the theater with the exception of a small number of troops engaged in training and advising Iraqi military, police, and political bodies (although military advisors embedded with Iraqi military units are under General Odierno's command). Certain logistics capabilities, likewise, fall under a separate command.

115 Department of Defense Press Briefing with Commanding General Multi-National Division-Baghdad and 1st Cavalry Division Maj. Gen. Joseph Fil Jr., February 16, 2007.

116 Department of Defense Special Briefing with Multi-National Corps-Iraq Commander Lieutenant General Ray Odierno, June 22, 2007. Two brigades would normally include around four-to-six battalions; General Odierno added individual battalions to brigade headquarters already in the city as well.

117 Department of Defense Press Briefing with Maj. Gen. William B. Caldwell IV, spokesman, Multi-National Force-Iraq, "Situational Update," February 21, 2007.

118 Department of Defense Press Briefing with Maj. Gen. William B. Caldwell IV, spokesman, Multi-National Force-Iraq, "Situational Update," February 21, 2007.

119 Multi-National Corps-Iraq Press Release No. 20070123-10, "New Combat Outpost Built to Thwart Crime in Ghazaliyah," 2nd Battalion, 12th Cavalry Regiment, January 23, 2007; 2nd Lieutenant Michael Daschle, "Living in the Neighborhood Has Advantages," *Dagger's Edge*, Vol. 1, Issue 8, February 17, 2007, 16.

120 Sgt. Mike Pryor, 82nd Airborne Division, "82nd Airborne Sets Up Shop in Adhamiyah," U.S. Federal News, February 9, 2007.

121 Kevin Maurer, "Meet the neighbors: An 82nd unit finds a Baghdad home," *Fayetteville Observer*, February 22, 2007.

122 Kevin Maurer, "Meet the neighbors: An 82nd unit finds a Baghdad home," *Fayetteville Observer*, February 22, 2007.

123 Michael Fumento, "Return to Ramadi," *The Weekly Standard*, November 27, 2006, 31.

124 Department of Defense Press Briefing with Maj. Gen. William B. Caldwell IV, spokesman, Multi-National Force-Iraq, "Situational Update," February 21, 2007.

125 Marc Santora; with Qais Mizher, "Iraqi Premier Admits Errors in Introducing Security Plan in Baghdad," *The New York Times*, February 6, 2007, A7.

126 Peter Grier, "Iraq security plan starts - with glitches," *Christian Science Monitor*, February 9, 2007, 3.

127 SPC L. B. Edgar, 7th MPAD, "Paratroopers stand up joint security station in Hurriyah," U.S. Federal News, February 12, 2007.

128 "Coalition, Iraqi Troops Start Clearing Sadr City," U.S. Federal News, March 4, 2007.

129 Department of Defense Press Briefing with Maj. Gen. William B. Caldwell IV, spokesman, Multi-National Force-Iraq, "Situational Update," February 21, 2007.

130 Department of Defense Press Briefing with Commanding General Multi-National Division-Baghdad and 1st Cavalry Division Maj. Gen. Joseph Fil Jr., February 16, 2007. General Fil also differentiated the Baghdad Security Operations from previous operations aiming to "clear, hold, and build." Only one of those, "clear," has a definition in military doctrine. "[C]learing involves...the elimination of enemy forces or any organized resistance against us. And that's

normally done in offensive way with a series of well-organized raids. 'Control' is where we maintain physical influence over an area to keep the enemy out and to put whatever conditions are necessary to move into the next phase, which is 'retain', which is where our friendly force remains there, keeps the enemy out, and allows the civilian population to develop." The non-military concepts of "hold" and "build," according to General Fil, did not involve "the application of force" and "the direct application of our soldiers and the Iraqi security forces to move into neighborhoods, to move into areas and to maintain their presence there full-time."

131   Area security is "a form of security operations conducted to protect friendly forces, installation routes, and actions within a specific area," Army FM 1-02, *Operational Terms and Graphics*.

132   Department of Defense Press Briefing with Commanding General Multi-National Division-Baghdad and 1st Cavalry Division Maj. Gen. Joseph Fil Jr., February 16, 2007.

133   Department of Defense Press Briefing with Maj. Gen. William B. Caldwell IV, spokesman, Multi-National Force-Iraq, "Situational Update," February 21, 2007.

134   Department of Defense Press Briefing with Col. Stephen Townsend, Commander 3rd Stryker Brigade Combat Team, 2nd Infantry Division, April 30, 2007.

135   Department of Defense Press Briefing with Col. Stephen Townsend, Commander 3rd Stryker Brigade Combat Team, 2nd Infantry Division, April 30, 2007.

136   The brigade thereby replaced several units that it had sent out to Ramadi and Baghdad. Department of Defense Special News Briefing with Colonel J. B. Burton, Commander, 2nd Brigade Combat Team, 1st Infantry Division, March 16, 2007.

137   One battalion from the 2nd Brigade Combat Team, 82nd Airborne Division, and another battalion from the 4th BCT, 1st ID in March; Department of Defense Special News Briefing with Colonel J. B. Burton, Commander, Dagger Brigade Combat Team, March 16, 2007.

138   Multi-National Corps—Iraq Release No. 20070319-08, "Fresh troops assume battle space in Baghdad," Multi-National Division-Baghdad PAO, March 19, 2007.

139   See Kimberly Kagan, "Enforcing the Law: The Baghdad Security Plan Begins, February 10-March 5, 2007" *Iraq Report*, March 15, 2007.

140   Department of Defense Press Briefing with Commanding General Multi-National Division-Baghdad and 1st Cavalry Division Maj. Gen. Joseph Fil Jr., February 16, 2007; Department of Defense Press Briefing with Maj. Gen. William B. Caldwell IV, spokesman, Multi-National Force-Iraq, "Situational Update,"

February 21, 2007. The Iraqi figures include 13,000 Iraqi Army soldiers, 20,000 Iraqi National Police, and 41,000 Iraqi police service troops (from General Fil's press conference).

141 Multi-National Corps-Iraq Release No. 20070301-01, "4ᵗʰ Brigade, 1ˢᵗ Infantry Division begins mission in Iraq," Multi-National Corps-Iraq PAO, March 1, 2007.

142 Department of Defense News Briefing with Commander, 4ᵗʰ Brigade Combat Team, 1ˢᵗ Infantry Division Col. Ricky Gibbs, May 25, 2007.

143 Department of Defense News Briefing with Commander, 4ᵗʰ Brigade Combat Team, 1ˢᵗ Infantry Division Col. Ricky Gibbs, May 25, 2007.

144 Department of Defense News Briefing with Commander, 4ᵗʰ Brigade Combat Team, 1ˢᵗ Infantry Division Col. Ricky Gibbs, May 25, 2007.

145 "Dempsey: Iraq Army deploying on time," United Press International, February 13, 2007.

146 "Dempsey: Iraq Army deploying on time," United Press International, February 13, 2007.

147 Sabrina Tavernise and John F. Burns, "The Bush Plan for Iraq; The War in Iraq; Iraqi government wary of buildup; Shiite leaders fear more troops will lead to a more assertive U.S. role," New York Times, January 11, 2007.

148 Louise Roug, "Maliki pledges to treat militants with an iron fist," Los Angeles Times, January 18, 2007, Home Edition, A1.

149 Leila Fadel and Zaineb Obeid, Mcclatchy-Tribune, "The War in Iraq; Al Sadr's militia lowers its profile; Anti-U.S. cleric tells his army to 'calm things down' after Bush orders increase in troops," The Houston Chronicle, January 14, 2007, 4 Star Edition, A22.

150 Leila Fadel and Zaineb Obeid, Mcclatchy-Tribune, "The War in Iraq; Al Sadr's militia lowers its profile; Anti-U.S. cleric tells his army to 'calm things down' after Bush orders increase in troops," The Houston Chronicle, January 14, 2007, 4 Star Edition, A22.

151 "Al Sadr faction ends boycott of parliament," The Irish Times, January 22, 2007, 11.

152 Ernesto Londono, "Key Aide To Sadr Arrested In Baghdad; Iraqi-Led Operation Part of Broader Push", The Washington Post, January 20, 2007, Final Edition, A15.

153 Associated Press, Washington Post, "The War in Iraq; Radical cleric's top aide under arrest, official says; Al Sadr's Jaysh al Mahdi reportedly in flux after U.S. steps up pressure on prime minister," The Houston Chronicle, January 19, 2007, 3 Star Edition, A14.

154 Associated Press, Washington Post, "The War in Iraq; Radical cleric's top aide

under arrest, official says; Al Sadr's Jaysh al Mahdi reportedly in flux after U.S. steps up pressure on prime minister," *The Houston Chronicle*, January 19, 2007, 3 Star Edition, A14; Ernesto Londono, "Key Aide To Sadr Arrested In Baghdad; Iraqi-Led Operation Part of Broader Push", *The Washington Post*, January 20, 2007, Final Edition, A15; Louise Roug, "Top Sadr Deputy is Arrested; Shiite leaders denounce the capture by U.S. and Iraqi troops and vow nationwide protests," *Los Angeles Times*, January 20, 2007 Saturday, Home Edition, A1.

155   Ernesto Londono, "Key Aide To Sadr Arrested In Baghdad; Iraqi-Led Operation Part of Broader Push", *The Washington Post*, January 20, 2007, Final Edition, A15.

156   Leila Fadel, "Baghdad security operation underway; Iraqi troops arrested a Health Ministry official charged by the U.S. command with corruption and with facilitating sectarian violence," *Star Tribune* (Minneapolis, MN), February 9, 2007, Metro Edition, 1A.

157   Richard A. Oppel, Jr., "Troops in Iraq Kill Official Who Worked For Shiite Cleric," *The New York Times*, February 6, 2007, Late Edition - Final, A8.

158   "Al Sadr faction ends boycott of parliament," *The Irish Times*, January 22, 2007, 11.

159   Borzou Daragahi, "Cooperative tone of Sadr surprises U.S.; The cleric's movement, long a foe of America, says it backs the new Iraq security plan.; Some doubt motives," *Los Angeles Times*, January 26, 2007, Home Edition, A1.

160   Joshua Partlow and Ernesto Londono, "Lie Low, Fighters Are Told; 'Try at All Costs' To Avoid Conflict With Americans," *The Washington Post*, February 1, 2007, Final Edition, A10.

161   Joshua Partlow and Ernesto Londono, "Lie Low, Fighters Are Told; 'Try at All Costs' To Avoid Conflict With Americans," *The Washington Post*, February 1, 2007, Final Edition, A10.

162   Times Wire Services, "Sadr aides deny the cleric is in Iran," *Los Angeles Times*, February 14, 2007, Home Edition, A6.

163   Plans to open a JSS in Sadr City were first publicly announced in the Department of Defense Press Briefing with Maj. Gen. William B. Caldwell IV, spokesman, Multi-National Force-Iraq, "Situational Update," February 21, 2007.

164   Sgt. Michael Garrett, 7th Mobile Public Affairs Detachment, "U.S. raids target insurgent strongholds," U.S. Federal News, February 15, 2007.

165   Leila Fadel, "Baghdad security operation underway; Iraqi troops arrested a Health Ministry official charged by the U.S. command with corruption and with facilitating sectarian violence," *Star Tribune* (Minneapolis, MN), February 9, 2007, Metro Edition, 1A.

166   Department of Defense Press Briefing with Maj. Gen. William B. Caldwell IV, spokesman, Multi-National Force-Iraq, "Situational Update," February 21, 2007.

167   Sgt. Mike Pryor, 82nd Airborne Division, "82nd Airborne Sets Up Shop in Adhamiyah," *Northwest Guardian*, February 15, 2007.

168   Multi-National Corps-Iraq Press Release No. 20070216-08 "New Baghdad Security Plan B-Roll; Operation footage available on DVIDS Hub," Multi-National Division - Baghdad PAO, February 16, 2007.

169   Multi-National Corps-Iraq Press Release No. 20070218-03, "Coalition Forces capture insurgent leader," February 18, 2007.

170   Multi-National Corps-Iraq Press Release No. 20070216-24, "Paratroopers crack down on extra-judicial killings," Multi-National Division-Baghdad PAO, February 16, 2007.

171   Sabrina Tavernise, "Iraqi Death Toll Exceeded 34,000 in 2006, U.N. Says," *The New York Times*, January 17, 2007, A1.

172   Multi-National Corps-Iraq, Press Release No. 20070215-05, "IA Captures Weapons Cache in Baghdad Mosque," February 15, 2007.

173   Multi-National Corps-Iraq, Press Release No. 20070221-25, "Iraqi Army Captures 2 Rogue JAM Cell Members During Raid," February 21, 2007.

174   Brian Murphy, Associated Press, "Baghdad raids nab leaders of key militia," *Newark Star-Ledger*, February 28, 2007, Final Edition, 1.

175   Damien McElroy, "New security strategy transforms battleground," *The Daily Telegraph*, March 1, 2007, 19.

176   Tina Susman, "Security Crackdown Widens to Shiite Slum; U.S. and Iraqi soldiers go door to door looking for weapons in the Sadr City neighborhood.; Troops ask politely," *Los Angeles Times*, March 5, 2007, Home Edition, A1; "Troops team up to clear Sadr City," Department of Defense News Service, March 5, 2007.

177   Multi-National Corps-Iraq, Press Release No. 20070306-13, "Clearing Sadr City MND-B general pleased with initial results," March 6, 2007.

178   Institute for the Study of War interview with Col. J. B. Burton, Commander, 2nd Brigade Combat Team, 1st Infantry Division, November 14, 2007.

179   Institute for the Study of War interview with Col. J. B. Burton, Commander, 2nd Brigade Combat Team, 1st Infantry Division, November 14, 2007.

180   Institute for the Study of War interview with Col. J. B. Burton, Commander, 2nd Brigade Combat Team, 1st Infantry Division, November 14, 2007.

181   Institute for the Study of War interview with Col. J. B. Burton, Commander, 2nd Brigade Combat Team, 1st Infantry Division, November 14, 2007.

182   "Coalition, Iraqi Troops Start Clearing Sadr City," U.S. Federal News, March 4, 2007.

183   Institute for the Study of War interview with Col. J. B. Burton, Commander, 2nd Brigade Combat Team, 1st Infantry Division, November 14, 2007.

184   Major Rob Parke, 3-2 SBCT Public Affairs Officer, Multi-National Corps-Iraq Release No. 20070322-01, "Iraqi and Coalition Soldiers begin clearing operations in the Mansour Security District," Multi-National Division-Baghdad PAO, March 22, 2007.

185   Donna Miles, "'Arrowhead Brigade' Commander Reports Operation Arrowhead Strike 9 Successes" Army News Service, Washington, May 01, 2007.

186   Department of Defense Press Briefing with Col. Stephen Townsend, Commander 3rd Stryker Brigade Combat Team, 2nd Infantry Division, Monday, 30 April 2007.

187   Institute for the Study of War interview with Col. J. B. Burton, Commander, 2nd Brigade Combat Team, 1st Infantry Division, November 14, 2007.

188   Institute for the Study of War interview with Col. J. B. Burton, Commander, 2nd Brigade Combat Team, 1st Infantry Division, November 14, 2007.

189   Institute for the Study of War Interview with Col. J. B. Burton, Commander, 2nd Brigade Combat Team, 1st Infantry Division, November 14, 2007.

190   Institute for the Study of War Interview with Col. J. B. Burton, Commander, 2nd Brigade Combat Team, 1st Infantry Division, November 14, 2007.

191   John Ward Anderson, "Sunni Insurgents Battle in Baghdad, Residents of Western Neighborhood Join Groups' Fight Against Al-Qaeda in Iraq," The Washington Post, June 1, 2007.

192   John Ward Anderson, "Sunni Insurgents Battle in Baghdad, Residents of Western Neighborhood Join Groups' Fight Against Al-Qaeda in Iraq," The Washington Post, June 1, 2007.

193   John Ward Anderson, "Sunni Insurgents Battle in Baghdad, Residents of Western Neighborhood Join Groups' Fight Against Al-Qaeda in Iraq," The Washington Post, June 1, 2007; "Sunni fighters take on Qaeda in Baghdad street," Agence France Presse, June 1, 2007.

194   Institute for the Study of War Interview with Col. J. B. Burton, Commander, 2nd Brigade Combat Team, 1st Infantry Division, November 14, 2007.

195   Institute for the Study of War Interview with Col. J. B. Burton, Commander, 2nd

Brigade Combat Team, 1ˢᵗ Infantry Division, November 14, 2007.

196   Douglas Birch, "Dramatic progress seen in Baghdad neighborhood," The Associated Press, November 8, 2007.

197   Bloggers Roundtable Interview with Colonel Ricky Gibbs, Commander of the 4ᵗʰ Brigade Combat Team, 1ˢᵗ Infantry Division, Multi-National Division-Baghdad, Topic: The Stand-up of the Iraqi Government; September 28, 2007; Department of Defense Press Briefing with Colonel Ricky Gibbs, Commander of the 4ᵗʰ Brigade Combat Team, 1ˢᵗ Infantry Division, Multi-National Division-Baghdad, May 25, 2007.

198   Multi-National Corps-Iraq Release No. 20070223-06, "MND-B troops engage weapons smugglers in SE Baghdad," Multi-National Division-Baghdad PAO, February 23, 2007.

199   Multi-National Corps-Iraq Release No. 20070228-08, "Iraqi Army Troops nab five insurgents with cavalry paratroopers supporting operation," 4ᵗʰ BCT (Abn.), 25ᵗʰ Infantry Division, Public Affairs, February 27, 2007.

200   Multi-National Corps-Iraq Release No. 20070228-08, "Iraqi Army Troops nab five insurgents with cavalry paratroopers supporting operation," 4ᵗʰ BCT (Abn.), 25ᵗʰ Infantry Division, Public Affairs, February 27, 2007.

201   Al-Hadi, Hadi. "Iraqi Police Announce the Capture of Two Gunmen in Saydiyah." Aswat al-Iraq News Service, February 13, 2007. Translation from Arabic.

202   Multi-National Corps-Iraq Release No. 20070321-11, "Soldiers build Combat Outpost in Baghdad B-Roll Troops construct COP in Furat District," Multi-National Division-Baghdad PAO, March 21, 2007; Sam Dagher, "Baghdad's Outposts Bring New Perils," The Christian Science Monitor, March 22, 2007.

203   Sam Dagher, "Baghdad's Outposts Bring New Perils," The Christian Science Monitor, March 22, 2007.

204   Department of Defense Press Briefing with General David Petraeus, Commander, Multi-National Force-Iraq, April 26, 2007; Maj. Kirk Luedeke, "General Petraeus Goes to Market, Chief U.S. military commander in Iraq visits the revitalized Dora Market," 4ᵗʰ Light Infantry Brigade, Combat Team Public Affairs, April 4, 2007.

205   Maj. Kirk Luedeke, "General Petraeus Goes to Market, Chief U.S. military commander in Iraq visits the revitalized Dora Market," 4ᵗʰ Light Infantry Brigade, Combat Team Public Affairs, April 4, 2007.

206   Multi-National Corps-Iraq Release No. 20070306-14, "Iraqi national police, emergency services respond to car bomb in southwestern Baghdad," Multi-National

Division-Baghdad PAO, March 6, 2007; Multi-National Corps-Iraq Release No. 20070307-09, "Car bomb kills 22 in southern Baghdad," Multi-National Division-Baghdad PAO, March 7, 2007.

207 Multi-National Corps-Iraq Release No. 20070313-24, "Insurgents target MND-B patrol with roadside bomb," March 13, 2007.

208 Multi-National Corps-Iraq Release No.20070325-06, "Iraqi Security Forces aid the victims of large car bomb," March 25, 2007, Follow-on Release to 20070324-10 - "Large Car-bomb in Southeast Baghdad," Multi-National Division - Baghdad PAO; Multi-National Corps-Iraq Release No. 20070324-12, "Large Car-bomb in Southeast Baghdad," Multi-National Division-Baghdad PAO, March 24, 2007.

209 Multi-National Corps-Iraq Release No. 20070329-02, "Iraqi Security Forces investigate car bomb attacks and help wounded," March 29, 2007.

210 Multi-National Corps-Iraq Release No. 20070313-12, "Raids seize weapons caches in southern Baghdad," Multi-National Division-Baghdad PAO, March 13, 2007; Multi-National Corps-Iraq Release No. 20070320-03, "National Police enter two mosques, seize weapons caches," Multi-National Division-Baghdad PAO, March 20, 2007; Multi-National Corps-Iraq Release No. 20070323-04, "Raid seizes weapons cache in southern Baghdad," March 23, 2007; Multi-National Corps-Iraq Release No. 20070323-03, "National police find weapons cache in mosque," March 23, 2007; Multi-National Corps-Iraq Release No. 20070403-06, "Weapons cache discovered in Bayaa," April 3, 2007.

211 Multi-National Corps-Iraq Release No. 20070405-02, "Roadside bomb strikes MND-B patrol," Multi-National Division-Baghdad Public Affairs, April 5, 2007; Multi-National Corps-Iraq Release No. 20070407-06, "MND-B patrol attacked in west Baghdad," Multi-National Division-Baghdad PAO, April 7, 2007; Multi-National Corps-Iraq Release No.20070411-11, "MND-B patrol attacked in southern Baghdad," Multi-National Division-Baghdad PAO, April 11, 2007; Multi-National Corps-Iraq Release No. 20070415-01, "MND-B patrol ends with small arms fire," Multi-National Division-Baghdad Public Affairs, April 15, 2007; Multi-National Corps-Iraq Release No. 20070416-16, "Explosively-formed projectile targets MND-B patrol," Multi-National Division-Baghdad Public Affairs, April 16, 2007; Multi-National Corps-Iraq Release No. 20070416-09, "MND-B patrol ends with small arms fire," Multi-National Division-Baghdad Public Affairs, April 16, 2007; Multi-National Corps-Iraq Release No. 20070416-08, "MND-B patrol targeted by IED strike," Multi-National Division-Baghdad PAO, April 16, 2007; Multi-National Corps-Iraq Release No. 20070419-04, "Small arms fire targets MND-B patrol," Multi-National Division-Baghdad PAO, April 19, 2007; Multi-National Corps-Iraq Release No. 20070421-11, "Roadside bomb, small arms fire targets MND-B patrol," April 21, 2007.

212 Multi-National Corps-Iraq Release No. 20070415-08, "National police and emergency services respond to twin car-bombing," April 15, 2007.

213 Multi-National Corps-Iraq Release No. 20070420-10, "MND-B Soldiers attacked from mosque; two insurgents killed," April 20, 2007.

214 Multi-National Corps-Iraq Release No. 20070420-10, "MND-B Soldiers attacked from mosque; two insurgents killed," April 20, 2007; Multi-National Corps-Iraq Release No. 20070420-11, "Correct the Record - Attack aviation fired 30mm rounds in firefight," Multi-National Division-Baghdad Public Affairs, April 20, 2007.

215 Multi-National Corps-Iraq Release No. 20070420-10, "MND-B Soldiers attacked from mosque; two insurgents killed," April 20, 2007.

216 Tina Susman, "Two Baghdad districts see no decline in sectarian 'cleansing'; Military officials say violence has eased, but the killings continue," *Los Angeles Times*, August 12, 2007; Multi-National Corps-Iraq Release No. 20070615-04, June 15, 2007, Iraqi fire department puts out electrical fire in Baghdad mosque, By Maj. Kirk Luedeke, 4th IBCT, 1st Inf. Div. PAO, Multi-National Division-Baghdad PAO.

217 Tina Susman, "Two Baghdad districts see no decline in sectarian 'cleansing'; Military officials say violence has eased, but the killings continue," *Los Angeles Times*, August 12, 2007.

218 Master Sgt. Dave Larsen, "Iraqi, U.S. Security Forces Focused on Rashid District," *Crossed Sabers*, Vol. I, Issue 13, May 28, 2007.

219 Multi-National Corps-Iraq Release No. 20070502-02, "Iraqi Special Operations Forces clash with insurgents in Baghdad; insurgent network disrupted," Multi-National Corps-Iraq PAO, May 2, 2007.

220 Maj. Kirk Luedeke, 4th IBCT, 1st Inf. Div. PAO, Multi-National Corps-Iraq Release No. 20070505-03, "MND-B troops thwart insurgent plans; discover truck bomb," Multi-National Division-Baghdad PAO, May 5, 2007; Multi-National Corps-Iraq Release No. 20070506-15, "Rashid clearing continues: troops seize EFP construction cache," Multi-National Division-Baghdad PAO, May 6, 2007; Multi-National Corps-Iraq Release No. 20070510-08, "Tips lead to twin car bomb discoveries," Multi-National Division-Baghdad PAO, May 10, 2007.

221 Multi-National Corps-Iraq Release No. 20070517-05, "Iraqi Army, EOD prevent car bomb tragedy in Bayaa," Multi-National Division-Baghdad PAO, May 17, 2007.

222 Sgt. 1st Class Rober Timmons and Pfc. Nathaniel Smith, 4th IBCT Public Affairs, "Dragon Fire West," *Dragon Fire*, Vol. I, Issue I, June 2007.

223   Multi-National Corps-Iraq Release No. 20070527-12, "Rashid clearing operations: Terrorist hunt moves to East Rashid," Multi-National Division-Baghdad PAO, May 27, 2007.

224   Multi-National Corps-Iraq Release No. 20070527-07, "Warrior Battalion defeats 18 IEDs in 48 hours," May 27, 2007.

225   Multi-National Corps-Iraq Release No. 20070604-08, "Arrests and multiple caches seized in Rashid," June 5, 2007.

226   Department of Defense Press Briefing with Colonel Ricky Gibbs, Commander of the 4th Brigade Combat Team, 1st Infantry Division, Multi-National Division-Baghdad, May 25, 2007.

227   Multi-National Corps-Iraq Release No. 20070502-07, "Roadside bomb targets MND-B patrol," May 2, 2007; Multi-National Corps-Iraq Release No. 20070503-07, "Insurgent attack targets MND-B Soldiers," May 3, 2007; Multi-National Corps-Iraq Release No. 20070506-14, "Roadside bomb strikes MND-B patrol," May 6, 2007; Multi-National Corps-Iraq Release No. 20070518-06, "MND-B units attacked during operations," May 18, 2007; Multi-National Corps-Iraq Release No. 20070523-10, "MND-B patrol receives small arms fire," May 23, 2007; Multi-National Corps-Iraq Release No. 20070525-02, "MND-B patrol struck by roadside bomb," May 25, 2007; Multi-National Corps-Iraq Release No. 20070526-12, "Roadside bomb strikes MND-B patrol," May 26, 2007; Multi-National Corps-Iraq Release No. 20070527-01, "Roadside bomb strikes MND-B patrol," May 27, 2007; Multi-National Corps-Iraq Release No. 20070529-10, "MND-B patrol targeted by roadside bomb," May 29, 2007; Multi-National Corps-Iraq Release No. 20070601-14, "Soldier dies of wounds from IED strike," June 1, 2007; Multi-National Corps-Iraq Release No. 20070531-04, "MND-B patrol struck by roadside bomb," May 31, 2007; Multi-National Corps-Iraq Release No. 200700601-04, "MND-B patrol targeted by small arms fire," June 1, 2007.

228   Multi-National Corps-Iraq Release No. 20070529-08, "Iraqi, Coalition Forces respond to Rashid suicide car bomb," May 29, 2007.

229   Multi-National Corps-Iraq Release No. 20070530-16, "Southern Baghdad Mosque Attacked," May 30, 2007.

230   U.S., Iraqi Forces Make ` High-Value' Arrest, Kill 30, Robin Stringer, Oct. 9 2006 (Bloomberg)

231   Babak Dehghanpisheh, "Iraq's New Guns for Hire; under Seige in Baghdad, Fighters from Moqtada al Sadr's Jaysh al Mahdi Are Going Freelance, and They're Already Spreading Havoc to Once Calm Parts of the Country," *Newsweek*, May 7, 2007.

232   Multi-National Corps-Iraq Release No. 20070406-17, "Operation Black Eagle

begins in Ad Diwaniyah," April 6, 2007.

233 "Isf, Coalition Forces Successfully Conducted Lynx Claw," U.S. Federal News, June 4, 2007.

234 Kim Gamel, "U.S. Military Reports 14 More Soldiers Killed in Deadly 3 Days in Iraq," Associated Press, June 4, 2007.

235 Patrick Gaughen, "The Fight for Diwaniyah," Institute for the Study of War Backgrounder #17, January 6, 2008.

236 Lauren Frayer, Associated Press, "U.S. Seeks Gains in Shiite Militia Rifts," May 15, 2007 - 5:06pm.

237 James Kitfield, "Success of Iraq Surves Rests on Ability to Suspend Cycle of Violence," *National Journal*, July 17, 2007.

238 Army FM 3-0, *Operations*, 4-83 - 4-94. Doctrine also recognizes "sustaining operations," the category into which combat service support, such as logistics and base security, falls.

239 Army FM 3-0, *Operations*, 4-86 - 4-89.

240 Bing West, *No True Glory: A Frontline Account of the Battle of Fallujah* (New York: Bantam Books, 2005), xv-xvi.

241 Jim Michaels, "In Ramadi, the force isn't huge but the task is," *USA Today*, August 29, 2006.

242 Department of Defense News Briefing with Commanding General Multi-National Force-West, II Marine Expeditionary Force (Forward) Maj. Gen. W. E. Gaskin, March 30, 2007.

243 Staff Sgt. Tracie G. Kessler, 2nd Marine Division, "Engineers finds weapon caches along Euphrates," Barwana, Iraq, Marine Corps News (online), February 24, 2007.

244 Multi-National Corps-Iraq Press Release No. 20061213-01, Dec. 13, 2006, "Ramadi police battle insurgent ambush," Multi-National Corps-West PAO.

245 Department of Defense News Briefing with Colonel Sean MacFarland, July 14, 2006; Jim Michaels, "In Ramadi, the force isn't huge but the task is," *USA Today*, August 29, 2006.

246 Department of Defense News Briefing with Colonel Sean MacFarland, July 14, 2006.

247 Department of Defense News Briefing with Colonel Sean MacFarland, July 14, 2006.

248 Kim Murphy, Times Staff Writer, "Tribes Heed Call to Join Battle for Iraq; Maliki

enlists the Sunni groups in an attempt to clear insurgents from Al Anbar province," *Los Angeles Times*, October 5, 2006, Home Edition, A9.

249 Department of Defense News Briefing with Colonel Sean MacFarland, July 14, 2006.

250 Jim Michaels, "In Ramadi, the force isn't huge but the task is," *USA Today*, August 29, 2006; Department of Defense News Briefing with Colonel Sean MacFarland, July 14, 2006.

251 Department of Defense News Briefing with Colonel Sean MacFarland, July 14, 2006.

252 Department of Defense News Briefing with Colonel Sean MacFarland, July 14, 2006.

253 Department of Defense News Briefing with Colonel Sean MacFarland, July 14, 2006.

254 Joshua Partlow, Washington Post Foreign Service, "Sheiks Help Curb Violence in Iraq's West, U.S. Says; Others See Peril in Tribal Confederation," *The Washington Post*, January 27, 2007, Final Edition, A13.

255 Multi-National Force-Iraq Press Release A061021a, "One terrorist killed and seven detained in Ramadi," October 21, 2006.

256 Department of Defense News Briefing with Colonel Sean MacFarland, July 14, 2006.

257 Department of Defense News Briefing with Colonel Sean MacFarland, July 14, 2006.

258 Tony Perry, Times Staff Writer, "A two-pronged approach in Ramadi neighborhood; Iraqi forces search for insurgents as U.S. troops build a police station," *Los Angeles Times*, January 5, 2007, Home Edition, A3.

259 David Wood, "Marines Locked in Anbar Standoff; Al-Qaida Insurgency Called Well-Financed, Well-Led and Elusive," *The Baltimore Sun*, January 2, 2007, Final Edition, 1A.

260 Jim Michaels, "In Ramadi, the force isn't huge but the task is," *USA Today*, August 29, 2006.

261 Multi-National Corps-Iraq Press Release, No. 20060818-01, "Most successful Iraqi Police recruiting drive," August 18, 2006.

262 Joshua Partlow, Washington Post Foreign Service, "Sheiks Help Curb Violence in Iraq's West, U.S. Says; Others See Peril in Tribal Confederation," *The Washington Post*, January 27, 2007, Final Edition, A13.

263 Kim Murphy, Times Staff Writer, "Tribes Heed Call to Join Battle for Iraq; Maliki

enlists the Sunni groups in an attempt to clear insurgents from Al Anbar province," *Los Angeles Times*, October 5, 2006, Home Edition, A9.

264   Kim Murphy, Times Staff Writer, "Tribes Heed Call to Join Battle for Iraq; Maliki
enlists the Sunni groups in an attempt to clear insurgents from Al Anbar province," *Los Angeles Times*, October 5, 2006, Home Edition, A9.

265   Kim Murphy, Times Staff Writer, "Tribes Heed Call to Join Battle for Iraq; Maliki
enlists the Sunni groups in an attempt to clear insurgents from Al Anbar province," *Los Angeles Times*, October 5, 2006, Home Edition, A9.

266   Multi-National Corps-Iraq Release No. 20061029-04, "Coalition Forces establish
new security station in Ramadi," October 29, 2006.

267   Multi-National Corps-Iraq Release No. 20061029-04, "Coalition Forces establish
new security station in Ramadi," October 29, 2006; Kim Murphy, Times Staff
Writer, "Tribes Heed Call to Join Battle for Iraq; Maliki enlists the Sunni groups
in an attempt to clear insurgents from Al Anbar province," *Los Angeles Times*,
October 5, 2006, Home Edition, A9.

268   Multi-National Corps-Iraq Release No. 20061013-05, "Operation Dealer Discovers SVBIEDs, Large Weapons Cache in Western Ramadi," October 13, 2006.

269   Multi-National Force-Iraq Press Release A061102a, "Air Strike Kills Terrorists
East of Ramadi," November 2, 2006.

270   Multi-National Force-Iraq Press Release A061108a, "Four terrorists killed, 48
detained in Ramadi raid," November 8, 2006.

271   Multi-National Corps-Iraq Release No. 20061029-04, "Coalition Forces establish
new security station in Ramadi," October 29, 2006.

272   Department of Defense News Briefing with Colonel Sean MacFarland, July 14,
2006.

273   Kim Murphy, Times Staff Writer, "Tribes Heed Call to Join Battle for Iraq; Maliki
enlists the Sunni groups in an attempt to clear insurgents from Al Anbar province," *Los Angeles Times*, October 5, 2006, Home Edition, A9.

274   Department of Defense News Briefing with Colonel Sean MacFarland, July
14, 2006; Kim Murphy, Times Staff Writer, "Tribes Heed Call to Join Battle for
Iraq; Maliki enlists the Sunni groups in an attempt to clear insurgents from Al
Anbar province," *Los Angeles Times*, October 5, 2006, Home Edition, A9; Michael
Fumento, "Return to Ramadi," *The Weekly Standard*, November 27, 2006, 27.

275   Multi-National Corps-Iraq Release No. 20061216-04, "Water pump station in
heart of Ramadi repaired," December 16, 2006.

276   Multi-National Corps-Iraq Release No. 20061111-01, "Iraqi Police drive recruits

400 in Ramadi, 1st Brigade Combat Team, 1st Armored Division PAO," November 11, 2006.

277   Multi-National Corps-Iraq Release No. 20070108-11, "Iraqi Police Take Supplies to School in Ramadi," January 8, 2007.

278   Multi-National Corps-Iraq Release No. 20070108-11, "Iraqi Police Take Supplies to School in Ramadi," January 8, 2007; "The Jim Lehrer Show," Interview with General David Petraeus, U.S. Army, Commanding General, Multinational Force-Iraq; Subject: The Situation in Iraq; Interviewer: Jim Lehrer; Wednesday, April 3, 2007.

279   Multi-National Corps-Iraq Release No. 20070111-04, "Hundreds of Ramadi Residents Join the Police," January 11, 2007.

280   David Wood, "Marines Locked in Anbar Standoff; Al-Qaida Insurgency Called Well-Financed, Well-Led and Elusive," The Baltimore Sun, January 2, 2007, Final Edition, 1A.

281   Multi-National Corps-Iraq Release No. 20061111-01, "Iraqi Police drive recruits 400 in Ramadi, 1st Brigade Combat Team, 1st Armored Division PAO," November 11, 2006.

282   Multi-National Corps-Iraq Release No. 20070111-04, "Hundreds of Ramadi Residents Join the Police," January 11, 2007.

283   Multi-National Corps-Iraq Release No. 20061111-01, "Iraqi Police drive recruits 400 in Ramadi, 1st Brigade Combat Team, 1st Armored Division PAO," November 11, 2006.

284   Multi-National Corps-Iraq Release No. 20070111-04, "Hundreds of Ramadi Residents Join the Police," January 11, 2007.

285   Multi-National Corps-Iraq Release No. 20061024-02, "Iraqi Army assumes responsibility of Northern Ramadi," October 24, 2006.

286   Multi-National Corps-Iraq, No. 20061125-07, "IA conducts census, security operations in Ramadi," 1st Brigade Combat Team, 1st Armored Division PAO, November 25, 2006,

287   Multi-National Corps-Iraq Release No. 20070111-04, "Hundreds of Ramadi Residents Join the Police," January 11, 2007.

288   MNC-I, Release No. 20061127-01, "Four Civilians Injured in Ramadi," Multi-National Corps-West PAO, November 27, 2006.

289   Multi-National Corps-Iraq Release No. 20061219-07, "IA Soldiers Capture 2 Insurgents near Ramadi," December 19, 2006.

290   Multi-National Corps-Iraq Release No. 20061220-14, "Ramadi Residents

Wounded and Killed by Terrorists," December 20, 2006.

291 Multi-National Corps-Iraq Release No. 20061228-21, "Insurgents kill woman, policeman, wound children in attack in Ramadi," December 28, 2006.

292 Multi-National Corps-Iraq Release No. 20070114-03, "Operation Squeeze Play makes Ramadi safer Multi-National Force," January 14, 2007.

293 Multi-National Corps-Iraq Release No. 20070114-03, "Operation Squeeze Play makes Ramadi safer Multi-National Force," January 14, 2007.

294 Multi-National Corps-Iraq Release No. 20061221-05, "Iraqi Police find IEDs inside government buildings in Ramadi," December 21, 2006.

295 Multi-National Corps-Iraq Release No. 20070108-05, "Ramadi Police capture insurgents in Ta'meem," January 8, 2007.

296 Multi-National Corps-Iraq Release No. 20070111-04, "Hundreds of Ramadi Residents Join the Police," January 11, 2007.

297 Multi-National Corps-Iraq Release No. 20070118-09, "New Iraqi police station under construction in Ramadi," January 18, 2007.

298 Multi-National Corps-Iraq Release No. 20070123-12, "Ramadi security forces come together to discuss future," January 23, 2007.

299 Multi-National Corps-Iraq Release No. 20070206-03, "Iraqi Police in Ramadi discover large weapons cache," February 6, 2007.

300 Multi-National Corps-Iraq Release No. 20061213-01, "Ramadi police battle insurgent ambush," Multi-National Corps-West PAO, December 13, 2006.

301 Multi-National Corps-Iraq Release No. 20070130-04, "Emergency Response Unit compound in Ramadi attacked by SVBIED," January 30, 2007.

302 Multi-National Corps-Iraq Release No. 20070130-04, "Emergency Response Unit compound in Ramadi attacked by SVBIED," January 30, 2007.

303 Department of Defense News Briefing with Commanding General Multi-National Force-West, II Marine Expeditionary Force (Forward) Maj. Gen. W. E. Gaskin, March 30, 2007.

304 Matt Millham, "Commander of the 1st Brigade Combat Team credits Iraqis for Ramadi turnaround," *Stars and Stripes*, European edition, March, 6, 2007.

305 Monte Morin, "'Raider Brigade' takes over Ramadi; Ceremony marks end of 1-1AD's battle to stabilize volatile city," *Stars and Stripes*, Mideast edition, February 19, 2007.

306 Monte Morin, "'Raider Brigade' takes over Ramadi; Ceremony marks end of 1-1AD's battle to stabilize volatile city," *Stars and Stripes*, Mideast edition, February

19, 2007.

307 Department of Defense News Briefing with Commanding General Multi-National Force-West, II Marine Expeditionary Force (Forward) Maj. Gen. W. E. Gaskin, March 30, 2007.

308 Kim Gamel, Associated Press, "Two die in gas attacks in Iraq," *The Star Ledger* (Newark, New Jersey), March 18, 2007, Final Edition, 5.

309 Brian Murphy, Associated Press, "Iraq gas tanker blasted in new twist to violence," *The Star Ledger* (Newark, New Jersey), February 21, 2007, Final, 6.

310 Borzou Daragahi, Times Staff Writer, "Another chlorine gas bomb attack in Iraq; For the second day in a row, a crude chemical weapon is used to target civilians, killing two; 40 die in other violence," *Los Angeles Times*, February 22, 2007, Home Edition, A8.

311 Peter Spiegel, Times Staff Writer, "The Conflict in Iraq: Another Rape Allegation; Discovery of Chemical Weaponry; Raided arms 'factory' had gas canisters, U.S. says; Announcement comes after recent attacks involving chlorine," *Los Angeles Times*, February 23, 2007, Correction Appended, Home Edition, A4.

312 Alexandra Zavis, "U.S. and Iraqi troops kill 8 during intense Anbar firefight," *Los Angeles Times*, March 22, 2007, Final, 8.

313 Lauren Frayer and Kim Gamel, Associated Press, "Maliki asks Sunni leaders' help to vanquish insurgents," *The Star Ledger* (Newark, New Jersey), March 14, 2007, 3.

314 Kirk Semple, "Iraq Premier Meets Leaders In Area Torn by Insurgency," *New York Times*, March 14, 2007, Correction Appended, Late Edition - Final, A10.

315 Kirk Semple, "Iraq Premier Meets Leaders In Area Torn by Insurgency," *New York Times*, March 14, 2007, Correction Appended, Late Edition - Final, A10.

316 Kirk Semple, "Iraq Premier Meets Leaders In Area Torn by Insurgency," *New York Times*, March 14, 2007, Correction Appended, Late Edition - Final, A10.

317 Kirk Semple, "Iraq Premier Meets Leaders In Area Torn by Insurgency," *New York Times*, March 14, 2007, Correction Appended, Late Edition - Final, A10.

318 Sudarsan Raghavan, Washington Post Foreign Service. "Maliki, Petraeus Visit Insurgent Hotbed in Iraq; Premier's First Official Trip to Ramadi Urged by Top U.S. Commander in Iraq," The Washington Post, March 14, 2007, Suburban Edition, Maryland, A9.

319 Kim Gamel, Associated Press, "Two die in gas attacks in Iraq," *The Star Ledger* (Newark, New Jersey), March 18, 2007, Final Edition, 5.

320 Kim Gamel, Associated Press, "Two die in gas attacks in Iraq," *The Star Ledger*

(Newark, New Jersey), March 18, 2007, Final Edition, 5.

321 Alexandra Zavis, "U.S. and Iraqi troops kill 8 during intense Anbar firefight," *Los Angeles Times*, March 22, 2007, Final, 8.

322 Multi-National Corps-Iraq Release No. 20070325-02, "Suicide Truck Bomb Captured in Ramadi," March 25, 2007.

323 Multi-National Corps-Iraq Release No. 20070328-11, "Fallujah Government Center attacked by chlorine truck bombs," March 28, 2007.

324 Department of Defense News Briefing with Colonel John Charlton, Commander of the 1st Brigade, 3rd Infantry Division, March 13, 2008.

325 Max Boot, "An Iraq Success Story," *Los Angeles Times*, April 24, 2007.

326 Headquarters, United States Central Command, Release number 07-01-03P, 3/21/2007, "Iraqi Police Clear Central Ramadi."

327 Multi-National Corps-Iraq Release No. 20070326-01, "Clearing Operations Begin in Ramadi," Multi-National Force-West PAO, March 26, 2007.

328 Department of Defense Bloggers Roundtable with Colonel John Charlton, Commander of the 1st Brigade, 3rd Infantry Division, August 3, 2007.

329 Multi-National Corps-Iraq Release Number 20070504-17, "Operation Forsythe Park update," Multi-National Force-West PAO, May 4, 2007.

330 Multi-National Corps-Iraq Release Number 20070504-17, "Operation Forsythe Park update," Multi-National Force-West PAO, May 4, 2007.

331 Multi-National Corps-Iraq Release Number 20070504-17, "Operation Forsythe Park update," Multi-National Force-West PAO, May 4, 2007.

332 Max Boot, "An Iraq Success Story," *Los Angeles Times*, April 24, 2007.

333 Department of Defense News Briefing with Colonel John Charlton, Commander of the 1st Brigade, 3rd Infantry Division, March 13, 2008.

334 Department of Defense News Briefing with Colonel John Charlton, Commander of the 1st Brigade, 3rd Infantry Division, March 13, 2008.

335 Department of Defense News Briefing with Colonel John Charlton, Commander of the 1st Brigade, 3rd Infantry Division, March 13, 2008.

336 Department of Defense News Briefing with Colonel John Charlton, Commander of the 1st Brigade, 3rd Infantry Division, March 13, 2008.

337 Multi-National Corps-Iraq Press Release No. 20070413-08, "JCC hosts town council meeting," Multi-National Force-West PAO, April 13, 2007.

338 Department of Defense News Briefing with Colonel John Charlton, Commander of the 1st Brigade, 3rd Infantry Division, March 13, 2008.

339   Department of Defense Bloggers Roundtable with Colonel John Charlton, Commander of the 1st Brigade, 3rd Infantry Division, August 3, 2007.

340   Ann Scott Tyson, "A Deadly Clash at Donkey Island; On a Routine Night Patrol Near Ramadi, U.S. Troops Stumble Upon a Camp of Heavily Armed Insurgents Poised to Retake the City," *The Washington Post*, August 19, 2007.

341   Ann Scott Tyson, "A Deadly Clash at Donkey Island; On a Routine Night Patrol Near Ramadi, U.S. Troops Stumble Upon a Camp of Heavily Armed Insurgents Poised to Retake the City," *The Washington Post*, August 19, 2007.

342   Ann Scott Tyson, "A Deadly Clash at Donkey Island; On a Routine Night Patrol Near Ramadi, U.S. Troops Stumble Upon a Camp of Heavily Armed Insurgents Poised to Retake the City," *The Washington Post*, August 19, 2007.

343   Department of Defense Bloggers Roundtable with Colonel John Charlton, Commander of the 1st Brigade, 3rd Infantry Division, August 3, 2007.

344   Department of Defense News Briefing with Colonel John Charlton, Commander of the 1st Brigade, 3rd Infantry Division, March 13, 2008.

345   Department of Defense News Briefing with Colonel John Charlton, Commander of the 1st Brigade, 3rd Infantry Division, March 13, 2008.

346   Colonel David Sutherland, Commander, Greywolf Brigade Combat Team, Interview with the Institute for the Study of War, October 25, 2007.

347   Colonel David Sutherland, Commander, Greywolf Brigade Combat Team, Interview with the Institute for the Study of War, October 25, 2007.

348   Colonel David Sutherland, Commander, Greywolf Brigade Combat Team, Interview with the Institute for the Study of War, October 25, 2007.

349   Colonel David Sutherland, Commander, Greywolf Brigade Combat Team, Interview with the Institute for the Study of War, October 25, 2007.

350   Colonel David Sutherland, Commander, Greywolf Brigade Combat Team, Interview with the Institute for the Study of War, October 25, 2007.

351   Colonel David Sutherland, Commander, Greywolf Brigade Combat Team, Interview with the Institute for the Study of War, October 25, 2007.

352   Joshua Partlow, Washington Post Foreign Service, "U.S. Bolstering Force in Deadly Diyala; Violence Against Troops Has Risen Sharply," *Washington Post*, Monday, April 16, 2007, A11.

353   Department of Defense Briefing, January 22, 2007, Federal News Service: Joint Press Conference with Colonel David Sutherland, Commander of 3rd BCT, 1st Cavalry Division, et. al., Combined Press Information Center, Baghdad, Iraq.

354   Department of Defense Briefing, January 22, 2007, Federal News Service: Joint

Press Conference with Colonel David Sutherland, Commander of 3ʳᵈ BCT, 1ˢᵗ Cavalry Division, et. al., Combined Press Information Center, Baghdad, Iraq.

355 Department of Defense Briefing, January 22, 2007, Federal News Service: Joint Press Conference with Colonel David Sutherland, Commander of 3ʳᵈ BCT, 1ˢᵗ Cavalry Division, et. al., Combined Press Information Center, Baghdad, Iraq.

356 Alexandra Zavis, "Insurgents prove slippery in U.S.-Iraqi hunt in rural east," *Los Angeles Times*, January 6, 2007, Home Edition, A3.

357 Department of Defense Briefing, January 22, 2007, Federal News Service: Joint Press Conference with Colonel David Sutherland, Commander of 3ʳᵈ BCT, 1ˢᵗ Cavalry Division, et. al., Combined Press Information Center, Baghdad, Iraq.

358 Department of Defense Briefing, January 22, 2007, Federal News Service: Joint Press Conference with Colonel David Sutherland, Commander of 3ʳᵈ BCT, 1ˢᵗ Cavalry Division, et. al., Combined Press Information Center, Baghdad, Iraq.

359 Department of Defense Briefing, January 22, 2007, Federal News Service: Joint Press Conference with Colonel David Sutherland, Commander of 3ʳᵈ BCT, 1ˢᵗ Cavalry Division, et. al., Combined Press Information Center, Baghdad, Iraq.

360 Department of Defense Briefing, January 22, 2007, Federal News Service: Joint Press Conference with Colonel David Sutherland, Commander of 3ʳᵈ BCT, 1ˢᵗ Cavalry Division, et. al., Combined Press Information Center, Baghdad, Iraq.

361 Alexandra Zavis, "U.S. launches air assault on Sunni Haven; the attack escalates the joint operation with Iraqi troops into Diyala province. Ground forces kill 21 suspected militants," *Los Angeles Times*, January 8, 2007, Home Edition, A3.

362 Department of Defense Briefing, January 22, 2007, Federal News Service: Joint Press Conference with Colonel David Sutherland, Commander of 3ʳᵈ BCT, 1ˢᵗ Cavalry Division, et. al., Combined Press Information Center, Baghdad, Iraq.

363 Alexandra Zavis, "The Conflict in Iraq: Troop Increase; Diyala Offensive; Executions; Escapee's Story; Diyala offensive gets caked in mud; U.S. and Iraqi troops on the hunt for insurgents hit adverse conditions," *Los Angeles Times*, Home Edition, January 9, 2007, A7.

364 Department of Defense Briefing, January 22, 2007, Federal News Service: Joint Press Conference with Colonel David Sutherland, Commander of 3ʳᵈ BCT, 1ˢᵗ Cavalry Division, et. al., Combined Press Information Center, Baghdad, Iraq.

365 Alexandra Zavis, "U.S.-Iraqi Assault Hits Sunni Haven; The offensive, a test of national troops, targets an isolated area where violence is on the rise; Guerrillas are Prepared," *Los Angeles Times*, January 5, 2007, Home Edition, A1.

366 Alexandra Zavis, "U.S.-Iraqi Assault Hits Sunni Haven; The offensive, a test of national troops, targets an isolated area where violence is on the rise; Guerrillas

are Prepared," *Los Angeles Times*, January 5, 2007, Home Edition, A1; Alexandra Zavis, "Insurgents prove slippery in U.S.-Iraqi hunt in rural east," *Los Angeles Times*, January 6, 2007, Home Edition, A3; Alexandra Zavis, "U.S. launches air assault on Sunni Haven; the attack escalates the joint operation with Iraqi troops into Diyala province. Ground forces kill 21 suspected militants," *Los Angeles Times*, January 8, 2007, Home Edition, A3.

367 Alexandra Zavis, "Insurgents prove slippery in U.S.-Iraqi hunt in rural east," *Los Angeles Times*, January 6, 2007, Home Edition, A3.

368 Alexandra Zavis, "U.S. launches air assault on Sunni Haven; the attack escalates the joint operation with Iraqi troops into Diyala province. Ground forces kill 21 suspected militants," *Los Angeles Times*, January 8, 2007, Home Edition, A3; Alexandra Zavis, "The Conflict in Iraq; Iran's Influence; Operation in Diyala; Joint assault amid canals resumes; U.S. and Iraqi troops mounting an offensive in Diyala province find arms caches and tunnels but few insurgents," *Los Angeles Times*, January 12, 2007, Home Edition, A10.

369 Alexandra Zavis, "Insurgents prove slippery in U.S.-Iraqi hunt in rural east," *Los Angeles Times*, January 6, 2007, Home Edition, A3; Alexandra Zavis, "The Conflict in Iraq: Troop Increase; Diyala Offensive; Executions; Escapee's Story; Diyala offensive gets caked in mud; U.S. and Iraqi troops on the hunt for insurgents hit adverse conditions," *Los Angeles Times*, Home Edition, January 9, 2007, A7.

370 Alexandra Zavis, "The Conflict in Iraq; Iran's Influence; Operation in Diyala; Joint assault amid canals resumes; U.S. and Iraqi troops mounting an offensive in Diyala province find arms caches and tunnels but few insurgents," *Los Angeles Times*, January 12, 2007, Home Edition, A10.

371 Alexandra Zavis, "U.S. launches air assault on Sunni Haven; the attack escalates the joint operation with Iraqi troops into Diyala province. Ground forces kill 21 suspected militants," *Los Angeles Times*, January 8, 2007, Home Edition, A3.

372 Alexandra Zavis, "The Conflict in Iraq; Iran's Influence; Operation in Diyala; Joint assault amid canals resumes; U.S. and Iraqi troops mounting an offensive in Diyala province find arms caches and tunnels but few insurgents," *Los Angeles Times*, January 12, 2007, Home Edition, A10.

373 Alexandra Zavis, "The Conflict in Iraq; Iran's Influence; Operation in Diyala; Joint assault amid canals resumes; U.S. and Iraqi troops mounting an offensive in Diyala province find arms caches and tunnels but few insurgents," *Los Angeles Times*, January 12, 2007, Home Edition, A10.

374 Department of Defense Briefing, January 22, 2007, Federal News Service: Joint Press Conference with Colonel David Sutherland, Commander of 3rd BCT, 1st Cavalry Division, et. al., Combined Press Information Center, Baghdad, Iraq.

375 Alexandra Zavis, "The Conflict in Iraq; Iran's Influence; Operation in Diyala; Joint assault amid canals resumes; U.S. and Iraqi troops mounting an offensive in Diyala province find arms caches and tunnels but few insurgents," *Los Angeles Times*, January 12, 2007, Home Edition, A10.

376 Multi-National Corps-Iraq Release No. 20070131-02, "Troops discover caches in Diyala province," Multi-National Division-North PAO, January 31, 2007.

377 Department of Defense Briefing, January 22, 2007, Federal News Service: Joint Press Conference with Colonel David Sutherland, Commander of 3rd BCT, 1st Cavalry Division, et. al., Combined Press Information Center, Baghdad, Iraq.

378 Kim Gamel, "Bomb strikes in Iraq kills at least 29 during Ashoura ceremonies," Associated Press, January 30, 2007; Deutsche Presse-Agentur, "At least 12 Iraqis killed, 23 wounded in a blast in Khanaqin," January 30, 2007.

379 "Iraqi, Coalition Troops Treat Wounded in Attack," U.S. Federal News, January 31, 2007.

380 "Leadership Discusses Security, Services in Balad Ruz," U.S. Federal News, February 3, 2007.

381 "Five Insurgents Killed, 12 Suspects Caught in Iraq Operations," American Forces Press Service, Washington, February 23, 2007.

382 "Airstrike Kills Terrorist; Iraqi Soldiers Respond to Baghdad Bombings," *Congressional Quarterly*, December 6, 2006.

383 Press Briefing with Colonel David W. Sutherland, 3rd Brigade Combat Team, 1st Cavalry Division Commander and Major General Shakir Halail Husain, 5th Iraqi Division Commander, Operational Update, March 16, 2007.

384 Richard Oppel and Iraqi Employees of the New York Times, "Attacks Surge as Iraqi Militants Overshadow City," *The New York Times*, April 15, 2007.

385 Multi-National Corps-Iraq Release No. 20070313-09, "Stryker Battalion arrives in Diyala Province," MND-North PAO, March 13, 2007.

386 Richard Oppel and Iraqi Employees of the New York Times, "Attacks Surge as Iraqi Militants Overshadow City," *The New York Times*, April 15, 2007.

387 Press Briefing with Colonel David W. Sutherland, 3rd Brigade Combat Team, 1st Cavalry Division Commander and Major General Shakir Halail Husain, 5th Iraqi Division Commander, Operational Update, March 16, 2007.

388 Multi-National Corps-Iraq Release No. 20070320-05, "Strykers discover cache in Diyala palm groves," MND-North PAO, March 20, 2007.

389 Sgt. Armando Monroig, 5th Mobile Public Affairs Detachment, Multi-National Force-Iraq, "Joint operation disrupts anti-Iraqi forces," March 30, 2007; Multi-

National Corps-Iraq Release No. 20070402-11, "Iraqi Security Forces, Cavalry discover extremist training camp," MND-North PAO, April 2, 2007; Multi-National Corps-Iraq Release No. 20070408-02, "Joint operation clears terrorists from Diyala River Valley," April 8, 2007.

390 Sgt. Armando Monroig, 5ᵗʰ Mobile Public Affairs Detachment, Multi-National Force-Iraq, "Joint operation disrupts anti-Iraqi forces," March 30, 2007.

391 Multi-National Corps-Iraq Release No. 20070402-11, "Iraqi Security Forces, Cavalry discover extremist training camp," MND-North PAO, April 2, 2007.

392 Multi-National Corps-Iraq Release No. 20070408-02, "Joint operation clears terrorists from Diyala River Valley," April 8, 2007.

393 Multi-National Corps-Iraq Release No. 20070408-02, "Joint operation clears terrorists from Diyala River Valley," April 8, 2007.

394 Multi-National Corps-Iraq Release No. 20070330-17, "Three suicide VBIEDs target Khalis population," MND-North PAO, March 30, 2007.

395 Richard Oppel and Iraqi Employees of the New York Times, "Attacks Surge as Iraqi Militants Overshadow City," The New York Times, April 15, 2007.

396 Joshua Partlow, Washington Post Foreign Service, "U.S. Bolstering Force in Deadly Diyala; Violence Against Troops Has Risen Sharply," The Washington Post, April 16, 2007, A11.

397 Staff Sgt. Antonieta Rico, 5ᵗʰ Mobile Public Affairs Detachment, "Stryker Battalion restores market security," Multi-National Force-Iraq, April 16, 2007.

398 Staff Sgt. Antonieta Rico, 5ᵗʰ Mobile Public Affairs Detachment, "Effort under way to clear market," Northwest Guardian, April 19, 2007.

399 Staff Sgt. Antonieta Rico, 5ᵗʰ Mobile Public Affairs Detachment, "Soldiers in Baqouba keep pressure on Al-Qaida in Iraq, April 23, 2007.

400 Multi-National Corps-Iraq Release No. 20070412-03, "Iraqi Army, Iraqi Police, Coalition force members deny enemy territory in Buhriz," MND-North PAO, April 12, 2007.

401 Staff Sgt. Antonieta Rico, 5ᵗʰ Mobile Public Affairs Detachment, "Soldiers in Baqouba keep pressure on Al-Qaida in Iraq, April 23, 2007.

402 Joshua Partlow, Washington Post Foreign Service, "U.S. Bolstering Force in Deadly Diyala; Violence Against Troops Has Risen Sharply," The Washington Post, April 16, 2007, A11.

403 Multi-National Corps-Iraq Release No. 20070423-02, "Coalition Forces see progress in Diyala River Valley," Multi-National Division-North PAO, April 23, 2007.

404 Multi-National Corps-Iraq Release No. 20070423-02, "Coalition Forces see

progress in Diyala River Valley," Multi-National Division-North PAO, April 23, 2007.

405 Multi-National Corps-Iraq, Release No. 20070425-01, "SVBIEDs target Coalition patrol base in Diyala province," Multi-National Division-North PAO, April 25, 2007.

406 CENTCOM Release No. 07-01-03, "Diyala leadership to fix fuel shortage in province," March 21, 2007.

407 Multi-National Corps-Iraq Release No. 20070423-13, "VBIED detonates near Diyala's provincial council headquarters," Multi-National Division-North PAO, April 23, 2007.

408 Multi-National Corps-Iraq Release No. 20070423-13, "VBIED detonates near Diyala's provincial council headquarters," Multi-National Division-North PAO, April 23, 2007.

409 "Sheiks sign peace agreement," MND-North PAO, May 3, 2007.

410 Multi-National Corps-Iraq Release No. 20061210-09, Sheiks continue discussions of security, stability for Diyala, Multi-National Division-North PAO, Dec. 10, 2006.

411 Colonel David Sutherland, Commander, Greywolf Brigade Combat Team, Interview with the Institute for the Study of War, October 25, 2007. The Shia Endowment and the Sunni Endowment are government entities in Iraq responsible for caring for Shia and Sunni religious institutions, respectively.

412 "Sheiks sign peace agreement," MND-North PAO, May 3, 2007; "Greywolf: Making a Difference," slides provided by 3-1 Cavalry PAO, October 25, 2007.

413 "Diyala sheiks meet to address concerns," Multi-National Division-North PAO, May 26, 2007.

414 "Diyala sheiks meet to address concerns," Multi-National Division-North PAO, May 26, 2007.

415 Multi-National Corps-Iraq Release No. 20070606-14, "Diyala Support Committee meets in Baqouba," MND-North PAO, June 6, 2007.

416 Damien Cave with Ali Adeeb and Qais Mizher, "Bombing at Iraqi Ministry Wounds 2 Top Officials," *The New York Times*, Late Edition, February 27, 2007.

417 Ammar Karim, "Shell-Shocked Baghdad Wakes to New Bomb," Agence France Presse, February 13, 2007.

418 Edward Wong and Wissam A. Habeeb, "Baghdad Car Bomb Kills 20 on Bookseller's Row," *The New York Times*, March 6, 2007.

419 Multi-National Corps-Iraq Release No. 20070122-09, "Al-Tair-rah Square targeted

by double car bombs," January 22, 2007; Multi-National Corps-Iraq Release No.20070126-03, "Motorcycle bomb strikes Iraqi shoppers," January 26, 2007; "Many die in Iraq pet market blast," *BBC News*, January 26, 2007; Multi-National Corps-Iraq Release No. 20070204-04, "Truck Bomb Blast Rocks Rusafa," February 4, 2007; Multi-National Corps-Iraq Release No. 20070206-06, "Nine Iraqis killed in two car bomb attacks in eastern Baghdad," February 6, 2007; Damien Cave, "Two Markets Bombed in Central Baghdad, Killing at least 67 and Wounding 155," *The New York Times*, February 13, 2007.

420 Sudarsan Raghavan and Saad al-Izzi, "Visiting Iraq, McCain Cites Progress on Safety Issues," *The Washington Post*, April 2, 2007; Department of Defense Special Briefing with General David Petraeus, Commander, Multi-National Force-Iraq, Topic: Update on Security Operations in Iraq, Location: Pentagon Briefing Room, Arlington, VA, April, 26, 2007.

421 Multi-National Force-Iraq Release A070322c, "Network leaders captured over last three days," March 22, 2007.

422 Brian Bennett, "Al-Qaeda Sends a Message," *Time*, April 12, 2007.

423 Multi-National Corps-Iraq Release No. 20070418-22, "131 dead, more than 160 wounded by multiple car bomb attacks in Baghdad," April 18, 2007.

424 Joshua Partlow, "More than 100 killed in Baghdad, Nearby Town," *The Washington Post*, March 30, 2007.

425 Multi-National Corps-Iraq Release No. 20070326-04, "Suspected Suicide Car Bomb Ring Leader Captured," Multi-National Division-Baghdad PAO, March 26, 2007; Multi-National Corps-Iraq Release No. 20070326-05, "Second Suspected Car Bomb Cell Leader Captured," Multi-National Division-Baghdad PAO, March 26, 2007.

426 Multi-National Corps-Iraq Release No. 20070404-10, "Iraqi Forces conduct raid in Baghdad," April 4, 2007.

427 Multi-National Corps-Iraq Release No. 20070604-02, "Construction complete on 'Safe Neighborhood' project in Adhamiyah," June 4, 2007; Tina Susman, "Military officials defend new barrier in Baghdad," *Los Angeles Times*, April 24, 2007.

428 Multi-National Corps-Iraq Release No. 20070604-02, "Construction complete on 'Safe Neighborhood' project in Adhamiyah," June 4, 2007.

429 Multi-National Corps-Iraq Release No. 20070310-09, "Iraqi Army stops car bomb from entering Sadr City," Multi-National Division-Baghdad PAO, March 10, 2007.

430 Multi-National Corps-Iraq Release No. 20070331-12, "Car Bomb Explodes in Sadr City," Multi-National Division-Baghdad PAO, 2nd BCT, 82nd Abn. Div. Public

Affairs, March 31, 2007.

431 Multi-National Corps-Iraq Release No. 20070406-03, "Car Bomb Explodes Outside Sadr City Joint Security Station," Multi-National Division-Baghdad Public Affairs, 2nd BCT, 82nd Abn. Div. Public Affairs, April 6, 2007.

432 As demonstrated above and stated in "The Jim Lehrer Show," Interview with General David Petraeus, U.S. Army, Commanding General, Multi-National Force-Iraq; Subject: The Situation in Iraq; Interviewer: Jim Lehrer; April 4, 2007.

433 Southwest of Baghdad, U.S. forces detained associates of a Libyan foreign fighter facilitator, suggesting that his network operated in that arc. Multi-National Force-Iraq Release No. A070525b, "Coalition Forces Nab 20 Suspected Al-Qaeda Terrorists," Multi-National Force-Iraq CPIC, May 25, 2007. In addition, U.S. forces found an enormous weapons cache (a "supermarket" type that usually feeds smaller, local caches) in a rural area between Iskandariyah and the Euphrates River.

434 The first edition of the *Iraq Report*, "From New Way Forward to New Commander," traced the movement of insurgents around the belts and from the belts into Baghdad in early 2007.

435 Multi-National Corps-Iraq Release No. 20070408-04, "Three known insurgents detained," Multi-National Division-Baghdad PAO, April 8. 2007.

436 Multi-National Corps-Iraq Release No. 20070428-13, "US, Iraqi Raid in Mahmudiyah Nets Iranian-marked Rockets, Mortars," Multi-National Division-Center PAO, April 28, 2007.

437 Multi-National Corps-Iraq Release No. 20070430-21, "Iraqi Soldiers Find VBIED in Mahmudiyah Area," Multi-National Division-Center PAO, April 30, 2007.

438 Multi-National Corps-Iraq Release No. 20070611-01, "Coalition Checkpoint Attacked," Multi-National Division-Center PAO, June 11, 2007.

439 Multi-National Corps-Iraq Release No. 20070515-09, "Search for Missing Soldiers Continues," Multi-National Division-Center PAO, May 15, 2007.

440 It is not clear from open sources whether al Qaeda traveled primarily in a counterclockwise movement, flowing from Anbar to Salman Pak (and from there to Tarmiyah), or in a clockwise movement, flowing from Salman Pak to Fallujah (and from there to Tarmiyah).

441 Press briefing by Major General Rick Lynch, Multi-National Division-Center, Topic: Operation Marne Torch, Location: The Combined Press Information Center, Baghdad, Iraq, June 24, 2007.

442 Press briefing by Major General Rick Lynch, Multi-National Division-Center,

Topic: Operation Marne Torch, Location: The Combined Press Information Center, Baghdad, Iraq, June 24, 2007.

443 Department of Defense Special Briefing with Multi-National Corps-Iraq Commander Lieutenant General Ray Odierno, June 22, 2007.

444 Department of Defense Special Briefing with Multi-National Corps-Iraq Commander Lieutenant General Ray Odierno, June 22, 2007. One indication of this connection between Salman Pak and Baghdad may be found in the flow of "extremists" (whether al Qaeda or Shia militia) through a checkpoint on the highway near Salman Pak, though the significance of this particular event is only conjecture. Multi-National Corps -Iraq Release No. 20070506-07, "Iraqi National Police Coordinates With 1-15 Infantry to Combat Extremists," Multi-National Corps-Iraq PAO, May 6, 2007.

445 Multi-National Force-Iraq Release No. A070403b, "Four-Day Operation Results in Eight Terrorists Killed; Several Weapons, Explosives Caches Destroyed," Multi-National Force-Iraq CPIC, April 3, 2007.

446 Such as a reconnaissance into Dura-iyah; Multi-National Corps-Iraq Release No. 20070517-08, "1-15 Infantry Conducts Operation Beach Yellow," Multi-National Division-Center PAO, May 17, 2007.

447 Multi-National Force-Iraq, Release No. A070414a, "Al-Qaeda Military Emir, 16 Other Suspects Detained in Raids," Multi-National Force-Iraq CPIC, April 14, 2007.

448 Press briefing by Major General Rick Lynch, Multi-National Division-Center, Topic: Operation Marne Torch, Location: The Combined Press Information Center, Baghdad, Iraq, June 24, 2007.

449 Press briefing by Major General Rick Lynch, Multi-National Division-Center, Topic: Operation Marne Torch, Location: The Combined Press Information Center, Baghdad, Iraq, June 24, 2007.

450 Press briefing by Major General Rick Lynch, Multi-National Division-Center, Topic: Operation Marne Torch, Location: The Combined Press Information Center, Baghdad, Iraq, June 24, 2007.

451 Department of Defense News Briefing, Pentagon, Presenter: Commander, 4th Brigade Combat Team, 1st Infantry Division Col. Ricky Gibbs, May 25, 2007.

452 Department of Defense News Briefing with Multi-National Corps-Iraq Commander Lieutenant General Ray Odierno, February 22, 2007.

453 The emir was positively identified as Muhammad Abdullah Abbas al Issawi, also known as Abu Abd al Sattar and Abu Akram. He also used boys, twelve and thirteen years old, as vehicle bomb drivers. Multi-National Force-Iraq Release

No. A070425b, "Al-Qaeda in Iraq Security Emir Killed," Multi-National Force-Iraq CPIC, April 25, 2007.

454 Multi-National Force-Iraq Release No. A070503b, "11 Suspected Terrorists Detained," Multi-National Force-Iraq CPIC, May 3, 2007.

455 Department of Defense Special Briefing with Multi-National Corps-Iraq Commander Lieutenant General Ray Odierno, June 22, 2007.

456 Multi-National Corps-Iraq Release No. 20070428-12, "Marines Destroy Truck Bomb near Karmah," Multi-National Force-West PAO, April 28, 2007.

457 Multi-National Force-Iraq Release No. A070511a, "Coalition Interrupts Terrorist Training, Terrorists Killed," Multi-National Force-Iraq CPIC, May 11, 2007.

458 Multi-National Force-Iraq Release No. A070514a, "Coalition Forces Detain 11 Suspects, Destroy Cache," Multi-National Force-Iraq CPIC, May 14, 2007.

459 Multi-National Force-Iraq Release No. A070516a, "Four Terrorists Killed, 30 Suspects Detained in Overnight Raids," Multi-National Force-Iraq CPIC, May 16, 2007.

460 Multi-National Force-Iraq Release No. A070521c, "3 Suspected Al-Qaeda Cell Leaders, 9 Others Detained," Multi-National Force-Iraq CPIC, May 21, 2007.

461 Multi-National Force-Iraq Release No. A070522a, "12 Iraqi Hostages Freed in Follow-on Operation," Multi-National Force-Iraq CPIC, May 22, 2007.

462 Multi-National Force-Iraq Release No. A070604b, "Terrorist Leader, Network Members Captured," Multi-National Force-Iraq CPIC, June 4, 2007.

463 Multi-National Corps-Iraq Release No. 20070504-17, "Operation Forsythe Park Update," Multi-National Force-West PAO, May 4, 2007.

464 Multi-National Corps-Iraq Release No. 20070603-14, "Iraqi Army Soldiers Kill Two Insurgents, Capture Another Near Balad," Multi-National Corps-Iraq PAO, June 3, 2007; Multi-National Corps-Iraq Release No. 20070616-12, "Raid on Suspected Safe House Near Samarra," Multi-National Corps-Iraq PAO, June 16, 2007.

465 Joint Press Conference with Secretary of Defense Robert Gates, U.S. Ambassador to Iraq Ryan Crocker, and Multi-National Force-Iraq Commander General David Petraeus, June 16, 2007.

466 Department of Defense Special Briefing with Multi-National Corps-Iraq Commander Lieutenant General Ray Odierno, June 22, 2007. Two brigades would normally include around four-to-six battalions; General Odierno added individual battalions to brigade headquarters already in the city as well.

467 Department of Defense Special Briefing with Multi-National Corps-Iraq

Commander Lieutenant General Ray Odierno, June 22, 2007.

468 Department of Defense News Briefing, Pentagon, Presenter: Commanding General of Multi-National Division-Baghdad and 1st Cavalry Division Maj. Gen. Joseph Fil, Jr., June 29, 2007.

469 Department of Defense Special Briefing with Multi-National Corps-Iraq Commander Lieutenant General Ray Odierno, June 22, 2007.

470 "The Jim Lehrer Show," Interview with General David Petraeus, U.S. Army, Commanding General, Multi-National Force-Iraq; Subject: The Situation in Iraq; Interviewer: Jim Lehrer; April 4, 2007.

471 "The Jim Lehrer Show," Interview with General David Petraeus, U.S. Army, Commanding General, Multi-National Force-Iraq; Subject: The Situation in Iraq; Interviewer: Jim Lehrer; April 4, 2007.

472 "The Jim Lehrer Show," Interview with General David Petraeus, U.S. Army, Commanding General, Multi-National Force-Iraq; Subject: The Situation in Iraq; Interviewer: Jim Lehrer; April 4, 2007.

473 Department of Defense News Briefing with Multi-National Division-Baghdad Commander Major General Joseph Fil, February 16, 2007.

474 "Span-of-control" is the term that the military uses to describe the number of subordinates a commander controls, as there is a limit to how many different subordinate units one person can command and his headquarters can control. As a rule of thumb, a good commander cannot effectively control more than five major subordinate units engaged in active operations at a time.

475 Multi-National Corps-Iraq Release No. 20070402-02, "3rd Infantry Division (Headquarters) arrives in Iraq" April 2, 2007.

476 Department of Defense News Briefing with Multi-National Division-Baghdad Commander Major General Joseph Fil, February 16, 2007. Lieutenant General Odierno (not Major General Fil) would have made the request for an additional Division Headquarters of General Petraeus, and he in turn would have asked the Army or the Joint Staff.

477 General Petraeus' and Lieutenant General Odierno's initial evaluation of the belts' importance is implicit in General Fil's comments. The deployment of the Stryker brigade to reinforce Diyala in March (which General Petraeus said was part of a chase or squirt, "The Jim Lehrer Show," Interview with General David Petraeus, U.S. Army, Commanding General, Multi-National Force-Iraq; Subject: The Situation in Iraq; Interviewer: Jim Lehrer, April 4, 2007) was not the genesis of the battle for the belts.

478 Press briefing by Major General Rick Lynch, Multi-National Division-Center,

Topic: Operation Marne Torch, Location: The Combined Press Information Center, Baghdad, Iraq, June 24, 2007.

479 Department of Defense Press Briefing with Multi-National Corps-Iraq Commander Lieutenant General Ray Odierno, May 31, 2007.

480 Joint Press Conference with Secretary of Defense Robert Gates, U.S. Ambassador to Iraq Ryan Crocker, and Multi-National Force-Iraq Commander General David Petraeus, June 16, 2007.

481 Multi-National Corps-Iraq Release No. 20070528-03, "3rd Combat Aviation Brigade Arrived in Iraq 3rd CAB PAO Release," Multi-National Division-Center PAO, May 28, 2007.

482 Multi-National Corps-Iraq Release No. 20070605-03, "Helicopters Conduct Air Strike," Multi-National Division-Center PAO, June 5, 2007; Multi-National Corps-Iraq Release No. 20070606-13, "1-15 Inf. Conducts Air Assault Mission, Destroys Enemy Cache," Multi-National Division-Center PAO, June 6, 2007.

483 Department of Defense Special Briefing with Multi-National Corps-Iraq Commander Lieutenant General Ray Odierno, June 22, 2007.

484 Department of Defense Special Briefing with Multi-National Corps-Iraq Commander Lieutenant General Ray Odierno, June 22, 2007.

485 Lieutenant General Raymond Odierno, MNC-I, interview with John Roberts, CNN's "American Morning," June 20, 2007.

486 Department of Defense Special Briefing with Multi-National Corps-Iraq Commander Lieutenant General Ray Odierno, June 22, 2007.

487 There were six named operations in the Baqubah area of operations (called AO Regular by U.S. forces), and four in the arc north and east of the city (AO Charger). "Greywolf: Making a Difference," slides provided by 3-1 Cavalry PAO, October 25, 2007.

488 Joshua, Partlow, Washington Post Foreign Service, "Troops Take Embattled Baqubah Bit by Bit, U.S. Commander Says," *Washington Post*, Tuesday, June 26, 2007; Michael R. Gordon, "U.S. Seeks to Block Exits for Iraq Insurgents," *The New York Times*, Tuesday, June 20, 2007.

489 Alissa J. Rubin and Graham Bowley, "At Least 12 U.S. Troops Killed in Iraq in 2 Days," *The New York Times*, June 21, 2007.

490 Lauren Frayer, "Soldiers roll on Baqubah, 22 enemy dead," *The Associated Press*, Tuesday, June 19, 2007; MNC-I Release No. 2007623-01, "CF, ISF searches yield torture chamber, bomb-rigged houses in Baqouba,"MND-North PAO, June 23, 2007; MNC-I Release No. 20070624-01, "ISF and CF deliver food and water to people in Baqouba,"MND-North PAO, June 24, 2007; MNC-I Release No. 20070625-01, "ISF,

CF discover execution house, illegal prison in Baqouba,"Multinational Division North-PAO, June 25, 2007.

491 Alexandra Zavis, "Militants' Baqubah fiefdom is liberated," *Los Angeles Times*, June 26, 2007.

492 Lauren Frayer, "U.S. Makes Improbable Sunni Ally in Iraq," *Associated Press*, June 23, 2007; Joe Klein, "Iraq; Turning on al-Qaeda in Baqubah," *Time Magazine*, Thursday, Jun. 21, 2007; Michael R. Gordon, "U.S. Seeks to Block Exits for Iraq Insurgents," *New York Times*, June 20, 2007.

493 MNC-I Release No. 20070605-02, "Iraqi Army forces detain two suspected al-Qaeda insurgents in Diyala Province." MNC-Iraq PAO, June 5, 2007.

494 Michael R. Gordon, "U.S. Seeks to Block Exits for Iraq Insurgents," *New York Times*, June 20, 2007.

495 Michael R. Gordon, "U.S. Seeks to Block Exits for Iraq Insurgents," *New York Times*, June 20, 2007.

496 Lauren Frayer, "Odierno: 80% of al-Qaida leaders fled Baqubah," *Associated Press*, Friday, June 22, 2007.

497 Michael R. Gordon, "For G.I.'s in Iraq, a Harrowing Day Facing a Trap," *New York Times*," June 26, 2007.

498 Michael R. Gordon, "For G.I.'s in Iraq, a Harrowing Day Facing a Trap," *New York Times*," June 26, 2007.

499 Joe Klein, "Iraq; Turning on al-Qaeda in Baqubah," *Time Magazine*, Thursday, Jun. 21, 2007; Lauren Frayer, "U.S. Makes Improbable Sunni Ally in Iraq," *Associated Press*, June 23, 2007; Joshua Partlow, "Troops Take Embattled Baqubah Bit by Bit, U.S. Commander Says," *Washington Post*, Tuesday, June 26, 2007, Page A17.

500 Joshua Partlow, "Troops Take Embattled Baqubah Bit by Bit, U.S. Commander Says," *Washington Post*, Tuesday, June 26, 2007, Page A17.

501 MNC-I Release No. 20070624-01, "ISF and CF deliver food and water to people in Baqouba,"MND-North PAO, June 24, 2007.

502 MNC-I Release No. 20070718-09, "Coalition Forces take offensive into eastern Baqouba," MND-North PAO, July 18, 2007; MNC-I Release No. 20070720-14, "GOI working to bring services back to Diyala," MND-North PAO," July 20, 2007.

503 MNC-I Release No. 20070803-05, "Local leaders meet to discuss issues affecting Baqouba," MND-North PAO, August 3, 2007.

504 MNC-I Release No. 20070801-04, "IA, Stryker leaders assess progress in Baqouba," MNC-Iraq PAO, August 1, 2007.

505 MNC-I Release No. 20070803-05, "Local leaders meet to discuss issues affecting

Baqouba," MND-North PAO, August 3, 2007.

506   MNC-I Release No. 20070705-08, "Baqouba Tribal Council meets to address concerns," MND-North PAO , July 5, 2007.

507   MNC-I Release No. 20070713-03, "Ubaidi, Anbakia tribes sign peace agreement in Diyala," MND-North PAO, July 13, 2007.

508   MNC-I, Release No. 20070709-07, "'Arrowhead Ripper' continues to deny terrorists resources," MND-North PAO, July 9, 2007.

509   MNC-I Release No. 20070718-09, "Coalition Forces take offensive into eastern Baqouba," MND-North PAO, July 18, 2007.

510   MNC-I Release No. 20070811-05, "Baqouba Guardians help secure city," MND-North PAO, August 11, 2007.

511   MNC-I Release No. 20070811-05, "Baqouba Guardians help secure city," MND-North PAO, August 11, 2007.

512   MNC-I Release No. 20070816-07, "Baqouba Guardians with IP repel al-Qaeda attack," MND-North PAO, August 16, 2007.

513   MNC-I Release No. 20070804-05, "Air assault south of Baqouba destroys four VBIEDs," MND-North PAO, August 4, 2007.

514   MNC-I Release No. 20070810-06, "Operation William Wallace clears Abu Tina," MND-North PAO, August 10, 2007.

515   John F. Burns, "Militants Said to Flee Before U.S. Offensive," *New York Times*, June 23, 2007; Alexandra Zavis, "Militants' Baqubah fiefdom is liberated," *Los Angeles Times*, June 26, 2007.

516   Joshua Partlow, "Troops Take Embattled Baqubah Bit by Bit, U.S. Commander Says," *Washington Post*, Tuesday, June 26, 2007, Page A17.

517   MNC-I Release No.20070724-02, "Khalis tribal leaders sign peace agreement," MND-North PAO, July 24, 2007; MNC-I Release No. 20070226-12, "Iraqi Army, Coalition Forces disrupt terrorist cells in Titten,"

MND-North PAO, Feb. 26, 2007.

518   Department of Defense Special Briefing with Col. Brian Jones, Commander, 3rd BCT, 4th Infantry Division, August, 4 2006.

519   Colonel David Sutherland, Interview with the Institute for the Study of War, October 25, 2007; MNF-I Release No. A070222b, "IA and CF detain Iraqi Police official in Baqubah," Baghdad, Iraq, February 22, 2007.

520   "Greywolf: Making a Difference," slides provided by 3-1 Cavalry PAO, October 25, 2007.

521 MNC-I Release No. 20071006-01, "Iraqi Special Operations Forces, U.S. Special Forces detain extremist company commander," Multi-National Corps-Iraq PAO, October 6, 2007.

522 MNC-I Release No. 20070226-01, "Iraqi Police, Coalition Forces Discover Large EFP Cache," MND-North PAO, Feb. 26, 2007.

523 MNF-I Release A070727a, "Coalition Forces Detain Four Suspected Special Groups Terrorists," July 27, 2007; MNF-I Release A070902a, "Coalition Forces detain seven suspected weapons facilitator," Sep. 2, 2007.

524 MNF-I Press Release A071005a, "Coalition Forces target Special Groups member, kill 25 terrorists," Oct. 5, 2007.

525 MND-I Release No. 20071006-01, "Iraqi Special Operations Forces, U.S. Special Forces detain extremist company commander," Multi-National Corps-Iraq PAO, October 6, 2007.

526 MNF-I Release A070720a, "Coalition Forces Capture High Value Terrorist with Ties to IRGC-QF," July 20, 2007.

527 Staff Sgt. Russell Bassett, "CLC Tip Leads to Massive EFP, Explosives Cache," DVIDs, October 25, 2007.

528 MNC-I Release No. 20061206-07, "VBIED, drive-by attack kills three, wounds four including children," Dec. 6, 2006; MNC-I Release No. 20070106-01, "VBIED targets IA soldiers in Khalis," MND-North PAO, June 6, 2007; MNC-I Release No. 20070206-05, "Coalition force members treat citizens, IP targeted in Khalis explosion," MND-North PAO, Feb. 6, 2007; MNC-I Release No. 20070330-17, "Three suicide VBIEDs target Khalis population," MND-North PAO, March 30, 2007; MNC-I Release No. 20070501-02, "Suicide bomber attacks funeral in Khalis," MND-North PAO, May 1, 2007.

529 Amran Awad, "Explosion of Two Car Bombs on Concrete Carrier Convoy in Khalis," *Aswat al-Iraq News Service*, May 5, 2007, Translation from Arabic.

530 Amran Awad, "Mortar Attacks on Village North of Khalis," *Aswat al-Iraq News Service*, May 1, 2007, Translation from Arabic; Amran Awad, "Explosion of Two Car Bombs on Concrete Carrier Convoy in Khalis," *Aswat al-Iraq News Service*, May 2, 2007, Translation from Arabic; Amran Awad, "Death of Two Civilians in Mortar Attack in Khalis," *Aswat al-Iraq News Service*, May 4, 2006, Translation from Arabic.

531 Amran Awad, "Death of Five Civilians in Clashes West of Hebheb," *Aswat al-Iraq News Service*, May 5, 2007, Translation from Arabic.

532 Richard A. Oppel Jr. and Khalid Al-Ansary, The New York Times Media Group, Karim Hilmi and Muhanad Seloom contributed reporting from Baghdad, and

Iraqi employees contributed from Diyala and Mosul, "At least 18 die in truck bomb blast near Fallujah," *The International Herald Tribune,* June 6, 2007; Amran Awad, "Gunmen Kidnap Seven University Students North of Baghdad." *Aswat al-Iraq News Service,* June 7, 2007, Translation from Arabic.

533 MNC-I Release No. 20070623-06, "Iraqi Army kill al-Qaeda gunmen during checkpoint attack," MND-North PAO, June 23, 2007; MNC-I Release No. 20070622-12, "Coalition Forces kill 17 al-Qaeda gunmen near Khalis," MND-North PAO, June 22, 2007.

534 Hussein Kadhim, McClatchy Newspapers, "Roundup of violence in Iraq," *McClatchy-Tribune News Service,* June 21, 2007.

535 MNC-I Release No. 20070622-12, "Coalition Forces kill 17 al-Qaeda gunmen near Khalis," MND-North PAO, June 22, 2007.

536 MNC-I Release No. 20070622-12, "Coalition Forces kill 17 al-Qaeda gunmen near Khalis," MND-North PAO, June 22, 2007.

537 MNC-I Release No. 20070628-06, "Khalis Police disrupt village firefight,"MND-North PAO, June 28, 2007; location of village: Aswat al-Iraq News Service. "Death of Two Civilians in Mortar Attack in Khalis." Amran Awad. 5/4/07.

538 MNF-I Release A070624a, "Coalition operation uncovers multiple caches," Baghdad, Iraq, June 24, 2007.

539 Department of Defense Bloggers roundtable with Lieutenant Colonel Andrew Poppas, Commander, 5th Squadron 73rd Cavalry 82nd Airborne, "Operation Ithaca via Teleconference from Iraq," Tuesday, July 17, 2007.

540 "Greywolf: Making a Difference," slides provided by 3-1 Cavalry PAO, October 25, 2007.

541 MNF-I Release A070704a, "Coalition Forces kill 25, detain 5 and uncover caches in Diyala," July 4, 2007.

542 MNC-I Release No. 20070703-04, "CF destroy homemade explosives factory," MND-North PAO, July 3, 2007. The press release locates the village in the Diyala River Valley, but spells it "Mikbisa," which seems to be a typographical error. See the follow-up release: MNF-I Release A070704a, "Coalition Forces kill 25, detain 5 and uncover caches in Diyala," July 4, 2007.

543 Sam Dagher, "US faced with Iraqi Army turncoats," Christian Science Monitor, July 10, 2007.

544 Sam Dagher, "US faced with Iraqi Army turncoats," Christian Science Monitor, July 10, 2007.

545   Sam Dagher, "US faced with Iraqi Army turncoats," *Christian Science Monitor*, July 10, 2007.

546   MNC-I Release No. 20071006-01, "Iraqi Special Operations Forces, U.S. Special Forces detain extremist company commander," MNC-Iraq PAO, October 6, 2007.

547   MNC-I Release No. 20071006-01, "Iraqi Special Operations Forces, U.S. Special Forces detain extremist company commander," MNC-Iraq PAO, October 6, 2007.

548   Department of Defense Bloggers roundtable with Lieutenant Colonel Andrew Poppas, Commander, 5th Squadron 73rd Cavalry 82nd Airborne, "Operation Ithaca via Teleconference from Iraq," Tuesday, July 17, 2007; for the identity of the village to which the displaced persons fled, see MNF-I Feature Story, Pfc. Ben Fox, 3rd Brigade Combat Team, 1st Cavalry Division, "Operation Olympus opens route, secures towns," July 28, 2007.

549   Department of Defense Bloggers roundtable with Lieutenant Colonel Andrew Poppas, Commander, 5th Squadron 73rd Cavalry 82nd Airborne, "Operation Ithaca via Teleconference from Iraq," Tuesday, July 17, 2007.

550   Gerry J. Gilmore, American Forces Press Service, "Operation Ithaca' Surprises, Pummels, al Qaeda Forces," *Defense Link*, Jul 18, 2007.

551   Gerry J. Gilmore, American Forces Press Service, "Operation Ithaca' Surprises, Pummels, al Qaeda Forces," *Defense Link*, Jul 18, 2007.

552   MNC-I Release No. 20070715-07, "Setback for al-Qaida operatives in Diyala," MND-North PAO, July 15, 2007; Department of Defense Bloggers roundtable with Lieutenant Colonel Andrew Poppas, Commander, 5th Squadron 73rd Cavalry 82nd Airborne, "Operation Ithaca via Teleconference from Iraq," Tuesday, July 17, 2007.

553   Pfc. Ben Fox, 3rd Brigade Combat Team, 1st Cavalry Division, "Operation Olympus opens route, secures towns," MNF-I Feature Story, Jul 28, 2007.

554   Pfc. Ben Fox, 3rd Brigade Combat Team, 1st Cavalry Division, "Operation Olympus opens route, secures towns," MNF-I Feature Story, Jul 28, 2007.

555   Pfc. Ben Fox, 3rd Brigade Combat Team, 1st Cavalry Division, "Operation Olympus opens route, secures towns," MNF-I Feature Story, Jul 28, 2007.

556   MNC-I Release No. 20070713-03, "Ubaidi, Anbakia tribes sign peace agreement in Diyala," MND-North PAO, July 13, 2007. The Iraq Report uses "district" to convey the Iraqi *qada*, a subdivision of a province most equivalent to an American county. The Iraq Report uses "city" or "municipality" to describe the municipal level of government, the Iraqi *nahia*. Khalis is both a *nahia* and a *qada*.

557 Colonel David Sutherland, Civilian Defense Experts Conference Call, November 9, 2007.

558 "Greywolf: Making a Difference," slides provided by 3-1 Cavalry PAO, October 25, 2007. The cooperation of Obeidis from Dojima also corresponds temporally with attempts to kidnap students: Amran Awad, "Gunmen Kidnap Seven University Students North of Baghdad," Aswat al-Iraq News Service, June 7, 2007, Translation from Arabic; Richard A. Oppel Jr. and Khalid Al-Ansary, The New York Times Media Group, and Iraqi employees contributed from Diyala and Mosul, "At least 18 die in truck bomb blast near Fallujah," *The International Herald Tribune*, June 6, 2007.

559 Colonel David Sutherland, Civilian Defense Experts Conference Call, November 9, 2007.

560 Sheikh Majeed al Bayati was kidnapped by a major criminal militia leader in Baghdad in late October, perhaps illustrating the militia's assessment of his activities. See "7 freed tribal chiefs arrive in Diyala," Aswat Aliraq, October 31, 2007. Rogue JAM leader, Arkhan Hasnawi, kidnapped Sheikh Majeed and others in Sha'ab after they attended a reconciliation meeting in the (JAM-guarded) al Rashid hotel. Arkhan Hasnawi offered to release the others (Shia) for ransom, but not Sheikh Majeed and the other Bayati (the Sunni). The Iraqi Security Forces later rescued all the hostages but one, who had been killed. According to Sutherland, none of the individuals captured participated in Diyala reconciliation talks with Greywolf. See Colonel David Sutherland, Civilian Defense Experts Conference Call, November 9, 2007.

561 "Greywolf: Making a Difference," slides provided by 3-1 Cavalry PAO, October 25, 2007. Fifteen Sunni and Shia tribal leaders in the Khalis district met with U.S. and Iraqi Army commanders, provincial director of police, the mayor of Khalis, the Khalis police chief, the Khalis Emergency Response Force commander, and Khalis city council members.

562 "Tribal Leaders continue reconciliation efforts across Diyala," MND-N Public Affairs, August 4, 2007.

563 "Greywolf: Making a Difference," slides provided by 3-1 Cavalry PAO, October 25, 2007; some points paraphrased.

564 Colonel David Sutherland, Civilian Defense Experts Conference Call, November 9, 2007.

565 "Leaders of Diyala River Valley recommit to reconciliation," Multi-National Division-North, Public Affairs Office, September 9, 2007.

566 Colonel David Sutherland, Commander, Greywolf Brigade Combat Team, Interview with the Institute for the Study of War, October 25, 2007.

567   Colonel David Sutherland, Commander, Greywolf Brigade Combat Team, Interview with the Institute for the Study of War, October 25, 2007.

568   Hamid Ahmed, "Mortars, Bombs in Iraq's North Kill 11," *Associated Press*, August 18, 2007; MNC-I Release No. 20070819-04, "Three killed, 22 wounded in Khalis market attack," Multi-National Division-North PAO, August 19, 2007.

569   MNC-I Release No. 20070822-04, "Khalis protest a sign of democracy in Diyala," Multi-National Division-North PAO, August 22, 2007.

570   MNC-I Release No. 20070828-02, "33 insurgents killed, Khalis waterway open," Multi-National Division-North PAO, August 28, 2007; The release states that a ZU was discovered, but the weapon was probably a ZSU. For the relative location of Gobia and Khalis, see Steven R. Hurst, "1 million Shiites ordered out of Karbala after violence; U.S., Iraqi forces kill 33 militants," *Associated Press*, August 28, 2007.

571   Colonel David Sutherland, Commander, Greywolf Brigade Combat Team, Interview with the Institute for the Study of War, October 25, 2007.

572   "Gunmen from the Mahdi Militia Kidnap Member of the Emergency Battalion in Khalis," Iqraa Press, September 8, 2007l; "Bluetooth Clip Provokes Fear in Khalis," Iqraa Press, September 8, 2007; "Death of Three and One Other Wounded from the relatives of a Tribal Leader in Khalis," Aswat al-Iraq News Service, September 12, 2007; "Jaysh al-Maydi Kidnaps Man near the Khalis Bank and Leaves his Body near the Industrial Area," Iqraa Press , September 21, 2007.

573   "Battles Between Al-Qaeda and Men of the Awakening in Hebheb in the Khalis Qadaa," *Igraa Press*, October 15, 2007; "Iraqi police find bodies in Baghdad, Diyala; gunmen blow up bridge in Ba'qubah," *BBC*, October 15, 2007; Zuhair al-Ubaydi "14 Mortar Rounds Fall on Khalis Qadaa this morning." *Iqraa Press*, October 19, 2007; Zuhair al-Ubaydi, "Kidnapping of Six Civilians from One Family in the Al-Aswad area in Qadaa Khalis" *Iqraa Press*, October 25, 2007.

574   Zuhair al-Ubaydi, "Three Gunmen Killed Near Al-Aswad in Khalis Qadaa," *Iqraa Press*, October 15, 2007; Muneer Ahmed and Zuhair al-Ubaydi, "Martyrdom and Wounding of Three Civilians in Armed Attacks," *Iqraa Press*, October 17, 2007; Zuhair al-Ubaydi, "Death of Gunmen and Arrest of Another, Freeing of Kidnappees in Khalis," *Iqraa Press*, October 22, 2007.

575   "Greywolf: Making a Difference," slides provided by 3-1 Cavalry PAO, October 25, 2007; Haidar Muhammad,. "National Reconciliation Conference in Khalis," *Igraa Press*, October 16, 2007.

576   MNF-I Release A070919b, "Coalition Forces kill one terrorist, detain 7 suspects," Sept. 19, 2007; MNC-I Release No. 20071002-10, "Coalition Forces detain terrorist

leaders responsible for IED/EFP attacks in Diyala," MND-North PAO, October 2, 2007.

577 MNF-I Release A070727a, "Coalition Forces Detain Four Suspected Special Groups Terrorists," July 27, 2007; MNF-I Release A070804b, "Coalition Forces Kill Four Suspected Secret Cell Terrorists, Detain Eighteen," Aug. 4, 2007; MNF-I Release A070820a, "Coalition Forces Kill Eight, Detain Three, Capturing a Special Groups Leader and Smuggler of Iranian Weapons," August 20, 2007; MNF-I Release A070902a, "Coalition Forces detain seven suspected weapons facilitators," Sep. 2, 2007.

578 MNF-I Press Release A071005a, "Coalition Forces target Special Groups member, kill 25 terrorists," October 5, 2007.

579 Colonel David Sutherland, Commander, Greywolf Brigade Combat Team, Interview with Katerina Kratovac, September 18, 2007.

580 Colonel David Sutherland, Commander, Greywolf Brigade Combat Team, Interview with Katerina Kratovac, September 18, 2007.

581 DoD Press Briefing with Army Lieutenant General Ray Odierno, Commander, Multinational Corps-Iraq, on Ongoing Security Operations in Iraq, August 17, 2007.

582 DoD Press Briefing with Army Lieutenant General Ray Odierno, Commander, Multinational Corps-Iraq, on Ongoing Security Operations in Iraq, August 17, 2007.

583 MNC-I Release No. 20070814-06, "Operation Lightning Hammer pursues al-Qaeda," MND-North PAO, August 14, 2007.

584 Colonel David Sutherland, Commander, Greywolf Brigade Combat Team, Interview with the Institute for the Study of War, October 25, 2007.

585 Colonel David Sutherland, Commander, Greywolf Brigade Combat Team, Interview with the Institute for the Study of War, October 25, 2007.

586 "Greywolf: Making a Difference," slides provided by 3-1 Cavalry PAO, October 25, 2007; MNC-I Release No. 20070824-11, "Iraqi citizens, police stand up to Al-Qaeda attack," Multi-National Division-North PAO, August 24, 2007; "Qaeda and Iraq militants clash," News24, August 23, 2007, Available at: <http://www.news24.com/News24/World/Iraq/0,,2-10-1460_2169807,00.html>.

587 "Greywolf: Making a Difference," slides provided by 3-1 Cavalry PAO, October 25, 2007.

588 Colonel David Sutherland, Commander, Greywolf Brigade Combat Team, Interview with the Institute for the Study of War, October 25, 2007.

589 Colonel David Sutherland, Commander, Greywolf Brigade Combat Team, Interview with the Institute for the Study of War, October 25, 2007.

590 Colonel David Sutherland, Commander, Greywolf Brigade Combat Team, Interview with the Institute for the Study of War, October 25, 2007.

591 MND-N Release No. 20071029-01, "Task Force Iron Soldiers discover significant caches," Multi-National Division-North PAO, October 29, 2007.

592 Colonel David Sutherland, Commander, Greywolf Brigade Combat Team, Interview with the Institute for the Study of War, October 25, 2007.

593 "Tammimi, Jibouri tribes uphold reconciliation in Diyala," MNF-I Daily Story, October 29, 2007.

594 Colonel David Sutherland, Commander, Greywolf Brigade Combat Team, Interview with the Institute for the Study of War, October 25, 2007.

595 "AQI: Increasingly extreme behavior," Multi-National Forces-Iraq, November 22, 2007.

596 "Greywolf: Making a Difference," slides provided by 3-1 Cavalry PAO, October 25, 2007.

597 MNC-I Release No. 20070913-05, "Released detainees pledge to uphold Rule of Law in Baqouba," Multi-National Division-North PAO, September 13, 2007.

598 Colonel David Sutherland, Commander, Greywolf Brigade Combat Team, Interview with Katerina Kratovac, September 18, 2007.

599 Colonel David Sutherland, Commander, Greywolf Brigade Combat Team, Interview with Katerina Kratovac, September 18, 2007.

600 DoD News Briefing with Maj. Gen. Mixon, Commander, Multi-National Division-North, October 26, 2007.

601 Colonel David Sutherland, Commander, Greywolf Brigade Combat Team, Interview with the Institute for the Study of War, October 25, 2007.

602 "Greywolf: Making a Difference," slides provided by 3-1 Cavalry PAO, October 25, 2007.

603 Iqraa Press. "Battles Between Al-Qaeda and Men of the Awakening in Hebheb in the Khalis Qadaa." [Special - No correspondent]. October 14, 2007; Iqraa Press. "National Reconciliation Conference in Khalis." Haidar Muhammad, October 16, 2007.

604 Press Conference: Lt. Gen. Abud Qanbar and Lt. Gen. Raymond T. Odierno, September 20, 2007.

605 Colonel David Sutherland, Commander, Greywolf Brigade Combat Team, Interview with Katerina Kratovac, September 18, 2007.

606 Colonel David Sutherland, Commander, Greywolf Brigade Combat Team, Interview with the Institute for the Study of War, October 25, 2007.

607 Colonel David Sutherland, Commander, Greywolf Brigade Combat Team, Interview with the Institute for the Study of War, October 25, 2007.

608 Department of Defense News Briefing, Pentagon, Presenter: Commanding General of Multi-National Division Baghdad and 1st Cavalry Division Maj. Gen. Joseph Fil, Jr., June 29, 2007.

609 Department of Defense News Briefing, Pentagon, Presenter: Commanding General of Multi-National Division Baghdad and 1st Cavalry Division Maj. Gen. Joseph Fil, Jr., June 29, 2007.

610 Department of Defense News Briefing, Pentagon, Presenter: Commanding General of Multi-National Division Baghdad and 1st Cavalry Division Maj. Gen. Joseph Fil, Jr., June 29, 2007.

611 Wesley Morgan, "Backgrounder #4, Order of Battle," July 1, 2007, www.understandingwar.org.

612 Patrick Gaughen, "Baghdad Neighborhood Project: Saydiyah," Backgrounder #15, Institute for the Study of War, November 21, 2007.

613 RN 20070621-07, "Marne Torch continues clearing insurgent safe havens," June 21, 2007.

614 Department of Defense Press Briefing with Colonel Terry R. Ferrell, Commander, 2nd Brigade Combat Team, 3rd Infantry Division, Multi-National Division-Center, December 3, 2007.

615 Colonel Terry Ferrell, Commander 2nd Brigade, 3rd Infantry Division. *DoD News Briefing.* 12/3/2007.

616 Colonel Terry Ferrell, Commander 2nd Brigade, 3rd Infantry Division. *DoD News Briefing.* 12/3/2007

617 Interview with Colonel Terry Ferrell, Commander 2nd Brigade Combat Team, 3rd Infantry Division. *Institute for the Study of War.* 1/22/2008.

618 Interview with Colonel Terry Ferrell, Commander 2nd Brigade Combat Team, 3rd Infantry Division. *Institute for the Study of War.* 1/22/2008.

619 Department of Defense Press Briefing with Colonel Terry Ferrell, Commander 2nd Brigade, 3rd Infantry Division, December 3, 2007; Department of Defense Bloggers Roundtable with Colonel Terry Ferrell, Commander 2nd Brigade, 3rd Infantry Division, February 14, 2008; Interview with Colonel Terry Ferrell,

Commander 2nd Brigade Combat Team, 3rd Infantry Division, Institute for the Study of War, January 22, 2008.

620 Interview with Colonel Terry Ferrell, Commander 2nd Brigade Combat Team, 3rd Infantry Division. Institute for the Study of War, January 22, 2008.

621 Colonel Dan Ball, Commander Combat Aviation Brigade, 3rd Infantry Division. Department of Defense Bloggers Roundtable, December 20, 2007.

622 Multi-National Division-Center Public Affairs Officer. Release No. 20070716-05: "MND-C begins new offensive operations." July 16, 2007.

623 Multi-National Corps-Iraq Public Affairs Officer. Release No. 20070713-21 "U.S. Special Forces apprehend high-level Al-Qaeda cell leader." July 13, 2007.

624 Multi-National Force - Iraq Public Affairs Officer. Release A070714a "Al-Qaeda cell leader, 17 suspected bombers captured." July 14, 2007.; Lieutenant General Ray Odierno, Commanding General, Multi-National Corps - Iraq. *DoD News Briefing*. July 19, 2007.

625 Drew Brown. "New Offensive Nets Little at Start." *Stars and Stripes*. August 17, 2007.

626 Multi-National Division-Center Public Affairs Officer. Release No. 20070918-01: "Marne Husky ends with capture of insurgent." September 18, 2007.

627 Interview with Colonel Dan Ball, Commander Combat Aviation Brigade, 3rd Infantry Division. Institute for the Study of War. 1/8/2008.

628 Michael Gordon, "The Former-Insurgent Counterinsurgency," *The New York Times*, September 2, 2007.

629 Department of Defense Bloggers Roundtable with Colonel Terry R. Ferrell, Commander, 2nd Brigade Combat Team, 3rd Infantry Division, Multi-National Division-Center, October 16, 2007.

630 Interview with Colonel Terry Ferrell, Commander 2nd Brigade Combat Team, 3rd Infantry Division. Institute for the Study of War. January 22, 2008.

631 Interview with Colonel Dan Ball, Commander Combat Aviation Brigade, 3rd Infantry Division. Institute for the Study of War. January 8, 2008.

632 Ibid.

633 Ibid., MNF-I RN 20070910-05, "In 24-hr battle, Hawr Rajab turns on al-Qaeda," September 10, 2007.

634 Colonel Terry Ferrell, Commander 2nd Brigade Combat Team, 3rd Infantry Division. DoD Bloggers Roundtable. October 16, 2007.

635   Colonel Terry Ferrell, Commander 2nd Brigade Combat Team, 3rd Infantry Division. DoD Bloggers Roundtable. October 16, 2007.

636   Colonel Terry Ferrell, Commander 2nd Brigade Combat Team, 3rd Infantry Division. DoD Bloggers Roundtable. October 16, 2007.

637   Colonel Terry Ferrell, Commander 2nd Brigade Combat Team, 3rd Infantry Division. DoD Bloggers Roundtable. October 16, 2007.

638   Colonel Terry Ferrell, Commander 2nd Brigade Combat Team, 3rd Infantry Division. DoD Bloggers Roundtable. October 16, 2007.

639   Colonel Terry Ferrell, Commander 2nd HBCT, 3rd Infantry Division on January 22, 2008.

640   Colonel Terry Ferrell, Commander 2nd Brigade, 3rd Infantry Division. DoD News Briefing. December 3, 2007.

641   Hendren, John. "Troops Killed in Battle for the Border; The deaths in western Iraq come as American forces fight for control of the area, believed to be a foreign supply route for the insurgency." Los Angeles Times. August 3, 2005; Louise Roug, "Shiites Observe Holy Day Amid Heavy Security." Los Angeles Times. March 21, 2006; "Breaking: 3 Car Bombs in Abu Disheer," Buratha News Service. March 31, 2006. Translation from Arabic.; "Body of Kidnapped Shi'a Child from Abu Disheer Found," Buratha News Service. May 25, 2006. Translation from Arabic.; "Mortar Attack on Popular Market in Abu Disheer," Buratha News Service. May 28, 2006. Translation from Arabic.; "16 Mortar Shells Target Abu Disheer," Buratha News Service. May 31, 2006. Translation from Arabic.; "Sectarian Crimes Against the People of Abu Disheer and the Terrorist Forces Present in Hawr Rajab and Arab Jabour," Buratha News Service. June 2, 2006. Translation from Arabic.; "8 mortar rounds and 120mm rockets fall on Abu Disheer," Buratha News Service. June 10, 2006. Translation from Arabic.; "Abu Disheer Targeted for 5th Consecutive Day," Buratha News Service. June 13, 2006. Translation from Arabic.; "Sectarian Rockets in Abu Disheer," Buratha News Service. June 18, 2007. Translation from Arabic.; "Violent Clashes in Abu Disheer Area," Buratha News Service. July 20, 2006. Translation from Arabic.; "Explosion of Sectarian Car Bomb," Buratha News Service. September 9, 2006. Translation from Arabic.; "Twenty Civilians Wounded in Mortar Attack on Abu Disheer," Buratha News Service. October 3, 2006. Translation from Arabic.; "Two Mortar Rounds Fall on Abu Disheer," Buratha News Service. October 24, 2006. Translation from Arabic.; "Three Martyred and 18 Wounded from Ahl al-Beit in Terrorist Rocket Attack on Abu Disheer," Buratha News Service. October 28, 2007. Translation from Arabic.

642 "Permission of Militias or Gunmen a Condition of Changing Residence in Baghdad," Al-Hayat, February 7, 2007. Translation from Arabic.

643 Patrick Gaughen, "Baghdad Neighborhood Project: Saydiyah," Backgrounder #15, Institute for the Study of War, November 21, 2007.

644 Patrick Gaughen, "Baghdad Neighborhood Project: Saydiyah," Backgrounder #15, Institute for the Study of War, November 21, 2007; James Glanz and Alissa Rubin, "Future Look of Iraq Complicated by Internal Migration," The New York Times, September 19, 2007; Husayn. Ali, "New Experiment for US Forces in Confronting Al-Qaeda; Peacekeeping Meetings Between Sunni and Shia Neighborhoods," Al-Hayat, September 14, 2007. Translation from Arabic; Radio Sawa, "Tawafuq Front Emphasizes its Thanks to the People of Abu Disheer for Taking in the Sunni Families that were Forced out of Hawr Rajab by Al-Qaeda," September 13, 2007. Translation from Arabic.

645 Patrick Gaughen, "Baghdad Neighborhood Project: Saydiyah," Backgrounder #15, Institute for the Study of War, November 21, 2007.

646 Patrick Gaughen, "Baghdad Neighborhood Project: Saydiyah," Backgrounder #15, Institute for the Study of War, November 21, 2007.

647 DoD Bloggers Roundtable with Col. John Riscassi, Commander, 2nd Stryker Cavalry Regiment, 25th Infantry Division, January 10, 2007.

648 Release No. 20070916-11, "Clearing Continues: Dragons and Dragoons begin Operation Dragon Talon II in Rashid, September 16, 2007.

649 Bloggers Roundtable with Col. Ricky Gibbs, Commander, 4th Brigade, 1st Infantry Division, September 28, 2007.

650 DoD Bloggers Roundtable with Col. John Riscassi, Commander, 2nd Stryker Cavalry Regiment, 25th Infantry Division, January 10, 2007.

651 Ibid.

652 DoD Press Briefing with General Joseph Fil, Commander, Multi-National Division-Baghdad, December 17, 2007.

653 Bloggers Roundtable with Col. Ricky Gibbs, Commander, 4th Brigade, 1st Infantry Division, September 28, 2007.

654 DoD Press Briefing with General Joseph Fil, Commander, Multi-National Division-Baghdad, December 17, 2007.

655 Michael R. Gordon, "Deadliest Bomb in Iraq is Made by Iran, U.S. Says," The New York Times, February 10, 2007, A6.

656 Dan Darling, "General Panic: Meet Brigadier General Qassem Suleimani, the

Commander of Iran's Anti-American Qods Force," *The Weekly Standard*, October 5, 2005.

657 Sean D. Naylor, "Iran Deeply Involved in Iraq, Petraeus Says," *Army Times*, May 24, 2007.

658 Angel Rabasa, *Beyond Al-Qaeda*, 2 vols., vol. 2 (Santa Monica, CA: Rand Corporation, 2006), 11-14.

659 Andrew Exum, "Comparing and Contrasting Hizballah and Iraq's Militias," in *Policy Watch* #1197 (The Washington Institute for Near East Policy, 2007).

660 Department of Defense Press Briefing with Multi-National Corps-Iraq Commander Lt. Gen. Ray Odierno, Topic: Ongoing Security Operations in Iraq, Location: Pentagon Briefing Room, Arlington, VA, August 17, 2007.

661 Michael Ware, "Inside Iran's Secret War for Iraq," *Time Magazine*, August 15, 2005.

662 Michael Ware, "Inside Iran's Secret War for Iraq," *Time Magazine*, August 15, 2005.

663 Edward T. Pound, "Special Report: The Iran Connection," *U.S. News and World Report*, November 14, 2004. The article notes that U.S. intelligence sources could not confirm that the fatwa had come from Iranian clerics, "but they believe it was credible."

664 Michael Ware, "Inside Iran's Secret War for Iraq," *Time Magazine*, August 15, 2005. Ware did not use the term "explosively-formed projectile," which was not yet then common currency, but the weapon he described was probably what is now known as an EFP.

665 Edward T. Pound, "Special Report: The Iran Connection," *U.S. News and World Report*, November 14, 2004.

666 Michael Ware, "Inside Iran's Secret War for Iraq," *Time Magazine*, August 15, 2005.

667 Michael Ware, "Inside Iran's Secret War for Iraq," *Time Magazine*, August 15, 2005.

668 Babak Dehghanpisheh, Melinda Liu, and Rod Norland, "We Are Your Martyrs," *Newsweek*, April 19, 2004. Mohammad Baqir al Hakim was the older brother of Abdul Aziz al Hakim, the current head of SCIRI (now renamed the Supreme Iraqi Islamic Council, or ISCI).

669 Edward T. Pound, "Special Report: The Iran Connection," *U.S. News and World Report*, November 14, 2004.

670 Kenneth Katzman, "Iran's Influence in Iraq," CRS Report for Congress, November 15, 2005.

671 Edward T. Pound, "Special Report: The Iran Connection," *U.S. News and World Report*, November 14, 2004.

672 Edward T. Pound, "Special Report: The Iran Connection," *U.S. News and World Report*, November 14, 2004.

673 Edward T. Pound, "Special Report: The Iran Connection," *U.S. News and World Report*, November 14, 2004.

674 Michael Ware, "Inside Iran's Secret War for Iraq," *Time Magazine*, August 15, 2005.

675 Michael Ware, "Inside Iran's Secret War for Iraq," *Time Magazine*, August 15, 2005.

676 677 Press Briefing by Multi-National Force-Iraq Deputy Chief of Staff for Strategic Effects Brigadier General Kevin Bergner, Topic: Security Operations in Iraq, Location: The Combined Press Information Center, Baghdad, Iraq, July 2, 2007.

678 Babak Dehghanpisheh, "Iraq's New Guns for Hire; under Seige in Baghdad, Fighters from Moqtada al Sadr's Jaysh al Mahdi Are Going Freelance, and They're Already Spreading Havoc to Once Calm Parts of the Country," *Newsweek*, May 7, 2007.

679 Multi-National Corps-Iraq Release No. 20070814-07, "Iraqi Army, U.S. Special Forces detain high-value rogue JAM Special Groups leader," August 14, 2007.

680 Multi-National Corps-Iraq Release No. 20070807-14, "Iraqi Army, U.S. Special Forces detain suspected rogue JAM recruiter; ISOF detain suspected Al-Qaeda emir," August 7, 2007; Multi-National Corps-Iraq Release No. 20070716-17, "Iraqi Army, Coalition Forces detain insurgent linked to Iranian IEDs," July 16, 2007.

681 Press Briefing with Multi-National Force-Iraq Deputy Chief of Staff for Strategic Effects Brigadier General Kevin Bergner, Security Operations in Iraq.

682 Multi-National Corps-Iraq Release No. 20070814-07, "Iraqi Army, U.S. Special Forces detain high-value rogue JAM Special Groups leader," August 14, 2007.

683 Press Briefing with Multi-National Force-Iraq Deputy Chief of Staff for Strategic Effects Brigadier General Kevin Bergner, Security Operations in Iraq.

684 Press Briefing with Multi-National Force-Iraq Deputy Chief of Staff for Strategic Effects Brigadier General Kevin Bergner, Security Operations in Iraq.

685 Hajji Yusif presumably works directly for the Qods Force Commander, General Qassim Sulleimani, but their precise relationship is not specified in the U.S. military's documentation. Press Briefing with Multi-National Force-Iraq Deputy Chief of Staff for Strategic Effects Brigadier General Kevin Bergner, Security Operations in Iraq.

686   Press Briefing with Multi-National Force-Iraq Deputy Chief of Staff for Strategic Effects Brigadier General Kevin Bergner, Security Operations in Iraq.

687   Press Briefing with Multi-National Force-Iraq Deputy Chief of Staff for Strategic Effects Brigadier General Kevin Bergner, Security Operations in Iraq.

688   Karin Bruillard, "Ex-Sadr Aide Held in American Deaths," *The Washington Post,* April 23, 2007.

689   Press Briefing with Multi-National Force-Iraq Deputy Chief of Staff for Strategic Effects Brigadier General Kevin Bergner, Security Operations in Iraq.

690   Michael R. Gordon and Dexter Filkins; Mark Mazzetti contributed reporting from Washington, and Hosham Hussein from Baghdad, "Hezbollah Helps Iraq Shiite Army, U.S. Official Says," *The New York Times,* November 28, 2006, Late Edition - Final A1.

691   Edward T. Pound, "Special Report: The Iran Connection," *U.S. News and World Report,* November 14, 2004.

692   Press briefing with Major General Rick Lynch, Multinational Division-Center, Topic: Operation Marne Torch, Location: The Combined Press Information Center, Baghdad, Iraq, June 24, 2007.

693   Robert H. Reid, "US general says Iranian-origin weapons turning up in Sunni insurgent hands" Associated Press, May 6, 2007; Department of Defense News Briefing with Col. Ricky Gibbs, Commander, 4th Brigade Combat Team, 1st Infantry Division, May 25, 2007

694   Multi-National Force-Iraq Release No. A070525b, "Coalition Forces Nab 20 Suspected Al-Qaeda Terrorists," Multi-National Force-Iraq CPIC, May 25, 2007.

695   Press briefing with Major General Rick Lynch, Multinational Division-Center, Topic: Operation Marne Torch, Location: The Combined Press Information Center, Baghdad, Iraq, June 24, 2007.

696   "2nd Brigade Soldiers have the mission of defeating insurgent activity, denying the enemy sanctuary and preventing terrorist elements from moving accelerants from the Arab Jabour area into Baghdad," according to Multi-National Corps-Iraq Release No. 20070618-03, "Marne Torch Commences in Areas South of Baghdad," Multi-National Division-Center PAO, June 18, 2007. See also: Multi-National Force-Iraq Release No. A070523b, "Four Terrorists Killed; Tied to IED Production," Multi-National Force-Iraq CPIC, May 23, 2007.

697   Press briefing with Major General Rick Lynch, Multinational Division-Center, Topic: Operation Marne Torch, Location: The Combined Press Information Center, Baghdad, Iraq, June 24, 2007.

698   Press briefing with Major General Rick Lynch, Multinational Division-Center,

Topic: Operation Marne Torch, Location: The Combined Press Information Center, Baghdad, Iraq, June 24, 2007.

699 Kim Gamel, "U.S. troops destroy boats and target roadside bomb routes south of Baghdad," Associated Press Writer, June 26, 2007.

700 Kim Gamel, "U.S. troops destroy boats and target roadside bomb routes south of Baghdad," Associated Press Writer, June 26, 2007.

701 Department of Defense Press Briefing with Commander, 4th Brigade Combat Team, 1st Infantry Division Col. Ricky Gibbs, May 25, 2007.

702 United States Army Special Operations Command News Service Release No. 070716-06, "Iraqi Forces Detain Al Qaeda Leader and EFP Facilitator in Samarra," July 16, 2007.

703 Multi-National Force-Iraq Press Release A071002a, "Coalition Forces disrupt al-Qaeda network: one killed, 10 detained," October 2, 2007.

704 Michael Ware, "Inside Iran's Secret War for Iraq," *Time Magazine*, August 15, 2005.

705 Press Briefing with Multi-National Force-Iraq Deputy Chief of Staff for Strategic Effects Brigadier General Kevin Bergner, Security Operations in Iraq.

706 Nelson Hernandez and K.I. Ibrahim, "Top Shiites Nominate a Premier for Iraq; Al-Maliki Opposed Hussein and the U.S.-Led Invasion," *The Washington Post*, April 22, 2006.; Sabrina Tavernise et al., "A Novice, but Outspoken; Jawad Al-Maliki," *The New York Times*, April 23, 2006.

707 Press Briefing with U.S. Ambassador Ryan Crocker, Location: The Combined Press Information Center, Baghdad, Iraq, August 21, 2007.

708 Sudarsan Raghavan and Robin Wright, "Iraq Expels 2 Iranians Detained by U.S., American Defense Official Calls Release 'Obviously Troubling,'" *The Washington Post*, December 30, 2006.

709 Sudarsan Raghavan and Robin Wright, "Iraq Expels 2 Iranians Detained by U.S., American Defense Official Calls Release 'Obviously Troubling,'" *The Washington Post*, December 30, 2006.

710 Multi-National Corps-Iraq Release No. A070114a, "Coalition targets Iranian influence in Northern Iraq," January 14, 2007.

711 Multi-National Force-Iraq Release A070920b, "Coalition Forces arrest Iranian Quds Force officer," September 20, 2007.

712 Multi-National Force Iraq Release A070618a, "Coalition Forces disrupt Secret Cell terrorist network," June 18, 2007.

713 Department of Defense News Briefing with Multi-National Division-Center

and 3rd Infantry Division Commander Maj. Gen. Rick Lynch, Topic: Operation Marne Husky, Location: Pentagon, Arlington, VA, August 24, 2007.

714 Human Rights Bureau of Democracy, and Labor, "Iraq," in Country Reports on Human Rights Practices 2006 (U.S. Department of State, 2007).

715 Kim Gamel, "Iraq Official Is Accused of Aiding Massacres," *Newark Star-Ledger*, February 9, 2007.

716 "Ia, Mnd-B Soldiers Act on Tip, Cordon Off Moh to Look for Kidnap Victims," U.S. Federal News, August 13, 2006.

717 Thomas Wagner, "Political Humorist Slain as Iraqi Death Toll Soars," *Newark Star-Ledger*, November 21, 2006.

718 Thomas Wagner, "Political Humorist Slain as Iraqi Death Toll Soars," *Newark Star-Ledger*, November 21, 2006.

719 Bassem Mroue and Qassim Abdul-Zahra, "Iraq Loses $8 Billion through Corruption," Associated Press Online, April 4, 2007; Damien Cave, "Iraq Raid Attempts to Cut Jaysh al Mahdi Link," *The International Herald Tribune*, February 9, 2007.

720 Alissa J. Rubin, "Trial of 2 Shiite Ex-Officials Test's Iraq's Judicial System," *The New York Times*, March 3, 2008,Late Edition - Final, Section A.

721 Alissa J. Rubin, "Trial of 2 Shiite Ex-Officials Test's Iraq's Judicial System," *The New York Times*, March 3, 2008,Late Edition - Final, Section A.

722 Joshua Partlow and Bassam Sebti, "Gunmen Kidnap Scores of Iraqis; Hussein Lawyer Slain," *The Washington Post*, June 21, 2006.

723 Associated Press, "Gunmen Release Iraq Electricity Official," The Associated Press, July 4, 2006; Associated Press, "Gunmen in Baghdad Kidnap Iraqi Diplomat Specializing in Iranian Relations," The Associated Press, July 11, 2006.

724 Ryan Lenz, "Iraqi Games Chief Part of Mass Kidnap," *The Sunday Mail* (Australia), July 16, 2006.

725 Sudarsan Raghavan, "In Iraqi Colleges, Fear for an Already Shrunken Realm; Mass Kidnapping Seen Likely to Boost Educators' Exodus," *The Washington Post*, November 16, 2006.

726 John F. Burns et al., "Dozens Abducted in Brazen Raid on Iraq Ministry," *The New York Times*, November 15, 2006.

727 Sudarsan Raghavan, "In Iraqi Colleges, Fear for an Already Shrunken Realm; Mass Kidnapping Seen Likely to Boost Educators' Exodus," *The Washington Post*, November 16, 2006.

728 John F. Burns et al., "Dozens Abducted in Brazen Raid on Iraq Ministry," *The New York Times*, November 15, 2006.

729 Mark Kukis, Mazin Ezzat, and Bobby Ghosh, "An Ambush in Karbala," *Time Magazine*, July 26, 2007.

730 Press Briefing with Multi-National Force-Iraq Deputy Chief of Staff for Strategic Effects Brigadier General Kevin Bergner, Security Operations in Iraq.

731 Press Briefing with Multi-National Force-Iraq Deputy Chief of Staff for Strategic Effects Brigadier General Kevin Bergner, Security Operations in Iraq.

732 Press briefing with Secretary of Defense Robert Gates, U.S. Ambassador to Iraq Ryan Crocker and Multi-National Force-Iraq Commander Gen. David Petraeus, Location: The U.S. Ambassador's Residence, Baghdad, Iraq, June 16, 2007.

733 Press briefing with Secretary of Defense Robert Gates, U.S. Ambassador to Iraq Ryan Crocker and Multi-National Force-Iraq Commander Gen. David Petraeus, Location: The U.S. Ambassador's Residence, Baghdad, Iraq, June 16, 2007.

734 Multi-National Corps-Iraq Release No. 20070718-16, "Update: Detainee captured June 28 identified," July 18, 2007.

735 Press Briefing with Multi-National Force-Iraq Deputy Chief of Staff for Strategic Effects Brigadier General Kevin Bergner, Security Operations in Iraq, Slide 4.

736 Press Briefing with Major General William Caldwell, Spokesman, Multi-National Force-Iraq and Major Marty Webber, Explosive Ordnance Disposal Expert, Topic: Iraq Operational Update Briefing, Location: The Combined Press Information Center, Baghdad, Iraq, February 14, 2007.

737 Press Briefing with Major General William Caldwell, Spokesman, Multi-National Force-Iraq and Major Marty Webber, Explosive Ordnance Disposal Expert, Topic: Iraq Operational Update Briefing, Location: The Combined Press Information Center, Baghdad, Iraq, February 14, 2007.

738 Michael Ware, "Inside Iran's Secret War for Iraq," *Time Magazine*, August 15, 2005.

739 Press Briefing with Multi-National Force-Iraq Deputy Chief of Staff for Strategic Effects Brigadier General Kevin Bergner, Security Operations in Iraq.

740 For example, Multi-National Corps-Iraq Release A070816b, "Coalition Forces Kill Three, Detain Six, Capturing a High-Priority Special Groups Weapons Smuggler," August 16, 2007.

741 Media roundtable with Maj. Gen. William Caldwell IV, MNF-I spokesman, and Maj. Marty Weber, 79th Explosive Ordnance Disposal Unit, April 11, 2007; "U.S. vs. Iran: Cold War, Too," Robin Wright, *The Washington Post*, July 29, 2007, Regional Edition, B01.

742 Thomas Harding, "Iraqi Insurgents Using Austrian Rifles from Iran," *Telegraph*, February 2, 2007.

743 Thomas Harding, "Iraqi Insurgents Using Austrian Rifles from Iran," *Telegraph*, February 2, 2007.

744 Thomas Harding, "Iraqi Insurgents Using Austrian Rifles from Iran," *Telegraph*, February 2, 2007.

745 Thomas Harding, "Iraqi Insurgents Using Austrian Rifles from Iran," *Telegraph*, February 2, 2007.

746 Babak Dehghanpisheh, "Iraq's New Guns for Hire; under Seige in Baghdad, Fighters from Moqtada al Sadr's Jaysh al Mahdi Are Going Freelance, and They're Already Spreading Havoc to Once Calm Parts of the Country," Newsweek, May 7 2007; Department of Defense News Briefing with Multi-National Division-Center and 3rd Infantry Division Commander Maj. Gen. Rick Lynch, Topic: Operation Marne Husky, Location: Pentagon, Arlington, VA, August 24, 2007.

747 Department of Defense Civilian Defense Experts Conference Call with Brigadier General Edward Cardon, Deputy Commander for Support, Multi-National Division-Center, July 19, 2007.

748 Department of Defense Civilian Defense Experts Conference Call with Brigadier General Edward Cardon, Deputy Commander for Support, Multi-National Division-Center, July 19, 2007; Babak Dehghanpisheh, "Iraq's New Guns for Hire; under Seige in Baghdad, Fighters from Moqtada al Sadr's Jaysh al Mahdi Are Going Freelance, and They're Already Spreading Havoc to Once Calm Parts of the Country," *Newsweek*, May 7 2007; Associated Press, "Iran Sealing Iraq Border after Detention of 2 Al-Qaida Suspects," The Associated Press, February 7, 2007.

749 "Protests after U.S. Troops Detain Iraq Shiite Leader," Agence France Presse, English, February 24, 2007.

750 "Iraqi Army Detains Two Wasit Provincial Officials on Suspicion of Smuggling Ieds," U.S. Federal News, January 19, 2007; Kut has also been an area in which rogue Jaysh al Mahdi have operated against Iraqi Security Forces (Multi-National Corps-Iraq Release No. 20070716-17, "Ambush disrupted; two extremists killed," July 16, 2007.)

751 Multi-National Force-Iraq Release A070808b, "Coalition Forces Kill 30 Special Groups Cell Terrorists, detain 12," August 8, 2007; The roads from Kut also extend southeast to Diwaniyah, the capital of Qadisiyah, and east to the major Shia cities of Hillah, Karbala, and Najaf.

752 Ravi Nessman, "U.S. Military Frees 42 Captives Kidnapped by Al-Qaida in Raid

on Hide-out in Iraq's Northeast," The Associated Press Worldstream, May 28 2007.

753 Hamid Ahmed. "Iraqi Police: Clashes Continue Between Iraqi Forces and Jaysh al Mahdi Fighters in South." Associated Press Worldstream, June 19 2007.

754 Multi-National Corps-Iraq Release No. 20070627-13, "Iraqi Army destroys weapons cache near Nasiriyah," June 27, 2007.

755 Multi-National Force-Iraq Press Briefing, Media roundtable with Major General William Caldwell, Spokesman for Multinational Force Iraq; and Major Marty Weber, 79th Explosive Ordnance Disposal Unit, Topic: Operational Update, Location: The Combined Press Information Center, Baghdad, Iraq, April 11, 2007.

756 Multi-National Corps-Iraq Release No. 20070630-04, "Iraqi Special Operation Forces detain insurgent leader," June 30, 2007.

757 Multi-National Corps-Iraq Release No. 20070630-04, "Iraqi Special Operation Forces detain insurgent leader," June 30, 2007; Multi-National Corps-Iraq Release No. 20070718-16, "Update: Detainee captured June 28 identified," July 18, 2007.

758 Multi-National Force-Iraq, Release No. A070618a, "Coalition Forces disrupt Secret Cell terrorist network," June 18, 2007.

759 Press Briefing with Multi-National Force-Iraq Deputy Chief of Staff for Strategic Effects Brigadier General Kevin Bergner, Security Operations in Iraq, July 2, 2007.

760 See Kimberly Kagan, " From 'New Way Forward' to New Commander, January 10-February 10, 2007" Iraq Report (www.understandingwar.org), March 1, 2007; and Kimberly Kagan, "The Battle for Diyala, February 11-April 25, 2007" Iraq Report (www.understandingwar.org), May 7, 2007; to review the operations in Balad Ruz and Turki Village.

761 The exact date of his meeting in Diyala has not been published. He was captured on March 20, 2007; he recorded the meeting in the twenty-two page personal diary that U.S. forces found when they captured him; and he was on his fourth trip to Iraq since May 2006.

762 Special Defense Department Briefing with Major General Benjamin Mixon, Commander, Multinational Division-North and the 25th Infantry Division; Colonel James Trogdon, Engineer Commander, Task Force Lightning, Topic: Ongoing Security Operations In Iraq, March 9, 2007.

763 Multi-National Corps-Iraq Release No. 20070820-06, "Iraqi Forces, U.S. Special Forces Battle Insurgents, Kill 8 Terrorists," August 20, 2007.

764 Multi-National Force-Iraq Release A071031b, "Coalition Forces capture targeted

Special Groups member, eleven others detained," October 31, 2007; Multi-National Force-Iraq Release A071108a, "Coalition Forces capture Special Groups leader, five others detained," November 8, 2007.

765 Department of Defense Special Briefing with Lieutenant General Ray Odierno, U.S. Army, Commander, Multi-National Corps-Iraq, Topic: Operation Phantom Thunder, Location: Pentagon Briefing Room, Arlington, VA, June 22, 2007.

766 Department of Defense Press Briefing with Major General Joseph Fil Jr., Commanding General of Multi-National Division-Baghdad and 1st Cavalry Division, Location: Pentagon Briefing Room, Arlington, VA, June 29, 2007.

767 Department of Defense Press Briefing with Multi-National Corps-Iraq Commander Lieutenant General Ray Odierno, Topic: Ongoing Security Operations in Iraq, Location: Pentagon Briefing Room, Arlington, VA, August 17, 2007.

768 Press Briefing with Multi-National Force-Iraq Deputy Chief of Staff for Strategic Effects Brigadier General Kevin Bergner, Security Operations in Iraq, July 2, 2007.

769 Press Briefing with Multi-National Force-Iraq Deputy Chief of Staff for Strategic Effects Brigadier General Kevin Bergner, Security Operations in Iraq, July 2, 2007.

770 Lauren Frayer, "U.S. soldiers find tips flowing from rifts within powerful Shiite militia run by young cleric," Associated Press Worldstream, May 16, 2007; Babak Dehghanpisheh, "Iraq's New Guns for Hire; under Seige in Baghdad, Fighters from Moqtada al Sadr's Jaysh al Mahdi Are Going Freelance, and They're Already Spreading Havoc to Once Calm Parts of the Country," Newsweek, May 7 2007.

771 Lauren Frayer, "U.S. soldiers find tips flowing from rifts within powerful Shiite militia run by young cleric," Associated Press Worldstream, May 16, 2007.

772 Sean D. Naylor, "Iran Deeply Involved in Iraq, Petraeus Says," *Army Times*, May 24, 2007. It is in this context that General Petraeus stated that the Qods Force reports to the Iranian supreme leader Ayatollah Ali Khamenei.

773 Multi-National Corps-Iraq Release No. 20070815-08, "Iraqi Army, U.S. Special Forces detain Shi'a extremist leader," August 15, 2007.

774 Multi-National Force-Iraq Release A070814b, "Coalition Forces Kill Four Terrorists, Detain Eight in Search for Militant Extremist Leader, August 14, 2007.

775 Department of Defense Press Briefing with Multi-National Corps-Iraq Commander Lieutenant General Ray Odierno, Topic: Ongoing Security Operations in Iraq, Location: Pentagon Briefing Room, Arlington, VA, August 17, 2007.

776 Department of Defense Press Briefing with Multi-National Corps-Iraq

Commander Lieutenant General Ray Odierno, Topic: Ongoing Security Operations in Iraq, Location: Pentagon Briefing Room, Arlington, VA, August 17, 2007.

777 Department of Defense Press Briefing with Multi-National Corps-Iraq Commander Lieutenant General Ray Odierno, Topic: Ongoing Security Operations in Iraq, Location: Pentagon Briefing Room, Arlington, VA, August 17, 2007.

778 Press Briefing with Ambassador Ryan Crocker, U.S. Ambassador to Iraq, Topic: Following the Meeting with the Iranian and Iraqi Ambassador, Location: The Combined Press Information Center, Baghdad, Iraq, May 29, 2007.

779 U.S. Department of State Daily Press Briefing with Spokesman Sean McCormack, Location: Washington, D.C., June 27, 2007.

780 Press Briefing with Ambassador Ryan Crocker, Topic: Second Round of U.S.-Iranian-Iraqi discussions, Location: The Combined Press Information Center, Baghdad, Iraq, July 24, 2007.

781 U.S. Department of State Daily Press Briefing with Spokesman Sean McCormack, Location: Washington, D.C., August 8, 2007.

782 Multi-National Force-Iraq Release A070816b, "Coalition Forces Kill Three, Detain Six, Capturing a High-Priority Special Groups Weapons Smuggler," August 16, 2007.

783 Multi-National Force-Iraq Release A070722a, "Coalition Forces Detain Two Suspected Weapons Smugglers," July 22, 2007.

784 Department of Defense News Briefing with Multi-National Division-Center and 3rd Infantry Division Commander Maj. Gen. Rick Lynch, Topic: Operation Marne Husky, Location: Pentagon, Arlington, VA, August 24, 2007.

785 Associated Press, "Poland to Move Troops into One Base in Iraq," Associated Press Worldstream, June 8, 2007.

786 Associated Press, "Georgian Parliament Approves Major Increase in Iraq Contingent," Associated Press Worldstream, June 8, 2007.

787 Department of Defense News Briefing with Multi-National Division-Center and 3rd Infantry Division Commander Maj. Gen. Rick Lynch, Topic: Operation Marne Husky, Location: Pentagon, Arlington, VA, August 24, 2007.

788 "Building upon a series of coordinated operations efforts that began with the raid in al Amarah in June, [June 18], Coalition Forces continue to attack the supply chain of illicit materials being shipped from Iran. Intelligence reports indicate that the targeted individual in last night's raid acts as a proxy between the Iranian Revolutionary Guard Corps-Qods Force and the Iraqi EFP network. Reports also indicate that he assists with the facilitation of weapons and EFP

shipments into Iraq as well as the transfer of militant extremists to Iran for training." Multi-National Corps-Iraq Release A070808b, "Coalition Forces Kill 30 Special Groups Cell Terrorists, detain 12," August 8, 2007.

789 Operations in Kharnabat (Multi-National Corps-Iraq Release A070720a, "Coalition Forces Capture High Value Terrorist with Ties to IRGC-QF," July 20, 2007) and Qasarin (Multi-National Corps-Iraq Release A070727a, "Coalition Forces Detain Four Suspected Special Groups Terrorists," July 27, 2007).

790 James Kitfield, "Success of Iraq Surves Rests on Ability to Suspend Cycle of Violence," *National Journal*, July 17, 2007.

791 Multi-National Corps-Iraq Release No. 20070815-07, "Iraqi Special Operations Forces, U.S. Special Forces detain rogue JAM brigade leader, three cell members," August 15, 2007.

792 Multi-National Force-Iraq Release A070731b, "Coalition Forces Capture Three Suspected Terrorists with Ties to IRGC-QF," July 31, 2007.

793 Multi-National Corps-Iraq Release No. 20070825-10, "ISOF, U.S. Special Forces detain nine extremist militants in Baghdad," August 25, 2007.

794 Multi-National Corps-Iraq Release No. 20070824-10, "MND-B troops engage militiamen, find cache," August 24, 2007.

795 Multi-National Corps-Iraq Release No. 20070820-06, "Iraqi Forces, U.S. Special Forces Battle Insurgents, Kill 8 Terrorists," August 20, 2007.

796 Multi-National Corps-Iraq Release No. 20070726-06, "Iraqi Security Forces, U.S. Special Forces detain rogue Jaysh al Mahdi leader," July 26, 2007.

797 Multi-National Corps-Iraq Release No. 20070727-08, "Iraqi Army, U.S. Special Forces detain rogue Jaysh al Mahdi cell leader," July 27, 2007.

798 Multi-National Corps-Iraq Release No. 20070808-04, "U.S. Special Forces, Iraqi SOF detain eight, kill one in air-strike," August 8, 2007.

799 Multi-National Corps-Iraq Release No. 20070813-08, "Iraqi, U.S. Special Forces detain key rogue JAM leader, capture Al Qaeda in Iraq medic," August 13, 2007.

800 Multi-National Corps-Iraq Release No. 20070819-02, "Iraqi Forces, U.S. Special Forces dismantle sniper cell, detain three, kill one in Baghdad," August 19, 2007.

801 Multi-National Corps-Iraq Release No. 20070820-06, "Iraqi Forces, U.S. Special Forces Battle Insurgents, Kill 8 Terrorists," August 20, 2007.

802 Department of Defense Press Briefing with Multi-National Corps-Iraq Commander Lieutenant General Ray Odierno, Topic: Ongoing Security Operations in Iraq, Location: Pentagon Briefing Room, Arlington, VA, August 17, 2007.

803 Multi-National Corps-Iraq Release No. 20070807-14, "Iraqi Army, U.S. Special

Forces detain suspected rogue JAM recruiter; ISOF detain suspected Al-Qaeda emir," August 7, 2007; Multi-National Corps - Iraq Release No. 20070814-07, "Iraqi Army, U.S. Special Forces detain high-value rogue JAM Special Groups leader," August 14, 2007.

804 Multi-National Corps-Iraq Release No. 20070815-08, "Iraqi Army, U.S. Special Forces detain Shi'a extremist leader," August 15, 2007.

805 General David H. Petraeus, Commander, Multi-National Force-Iraq, "Report to Congress on the Situation in Iraq," 8-9 April 2008, p. 2 and slide 2.

806 "The Surge in Iraq: One Year Later," by Lt. Gen. Raymond T Odierno, Heritage Lecture #1068, March 13, 2008; available at http://www.heritage.org/Research/NationalSecurity/hl1068.cfm.

807 The Surge in Iraq: One Year Later," by Lt. Gen. Raymond T Odierno, Heritage Lecture #1068, March 13, 2008; available at http://www.heritage.org/Research/NationalSecurity/hl1068.cfm.

808 "The Surge in Iraq: One Year Later," by Lt. Gen. Raymond T Odierno, Heritage Lecture #1068, March 13, 2008; available at http://www.heritage.org/Research/NationalSecurity/hl1068.cfm.

809 General David H. Petraeus, Commander, Multi-National Force-Iraq, "Report to Congress on the Situation in Iraq," 8-9 April 2008, slide 7.

■ ■ ■ Index

THE OXFORD SHAKESPEARE

All's Well that Ends Well
Anthony and Cleopatra
As You Like It
The Comedy of Errors
The Complete Sonnets
  and Poems
Coriolanus
Cymbeline
Hamlet
Henry V
Henry IV, Part 1
Henry IV, Part 2
Henry VI, Part One
Henry VI, Part Two
Henry VI, Part Three
Julius Caesar
King Henry VIII
King John
King Lear
Love's Labour's Lost

Macbeth
Measure for Measure
The Merchant of Venice
The Merry Wives of Windsor
A Midsummer Night's Dream
Much Ado About Nothing
Othello
Pericles
Richard II
Richard III
Romeo and Juliet
The Taming of the Shrew
The Tempest
Timon of Athens
Titus Andronicus
Troilus and Cressida
Twelfth Night
The Two Gentlemen of Verona
The Two Noble Kinsmen
The Winter's Tale

OXFORD WORLD'S CLASSICS

WILLIAM SHAKESPEARE

Love's Labour's Lost

Edited by
G. R. HIBBARD

OXFORD
UNIVERSITY PRESS

OXFORD

UNIVERSITY PRESS

Great Clarendon Street, Oxford OX2 6DP

Oxford University Press is a department of the University of Oxford.
It furthers the University's objective of excellence in research, scholarship,
and education by publishing worldwide in

Oxford New York

Auckland Bangkok Bogotá Buenos Aires Cape Town Chennai
Dar es Salaam Delhi Hong Kong Istanbul Karachi Kolkata
Kuala Lumpur Madrid Melbourne Mexico City Mumbai Nairobi
São Paulo Shanghai Singapore Taipei Tokyo Toronto

Oxford is a registered trade mark of Oxford University Press
in the UK and in certain other countries

Published in the United States
by Oxford University Press Inc., New York

© Oxford University Press 1990

The moral rights of the author have been asserted

Database right Oxford University Press (maker)

First published 1990 as an Oxford University Press paperback
and simultaneously in a hardback edition
First published as a World's Classics paperback 1994
Reissued as an Oxford World's Classics paperback 1998
Reissued 2008

British Library Cataloguing in Publication Data

Data available

Library of Congress Cataloging in Publication Data

Shakespeare, William, 1564–1616.
Love's labour's lost / edited by G. R. Hibbard.
(Oxford world's classics)
Includes index.
1. Hibbert, G. R. (George Richard), 1915–   . II. Title.
III. Series: Shakespeare, William, 1564–1616. Works. 1982.
PR2822.A2H7 1990 822.3'3—dc19 89–30056

ISBN 978–0–19–953681–8

6

Printed in Great Britain by
Clays Ltd, St Ives plc

PREFACE

I AM particularly indebted to John Caldwell for contributing 'A Note on the Music', to Christine Buckley and Frances Whistler for their help in dealing with the Illustrations, and, above all, to Stanley Wells for many useful suggestions and some even more useful, not to say necessary, cautions.

G. R. HIBBARD

CONTENTS

LIST OF ILLUSTRATIONS

viii

INTRODUCTION

In 1598, the year in which the earliest extant text we have of
Love's Labour's Lost appeared in print, an emphatically minor
poet, Robert Tofte, published his very long and very lugubrious
work entitled *Alba: The Month's Mind of a Melancholy Lover*.
Bearing the discouraged and discouraging motto *Spes, Amor, &
Fortuna valete* ('Farewell to hope, to love, and to fortune') on its
title-page, and running to three parts, it is an unrelieved outpouring of woe. Written in the same six-line stanza form as *Venus and
Adonis*, it belongs in all other respects to the tradition of the
conventional Elizabethan sonnet sequence. In love with a lady
who disdains his advances, the poet laments his unfortunate
state. Its main interest today is an extraneous one: it contains one
of the two earliest references we have to *Love's Labour's Lost*.
Occurring in the Third Part of the poem, the relevant passage
runs thus:

> *Love's Labour Lost*, I once did see a play,
> Yclepèd so, so callèd to my pain,
> Which I to hear to my small joy did stay,
> Giving attendance on my froward dame.
>> My misgiving mind presaging to me ill,
>> Yet was I drawn to see it 'gainst my will.
>
> This play no play but plague was unto me,
> For there I lost the love I likèd most;
> And what to others seemed a jest to be,
> I, that (in earnest) found unto my cost.
>> To everyone (save me) 'twas comical,
>> Whilst tragic-like to me it did befall.
>
> Each actor played in cunning wise his part,
> But chiefly those entrapped in Cupid's snare;
> Yet all was feignèd, 'twas not from the heart;
> They seemed to grieve, but yet they felt no care.
>> 'Twas I that grief indeed did bear in breast,
>> The others did but make a show in jest.
>
> Yet neither feigning theirs, nor my mere truth,
> Could make her once so much as for to smile;

> Whilst she, despite of pity mild and ruth,
> Did sit as scorning of my woes the while.
>   Thus did she sit to see Love lose his love,
>   Like hardened rock that force nor power can move.
>
>   (Sig. G5)

It is possible, of course, that Tofte's visit to the theatre is a piece of fiction, but this seems unlikely because there is evidence in the poem to suggest that he was something of a playgoer. He refers to Tamburlaine, echoes *The Spanish Tragedy* twice, and *Romeo and Juliet* at least once.[1] But, whether factual or fictional, this account strongly suggests that Tofte had in mind a performance at one of the public theatres, rather than one at court or at the home of a great man. Had the occasion been a distinguished one, he would almost certainly have mentioned it. As it stands, however, it all sounds decidedly familiar, an Elizabethan version, as Hugh Hunt observes,[2] of today's young man who takes his girl-friend to the cinema. The matter is of some importance, for it has often been maintained that the playwright composed this comedy with a coterie audience in view. Only those with a good education and some close acquaintance with courtly life and manners would, it has been argued, have been able to understand and enjoy the 'sets of wit' and the sustained word-play with which it is so liberally studded. Support for this idea was found in the statement on the title-page of the Quarto of 1598 to the effect that the play had been presented before the Queen 'this last Christmas', and in the fact that it was acted before Queen Anne, at the Earl of Southampton's house in the Strand, in January 1605 (Chambers, *William Shakespeare*, ii. 330–2). There is, however, nothing particularly unusual about either performance. *The Merry Wives of Windsor*, as published in 1602, proclaims on its title-page that it had been put on before the Queen; and a letter from Sir Walter Cope to Lord Cranborne says explicitly that Richard Burbage, the leading actor in Shakespeare's company, recommended *Love's Labour's Lost* as the most suitable play the King's Men could stage to entertain Queen Anne, because it was full of 'wit and mirth' (ibid.). Moreover, the title-page of the Second Quarto, published in 1631, states that the comedy had been acted by the King's Men both 'at the Blackfriars and the Globe', which implies, incidentally, that it

---

[1] Sigs. A4, E1ᵛ, G6ᵛ, E1ᵛ.   [2] Old Vic Prefaces (1954), p. 9.

still had an appeal for a popular audience in 1609 or thereafter, since it was not until 1609 that the company began to act in the Blackfriars playhouse. Indeed, it may, for all we know, have still been in the repertory of the King's Men in the 1630s.

Then, in 1642, the theatres were closed, and remained closed until after the Restoration. When they reopened, many of Shakespeare's plays were revived, but *Love's Labour's Lost*, although it was allotted to Sir Thomas Killigrew in a list of January 1669,[1] was not among them. In fact, it was not to be staged again for the best part of two hundred years. During this long eclipse an adaptation of it entitled *The Students* was published in 1762; but there is no evidence that it ever reached the stage. It did not deserve to; and its author—'Our bard, advent'ring to the comic land', as he calls himself in the Prologue—was right to remain anonymous. *The Students* is a travesty rather than an adaptation of the original. Inept, vulgar, tasteless, and foolish, it had nothing to recommend it to the theatre managers of the day, or of any other day.

Those same theatre managers also had their own reasons for not trying to put on the comedy itself as Shakespeare left it; and Doctor Johnson tells us what their main objections to it could have been. In an over-view of the play that is more perceptive and generous than anything previously written about it he has this to say:

In this play, which all the editors have concurred to censure and some [Pope among them] have rejected as unworthy of our poet, it must be confessed that there are many passages mean, childish, and vulgar; and some which ought not to have been exhibited, as we are told they were, to a maiden queen. But there are scattered through the whole many sparks of genius; nor is there any play that has more evident marks of the hand of Shakespeare.[2]

There can be little doubt as to what Johnson was thinking of when he referred to passages 'mean, childish, and vulgar'. Like his age in general and the ages before it right back to the Restoration, he had a poor opinion of puns and of Shakespeare's

---

[1] Allardyce Nicoll, *A History of English Drama 1660–1900*, 6 vols. (Cambridge, 1923), i. 354.

[2] *Dr Johnson on Shakespeare*, ed. W. K. Wimsatt (Harmondsworth, 1969), p. 108.

fondness for them. In a famous passage in his *Preface* of 1765 he writes:

A quibble is to Shakespeare what luminous vapours are to the traveller; he follows it at all adventures; it is sure to lead him out of his way and sure to engulf him in the mire. It has some malignant power over his mind, and its fascinations are irresistible ... A quibble, poor and barren as it is, gave him such delight that he was content to purchase it by the sacrifice of reason, propriety, and truth. A quibble was to him the fatal Cleopatra for which he lost the world and was content to lose it. (Ibid., p. 68)

Those words are an eloquent climax to a chorus of indictment that had been swelling for almost a century ever since Dryden in his *Essay of Dramatic Poesy* (1668) had written of Shakespeare's 'comic wit degenerating into clenches'.[1] In such a climate of opinion *Love's Labour's Lost*, in which puns are omnipresent and an essential part of the play's very being, stood little chance of a sympathetic reception. Furthermore, to an age which, from the time of Pope onwards and increasingly with the onset of Romanticism, was coming to regard the creation of highly individualized characters who grow and develop in response to experience as Shakespeare's supreme achievement, the comedy had little to offer; a couple of eccentrics in Armado and Holofernes, and, in the main plot, Biron and the Princess.

Nevertheless, two hundred years after the play's disappearance from the English stage, something spurred Madame Vestris and her husband Charles James Mathews to put *Love's Labour's Lost* on at Covent Garden in 1839. It was a lavish production, complete with gorgeous costumes and an elaborate *mise-en-scène* that was much admired;[2] but the couple made a terrible mistake. They had just taken over the theatre, and for this, their first production in it, they closed the shilling gallery. As a result there was something like a riot on the first night, with indignant theatre-goers making their protest against the move by damning the play. After this inauspicious opening the production ran for only eight more nights before it was taken off. Hitherto two obstacles had stood in the way of any proper appreciation of the play either in the theatre or in the study: the notion that it was

[1] *Essays of John Dryden*, ed. W. P. Ker, 2 vols. (Oxford, 1900), i. 80.
[2] See George C. D. Odell, *Shakespeare from Betterton to Irving*, 2 vols. (New York, 1920), ii. 222–3.

recalcitrantly Elizabethan in its reliance on word-play, and therefore 'not for all time'; and that it was not a play of characters. Now to these was added a third: it had not gone well on the stage. *Love's Labour's Lost* was caught, as it were, on the horns of a dilemma. Because it was thought of in this way, it was only rarely performed in the later nineteenth and early twentieth centuries, and, when it was staged, it was either by amateur actors —George Bernard Shaw saw such a production in 1886[1]—or by professionals who had no real faith in it.

One exception must, however, be made to this generalization— an essay on the play by Walter Pater, first published in 1878 and subsequently included in his *Appreciations, with an Essay on Style* of 1889.[2] Deeply interested in style—'the fancy so many of us have for an exquisite and curious skill in the use of words', as he calls it—Pater does justice to the play's 'curious foppery of language' and Shakespeare's ambivalent attitude towards it, especially as it appears in the speeches of Biron; but he says practically nothing about the comedy as a comedy. One is left wondering whether he had ever seen it, or, indeed, had any opportunity to see it.

Such were the fortunes of *Love's Labour's Lost* up to 1927. But in that year they changed radically and for the better, since it saw the publication of the most appreciative and influential piece on the comedy that had ever appeared, Harley Granville-Barker's *Preface* to it. Significantly the essay begins with an apology that shows the power the objections to the play cited above were still capable of exerting.

Here is a fashionable play; now, by three hundred years, out of fashion. Nor did it ever, one supposes, make a very wide appeal. It abounds in jokes for the elect. Were you not numbered among them you laughed, for safety, in the likeliest places. A year or two later the elect themselves might be hard put to it to remember what the joke was.[3]

Furthermore, Granville-Barker, like most scholars and critics at the time, thought of *Love's Labour's Lost* as very early Shakespeare. He writes of 'the dramatist learning his art', calls him 'a clever young man', and refers to the play as his 'earliest essay'. Yet

---

[1] *Shaw on Shakespeare*, ed. Edwin Wilson (Harmondsworth, 1969), pp. 33–5.

[2] Repr. 1910, pp. 161–9.

[3] *Prefaces to Shakespeare, First Series* (1927), p. 1.

despite these preconceptions he succeeds in getting to the heart of the comedy as no one before him had done, and he does so because he looks at it as a piece of theatre designed for the Elizabethan stage. He heads his first section on it 'The Producer's Problem', and moves on thence to 'The Method of the Acting', insisting on the need for the actor to let the words speak for themselves, as it were. Recognizing, as Shaw had done before him,[1] that the verse has its own authentic music, he goes on to say:

if the music is clear and fine, as Elizabethan music was, if the costumes strike their note of fantastic beauty, if, above all, the speech and movements of the actors are fine and rhythmical too, then this quaint medley of mask and play can still be made delightful. But it asks for style in the acting. The whole play, first and last, demands style. (p. 14)

His words did not go unheeded. In 1932 Tyrone Guthrie, who had read the *Prefaces* with attention,[2] put on *Love's Labour's Lost* at the Westminster, doing it in a style that led J. C. Trewin to remark: 'It was this production of the young comedy, so picked, so spruce, so peregrinate, a festival of words, that would take him one day to the Old Vic'.[3] The 'one day' was not long in coming. The Old Vic production followed in 1936. It was, to quote Trewin once more:

[an] elegant revival—two pavilions, a fountain, wrought-iron gates—with Ernest Milton's Armado to strut, a moulting peacock, across the turf, Alec Clunes in Berowne's silken terms precise, and Michael Redgrave ... as Ferdinand of Navarre. (Ibid., p. 163)

But the greatest tribute to Guthrie's achievement came from Dover Wilson who, with his characteristic generosity of spirit, wrote of the production:

it revealed [the play] as a first-rate comedy of the pattern kind—so full of fun, of *permanent* wit, of brilliant and entrancing situation, that you hardly noticed the faded jesting and allusion, as you sat spell-bound and drank it all in. It was a thrilling production, Shakespearian criticism of the best kind, because a real piece of restoration ... Mr. Guthrie not only gave me a new play, the existence of which I had never suspected, which indeed had been veiled from men's eyes for three centuries, but he set me

---

[1] *Op. cit.*, p. 135.
[2] Tyrone Guthrie, *A Life in the Theatre* (1959), p. 108.
[3] J. C. Trewin, *Shakespeare on the English Stage 1900–1964* (1964), p. 133.

at a fresh standpoint of understanding and appreciation from which the whole of Shakespearian comedy might be reviewed in a new light.[1]

Having paid this homage to Guthrie, Wilson added to it when, in 1962, he published a second and revised version of his original edition of 1923. There he says:

I had spent two years upon this edition, but Guthrie's production, which I saw in company with Alfred Pollard, convinced me that I was then beginning to understand the play for the first time, an education continued later under Peter Brook's tuition. The striking impression left in both cases was one of a ballet-like speed, tip-toe delicacy, and kaleidoscopic shifts of colour, all in the text when rightly conceived, and culminating in the grim shock of the entry of a messenger of Death, clad in black from head to foot. (pp. lxi–lxii)

The production by Peter Brook that Dover Wilson refers to followed ten years after Guthrie's. It took place at Stratford-upon-Avon in 1946, and in very different circumstances. The Second World War had just come to an end. Wittingly or unwittingly, Brook took Granville-Barker's advice. He put on the comedy in style and with style, setting it in the world of Watteau. It emerged in the theatre as a bright scintillating jewel of a play that also had its own peculiar, shifting, shadowy depths. It seemed to reflect the mood of euphoria, flecked with dark memories of the conflict now over and apprehensions about the future, that was so characteristic of Britain at the time. In a letter to J. C. Trewin, John Harrison, who played Longueville, had this to say about the first night:

Nobody outside the theatre had heard much about the production; there had been little publicity for Brook, and the audience assembled in noticeable calm. Three hours later, anyone late on the Bancroft meadow would have guessed at something uncommon. From a Stratford failure the mourners file out quietly, but any success is talked volubly through the streets, as *Love's Labour's Lost* would be all that summer.[2]

In fact, so great was the production's popularity that it was retained in the company's repertory for the following year.

One question remained unanswered: how far was the rising reputation of *Love's Labour's Lost* in the theatre to be attributed to

[1] *Shakespeare's Happy Comedies* (1962), p. 64.

[2] J. C. Trewin, *Peter Brook: A Biography* (1971), p. 25.

1. The Forester (Leo McKern) points out to the Princess (Angela Baddeley) a suitable location from which to shoot deer, in Hugh Hunt's 1949 production for the Old Vic company. Looking on are her lords (including Boyet, played by Walter Hudd, in embroidered gauntlets) and her ladies (Yvonne Mitchell as Katherine, Diana Churchill as Rosaline, and Jane Wenham as Maria).

the genius of Guthrie and Brook, rather than to any inherent qualities of the comedy itself? The answer was not long in coming. In the autumn of 1949 Hugh Hunt took over the direction of the Old Vic company, then acting at the New Theatre, and boldly began the season with a revival of the play. He did not, however, give it an eighteenth-century setting and costumes, as Guthrie and Brook had done. Instead, he chose to dress it in Elizabethan costumes, which worked equally well. Once again the production proved an unqualified success, with Michael Redgrave as Biron, Diana Churchill as Rosaline, Mark Dignam as Holofernes, and Miles Malleson as Sir Nathaniel. In the course of a little over twenty years *Love's Labour's Lost* had ceased to be a theatrical liability, something to be put on occasionally at Stratford more out of a sense of duty than anything else, and had become a beckoning opportunity for directors to test their interpretative insights and for actors to show off their professional skills. The part of Armado in particular has become a much coveted one.

2. The arrival of Marcadé in Hugh Hunt's production. The Princess and her ladies are still watching the impending combat between Costard (George Benson) and Armado (Baliol Holloway), while almost everyone else has noticed the presence of Marcadé (Richard Walter). Holofernes (Mark Dignam) and Nathaniel (Miles Malleson) are to left and right of the messenger.

Since 1949 *Love's Labour's Lost* has never looked back. At Stratford-upon-Avon, where it has become something of a favourite, it has been put on at least once in every decade, and as many as four times in the seventies, i.e. as often as it was played there in the entire fifty years from 1885 to 1934. Still more remarkable has been its success elsewhere. Who, for instance, even in the magical summer of 1946, would have dreamed that little more than thirty years later there would be no fewer than three separate productions of it in a single year in the western United States alone? Yet so it was. In 1980 it was staged at the Old Globe Theatre in San Diego, California, at Boulder, Colorado in a manner that Michael Mullin described as 'superb',[1] and at the Oregon Festival in Ashland, three places where it had already been produced in 1972, 1971, and 1972 respectively.

Part at least of the attraction the comedy has had for the modern director and indirectly through him for a modern

---

[1] *Shakespeare Quarterly*, 32 (1981), 243–5; p. 244.

audience lies in the unfinished state (see Introduction, pp. 57–65) in which the text has come down to us, a state particularly evident in the sparse and often sketchy nature of its stage directions. It not merely allows great freedom in interpreting such hints as the playwright chooses to give but it also positively demands that the director exercise his own inventiveness by supplying them where they do not exist at all. The great dramatic moment, to which all that goes before it, and especially the first seven lines, leads up, is, of course, the entrance of Marcadé a little more than two hundred lines from the end. But Shakespeare says nothing about the way in which that entrance is to be managed. The careful directions he provides, first to prepare for and then to accompany the arrival of Fortinbras at the end of *Hamlet*, are not to be found here. The director has a free hand. Peter Brook chose to herald the messenger's coming with a slow dimming of the lights and a long pause, a method that for a time became almost a tradition. At the National Theatre in 1969, however, Sir Laurence Olivier went another way to work. His Marcadé appeared suddenly 'as if from nowhere [as death so often does] in the *mêlée* of rustic actors and patrician audience'.[1] It, in turn, was an innovation that appears to have caught on. In 1973 David Jones produced the play at the Royal Shakespeare Theatre and handled this crucial moment in a fashion that led Richard David to write: 'it was not the traditional *coup de théâtre* ... [Marcadé] made his way through a scuffling crowd that had been made as undignified as possible'.[2]

A similar uncertainty lying ready and waiting to be exploited by the imaginative and enterprising director is that neither the Quarto of 1598 nor the Folio of 1623 offers any guidance as to who is to sing Spring's song and who Winter's. Most directors have preferred to hand these lyrics over to the rustics, but there have been occasions when the entire cast has joined in; and John Barton at Stratford-upon-Avon in 1978 had them 'spoken (not sung) with quiet ease, reinforced by the note of a genuine owl somewhere in the twilight'.[3] Not the least interesting and significant of the many experiments in staging that this highly experimental comedy has given rise to was Barry Kyle's casting of Josette Simon, a black actress, in the role of Rosaline at the same

[1] Robert Speaight, *Shakespeare Quarterly*, 20 (1969), 435–41; p. 440.
[2] *Shakespeare in the Theatre* (1978), p. 130.
[3] J. C. Trewin, *Shakespeare Quarterly*, 30 (1979), 151–8; p. 155.

3. The dialogue of the owl and the cuckoo at the play's close, in David Jones's Royal Shakespeare Theatre production of 1973. Sir Nathaniel (Jeffery Dench) sings Ver's song, watched by the Queen (Susan Fleetwood) and the King (Bernard Lloyd), standing centre, and Rosaline (Estelle Kohler) seated at their feet. Annette Badland, as an unnamed villager, sang Hiems' song.

theatre in 1984. Though not conforming to the letter of the text, it was wholly in keeping with the spirit of the play, which so firmly asserts the superiority in good sense and maturity of understanding, at least where matters of the heart are concerned, of young women over young men.

By the time Hugh Hunt's *Love's Labour's Lost* had run its course, it was already abundantly clear that there was nothing freakish, out of the way, or unaccountable about the change in the play's fortunes. It appealed to playgoers of the late forties— and has continued to appeal to playgoers since—because it is, in many ways, a remarkably 'modern' work of art. In a world that was exploring and enjoying the work of James Joyce its reliance on the pun had ceased to be an irritant and become a positive asset. Good puns were being recognized for what they are, a means of bringing two diverse kinds of experience into a sudden, unexpected, and illuminating juxtaposition with one another. Nor, to the reader of *Ulysses*, was there anything unduly ostentatious and jarring about the comedy's recourse to rare and learned words, some of them nonce-words. The great revival of interest in the poetry of the metaphysicals, together with its impact on the poetry of men such as T. S. Eliot, had altered our attitude to 'conceited' language in general. Most important of all, however, the pioneer work of men like William Poel and Granville-Barker in discovering and then advocating the virtues of the bare Elizabethan stage, and especially of the intimacy between players and audience to which it lent itself so well, was beginning to bear fruit in the theatre. Elaborate scenery was being discarded in revivals of plays by Shakespeare and his contemporaries in favour of a single non-representational set that would serve for the entire performance. With the disappearance of the change-able scenery went the time wasted in changing it and the con-sequent loss of continuity and momentum that it had entailed. The 'ballet-like speed' that so impressed Dover Wilson in 1936 would not have been possible on the nineteenth-century stage. There was, furthermore, a growing awareness on the part of producers that Elizabethan and Jacobean plays did not lend them-selves readily to the 'realism' both in setting and in acting that had been so dominant in the theatre for so long. Guthrie de-scribes what was happening:

I began to see wherein for me the real magic of the theatre lay. It was, I discovered, charming, interesting and exciting not the nearer it ap-proached 'reality', but the further it retreated into its own sort of artifice.[1]

About no play in the Shakespeare canon is this truer than it is about *Love's Labour's Lost*. Consciously 'artificial', in the best sense of that word, from first to last, it gains immeasurably from productions that concentrate on, bring out, and even heighten its artificiality. Since 1949 the 'sparks of genius' that Doctor Johnson detected in the play have been recognized for what they really are, a brilliantly dazzling display of poetic and theatrical virtuosity.

The Play

Love's Labour's Lost is exceptional among the comedies Shake-speare wrote prior to 1602, or thereabouts, in at least three respects: death plays a direct and highly significant part in it; as its title proclaims, it neither includes, nor concludes with, a marriage or marriages; and it has little or nothing to offer in the

[1] *A Life in the Theatre*, p. 180.

way of a story. Essentially, all that happens in it is that the young King of Navarre and three of his courtiers solemnly vow to abjure all contact with women and devote themselves to a course of study that will occupy them for the next three years. In their brash and ill-considered enthusiasm they have, however, overlooked the fact that the Princess of France, accompanied by three of her ladies, is about to arrive at the court of Navarre on an embassy from her 'sick, and bedrid father'. Predictably and promptly the four men break their new-made vows by falling in love and abandoning the profits of learning for the pleasures of wooing. To further their purpose they seek to entertain and impress the four women, first with a masque and then with a pageant. Neither device works. Then, when the hilarity created by the ludicrously inept pageant is at its height, the unexpected suddenly breaks in and takes over the fragile ephemeral world of the royal park. A messenger, Monsieur Marcadé, arrives from France with the news that the father of the Princess has died. 'The scene begins to cloud.' The revelry comes to an abrupt end. Inconsiderately and unfeelingly the four men still try to persist with their wooing. But the Princess, now Queen of France, will have none of it. Uncertain about the men's sincerity, as well they might be after this gratuitous display of male single-mindedness, she and her ladies set their lovers tasks that will take a year to complete and will reveal whether the men's professions of devotion are to be trusted or not. The King and his courtiers accept these conditions, and the two parties go their separate ways, having agreed to meet again after a twelvemonth and a day. Biron, the most vocal of the men, underlines the anomaly of this conclusion and, simultaneously, the self-conscious nature of the comedy by saying: 'Our wooing doth not end like an old play :| Jack hath not Jill.'

Such complications as there are spring from those well-worn devices of the comic scene, the conversation overheard, the use of masks to conceal identities, and letters mistakenly delivered to the wrong recipients. As for the sub-plot, it is so slight, turning as it does on the efforts of the 'fantastical Spaniard' Don Adriano de Armado to win the love of the country maid Jaquenetta, that it can hardly be described as a sub-plot at all. It might better be called a parodic counterpoint to the main business of the comedy.

This slenderness of intrigue is not only one of the play's most striking and unusual features but also one of its most positive assets. No longer faced with the difficulties he had encountered when writing *The Two Gentlemen of Verona*, for instance, where he had sought to cram a long and complicated story into the brief traffic required by the stage, with a consequent loss of adequate motivation and explanation, especially in the last act, Shakespeare was now free to enjoy himself by centring his attention on other and more exciting things, including lively displays of wit, the exploration of ideas and attitudes, the development of themes, and playing games with words. He seized the opportunity with an eager and exuberant assurance. In contrast to *The Two Gentlemen of Verona*, where there is a pronounced element of huddle about the ending, *Love's Labour's Lost* is, as befits its holiday nature, remarkable for its leisurely pace and amplitude of statement. It is the longest of the comedies he wrote before 1602,[1] and also the most stylized of them.

The stylization is particularly clear in the formal groupings of the characters. There is, to misquote Thomas Sprat, 'an almost mathematical symmetry' about it. Of the King's three courtiers and fellow-students, two, Longueville and Dumaine, are the courtiers of convention. They follow the King's lead in all they say and do, and, for the reader, as distinct from the playgoer, are not easily or readily distinguishable from one another. The other, Biron, is not in the least conventional. Of an independent nature, much in love with paradox, and taking a positive delight in being different and disruptive, he can think and act for himself, criticize himself as well as others, and, above all, speak eloquently on any topic that comes his way. His is the largest role by far; he utters between a fifth and a quarter of the play's total number of lines. The three women in attendance on the Princess correspond exactly to the three courtiers. Two of them, Maria and Katherine, are fashionable beauties, that is to say blondes, fitting matches for Longueville and Dumaine. The third, Rosaline, is not a conventional beauty at all. Like the 'dark lady' of the Sonnets, she is a brunette, or, in the vivid word-picture Biron paints of her in his soliloquy at the end of 3.1:

> A whitely wanton with a velvet brow,
> With two pitch-balls stuck in her face for eyes.

---

[1] See *The Complete Pelican Shakespeare*, ed. Alfred Harbage (1969), p. 31.

4. The Princess of France (Emily Richard, far right) attended by her ladies, Katherine (Kate Buffery), Rosaline (Josette Simon), and Maria (Alison Rose), and by Boyet (Harold Innocent), in the 1984 Royal Shakespeare Theatre production, directed by Barry Kyle.

5. Sir Nathaniel (Timothy West) reads Biron's letter mistakenly given to Jaquenetta (Patsy Byrne). Tony Church as Holofernes looks over his shoulder, and Costard (Tim Wylton, right) shows mild interest, but the scene's verbal displays send Dull (David Waller) to sleep; from John Barton's 1965 production at the Royal Shakespeare Theatre.

The wittiest, though by no means the most sensible and judicious of the women—that role is reserved for the Princess—Rosaline is obviously the right match for Biron. It goes almost without saying that in this highly formal world the King falls in love with the Princess at first sight. One courtly figure remains, the French lord Boyet. In attendance on the Princess, and at least middle-aged if not old, he acts as an intermediary between the two groups, carrying messages, picking up bits of intelligence, and engaging in badinage with men and women alike. Much interested in match-making and gossip, he is a sort of seedy run-down Cupid, 'Cupid's grandfather', as Katherine calls him at 2.1.253.

A similar kind of grouping appears among the characters of the sub-plot. On the one side are the fantastical pretenders to fashion or learning: Armado, Holofernes, and Sir Nathaniel. All three are well-established stage types, or rather, by the time the play is over, wonderfully original variants on established stage types that go back ultimately to the Italian *commedia dell'arte*, the Braggart, the Pedant, and the *Zani*. Over against these three are set their antitheses, the genuine country folk: Costard, the clown in the sense of rustic; Dull, the village constable; and Jaquenetta the dairymaid. Having no inflated notions about themselves and their own importance, these three can see through those who have, and show no hesitation about saying what they think. And, finally, standing between these two groups is the figure of Moth, Armado's page. Precociously knowledgeable about the love-game, though as yet too young to practise it, Moth takes an impish Cupid-like delight in puncturing pretensions, and finds a natural ally in Costard, who proudly recognizes their kinship in this respect by saying to him:

O, an the heavens were so pleased that thou wert but my bastard, what a joyful father wouldst thou make me! Go to, thou hast it *ad dunghill*, at the fingers' ends, as they say. (5.1.66–9)

The formal groupings are one with and inseparable from both the conduct of the action and of the dialogue. The entire play can usefully be viewed as a country-dance, which the *OED* defines as 'A dance practised by country-people, usually in the open air ... applied to dances in which an indefinite number of couples stand up face to face in two long lines'. The dance that is the play does, indeed, take place, as stage designers have been quick to recog-

6. An aspect of the passion for elaborate and symmetrical patterning in the artificial shaping of nature—a recurrent theme in Renaissance culture—is the formal knot-garden; Armado refers to Navarre's 'curi-ous-knotted garden' (1.1.240). This design from Thomas Hill's *The Gardener's Labyrinth* (1577) is, in fact, the horticultural equivalent of one of Armado's speeches.

nize, in the open air, somewhere just outside the gates that bar the way to the royal residence, from which the Princess and her ladies are excluded by the King's vow and edict. The first act introduces all the male characters of any consequence, apart from Holofernes and Sir Nathaniel, and one minor female figure, Jaquenetta the dairymaid, whose mere presence has proved too great a temptation to Costard and deprived him of his liberty. But as yet the King and his fellow-votaries have no partners and have solemnly sworn not to have any for the next three years. The second act, however, introduces the Princess and her ladies to line up, as it were, outside the forbidden gates. In due course the King's party appears to bid the Princess welcome, and there-upon the two lines break up into four discrete couples. The couples do not actually dance, but the metaphorical dance that is the play has obviously begun. Eventually the men return to the King's house, leaving the women and Boyet to discuss what has happened.

The two groups do not meet again until the last scene, where the women are the first to appear, busy displaying to one another the costly 'favours' they have received from the men, and also sharply criticizing the love-letters that have accompanied those 'favours'. Told by Boyet that the King and his 'book-men' are about to descend on them in order 'to parley, court, and dance' (5.2.122), the Princess devises a counter-strategy. Again the men arrive, this time disguised as Muscovites. Again the two lines become four separate couples; but these couples are wrong couples. Deceived by the fact that the women have exchanged 'favours' with one another, each man woos a lady who is not the lady he thinks she is, while the other three couples converse apart. Finally the men go, leaving the ladies to crow over their discomfiture. The men are not absent for long. Coming back undisguised to the ladies who have now removed their masks and are wearing the 'favours' that are rightly theirs, the King and his party are exposed to mockery and have to admit defeat. The men and the women then sit down to watch the Pageant of the Nine Worthies until it is interrupted by the arrival of Monsieur Marcadé. Now, for the last time, the men and the women split into four separate pairs, each of which holds the centre of the stage for a time, while the other three pairs converse apart, until the final agreement is reached to renew the dance in a year and a day.

The stylization so evident in these scenes is reinforced by yet another feature of the play: its recourse to what might not unfittingly be called the parade-ground technique of action and dialogue. There are signs of it early in the first scene when Longueville and Dumaine immediately give their assent to the King's plans and put their names to the document he presents them with. Biron, however, the subversive recruit, does not follow suit for a long time, and thus breaks the pattern. It reasserts itself soon after the opening of 2.1, when the Princess asks her followers:

> Who are the votaries, my loving lords,
> That are vow-fellows with this virtuous Duke?

Thereupon, each of her ladies in turn admits her acquaintance with one of the King's lords and gives a character sketch of him. Later in the same scene, after the King and his men have left the stage, the three lords return to it, one succeeding another, so that each can ask Boyet for the name of the lady he feels drawn to.

By this time it is clear that Shakespeare is playing with and trying out one of the oldest and most effective of comic devices, that of first raising and then satisfying certain expectations in the minds of his audience. The third scene of the fourth act is probably the most extended and hilarious exploitation of the device in the whole of his work. It begins with the entry of Biron, carrying a paper in his hand and soliloquizing on his own state. Ruefully he admits that he is in love, calls himself a fool for being so, and concludes by saying:

Well, she [Rosaline] hath one o' my sonnets already. The clown bore it, the fool sent it, and the lady hath it. Sweet clown, sweeter fool, sweetest lady! By the world, I would not care a pin if the other three were in.

In fact, as the audience knows but Biron does not, the letter has not reached Rosaline. Wrongly delivered by Costard to Jaquenetta, it is now on its way to the King. Nevertheless, at this point Biron's wish begins to be satisfied. The King enters, carrying a sonnet he has written to the Princess. Biron promptly makes himself scarce, either by climbing a tree or standing aside, in order to overlook and overhear the King, who proceeds to read out his poem. As the King finishes his reading, he sees Longueville coming, and, in his turn, stands aside. Longueville too has a sonnet, which he reads aloud, and he also steps aside as Dumaine appears on the scene to read his lyric, addressed to the 'most divine Kate'. Having read it out, he goes on to wish that the other three men were also in love. His wish is granted. The sequence of events we have witnessed so far immediately goes into reverse, as it were. Longueville comes out of hiding to chide Dumaine for falling in love. He is followed by the King who chides both of them. But the King's moment of triumph is short-lived, for Biron comes forward to gloat and crow over the three of them. He does it with such abandon and gusto that the King has already begun to suspect him of insincerity when Costard and Jaquenetta appear, bringing with them Biron's sonnet to Rosaline. Their arrival puts an end to his scoffs and taunts, forcibly converting him from seemingly tyrannical foe of love to ardent apologist for it.

When acted with the aplomb and timing it demands, the scene

is irresistibly funny, a text-book demonstration of the validity of Bergson's theory of laughter, that it is triggered by the spectacle of men behaving like machines. But, as Bottom nearly says, it does 'ask some skill in the true performing of it', in order to make the Elizabethan conventions of soliloquy and aside intelligible and acceptable to a modern audience. In the production Shaw saw in 1886 professional experience was sadly lacking, and its absence at this crucial point presented him with an easy target. He wrote:

The only absolutely impossible situation was that of Biron hiding in the tree to overlook the king, who presently hides to watch Longaville, who in turn spies on Dumain; as the result of which we had three out of the four gentlemen shouting 'asides' through the sylvan stillness, No. 1 being inaudible to 2, 3, and 4; No. 2 audible to No. 1, but not to 3 and 4; No. 3 audible to 1 and 2, but not to No. 4; and No. 4 audible to all the rest, but himself temporarily stone deaf. Shakespear has certainly succeeded in making this arrangement intelligible; but the Dramatic Students' stage manager did not succeed in making it credible.[1]

The answer to Shaw's objection that the stage manager failed to make the scene credible is, of course, that if the stage manager tried to do any such thing he was attempting the impossible, since Shakespeare had never meant it to be credible, in the sense of probable or plausible. The scene is a superb piece of artifice designed to amuse and to entertain, which is precisely what it does, because everything that happens in it, right down to the arrival of Costard and Jaquenetta, is completely predictable. From the moment Biron sees the King approaching we know substantially what is to follow, and we enjoy seeing our expectations realized. Shakespeare himself was evidently delighted with the effect, for he goes on to repeat it twice over in the last scene. We know before the masque of Muscovites begins that it is bound to fall flat on its face, just as we know that the Pageant of the Nine Worthies will be a triumph of incompetence.

What we do not know is that the sense of security we are made to feel through so much of the play's course is a false one. Shakespeare has his surprises in store for us; and surprise can be devastating when it intrudes into what has, so far, seemed a wholly predictable world and action. A hint of what is to come is given early in the long final scene. The Princess and her ladies are

[1] *Shaw on Shakespeare*, p. 135.

talking and jesting about the gifts they have received from the King and his men, and also about the influence of Cupid, whom Katherine describes as 'a shrewd unhappy gallows'. To this outburst Rosaline replies: 'You'll ne'er be friends with him; a killed your sister.' And Katherine then completes the little story by saying: 'He made her melancholy, sad, and heavy, | And so she died.' A momentary breath of cold air sends a ripple over the brilliant surface of witty badinage. It is almost, but not quite, forgotten by the time the Pageant of the Nine Worthies is played, which also brings its surprises with it. Exasperated beyond measure, as he has every right to be, by the outrageous abuse heaped on him by the courtiers, Holofernes turns on his tormentors to administer the rebuke their bad behaviour deserves: 'This is not generous, not gentle, not humble' (5.2.621). The foolish overbearing pedant we have seen hitherto has been transformed into a master of manners. Similarly, Armado the braggart, subjected to the same kind of insults, speaks up bravely, nobly, and humanely in defence of the dead Hector whom he is impersonating. 'The sweet war-man', he tells his unruly auditors, 'is dead and rotten. Sweet chucks, beat not the bones of the buried. When he breathed, he was a man' (5.2.651-3). Depths we had not expected are being sounded. And then, to crown these revelations, comes the great *coup de théâtre*, the unheralded entry of Monsieur Marcadé, to announce the death of the King of France. His news acts as a chilling shock, made all the more powerful by the stark simplicity of what he says: twenty-eight simple words, none of them more than a disyllable, in a blank verse that is very close to prose. Paradoxically yet rightly the most important moment in this play so concerned with words is almost wordless.

In fact—and this is yet another instance of the conscious artifice that informs the entire comedy—there is not much blank verse in *Love's Labour's Lost*. Like *A Midsummer Night's Dream*, its only rival in this respect, it prefers to rely on rhyme. About sixty-five per cent of its total lines are in verse, but of these no more than a third are in blank verse. The rest are rhymed in a wide variety of ways. Heroic couplets are common, especially in the 'sets of wit' that the courtiers and the ladies engage in. So are sonnets. There are, if one includes the first fourteen lines in which the King sets out his plans and the fifteen lines in which he describes Armado (1.1.161–75), no fewer than five of them. Moreover, they are easily and invitingly detachable. *Love's Labour's Lost* was the first of Shakespeare's plays to provide material for the anthologists of the day. Biron's sonnet (4.2.104–17), Longueville's sonnet (4.3.58–71), and Dumaine's dainty lyric (4.3.99–118) all appeared in a miscellany entitled *The Passionate Pilgrim*, published by William Jaggard in 1599, and Dumaine's lyric yet again in the great collection entitled *England's Helicon*, which came out in 1600. In addition quatrains in alternate rhyme are common. It is in these measures and, of course, in blank verse that the courtly figures discourse and express themselves. The other characters, as befits their station, resort to more popular kinds of verse: ballad metre, 'fourteeners', poulter's measure, and the like, together with the shambling brokenbacked couplets, that almost cry out to be intoned in a parsonic manner, through which Sir Nathaniel voices his sense of his own superiority to Constable Dull, whose 'ignorance' he cites as the text for what amounts to a miniature sermon (4.2.24–32). In general, however, they stick to prose, of which they have almost a monopoly; and a most extraordinary prose it proves to be, at least in the mouths of Armado and Holofernes, absurd in its excesses and affectations and delightful in its absurdity.

The play opens on a confident full-throated note. The King's initial speech has a heroic ring to it. His lines sound a clarion call to endeavour, to labour. But the labour he has in mind is none of Cupid's. Like Hercules at the parting of the ways, he has, according to what he says, chosen the rough and arduous road that leads to virtue in preference to the smooth and easy road that leads to pleasure.[1] The pursuit of fame is, he asserts, the right and proper end of living, and true fame is to be sought and won through an austere course of study that will turn the court of Navarre into 'a little academe' and make it 'the wonder of the world'. Fourteen lines, that are both in structure and effect a sonnet in blank verse, suffice to set the scene firmly in the world of the Renaissance typified by the *Accademia Platonica* of Florence which Cosimo de' Medici had established in the mid fifteenth century. The King's ambition is evidently to become the philo-

[1] See Erwin Panofsky, *Hercules am Scheidewege* (Leipzig, 1930).

sopher-king, the ideal ruler of Plato's imagined commonwealth; and it has to be admitted that the programme he outlines represents a far better and more civilized way of earning fame than that which had so strong an appeal for most monarchs and princes of the time. This said, however, it is already plain that the King's plans, especially after more detail about them emerges, rest on an unrealistic view of human nature in general and of his own nature in particular. He is obviously indulging in wishful thinking when he addresses his fellow-students as 'brave conquerors'. They may indeed be warring against their 'affections', meaning 'passions', but they are far from having overcome them. The Archpoet of the late twelfth century could have told him better:

> *Res est arduissima*
> *vincere naturam,*
> *in aspectu virginis*
> *mentem esse puram;*
> *iuvenes non possumus*
> *legem sequi duram,*
> *leviumque corporum*
> *non habere curam.*[1]

For all its vigour and the rich resounding language in which it is couched, the King's speech is distinctly hollow; and its hollowness is underlined by the casual unthinking manner in which Longueville and Dumaine accept the conditions it lays down. Like the King himself, they seem to regard a thing well said as a thing well done.

It is all very high-minded, not to say high-falutin, and badly out of touch with the hard facts of life. The academy is a flimsy structure, carefully designed to be easily knocked down. Biron, a born wrecker, finds the temptation to begin that process irresistible. Equipped with some sense of, and some respect for, facts, he

[1] Quoted from Helen Waddell, *The Wandering Scholars* (Harmondsworth, 1954), pp. 252–3. Miss Waddell (p. 177) translates the lines thus:

> Hard beyond all hardness, this
>   Mastering of Nature:
> Who shall say his heart is clean,
>   Near so fair a creature?
> Young are we, so hard a law,
>   How should we obey it?
> And our bodies, they are young,
>   Shall they have no say in't?

puts the case for natural behaviour. Unlike the three previous speeches, his first contribution to the play's exposition, in which he reminds the others of precisely what they are committing themselves to—a series of 'barren tasks, too hard to keep: | Not to see ladies, study, fast, not sleep'—evolves along neat logical lines. The items in it are ticked off one by one, and the list is punctuated by the recurring refrain: 'The which I hope is not enrollèd there'.

Hitherto the dialogue has been conducted in blank verse, apart from the concluding lines to each speech, which have taken the form of a couplet. Now, however, as an argument develops between Biron and the King, blank verse gives way to couplets, the right vehicle for snip-snap repartee in which the participants seek to score points off one another, until Biron produces a definition of the proper end of study which, if accepted by the others, would turn the whole idea of the academy upside down and inside out, leading the King to say:

> These be the stops that hinder study quite,
> And train our intellects to vain delight.
>
> (1.1.70–1)

Hereupon, Biron, taking this statement as a challenge to his dialectical virtuosity, and slipping easily into quatrains in alternate rhyme, which allow of a more fluid movement than do end-stopped couplets, catches up the King's last two words and expatiates on them for the next twenty lines. At first sight it may well seem that he is using far more words than are necessary, especially as some of them are the same words, though employed in senses that are constantly shifting. The whole outpouring appears to be wide open to the charge Sir Francis Bacon would soon bring against the Renaissance Latinists, whom he would accuse of paying more attention to 'copie' [i.e. copiousness] than 'weight', and then go on to say: 'Here therefore is the first distemper of learning, when men study words and not matter'.[1] Doctor Johnson was certainly of this opinion. Picking out the line 'Light, seeking light, doth light of light beguile', he comments:

The whole sense of this gingling declamation is only this, that *a man by too close study may read himself blind*, which might have been told with less obscurity in fewer words.[2]

---

[1] *The Advancement of Learning*, ed. William Aldis Wright (Oxford, 1900), p. 30.
[2] *Johnson on Shakespeare*, ed. Walter Raleigh (Oxford, 1908), p. 86.

But might it? Is not the total significance of the line richer than Johnson allows? What Biron is saying runs something like this: 'A man seeking for understanding solely by reading books fails to find the illumination he looks for. Instead, he becomes muddled and confused, and, ultimately goes blind.' The play on the word *light* enforces the paradox that the misguided effort defeats the attainment of the laudable objective it has in view.

Doctor Johnson should have cheered. The sentiments are very much his. He found fault with Milton for looking at life 'through the spectacles of books', and in his *Rasselas* the sage, Imlac, tells the Abyssinian prince: 'It seems to me, that while you are making the choice of life you neglect to live.'[1] But Johnson was put off by the word-play. Nevertheless, that word-play is an extremely important element in the comedy. From this point onwards there is one reference after another to *light*, *eyes*, and *books*. The interplay between them is complex and subtle, but, broadly speaking, their main significance is much as follows: light is understanding, and especially understanding of life; but it is also that which enables us to see, in the metaphorical as well as the literal sense of that word, and that which dazzles us and makes us incapable of seeing when there is too much of it. The eye is, of course, the organ through which light is perceived, but, where men and women in love are concerned, it is also, in the sense of the beloved's eye, the book that is studied and interpreted, sometimes rightly and sometimes wrongly.

Biron's manner of expressing all this is clever, intricate, and ostentatiously artificial; but his message is plain, simple, and sensible, a plea for the exercise of common sense and for heeding the promptings of nature. When the King accuses him of being a kill-joy, because he is so critical of the forcing-house that the academy threatens to become, his answer comes back clearly and unequivocally:

> Why should proud summer boast
> Before the birds have any cause to sing?
> Why should I joy in any abortive birth?
> At Christmas I no more desire a rose
> Than wish a snow in May's new-fangled shows,
> But like of each thing that in season grows.
>
> (I.I.I02-7)

---

[1] *Johnson: Prose and Poetry*, selected by Mona Wilson (1950), pp. 837 and 444-5.

Far more simple and direct than anything Biron has said hitherto, these lines announce a theme that will continue to run as a sort of bass through the rest of the play's course and finally emerge as its dominant strain in the songs of Spring and Winter with which the comedy ends: a deep feeling for the connections between the human world and the world of nature, together with a recognition of the vital importance of seasonal rhythms. If it is to succeed, a proposal, including a proposal of marriage, must be rightly timed. By the end of the play, the four men are just beginning to learn this. The women have known it from the start.

But, while *Love's Labour's Lost* shares this concern with Shakespeare's other comedies, the movement of its action is, in one respect at least, unique. Instead of ending with the coming into being of a new society, it concludes with a reversion to a much older one. Beginning by trying to fit himself for the role of philosopher–king, Navarre, and his lords with him, finally accepts that of the medieval knight who wins the hand of his lady by service. The magical phrase 'a twelvemonth and a day', so reminiscent of *Sir Gawaine and the Green Knight*, 'The Wife of Bath's Tale', and romance in general, occurs twice in the last hundred lines of *Love's Labour's Lost*, and nowhere else in the whole of Shakespeare's writings.

It is, appropriately enough, Biron, the man with whom facts count, who now notices and points out that one part of the King's Utopian dream is already out of date and impracticable. Since the Princess of France is already on her way to Navarre to negotiate about matters of state, the King must perforce break his newly-taken oath not to talk with a woman for the next three years. From this moment the idea of the academy, already badly shaken, is in ruins, though the men are reluctant to admit it. It is plain, as it should have been from the first, that the King cannot abandon his royal duties and obligations in favour of living as a recluse without making proper arrangements for the conduct of affairs during his retirement from public life. Trying to make the best of a bad job, Navarre pleads necessity as a reason for infringing his own decree; and Biron draws the logical consequences:

> Necessity will make us all forsworn
> > Three thousand times within this three years' space;
> For every man with his affects is born,
> > Not by might mastered, but by special grace.

> (1.1.148–51)

Much of the subsequent development of the action, and of the play's total significance, is implicit in those lines. *Love's Labour's Lost*, for most of its course, dances lightly on its way; there is nothing solemn or portentous about it; but, like all good comedy, it is not without its serious concerns. Foremost among them are two: first, the conviction that man is a passional being, incapable of controlling his 'affects', his instinctive urges and desires, without divine assistance; and, secondly, the recognition that oaths, the bonds of civil society, are, or at least should be, binding. They are not to be taken rashly and then brushed aside casually, as the King seems to think, or made in the full knowledge that they will not be kept, which is what Biron does when, in complete defiance of his own èminently rational demurs, he sets his name to the articles.

With the matter of the oath-taking settled for the time being, a fresh interest is needed. Biron opens the way for it by asking: 'is there no quick recreation granted?' The King replies by giving a full-length 'character' of Armado in which he describes that 'refinèd traveller of Spain' as

> One who the music of his own vain tongue
> Doth ravish like enchanting harmony.
>
> (1.1.165–6)

The words apply equally well to the four students, and particularly well to Biron; but blissfully blind to this fact, the King goes on to say:

> How you delight, my lords, I know not, I,
> But I protest I love to hear him lie,
> And I will use him for my minstrelsy.

The minstrel was, among other things, the story-teller; and the stories the King apparently expects Armado to relate are tall stories of the kind Falstaff would soon be telling, tales of great deeds done and daring enterprises about to be undertaken—all of them fictional and having no more substance than the boasts made about the 'invincible' Spanish Armada with which both Armado's name and his nationality connect him. Biron approves of the plan, characterizing Armado as 'A man of fire-new words, fashion's own knight', and Longueville adds his mite of expository information:

> Costard the swain and he shall be our sport,
> And so to study three years is but short.
>
> (1.1.178-9)

From all this it would appear that the King and his followers are arranging a programme of entertainment for themselves, which we shall see carried into action. That impression is seemingly confirmed at once, for, pat on the cue provided by his name, Costard makes his entry, escorted by Constable Dull who has him in custody and bears a letter for the King recounting the heinous offence with which Costard is charged. It is, one notes admiringly, marvellously right that we should hear Armado, the author of the letter, before we actually see him, for the essence of the man is in what he says, or rather in his way of saying it.

The reading-out of the letter is delayed by Costard, who insists on giving his own version of his misdemeanour. Employing the legal terminology and the verbal quibbles he regards as proper for the occasion, much as the Gravedigger would do in *Hamlet* five or six years later, he reveals that he was caught in the act of consorting with Jaquenetta in the royal park, an action which he stoutly defends on the grounds that it was perfectly natural. The preposterousness of the academy and, still more, of the King's attempt to force its restrictions on his dependents, is emphatically underscored. Eventually, however, the letter is read out by the King, while his rehearsal of its polysyllabic periphrases is punctuated by terse monosyllabic interruptions from Costard. So far as matter goes, the letter adds nothing whatever to Costard's own account of his delinquency, but the manner of it is utterly different. Armado, to impress the King with his dutiful devotion, and, as he hopes, to elevate the clown's 'hearkening after the flesh' into a major crime, uses dozens of words to say what Costard says in one.

The letter is deliciously and consistently ridiculous. But what, precisely, is Shakespeare, as distinct from Armado, doing in it? He is, surely and above all else, enjoying himself enormously. The missive is written *con amore*; its composition a labour of love. Fvery word in it has been chosen with care and discrimination; every construction elaborated in conformity with a set pattern.

Often labelled satire, it is really nothing of the kind. The play-wright's aim is not to attack the extravagant copiousness of much Elizabethan narrative prose, especially of the pastoral variety, and destroy it by concentrating on its absurdities, but rather to build up, in a spirit of creative play, an insubstantial and fantastic edifice of words and figures of speech, which he and his audience in the theatre can then stand back from and admire with amused amazement as they see so much being made out of so little. If Shakespeare himself played a part, as seems quite likely, in the early performances of *Love's Labour's Lost*, it should have been that of Armado.

By the time the first scene is over, we think we know how Armado will continue to be used. The King and his party will encourage him to indulge his fondness for unrelenting circum-locution, something we have now heard him doing, and his compulsion to brag and tell lies, something we have been told he does but have not yet heard him doing, and will find enter-tainment in his posturings. In fact, we are quite wrong on both counts. It is true that Boyet, the know-all attendant on the Princess, keeps up the fiction by telling her in the fourth act:

> This Armado is a Spaniard that keeps here in court,
> A phantasime, a Monarcho, and one that makes sport
> To the Prince and his book-mates.
>
> (4.1.97–9)

But the fact remains that Armado never appears on stage with the King and his courtiers until about four hundred lines from the end of the play, and, when he does so, it is to hand the King the 'plot' or programme, as it would be today, for the Pageant of the Nine Worthies which he has commissioned and in which he is about to take part. Moreover, he does not brag in the manner the King has led us to expect he will. He talks, and writes, in high-flown terms that are admirably sustained, some of them fire-new from the neological mint, some of them bits of treasure-trove from the ancient fields of romance, but he tells no boasting tales either about himself or others. The nearest he comes to doing so is when he insinuates, in 5.1, that he is on intimate terms with the King. Shakespeare, it seems clear, changed his mind about Armado. Having written that first letter, he knew that he wanted to compose more letters and speeches in the same exuberantly

7. John Neville as Don Armado in the Stratford, Ontario production of 1984, directed by Michael Langham.

fantastic vein. He therefore jettisoned the notion of Armado as the braggart of theatrical tradition, and turned him into a brilliant parody of the King and his followers. Like them, Armado falls in love, thus breaking his promise to 'study three years' with them; like them, he writes a love letter to the idol of his affections; and, most significant of all, he puts his trust in words and their power to move and prove. He even has a tiny court of his own. It consists solely of his page Moth, who is as critical of his master's poses and plans as Biron is of the King's, and who, again like Biron, is much given to word-play.

The second scene of the first act, where we actually see Armado in person, is in no small measure a preview of much that will follow in the main action. Already in love with Jaquenetta, the Spaniard has adopted the melancholy pose thought proper to that condition. Confessing his love, he asks Moth to provide some precedents for such unsoldierly behaviour, much as the King will ask Biron to find some justification for his falling in love in 4.3; and, when Jaquenetta herself appears, he declares his love for her and is rebuffed by her, much as Biron will be rebuffed by Rosaline in 2.1. Similarly the superb self-regarding soliloquy with which he closes 1.2 anticipates the way in which all the students will become sonneteers, while at one point—so thin is the line that separates the mock-heroic from the true heroic—it even has more than a touch of Othello's farewell to his 'occupation' (*Othello* 3.3.352–62) when it ends thus:

Adieu, valour; rust, rapier; be still, drum; for your manager is in love; yea, he loveth. Assist me, some extemporal god of rhyme, for I am sure I shall turn sonnet. Devise, wit; write, pen; for I am for whole volumes in folio.

Like his letter to the King, Armado's soliloquy is an ostentatious parade of affectation. It says little; but that little is, in its own peculiar manner, exquisitely phrased and cadenced. It has musical properties and affinities. Grammar is transformed into notes on a scale as the positive *base* inevitably leads on to the comparative *baser*, and that, in turn, to the superlative *basest.* Furthermore, the triple pattern thus established is renewed in 'Love is a familiar; Love is a devil. There is no evil angel but Love', and again in 'Adieu, valour; rust, rapier; be still, drum'. In Armado's case the style—and he has style—is indeed the man, and it comes into full flower in the letter he writes to Jaquenetta, which is read out by Boyet in 4.1. In it the pattern of graduated triple repetition is dominant, and even acquires a classical sanction when Armado takes over Caesar's '*Veni, vidi, vici*', a statement so laconic that it provides the material for his next twenty lines or so as he translates it into his own idiosyncratic kind of English. But this dominant triple rhythm is now complicated by the interplay with it of double antitheses, such as 'The magnanimous and most illustrate King Cophetua set eye upon the penurious and indubitate beggar Zenelophon', and 'I am the King, for so stands the comparison; thou the beggar, for so witnesseth thy lowliness'. The letter might well be described as variations on a theme by Caesar.

Armado's part, then, changes and grows as Shakespeare first perceives and then realizes and exploits the possibilities latent in it. It also seems to have led him to the creation of two other figures, who were not, perhaps, envisaged in his original conception of the comedy—Holofernes the pedant, and Sir Nathaniel the curate. They, unlike Armado, are not introduced by character sketches that precede their appearance on stage. Indeed, there has not been so much as a hint of their existence before they suddenly pop up, as it were, in the stage direction that initiates the action of 4.2, that is to say about one third of the way through the play, and not long after the disappearance from it of the two nameless lords attending on the Princess. Called for by the stage direction that opens 4.1, these two speak not a word in the scene and make their exit from it, along with the Princess, about forty lines before it ends. It looks very much as though Shakespeare phased them out because by this time he had come to see that he could make much better use of the two actors playing these supernumerary parts by giving them new roles. The introduction of the parson and the schoolmaster has a double effect. First, it fills out and completes the village community, represented hitherto by Costard, Dull, and Jaquenetta; and, secondly and more importantly, it provides the playwright with the means to carry much further that exploration and exploitation of linguistic fads and eccentricities which he had begun through his creation of Armado.

A talker, if he is to show his paces—and both Armado and Holofernes are bent on doing so—must have an audience. Armado is furnished with a sharply critical one in Moth; Holofernes with an effusively adulatory one in Sir Nathaniel. Both talkers are expert in making much of little; but their ways of doing it differ widely. The Spaniard's great stand-by is the periphrasis; whereas the pedant relies mainly on the synonym, of which George Puttenham had remarked in his *The Art of English Poesy* (1589) that an abundance of them 'doth much beautify and enlarge the matter'.[1] The first speech Holofernes makes shows conclusively that he is of the same mind as Puttenham. Addressing Sir Nathaniel, he says:

The deer was, as you know, in blood, *sanguis*, ripe as the pomewater, who now hangeth like a jewel in the ear of *caelum*, the sky, the welkin, the heaven, and anon falleth like a crab on the face of *terra*, the soil, the land, the earth. (4.2.3–7)

Armado, it is true, also makes play with synonyms on occasions, as when he writes, for instance, of the ink 'which here thou

[1] Ed. Gladys D. Willcock and Alice Walker (Cambridge, 1936), p. 215.

viewest, beholdest, surveyest, or seest' (1.1.238–9), but with him they are only one item in a large store of decorative devices. Holofernes, however, is a speaking dictionary, and a polyglot dictionary at that. Moreover, he has a head full of Latin tags and familiar quotations, prefers long Latinate words of the inkhorn variety to plain English terms, and finds lists irresistible. Yet figure of fun though he is, he too, like Armado, has his moments of felicity that bring him close to his creator. When he graciously accepts the curate's praise of his painfully excogitated lines on the death of the deer, he hymns his own inventive faculty in a way that suggests he has the root of the matter in him, and that looks forward to Falstaff's tribute to the stimulating effect sack can have on the imagination (*2 Henry IV* 4.2.93–9); and his admiring quibbling reference to Ovid may well express something of Shakespeare's own attitude to the Roman poet whose work meant so much to him:

for the elegancy, facility, and golden cadence of poesy ... Ovidius Naso was the man. And why indeed 'Naso' but for smelling out the odoriferous flowers of fancy, the jerks of invention? (4.2.121–4)

Improvisation, so evident in Shakespeare's treatment of Armado and in his invention of Holofernes and Sir Nathaniel, has also left its mark on the play as a whole. Both the masque of Muscovites and the Pageant of the Nine Worthies look very much like afterthoughts, as distinct from integral parts of the playwright's original plan. A mere glance at the way in which similar material is handled in *A Midsummer Night's Dream* is instructive. In it the 'tedious brief scene of young Pyramus | And his love Thisbe: very tragical mirth' (5.1.56–7) is an essential part of the structure, something built into it from the outset. Within a dozen lines of the opening Theseus orders Philostrate to 'Stir up the Athenian youth to merriments'; and no sooner is the first scene over than a consequence of that order is before our eyes as the mechanicals gather to discuss their play and take up the roles Quince has allotted them. The masque in *Love's Labour's Lost*, on the other hand, is never so much as mentioned until the end of the climactic scene 4.3, where the King suggests that he and his men devise some entertainment for the Princess and her ladies, and Biron, being a little more specific, sees four possibilities: 'revels, dances, masques, and merry hours' (4.3.354). Even so, however, the final scene is well advanced before the audience learns that a masque has been decided on. As for the Pageant, the first we hear about it is in 5.1, when Armado asks the schoolmaster for his assistance in providing the King with 'some delightful ostentation, or show, or pageant, or antic, or firework'. *Love's Labour's Lost* exerts a peculiar fascination of its own because it positively invites one to look over Shakespeare's shoulder, as it were, and watch him in the act of composition, coping with difficulties as they arise.

Yet the main outlines of the play, and especially of the closely interrelated conflicts with which it deals, never waver. So definite are they that they almost cry out to be formulated in abstract terms. The dominant motif is that of antithesis and reversal. Already present in the first scene, it becomes crystal clear in the second where it takes visual form as the tiny page Moth, whose diminutive stature is insisted on throughout, and his tall gaunt master, as most producers rightly make him, appear on stage for the first time. Between them these two form 'a little academe' of their own as well as a little court. But in this school the relationship of teacher to taught is inverted. It is Moth who instructs and provides the examples and definitions—'Define, define, well-educated infant', says Armado to him at one point (1.2.90); while the boy addresses his master as 'Negligent student' at another (3.1.32)—and the definitions themselves are much concerned with hair-splitting. Logic flourishes, especially in its extreme form, arithmetic, and so does paradox, as when Moth 'proves' that lead, far from being 'a metal heavy, dull, and slow', is 'swift' (3.1.54–9). But Moth's most telling way of going to work is by repeating and, in the process, reversing whatever Armado says, as he does in the following exchange:

ARMADO How canst thou part sadness and melancholy, my tender juvenal?

MOTH By a familiar demonstration of the working, my tough señor.

ARMADO Why tough señor? Why tough señor?

MOTH Why 'tender juvenal'? Why 'tender juvenal'?

ARMADO I spoke it, tender juvenal, as a congruent epitheton appertaining to thy young days, which we may nominate tender.

MOTH And I, tough señor, as an appertinent title to your old time, which we may name tough.

(1.2.7–15)

The incisive and insistent pattern set up by these exchanges is the very backbone of the comedy's dialogue, running right through it to culminate in the perfectly balanced songs with which Spring and Winter take up an old dispute that neither can win. *Love's Labour's Lost* is, in fact, the dramatization of a whole collection of closely interrelated oppositions: young men versus young women; artifice versus nature; study versus love; Plato versus Ovid; books versus eyes; words versus deeds; and deliberately cultivated neologizing speech versus plain idiomatic speech.

The most important of these 'contraries', as William Blake might have called them, is the first, the battle of the sexes. Implicit in the King's opening speech, and made quite explicit in the first two articles of his edict, is the notion of women as the enemy. From this point onwards the relationship between the two sexes is repeatedly seen and referred to by both sides as a kind of warfare. The dialogue is shot through and through with military terminology in a manner that goes back at least as far as Ovid, who had begun the ninth elegy of his First Book with the words '*Militat omnis amans, et habet sua castra Cupido*',[1] and then developed the analogy between the lover and the soldier through the rest of his poem. This use of the language of war becomes even more pronounced in the soliloquy with which Biron concludes 3.1, and reaches a sustained climax, that carries over into 5.2, at the end of 4.3. There the King, swept off his feet by Biron's eloquent praise of love, cries out: 'Saint Cupid, then! And, soldiers, to the field!', to which Biron himself adds:

> Advance your standards, and upon them, lords!
> Pell-mell, down with them! But be first advised
> In conflict that you get the sun of them.
>
> (4.3.342–4)

In its bawdy innuendo that speech sounds more like the prelude to a rape of the Gallic women than to a masque—soon to become a massacre—of Muscovites. The women are more than equal to the challenge. Told by Boyet, whom she addresses as 'scout', that the men are approaching 'Armèd in arguments', the Princess responds by saying 'Saint Denis to Saint Cupid!' (5.2.81–8).

The war is, as Boyet says, waged with arguments and with

[1] Every lover is a soldier, and Cupid has his tents.

repartee. Whenever the men and women meet wit combats ensue, usually in the form of stichomythic thrusts, parries, and counterthrusts. Words become weapons, and very sharp weapons at that. Boyet sums up this aspect of it all when he remarks:

> The tongues of mocking wenches are as keen
>   As is the razor's edge invisible,
> Cutting a smaller hair than may be seen;
>   Above the sense of sense, so sensible
> Seemeth their conference; their conceits have wings
> Fleeter than arrows, bullets, wind, thought, swifter things.
>
> (5.2.256–61)

As the last line and a half make plain, words can be missiles as well as swords and daggers. Moreover, the women, like the men, play war-games to keep their hands in, as it were. They spend much of their time whetting their wits on one another's and on Boyet's; while Biron, from the very outset, is always ready to take on his fellow-students, or even himself. In speech after speech, whether it be a soliloquy such as that with which he ends 3.1, a diatribe, such as his castigation of the other three in 4.3, or his two flyting attacks on Boyet in 5.2, he piles up dismissive item on dismissive item in what becomes a positive hailstorm of picturesque abuse, made up to a large extent of freshly coined compound nouns. *Carry-tale*, for which the *OED* can find only one precedent, together with *please-man*, *mumble-news*, and *trencher-knight*, for which it can cite none, and *zany*, borrowed either from the French or the Italian, all appear in the course of a mere two lines (5.2.463–4).

The linguistic vigour and fertility so evident in these lines and in the entire speech from which they come is, of course, typical of the play as a whole. *Love's Labour's Lost* contains, as Alfred Hart showed more than forty years ago,[1] a larger number of new words—new in the sense that Shakespeare had not used them before—than any other play, with the single exception of *Hamlet*, that he wrote; and *Hamlet*, it has to be remembered, is nearly half as long again as the comedy. Armado and Holofernes between them are responsible for the majority of these new words; but Biron is the third most important contributor to the total; and,

---

[1] 'Vocabularies of Shakespeare's Plays' and 'The Growth of Shakespeare's Vocabulary', *RES* 19 (1943), 128–40 and 242–54.

while their new words smell of the inkhorn, his do not. They appear as natural growths from the native soil of plain English usage. They need no gloss and have never needed one.

In this respect they tie up with and complement another less noticed yet equally striking feature of Biron's speech, his recourse to proverbial lore, which tends to be the language of common experience and common sense. The figures concerning this phenomenon, as set out by R. W. Dent in his *Shakespeare's Proverbial Language*,[1] are highly illuminating. *Love's Labour's Lost*, with a total of 189, makes more use of proverbs than does any other of the comedies, its nearest rival being *Twelfth Night*, with 150, and is outdone by only two of the other plays, both of them tragedies: *King Lear*, with 197, and *Romeo and Juliet*, with 223. No fewer than 47 of these proverbial phrases by my count, i.e. one quarter, come from the lips of Biron.

The range and variety of Biron's vocabulary are a pointer to what is simultaneously his main strength and his main weakness. A true child of the Renaissance, he sets great store, as do his fellow-students, by eloquence, which Samuel Daniel would soon invoke in his *Musophilus* (1599) in the following terms:

> Power above powers, O heavenly *Eloquence*,
>   That with the strong rein of commanding words,
>   Dost manage, guide, and master th'eminence
>   Of men's affections, more than all their swords.[2]

Like Daniel, the four young men regard the power of words as unlimited. Having fallen in love, they all turn to the writing of verse as the recognized and appropriate means of persuading the ladies to love them in return. Moreover, all four think that words, properly handled, can prove anything, even that black is white. It is true that when Biron says of the dark Rosaline, 'I'll prove her fair, or talk till doomsday here' (4.3.271), the other three protest against his sophistry, but within a dozen lines the King is requesting him to do the impossible: ' good Biron, now prove | Our loving lawful and our faith not torn'. It is an absurd demand. The men have broken their initial vows; and nothing they can do will alter that fact. Still less will anything they can say. Costard knows better. He is not taken in when Armado gives him three

[1] Berkeley, Los Angeles, London, 1981, pp. 3–4.

[2] *Poems and 'A Defence of Ryme'*, ed. A. C. Sprague (1950), p. 96, ll. 939–42.

farthings by way of 'remuneration'. For him three farthings remain three farthings, despite the imposing, six-syllable, Latinate name Armado chooses to give them, and, as such, elevenpence farthing inferior to Biron's two-syllable 'guerdon' of one shilling (3.1.127–38).

Nevertheless, Biron complies with the King's request, and puts on a sparkling display of rhetorical and, it must in fairness be added, poetical pyrotechnics, that grows out of his similar performance at the play's opening (1.1.72–93). Addressing his fellows as 'affection's men-at-arms', and thus implying that they have now enlisted under the banners of those same natural impulses they originally set out to 'conquer', he begins by arguing along pseudo-logical lines. But as he warms to his work, and moves on to the subject of women's eyes, the prompters of love, his verse takes off, so to speak. It becomes musical, singing with lyrical grace and rhapsodical fervour, and rising to a climax in the lines:

> For valour, is not Love a Hercules,
> Still climbing trees in the Hesperides?
> Subtle as Sphinx, as sweet and musical
> As bright Apollo's lute, strung with his hair;
> And when Love speaks, the voice of all the gods
> Make heaven drowsy with the harmony.

$$(4.3.315-20)$$

There is more than a touch of Marlowe about it all, of the Marlowe who had written of men's souls 'Still climbing after knowledge infinite', and of the poet ever searching for the perfect word and image that always elude him (*1 Tamburlaine* 2.1.24 and 5.2.98–110). But it also has its own peculiar 'Promethean fire', with *Promethean* meaning 'life-infusing', as it does again in *Othello*, at 5.2.12, the only other place where the word appears in Shakespeare's writings. Having soared into the empyrean, however, Biron must eventually come back to earth. He does so by returning to the dialectical legerdemain with which he began, and by concluding with the rhetorical question, 'Who can sever love from charity?', that assumes the answer 'No one', but really deserves the answer 'Anyone who knows the difference between pagan *amor* and Christian *caritas*'.

For a moment Biron is as much intoxicated by his own virtuosity as are the other three, but before the scene is over he has begun to sober down. Nevertheless, much has yet to happen to bring him to a proper understanding of the limits of language. Even after the masque of Muscovites has turned into a fiasco, he still attempts to win Rosaline's love by harping on his favourite conceit about *eyes*, *light*, and the dazzling effect of the *sun* (5.2.374–6); and it is not until the women reveal that they knew all along who the masquers were that he begins at last to see something of the inadequacy of words. The palinode in which he does so: 'Thus pour the stars down plagues for perjury ... sans crack or flaw' (5.2.394–415), is a superbly paradoxical performance by a master of paradox. Biron rejects verbal artifice, to which he has hitherto pinned his faith, in favour of plain homespun language, or so at least he says. Yet the terms in which he does it are a compelling demonstration of the force and energy figurative speech is capable of. Its power to wound is vividly conjured up in the four lines he devotes to Rosaline's wit:

> Here stand I, lady, dart thy skill at me,
>   Bruise me with scorn, confound me with a flout,
> Thrust thy sharp wit quite through my ignorance,
>   Cut me to pieces with thy keen conceit.

But so also is its capacity to delight. The sensuous pleasure to be derived from it becomes palpable in the soft rich materials with which he clothes his figures, 'Taffeta phrases, silken terms precise', and so on. In love with them still, he lingers fondly over them in the very act of abjuring them, and then undercuts all he has said so far by his inability to resist the attractions of the gallicism *sans*.

Even at this late stage Biron is far from cured of his infatuation with words. He will still go on to make his abusive attack on Boyet (5.2.460–81); to preface an appeal to the ladies with the statement, 'Honest plain words best pierce the ear of grief', and then launch into yet another word game, playing upon *eyes* and juggling with the meanings of the words *false* and *true* (5.2.743–64). Moreover, in the very speech where he finally capitulates and asks Rosaline to 'Impose some service' on him he is still talking about 'the window of my heart, mine eye'. Only when she has laid down her conditions does he admit that there are indeed things that words cannot do:

> To move wild laughter in the throat of death?
> It cannot be, it is impossible.
> Mirth cannot move a soul in agony.
>
> (5.2.837–9)

Biron is obviously the dominant figure among the men, their leader, as they acknowledge when the King, seconded by Longueville and Dumaine, calls on him to 'prove' that they have not been guilty of perjury. He is also the most interesting of them, because he has a certain complexity. Capable, on the one hand, of genuine poetic flight, notably in his hymn to love, he can, on the other, be self-critical, making himself the object of his own wry mockeries, and even cynical. There are times, particularly in the soliloquy with which he ends 3.1 and in its companion soliloquy with which he opens 4.3, when he reminds one of the young John Donne who was a student at Lincoln's Inn between 1592 and 1594, where he may have written such poems as 'Woman's Constancy' and 'The Triple Fool'.[1] In the first Donne plays tricks with the words 'true' and 'false' much as Biron does at 5.2.760–4, while he begins the second with the lines:

> I am two fools, I know,
> For loving and for saying so
> In whining poetry.

I am not suggesting that Biron is to be identified with Donne, but rather that the roundness his character takes on may owe something to the contacts Shakespeare seems to have had with the young men of the Inns of Court in the early 1590s (see pp. 45–7), which was also, interestingly enough, the time when, according to Sir Richard Baker, Donne was 'a great visitor of ladies, a great frequenter of plays, a great writer of conceited verses'.[2] If the playwright ever depicted a typical Inns of Court man, then Biron is he.

Biron's counterpart among the women and, simultaneously, his antithesis is not, as one would expect, Rosaline. She is altogether too much like him, especially when she looks forward with such keen anticipation to 'torturing' him (5.2.60–8), to fulfil that role. The opposing voice to his is that of the Princess, who, unlike the King, exerts a natural unquestioned authority

[1] See R. C. Bald, *John Donne: A Life* (Oxford, 1970), p. 71.
[2] Quoted from Bald, p. 72.

over her followers. It is a quiet reasonable voice, free from the assertive argumentativeness that characterizes so many of Biron's speeches, but it is also firm and confident. The first exchange between her and the King tells us much. 'Fair Princess, welcome to the court of Navarre', says he, mouthing the polite formula he thinks appropriate to the occasion and, no doubt, expecting a similar formula in return. He does not receive it. Instead, the Princess replies: ' "Fair" I give you back again, and welcome I have not yet' (2.1.91–2). It is already clear that for her words are not things to be twisted, turned, and given as much or as little weight as the speaker chooses. They should be the instruments of society, the servants of truth, and correspond with facts. Forced into facing his own discourtesy, Navarre tries to gloss it over, but only succeeds in making it worse, as the Princess points out by saying:

> I hear your grace hath sworn out housekeeping.
> 'Tis deadly sin to keep that oath, my lord,
> And sin to break it.
>
> (2.1.103–5)

Her clear-eyed perception of the dilemma the men are now in and the attitude she adopts towards it remain hers to the end. When the King, having decided to abandon his initial position, eventually invites her to enter his court, her answer is as unequivocal and uncompromising as it was at their first interview:

> This field shall hold me, and so hold your vow.
> Nor God nor I delights in perjured men.
>
> (5.2.345–6)

A mirror of manners—her reception of the Pageant in particular is a rebuke to the uncouth and unruly responses to it of the King's men—the Princess is the standard by which the men are measured and found wanting. She is the play's still centre, exercising an influence on its outcome and characters that goes far beyond anything the mere size of her part might lead one to expect.

Love, the mischievous amoral Dan Cupid, who thinks women are to be won 'with revels, dances, masques, and merry hours', and, above all else, with sophistries and flatteries, stands no chance of prevailing against one for whom 'the right true end of love' is marriage, and marriage 'a world-without-end bargain'.

As Ver, '[maintained] by the cuckoo', and Hiems, 'maintained by the owl', renew an ancient debate, we are transported out of the rarefied atmosphere and artificial ambience of the royal park into the genuine countryside. The 'war of wits' is over; and with it have gone the sharp ripostes, the dazzling word-play so like sword-play, the puns, the 'taffeta phrases', the 'silken terms precise', the lexicographical lists, and the circling periphrases. Specious dialectic no longer rears its head. From a world in which words have an almost independent life of their own, fighting and dancing with one another, we move into another where they are intimately related to the things they denote—flowers, birds, the wind that blows, the cold that freezes, and simple yet essential human activities. The two seasons, like the two sexes, not only oppose one another but also balance one another. Spring is a time of love and delight, but it also brings its attendant misgivings typified by the voice of the cuckoo. Winter is a time of coughs and red noses, but it also has its compensations, the roasted crab-apples hissing in the bowl and the merry note of the staring owl. The two songs, so antiphonally connected, establish the point of balance on which the play has come to rest.

The Date and 'Sources'

The earliest text of *Love's Labour's Lost* that we have, the First Quarto, was published, its title-page tells us, in 1598, and thus provides a definite *terminus ad quem* for the date of its composition. That same title-page also states that the play had been 'presented before her Highness this last Christmas'. At first sight this looks like a reference to the Christmas of 1597, thus pushing the latest time for composition back by a year; but then one realizes that the First Quarto might have come out during the first three months of what we now call 1599, so that the Christmas in question could still be that of 1598. One other bit of external evidence can be gleaned from the title-page. It says that the text it offers has been 'Newly corrected and augmented', thus implying that there had been a previous edition which could not conceivably have been published later than 1598. If there had been, however, no copy of it has ever come to light. The two earliest mentions of the play—one in Robert Tofte's *Alba*, cited at pages 1–2, and the other in Francis Meres's *Palladis Tamia* (see pp. 81–2)— do not help in establishing any other date by which it must have been written, since both occur in works first published in 1598. Some scholars have argued that the word 'once' in the first line of Tofte's account of his visit to the theatre means 'a long time ago', but, in view of what he says about his experience there, 'on a particular occasion' seems a far more likely interpretation of it.

In these circumstances internal evidence becomes all important, and it, by its very nature, tends to be subjective. It is obviously so in the opinion hazarded by Charles Gildon in 1710, which runs thus: 'since it is one of the worst of Shakespeare's Plays, nay I think I may say the very worst, I cannot but think it is his first' (Furness, p. 327). Not all critics of the eighteenth century were so ready to condemn the comedy as Gildon was, but most of them did concur with him in regarding it as very early, i.e. as belonging to 1590 or thereabouts. Edmond Malone, the first scholar to make 'An Attempt to ascertain the Order in which the Plays of Shakespeare were written' (1778), pointed the way to a more objective method. Taking a high incidence of rhymed verse as an index to plays composed early in the playwright's career, he began by suggesting 1591 as the date of *Love's Labour's Lost*, but then later revised it to read 1594, though he still thought of the play as 'one of [Shakespeare's] earliest essays' in the writing of comedy (Furness, p. 328). It was, however, the notion of earliness, rather than the specific date of 1594, that appealed to scholars and critics in the nineteenth century and well on into the twentieth. Then, as the play began to rise in critical estimation, its chronological place in the canon was assessed afresh with results that are well summarized by E. K. Chambers in his *William Shakespeare*, where he writes of *Love's Labour's Lost*: 'The versification is extremely adroit, and certainly not that of a beginner. I regard the play as the earliest of the lyrical group which includes *Midsummer Night's Dream*, *Romeo and Juliet*, and *Richard II*, and I put it in 1595' (i. 335).

There are verifiable grounds for bringing these four plays together and thinking of them as a separate group. They are not only lyrical, as Chambers says, but also their lyricism is evident in the extensive use they make of rhyme. No fewer than 43.1 per cent of the total lines in *Love's Labour's Lost* and 45.5 per cent of those in *A Midsummer Night's Dream* are rhymed. No other of Shakespeare's comedies comes anywhere near to approaching them in this respect. Their closest rival is *The Comedy of Errors*, with 21.5 per cent. Similarly, *Richard II* has far more rhymed verse—19.1 per cent—than any other of the history plays; and *Romeo and Juliet*, with 16.6 per cent, more than any other of the tragedies (the figures are taken from Harbage, p. 31).

Other links between the four plays reinforce the idea that they are connected with one another and belong to roughly the same stage in the playwright's career. Those connecting *Love's Labour's Lost* with *A Midsummer Night's Dream* are particularly strong, and do much to suggest that the latter play grew, to some extent, out of the former. Both contain a play-within-the-play, or rather, in the case of *Love's Labour's Lost*, shows-within-the-play, in their last acts. But, while the Masque of Muscovites and the Pageant of the Nine Worthies look like bits of improvisation on the part of the playwright, the 'tedious brief scene of young Pyramus | And his love Thisbe' has been carefully prepared for from the very opening of *A Midsummer Night's Dream*. Moreover, Shakespeare himself positively invites us to contrast these two comedies with one another. Near the end of *Love's Labour's Lost* Biron remarks: 'Our wooing doth not end like an old play: | Jack hath not Jill'; whereas Robin Goodfellow concludes the third act of *A Midsummer Night's Dream* with the words:

> Jack shall have Jill,
> Naught shall go ill,
> The man shall have his mare again, and all shall be well.

Whether or not 'Pyramus and Thisbe' is meant as a burlesque of *Romeo and Juliet*, the temptation to see it as one is strong; and there is a distinct possibility that Rosaline in *Love's Labour's Lost* grew out of the unseen presence, also called Rosaline, who haunts the opening scene of the tragedy. As for *Richard II*, its hero is as eloquent as Biron, puts his trust in words, as Biron does, and eventually discovers their inadequacy as a means of dealing with the practical difficulties of life.

Assuming, then, that the four plays are indeed a group, and that, as seems likely, either *Love's Labour's Lost* or *Romeo and Juliet* is the earliest of them, what light does this throw on the date when *Love's Labour's Lost* came into being? It seems to show that

all four had been produced by 1597, for in that year two of them—
Romeo and Juliet and *Richard II*—appeared in print, each bearing on
its title-page the statement that it had been publicly acted by
Shakespeare's company, and, in the case of *Romeo and Juliet*, 'often
(with great applause)', which almost certainly implies that it had
been in existence for some considerable time before that date.
Indeed, had that First Quarto been a legitimate publication, as the
First Quarto of *Richard II* was, printing a text obtained from the
company, it would be possible to say, with a fair measure of
certainty, that the play was considerably more than a year old.
Elizabethan acting companies did not normally allow their plays to
be printed until well after they had ceased to draw an audience.
The case of Ben Jonson is an interesting one in this connection, for
he, unlike most of his fellow-dramatists, saw to it that the printed
versions of his plays specified the year in which a particular drama
was first put on. Of the nine plays he wrote between 1598 and
1611, only *Catiline*, the last of them, came out in the same year as
that in which it was first staged; and it, significantly, had been a
complete flop. It seems reasonable, therefore, to think that the
group of Shakespeare's plays to which *Love's Labour's Lost* belongs
had been written by 1596 at the latest.

Is there, then, a date before which these four plays are unlikely
to have been written? There is such a date, and it is the spring of
1594, for it was not until then that the worst outbreak of plague
in the whole of Elizabeth's reign came to an end. It had begun in
August 1592, and had kept the theatres closed, except for brief
intervals, for the best part of two years. During this time acting
companies fell into disarray and broke up, while Shakespeare
himself devoted some at least of his energies to the writing of his
two narrative poems: *Venus and Adonis*, published in 1593, and
The Rape of Lucrece, published in 1594. With the end of the plague
came a time of reorganization and rebuilding in the acting
profession; and Shakespeare became a 'sharer' in a newly formed
company, the Lord Chamberlain's Men, as they were called, with
which he was to remain for the rest of his career. *Love's Labour's
Lost*, which frequently echoes both narrative poems, could well
have been one of the first plays he wrote for this new company;
and the date 1594–5 the likeliest for its composition.

An even more precise dating would be possible if only it could
be shown conclusively that Shakespeare was indebted to the

8. *Maroccus Extaticus*, a pamphlet celebrating the many talents of Moth's 'dancing horse' (1.2.53), was published in 1595, at roughly the same time as the first performances of *Love's Labour's Lost*.

Gray's Inn Revels of Christmas 1594–5 for the idea of the Masque of Muscovites in 5.2 of his comedy. On this particular occasion the Revels were of an unusually elaborate kind; and the Lord Chamberlain's Men were almost certainly involved in them. On the night of 28 December the Lord of Misrule at Gray's Inn, or Prince of Purpoole as he was called, received an 'Ambassador' from the Inner Temple in what was evidently meant to be a scene of mock-pageantry. However, as might be expected of ceremonies presided over by a Lord of Misrule, things got out of hand. The audience invaded the stage; and the 'Ambassador' left in a huff, taking his train with him.

After their departure the throngs and tumults did somewhat cease, although so much of them continued as was able to disorder and confound any good inventions whatsoever. In regard whereof, as also for that the sports intended were especially for gracing of the *Templarians*, it was thought good not to offer any thing of account, saving dancing and revelling with gentlewomen; and after such sports, a Comedy of Errors (like to *Plautus* his *Menechmus*) was played by the players. So that night was begun, and continued to the end, in nothing but confusion and errors; whereupon, it was ever afterwards called, *The Night of Errors*.[1]

[1] *Gesta Grayorum 1688*, ed. W. W. Greg (Oxford, 1915), p. 22.

The comedy must have been *The Comedy of Errors*, and the 'players' of it the Lord Chamberlain's Men.

A few days later, on Twelfth Night, a further entertainment was put on. In it another 'Ambassador', purporting to come from 'the mighty Emperor of Russia and Muscovy', appeared on stage at Gray's Inn, 'in attire of Russia, accompanied with two or three of his own country, in like habit', to praise some English knights for having defeated some Bigarian and Negro-Tartars who had invaded the Emperor's dominions.[1] The likelihood of a connection between the Revels and *Love's Labour's Lost* becomes a near-certainty at this point, for when the men make their entrance in 5.2, disguised as Muscovites, they are preceded by '*blackamoors with music*'; but the question of who borrowed from whom still remains open, and there seems to be no way of arriving at a definite answer to it. Moreover, the Masque of Muscovites is simply an episode in the comedy, it does not provide the overall structure of it, and in this respect, as well as in its inconclusiveness, it is typical of the 'sources' that have been, at one time or another, suggested for the play.

It is, for instance, quite likely but far from certain that the initial idea of four young men withdrawing from the world for a time in order to study reached Shakespeare through Pierre de la Primaudaye's *L'Académie française*, first published in 1577, and translated into English by T. Bowes in 1586. Dedicating his work to Henry III of France, de la Primaudaye writes of four young gentlemen of Anjou who were placed under the tuition of a master in order that they might learn Latin, Greek, and, above all, 'the moral philosophy of ancient sages and wise men', thus becoming familiar with 'the doctrine of good living'. These young men do not, however, take any rash oaths; and, when their studies are interrupted, it is not by the appearance of ladies in their retreat, but by an outbreak of civil war (Bullough, i. 434–5).

In fact, no source in the proper sense of that word, i.e. a story or record of a series of events that corresponds with the main outlines of Shakespeare's plot, has been discovered, or seems likely to be. The latest attempt to suggest one, that by Glynne Wickham in his article '*Love's Labour's Lost* and *The Four Foster Children of Desire*, 1581',[2] falls down on two counts at least.

---

[1] Ibid., pp. 45–6.
[2] *Shakespeare Quarterly*, 36 (1985), 49–55.

There is nothing in the entertainment, put on in the tiltyard at Whitehall about fourteen years before the comedy was written, to correspond to the death of the King of France, which is the climactic event in Shakespeare's play. Furthermore, one cannot have it both ways. If, as Wickham argues, *Love's Labour's Lost* is the playwright's 'riposte to Sidney's strictures on "mongrel tragi-comedy" ', a deliberate and defiant mingling of kings and clowns, then it should, to be consistent, also make fun of the neo-classical unities of time and place, since the popular drama's complete disregard of them counted for at least as much in Sidney's attack on it as did its 'mongrel' nature. In fact, however, the comedy, either by accident or design, observes both these 'unities', and its doing so cannot be casually dismissed as mere 'lip-service'.

It is in perfect keeping with the general nature of this particular comedy, so preoccupied with the *cacoethes loquendi*, which it simultaneously indulges and holds up to ridicule, that the one source for it about which one can reasonably feel certain should account for no more than a name, and that the name of a minor character who, nevertheless, has a decisive effect on the play's outcome and whose importance for the whole is in inverse proportion to the size of his part—a mere twenty-eight words. Monsieur Marcadé, as J. M. Nosworthy[1] and Anne Barton[2] recognized and pointed out independently of each other, had his origins in a play by Robert Wilson, *The Cobbler's Prophecy*, first published in 1594 but probably composed several years earlier. Samuel Schoenbaum dates it *c.*1589–1594. In this comedy the god Mercury plays a large part; but Ralph the Cobbler, who has evidently not enjoyed the benefit of a grammar-school education, refers to him as 'Markedy' (lines 129, 169), 'Markedie' (lines 242, 652), and 'Merkedy' (line 1356).[3] 'Here then', writes Nosworthy, 'is the apparent source from which Shakespeare derived his name for a human *deus ex machina* who, at the same time, transparently fulfils two of the functions of the god Mercury—those of the messenger and psychopomp' (p. 109). But, while the debt to Wilson is there, it sheds no fresh light on the date of *Love's Labour's Lost*, since Shakespeare could well have

[1] 'The Importance of Being Marcade', *Shakespeare Survey 32* (1979), 105–14.

[2] *The Times Literary Supplement*, 24 November 1978.

[3] Malone Society Reprint (Oxford, 1914).

seen a performance of *The Cobbler's Prophecy* long before its appearance in print in 1594.

One large question remains: how far is *Love's Labour's Lost* a topical comedy, dealing with and reflecting on persons and events contemporary with it? In part at least it is. It stands alone among Shakespeare's plays in that some of the leading characters in it are, nominally at any rate, historical figures who were walking this earth at the time when it was written. The King is, in some respects, Henry of Navarre (1553–1610), who had become Henry IV of France on the assassination of Henry III in 1589 and had eventually, after a protracted struggle with the Catholic League and with Spain, made his own position secure and brought peace to a land that had been torn by religious wars ever since 1562 by abjuring Protestantism and becoming a Catholic in 1593. Even then, however, he had to wait another two years before the Pope finally lifted the sentence of excommunication which had been in force against him for the previous ten years. The fact that the King of Navarre in the play is called Ferdinand, not Henry, would in no way have hindered this identification by the original audiences, since the name Ferdinand never occurs in the dialogue, being found only in some of the stage directions and speech headings.

The King's fellow-students also had their counterparts in real life. The Duc de Longueville fought for the King during the later stages of the religious wars; and so did two Birons, father and son. Which of the two Shakespeare had in mind is not altogether clear. Armand de Gontaut, Baron de Biron, was killed in 1592, by which time he was sixty-eight years old, whereas his son Charles de Gontaut, Duc de Biron, was only thirty. If the play belongs to 1594–5, the son seems the more likely of them. Dumaine is the odd man out in this company, though he, like Henry himself, had already appeared, under precisely this name, on the English stage in Marlowe's *The Massacre at Paris* (1593). Historically he was Charles de Lorraine, Duc de Mayenne (1554–1611), who had taken over the leadership of the Catholic League after the assassination of his elder brother, Henry, Duc de Guise, in 1588. The most inveterate of Henry IV's opponents, he carried on the struggle until January 1596, when he at last made his peace with the King. The Dumaine of the play is and, equally evidently, is not de Mayenne. Similarly, the Princess of France is and is not

Marguerite de Valois, whom Henry married in 1572. Shallow, frivolous, and morally lax, Marguerite was almost the obverse of Shakespeare's Princess; and her marriage to Henry was one of convenience not of affection and esteem.

In *Love's Labour's Lost* there is not so much as a hint of the horrors and the savagery of the religious wars. Set in a sunlit park, the only war it dramatizes is that of the sexes. There is something of the pastoral about it all, including the intrusion of the *memento mori*, with its message *et ego in Arcadia vixi*, represented by Monsieur Marcadé. Yet the action it deals with has its historical side. Most of Henry IV's life was spent in warfare and business of state. He was already serving as a soldier and taking part in battles at the tender age of fourteen. Nevertheless, he did enjoy one holiday. In 1576, after spending the four years that followed the St. Bartholomew's Day massacre of 1572 as a virtual prisoner at the French court in Paris, he escaped and made his way back to south-western France and Navarre. And there, in 1578, he was visited at his ancestral home of Nérac by Marguerite, from whom he had been separated for the best part of three years. At Nérac Henry, who resumed conjugal relations with his wife for a time, passed his days in hunting, playing tennis, paying visits, and pursuing women. The vows he makes at the opening of Shakespeare's play—'Not to see ladies, study, fast, not sleep'— would have met with nothing but derision from him. Marguerite brought with her not only her mother Catherine de Medici but also, knowing her husband's tastes and proclivities, a train of beautiful young women, including a former mistress of his with whom he renewed his relationship and the fair Victoria d'Ayole Dayolle, whom he soon made his mistress. Marguerite did not mind, since the arrangement left her free to enjoy herself with young men of her own choice. In fact, as Lord Russell of Liverpool puts it, 'the royal couple lived their own lives and had their own lovers and mistresses, and there was no secret about it'.[1] In the evenings there was dancing and performances of Italian comedies. In 1582, however, Marguerite returned to the court in Paris; and soon thereafter Henry had to resume his campaigning.

It seems likely that the festive atmosphere of life at Nérac— even though Shakespeare could only have learned about it

---

[1] *Henry of Navarre* (1969), p. 58.

through gossip and rumour—contributed something to the festive nature of his comedy, which can be seen as a delicate, glancing comment on that life. Nor would an Elizabethan audience in the mid-1590s have missed the parallel between the men's perjuries in the play and Henry IV's abjuring of Protestantism in 1593, an action that came in for some harsh censure in England, where he had hitherto been regarded as something of a hero, and from which he had received a measure of support in the shape of military forces as well as money.

But, while Shakespeare positively invites his audience to identify the King and his three courtiers with living figures by the names he gives them, this cannot be said about the characters in his sub-plot, where the names are patently fictional. Nevertheless, this fact has not deterred scholars and critics from making erudite guesses and even assertions. As early as 1747 William Warburton wrote: 'By Holofernes is designed a particular character, a pedant and schoolmaster of our author's time, one John Florio, a teacher of the Italian tongue in London' (Furness, p. 351). Warburton's description of Florio is deliberately slanted to make the identification fit. Florio was indeed a schoolmaster, in the sense that he taught Italian, but far from being a pedant, he was a man of great distinction, the author of, among other things, an Italian–English dictionary, entitled *A World of Words*, published in 1598, and the translator of Montaigne's *Essays*, which came out in 1603. Enjoying the patronage of men such as the Earl of Pembroke and the Earl of Southampton, and eventually becoming tutor to Prince Henry, the son of James I, Florio is a far cry indeed from Shakespeare's country dominie, who is, according to Warburton, a satirical portrait of him. Doctor Johnson was 'inclined to doubt' the whole idea, as were many others, but once started speculation continued throughout the eighteenth and the greater part of the nineteenth century, until, in 1884, it reached the heights of irresponsible absurdity in F. G. Fleay's article 'Shakespeare and Puritanism'.[1] Fleay dismissed Warburton's identification as a 'crude theory' deserving 'no consideration', but then proceeded to add: 'it does not follow that there is no truth in the notion that he [Holofernes] represents somebody. If he does, however, the whole group to which he belongs must also be

[1] *Anglia*, 7 (1884), 223–31.

personal portraits' (Furness, p. 7). Thinking, as most critics did at the time, that *Love's Labour's Lost* was written in 1590, Fleay had looked around for a suitable historical event with which to connect it, and had, he thought, found it in the Martin Marprelate controversy of 1588–90. Holding that Shakespeare at this stage in his career was on the side of Martin and the Puritans, Fleay identified the characters of the sub-plot with those who wrote against Martin or acted in plays attacking him. Armado becomes a caricature of John Lyly; Holofernes of Thomas Cooper, the Bishop of Winchester; Sir Nathaniel of Robert Greene; Costard of the actor William Kempe; Moth of Thomas Nashe; and Anthony Dull of Anthony Munday. Jaquenetta, however, true to her character, proved more than a match even for Fleay's misplaced ingenuity, so he quietly ignored her.

Fleay's wild guessing had at least one salutary effect: it put an end for a time to the merry game of unmasking the characters; but not for good and all. In 1923, nearly forty years after the appearance of his article, Sir Arthur Quiller-Couch and John Dover Wilson published their Cambridge edition of the play, and in their Introduction to it, after asserting confidently and twice over their conviction that *Love's Labour's Lost* was written 'as a *topical* play' (pp. xvi and xviii), they continued thus:

if the Marprelate Controversy be extended over the dispute between Gabriel Harvey and Thomas Nashe, which grew out of it, Fleay's general aim was perhaps not wholly wide, and one of his arrows (we are convinced) hit the mark. 'Is not Moth,' he asks, 'Thomas Nashe, "the young juvenal," the tender boy, the ready pamphleteer, the sarcastic satirist?' To this we answer, 'Yes, and almost beyond a doubt.' (p. xx)

Wilson still maintained this position in the Preface to his second edition, published in 1962 (p. xiii); so it seems worth while to examine the 'proofs' he and Quiller-Couch originally offered for their assertion. First, they quote Moth's speech at 3.1.10–23, which, they say, is in Nashe's manner. So it is, especially in its sustained use of reductive comparisons and its headlong pace; but the passage remains an isolated one; Moth never speaks in this vein again or at this length. His normal mode of discourse is made up of sharp questions and quick answers. As further evidence the two editors point to the dialogue that opens 1.2, in which Armado addresses his page as 'my tender Juvenal', and

Moth retorts by addressing him as 'my tough segñor', thus leading in to a 'set of wit' in which the two phrases are bandied to and fro. Of this they say:

Now some have disputed that Nashe is the 'young Iuuenall, that byting Satyrist' referred to by Greene in the famous passage of *A Groatsworth of Wit* (1592) wherein he warns his fellow-dramatists against the 'Upstart Crow': but there can be no question that Meres hails him as 'sweet Tom,' and 'gallant young Juvenal' in his *Wit's Treasurie* (1598) ... The epithet 'tender', moreover, is not to be overlooked. Neshe was a recognized variant of the surname Nashe, and 'nesh' or 'nash' at that time = 'soft, delicate, pitiful, tender.' (p. xxii)

To this they add: 'Puns upon "purse", "pen", "penny" obtrude themselves throughout the play when Moth is assailed or retorts: all of them meaningless (so far as we can discover) unless referable to Nashe's *Pierce (i.q. Purse) Penilesse.*' Then comes the 'clue' provided by Hercules' killing of 'Cerberus, that three-headed Canis', which they interpret as a reference to 'Nashe's prowess in 1589 against the three-headed Martin—Martin Marprelate, Martin Senior and Martin Junior' (p. xxiii). And, finally, to clinch the argument comes 'the discovery ... that "Moth" is, by Elizabethan spelling, just Nashe's familiar Christian name reversed.'

It is all very erudite and ingenious, no doubt, but what has it to do with *Love's Labour's Lost*, a play written for a theatre audience in the mid-1590s, not for a group of scholars spending their days in the British Museum in the 1920s? Greene's pamphlet is 'famous'—or 'infamous'—now for its attack on Shakespeare, the first reference we have to him as a dramatist, and it did cause something of a stir in its own day. But that stir seems to have been short-lived. Published first in 1592, the pamphlet did not go into a second edition until 1596, which means that probably not more than 500 copies of it were in circulation when Shakespeare wrote his play.[1] The likelihood that any significant number of people in the earliest audiences would be reminded of Greene's advice to Nashe is, therefore, small. Nor is there any good reason for thinking that a theatre-goer of the day would say 'Nashe' on hearing the word 'tender' applied to Moth. In fact, Nashe, as his

[1] See Edwin H. Miller, *The Professional Writer in Elizabethan England* (Cambridge, Mass., 1959), p. 155.

opponents were quickly made to realize, was anything but tender. As for the 'Puns upon "purse", "pen", "penny" [that] obtrude themselves ... when Moth is assailed or retorts', 'purse' occurs once only (5.1.66) with no punning intent that I can see, while 'pierced' and 'piercing' (4.2.81–5) belong to a scene in which Moth has no part. 'Pen(s)' are more plentiful, but again I see no punning on them, nor do I find any in the three uses of 'penny' (3.1.25, 135; and 5.1.63). Moreover, if the statement were true, which it patently is not, it would prove nothing. Proverbs about purses and pennies were part of the small change of daily intercourse in Shakespeare's England. Still less likely is it that anyone would have exclaimed 'Martin!' on hearing of the 'three-headed Canis', or thought of Thom spelled (more or less) backwards at a mention of Moth.

Plays do not work in the way the Cambridge editors seem to have imagined. There is, as it happens, a trilogy in which Nashe does appear. The work of an anonymous author, it was written for a special audience, the students of Cambridge University in general and of St. John's College in particular, Nashe's own college. There the first play, *The Pilgrimage to Parnassus*, was put on at Christmas 1598–9; the second, *The First Part of the Return from Parnassus*, at Christmas 1599–1600; and the third, *The Second Part of the Return from Parnassus* at Christmas 1601–2, and again at Christmas 1602–3. One of the leading characters in it, Ingenioso, who appears in all three parts, was identified with Nashe by Fleay as long ago as 1891.[1] Characteristically Fleay offered little evidence. There is, however, no shortage of it, and it is set out in detail by the play's most recent editor, J. B. Leishman, who devotes nine pages of his Introduction to it.[2] It is essentially of two kinds:

firstly, the fact that much that we hear of and from Ingenioso corresponds very closely with the known facts of Nashe's life; secondly, the fact that the author of the Parnassus Plays reveals a very close acquaintance with his writings, modelling ... numerous passages upon them, and sometimes borrowing from them whole phrases, a large number of which he puts in the mouth of Ingenioso. (p. 72)

Leishman's identification of Ingenioso with Nashe is a solid structure on a firm foundation. Compared with it, the Cambridge

---

[1] *A Biographical Chronicle of the English Drama*, 2 vols. (1891), ii. 348.

[2] *The Three Parnassus Plays* (1949).

editors' identification of Moth with Nashe has no more foundation than the proverbial castle in the air.

They have an even more insubstantial foundation for their
main and very influential contention to which their suggested
Moth–Nashe connection is but a prelude. It consists of four words
only, which are, as they print them, 'the School of Night'. They
occur in the great climactic scene 4.3, and they are spoken by the
King. Biron has been rhapsodizing about Rosaline's dark beauty
and has concluded his speech with the following words, quoted
here in the spelling and punctuation of the Quarto:

> O who can giue an oth? Where is a booke?
> That I may sweare Beautie doth beautie lacke,
> If that she learne not of her eye to looke:
> No face is fayre that is not full so blacke.

Outraged by this piece of sophistry, the King retorts:

> O paradox, Blacke is the badge of Hell,
> The hue of dungions, and the Schoole of night ...
>   (4.3.247–52)

Many editors ever since the time of Theobald had been troubled
by the word 'Schoole' in this context and had sought to emend it
in various ways, none of them really convincing. Quiller-Couch
and Dover Wilson, however, let it stand because they thought it
'not only right but illuminating' (p. xxix), provided that the
punctuation of the relevant lines was altered and the word 'night'
given an initial capital. So in their edition the two lines read:

> O paradox! Black is the badge of hell,
> The hue of dungeons and the School of Night.

The King's three parallel statements have been reduced to two,
with the second of them now meaning 'Black is the hue of
dungeons and (also the hue of) the School of Night'. The
troublesome 'Black is ... the school of night' has been eliminated,
provided, that is, that there was something called 'the School of
Night'. Quiller-Couch and Dover Wilson were convinced that
there was. Adopting a theory first set out by Arthur Acheson in
his *Shakespeare and the Rival Poet* (1903), they agreed with him
'that a School of Night really existed, that Chapman's *Shadow of
Night* (1594) was a product of this School, and that the Academe

of Navarre is Shakespeare's satire upon it' (p. xxx). Their grounds for doing so, even though no other reference to 'the School of Night' has ever been found, amount to this: that there was what the Jesuit Robert Parsons, writing in 1592, had dubbed 'Sir Walter Ralegh's school of atheism', a group of men deeply interested in mathematics, astronomy, and unorthodox speculation. As well as Ralegh, who was its leader, it included George Chapman, the Earl of Derby, the Earl of Northumberland, Sir George Carey, Matthew Roydon, Thomas Harriot the famous mathematician, and, possibly, Christopher Marlowe. Opposed to this group, the Cambridge editors hypothesize, was another that included Shakespeare's patron the Earl of Southampton, Southampton's friend the Earl of Essex, and, of course, Shakespeare himself. Whereas the first group was devoted to abstract and arcane ideas and set a high value on the study of books, the second favoured common sense and natural behaviour. Biron sums up the essential opposition for us when he dismisses close study as 'leaden contemplation' and states his preference for a doctrine derived 'from women's eyes'.

How an audience could possibly have gathered all this from a single mention of 'the school of night' is something the Cambridge editors do not explain. Nevertheless, the notion was widely accepted among scholars, especially after it had been developed in much greater detail and with far more circumspection by Frances A. Yates in her *A Study of 'Love's Labour's Lost'* (Cambridge, 1936), and held the field until 1941, when it was decisively challenged by E. A. Strathman. Engaged at the time on his very important work *Sir Walter Ralegh: A Study in Elizabethan Skepticism*,[1] Strathman published some interim findings in the form of an article entitled 'The Textual Evidence for "The School of Night" '.[2] In it, after meticulously examining the evidence used by the Cambridge editors, he concludes thus:

That Chapman's *Shadow of Night* and the speeches of Berowne present contrasting philosophies is true; that Ralegh and Northumberland were patrons of scientific learning is true; that the Ralegh coterie was accused of unorthodox beliefs is true. But there is no independent evidence ... to establish the Q reading 'Schoole of night' as an allusion to Ralegh and his associates. (p. 186)

[1] New York, 1951.
[2] *Modern Language Notes*, 56 (1941), 176–86.

The final blow to the whole tottering edifice of conjecture and speculation came in 1956 when C. J. Sisson pointed out that 'a plain sense resides in the original [reading], which in fact offers no crux. *Black is the school of night*, in the sense that night is the scholar or pupil of blackness, darkness ...'[1] It might be added that the idea of student and teacher lying behind the statement has already been adumbrated in Biron's assertion: 'beauty doth beauty lack, | If that she [beauty] learn not of her [Rosaline's] eye to look' (4.3.248–9), and is repeated and endorsed when he refers to the ladies as 'beauty's tutors' (4.3.298).

The Text

The earliest text we have of *Love's Labour's Lost* is a quarto of 1598, henceforward referred to as Q, of which fourteen copies have survived.[2] Its title-page, reproduced here in facsimile, is of considerable interest on several scores. First, the description of the play that it offers is a remarkably accurate one, for the most distinctive feature of this comedy is precisely its 'pleasant conceited', meaning 'delightfully clever and witty', quality. Secondly, the title-page carries Shakespeare's name, something none of his plays published before it does; and, thirdly, it makes two further statements, both designed to catch the prospective purchaser's interest and attention: one of them, if taken literally, patently untrue, and the other tantalizingly unverifiable. The text of Q cannot be a faithful version of the comedy 'As it was presented before her Highnes | this last Christmas', because it is, as it stands, unactable; and if the words 'Newly corrected and augmented' are intended to imply, as many scholars think they are, that there had been an earlier and, perhaps, inferior quarto, as they undoubtedly do on the title-page of the Second Quarto of *Romeo and Juliet* (1599), which claims its text to be '*Newly corrected, augmented, and | amended*', they can neither be completely verified nor completely refuted, since no copy of any such quarto has ever come to light.

Q is unactable for a number of reasons. First, it is plagued by a superfluity and confusion of names. Of its twenty characters, only

---

[1] *New Readings in Shakespeare* (Cambridge, 1956), p. 115.

[2] Their locations are given by Paul Werstine in his 'Variants in the First Quarto of *Love's Labor's Lost*', *Shakespeare Studies*, 12 (1979), 35–47.

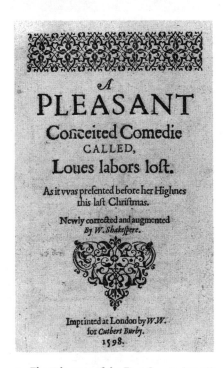

The title-page reads:

A
PLEASANT
Conceited Comedie
CALLED,
Loues labors loſt.

As it vvas preſented before her Highnes
this laſt Chriſtmas.

Newly correſted and augmented
By W. Shakeſpere.

Imprinted at London by *W.W.*
for *Cutbert Burby.*
1598.

9. The title-page of the First Quarto (1598).

six—Longueville, Dumaine, Biron, Boyet, the Forester, and Marcadé—have each a single consistent speech-prefix for their parts. The others come on, speak their lines, and go off again under various names and titles. The King, for instance, makes his initial entry at the play's opening as 'Ferdinand K. of Nauar'; and his first speech is headed '*Ferdinand.*' After that he is '*Ferd.*' or '*Fer.*' for the rest of the scene. On his next appearance, however, at 2.1.89.1, he is '*Nauar.*', and, for his subsequent speeches, '*Nauar.*' or '*Nau.*', until, at line 127, he suddenly becomes '*Ferd.*' once more and remains so up to his exit line which is headed '*Nau.*' He is not seen again until 4.3, where, at line 19.2, the direction reads: '*The King entreth*'. His first words are headed '*King.*'; and '*King.*' or '*Kin.*' he then continues to be to the end of the play. There are also, it is worth noting, four occasions in the first two acts when other characters refer to him as 'the Duke'. In similar fashion the Princess is '*Princesse*' when she makes her initial entrance at the beginning of 2.1; but her first speech is

58

headed '*Queene.*', a title that is not properly hers until she hears the news of her father's death in 5.2. For her second speech in 2.1 she becomes '*Prince.*', and thereafter, to the end of the scene, her speech-prefixes are abbreviations of '*Princesse*'. It is under this title that she comes on at the opening of 4.1; but the first speech she makes after doing so is prefixed '*Quee.*', and '*Queen.*' or '*Quee.*' she remains for the rest of the play, except at 5.2.552, where her speech thanking Costard for his performance in the role of Pompey is headed '*Lady.*' Even such minor figures as Dull and Jaquenetta enjoy the luxury of two other names apiece in stage directions and speech-prefixes: he is also '*Anthonie*' and '*Constable*', while she is also '*Maid*' and '*Wench*'.

Such variations in nomenclature as these are, of course, common enough in a dramatist's early drafts, where he is naturally more concerned with a character's relation to others on stage than with that character's often arbitrary personal name, and they strongly suggest that Q represents the play in a pre-performance state, before the speech-prefixes and the like had been regularized by the bookkeeper. Confirmation that such is indeed the case is provided by a characteristic feature of the stage directions noted and documented by W. W. Greg. 'Everywhere', he writes, 'they illustrate the author's uncertainty how to describe his characters and, particularly in the last act, his vague definition of groups' (*SFF*, p. 221). Typical examples of the phenomenon he has in mind, all culled from the final scene, are the following: '*Enter the Ladyes*' (5.2.0.1); '*Enter the King and the rest*' (l. 309.1); '*Enter the Ladies*' (l. 336.1); and '*Enter all*' (l. 871.1), where '*all*' must mean 'all those members of the cast who are not already on stage'.

This multiplicity of names would not, of course, in itself make the play impossible to stage. Moth, for example, should have no difficulty in answering to the call '*Boy*' as well as the call '*Page*'; but things would obviously run more smoothly if he had but one of them to keep in mind. It is the confusion of names that is really damaging. It appears in its simplest and most readily explicable form at 5.2.242–55, a 'set of wit' in which the players are Katherine and Longueville. There can be no question about their identity, since their duologue begins at a point where the three other mismatched couples—Rosaline and the King, the Princess and Biron, and Maria and Dumaine—having played their 'sets', are all busy talking to one another. Nevertheless, every one of Katherine's speeches has the prefix, either in full or abbreviated, of '*Maria.*' The mistake cannot be the compositor's. There is no likelihood of a manuscript '*Kath.*' being read as '*Maria.*'. The error must, therefore, be the author's. Shakespeare has allowed his pairing of Longueville and Maria, which is right for the rest of the play, to obscure the fact that at this point Longueville is speaking, not to Maria, but to Katherine disguised as Maria. It is a mistake which can easily be corrected, but it must be put right before the play can be staged.

Much more serious is the muddle in 2.1 over the names of two of the ladies in attendance on the Princess. When they first speak, all three of the ladies do so as nameless numbers. 1. *Lady* gives an admiring character sketch of Longueville, whom she met at a 'marriage feast' celebrating the union of 'L. *Perigort* and the bewtious heire | of *Jaques Fauconbridge*'; 2. *Lady* does the same thing for Dumaine, whom she saw 'at the Duke *Alansoes* [Alençon's] once'; and 3. *Lady* for Biron, who was with Dumaine on that occasion.

At this point the King and his three courtiers appear; and the Princess wastes no time in making it amply clear that she is highly displeased by the King's decision to lodge her and her ladies 'in the field'. She then goes on to present him with a letter from her father that is, we later discover, both long and complicated; and in order to give Navarre at least a token time in which to read and digest it Shakespeare has Biron make advances to one of the attendant ladies, whose speech-prefix is '*Kather.*' or '*Kath.*', in an attempt to establish her identity as someone he danced with 'in *Brabant* once'. She, however, skilfully parries his probes until, thwarted in his efforts, he gives up. As this encounter ends, the King and the Princess spend the next fifty lines or so in arguing about the rather tiresome business of Aquitaine; and, when they have done, the King makes his exit, which is clearly marked, and presumably takes Dumaine with him, for some twelve lines later that character is required to enter. It also looks as though Longueville too leaves. Biron, however, remains on stage to take part in a duologue with a lady whose speech-prefix is '*Ros.*' Like his earlier exchanges with Katherine, these are made up of stichomythic thrust and parry that begins as prose but then slips into three-beat couplets. In fact, this set of wit looks like a continuation of the previous one, except for the difference in the lady's name. It concludes with Biron making his exit. A piece of formal patterning of the kind so frequent in this comedy follows. No sooner has Biron gone than Dumaine returns to ask Boyet: 'What Ladie is that same?' To this Boyet replies: 'The heire of *Alanson*, *Rosalin* her name', thus equating her with '2. *Lady*.' Satisfied, Dumaine goes off. He is immediately succeeded by Longueville enquiring about the name of another Lady whom he refers to as 'she in the white'. Some verbal sparring ensues, but eventually Boyet replies: 'She is an heire of *Falconbridge*', i.e. '1. *Lady*.', or, as she will be named at line 213, '*Lady Maria*.'. Finally, to complete the sequence, Biron comes back to put his query: 'Whats her name in the capp?', to which Boyet answers: '*Katherin* by good happ.'

All now seems clear, or nearly so. '1. *Lady*.', acquainted with Longueville, is Maria; '2. *Lady*.', acquainted with Dumaine, is Rosaline; and '3. *Lady*.', acquainted with Biron, is Katherine. But we are left with the awkward question of why the lady whom Biron addresses in his second battle of wits with a woman, which reads so much like a continuation of his first, should be called Rosaline not Katherine. It looks as though the playwright is dithering over the two names; and confirmation that such is indeed the case is provided by what follows. After Biron has gone the next speaker is '*Lady Maria*.', and at line 217 '*Lady Ka*.' joins in, but then for the rest of the scene the three personal names disappear completely and are replaced by such indeterminate prefixes as '*La*.', '*Lad*.', '*Lad*. 2', and '*Lad*. 3.' Then, at 3.1.161, Biron entrusts Costard with the delivery of a letter addressed to Rosaline. After that there is no more confusion of the two names Rosaline and Katherine. Shakespeare has at last made up his mind. Beginning by thinking, perhaps, that the name of the heroine of *The Taming of the Shrew* would be the right name for a woman capable of holding her own with Biron, he then allows Rosaline, the name of the 'pale hard-hearted wench' with the black eyes in *Romeo and Juliet* (2.3.4 and 13), to take over for a few moments at 179–90, and then completely at 3.1.161. Having settled the matter, he presses on with his play, leaving the tidying-up to be done in a fair copy which has, by this time, become indispensable.

This seems the simplest and most likely solution to the

problem and therefore dictates the course followed in this edition, where 'Rosaline' replaces 'Katherine' at 114–25 and 208 and 'Katherine' replaces 'Rosaline' at 193. But there are other ways of dealing with the 'tangle', as it has often been called. Dover Wilson, building on a suggestion by Capell, and on an elaboration of that suggestion by H. B. Charlton,[1] takes the view that Shakespeare initially intended the three ladies to wear masks— the Katherine of Q certainly has one, whether she is wearing it or not, at 122–3—but then, to avoid anticipating the use of mistaken identities in 5.2, dropped the idea and with it both the duologue between Biron and Katherine at 113–26 and that between Biron and Rosaline at 178–91. However, the compositor failed to recognize his cancellation marks and so printed what he should have suppressed. There are at least two difficulties in the way of accepting this explanation: first, there is no direction for the ladies to mask; and, secondly, there is nothing in the form of action or dialogue to cover the King's perusal of the letter.

John Kerrigan's treatment of the crux comes nearer to that adopted in this edition.[2] He holds that Shakespeare in his first draft wrote the exchanges between Biron and Katherine because at this stage he meant to pair the two of them. Then, having decided that Rosaline would, after all, be a better name for Biron's love, he wrote the second duologue on a separate sheet of paper to take the place of the first. The compositor, however, printed both, instead of replacing the first with the second as he should have done. In keeping with this hypothesis, Kerrigan prints the second duologue where the first stands in Q, and relegates the first to the commentary. This procedure effectively disposes of the business of masking but also creates difficulties of its own. The symmetry, so evident in exchanges between Biron and a lady while the King reads the letter and further exchanges between Biron and a lady after the meeting between the King and the Princess is over, is destroyed. Moreover, Kerrigan leaves himself with some awkward stage business: he has to give Dumaine an exit along with the King in order to bring him back on stage immediately.

Stanley Wells, in his edition of the play for the *Complete Oxford*

---

[1] *Love's Labour's Lost*, ed. John Dover Wilson and Sir Arthur Quiller-Couch (Cambridge, 1923), p. 119.

[2] 'Shakespeare at Work: The Katherine–Rosaline Tangle in *Love's Labour's Lost*' *RES*, NS 33 (1982), 129–36.

Shakespeare, takes much the same line about the issue as does this edition, which is much indebted to his, but with some important differences in the way of explanation. He thinks that 'in writing the lines as they stand in Q, Shakespeare paired Biron with Katherine and at a later stage, having decided on a change of name, altered the prefix correctly at [180–93], but failed to make the necessary changes elsewhere' (*TC*, p. 271). It is, of course, possible that this is what happened, but it seems unlikely. Revision and a failure to revise make awkward bedfellows. As an alternative to this theory he goes on to suggest that 'the second duologue may be a later addition composed to give further prominence to Biron and Rosaline after Shakespeare had made his final decision about her name' (ibid.). This also could be true; but symmetry is such a marked feature of the play that two matching duologues could well have been part of its original structure. On the whole, then, the notion of authorial havering over the two names accounts for more than any other hypothesis and accounts for it more readily and economically.

Further troubles with nomenclature are still to come. There is a very bad muddle in 4.2, and again at one point in 5.1, over the names of the Curate and the Schoolmaster. They make their first entrance at the opening of 4.2, where the stage direction reads: 'Enter *Dull, Holofernes,* the *Pedant* and *Nathaniel*', an ambiguous statement in itself, since it is not clear whether it covers four characters or only three. In fact, it covers three because Holofernes and the Pedant are one and the same. There is some slight irregularity in the speech-prefixes to begin with. Nathaniel, the first to speak, does so as '*Nat.*'; but his second speech is headed '*Curat Nath.*'; and Holofernes says his first line as '*Ped.*' After that, however, all is plain sailing up to line 64, with the speeches of the three characters involved headed '*Holo.*', '*Nath.*', and '*Dul.*' respectively. Then, suddenly and for no apparent reason, everything goes wrong. At line 65 a speech that clearly belongs to Holofernes is headed '*Nath.*', while the reply to it, which should be Nathaniel's, is headed '*Holo.*' From this point onwards, for the next eighty lines or so, every speech assigned to Nathaniel really belongs to Holofernes and *vice versa*. But there are also two speeches by the Schoolmaster which carry the prefixes '*Pedan.*' and '*Ped.*'; and in both cases (118–19 and 134–40) the assignment is correct. There are, moreover, other curious irregularities and puzzles. At line 104, where the Curate starts to read Biron's sonnet, there is no speech-prefix at all, though one is badly needed; and, when the reading is over, the Schoolmaster, now speaking as '*Pedan.*', makes a two-line comment on it which is rightfully and properly his, but then loses his next seven lines to '*Nath.*' Furthermore, at line 120, where the prefix is '*Ped.*', he actually addresses Nathaniel as 'Sir *Holofernes*', something he will do again at 5.1.107. It is not until line 146 that the scene gets back on course through a series of exchanges in which the Schoolmaster is consistently '*Ped.*' or '*Peda.*' and properly addresses the Curate as 'Sir *Nathaniel*' (l. 148).

The simplest and, in many ways, the most attractive solution to the puzzle is Gary Taylor's. He thinks 'that as Shakespeare composed the second half of his play he became muddled about the clergyman's and schoolmaster's names and, to make things easier for himself, used occupational names instead' (Kerrigan, p. 192). This suggestion works perfectly for 5.1 and 5.2, where the speech-prefixes for Holofernes and Nathaniel are rightly and consistently *Pedant* and *Curate* respectively; but it does not explain how Shakespeare could suddenly become confused about the personal names of the two characters roughly one third of the way through 4.2 after using them quite correctly up to that point. At least it does not do so for those who think of Shakespeare as a playwright who did his composing while sitting in his study, if he ever had one, and who looked back carefully over what he had written already. It might well have happened, however, that having written the first third of 4.2, he realized how best to continue the scene while he was away from his lodgings in London, touring somewhere in the provinces perhaps, reached for the nearest sheet of paper, and jotted the continuation down, caring little whether he had the names right or wrong, since he knew any necessary adjustment could be made in the fair copy.

The confusion of names is not the only confusion in the relevant part of 4.2. Two of Jaquenetta's speeches in it cannot be reconciled with one another. At line 88 she asks the Curate, whom she addresses as 'Good M. Parson', to 'be so good as read me this letter, it was geuen me by *Costard*, and sent me from *Don Armatho*'. Later, however, when the Schoolmaster asks her: 'Was this directed to you?', she replies: 'I sir from one mounsier *Berowne*, one of the strange Queenes Lordes' (128–9). This answer is, as it stands and where it stands, sheer nonsense. It not only contradicts her previous statement but is also badly astray in its description of Biron. It looks, in fact, like a garbled version of Holofernes' comment in the next speech, where he says: 'this *Berowne* is one of the Votaries with the King, and here he hath framed a letter to a sequent of the stranger Queenes' (134–6). It would be in keeping with the general character of Q for Shakespeare to have written Jaquenetta's speech as it stands, then to have recognized its inconsistency with her earlier answer and cancelled the words after 'I sir' with a marking unknown to the compositor, who, consequently, left them standing.

That possibility is made all the likelier by what can now be regarded as a fortunate and enlightening accident: at least two passages in the play are duplicated. First in 4.3, and then again in 5.2, what is evidently a false start is followed, immediately in the first case and fifteen lines later in the second, by a revised and much expanded version of the same matter, which is, in both instances, manifestly superior to the first shot. The writing of the new versions should have led, of course, to the deletion of the false starts; but, either because Shakespeare in the heat of composition failed to mark them for deletion, or because he used for that purpose theatrical markings familiar to the bookkeeper but not to the compositor, they survived, and are to be found in Appendix A to this edition. They have their own peculiar fascination, since a comparison between them and the final versions enables us to observe Shakespeare at work, changing his mind, and changing it for the better, charging Biron's initial praise of women's eyes with mythological matter that transforms it into a glowing hymn to Love, and converting five rather tame lines, in which Rosaline lays down the conditions on which she will accept Biron, into a much more detailed and harsher sentence moved into a position where it ceases to be a mere item in a list of such conditions and becomes, instead, a fitting and powerful climax to that list.

All the features of Q dealt with so far not only make it unactable but also point unequivocally in one direction—to the author's foul papers as the 'copy' from which it was set up. So do the strange and unusual spellings with which it is replete, and which led Dover Wilson to describe it as 'a mine for students of Shakespearian spelling' and to compile 'a brief list of the archaic and peculiar forms' to be found in it (p. 103). Some of his examples do not, it should be pointed out, stand up to a close scrutiny. The form 'bed-red' (1.1.137), for instance, is not only older than 'bed-rid', which has now displaced it, but persisted, according to *OED*, into the eighteenth century, while 'deus' (1.2.46) for 'deuce' was still current in the nineteenth. Other seemingly odd spellings look more like compositorial errors than authorial idiosyncrasies: 'dooters', i.e. 'doters', at 4.3.257, is probably the result of a misreading of 'doaters'; and 'rayse' (4.3.26) could well come from a transposition by the compositor of the last two letters in 'rayes'. All the same, there is a considerable residue of what might fittingly be called 'racked ortagriphie' (5.1.19); and it can be added to. Very strange indeed, for example, are 'abhortive' (1.1.104) and 'mouce' (5.2.19), spellings not recognized at all by *OED* because in the Folio text of the play, on which it relies, they have already been corrected to 'abortive' and 'mouse'. Moreover, at least one word in Wilson's list, 'annothanize' (4.1.67), which he regards as a partial misprint of 'anothomize', found at Q *2 Henry IV*, Ind.21, could well be a Shakespearian coinage, combining the senses of 'anatomize', i.e. 'analyse', and 'annote', i.e. 'explain', a word not used elsewhere by Shakespeare himself but current in his day.

So far, then, the case for authorial foul papers as the 'copy' from which Q was set seems a wholly convincing one. There is, however, a large obstacle in the way of its acceptance: the four words 'Newly corrected and augmented' which appear on its title-page. Five other plays by Shakespeare came out in quartos that carried some such statement on their title-pages: *Romeo and Juliet* Q2 (1599), 'Newly corrected, augmented, and amended'; *1 Henry IV* Q2 (1599), 'Newly corrected'; *Richard III* Q3 (1602), 'Newly augmented'; *Hamlet* Q2 (1604–5), 'Newly imprinted and enlarged to almost as much againe as it was, according to the true and perfect Coppie'; and the two-part play of *The Whole Contention* Q3 (1619), 'newly corrected and enlarged'. But, though they look similar, these claims, when examined, vary greatly in their validity, ranging from the blatantly misleading to the almost mathematically accurate. At one end of the scale, *Richard III* Q3, purporting to be 'Newly augmented', has no augmentation whatsoever. It is simply a reprint of Q2 (1598), which is, in its turn, a reprint of Q1 (1597). At the other, *Hamlet*

Q2 is indeed nearly twice as long as *Hamlet* Q1 (1603). In fact, 'Newly corrected and augmented', or 'enlarged', seems to have been a rather elastic formula, but a formula used only in connection with plays that had already appeared in print, irrespective of whether that earlier appearance had been as a good quarto, like *1 Henry IV* Q1 (1597), as a 'goodish' quarto, like *Richard III* Q1 (1597), or as a bad quarto, like *Romeo and Juliet* Q1 (1597) and *Hamlet* Q1 (1603). It may, therefore, reasonably be assumed that, even though so far as we know, no copy of it has survived, there had been an edition of *Love's Labour's Lost* prior to the publication of the quarto of 1598.

In these circumstances, we do not and cannot know for a certainty whether the lost quarto was good or bad. However, most scholars, following the lead given by A. W. Pollard in 1909,[1] have inclined to the latter alternative, for three reasons: first, Q *Love's Labour's Lost* and *Romeo and Juliet* do resemble one another in the claims they make on their title-pages; secondly, neither of them was entered on the Stationers' Register; and, thirdly, both came from the house of the same publisher. Nevertheless, their case is not so strong as it looks at first sight. There is what could well be a significant difference between the wording on the title-page of *Romeo and Juliet* Q2 and that on the title-page of Q *Love's Labour's Lost*: the latter does not say, as *Romeo and Juliet* Q2 does, that the text it offers has been 'amended', which, in this context, should mean something like 'substantially altered for the better', as indeed the text of *Romeo and Juliet* Q2 has been when compared with that of Q1. Had it been possible to make such a claim for the 1598 quarto of *Love's Labour's Lost*, it seems likely that Cuthbert Burby, the publisher of both the quartos concerned, would have made it. Furthermore, it does not follow that because *Romeo and Juliet* Q1, not entered in the Stationers' Register, was a bad quarto, the lost edition of *Love's Labour's Lost*, also not entered, must likewise have been bad. It has to be remembered 'that many books were quite openly and regularly published without entrance', and that 'the proportion of works published that were entered ... appears to have been on the average about two-thirds' (Greg, *SFF*, pp. 34–5).

The question of whether the lost quarto was good or bad

---

[1] *Shakespeare's Folios and Quartos* (1909), pp. 70–1.

cannot, it should now be clear, be decided on the strength of analogies alone. If a stress on the analogy of Q with *Romeo and Juliet* Q2 leads to the conclusion that it was bad, a stress on the analogy with *1 Henry IV* Q2 leads to the opposite conclusion, that it was good. Something more objective in the form of evidence is badly needed. Fortunately, a splendid start in providing it has been made by Paul Werstine in a meticulously documented and very persuasive study published in 1984.[1] His point of departure is the fact that twenty books printed between 1598 and 1600 in the shop of William White, the '*W.W.*' of the Q title-page, have survived. Twelve of them were printed from manuscript, while four, including three plays—Shakespeare's *The True Tragedy of Richard Duke of York* Q2 (1600), George Peele's *The Famous Chronicle of King Edward I* Q2 (1599), and Thomas Kyd's *The Spanish Tragedy* Q3 (1599)—were reprints. There were also three editions of Samuel Rowlands's *The Letting of Humour's Blood* (1600), which Werstine excludes from his survey, since he is not sure whether they were set from manuscript or not, and, finally, the 1598 quarto of *Love's Labour's Lost*. A careful analysis of some of the spellings in the seventeen works he considers leads Werstine to conclude that White's compositors 'demonstrated nearly absolute consistency in maintaining their preferences for the spellings of a number of common words whenever they worked from manuscript copy. Only when they were faced with printed copy did their constancy waver as they transferred from printed books spellings that they almost never used in setting from manuscript' (pp. 54–5). For example, the word *any* occurs 283 times in the books set from manuscript, and on 282 of these occasions it is spelled *any*; only once does the alternative spelling *anie* appear. In the reprints and in Q *Love's Labour's Lost*, however, the tally is a different one. In *The Spanish Tragedy* Q3 the ratio of *any* to *anie* is 10/4, in *The Famous Chronicle* it is 22/2, and in Q *Love's Labour's Lost* 10/2. Similarly, the ratio of *eye* to *eie* in works set from manuscript is 117/3, whereas it is 8/7 in the *True Tragedy*, 9/10 in *The Famous Chronicle*, 17/9 in *The Spanish Tragedy*, and 63/10 in *Love's Labour's Lost*. Three other common words—*fayth/faith*, *many/manie*, and *very/verie*—tell much the

[1] 'The Editorial Usefulness of Printing House and Compositor Studies', *Play-Texts in Old Spelling*, ed. G. B. Shand and Raymond C. Shady (New York, 1984), pp. 35–64.

same story, as does the less common word *mayd(en)/maid(en)*. As Werstine puts it with modest caution, 'While six pairs of spelling variants from *LLLQ1* are too few for any conclusive demonstration that *LLLQ1* is a reprint of an earlier quarto, they are enough to indicate that *LLLQ1* may be a reprint' (pp. 57–8). And this possibility opens up another, for 'if the first printing of *LLL* served as copy for the entire first extant quarto, the first printing must have been a good quarto, not a bad one', providing 'a better, not a worse, text of the play' (p. 61).

Before Werstine's paper came out in its final form his intimate knowledge of White's printing house, and of all the extant copies of Q, evident in his article 'Variants in the First Quarto of *Love's Labour's Lost*',[1] had enabled him to deal decisively with the view expressed by George R. Price,[2] to the effect that any hypothesis suggesting the use of printed copy in the setting-up of Q is 'untenable' (p. 434). Price gives two reasons for his verdict: first, 'the difficulties experienced by the compositors [of Q] in casting off, as revealed by irregularities in the setting of the pages', which, he thinks, could not have occurred had they been setting from print; and, secondly, 'the very abundance of the typographical errors left uncorrected'. Replying to this statement,[3] Werstine points out that 'exactly the same irregularities in the setting of pages appears in White's reprint of *The True Tragedie*. If faulty casting off drove White's compositor to limit A4 of *LLLQ1* to thirty-six lines [instead of the normal thirty-eight] in order to avoid setting a centered stage direction at the bottom of the page, an error in casting off forced the compositor of C3 of *The True Tragedie* to set only thirty-five lines to avoid ending that page with a stage direction'. As for the 'abundance of typographical errors' in Q, Werstine, who counts sixty-seven of them, shows that this total is very much in keeping with those to be found in the three plays that are reprints. 'White's compositors', he writes, 'introduced at least sixty-eight such errors into the reprint of *Edwarde the first*, seventy-four into the reprint of *The True Tragedie*, and fifty-nine into the reprint of *The Spanish Tragedie*' (p. 494).

A third theory about the nature of the copy used in the setting

---

[1] *Shakespeare Studies*, 12 (1979), 35–47.
[2] 'The Printing of *Love's Labour's Lost* (1598)', *Papers of the Bibliographical Society of America*, 72 (1978), 419–34.
[3] *Papers of the Bibliographical Society of America*, 73 (1979), 493–4.

of Q is set forth by Manfred Draudt in his 'Printer's Copy for the Quarto of *Love's Labour's Lost* (1598)'.[1] His hypothesis is that the copy was mixed, some of it printed, the rest manuscript. He sees the quarto as falling into two parts: Acts 1 to 3, occupying sheets A to C/D, and Acts 4 and 5, occupying sheets C/D to K. Accepting, but not verifying, Price's statement that sheets A, B, and C are passably free of errors, but with D the remaining sheets become much worse, he argues that this 'worsening' is due to a change-over from printed copy to manuscript copy which the compositors found much harder to cope with. In fact, however, as Werstine conclusively shows, many of the errors in question are of a kind that compositors are prone to—transposition of letters, and the like—and are not to be attributed to any difficulties caused by a puzzling handwriting ('Editorial Usefulness', p. 52). Moreover—and this observation is crucial—the crop of errors in Q, says Werstine, can be paralleled by 'scores of similar errors ... in books set by White's compositors from clear printed copy' (p. 53).

It is hard to escape the conclusion that Draudt has been over-impressed by the similarities in wording between the title-page of Q and the title-page of *Romeo and Juliet* Q2, especially as he pushes that analogy to include *Hamlet* Q2 as well. His basic assumption is that because *Romeo and Juliet* Q2 was printed mainly from manuscript but with some use of Q1, and because *Hamlet* Q2, though printed from manuscript, was affected to some degree by Q1, which the printers consulted, Q *Love's Labour's Lost* must have had much the same kind of printing history and depended in part on the lost quarto, which, again by reason of analogy, he takes to have been 'bad'. Nowhere does he so much as mention the possibility that it could equally well have been good.

Of the three hypotheses, Werstine's, resting as it does on patiently gathered verifiable evidence, seems by far the most persuasive and acceptable. Moreover, it can be supported by considerations other than those already taken into account. The recognized bad quartos of Shakespeare's plays, different though they are in other respects, have one thing in common: all of them present versions of plays that are very decidedly plays of action, with a pronounced story interest; and the general tendency of the

[1] *The Library*, VI, 3 (1981), 119–31.

bad quartos is to increase the emphasis on action by cutting or entirely dispensing with passages of narration, description, or reflection. But *Love's Labour's Lost* is not a play of this kind at all. It has less story interest than any other play that Shakespeare ever wrote. Reduced to its action alone, it would offer thin fare indeed. Closely connected with this consideration is another. The bad quartos are bad because the texts they present are not directly and immediately related to the author's manuscript or to any authoritative transcript of that manuscript. All of them rest on reports, on what one or more people could remember of the words spoken on the stage. But any reporter who knew his business would have seen at once that *Love's Labour's Lost* was not a play that lent itself readily to memorial reconstruction. Both its unusual vocabulary and, still more, its intricate word-play would have militated against its being recalled with any precision. But these same qualities might well have made a sound version of it, legitimately acquired from the company, very attractive to a reader. From its pages he would have been able to work out at his leisure the fine details of many an exchange which had caught his attention but eluded his full comprehension when spoken in the theatre.

The most reasonable and acceptable theory with regard to the copy for Q is that set out by Stanley Wells, who writes:

Although the use as copy of a mixture of bad quarto and foul papers cannot be disproven, it remains to be proven, and all evidence so far produced is compatible with the simpler hypothesis that Q is a straight reprint of a lost 'good' quarto, itself set directly from Shakespeare's foul papers.[1]

Three attempts have been made to identify the compositor or compositors responsible for setting Q. Draudt thinks that only one was involved, but gives no reason for so thinking ('Printer's Copy', pp. 121–2). Price, on the other hand, bringing a whole battery of tests into play, eventually but rather hesitantly concludes that the work was carried out by three compositors, of whom the first set seventeen pages, the second thirty-two pages, and the third twenty-five pages. But both the criteria he uses and the way in which he applies them have met with some damaging criticism from Werstine ('Editorial Usefulness', pp. 42–54), who

[1] *William Shakespeare: A Textual Companion* (Oxford, 1986), p. 270.

has made his own identifications which do not correspond at all with Price's, apart from the fact that he too thinks that three compositors worked on the setting of Q. Relying for his evidence on the well-tried test of preferred spellings, Werstine finds that William White employed five workmen in all during the years 1598 to 1600. Two of them had no hand whatever in the composing of Q, while another, whom he labels R, was responsible for one page only—B1 (1.1.221–66). The remainder of the work was, he thinks, divided very unequally between Compositor S and Compositor T, with S setting a mere seven pages—A2–3ᵛ (1.1.143) and F1–2 (4.3.181–7)—and thus leaving sixty-six pages out of the total of seventy-four to Compositor T.

These findings ('Editorial Usefulness', pp. 37–8), backed up, as they are, by a mass of detail, carry far more conviction than do Price's; and, in their suggestion that one compositor set more than nine-tenths of the text, are consonant with what is, perhaps, the most marked characteristic of Q as a piece of printing: 'its uniform badness', as Dover Wilson called it more than sixty years ago. So struck was he by the sheer incompetence of the workmanship that he remarked, 'it is charitable to suppose that the printing-office was hardly in working order when the job was begun'—White had only recently acquired his business at the time—and then went on to express his belief that the task was carried out by one man alone, since such a botched job could 'hardly be the product of two men setting up alternately'. As for the compositor concerned, Wilson labels him 'the veriest tyro at his craft', and writes of his 'prentice-hand' (p. 100).

This 'prentice-hand' betrays itself, Wilson notes, in several different kinds of elementary error. First, the text is plastered with 'literals', especially in the form of turned letters or foul case. Here are some examples chosen from the beginning and the ending of the play: 'publibue' for 'publique' (1.1.130), 'inchannting' for 'inchaunting' (1.1.166), 'Contempls' for 'Contempts' (1.1.188), 'Gfficer' for 'Officer' (1.1.258), 'Conqueronr' for 'Conquerour' (5.2.567), 'Flder' for 'Elder' (5.2.599), '*Eeter*' for '*Enter*' (5.2.623.1), 'interrnpptest' for 'interrupptest' (5.2.706), and 'rherefore' for 'therefore' (5.2.779). Secondly, missing letters are common. Q has 'thee' for 'three' (1.1.24), 'pome' for 'pompe' (1.1.31), 'wost' for 'worst' (1.1.269), 'prosperie' for 'prosperitie' (1.1.300), 'measue' for 'measure' (5.2.222), 'Loke' for 'Looke'

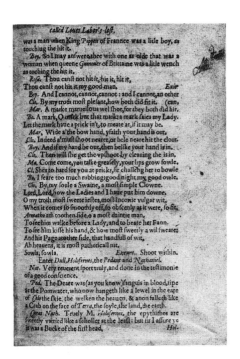

10. Sig. D4 of the First Quarto.

(5.2.251), 'thy' for 'they' (5.2.500), and 'intiled' for 'intitled' (5.2.800). Thirdly, the punctuation is anything but helpful. As Wilson says, it is 'not only frequently absurd but greatly over-weighted throughout, especially in the matter of full-stops, which occur in great profusion' (p. 104). There is no need to go further than the first page of Q (1.1.1.–30) to verify the accuracy of this observation. There line 5 ends with 'buy:' at a point where no stop at all is needed and where the colon is positively distracting. The same thing can be said about 'desires.' at the end of line 10 and about 'delyghts:' at the end of line 29. Even pages that have, as Werstine shows ('Variants', pp. 39–40), been subjected to some scrutiny, still contain glaring errors. Signature D4 will serve to make the point: see Fig. 10. In line 10, the proof-reader rightly and properly changed 'hid hit', the uncorrected reading, to 'did hit', and, in a pernickety mood, altered 'a' to 'a'' twice in consecutive lines (13 and 14). Yet he allowed far more serious mistakes to stand. Having replaced 'hid' with 'did', he still failed

73

to complete the line he was setting. The correct reading, dictated by sense, rhythm, and rhyme, is 'did hit it'; but the compositor, having no space left in his line, or in the line above, or in the line below, for the recalcitrant 'it', adopted the Procrustean solution to his difficulty by leaving 'it' out entirely, just as, for precisely the same reason, he omitted the full stop that should close line 18. Moreover, two other errors remain uncorrected. At line 16, the compositor has picked up the words 'is in' from the end of the previous line and used them again, instead of printing 'pin', as he should have done. And, finally, at line 28, he has omitted the word 'a' from the phrase 'it is a most patheticall nit'.

The general badness of Q as a specimen of the printer's craft raises two important questions. First, how far was it proof-read and corrected; and, secondly, how far is it to be trusted when it presents bad Latin and garbled Italian? The answer to the first question is that it was certainly subjected to proof-reading in parts. As long ago as 1957, W. W. Greg, in the introduction to his facsimile edition of Q,[1] listed seven known variants, due to stop-press correction. The full extent of the corrective process, in so far as it can be determined, was not established, however, until 1979, when Paul Werstine published his valuable study 'Variants in the First Quarto of *Love's Labor's Lost*'. In it he demonstrates that seven of the play's nineteen formes were proof-read: the outer forme of sheet A, and both the inner formes and the outer formes of sheets C, D, and E. Whether proof-reading continued beyond the end of E it is impossible to say, since no extant copy of Q shows any variants from the rest after this point.

Noting that the corrections, which are collated in this edition, fall into two groups, being scanty in outer A and in C but more numerous in D and E, Werstine deduces, fairly enough, that editors should be circumspect about emending words and passages in D and E, and agrees with those, such as H. H. Furness and Richard David, who hold that it is the characters, not the printer, who are responsible for 'the grossest corruptions of foreign languages in the play' (p. 42). However, a further look at the facsimile of D4 makes one question the validity of this latter view. In the first line he speaks the Pedant, as he is called at this point, remarks that the deer the Princess shot was 'sanguis in

---

[1] Shakespeare Quarto Facsimiles, No. 10 (Oxford, 1957).

blood'. The words are sheer nonsense, of course, and have been much discussed, yet they admit of a simple explanation: the compositor, trying to carry too much in his head, has transposed 'sanguis' and 'in blood'. The right reading (see Commentary) is 'in blood, sanguis', which makes perfect sense and is couched in what we soon come to recognize as Holofernes' personal idiom. Moreover, this is not an isolated instance of Compositor T's tendency to transpose. At 4.3.173, the King says bitterly to Biron: 'Are we betrayed thus to thy over-view?', to which Biron replies in Q: 'Not you by me, but I betrayed to you', an answer which, as Capell noticed, is more to the point and takes on the right antithetical bite if it reads: 'Not you to me, but I betrayed by you'. Nor does Compositor T restrict his transposing habit to single words and phrases. On one occasion at least (5.2.876–7) he transposes whole lines, printing the second and third lines of the cuckoo song in reverse order. Even '*Celo*' in the same initial speech, which many have seized on as evidence of the schoolmaster's incompetence as a Latinist because it is in the wrong case, the ablative instead of the nominative, could equally well be 'a misreading of a manuscript "*Celū*" ("e" was acceptable in renaissance Latin for "ae", and the tilde over the "u" stood for "m")' (Kerrigan, pp. 188–9). Furthermore, it is abundantly clear that the worst piece of corruption in the entire text is compositorial, and in no way reflects badly on Holofernes. At 5.1.26, Nathaniel, in answer to a question put to him by Holofernes, replies: '*Laus deo, bene intelligo.*' It is good grammatical Latin, yet it is met with what must be a reproof, that runs thus: '*Bome boon for boon prescian*, a little scratcht, twil serue.' Whatever those first four words are supposed to mean, they certainly cannot be the words Shakespeare gave Holofernes to speak. Indeed, it is not even clear what language or languages they are intended to represent. This passage alone—and it does not stand alone, for Holofernes has already been saddled with another piece of gibberish on the subject of Venice at 4.2.95–6—is sufficient in itself to make one sceptical, as Dover Wilson had become in his second edition of 1962 (pp. viii–xi), of the view that errors in the use of foreign languages are deliberately designed by the playwright to expose the emptiness of their speakers' pretensions to learning. It also leaves one equally sceptical about the title-page's claim that the text has been 'Newly corrected'. Such correction as it has undergone can only have been of the most cursory and casual kind.

What, then, is the validity of 'augmented'? In one sense, it is indubitably and demonstrably true. The evidence is there in the two duplicated passages. At 4.3.293, twenty-three lines of a first draft have been expanded into a revised version of forty-eight lines; and at 5.2.819 the thirty-five lines of dialogue between Biron and Rosaline that follow are clearly meant to replace a mere six lines of dialogue between them that began originally at 5.2.805. Whether these revised lines are the augmentations that whoever was responsible for the wording on the title-page had in mind it is not possible to say; but they do raise two crucial and interrelated questions. First, are they, as Dover Wilson (p. 125) averred, part of 'a drastic revision' of the play as originally composed; and, secondly, when were they written? Like most critics before him, Wilson had no doubt that there was such a revision and that it was made in preparation for the performance the Queen saw during the Christmas season of 1597–8. Yet, as has already been demonstrated at some length (pp. 57–65), if there was such a revision and it resulted in the text of Q, it still left the play unactable. To this editor, as to Chambers (*William Shakespeare*, i. 335) and Greg (*SFF*, p. 220), both the first version of 4.3.293–340 and the first version of 5.2.805–53 look like 'false starts', which Shakespeare had no sooner written than he recognized their inadequacy, and promptly replaced them with fuller and better versions. They belong naturally with so much else in the play that bears witness to the playwright's discovery of his comedy as he proceeds with the writing of it: his difficulty in deciding on the right names for two of the ladies, for instance, and his introduction of three French lords into the cast at the opening of 2.1, only to find that one of them, Boyet, is enough for his purposes, whereupon he unobtrusively drops the other two before the end of 4.1.

Nevertheless, the notion that there was a revision of some kind in 1597 has been slow to die, largely owing to an influential article by J. W. Lever, published in 1952.[1] In it Lever argues, in a way many have found convincing, that the first stanza of the spring-song at the end of the play was heavily indebted to a

---

[1] 'Three Notes on Shakespeare's Plants', *RES*, NS 3 (1952), 117–29.

passage in John Gerard's *Herbal*, which first appeared in 1597. Abbreviated, the relevant passage in that work runs thus:

Milk-white Lady-smocks hath stalks rising immediately from the root ... The flowers grow at the top, made of four leaves of a yellowish colour. .... These kinds of cuckoo-flowers grow in moist meadows, [and they flower] in April and May when the cuckoo doth begin to sing her pleasant notes without stammering. ... They are commonly called in Latin *flos Cuculi*, for the reason aforesaid ... it is called ... in English cuckoo-flowers; in Norfolk, Canterbury bells; at the Nantwich in Cheshire, where I had my beginning, Lady-smocks, which hath given me cause to christen it after my country fashion.[1]

From this statement Lever deduced 'that the Cheshire name "Lady-smocks" came into standard English through Gerarde's idiosyncrasy, and that Shakespeare took it straight from the *Herball*', along with 'the meadows', and so on.

So things stood until 1982, when John Kerrigan demolished the whole theory in his '*Love's Labor's Lost* and Shakespearean Revision',[2] where, starting from Mats Rydén's noticing that the word 'Lady-smocks' was already in literary use by 1593,[3] when it appeared in Michael Drayton's *The Shepherd's Garland*,[4] Kerrigan comes to the irrefutable conclusion 'that if one Warwickshire man [Drayton] could write about "Lady-smocks" in the early to mid-1590s, another [Shakespeare] surely could' (p. 339). Shakespeare's lines are then, as one instinctively feels, the fruit of his observation, not of his reading. They throw no light on the date of the play or on the question of whether it was revised or not.

So far, then, it is clear that Q must be the control-text for an edition of the comedy, since the copy from which it was set was either the author's foul papers or the lost Quarto which had itself been set from those same foul papers. But there is a complication. The next appearance of *Love's Labour's Lost* in print, after 1598, was in the First Folio edition of Shakespeare's plays, hence-forward referred to as F, published in 1623, seven years after the playwright's death, where it occupies pages 122–44 of the

---

[1] Book II, Chap. xviii, p. 203.

[2] *Shakespeare Quarterly*, 33 (1982), 337–9.

[3] 'Shakespeare's Cuckoo-buds', *Studia Neophilologica*, 49 (1977), 25–7.

[4] 'The Fourth Eclogue', l. 153; *Poems of Michael Drayton*, ed. John Buxton (1953), i. 58. 153.

comedies (signatures L1ᵛ–M6ᵛ); and the text printed in F, though manifestly set from a copy of Q, differs in some significant ways from that of Q. The most obvious and immediately perceptible of these differences, though by no means the most important, is summarized thus by W. W. Greg:

F introduces a division into acts only (misprinting the fifth 'Actus Quartus') of monstrously disproportionate lengths—509, 257, 207, 710, and 1104 lines respectively. Probably it was made at the time of printing, for in this case the note 'Finis Actus Primus' ... looks as though it had been added merely to fill up the space at the foot of a column. (*SFF*, p. 223)

The act divisions of F are patently absurd. Nevertheless, they have been preserved in this edition, along with the scene divisions introduced by editors in the eighteenth century, purely for convenience of reference.

The other major difference between F and Q, and by far the most important one, is that F adds six words, 'You that way; we this way', to the very end of the play and assigns them, together with the entire speech they conclude, to Armado, whereas Q's enigmatic final comment, 'The words of Mercury are harsh after the songs of Apollo', is not assigned to anyone. To many critics 'You that way; we this way', endorsing the fact that this comedy ends with partings not unions, has seemed the perfect conclusion. But what authority does it have? Is this addition the work of Shakespeare himself, or is it, as Greg unhesitatingly asserts, 'the editor's desperate attempt to fit the final words of Q into the structure of the play' (*SFF*, p. 223)?

To reach any kind of conclusion about the authenticity of those final words peculiar to F and of the other variants from Q that it offers, it is necessary to take a closer look at F as a whole. That it was indeed set from a copy of Q is beyond doubt. The proof is, as Dover Wilson acutely pointed out (p. 186), that it prints the word 'venewe', at 5.1.55, as though it were two words, 'vene we', thus perpetuating an error that originates in Q, where it was caused by the accidental loosening and shifting of the type after it had been set. For more evidence of the dependence of F on Q, one need only turn to F's treatment of Q's D4 (see Figure 10). F repeats at least three of Q's patent mistakes: 'did hit' for 'did hit it', 'the is in' for 'the pin', and 'it is most' for 'it is a most' (4.1.128, 135, and 147). Moreover, F adds two gratuitous errors of its own. It shifts the stage direction '*Exit*' from the end of Rosaline's speech at line 125 to the end of Boyet's speech at line 127, where it is clearly out of place, since he remains on stage; and it omits the word 'And' from the beginning of that same speech. At the same time, however, it makes good one omission from Q by supplying the full-stop that is needed at the end of line 137.

The Folio compositor responsible for setting its version of Q's D4, Compositor D,[1] was also guilty of omitting nine lines of dialogue, 80–8, from 3.1. One can see how it came about. It occurs in the course of the exchanges between Armado and Moth in which the jingle, 'The fox, the ape, and the humble-bee | Were still at odds, being but three', is spoken no fewer than three times in a mere twelve lines. Faced with this repetitive pattern, D allowed his eye to skip from the words introducing the first instance to those introducing the third. This is not to say, however, that omission is the prerogative of Compositor D. His fellow-worker C, for example, leaves out the word 'quite' (1.1.27) on the first page; while B completely ignores the moving sentence, 'When he breathed, he was a man' (5.2.652–3), in Armado's spirited defence of the dead Hector.

The Folio compositors also imported other kinds of corruption into their text. They are prone to modernize. At 1.1.130 D turns 'can possible' into 'shall possibly', and at 1.1.157 'other' into 'others'; while C, for his part, changes 'a' to 'he', and thus starts a trend towards the less colloquial which becomes quite pronounced. Moreover, all three are ready to alter a word, or even leave it out altogether, in order to justify a line of type. For this reason C replaces 'fitteth' (1.2.40) with 'fits'; D reduces 'Maister, will' (3.1.7) to 'Will'; and B cuts 'to her thither' down to size by omitting 'thither' (5.2.312). They are also given to transposing words. At 1.2.164–5 C prints 'yet *Sampsoun* was' for 'Yet was *Sampsoun*', and at 2.1.175 'we shall' for 'shall we'; and B, at 5.2.324, turns 'kist his hand, a way' into 'kist away his hand'.

These examples—a few out of many—confirm that MacD. P. Jackson is right when he generalizes to the following effect: 'The

[1] F was set by three compositors, working as follows: C set L1ᵛ, D set L2, C set L2ᵛ–L4, D set L4ᵛ–6ᵛ, C set M1–3ᵛ, B set M4–6ᵛ. See Charlton Hinman, *The Printing and Proof-Reading of the First Folio of Shakespeare*, 2 vols. (Oxford, 1963), ii. 514.

similarities between the three compositors are more notable than the differences. Each corrupted the text with definite errors or with unauthorized alterations at the rate of about six per Folio page.'[1] And, since *Love's Labour's Lost* occupies 23 Folio pages, Jackson's count of corruptions in F, 138, corresponds almost exactly with the total of 137 arrived at by Dover Wilson (p. 189). Wilson notes further that F allows no fewer than 59 errors in Q to stand while making sound corrections of some 117 errors in that text, most of the mistakes concerned being of a kind that an experienced workman would recognize at once: 'missing, transposed, or wrong letters'. Even some of F's more striking changes, such as 'Importunes' for Q's 'Importuous' (2.1.32), 'vnpeopled' for 'vnpeeled' (2.1.88), 'indiscreet' for 'indistreel' (4.2.29), and the like, would not be beyond these compositors' capability and purview.

There are also, however, other alterations that can hardly have originated with the printers. Wilson puts the matter thus: 'No compositor would have changed "Clymbe ore the house to vnlocke the little gate" (Q.) into "That were to clymbe ore the house to vnlocke the gate" (F.), which occurs at 1.1.109'; and he then goes on to list 'seven other variants of the same kind'. They are 'parts' for 'peerelsse' (2.1.44), 'stab'd' for 'stable' (5.2.80), 'Ioue' for 'God' (l. 316), 'Zanie' for 'saine' (l. 463), 'manager' [it should be 'manage'] for 'nuage' (l. 482), 'doth least' for 'doth best' (l. 513), and 'euer' for 'herrite' (l. 804). It is, perhaps, not purely coincidental that the last six of these alterations occur in the final scene of the play, and the last five of them in the stint that was set by Compositor B, who has become almost notorious for his high-handed treatment of copy. But, however that may be, it seems clear that the copy of Q used by the printers of F had undergone some annotation before it went to them from the playhouse.

What is not clear is whether the annotator consulted a playhouse manuscript in making his alterations. The evidence is contradictory. In substituting 'Ioue' for 'God' he could well have been using his own initiative, since all he was doing was to bring the text into line with the requirements of the Act of 1606 prohibiting profanity on the stage, something he signally failed to do with the other twenty instances of 'God' in Q; but in replacing

---

[1] MacD. P. Jackson, 'Compositors B, C, and D, and the First Folio Text of *Love's Labour's Lost*', *Papers of the Bibliographical Society of America*, 72 (1978), 61–5.

'herrite' with 'euer' he must have been guessing; and why he chose to alter his text at 1.1.109 is beyond the wit of man. Yet the other five changes, assuming that the word he substituted for the unintelligible 'nuage' was indeed 'manage' which Compositor B misread as 'manager', are all sound. On balance, therefore, it does look as though he had access, when he chose to avail himself of it, to a better text than that provided by Q, and that he did turn to it when scanning the last part of Q, to which he paid more attention than he seems to have done to the rest of it. In these circumstances the case for the authenticity of F's final sentence becomes a strong one.[1]

In view of what has been said already (pp. 60–3) about the confusion of names in 2.1, it would be helpful to the case set out there if the same claim to authenticity could be made for F's alteration of the speech-prefix '*Kather⟨ine⟩*' at lines 114–25 to '*Rosa⟨line⟩*'. Unfortunately, it cannot. The other changes of speech headings in F forbid it, for they are either obvious corrections of mis-spellings in Q, such as '*Clo.*' for that text's '*Col.*' (1.1.286), or the abortive effort in 1.2 to regularize '*Armado*' to '*Braggart*' and the equally abortive attempt to provide personal names for Q's indecisive '*Lad.*', '*Lad. 2.*', '*Lad. 3.*', '*Lad.*', and '*Lad.*' in the closing lines of 2.1.

Behind the text of *Love's Labour's Lost*, as we have it in the Quarto of 1598, lurks the ghost of an earlier 'lost' quarto. It is in keeping with the comedy's teasing ending and with its pronounced symmetry of form that behind it there lurks another ghost, that of a 'lost' play by Shakespeare entitled *Love's Labour's Won*. The only evidence, prior to 1953, that it ever existed was provided by its appearance in the celebrated list of Shakespeare's works given by Francis Meres in his *Palladis Tamia: Wit's Treasury* of 1598, where Meres writes:

As *Plautus* and *Seneca* are accounted the best for Comedy and Tragedy among the Latines: so *Shakespeare* among the English is the most excellent in both kinds for the stage; for Comedy, witnes his *Gentlemen of Verona*, his *Errors*, his *Loue labors lost*, his *Loue labours wonne*, his *Midsummers night dreame*, & his *Merchant of Venice*: for Tragedy his *Richard the 2. Richard the 3. Henry the 4. King Iohn, Titus Andronicus* and his *Romeo* and *Iuliet*. (Quoted from Chambers, *William Shakespeare*, ii. 194)

[1] See Stanley Wells, 'The Copy for the Folio Text of *Love's Labour's Lost*', *RES*, NS 33 (1982), 137–47.

However, no copy of *Love's Labour's Won* has ever come to light; and up to 1953 scholars tended to think that there were three possible explanations for Meres's statement. First, and most likely, that *Love's Labour's Won* was simply some other known comedy by Shakespeare under another name: *The Taming of the Shrew*, for instance, or *Much Ado About Nothing*, neither of them in Meres's list. Secondly, there was the possibility that *Love's Labour's Won* was merely an alternative title for *Love's Labour's Lost* itself, and that Meres had failed to realize this. Thirdly, it was suggested that Meres had invented the title *Love's Labour's Won* in order that he might have six comedies to balance the six 'tragedies' he cites.

Then, late in 1953, two leaves of paper, covered with Elizabethan handwriting, were found in the backing used to strengthen the spine of a copy of Thomas Gataker's *Certaine Sermons* published in 1637–8. Happily, this find was shown at once to the well known American scholar T. W. Baldwin, who immediately recognized its significance, proceeded to work on it, and, two years later, published an exhaustive account of his findings: *Shakspere's 'Love's Labor's Won'* (Carbondale, 1957). The leaves were, he discovered, from the ledger of a stationer in Exeter, and the jottings noted various items the stationer had sold during the month of August 1603, together with a list of books he had in stock at the time. Part of that list was made up of '[inte]rludes & tragedyes', and it concludes with the following items:

> marchant of vennis
> taming of a shrew
> knak to know a knave
> knak to know an honest man
> loves labor lost
> loves labor won.

In print by 1603 at the very latest, *Love's Labour's Won* was no fictitious play invented by Meres for the sake of symmetry; nor can it have been an alternative name for *The Taming of a/the Shrew*, or *The Merchant of Venice*, or *Love's Labour's Lost* itself. It was also distinct, Meres's testimony assures us, from *The Two Gentlemen of Verona*, *The Comedy of Errors*, and *A Midsummer Night's Dream*. There is no other comedy thought to have been written by Shakespeare before 1598 with which to equate it. It seems beyond doubt, therefore, that it did exist, that it was published, and that it has since disappeared. Further than that it is not possible to go.

EDITORIAL PROCEDURES

FOR the reasons set out in the Introduction the control text for this edition is the Quarto of 1598, since it was printed either from Shakespeare's manuscript or from a lost quarto based on that same manuscript. It is further assumed that the manuscript in question must have been in the form of 'foul papers', that is to say in a state from which a 'fair copy', suitable for use as a prompt-book and the drawing up of actors 'parts', could be made and would have to be made before the play could be staged. On the hypothesis that the text of F, which is in all essentials a reprint of Q, may have been influenced by some cursory and unsystematic consultation of such 'fair copy', some of its readings, including its last line, which does not appear at all in Q, are adopted here, but, apart from its corrections of obvious printers' errors, only very rarely. It is, however, substantially collated. So far as words and passages in foreign languages, and especially in Latin, are concerned, errors in them have been corrected because, to this editor, they look far more like compositorial mistakes than an attempt on the part of the playwright to pillory Holofernes' Latin as bad. Pedants are often tiresomely pernickety but rarely wildly inaccurate.

The general principles governing the modernization of the text are those set out by Stanley Wells in his *Modernizing Shakespeare's Spelling* (Oxford, 1979); and, in keeping with them, passages from authors of the sixteenth and early seventeenth centuries, quoted in the introduction and commentary, have also been modernized even when they have been taken from editions using old spelling. Old spellings are, however, retained in documentary evidence, for much of the matter dealt with in that part of the introduction devoted to the text, and in the collations, where the lemma takes the modernized form but the rest of the entry is given in the original spelling.

Since directions such as 'aside' or 'to' another character, together with act and scene divisions, are all editorial, they are not attributed in the collations. Changes or variations in the punctuation are noted only where they are significant. Speech headings have been silently normalized.

85

Quotations from the Bible are taken, unless otherwise stated, from the Bishops' Bible of 1568. References to other works by Shakespeare are keyed to Oxford.

Words are normally defined only when they first appear or when they convey a significantly different meaning from that which they had on their first appearance. All words that are glossed are listed in the index.

Abbreviations and References

The following abbreviations are used in the textual part of the introduction, in the collations, and in the commentary. The place of publication is, unless otherwise specified, London.

EDITIONS OF SHAKESPEARE

Q	*A* PLEASANT Conceited Comedie CALLED, Loues labors lost. *As it was presented before her Highnes this last Christmas. Newly corrected and augmented By W. Shakespeare.* . . . 1598
Q2	Loues Labours lost. A WITTIE AND PLEASANT COMEDIE, As it was Acted by his Maiesties Seruants at *the* Blacke-Friers *and the* Globe. By WILLIAM SHAKESPEARE. . . . 1631.
F	The First Folio, 1623
F2	The Second Folio, 1632
F3	The Third Folio, 1663
F4	The Fourth Folio, 1685
Alexander	Peter Alexander, *Complete Works* (1951)
Cambridge	W. G. Clark and W. A. Wright, *Works*, The Cambridge Shakespeare, 9 vols. (Cambridge, 1863–6)
Capell	Edward Capell, *Comedies, Histories, and Tragedies*, 10 vols. (1767–8)
Collier	John Payne Collier, *Works*, 8 vols. (1842–4)
Collier 1853	John Payne Collier, *Plays* (1853)
Collier 1858	John Payne Collier, *Comedies, Histories, Tragedies, and Poems* (1858)
David	Richard David, *Love's Labour's Lost*, new Arden Shakespeare (1951)
Delius	Nikolaus Delius, *Werke*, 7 vols. (Elberfeld, 1854–61)

Dyce	Alexander Dyce, *Works*, 6 vols. (1857)
Furness	Horace Howard Furness, *Love's Labour's Lost*, A New Variorum Edition (Philadelphia, 1904)
Globe	W. G. Clark and W. A. Wright, *Works*, The Globe Edition (1864)
Halliwell	James O. Halliwell, *Works*, 16 vols. (1853–65)
Hanmer	Thomas Hanmer, *Works*, 6 vols. (Oxford, 1743–4)
Harbage	Alfred Harbage, *Complete Works*, The Pelican Shakespeare (1969)
Hart	H. C. Hart, *Love's Labour's Lost*, Arden Shakespeare (1906)
Hudson	H. N. Hudson, *Works*, 11 vols. (Boston, 1851–6)
Johnson	Samuel Johnson, *Plays*, 8 vols. (1765)
Johnson and Steevens	Samuel Johnson and George Steevens, *Plays*, 10 vols. (1778)
Johnson and Steevens 1785	Samuel Johnson, George Steevens, and Isaac Reed, *Plays*, 10 vols. (1785)
Keightley	Thomas Keightley, *Plays*, 6 vols. (1864)
Kerrigan	John Kerrigan, *Love's Labour's Lost*, New Penguin Shakespeare (Harmondsworth, 1982)
Knight	Charles Knight, *Works*, Pictorial Edition, 8 vols. (1838–43)
Malone	Edmond Malone, *Plays and Poems*, 10 vols. (1790)
Marshall	Henry Irving and Frank A. Marshall, *Works*, The Henry Irving Shakespeare, 8 vols. (1888–90)
Oxford	Stanley Wells and Gary Taylor, *Complete Works* (Oxford, 1986)
Pope	Alexander Pope, *Works*, 6 vols. (1723–5)
Pope 1728	Alexander Pope, *Works*, 10 vols. (1728)
Rann	Joseph Rann, *Dramatic Works*, 6 vols. (Oxford, 1786–94)
Ridley	M. R. Ridley, *Love's Labour's Lost*, The New Temple Shakespeare (1934)
Riverside	G. B. Evans (textual editor), *The Riverside Shakespeare* (Boston, 1974)
Rowe	Nicholas Rowe, *Works*, 6 vols. (1709)
Rowe 1714	Nicholas Rowe, *Works*, 8 vols. (1714)
Singer	Samuel Weller Singer, *Dramatic Works*, 10 vols. (1856)

Sisson	Charles Jasper Sisson, *Complete Works* (1954)
Steevens	George Steevens and Isaac Reed, *Plays*, 15 vols. (1793)
Theobald	Lewis Theobald, *Works*, 7 vols. (1733)
Theobald 1740	Lewis Theobald, *Works*, 8 vols. (1740)
Warburton	William Warburton, *Works*, 8 vols. (1747)
White	Richard Grant White, *Works*, 12 vols. (Boston, 1857–66)
Wilson	Sir Arthur Quiller-Couch and John Dover Wilson, *Love's Labour's Lost*, The New Shakespeare (Cambridge, 1923)
Wilson 1962	John Dover Wilson, *Love's Labour's Lost*, The New Shakespeare (Cambridge, 1962)

OTHER WORKS

Abbott	E. A. Abbott, *A Shakespearian Grammar*, second edition (1870)
Arcadia, The	Sir Philip Sidney, *The Countess of Pembroke's Arcadia*, ed. Albert Feuillerat (Cambridge, 1939)
Binns	J. W. Binns, 'Shakespeare's Latin Citations: the Editorial Problem', *Shakespeare Survey 35* (1982), 119–28
Bullough	Geoffrey Bullough, *Narrative and Dramatic Sources of Shakespeare*, 8 vols. (1957–75)
Chambers, *William Shakespeare*	E. K. Chambers, *William Shakespeare*, 2 vols. (Oxford, 1930)
Chapman	*The Plays of George Chapman*, ed. T. M. Parrott, 2 vols. (1910–14)
Chaucer	*The Works of Geoffrey Chaucer*, ed. F. N. Robinson (Boston, 1933)
Dent	R. W. Dent, *Shakespeare's Proverbial Language: An Index* (1981)
Farmer	Richard Farmer, in *Works*, ed. Johnson and Steevens (1773)
Grosart	*The Life and Complete Works ... of Robert Greene*, ed. A. B. Grosart, 15 vols. (1881–6)
Harvey Wood	The Plays of John Marston, ed. H. Harvey Wood, 3 vols. (1934–9)
Helicon	*England's Helicon* (1600)
Malcontent, The	*The Malcontent* [by] John Marston, ed. G. K. Hunter (1975)

Nashe	*The Works of Thomas Nashe*, ed. R. B. McKerrow (1904–10) ... With supplementary notes ... by F. P. Wilson, 5 vols. (Oxford, 1958)
OED	*The Oxford English Dictionary, being a corrected re-issue of A New English Dictionary on Historical Principles*, 13 vols. (Oxford 1933), and Supplements 1–3 (1972, 1976, 1982)
Onions	C. T. Onions, *A Shakespeare Glossary*, second edition revised (Oxford, 1966)
Partridge	Eric Partridge, *Shakespeare's Bawdy* (1968)
Pilgrim	*The Passionate Pilgrim* (1599)
Schmidt	Alexander Schmidt, *A Shakespeare Lexicon*, fourth edition (revised by G. Sarrazin), 2 vols. (Berlin and Leipzig, 1923)
Schoenbaum	*Annals of English Drama 975–1700*, by Alfred Harbage, revised by S. Schoenbaum (1964)
SFF	W. W. Greg, *The Shakespeare First Folio* (Oxford, 1955)
Shakespeare's England	*Shakespeare's England*, ed. C. T. Onions, 2 vols. (Oxford, 1932)
Sisson, *New Readings*	C. J. Sisson, *New Readings in Shakespeare*, 2 vols. (Cambridge, 1956)
TC	Stanley Wells and Gary Taylor with John Jowett and William Montgomery, *William Shakespeare: A Textual Companion* (Oxford, 1987)
Thomson	J. A. K. Thomson, *Shakespeare and the Classics* (1952)
Tilley	M. P. Tilley, *A Dictionary of the Proverbs in England in the Sixteenth and Seventeenth Centuries* (Ann Arbor, 1950)
Tyrwhitt	Thomas Tyrwhitt, *Observations and Conjectures upon Some Passages of Shakespeare* (1766)
Walker, W. S.	W. S. Walker, *A Critical Examination of the Text of Shakespeare*, 3 vols. (1860)
Webster	*The Works of John Webster*, ed. F. L. Lucas, 4 vols. (1927)
Wells, *Re-Editing*	Stanley Wells, *Re-Editing Shakespeare for the Modern Reader* (Oxford, 1984)

Love's Labour's Lost

THE PERSONS OF THE PLAY

FERDINAND, King of Navarre

BIRON
LONGUEVILLE ⎬ lords in attendance on the King
DUMAINE

THE PRINCESS OF FRANCE

ROSALINE
MARIA ⎬ ladies in attendance on the Princess
KATHERINE

BOYET, a French lord in attendance on the Princess

TWO OTHER FRENCH LORDS, also in attendance on the Princess

MONSIEUR MARCADÉ, a messenger

DON ADRIANO DE ARMADO, a braggart from Spain

MOTH, his page

HOLOFERNES, a schoolmaster

NATHANIEL, a curate

DULL, a constable

COSTARD, a rustic

JAQUENETTA, a dairymaid

A FORESTER

Attendants on the King

Love's Labour's Lost

―――――――――――

1.1 *Enter Ferdinand, King of Navarre, Biron, Longueville, and Dumaine*

KING

Let fame, that all hunt after in their lives,
Live registered upon our brazen tombs,
And then grace us in the disgrace of death;

Love's Labour's Lost] *A PLEASANT* Conceited Comedie CALLED, Loues labors lost. Q (*title-page*); *A pleasant conceited Comedie: called Loues Labor's lost* Q (*running titles*); Loues Labour's lost. F (*head-title; running titles*); Loues Labour lost. F (*table of contents*).
1.1.0.1 *Biron*] QF (Berowne)   0.1 *Longueville*] QF (Longauill)   1 KING] ROWE; *Ferdinand* QF

Love's Labour's Lost It is far from certain what Shakespeare intended his play to be called. Its name, as it appears on the title-page of Q, is 'Loues labors lost', which is ambiguous. It can mean either 'the labour of love is lost' or 'the lost labours of love'. However, the running title of Q— '*A pleasant conceited Comedie: called Loues Labor's lost*'—seems to settle the issue, especially as it has the support of F, where the running title is '*Loues Labour's lost*' and the head-title 'Loues Labour's Lost'. But there are complications. In the Catalogue of the plays included in F it is listed as '*Loues Labour lost*', and this is the name by which Robert Tofte refers to it in his *Alba* of 1598 (see Introduction, p. 1). Francis Meres, however, in his *Palladis Tamia: Wit's Treasury*, also published in 1598, calls it '*Loue labors lost*'. *Love's Labour's Lost* is probably right, but *Love's Labours Lost* has its attractions, particularly in a play where the name *Hercules* occurs no fewer than eleven times.

Like much else in the comedy, the title has a proverbial ring to it. 'To lose one's labour' (Tilley L9) goes back to the early 16th century; and Dent (L555.1) gives good reasons for thinking that although Shakespeare's title is the first recorded instance of the precise phrase it may well have been current earlier. *Love* is, of course, Cupid, who is mentioned more often in this play than in any other that Shakespeare wrote, though *Much Ado About Nothing*—another comedy with a

proverbial title—runs it close in this as in many other respects.

1.1.0.1 *Ferdinand, King of Navarre* There never was a king of Navarre called Ferdinand; and no one in the play ever refers to him by that name. It is used, however, in the speech-prefixes of 1.1 and 2.1. After that his speeches are headed '*King*'.
Biron See Introduction, p. 49. Shakespeare, like Nashe (ii.182), spells the name 'Berowne', and rhymes it with 'moon' (4.3.229).
Longueville See Introduction, p. 49. Spelling this name 'Longauill', 'Longauil', and 'Longauile', Shakespeare makes it rhyme with 'ill' (4.3.121), with 'compile' (4.3.131), and even extracts some puns on 'veal' and 'well' from it (5.2.247).
Dumaine See Introduction p. 49. The name is an Anglicized version of the Duc de Mayenne.

1.1.1–7 **Let … eternity** As many critics and commentators have noticed, there are marked similarities between these lines and some of the Sonnets, especially 19, 55, 63–5, and 100.
2 **brazen tombs** tombs bearing inscribed brass plates
3 **grace … death** make us honoured and admired even when we have been physically disfigured by death—a version of the Latin tag '*Vivit post funera virtus*' (Tilley V74). Compare *Lucrece* 1319–21: 'When sighs and groans and tears may grace the fashion | Of her disgrace,

95

When, spite of cormorant devouring Time,
Th'endeavour of this present breath may buy
That honour which shall bate his scythe's keen edge,
And make us heirs of all eternity.
Therefore, brave conquerors—for so you are,
That war against your own affections
And the huge army of the world's desires—   10
Our late edict shall strongly stand in force.
Navarre shall be the wonder of the world;
Our court shall be a little academe,
Still and contemplative in living art.
You three, Biron, Dumaine, and Longueville,
Have sworn for three years' term to live with me,
My fellow-scholars, and to keep those statutes
That are recorded in this schedule here.
Your oaths are passed, and now subscribe your names,
That his own hand may strike his honour down   20
That violates the smallest branch herein.

---

5 buy ∧] F2 ; ～ : QF   10 desires—] ROWE (*subs.*) ; ～. QF

the better so to clear her | From that suspicion which the world might bear her.'

4 **spite** in spite
  cormorant ravenous. For Shakespeare and his age the cormorant was an emblem of consuming greed.
  devouring Time 'Time devours all things' was proverbial (Tilley T326).
5 **Th'endeavour ... breath** our efforts while we are alive
6 **bate** blunt, dull
  his scythe's keen edge Erwin Panofsky has a fascinating chapter on the evolution of the figure of Father Time, complete with scythe or sickle, in his *Studies in Iconology* (Oxford, 1939; repr. New York and Evanston, 1962), pp. 69–93. It throws much light on this particular passage.
8 **brave conquerors** The King rashly but characteristically assumes that he and his fellow-students have already accomplished the arduous task on which they are only now about to embark.
9 **affections** passions, natural impulses

11 **late** recent
13 **academe** academy. Not used by Shakespeare in any other of his writings, this 'poetic' form of the older word *academy* appears to have originated in this passage. Imitations of Plato's Academy came into being first in Florence during the mid 15th century and then in other parts of Europe. *L'Académie française* by Pierre de la Primaudaye, a fictional account of such an institution published in 1577, had been translated into English by Thomas Bowes in 1586 under the title of *The French Academy* and was widely known. See Introduction p. 47.
14 **Still and contemplative in** calmly and steadily studying (hendiadys)
  living art The phrase seems to combine two ideas in one : (1) the art of living—the *ars vivendi* of the Stoic philosophers; (2) vital learning, learning that has a practical bearing on the whole business of living.
17 **keep** observe
  statutes terms, conditions
19 **passed** pledged
21 **branch** clause, detail

96

If you are armed to do as sworn to do,
Subscribe to your deep oaths, and keep it too.

LONGUEVILLE

I am resolved. 'Tis but a three years' fast.
The mind shall banquet though the body pine.
Fat paunches have lean pates, and dainty bits
Make rich the ribs but bankrupt quite the wits.

He signs

DUMAINE

My loving lord, Dumaine is mortified.
The grosser manner of these world's delights
He throws upon the gross world's baser slaves.   30
To love, to wealth, to pomp, I pine and die,
With all these living in philosophy.

He signs

BIRON

I can but say their protestation over.
So much, dear liege, I have already sworn,
That is, to live and study here three years.
But there are other strict observances:
As not to see a woman in that term,
Which I hope well is not enrollèd there;
And one day in a week to touch no food,
And but one meal on every day beside,   40
The which I hope is not enrollèd there;
And then to sleep but three hours in the night,
And not be seen to wink of all the day,

---

24 resolved] F (resolu'd); resolued Q   three] F; thee Q   27 bankrupt quite] Q (bancrout
quit); bankerout F   27.1 *He signs*] *not in* QF   30 slaves.] F (slaues:); ~ ∧ Q   31 pomp] Q
(pome), F   32.1 *He signs*] *not in* QF   43 day,] ROWE (*subs.*); ~. QF

22 **armed** prepared, ready
23 **deep** grave, serious
26 **Fat ... pates** i.e. fat-bellied men have poor
    headpieces. The idea was an old one, but
    Shakespeare's phrasing of it made it
    proverbial (Tilley P123). He contradicted
    it, of course, when he created Falstaff.
    bits morsels (synonymous with 'bites')
28 **mortified** dead to worldly pleasures
29 **manner** sort, kind
32 **With ... philosophy** i.e. finding a more
    than adequate substitute for love,

wealth, and pomp in the study of philosophy
37 **not to see a woman** David notes that
    Robert Greene, in his *The Royal Exchange*
    (1590), says: 'Plato admitted no auditor
    in his academy but such as while they
    were his scholars would abstain from
    women; for he was wont to say that the
    greatest enemy to memory was venery'
    (Grosart, vii. 314).
43 **wink of all** close one's eyes during the
    whole of

When I was wont to think no harm all night,
And make a dark night too of half the day,
Which I hope well is not enrollèd there.
O, these are barren tasks, too hard to keep:
Not to see ladies, study, fast, not sleep.

KING

Your oath is passed to pass away from these.

BIRON

Let me say no, my liege, an if you please.   50
I only swore to study with your grace,
And stay here in your court for three years' space.

LONGUEVILLE

You swore to that, Biron, and to the rest.

BIRON

By yea and nay, sir, then I swore in jest.
What is the end of study, let me know?

KING

Why, that to know which else we should not know.

BIRON

Things hid and barred, you mean, from common
          sense?

KING

Ay, that is study's god-like recompense.

BIRON

Come on then, I will swear to study so,
To know the thing I am forbid to know: 60

---

57 common] Q (cammon), F   59 Come on] F; Com'on Q

---

44 **think ... night** i.e. think there was no
harm in sleeping all the night—an allusion to the proverb 'He that drinks well
sleeps well and he that sleeps well thinks
no harm' (Tilley H169)

49 **pass away from** abandon, give up

50 **an if** if

54 **By yea and nay** 'a formula of asservera-
tion in the form of, and substituted for, an
oath' (*OED, yea*, 3b). This common oath,
derived from Matthew 5:37: 'let your
communication be Yea, yea; Nay, nay',
is applied equivocally by Biron to suggest
that he swore and did not swear.

57 **Things ... sense** There is a distinct echo
here, as David points out, of Ovid's
description of Pythagoras and his teach-

ings (*Metamorphoses*, xv. 60–272). In
Golding's translation (1565) the relevant
part of it relates how Pythagoras 'taught
his silent sort [group of disciples] | (Which
wondered at the heavenly words their
master did report) | The first foundation of
the world; the cause of everything; |
What Nature was, and what was God; |
whence snow and lightning spring; |
And whether Jove or else the winds in
breaking clouds do thunder; | What
shakes the earth; what law the stars do
keep their courses under; | And what-
soever other thing is hid from common
sense.'

57 **common sense** ordinary or untutored
perception (*OED*, 2c)

As thus—to study where I well may dine,
    When I to feast expressly am forbid;
Or study where to meet some mistress fine,
    When mistresses from common sense are hid;
Or, having sworn too hard-a-keeping oath,
Study to break it and not break my troth.
If study's gain be thus, and this be so,
Study knows that which yet it doth not know.
Swear me to this, and I will ne'er say no.

KING

These be the stops that hinder study quite,   70
And train our intellects to vain delight.

BIRON

Why, all delights are vain, but that most vain
Which, with pain purchased, doth inherit pain:
As painfully to pore upon a book
    To seek the light of truth, while truth the while
Doth falsely blind the eyesight of his look.
    Light seeking light doth light of light beguile;
So, ere you find where light in darkness lies,
Your light grows dark by losing of your eyes.
Study me how to please the eye indeed   80
    By fixing it upon a fairer eye,
Who dazzling so, that eye shall be his heed,

---

62 feast] THEOBALD; fast QF   72 but] Q; and F

65 **too hard-a-keeping oath** an oath that is
  too hard to keep
70 **stops** obstacles (*OED, sb.*² 7)
71 **train** entice, allure (*OED, v.*¹ 4)
73 **pain** (a) effort, pains (b) suffering
  purchased obtained, won
  inherit pain bring trouble and suffering
  with it
74 **As** for instance (Abbott 113)
  painfully laboriously, painstakingly
76 **falsely** treacherously
  his look [the eyesight's] ability to see. *His*
  is the normal form for the possessive of *It*
  as well as of *He* in Shakespeare (Abbott
  228).
77 **Light ... beguile** i.e. the eye seeking for
  intellectual illumination through reading
  robs itself of the power to see, or, as Dr
  Johnson puts it, 'a man by too close study
  may read himself blind'.
  Light Shakespeare can refer to the eyes as

light because it was believed in his day
that they emitted 'eyebeams' by means of
which they saw. Compare Donne's 'The
Ecstasy', ll. 8–9: 'Our eyebeams twisted,
and did thread | Our eyes upon one
double string'.
78 **darkness** obscurity (of learned books)
80 **Study me** study, I say. This is an instance
  of the so-called 'ethic dative' in which *me*
  originally meant 'for me'. By Shakespeare's time, however, it had become
  little more than a means by which the
  speaker drew attention to himself. See
  Abbott 220.
81 **a fairer eye** i.e. the eye of a beautiful girl
82–3 **Who ... by** i.e. and the man whose
  eyesight is thus made ineffective will find
  that fairer eye to be his salvation, since it
  will give real light to him whose eyesight
  was at first blinded by it.
82 **dazzling** To *dazzle* was 'to lose the faculty

And give him light that it was blinded by.
Study is like the heaven's glorious sun,
    That will not be deep-searched with saucy looks;
Small have continual plodders ever won,
    Save base authority from others' books.
These earthly godfathers of heaven's lights,
    That give a name to every fixèd star,
Have no more profit of their shining nights   90
    Than those that walk and wot not what they are.
Too much to know is to know naught but fame,
And every godfather can give a name.

KING

How well he's read, to reason against reading.

DUMAINE

Proceeded well, to stop all good proceeding.

LONGUEVILLE

He weeds the corn, and still lets grow the weeding.

BIRON

The spring is near when green geese are a-breeding.

DUMAINE

How follows that?

BIRON   Fit in his place and time.

---

of distinct and steady vision, especially
from gazing at too bright light' (*OED*, *v.*
1). Compare *Richard Duke of York* 2.1.25:
'Dazzle mine eyes, or do I see three suns?'

82 **heed** protection, means of safety
(Schmidt)

84–5 **heaven's ... looks** Compare the
proverbial saying 'He that gazes upon the
sun shall at last be blind' (Dent S971.1).

85 **saucy** insolent, presumptuous

86 **Small** little. Shakespeare often uses adjectives as nouns (Abbott 5).
plodders drudges, purveyors of second-
hand learning. This is the first instance of
the word cited by *OED*; but it also occurs
in *The Unfortunate Traveller* (1594),
where Nashe writes of some German
scholars: 'Gross plodders they were all,
that had some learning and reading, but
no wit to make use of it' (Nashe, ii. 251.
11–13).

88–9 **These ... star** i.e. astronomers, who
give names to stars in much the same
way as godparents name children when

they are baptized

91 **wot** know

92 **Too ... fame** i.e. men acquire knowledge,
in excess of anything they can make use
of, merely to show off

95 **Proceeded** argued (*OED*, *v.* 2b).
proceeding advancement (of learning)
(*OED*, *vbl. sb.* 4)

96 **weeds ... weeding** pulls up the wheat and
leaves the weeds to grow. *OED* (*vbl. sb.*
1c) offers no parallel to this unusual sense
of *weeding*; and the gloss it provides,
'That which is weeded out', is patently
wrong. It should read: 'That which
ought to be weeded out but is not'.

97 **The spring ... a-breeding.** *Green geese* are
geese hatched in the autumn and eaten
in the spring, particularly May, of the
following year. Proverbially giddy and
witless, they are also synonymous with
silly young fools. Biron seems to be
equating the triplet in double rhyme
uttered by his companions to the cackling
of mating geese.

98 **his** its

DUMAINE

In reason nothing.

BIRON   Something then in rhyme.

KING

Biron is like an envious sneaping frost,   100
    That bites the first-born infants of the spring.

BIRON

Well, say I am. Why should proud summer boast
    Before the birds have any cause to sing?
Why should I joy in any abortive birth?
At Christmas I no more desire a rose
Than wish a snow in May's new-fangled shows,
But like of each thing that in season grows.
So you, to study now it is too late,
Climb o'er the house to unlock the little gate.

KING

Well, sit you out. Go home, Biron. Adieu!   110

BIRON

No, my good lord, I have sworn to stay with you.
And though I have for barbarism spoke more
    Than for that angel knowledge you can say,
Yet, confident, I'll keep what I have sworn,
    And bide the penance of each three years' day.
Give me the paper, let me read the same,
And to the strict'st decrees I'll write my name.

---

104 any] QF; an POPE   abortive] Q (abhortiue), F   109 Climb ... gate] Q; That were to clymbe ore the house to vnlocke the gate F   110 sit] Q; fit F   114 sworn] QF; swore F2   117 strict'st] F2; strictest QF

99 **In ... rhyme** An allusion to the proverbial contrast between rhyme and reason (Dent R98.1).
100 **envious** malevolent
sneaping frost nipping frost. The King is quibbling on *rhyme* and *rime*. Shakespeare uses the rare word *sneap* on two other occasions only, both referring to the weather: *Lucrece* 333 and *Winter's Tale* 1.2.13.
101 **first-born infants of the spring** earliest buds and flowers. Compare *Hamlet* 1.3.39.
104 **abortive** premature (*OED*, A.1)
107 **like of** like, take pleasure in (Abbott 177)
109 **Climb ... gate** i.e. behave in a futile manner. To climb over the gate, especially if it is a 'little gate', in order to unlock the house makes good sense; but to reverse the process makes no sense at all. The expression sounds like a proverbial one, but there seems to be no record of such a proverb.
    In the Folio the line reads: 'That were to clymbe ore the house to vnlocke the gate'. See Introduction, pp. 80–1.
110 **sit you out** i.e. take no part in (our scheme). The phrase comes from card games.
112 **barbarism** wilful ignorance, anti-intellectualism
115 **each three years' day** i.e. each day of the three years

KING (*handing over a paper*)

How well this yielding rescues thee from shame.

BIRON (*reads*) 'Item: that no woman shall come within a
mile of my court.' Hath this been proclaimed?   120

LONGUEVILLE Four days ago.

BIRON Let's see the penalty. (*He reads*) 'On pain of losing
her tongue.' Who devised this penalty?

LONGUEVILLE Marry, that did I.

BIRON Sweet lord, and why?

LONGUEVILLE

To fright them hence with that dread penalty.

BIRON

A dangerous law against gentility.

(*He reads*) 'Item: if any man be seen to talk with a
woman within the term of three years, he shall endure
such public shame as the rest of the court can possible   130
devise.'

This article, my liege, yourself must break;

  For well you know here comes in embassy

The French King's daughter with yourself to speak—

  A maid of grace and complete majesty—

About surrender up of Aquitaine

  To her decrepit, sick, and bedrid father.

Therefore this article is made in vain,

  Or vainly comes th'admirèd Princess hither.

KING

What say you, lords? Why, this was quite forgot.   140

BIRON

So study evermore is overshot.

While it doth study to have what it would,

It doth forget to do the thing it should;

---

118 *handing over a paper*] *not in* QF   119 *reads*] *not in* QF   127 BIRON] THEOBALD
(*Berowne*); *continued to Longueville*, QF (*with 'Ber.' before l. 132*)   gentility] F (gentilitie);
gentletie Q   128 *He reads*] *not in* QF   130 public] Q (publibue), F   can possible] Q; shall
possibly F   133 embassy] Q (Embassaie), F   possibly F

124 **Marry** indeed (a weakened form of the
  oath 'by the Virgin Mary')
127 **A dangerous ... gentility** a decree that
  endangers good manners and civilized
  living
130 **possible** possibly (*OED*, *possible*, C)

133 **in embassy** as an ambassador
135 **complete** perfect. The accent is on the
  first syllable.
141 **is overshot** misses its mark by shooting
  over the top of the target; a proverbial
  phrase (Dent O91.1)

And when it hath the thing it hunteth most,
'Tis won as towns with fire—so won, so lost.

KING

We must of force dispense with this decree.
She must lie here on mere necessity.

BIRON

Necessity will make us all forsworn
    Three thousand times within this three years' space;
For every man with his affects is born,   150
    Not by might mastered, but by special grace.
If I break faith, this word shall speak for me:
I am forsworn 'on mere necessity'.
So to the laws at large I write my name;
    And he that breaks them in the least degree
Stands in attainder of eternal shame.
    Suggestions are to other as to me;
But I believe, although I seem so loath,
I am the last that will last keep his oath.
        He signs
But is there no quick recreation granted?   160

KING

Ay, that there is. Our court, you know, is haunted
    With a refinèd traveller of Spain,
A man in all the world's new fashion planted,
    That hath a mint of phrases in his brain,

---

152 speak] Q (speake); breake F   157 other] Q; others F   159.1 *He signs] not in* QF

145 **as towns with fire** i.e. like towns taken
    by assault but set on fire in the process
146 **of force** perforce, necessarily
147 **lie** stay, lodge
    mere absolute, sheer
150 **affects** passions
151 **Not ... grace** Compare the injunction in
    the Catechism following on the ten com-
    mandments and the lessons to be derived
    from them: 'My good Child, know this,
    thou art not able to do these things of
    thyself, nor to walk in the Command-
    ments of God, and to serve him, without
    his special grace'.
154 **at large** in general, as a whole
156 **in attainder of** condemned to, sentenced
    to (*OED*, 2a)
157 **Suggestions ... me** i.e. I am as suscepti-

ble to temptations as other men are. For
Shakespeare *suggestion* almost invariably
means *temptation*. See the examples given
by Schmidt.
159 **I ... oath** (a) I, the last to sign, will keep
    my oath the longest (b) I, the last to sign,
    am the least likely to keep my oath the
    longest. Biron, characteristically, is being
    deliberately ambiguous.
160 **quick recreation** lively sport, spritely
    diversion
161-2 **haunted | With** frequented by
162 **refinèd** polished, highly cultivated. *OED*
    (*ppl. a.* 2) cites this as its earliest example
    of the word in this sense.
163 **planted** invested, acknowledged (as an
    expert)

One who the music of his own vain tongue
  Doth ravish like enchanting harmony,
A man of compliments, whom right and wrong
  Have chose as umpire of their mutiny.
This child of fancy, that Armado hight,
  For interim to our studies shall relate   170
In high-born words the worth of many a knight
  From tawny Spain, lost in the world's debate.
How you delight, my lords, I know not, I,
But I protest I love to hear him lie,
And I will use him for my minstrelsy.

BIRON

Armado is a most illustrious wight,
A man of fire-new words, fashion's own knight.

LONGUEVILLE

Costard the swain and he shall be our sport,
And so to study three years is but short.

    Enter Constable Dull with a letter, and Costard

DULL Which is the Duke's own person?   180
BIRON This, fellow. What wouldst?

---

165 One] F; On Q   179.1 *Enter … Costard*] MALONE (*subs.*); *Enter a Constable with Costard with a letter.* QF   180 DULL] ROWE; *Constab.* Q; *Const.* F

165–6 **One … harmony** An elaborate version of 'He loves to hear himself speak' (Dent L563).

165 **who** whom. Shakespeare often neglects to inflect *who* (Abbott 274).

167 **compliments** fashionable manners, or, perhaps, accomplishments

168 **mutiny** strife, discord

169 **child of fancy** fantastical being
hight is called. This word, already archaic in Shakespeare's day, appears in two only of his other works: *A Midsummer Night's Dream* (5.1.138) and *Pericles* (15.18).

170 **For interim to** to make an interval in, to provide a relaxation from

171 **high-born** high-flown, lofty (perhaps 'high-borne')

172 **tawny** yellowish-brown (because sunburnt). Compare 'The ground indeed is tawny' (*Tempest* 2.1.59).
world's debate i.e. warfare to which the world is so prone

173 **How you delight** what gives you pleasure

175 **minstrelsy** Down to the end of the 16th century story-telling was part of the minstrel's repertoire (*OED, minstrel*, 2).

176 **wight** person. Much used by Pistol, this rather old-fashioned word seems to have had a smack of the absurd about it for Shakespeare.

177 **fire-new** newly coined, fresh from the mint. 'Fire-new' is itself an example of the phenomenon it describes; *OED*'s earliest citation of it is from *Richard III* 1.3.254: 'Your fire-new stamp of honour is scarce current.' It is typical of the whole temper of *Love's Labour's Lost* that while it ridicules some neologisms it is extremely rich in them.

178 **Costard** A *costard* was a large kind of apple and also a slang term for the *head*.
swain rustic labourer

180 **the Duke's own person** Since Armado, at 1.2.36, and the Princess, at 2.1.38, both refer to the King as the Duke, this slip is very likely to be Shakespeare's rather than Dull's.

DULL I myself reprehend his own person, for I am his
    grace's farborough. But I would see his own person in
    flesh and blood.

BIRON This is he.

DULL Señor Arm—Arm—commends you. There's villainy
    abroad. This letter will tell you more.

COSTARD Sir, the contempts thereof are as touching me.

KING A letter from the magnificent Armado.

BIRON How low soever the matter, I hope in God for high   190
    words.

LONGUEVILLE A high hope for a low heaven. God grant us
    patience!

BIRON To hear, or forbear laughing?

LONGUEVILLE To hear meekly, sir, and to laugh moder-
    ately, or to forbear both.

BIRON Well, sir, be it as the style shall give us cause to
    climb in the merriness.

COSTARD The matter is to me, sir, as concerning Jaquen-
    etta. The manner of it is, I was taken with the manner.   200

BIRON In what manner?

COSTARD In manner and form following, sir, all those

183 farborough] Q (Farborough); Tharborough F   186 Señor] OXFORD; Signeour Q;
Signeor F   188 COSTARD] ROWE; *Clo⟨wne⟩*. QF (*throughout the scene, except at ll. 219 and 221,
where Q and F read Cost⟨ard⟩*.)   contempts] Q (Contempls), F   194 laughing] CAPELL;
hearing QF

182 **reprehend** The word Dull has in mind is,
of course, *represent*. In his verbal blunders
he anticipates Dogberry in *Much Ado*.

183 **farborough** Dull's version of *tharborough*—the reading of F—itself a corruption of *thirdborough*, the lowest in rank of
petty constables. Ben Jonson, in his *A Tale
of a Tub*, includes in his list of 'The
Persons that act' a High Constable, a
Headborough, a petty Constable, and a
Thirdborough who is a tinker. Compare
The Taming of the Shrew Ind.1.10–11.

186 **commends you** What Dull should say is
'commends himself to you', a polite formula meaning 'greets you'.

188 **contempts** Costard means 'contents',
yet in a sense he is right, for Armado's
letter does express contempt for him.

189 **magnificent** splendid, impressive (*OED*,
adj. 4). The word, which Shakespeare
employs only here and at 3.1.171, is not
completely dismissive, but, rather, playfully ironical.

192 **A high ... heaven** i.e. 'high words are a
low sort of *heaven* to *hope* highly for'
(Kerrigan)

197–8 **the style ... climb** Biron puns on *style*
and *stile* as Benedick does in *Much Ado*
5.2.5–6, where he replies to Margaret's
request that he write her a sonnet by
saying: 'In so high a style, Margaret, that
no man living shall come over it'.

199 **to** about, with reference to

200 **taken with the manner** caught in the
act. *Manner* is an Anglicized form of the
Anglo-French legal word *mainour*, the
form in which it appears in *OED*, signifying 'hand-work'. Thence it came to mean
'the stolen thing which is found in a
thief's possession when he is arrested'
(*OED*, 1), and ultimately it was no longer
confined to theft but was applied to any
unlawful act.

202 **In manner and form following** Another
legal tag that found its way into common
parlance (Dent M631.1).

three. I was seen with her in the manor-house, sitting
with her upon the form, and taken following her into
the park, which, put together, is 'in manner and form
following'. Now, sir, for the manner—it is the manner
of a man to speak to a woman. For the form—in some
form.

BIRON For the 'following', sir?

COSTARD As it shall follow in my correction; and God   210
defend the right!

KING Will you hear this letter with attention?

BIRON As we would hear an oracle.

COSTARD Such is the simplicity of man to hearken after the
flesh.

KING (*reads*) 'Great deputy, the welkin's vicegerent, and
sole dominator of Navarre, my soul's earth's god, and
body's fostering patron'—

COSTARD Not a word of Costard yet.

KING 'So it is'—   220

COSTARD It may be so; but if he say it is so, he is, in telling
true, but so.

KING Peace!

COSTARD —be to me, and every man that dares not fight.

KING No words!

COSTARD —of other men's secrets, I beseech you.

KING 'So it is, besieged with sable-coloured melancholy, I

---

214 simplicity] Q (sinplicitie), F   216 *reads*] ROWE (*subs.*); *not in* QF   welkin's] Q (*welkis*), F
219, 221 COSTARD] QF (*Cost.*)   219 Costard] Q (*corr.*), F (*Costard*); Costart Q (*uncorr.*)

---

210 **correction** chastisement, punishment
(*OED*, 4)
210–11 **God defend the right** The standard
prayer made by a combatant before engaging in a trial by combat. Compare, for
instance, *Richard II* 1.3.101.
214 **simplicity** The Quarto reading 'sinplicitie' has been defended on the grounds
that it is a 'Freudian' slip; but there are
many literal errors in Q, and it is hard to
see how an actor can make the point. His
audience will hear the familiar word
'simplicity', no matter how careful his
enunciation is.
  hearken after listen to, follow the urgings
of
216 **welkin's vicegerent** heaven's deputy—
an inflated rendering of the orthodox

16th-century political doctrine to the
effect that 'Kings are gods on earth' (Dent
G275.1). Shakespeare does not use *vicegerent* elsewhere.
217 **dominator** ruler. The only other occur-
rence of *dominator* in Shakespeare is at
Titus Andronicus 2.3.31, where it appears
in an astrological context.
  earth's god god on earth
221–2 **in telling true** to tell the truth
222 **but so** merely so so, not worth much
226 **secrets** private concerns
227 **besieged with** beset by (Abbott 193)
  sable-coloured black (because *melancholy*
was supposed to result from an excess of
'black bile', one of the four *humours*, or
bodily fluids that determined a man's
temperament). See note at 1.2.76.

did commend the black oppressing humour to the most
wholesome physic of thy health-giving air; and, as I am
a gentleman, betook myself to walk. The time when?   230
About the sixth hour, when beasts most graze, birds
best peck, and men sit down to that nourishment which
is called supper. So much for the time when. Now for
the ground which—which, I mean, I walked upon. It is
yclept thy park. Then for the place where—where, I
mean, I did encounter that obscene and most preposterous event that draweth from my snow-white pen the
ebon-coloured ink which here thou viewest, beholdest,
surveyest, or seest. But to the place where. It standeth
north-north-east and by east from the west corner of thy   240
curious-knotted garden. There did I see that low-spirited
swain, that base minnow of thy mirth'—

COSTARD Me?

KING 'that unlettered small-knowing soul'—

COSTARD Me?

KING 'that shallow vassal'—

COSTARD Still me?

KING 'which, as I remember, hight Costard'—

242 minnow] QF (*Minow*); minion SISSON (*conj.* Johnson)   247 me?] F (mee?); mee. Q

228 **commend** commit, entrust (*OED, v.* 1)
  the black oppressing humour i.e. my
  melancholy
229 **physic** medicine
  as on my word as (*OED, adv.* 14). Compare *Richard II* 3.1.118–19: 'This swears
  he as he is a prince and just, | And as I
  am a gentleman I credit him'.
235 **yclept** called. Shakespeare uses this archaic word, fashionable among writers of
  the late 16th century, at two places only:
  here, and in Holofernes' speech at
  5.2.591.
236 **obscene** repulsive, disgusting
236–7 **preposterous** contrary to the natural
  order of things—something the 'event'
  Armado goes on to describe certainly is
  not
237 **snow-white pen** The *pen* is a goose-
  quill; and *snow-white* was a time-honoured cliché (Dent S591.1).
238 **ebon-coloured** black. The blackness of
  ebony was proverbial (Tilley E56a).
241 **curious-knotted garden** garden laid out
  in intricately designed beds of herbs and

flowers (*OED, knot, sb.*[1] 7). Compare
Richard II 3.4.47, where the Gardener
sees England as a ruined garden in which
the *knots* are *disordered*. For a diagram
of 'a proper knot', the horticultural
counterpart to almost any speech by
Armado, see Fig. 6.
241 **low-spirited** base (*OED, a.* a), not 'de-
  jected'; earliest instance cited by *OED*
242 **minnow** i.e. contemptible little object.
  Compare *Coriolanus* 3.1.92 where the
  hero refers to the Roman mob as 'min-
  nows'. Costard, whom Shakespeare
  seems to have imagined as a big man, is,
  for Armado, a 'minnow' in his unimpor-
  tance. This is *OED*'s earliest example of
  'minnow' in a figurative sense; but it
  dates *Love's Labour's Lost* 1588. As David
  points out, Nashe calls Richard Harvey
  'a little minnow' in his *Have With You
  to Saffron Walden* published in 1596
  (Nashe, iii. 80. 33–4).
244 **unlettered** illiterate
246 **vassal** slavish wretch, underling

COSTARD O, me!

KING 'sorted and consorted, contrary to thy established   250
    proclaimed edict and continent canon, wherewith?
    O with—but with this I passion to say wherewith'—

COSTARD With a wench.

KING 'with a child of our grandmother Eve, a female, or,
    for thy more sweet understanding, a woman. Him I—as
    my ever-esteemed duty pricks me on—have sent to
    thee, to receive the meed of punishment, by thy sweet
    grace's officer, Anthony Dull, a man of good repute,
    carriage, bearing, and estimation.'

DULL Me, an't shall please you. I am Anthony Dull.   260

KING 'For Jaquenetta—so is the weaker vessel called—
    which I apprehended with the aforesaid swain, I keep
    her as a vessel of thy law's fury, and shall, at the least of
    thy sweet notice, bring her to trial. Thine in all compli-
    ments of devoted and heart-burning heat of duty,

                              Don Adriano de Armado.'

BIRON This is not so well as I looked for, but the best that
    ever I heard.

KING Ay, the best for the worst.—But, sirrah, what say
    you to this?   270

COSTARD Sir, I confess the wench.

KING Did you hear the proclamation?

---

251 wherewith?] This edition; Which with QF; with, with THEOBALD   258 officer] Q
(Gfficer), F   260 DULL] ROWE; *Anth.* QF   262 keep] Q; keeper F   269 worst] Q (wost), F

---

250 **sorted and consorted** associated and
    accompanied
251 **continent canon** decree enjoining sex-
    ual restraint
251–2 **wherewith?** O Q, followed by F, reads
    '*Which with, ô*'. But this makes no sense.
    The assumption behind the emendation
    is that the compositor misread an abbre-
    viated form of 'where' as an abbreviated
    form of 'which'. 'Wherewith', meaning
    'with what' and repeated later, is in
    Armado's authentic manner.
252 **passion** grieve. Compare *The Two Gentle-
    men of Verona* 4.4.164–5: 'Madam, 'twas
    Ariadne, passioning | For Theseus' per-
    jury and unjust flight'.
257 **meed** reward
260 **an't** if it
261 **the weaker vessel** 'A woman is the

weaker vessel' was a commonplace of the
time (Dent W655). Biblical in origin, it
comes from I Peter 3: 7, where it is
restricted to the wife; it was extended to
women in general from at least as early as
1576. The word *vessel* came to mean
person because of its use in translations of
the Bible where the human body is
thought of as the container of the soul.
263–4 **at ... notice** i.e. immediately on
    receiving your orders
269 **the best for the worst** i.e. a superb
    example of the thoroughly bad—a varia-
    tion on the common saying 'The better
    the worse' (Dent B333)
271 **confess** acknowledge the truth of the
    accusation concerning. Compare *The
    Merchant of Venice* 4.1.178: 'Do you
    confess the bond?'

COSTARD I do confess much of the hearing it, but little of
    the marking of it.

KING It was proclaimed a year's imprisonment to be taken
    with a wench.

COSTARD I was taken with none, sir, I was taken with a
    damsel.

KING Well, it was proclaimed damsel.

COSTARD This was no damsel neither, sir; she was a   280
    virgin.

⌜KING⌝ It is so varied too, for it was proclaimed virgin.

COSTARD If it were, I deny her virginity. I was taken with a
    maid.

KING This maid will not serve your turn, sir.

COSTARD This maid will serve my turn, sir.

KING Sir, I will pronounce your sentence: you shall fast a
    week with bran and water.

COSTARD I had rather pray a month with mutton and
    porridge.   290

KING And Don Armado shall be your keeper.—
    My Lord Biron, see him delivered o'er;
    And go we, lords, to put in practice that
        Which each to other hath so strongly sworn.
            Exeunt King, Longueville, and Dumaine

BIRON
    I'll lay my head to any good man's hat
        These oaths and laws will prove an idle scorn.
    Sirrah, come on.

COSTARD I suffer for the truth, sir, for true it is I was taken

282 KING] F (*Fer.*); *Ber.* Q   292 delivered] F (deliuer'd); deliuered Q   294.1 *Exeunt ...
Dumaine*] *not in* QF

282 KING This is the reading of F, which
heads the speech '*Fer.*', whereas Q heads
it '*Ber.*' F is followed here because an
intrusion by Biron at this point would
break the pattern of the exchanges.
    is so varied provides for that variation

285 This maid ... turn i.e. your recourse to
the word 'maid' will not help you out of
your troubles

286 will serve my turn Costard neatly gives
the King's words a bawdy application.
Compare *Antony and Cleopatra* 2.5.58–9,
where Cleopatra, hearing from the Messenger that Antony is 'bound unto Octa-

via', asks, 'For what good turn?', and
receives the answer: 'For the best turn
i'th' bed.'

289–90 mutton and porridge mutton broth
(hendiadys). Costard is probably quibbling on *mutton* in the slang sense of
'whore'.

295 I'll ... hat A variant on the common
betting formula 'My cap (hat) to a noble
(etc.)' (Dent C63.1).

298 I suffer ... truth With lugubrious humour Costard casts himself for the role of
martyr.

with Jaquenetta, and Jaquenetta is a true girl. And
therefore welcome the sour cup of prosperity! Affliction   300
may one day smile again, and till then, sit thee down,
sorrow!   *Exeunt*

I.2   *Enter Armado and Moth, his page*

ARMADO Boy, what sign is it when a man of great spirit
grows melancholy?

MOTH A great sign, sir, that he will look sad.

ARMADO Why, sadness is one and the selfsame thing, dear
imp.

MOTH No, no, O Lord, sir, no.

ARMADO How canst thou part sadness and melancholy,
my tender juvenal?

300 prosperity] F (prosperitie); prosperie Q   Affliction] F; affliccio Q   301 till] Q; vntill F
sit thee down] Q; sit downe F   302.1 *Exeunt*] Q; *Exit* F
    1.2.0.1 *Moth*] QF; *Mote* KERRIGAN, OXFORD   I (*and throughout the scene*) ARMADO] Q
(*Armado, variously abbreviated*); *Arma⟨do⟩. at line I but thereafter Brag⟨gart⟩.* F   3 (*and
throughout the scene*) MOTH] ROWE;   *Boy.* QF;   KERRIGAN, OXFORD *read* MOTE

299 **true** good, honest
300 **prosperity** Costard's version of 'adver-
    sity'.
301–2 **sit ... sorrow.** This phrase, substan-
    tially repeated at 4.3.3–4, sounds very
    much like a proverb; but no source for it
    has yet been found. Shakespeare was
    soon to give the familiar phrase a power-
    ful tragic resonance in his *K. John*, where
    Constance, seating herself on the ground,
    says: 'Here I and sorrows sit; | Here is
    my throne; let kings come bow to it'
    (2.1.73–4).
1.2.0.1 **Moth** See Appendix D.
  1–2 **Boy ... melancholy?** The answer Ar-
    mado expects but does not receive is: 'It is
    an infallible sign that he is in love.' Ovid
    in his *Ars Amatoria*, i. 737–8, writes: '*Ut
    voto potiare tuo, miserabilis esto ; | Ut qui te
    videat, dicere possit, Amas.*' Francis Wol-
    ferston in his version of 1661 renders
    these lines thus: 'By looking melancholy
    you will prove | Successful; all will say,
    "This man's in love".'
  5 **imp** Originally a young shoot of a tree or
    plant, *imp* was then used of children,
    especially boys, with no derogatory im-
    plications. Eventually, however, it came
    to be restricted to 'imps of hell'.
    Shakespeare seems to have found it
    rather absurd or comic, for he puts it in
    the mouths of three characters only:

Armado, Holofernes (5.2.581), and En-
sign Pistol (*2 Henry IV* 5.5.42 and *Henry
V* 4.1.46).
6 **O Lord, sir** indeed, certainly. The phrase
    was almost meaningless, as Shakespeare
    emphasizes in *All's Well That Ends Well*
    2.2.13–57, where it is described as 'an
    answer will serve all men'.
7 **part** separate, distinguish between
8 **juvenal** youth, juvenile. Although *OED*
    can cite no example of *juvenile* before
    1625, and then only as an adjective, it is
    evident that Shakespeare had either the
    Latin *juvenilis* or the French *juvénile* in
    mind when thus turning the name of the
    great Roman satirist Juvenal into a com-
    mon noun. Compare his playing on the
    name of Ovid at 4.2.122. There is also a
    distinct possibility that he was thinking of
    Robert Greene's reference to, in all likeli-
    hood, Thomas Nashe in his *Greene's
    Groatsworth of Wit* (1592), where Greene
    writes of 'young Juvenal, that biting
    satirist, that lastly with me together writ
    a comedy' (Sig. F1). This does not mean
    that Moth is a portrait of Nashe. Armado
    uses the word again at 3.1.63; Flute
    employs it in *Dream* 3.1.89; and Falstaff
    in *2 Henry IV* 1.2.19. These are its only
    appearances in Shakespeare, all of them
    in comic contexts.

MOTH By a familiar demonstration of the working, my
    tough señor.   10

ARMADO Why 'tough señor'? Why 'tough señor'?

MOTH Why 'tender juvenal'? Why 'tender juvenal'?

ARMADO I spoke it, tender juvenal, as a congruent epithe-
    ton appertaining to thy young days, which we may
    nominate tender.

MOTH And I, tough señor, as an appertinent title to your
    old time, which we may name tough.

ARMADO Pretty and apt.

MOTH How mean you, sir? I pretty and my saying apt, or I
    apt and my saying pretty?   20

ARMADO Thou pretty, because little.

MOTH Little pretty, because little. Wherefore apt?

ARMADO And therefore apt, because quick.

MOTH Speak you this in my praise, master?

ARMADO In thy condign praise.

MOTH I will praise an eel with the same praise.

ARMADO What, that an eel is ingenious?

MOTH That an eel is quick.

ARMADO I do say thou art quick in answers. Thou heatest
    my blood.   30

MOTH I am answered, sir.

ARMADO I love not to be crossed.

MOTH *(aside)* He speaks the mere contrary—crosses love
    not him.

ARMADO I have promised to study three years with the
    Duke.

10, 11, *and* 16 señor] OXFORD; signeor Q; signeur F   13–14 epitheton] F2; apethaton Q;
apathaton F

  9 **familiar** readily intelligible (*OED, a.* 6c).
    working operation, application
10 **señor** punning on 'senior'
13–14 **congruent epitheton appertaining to**
    fitting expression to describe. *Epitheton* is
    the original Greek and late Latin form
    from which *epithet* derives. It is not used
    by Shakespeare elsewhere.
15 **nominate** name, call
16 **appertinent** belonging, appropriate
18 **Pretty and apt** pretty apt (hendiadys)
21 **pretty, because little** 'Little things are
    pretty' was proverbial (Dent T188).
25 **condign** well deserved (*OED, a.* 3)

27 **ingenious** talented, clever. Compare
    Richard III 3.1.153–4, where Richard
    says of the young Duke of York: 'O, 'tis a
    parlous boy, | Bold, quick, ingenious, for-
    ward, capable.'
28 **an eel is quick** proverbial (Dent E59)
29–30 **Thou ... blood** i.e. you make me
    angry (by misinterpreting what I say)
32 **crossed** contradicted (*OED, v.* 14c)
33 **mere contrary** i.e. absolute opposite (of
    the truth)
    crosses coins (because many had a cross
    stamped on one side: *OED, sb.* 20)

MOTH You may do it in an hour, sir.

ARMADO Impossible.

MOTH How many is one thrice told?

ARMADO I am ill at reckoning. It fitteth the spirit of a   40
tapster.

MOTH You are a gentleman and a gamester, sir.

ARMADO I confess both. They are both the varnish of a
complete man.

MOTH Then I am sure you know how much the gross sum
of deuce-ace amounts to.

ARMADO It doth amount to one more than two.

MOTH Which the base vulgar do call three.

ARMADO True.

MOTH Why, sir, is this such a piece of study? Now here is   50
three studied ere ye'll thrice wink; and how easy it is to
put 'years' to the word 'three', and study three years in
two words, the dancing horse will tell you.

ARMADO A most fine figure!

MOTH (*aside*) To prove you a cipher.

ARMADO I will hereupon confess I am in love; and as it is
base for a soldier to love, so am I in love with a base
wench. If drawing my sword against the humour of
affection would deliver me from the reprobate thought
of it, I would take desire prisoner, and ransom him to   60
any French courtier for a new-devised curtsy. I think

40 fitteth] Q; fits F   48 do] Q; *not in* F   50 here is] Q; here's F   51 ye'll] Q (yele); you'll F

39 **told** counted
42 **gamester** gambler
43 **varnish** finishing touch, polish
46 **deuce-ace** a throw of two and a throw of one in a dice game
48 **vulgar** ordinary people (*OED, sb.* 2a)
50 **piece** masterpiece. Compare *Winter's Tale* 4.4.32: 'a piece of beauty'.
51 **studied** thoroughly investigated, mastered
53 **the dancing horse** The horse in question is almost certainly the celebrated Morocco, mentioned by writers innumerable from 1591 onwards, and the subject of a pamphlet, *Maroccus Extaticus, or Bankes Bay Horse in a Trance* (1595). As well as being able to dance, Morocco could also count by beating out numbers

with his hoof. See Fig. 8.
54 **figure** (a) figure of speech, which is what Armado means (b) numeral, the sense in which Moth takes it
55 **cipher** nonentity, nothing. 'He is a cipher among numbers' was proverbial (Dent C391).
57 **base** unbefitting, morally reprehensible
57–8 **base wench** wench of low birth
58–9 **humour of affection** i.e. inclination to fall in love
59 **reprobate** depraved, sinful (*OED, a.* 2). Compare *Lucrece* 300–1: 'By reprobate desire thus madly led | The Roman lord marcheth to Lucrece' bed'.
61 **new-devised curtsy** i.e. latest thing in fashionable bows
61–2 **think scorn** disdain

scorn to sigh; methinks I should outswear Cupid.
Comfort me, boy. What great men have been in love?

MOTH Hercules, master.

ARMADO Most sweet Hercules! More authority, dear boy,
name more. And, sweet my child, let them be men of
good repute and carriage.

MOTH Samson, master. He was a man of good carriage,
great carriage, for he carried the town-gates on his back
like a porter, and he was in love.   70

ARMADO O well-knit Samson, strong-jointed Samson! I do
excel thee in my rapier as much as thou didst me in
carrying gates. I am in love, too. Who was Samson's
love, my dear Moth?

MOTH A woman, master.

ARMADO Of what complexion?

MOTH Of all the four, or the three, or the two, or one of the
four.

ARMADO Tell me precisely of what complexion.

MOTH Of the sea-water green, sir.   80

ARMADO Is that one of the four complexions?

MOTH As I have read, sir; and the best of them too.

ARMADO Green indeed is the colour of lovers. But to have a
love of that colour, methinks Samson had small reason
for it. He surely affected her for her wit.

---

62 **outswear** renounce, swear to do without.
Compare 2.1.103: 'I hear your grace
hath sworn out housekeeping.'

67 **carriage** behaviour, bearing

68 **carriage** power in carrying

69–70 **he carried ... porter**. The story of
how Samson carried off the gates of Gaza
is told in Judges 16: 3.

72 **rapier** Introduced from the Continent,
the rapier was the fashionable weapon in
England during the 1590s, and brought
with it a technical vocabulary that also
became fashionable with many and a
target for satire with many more. The
two attitudes are typified by Tybalt and
Mercutio in *Romeo and Juliet*.

76–81 **Of what complexion? ... one of the
four complexions?** The primary meaning
of *complexion* was *temperament*, as determined by the mixture of the four *humours*, blood, choler, phlegm, and black

bile, in a man's make-up. The notion is
still alive in the words *sanguine, choleric,
phlegmatic*, and *melancholy*. It was also
used, however, of the *humours* themselves; and, as these were supposed to
affect the colour of the skin, it eventually
acquired its modern meaning. Armado
uses it in its old sense, Moth in his modern
one.

80 **sea-water green** Moth seems to imply
that Delilah suffered from 'green-sick-
ness', i.e. chlorosis, a disease incident to
young women. He is certainly stuffing
Armado full of nonsense.

83 **Green ... lovers** David aptly refers to the
popular song 'Greensleeves'. The close
association of spring and its greenery
with love is a familiar feature of medieval
and 16th-century poetry.

85 **affected her for her wit** loved her for her
intelligence

MOTH It was so, sir, for she had a green wit.
ARMADO My love is most immaculate white and red.
MOTH Most maculate thoughts, master, are masked under
such colours.
ARMADO Define, define, well-educated infant.   90
MOTH My father's wit and my mother's tongue assist me!
ARMADO Sweet invocation of a child, most pretty and
pathetical!
MOTH

    If she be made of white and red,
      Her faults will ne'er be known,
    For blushing cheeks by faults are bred,
      And fears by pale white shown.
    Then if she fear or be to blame,
      By this you shall not know,
    For still her cheeks possess the same   100
      Which native she doth owe.

A dangerous rhyme, master, against the reason of
white and red.

ARMADO Is there not a ballad, boy, of the King and the
Beggar?
MOTH The world was very guilty of such a ballad some
three ages since, but I think now 'tis not to be found, or

---

88 maculate] Q; immaculate F   96 blushing] F2; blush-in QF

86 **green wit** immature childish mind. The
phrase was proverbial (Dent W563.1).
Compare *Winter's Tale* 3.2.180–1: 'Fan-
cies too weak for boys, too green and
idle | For girls of nine'.
88 **Most maculate** very impure (Shakespeare's only use of *maculate*)
90 **Define** i.e. explain what you mean
91 **My father's ... tongue** An ingenious
variation on two common expressions:
'mother-tongue' and 'mother-wit' (Dent
M1208.1 and .2).
93 **pathetical** moving, touching, appealing
99 **By this** i.e. from her complexion
100 **still** always
    possess the same i.e. retain the same
colour
101 **native she doth owe** is hers naturally
('owe' = 'own')
102–3 **A dangerous ... red** a little jingle
showing the danger of drawing conclu-

sions from *white*, which may merely be
ceruse, and *red*, which may be rouge
104–5 **a ballad ... Beggar** The ballad referred to is almost certainly the same as
that which Armado mentions again at
4.1.64–77, where he writes of 'King
Cophetua and the ... beggar Zenelophon'. The earliest surviving copy of it is
in Richard Johnson's *Crown Garland of
Golden Roses* (1612), where its title is 'A
Song of a Beggar and a King'. Thomas
Percy took it thence and reprinted it in his
Reliques of Ancient English Poetry (1765)
as 'King Cophetua and the Beggar-Maid'.
To judge from Moth's description of it, the
original ballad must have been far more
robust than Johnson's decorous version.
There are further allusions to the story in
Romeo (2.1.13–14), *Richard II* (5.3.78),
and *2 Henry IV* (5.3.103).

if it were, it would neither serve for the writing nor the
tune.

ARMADO I will have that subject newly writ o'er, that I   110
may example my digression by some mighty precedent.
Boy, I do love that country girl that I took in the park
with the rational hind Costard. She deserves well.

MOTH (*aside*) To be whipped—and yet a better love than my
master.

ARMADO Sing, boy. My spirit grows heavy in love.

MOTH (*aside*) And that's great marvel, loving a light
wench.

ARMADO I say, sing.

MOTH Forbear till this company be passed.   120

> *Enter Costard, Dull, and Jaquenetta*

DULL (*to Armado*) Sir, the Duke's pleasure is that you keep
Costard safe; and you must suffer him to take no
delight, nor no penance, but a must fast three days a
week. For this damsel, I must keep her at the park; she
is allowed for the dey-woman. Fare you well.

ARMADO (*aside*) I do betray myself with blushing.—Maid—

JAQUENETTA Man.

ARMADO I will visit thee at the lodge.

JAQUENETTA That's hereby.

ARMADO I know where it is situate.   130

JAQUENETTA Lord, how wise you are!

ARMADO I will tell thee wonders.

JAQUENETTA With that face?

---

116 love] Q (loue); ioue F   120.1 *Enter ... Jaquenetta*] THEOBALD; Enter *Clowne, Constable,
and Wench.* Q, F (*subs.*)   121 DULL] ROWE; *Const.* QF   122 suffer him to] Q; let him F   123
a] Q; hee F   125 dey-woman] F (Day-woman); Day womand Q   well.] Q; well. *Exit.* F
127–36 JAQUENETTA] ROWE; *Maide.* QF (*and throughout, variously abbreviated*)   133 that]
Q; what F

---

108 **serve** be acceptable
111 **example** excuse, justify by a precedent
    (*OED, v.* 3)
    digression transgression, going astray
    (*OED,* 1b)
113 **rational hind** yokel endowed with the
    faculty of reason
114 **whipped** Whipping was the punish-
    ment meted out to whores.
117 **light** (a) the opposite of *heavy* (line 116)
    (b) wanton
123 **penance** Dull's mistake for 'pleasance',
    a word Shakespeare uses in *Othello*

2.3.285.
    a colloquial form of *he*
125 **allowed for the dey-woman** approved to
    serve as the dairy-maid. The earliest
    citation of *dey-woman* in OED, not else-
    where in Shakespeare.
129 **hereby** close by. Since the rest of Ja-
    quenetta's answers are well worn bits of
    rustic repartee, 'That's hereby' should be
    of the same kind. But, if it is, its signifi-
    cance remains to be discovered.
133 **With that face?** Really?

115

ARMADO I love thee.

JAQUENETTA So I heard you say.

ARMADO And so farewell.

JAQUENETTA Fair weather after you.

⌈DULL⌉ Come, Jaquenetta, away.

⌈ *Exeunt Dull and Jaquenetta*⌉

ARMADO Villain, thou shalt fast for thy offences ere thou
be pardoned.   140

COSTARD Well, sir, I hope when I do it I shall do it on a full
stomach.

ARMADO Thou shalt be heavily punished.

COSTARD I am more bound to you than your fellows, for
they are but lightly rewarded.

ARMADO Take away this villain. Shut him up.

MOTH Come, you transgressing slave, away!

COSTARD Let me not be pent up, sir, I will fast being loose.

MOTH No, sir, that were fast and loose. Thou shalt to
prison.   150

COSTARD Well, if ever I do see the merry days of desolation
that I have seen, some shall see—

---

1 38 DULL] THEOBALD; *Clo.* QF   1 38.1 *Exeunt ... Jaquenetta*] THEOBALD; *Exeunt.* QF   141 (*and
for the rest of the scene*) COSTARD] ROWE; *Clo.* QF   146 ARMADO] Q (*Ar.*); *Clo.* F

1 35 **So ... say** A rough equivalent of 'you
don't say so'.

1 37 **Fair weather after you** proverbial (Tilley
W217)

1 38 DULL Both Q and F read '*Clo⟨wne⟩.*', and
both end the line with the stage direction
'*Exeunt.*' This direction cannot cover Armado, Moth, or Costard, since all three
remain behind to continue the scene. The
line must therefore, as Theobald was the
first to recognize, be spoken by Dull. It
looks as though the Q compositor misread
a manuscript '*Co.*', short for '*Constable*', as
'*Clo.*' His error was perpetuated by the F
compositor, who had already—either on
his own initiative or on that of the annotator—added an '*Exit.*' for Dull at the end of
1 25, where the Constable says 'Fare you
well', but then has to remain on stage
waiting for Jaquenetta, who is busy dealing with Armado's advances to her.

1 39 **Villain** (a) peasant (b) rogue

1 41–2 **do it ... stomach** Referring to the
proverb 'The belly that is full may well
fast' (Dent B289) and quibbling on the
phrase 'on a full stomach', meaning

'courageously'.

1 44 **fellows** servants

1 48 **pent up** (a) imprisoned (b) costive
loose (a) at liberty (b) loose in the bowels

1 49 **fast and loose** A cheating trick played by
gipsies and other vagrants. Compare
Antony 4.1 3.28–9, where Antony says
that Cleopatra 'Like a right gipsy hath at
fast and loose | Beguiled me to the very
heart of loss.' According to J. Brand in his
Popular Antiquities (1 873), the trick,
which he calls 'Pricking at the Belt', was
played thus: 'A leathern belt is made up
into a number of intricate folds, and
placed edgewise upon a table. One of the
folds is made to resemble the middle of a
girdle, so that whoever shall thrust a
skewer into it would think he held it fast
to the table; whereas, when he has so
done, the person with whom he plays
may take hold of both ends and draw it
away' (ii. 4 35). Quoted from Furness.

1 51 **desolation** Costard probably means *jubi-
lation*, just as by *silent* (l. 1 55) he means
loquacious and by *little* (l. 1 57) he means
much.

MOTH What shall some see?

COSTARD Nay, nothing, Master Moth, but what they look
upon. It is not for prisoners to be too silent in their
words, and therefore I will say nothing. I thank God I
have as little patience as another man, and therefore I
can be quiet.   *Exeunt Moth and Costard*

ARMADO I do affect the very ground, which is base, where
her shoe, which is baser, guided by her foot, which is   160
basest, doth tread. I shall be forsworn, which is a great
argument of falsehood, if I love. And how can that be
true love which is falsely attempted? Love is a familiar;
Love is a devil. There is no evil angel but Love. Yet was
Samson so tempted, and he had an excellent strength;
yet was Solomon so seduced, and he had a very good
wit. Cupid's butt-shaft is too hard for Hercules' club,
and therefore too much odds for a Spaniard's rapier.
The first and second cause will not serve my turn. The
passado he respects not, the duello he regards not. His   170
disgrace is to be called boy, but his glory is to subdue
men. Adieu, valour; rust, rapier; be still, drum; for

154 Master] F; M. Q   155 too] Q; *not in* F   158 *Exeunt ... Costard*] POPE (*subs.*); *Exit.* QF
164–5 was Samson] Q (was *Sampson*); *Sampson* was F   170 duello] F (*Duello*); *Duella* Q

159 **affect** love

159–61 **affect ... tread** 'To love (hate) the
ground another treads on' was proverbial (Dent G468).

162 **argument** proof

163 **is falsely attempted** i.e. one strives to
win by breaking one's vow (*OED, attempt, v.* 6). Compare *Timon of Athens*
1.1.127–8: 'This man of thine | Attempts
her love'.
familiar demon, evil spirit in attendance.
Compare *1 Henry VI* 3.6.7–8: 'But where
is Pucelle now? | I think her old familiar is
asleep'.

166 **Solomon so seduced** See 1 Kings 11:
1–3.

167 **butt-shaft** a kind of arrow employed in
target practice. Having a sharp head but
no barb, it would stick in the butt
(=mark), and could then be easily ex-
tracted from it. Compare *Romeo*
2.3.14–15, where Mercutio says that
Romeo has had 'the very pin of his heart
cleft with the blind bow-boy's butt-shaft'.

169 **The first and second cause** The 1590s
saw a positive spate of books dealing with

duelling and listing the reasons for issu-
ing a challenge. Touchstone makes
splendid fun of them in *As You Like It*
5.4.49–101. One of the earliest of these
treatises, *The Book of Honour and Arms*,
attributed to Sir William Segar and published in 1590, distinguishes the two
main justifications for engaging in a duel
thus: 'I say then that the causes of all
quarrel whereupon it behoveth to use the
trial of arms may be reduced into two: for
it seemeth to me not reasonable that any
man should expose himself to the peril of
death, save only for such occasions as do
deserve death. Wherefore whensoever
one man doth accuse another of such a
crime as meriteth death, in that case the
combat ought to be granted. The second
cause of combat is honour, because
among persons of reputation, honour is
preferred before life' (p. 22).

170 **passado** forward thrust with the sword,
one foot being advanced at the same time
(*OED*)
duello duelling code (first citation by
OED)

your manager is in love; yea, he loveth. Assist me, some
extemporal god of rhyme, for I am sure I shall turn
sonnet. Devise wit; write, pen; for I am for whole
volumes in folio.   *Exit*

2.1   *Enter the Princess of France, Rosaline wearing a cap,*
          Maria in white, and Katherine, with Boyet and two
          attendant lords

BOYET

Now, madam, summon up your dearest spirits.
Consider who the King your father sends,
To whom he sends, and what's his embassy:
Yourself, held precious in the world's esteem,
To parley with the sole inheritor
Of all perfections that a man may owe,
Matchless Navarre; the plea of no less weight
Than Aquitaine, a dowry for a queen.
Be now as prodigal of all dear grace
As Nature was in making graces dear   10
When she did starve the general world beside,
And prodigally gave them all to you.

PRINCESS

Good Lord Boyet, my beauty, though but mean,
Needs not the painted flourish of your praise.
Beauty is bought by judgement of the eye,

---

1 76 *Exit*] Q; *Exit. | Finis Actus Primus.* F
   2.1.0.1–3 *Enter ... lords*] This edition: *Enter the Princesse of Fraunce, with three attending*
Ladies and three Lordes Q, F (*subs.*)   2 Consider] Q (Cosider), F   I 3 PRINCESS] F2; *Queene.* QF

173 **manager** controller, master (*OED*, 1;
   earliest example cited)
174 **extemporal god of rhyme** god of 'unpre-
   meditated verse'
174–5 **turn sonnet** i.e. become 'all love and
   poetry from top to toe' (Schmidt). For
   Shakespeare and his age any poem of a
   lyrical and amatory kind was a *sonnet*.
2.1.0.1–2 *Rosaline ... white* See lines 195
   and 207.
  1 **dearest spirits** utmost resources of will
   and intellect. For *dearest*, meaning *ut-*
   most, compare *Hamlet* 1.2.181. Kerrigan
   makes the interesting suggestion that
   there may be a playful reference to the
   idea of conjuring up devils.

3 **embassy** message (*OED*, 2)
5 **inheritor** possessor, owner
6 **owe** own
7 **plea** claim, that which is pleaded for
   (*OED*, sb. 5). All *OED* examples of *plea* in
   this unusual sense are from Shakespeare.
9 **prodigal** lavish
   dear precious
10 **dear** costly
I I **starve ... beside** i.e. deprive the rest of the
   world of graces
I 3 **mean** average, moderate
14 **painted flourish** glossy ostentatious embellishment. 'A good face needs no paint'
   was proverbial (Dent F7).

Not uttered by base sale of chapmen's tongues.
I am less proud to hear you tell my worth
Than you much willing to be counted wise
In spending your wit in the praise of mine.
But now to task the tasker. Good Boyet,   20
You are not ignorant all-telling fame
Doth noise abroad Navarre hath made a vow,
Till painful study shall outwear three years,
No woman may approach his silent court.
Therefore to's seemeth it a needful course,
Before we enter his forbidden gates,
To know his pleasure; and in that behalf,
Bold of your worthiness, we single you
As our best-moving fair solicitor.
Tell him the daughter of the King of France,   30
On serious business craving quick dispatch,
Importunes personal conference with his grace.
Haste, signify so much, while we attend,
Like humble-visaged suitors, his high will.

BOYET

Proud of employment, willingly I go.

PRINCESS

All pride is willing pride, and yours is so.   *Exit Boyet*
Who are the votaries, my loving lords,
That are vow-fellows with this virtuous Duke?

20–1 Boyet, | You] Q; *Boyet,* | *Prin.* You F   32 Importunes] F; Importuous Q   34 humble-visaged] F (humble visag'd); humble visage Q   36.1 *Exit Boyet*] Q (*Exit Boy.*); *Exit* F (*both after l. 35*)

16 **uttered** offered for sale. Compare *Romeo*
5.1.66–7: 'Such mortal drugs I have, but
Mantua's law | Is death to any he that
utters them.'
  chapmen's merchants', traders'
17 **tell** (a) speak of (b) count, reckon
18 **counted** accounted, regarded as
20 **task the tasker** impose a task on the man
who has been setting tasks (the earliest
instance of *tasker* in this sense cited by
OED, not elsewhere in Shakespeare)
21 Wells sugggests that 'F's redundant
prefix "*Prin.*" may reflect a cut in performance of the scene's previous lines'.
  fame rumour
22 **noise abroad** 'broadcast', spread the

story
23 **outwear** wear out. Shakespeare uses
outwear only with reference to time.
25 **to's** to us (colloquial)
27 **in that behalf** on that account, for that
purpose (*OED*, *behalf*, 2c)
28 **Bold of** confident of, trusting in (*OED*, *a.*
6).
29 **best-moving** most persuasive, most eloquent
  fair solicitor just advocate, reliable agent
(*OED*, *solicitor*, 2)
32 **Importunes** (accented on the second syllable)
  conference conversation

FIRST LORD

Lord Longueville is one.

PRINCESS   Know you the man?

MARIA

I know him, madam. At a marriage feast   40
Between Lord Périgord and the beauteous heir
Of Jaques Falconbridge, solemnizèd
In Normandy, saw I this Longueville.
A man of sovereign parts, peerless he is esteemed,
Well fitted in arts, glorious in arms.
Nothing becomes him ill that he would well.
The only soil of his fair virtue's gloss—
If virtue's gloss will stain with any soil—
Is a sharp wit matched with too blunt a will,
Whose edge hath power to cut, whose will still wills   50
It should none spare that come within his power.

PRINCESS

Some merry mocking lord belike, is't so?

MARIA

They say so most that most his humours know.

PRINCESS

Such short-lived wits do wither as they grow.
Who are the rest?

39 FIRST LORD Lord Longueville] CAPELL; *Lor. Longauill* QF   40 MARIA] ROWE; I. *Lady.* Q, F
(*subs.*)   madam.] CAPELL (~ ;); ~ ∧ QF   41 Lord Périgord] OXFORD; L. *Perigort* QF
42 solemnizèd ∧] RANN; ~ . QF   44 sovereign parts, peerless] ALEXANDER; soueraigne
peerelsse Q; soueraigne parts F   45 Well ... arts] QF; In arts well fitted WHITE (*conj.*
Keightley)   50 wills] ROWE; ~ , QF   53 MARIA] ROWE; *Lad.* Q; *Lad.* I. F

41 **heir** heiress. *OED* gives no example of
heiress before 1659.
42 **solemnizèd** (accented on the second syllable)
44 **sovereign parts, peerless** Q reads 'soueraigne peerelsse'; F 'soueraigne parts',
The assumption behind the present reading is that the compositor of Q inadver-
tently omitted 'parts'. Then the annotator who prepared a copy of Q for the
printing of F noticed the omission and
wrote in the missing word which the
compositor of F took to be a correction of
'peerelsse'. The result is a six-foot line;
but *LLL* is a play of metrical variety.
45 **Well ... arms** This line would seem to be
Shakespeare's rendering of the well
known Latin tag *Tam Marti quam Mercu-
rio* which the poet George Gascoigne had

adopted as his motto.
45 **fitted in arts** qualified in intellectual pur-
suits
   glorious in arms famous in war
46 **Nothing ... well** 'anything he wants to
do well he does well and looks admirable
for it' (Kerrigan)
47 **soil** tarnish, stain
   gloss lustre
49 **matched** joined, paired
   blunt a will i.e. insensitive a readiness to
use it
50 **whose will still wills** i.e. and his will
invariably determines
51 **his** its
53 **most his humours know** best know his
moods
54 **Such ... grow** A version of 'Soon ripe
soon rotten' (Tilley R133). Compare 'So

KATHERINE

The young Dumaine, a well-accomplished youth,
Of all that virtue love for virtue loved;
Most power to do most harm, least knowing ill;
For he hath wit to make an ill shape good,
And shape to win grace, though he had no wit.   60
I saw him at the Duke Alençon's once;
And much too little of that good I saw
Is my report to his great worthiness.

ROSALINE

Another of these students at that time
Was there with him, if I have heard a truth.
Biron they call him, but a merrier man,
Within the limit of becoming mirth,
I never spent an hour's talk withal.
His eye begets occasion for his wit,
For every object that the one doth catch   70
The other turns to a mirth-moving jest,
Which his fair tongue, conceit's expositor,
Delivers in such apt and gracious words
That agèd ears play truant at his tales,
And younger hearings are quite ravishèd,
So sweet and voluble is his discourse.

PRINCESS

God bless my ladies! Are they all in love,

56 KATHERINE] ROWE; *2. Lad.* QF   60 he] Q; she F   61 Alençon's] JOHNSON and STEEVENS;
Alansoes QF   64 ROSALINE] F (*Rossa.*); *3. Lad.* Q   65 if] Q; as F

wise so young, they say, do never live
long' (*Richard III* 3.1.79).

57 **Of** by
58 **Most … ill** i.e. because he knows little or
nothing about the nature of evil, he has a
great potential for doing a lot of harm
59–60 **he … wit** 'his intelligence is such
that it would make up for an ugly body,
and his physical endowment is such that
it would make up for lack of brains'
(Riverside)
62 **much too little** far too short
63 **to** compared to (*OED*, A 18). Compare
Hamlet 1.2.139–40: 'So excellent a king,
that was to this | Hyperion to a satyr'.
66 **Biron … man** David tentatively suggests

that there is a pun here on *Berowne*, the
name as it is in Q, and *brown*, both
pronounced to rhyme with *moon*
(4.3.227 and 229). It seems highly likely,
for *brown* could mean *sombre*, as in *brown
study*, and would thus account for the
but.
68 **withal** with. This emphatic form of *with* is
used after the object at the end of a
sentence (Abbott 196).
69 **begets occasion** spots opportunities
72 **conceit's expositor** the expounder of
witty ideas (Shakespeare's sole use of
expositor).
74 **play truant at** i.e. abandon their pursuit
of serious matters in favour of listening to
76 **voluble** fluent

That every one her own hath garnishèd
With such bedecking ornaments of praise?

FIRST LORD

Here comes Boyet.

Enter Boyet

PRINCESS   Now, what admittance, lord?   80

BOYET

Navarre had notice of your fair approach,
And he and his competitors in oath
Were all addressed to meet you, gentle lady,
Before I came. Marry, thus much I have learnt:
He rather means to lodge you in the field,
Like one that comes here to besiege his court,
Than seek a dispensation for his oath
To let you enter his unpeopled house.
Here comes Navarre.

Enter the King, Longueville, Dumaine, and Biron

KING Fair Princess, welcome to the court of Navarre.   90

PRINCESS 'Fair' I give you back again, and welcome I have
    not yet. The roof of this court is too high to be yours,
    and welcome to the wide fields too base to be mine.

KING

You shall be welcome, madam, to my court.

PRINCESS

I will be welcome then. Conduct me thither.

---

80 FIRST LORD] Q (*Lord.*); *Ma⟨ria⟩.* F   88 unpeopled] F; vnpeeled Q   89 Here comes
Navarre] F; *Bo⟨yet⟩.* Heere comes *Nauar* Q   89.1 *Enter ... Biron*] QF (Enter *Nauar, Longauill,
Dumaine, & Berowne.*), *after l. 88*   90–110 KING] ROWE; *Nauar.* QF

78–9 **garnishèd ... bedecking ornaments**
    Compare *Henry V* 2.2.131: 'Garnished
    and decked in modest complement'.
80 **admittance** sort of reception (Schmidt)
81 **fair** Here, as so often in this play, where it
    is badly overworked, *fair* has no definite
    meaning but serves as a convenient filler
    to eke out the line.
82 **competitors** partners, associates (*OED*,
    2). This sense of *competitor* is much
    commoner in Shakespeare than its mod-
    ern sense.
83 **addressed** prepared, ready
84 **Marry** a mild oath, originally the name of
    the Virgin Mary
85 **field** (a) open country (b) battlefield

88 **unpeopled house** house inadequately
    staffed with servants. Shakespeare uses
    unpeopled again at *Richard II* 1.2.69 and
    As You Like It 3.2.123, and frequently
    has *people* for *servants*, as, for example, at
    Twelfth Night 2.5.56–7, where Malvolio
    says: 'Seven of my people with an obedi-
    ent start make out for him'.
        The Q reading 'vnpeeled' is almost
    certainly a misprint for a word that
    probably appeared in Shakespeare's
    manuscript as 'vnpeepled'. As Wilson
    notices and *OED* confirms, both 'peple'
    and 'peeple' were not uncommon 16th-
    century spellings of 'people'.
92 **The roof ... court** i.e. the sky

KING

Hear me, dear lady. I have sworn an oath—

PRINCESS

Our Lady help my lord! He'll be forsworn.

KING

Not for the world, fair madam, by my will.

PRINCESS

Why, will shall break it; will, and nothing else.

KING

Your ladyship is ignorant what it is.   100

PRINCESS

Were my lord so, his ignorance were wise,

Where now his knowledge must prove ignorance.

I hear your grace hath sworn out housekeeping.

'Tis deadly sin to keep that oath, my lord,

And sin to break it.

But pardon me, I am too sudden bold;

To teach a teacher ill beseemeth me.

Vouchsafe to read the purpose of my coming,

And suddenly resolve me in my suit.

She gives the King a document

KING

Madam, I will, if suddenly I may.   110

PRINCESS

You will the sooner that I were away,

For you'll prove perjured if you make me stay.

The King peruses the document

BIRON (*to Rosaline*)

Did not I dance with you in Brabant once?

⌈ROSALINE⌉

Did not I dance with you in Brabant once?

99 it; will,] CAPELL; it will, QF   109.1 *She ... document*] *not in* QF   112.1 *The ... document*]
not in QF   114–25 ROSALINE] F (*Rosa.*); *Kath⟨erine⟩.* Q

98 **by my will** willingly
99 **will** desire
102 **Where** whereas (Abbott 134)
   prove turn out to be
103 **sworn out housekeeping** renounced
   hospitality (*OED, housekeeping*, 2). Complaints about the decay of housekeeping,
   the kind of hospitality practised by Chaucer's Franklin, were common in

Shakespeare's day.
106 **sudden** rashly, inconsiderately
109 **suddenly** immediately
   resolve me in give me your answer to
   (*OED, v.* 11)
111 **You ... away** i.e. you will do it the more
   readily in order to have me go
113–26 **Did not I dance ... be gone** See
   Introduction, pp. 60–3.

BIRON

I know you did.

⌈**ROSALINE**⌉   How needless was it then

To ask the question!

BIRON   You must not be so quick.

⌈**ROSALINE**⌉

'Tis long of you that spur me with such questions.

BIRON

Your wit's too hot, it speeds too fast, 'twill tire.

⌈**ROSALINE**⌉

Not till it leave the rider in the mire.

BIRON

What time o'day?   120

⌈**ROSALINE**⌉

The hour that fools should ask.

BIRON

Now fair befall your mask.

⌈**ROSALINE**⌉

Fair fall the face it covers.

BIRON

And send you many lovers.

⌈**ROSALINE**⌉

Amen, so you be none.

BIRON

Nay, then will I be gone.

     ⌈*He leaves her*⌉

KING (*to the Princess*)

Madam, your father here doth intimate

The payment of a hundred thousand crowns,

Being but the one half of an entire sum

Disbursèd by my father in his wars.   130

126.1 *He leaves her*] *not in* QF   127 KING] F (*Kin.*); *Ferd.* Q   129 of] F; of, of Q

116 **quick** (a) impatient (*OED, a.* 22) (b) sharp, caustic (18b)

117–19 **'Tis ... mire** Proverbial—'Do not spur a willing horse', 'A free horse will soon tire', and 'To leave in the mire' (Dent H638, H642, M989).

117 **long of** owing to, because of (*OED, a.*²).
spur (a) urge on (b) interrogate (*OED, speer, v.*¹, of which *spur* was a variant spelling)

120 **What time o' day?** Biron asks a silly question in order to change the topic.

122 **fair befall** i.e. good luck to (*OED, befall, v.* 4e)

123 **Fair fall** may good befall (*OED, fall, v.* 46d)

125 **so** provided that, so long as

127 **intimate** notify us of, refer to

129 **entire** (stressed on the first syllable)

130 **his** i.e. the King of France's

But say that he, or we—as neither have—
Received that sum, yet there remains unpaid
A hundred thousand more, in surety of the which
One part of Aquitaine is bound to us,
Although not valued to the money's worth.
If then the King your father will restore
But that one half which is unsatisfied,
We will give up our right in Aquitaine,
And hold fair friendship with his majesty.
But that, it seems, he little purposeth,   140
For here he doth demand to have repaid
A hundred thousand crowns, and not demands,
On payment of a hundred thousand crowns,
To have his title live in Aquitaine,
Which we much rather had depart withal,
And have the money by our father lent,
Than Aquitaine, so gelded as it is.
Dear Princess, were not his requests so far
From reason's yielding, your fair self should make
A yielding 'gainst some reason in my breast,   150
And go well satisfied to France again.

PRINCESS

You do the King my father too much wrong,
And wrong the reputation of your name,
In so unseeming to confess receipt
Of that which hath so faithfully been paid.

KING

I do protest I never heard of it;
And if you prove it, I'll repay it back
Or yield up Aquitaine.

PRINCESS   We arrest your word.

139 friendship] Q (faiendship), F   141 demand] Q (pemaund), F   repaid] Q (repaide); repaie F
142 A] Q; An F   143 On] THEOBALD; One QF

131 **he** i.e. my father
  as neither have which neither of us has.
  For Shakespeare's use of *as* as a relative in
  parenthetical clauses, and of *neither* as a
  plural pronoun, see Abbott 111 and 12.
133 **surety** guarantee (*OED*, *sb.* 5)
134 **bound** mortgaged, secured
135 **valued ... worth** i.e. really worth the
  money it is supposed to secure
136 **restore** repay, give back to the true

owner
137 **unsatisfied** unpaid
142 **and not demands** i.e. does not demand
  as in equity he might
145 **had depart withal** would part with
147 **gelded** i.e. deprived of an essential part
  (*OED*, *v.*¹ 2)
154 **unseeming** not seeming (to be willing
  to) (Onions)
158 **arrest your word** seize your promise as

Boyet, you can produce acquittances
For such a sum from special officers   160
Of Charles, his father.
KING   Satisfy me so.
BOYET

So please your grace, the packet is not come
Where that and other specialties are bound.
Tomorrow you shall have a sight of them.

KING

It shall suffice me; at which interview
All liberal reason I will yield unto.
Meantime receive such welcome at my hand
As honour, without breach of honour, may
Make tender of to thy true worthiness.
You may not come, fair Princess, within my gates,   170
But here without you shall be so received
As you shall deem yourself lodged in my heart,
Though so denied fair harbour in my house.
Your own good thoughts excuse me, and farewell.
Tomorrow shall we visit you again.

PRINCESS

Sweet health and fair desires consort your grace.

KING

Thy own wish wish I thee in every place.
                    Exeunt the King, Longueville, and Dumaine
BIRON Lady, I will commend you to mine own heart.
ROSALINE Pray you, do my commendations; I would be
        glad to see it.   180

166 I will] Q; would I F   168 may ∧] F; ~, Q   170 within] Q; in F   177 KING] F
(*Kin.*); *Na.* Q   177.1 *Exeunt ... Dumaine*] CAPELL (*subs.*); *Exit.* QF   178–91 BIRON] Q (*Ber.*,
with '*Bar.*' at l. 185); *Boy⟨et⟩.* F   178 mine own] Q (my none); my owne F

security. Compare *Measure for Measure*
2.4.134: 'I do arrest your words.' *OED* (*v.*
12) cites no other instances of *arrest* in
this figurative sense; but, as David points
out, Shakespeare had been anticipated by
Sir Philip Sidney in his *Arcadia*, where
Artesia 'took the advantage one day
upon Phalantus' unconscionable prais-
ings of her ... to arrest his word as soon
as it was out of his mouth' (i. 99).

163 **specialties** special legal contracts under
      seal (*OED*, 7). Compare *Shrew* 2.1.126–7:

'Let specialties be therefore drawn be-
tween us, | That covenants may be kept
on either hand.'
166 **All liberal reason** 'any civilized argument' (Kerrigan)
169 **Make tender of** offer
172 **As that** (Abbott 109)
173 **harbour** quarters, lodgings (*OED*, *sb.*¹
      2)
176 **consort** accompany, go with
178 **commend** (a) commit (b) remember
179 **do my commendations** i.e. give it my
      greetings

BIRON I would you heard it groan.

ROSALINE Is the fool sick?

BIRON Sick at the heart.

ROSALINE

Alack, let it blood.

BIRON

Would that do it good?

ROSALINE

My physic says ay.

BIRON

Will you prick't with your eye?

ROSALINE

Non point, with my knife.

BIRON

Now God save thy life.

ROSALINE

And yours—from long living.   190

BIRON

I cannot stay thanksgiving.   *Exit*
 Enter Dumaine

DUMAINE (*to Boyet*)

Sir, I pray you a word. What lady is that same?

BOYET

The heir of Alençon, Katherine her name.

DUMAINE

A gallant lady! Monsieur, fare you well.   *Exit*
 Enter Longueville

LONGUEVILLE (*to Boyet*)

I beseech you a word. What is she in the white?

BOYET

A woman sometimes, an you saw her in the light.

LONGUEVILLE

Perchance light in the light. I desire her name.

---

182 fool] Q (foole); soule F 188 *Non point*] KERRIGAN; *No poynt* QF 191 *Exit*] QF; *retiring* CAPELL 193 Katherine] SINGER (*conj.* Capell); *Rosalin* QF 194 *Exit*] Q; *not in* F 194.1 *Enter Longueville*] F2; *not in* QF 196 an] Q (and); if F 197 name.] F; ~? Q

182 **fool** poor thing (*OED, sb.*[1] c)

184 **let it blood** bleed it

186 **physic** medical knowledge

188 *Non point* (a) not a bit, not at all (*OED, point, sb.*[1] 6b) (b) it's blunt. Both Q and F italicize *No poynt*, as they have it, to stress

the primacy of the French meaning. See Wells, *Re-Editing*, p. 26.

191 **stay thanksgiving** take the time to thank you properly

197 **light in the light** i.e. wanton when seen for what she really is

BOYET

She hath but one for herself; to desire that were a
shame.

LONGUEVILLE

Pray you, sir, whose daughter?

BOYET

Her mother's, I have heard.   200

LONGUEVILLE

God's blessing on your beard!

BOYET

Good sir, be not offended.
She is an heir of Falconbridge.

LONGUEVILLE

Nay, my choler is ended.
She is a most sweet lady.

BOYET

Not unlike, sir, that may be.   *Exit Longueville*
        Enter Biron

BIRON

What's her name in the cap?

BOYET

Rosaline, by good hap.

BIRON

Is she wedded or no?

BOYET

To her will, sir, or so.   210

BIRON

You are welcome, sir. Adieu.

BOYET

Farewell to me, sir, and welcome to you.   *Exit Biron*

---

201 on] Q; a F   206 *Exit Longueville*] Q; *after l. 205* F   208 Rosaline] SINGER; *Katherin* Q;
Katherine F   211 You] F; O you Q   212 *Exit Biron*] Q (*Exit Bero.*); *Exit* F

201 **God's ... beard** 'may'st thou have some
sense and seriousness more proportion-
ate to thy beard, the length of which suits
ill with such idle catches of wit' (Johnson).
206 **unlike** unlikely
209–10 **Is she ... so** 'To be wedded to one's
will' was proverbial (Tilley W392).

211 **You are welcome** at your service
(Schmidt). This is the reading of F. Q
begins the line with an intrusive 'O',
probably caught from the last letter of the
speech-prefix '*Bero⟨wne⟩*.'
212 **welcome to you** you are welcome to
go—proverbial (Tilley W259)

MARIA

That last is Biron, the merry madcap lord.

Not a word with him but a jest.

BOYET   And every jest but a word.

PRINCESS

It was well done of you to take him at his word.

BOYET

I was as willing to grapple as he was to board.

⌈ROSALINE⌉

Two hot sheeps, marry!

BOYET   And wherefore not 'ships'?

No sheep, sweet lamb, unless we feed on your lips.

⌈ROSALINE⌉

You sheep, and I pasture. Shall that finish the jest?

BOYET

So you grant pasture for me.

          ⌈*He tries to kiss her*⌉

⌈ROSALINE⌉   Not so, gentle beast.   220

My lips are no common, though several they be.

BOYET

Belonging to whom?

⌈ROSALINE⌉   To my fortunes and me.

PRINCESS

Good wits will be jangling; but, gentles, agree:

---

217 ROSALINE] This edition; *Lady Ka.* Q; *La. Ma.* F   sheeps, marry!] THEOBALD (*subs.*);
Sheepes marie. Q; Sheepes marie: F   BOYET And ... 'ships'?] Q; *continued to Rosaline* F
219, 221, 222 ROSALINE] This edition; *La⟨dy⟩.* QF   220 He ... her] CAPELL; *not in* QF
223 but, gentles,] THEOBALD; but ∧ gentles ∧ QF

213 **madcap** entertainingly wild and eccentric

215 **take him at his word** take him on at his own word-games

216 **grapple ... board** The language is that of a naval battle.

217 **hot sheeps** fiery, ardent sheep—almost a contradiction in terms in view of the sheep's reputed meekness and timidity. Katherine takes a poor view of the verbal battle between the two men.
sheeps ... 'ships' In his early comedies Shakespeare found this pun irresistible—compare *Two Gentlemen* 1.1.72–9 and *Comedy of Errors* 4.1.93–4—but then, mercifully, abandoned it.

219 **pasture** probably quibbling on 'pastor', meaning 'shepherd'

220 **So** provided

221 **My lips ... be** i.e. my lips are no common (pasture on which all the farmers of the village have the right to graze their stock) although they are, admittedly, pasture (but enclosed pasture in private ownership). See *OED, several, sb.* 2, and compare Sonnets 137.9–10: 'Why should my heart think that a several plot | Which my heart knows the wide world's common place?'
several (a) privately owned enclosed land (b) more than one (c) parted

223 **jangling** disputing, wrangling
gentles gentlefolk (*OED, sb.* 1c). Shakespeare and other playwrights of the time often addressed their audiences as 'gentles'. See, for instance, *Henry V* Pro.8.

This civil war of wits were much better used
On Navarre and his book-men, for here 'tis abused.

BOYET

If my observation, which very seldom lies
By the heart's still rhetoric disclosèd wi'th' eyes,
Deceive me not now, Navarre is infected.

PRINCESS With what?

BOYET

With that which we lovers entitle 'affected'.   230

PRINCESS Your reason?

BOYET

Why, all his behaviours did make their retire
To the court of his eye, peeping thorough desire.
His heart, like an agate with your print impressed,
Proud with his form, in his eye pride expressed.
His tongue, all impatient to speak and not see,
Did stumble with haste in his eyesight to be.
All senses to that sense did make their repair,
To feel only looking on fairest of fair.
Methought all his senses were locked in his eye,   240
As jewels in crystal for some prince to buy;
Who, tend'ring their own worth from where they were
        glassed,
Did point you to buy them along as you passed.

226–7 observation, which ... eyes,] F (obseruation (which ... eyes)); obseruation (which ...
eyes. Q   226 lies] Q (*corr.*), F; lyes? Q (*uncorr.*)   227 wi'th'] This edition; with QF
231 reason?] ROWE; ~. QF   232 did] Q; doe F   242 where] Q; whence F   243 point
you] Q; point out F

225 **book-men** scholars. Shakespeare's only
    other use of this word is at 4.2.33.
    abused put to a wrong use, misapplied
226–7 **lies | By** conveys a false impression
    about, is mistaken about. For *by* in the
    sense of 'about', 'concerning', see Abbott
    145, and compare *Merchant* 1.2.52–3:
    'How say you by the French lord, Mon-
    sieur Le Bon?'
227 **still rhetoric** dumb eloquence
    wi'th' by the (Abbott 193). Compare
    K. John 2.1.567–8: 'rounded in the ear |
    With that same purpose-changer'.
230 **affected** being in love
232–3 **Why ... desire** 'all his powers of
    expression were concentrated in his eye,
    and shared in the longing look he gave
    you' (David)
232 **retire** repair, withdrawal

233 **thorough** through
234 **with your print impressed** i.e. with a
    representation of you engraved on it
235 **Proud with his form** made proud by the
    form—the Princess's image—stamped
    on it
236 **impatient ... see** frustrated because of
    being limited to speaking and so unable
    to see
239 **looking** through looking
241 **crystal** crystal glass
242 **Who** and they (Abbott 259)
    tend'ring offering, proffering for accep-
    tance
    glassed enclosed in glass (*OED*, *v*. 2;
    earliest example of this sense, not used
    elsewhere by Shakespeare)
243 **point** direct (Onions)

His face's own margin did quote such amazes
That all eyes saw his eyes enchanted with gazes.
I'll give you Aquitaine, and all that is his
An you give him for my sake but one loving kiss.

PRINCESS

Come, to our pavilion. Boyet is disposed.

BOYET

But to speak that in words which his eye hath
        disclosed.
I only have made a mouth of his eye   250
By adding a tongue which I know will not lie.

⌈**MARIA**⌉

Thou art an old love-monger, and speakest skilfully.

⌈**KATHERINE**⌉

He is Cupid's grandfather, and learns news of him.

⌈**ROSALINE**⌉

Then was Venus like her mother, for her father is but
        grim.

BOYET

Do you hear, my mad wenches?

⌈**MARIA**⌉   No.

BOYET   What then, do you see?

⌈**MARIA**⌉

Our way to be gone.

BOYET   You are too hard for me.   *Exeunt*

---

249 BOYET] Q (*Bo.*); *Bro.* F   252 MARIA] CAPELL; *Lad.* Q; *Lad. Ro.* F   253 KATHERINE]
CAPELL; *Lad.* 2. Q; *Lad. Ma.* F   254 ROSALINE] ROWE; *Lad.* 3. Q; *Lad.* 2. F   255 MARIA]
ROWE; *Lad.* Q; *La.* 1. F   256 MARIA Our] This edition (*conj.* Wilson); *Lad.* 1, our Q; *Lad.* 2. 1,
our F

244 **His ... amazes** The idea of the face as a
    book is common in Shakespeare; com-
    pare *Macbeth* 1.5.61–2: 'Your face, my
    thane, is as a book where men | May read
    strange matters.' The *margin* frequently
    contained notes summarizing the con-
    tents of a paragraph or drawing the
    reader's attention to something of special
    interest, while to *quote* could mean to
    indicate by means of a pointing index
    finger in the *margin*.
    amazes extremes of admiration. Since
    amaze derives from *maze* (*sb.*), it probably
    suggested the word *enchanted* in the next
    line.
248 **disposed** inclined to be merry, in a

jocund mood (*OED*, *ppl. a.* 4b)
252 MARIA For the attribution of the ladies'
    speeches see Introduction, p. 61.
    love-monger dealer in love affairs (not
    used elsewhere in Shakespeare)
    skilfully expertly
255 **Do you hear** A formula for gaining
    attention, equivalent to the modern 'Lis-
    ten'.
    mad wenches high-spirited girls. 'Mad
    wenches' was something of a stock
    phrase (Dent W274.1).
256 MARIA Q reads '*Lad.*'; F '*Lad.* 2.' Follow-
    ing Wilson's suggestion, this edition as-
    sumes that Shakespeare wrote '*Lad.* 1.'
    which the compositor misread as '*Lad.* l'.

3.1 *Enter Armado and Moth*

ARMADO Warble, child, make passionate my sense of
    hearing.

MOTH ⌈*sings the song*⌉ 'Concolinel'.

ARMADO Sweet air! Go, tenderness of years, take this key,
    give enlargement to the swain, bring him festinately
    hither. I must employ him in a letter to my love.

MOTH Master, will you win your love with a French
    brawl?

ARMADO How meanest thou? Brawling in French?

MOTH No, my complete master; but to jig off a tune at the   10
    tongue's end, canary to it with your feet, humour it
    with turning up your eyelids, sigh a note and sing a
    note, sometime through the throat as if you swallowed
    love with singing love, sometime through the nose as if
    you snuffed up love by smelling love, with your hat
    penthouse-like o'er the shop of your eyes, with your

3.1.0.1 *Enter Armado and Moth*] ROWE; Enter *Braggart and his Boy.* Q; *Enter Braggart
and Boy.* | Song. F   1–63 ARMADO] ROWE; *Bra⟨ggart⟩.* QF   3–62 MOTH] ROWE; *Boy.* QF
3 *sings the song*] THEOBALD (*subs.*); *not in* QF   7 Master, will] Q; Will F   11 with your] Q;
with the F   12 eyelids] Q (eylids); eie F   13 throat as if] THEOBALD (*subs.*); throate, if Q;
throate: if F   14 singing love,] THEOBALD; singing loue ∧ Q; singing, loue ∧ F   through
the nose] F2; through: nose QF   15 love, with] F2; loue ∧ with QF

3.1.1 **make passionate ... hearing** i.e. assure
    that my sense of hearing is deeply affected
    by the passion of love (*OED, passionate, a.*
    4)

3 **Concolinel** The likeliest explanation of
    this strange word is that it is the title of
    Moth's song. If it is, it could well be a
    corruption of the Irish lyric '*Can cailin
    gheal*', pronounced 'Con colleen yal' and
    meaning 'Sing, fair maiden'. Compare
    Pistol's reference to another Irish song,
    '*Calin o custure me*', at *Henry V* 4.4.4.
    Alternatively, it might be the opening of
    some lost French song beginning '*Quand
    Colinelle*'.

5 **give enlargement to** free
    festinately immediately (only example
    cited by *OED*)

7–8 **French brawl** a kind of French dance
    resembling a cotillon (*OED, brawl, sb.*¹ 2).
    A dance in which 'the dancers move
    sideways and not forward', a *brawl* is
    staged in John Marston's *The Malcontent*
    (4.2.1–14).

10 **jig off a tune** sing a tune in the style of a

    jig (earliest example of *jig* as a verb in
    OED)

10–11 **at the tongue's end** proverbial (Tilley
    T413)

11 **canary** i.e. dance as if you were dancing
    the *canaries*. So called because it seems to
    have originated in the Canary Islands,
    the *canaries* was a quick and lively dance.
    OED cites this as its earliest instance of
    canary as a verb.
    humour it adapt yourself to it (*OED, v.* 2;
    earliest example of this meaning)

15–19 **with your hat ... painting** See the
    picture of the melancholy lover Inamo-
    rato in the frontispiece to Robert Burton's
    The Anatomy of Melancholy (1621).

16 **penthouse-like o'er the shop** Many Eliza-
    bethan shops had a stall, or *bulk*, as it was
    called, at their fronts for the display of
    wares. This stall was protected from the
    weather by a wooden *penthouse*, a kind of
    awning that could be raised during the
    day to provide a sloping roof and lowered
    at night.

arms crossed on your thin-belly doublet like a rabbit on
a spit, or your hands in your pocket like a man after the
old painting; and keep not too long in one tune, but a
snip and away. These are compliments, these are hu- 20
mours, these betray nice wenches that would be betrayed without these; and make them men of note—do
you note me?—that most are affected to these.

ARMADO How hast thou purchased this experience?

MOTH By my penny of observation.

ARMADO But O—but O—

MOTH 'The hobby-horse is forgot.'

ARMADO Call'st thou my love 'hobby-horse'?

MOTH No, master. The hobby-horse is but a colt, and your
love perhaps a hackney. But have you forgot your love? 30

ARMADO Almost I had.

MOTH Negligent student! Learn her by heart.

ARMADO By heart and in heart, boy.

17 thin-belly] F (thinbellie); thinbellies Q   22–3 note—do you note me?—that] HANMER
(subs.); note: do you note men that QF; note—do you note? *men*—that OXFORD   25 penny]
HANMER; penne QF   29 and] Q; and | and F

17 **arms crossed** Folded arms were regarded
as infallible signs of disappointed love. See
Two Gentlemen 2.1.17–19: 'you have
learned, like Sir Proteus, to wreath your
arms, like a malcontent'.
  your thin-belly doublet doublet cut to
emphasize the thinness of your belly
18 **after** in the manner of
18–19 **the old painting** It seems unlikely
that Moth has any particular painting in
mind. He appears, as Kerrigan points out,
to be thinking about the kind of painting
Borachio describes in his account of the
effect fashion can have on young men:
'sometimes fashioning them like Phar-
aoh's soldiers in the reechy painting,
sometime like god Bel's priests in the old
church window, sometime like the
shaven Hercules in the smirched, worm-
eaten tapestry' (*Much Ado* 3.3.128–32).
19–20 **a snip and away** a snatch and then
on to another. 'A snatch and away' was
proverbial (Tilley S587).
20 **compliments** gentlemanly accomplishments
20–1 **humours** fashionable affectations
(*OED, sb.* 6)
21 **betray** seduce (Schmidt)
  nice wanton (*OED, a.* 2a)
22 **of note** of eminence, of distinction

22–3 **do you note me?** are you paying
attention to me? Q, followed by F, reads
'do you note men', which yields no ready
sense.
23 **affected** inclined, given
24 **purchased** acquired (*OED, v.* 4). Moth
takes the word to mean 'bought'.
25 **penny** pennyworth (*OED*, 7). Q and F
read 'penne', but the connection with
'purchase' validates the emendation to
'penny'. Compare the title of Robert
Greene's pamphlet of 1592, *Greene's
Groatsworth of Wit bought with a million of
repentance.*
27 **The hobby-horse is forgot** Moth derisively
interprets Armado's sighs as part of the
line given in full in *Hamlet* 3.2.129, 'For
O, for O, the hobby-horse is forgot.' These
words seem to have been the refrain of a
popular ballad which has not survived.
The hobby-horse, a dancer got up to look
like a horse, was a very popular figure in
May-games and similar festivities.
28 **hobby-horse** Elizabethan slang for 'prostitute' (*OED*, 3b).
29 **colt** (a) young horse (b) lascivious man
(*OED*, 2c)
30 **hackney** (a) horse kept for hire (*OED, sb.*
2) (b) slang for 'whore' (*OED, sb.* 4)

MOTH And out of heart, master. All those three I will prove.

ARMADO What wilt thou prove?

MOTH A man, if I live; and this 'by', 'in', and 'without' upon the instant. 'By' heart you love her because your heart cannot come by her. 'In' heart you love her because your heart is in love with her. And 'out' of   40 heart you love her, being out of heart that you cannot enjoy her.

ARMADO I am all these three.

MOTH And three times as much more—(*aside*) and yet nothing at all.

ARMADO Fetch hither the swain. He must carry me a letter.

MOTH A message well sympathized—a horse to be ambassador for an ass.

ARMADO Ha, ha, what sayest thou?   50

MOTH Marry, sir, you must send the ass upon the horse, for he is very slow-gaited. But I go.

ARMADO The way is but short. Away!

MOTH As swift as lead, sir.

ARMADO Thy meaning, pretty ingenious?
Is not lead a metal heavy, dull, and slow?

MOTH

Minime, honest master, or rather, master, no.

---

37 and this] Q (*corr.*); (and this) F; and (this) Q (*uncorr.*)   55 Thy] F; The Q   57 *Minime*] Q (Minnime); F (*Minnime*)

35–6 **prove** (a) demonstrate (b) turn out to be

44–5 **And ... all** Continuing the lesson in arithmetic which he began at 1.2.39, Moth now observes that three noughts are nought, and so Armado is still the *cipher* that he was then.

48 **well sympathized** i.e. whose parts are in perfect harmony with one another (*OED, v.* 3c)

48–52 **a horse ... slow-gaited** The precise point of these exchanges is obscure. The ass was, of course, regarded as the type of stupidity, and so in some contexts was the horse—compare *1 Henry IV*

2.5.194–6: 'I tell thee what, Hal, if I tell thee a lie, spit in my face, call me horse.' So Moth may well be saying that one stupid creature (Costard) is the right messenger (*ambassador*) for another (Armado). *Slow-gaited* could, perhaps, mean 'slow in the uptake'.

54 **As swift as lead.** Moth's paradox is made up of two conventional similes: 'As heavy as lead' (Tilley L134) and 'As swift as a bullet' (Dent B719.1).

55 **ingenious** Shakespeare often uses adjectives as nouns. See Abbott 5.

57 *Minime* Latin for 'certainly not'

ARMADO

I say lead is slow.

MOTH   You are too swift, sir, to say so.

Is that lead slow which is fired from a gun?

ARMADO Sweet smoke of rhetoric!   60

He reputes me a cannon; and the bullet, that's he.

I shoot thee at the swain.

MOTH   Thump then, and I flee.   *Exit*

ARMADO

A most acute juvenal, voluble and free of grace!

By thy favour, sweet welkin, I must sigh in thy face.

Most rude melancholy, valour gives thee place.

My herald is returned.

>   *Enter Moth with Costard*

MOTH

A wonder, master! Here's a costard broken in a shin.

ARMADO

Some enigma, some riddle. Come, thy *l'envoi*—begin.

COSTARD No egma, no riddle, no *l'envoi*, no salve in the
mail, sir! O, sir, plantain, a plain plantain! No *l'envoi*,   70
no *l'envoi*, no salve, sir, but a plantain!

62 *Exit*] F2; *not in* QF   63 voluble] F; volable Q   66.1 *Enter Moth with Costard*] ROWE
(*subs.*); Enter *Page* and *Clowne*. QF   67–95 MOTH] ROWE; *Pag.* QF   69–140 COSTARD]
ROWE; *Clow⟨ne⟩.* QF   69–70 salve in the mail] MALONE (*after* Johnson; the F2); salue, in
thee male QF   70 O] Q; Or F   plain] Q (pline), F

60 **smoke** mist. Shakespeare, on several occasions, uses *smoke* to describe the insubstantial nature of words. Compare, for
instance, *Lucrece* 1027: 'This helpless
smoke of words doth me no right.'
62 **Thump** i.e. make a noise like a gun going
off
63 **acute** This is the earliest example cited by
OED (*a.* 7) of *acute* applied to the intellectual powers.
65 **gives thee place** yields its place to you
67 **Here's ... shin** here's a head with a graze
on its shin. 'To break one's shins' was
a common expression (Dent S342.1).
David, taking up a suggestion of John
Crow's, gives some good reasons for
thinking that the phrase could mean 'to
suffer a disappointment in love'.
68 **enigma** Shakespeare's only other use of
this word is at *Coriolanus* 2.3.90.
l'envoi The *envoi* was the concluding part
of a literary composition, the author's
parting words to it before sending it on its

way into the world. Armado, however, as
he tells us at lines 78–9, regards it as a
summary or explanation of what has
gone before.
69 **No egma ... *l'envoi*** Costard evidently
thinks Armado is ordering some outlandish remedies for his broken shin, and is
very alarmed at the prospect. Kerrigan
tentatively suggests that 'he confuses
enigma or *egma* with "enema", and
thinks that *l'envoi* has something to do
with the verb "to lenify" (that is "to
purge gently")'. Unfortunately *OED* has
no instance of 'enema' prior to 1681. It
therefore seems more likely that Costard
takes *enigma* to be some nostrum made
from eggs, and mishears *riddle* as 'rud-
dle', a variety of red ochre used for
marking sheep.
69–70 **salve in the mail** ointment or plaster
in the bag (carried by a quacksalver)
70 **plantain** The leaves of the plantain were
considered a good old remedy for bruises,

ARMADO By virtue, thou enforcest laughter; thy silly
thought my spleen; the heaving of my lungs provokes
me to ridiculous smiling. O, pardon me, my stars! Doth
the inconsiderate take *salve* for *l'envoi* and the word
'*l'envoi*' for a *salve*?

MOTH Do the wise think them other? Is not *l'envoi* a *salve*?

ARMADO

No, page. It is an epilogue or discourse to make plain
Some obscure precedence that hath tofore been sain.
I will example it: 80

The fox, the ape, and the humble-bee
Were still at odds, being but three.

There's the moral. Now the *l'envoi*.

MOTH I will add the *l'envoi*. Say the moral again.

ARMADO

The fox, the ape, and the humble-bee
Were still at odds, being but three.

MOTH

Until the goose came out of door,
And stayed the odds by adding four.

80–81 I ... four] Q; *not in* F

grazes, and the like. Compare *Romeo*
1.2.50–2: 'Your plantain leaf is excellent
for that. | —For what, I pray thee?—For
your broken shin.'

72 **silly** simple-minded, naïve

73 **spleen** i.e. uncontrollable mirth. The
spleen, it was thought, was the source of
both anger and merriment.

74 **ridiculous** derisive

74–6 **Doth ... salve?** As David succinctly
remarks, the answer to this question is
'yes'. Armado misinterprets Costard's
salve (*OED*, *sb.*¹) as *salve* (*OED*, *sb.*⁵),
meaning 'a greeting or salutation on
meeting' and derived from the Latin *salve*
i.e. 'hail!', 'greetings!', the exact opposite
of *l'envoi*.

75 **inconsiderate** thoughtless person (*OED*,
sb.)

79 **precedence** something, as Armado re-
dundantly explains, said before (*OED*,
2)—earliest example of the word in this
sense. Compare *Antony* 2.5.50–1: 'I do
not like "But yet"; it does allay | The
good precedence.'
sain said. This form of the past participle
was popular with poets of the 16th and

17th centuries because, perhaps, of the
readiness with which it lent itself, as
here, to rhyming.

80 **example** provide an example of (*OED*, *v.*
1)

81–94 **The fox ... four** There has been much
throwing about of brains—and of
names—in the many attempts that have
been made to extract topical significance
out of these lines. None, however, of the
'solutions' proposed has proved really
convincing. It seems far better therefore
to take the four lines of doggerel for what
they so obviously are, a miniature beast
fable, which, like the beast fable at large,
deals with the general rather than the
particular and with the self-evident
rather than the arcane.

82 **still** always
at odds (a) quarrelling (b) an odd number

83 **moral** The meaning of *moral* here, not
adequately covered by *OED*, appears to
be, as Schmidt glosses it, 'a truth proposed', or, in other words, 'a glimpse into
the obvious'. Compare *Dream* 5.1.120–1:
'A good moral, my lord: it is not enough
to speak, but to speak true.'

88 **stayed the odds** (a) settled the quarrel

Now will I begin your moral, and do you follow with
   my *l'envoi*.   90
    The fox, the ape, and the humble-bee
    Were still at odds, being but three.

ARMADO
    Until the goose came out of door,
    Staying the odds by adding four.

MOTH A good *l'envoi*, ending in the goose. Would you
   desire more?

COSTARD
    The boy hath sold him a bargain, a goose, that's flat.
    Sir, your pennyworth is good, an your goose be fat.
    To sell a bargain well is as cunning as fast and loose.
    Let me see: a fat *l'envoi*—ay, that's a fat goose.   100

ARMADO
    Come hither, come hither. How did this argument
      begin?

MOTH
    By saying that a costard was broken in a shin.
    Then called you for the *l'envoi*.

COSTARD True, and I for a plantain—thus came your
   argument in. Then the boy's fat *l'envoi*, the goose that
   you bought; and he ended the market.

ARMADO But tell me, how was there a costard broken in a
   shin?

MOTH I will tell you sensibly.

COSTARD Thou hast no feeling of it, Moth. I will speak that   110
   l'envoi.

101 ARMADO (Come ... argument] Q (*corr.*), F (*Ar.* Come ... argument); *Arm.* Come ... argumet
Q (*uncorr.*)   110 it, Moth. I] ROWE (*subs.*); it, *Moth*, I QF

(*OED*, *v.*[1] 28) (b) made the odd number
even

88 **adding** making the arithmetical sum add
up to

95 *l'envoi*, **ending in the goose** Moth's point
is that *l'envoi* ends in *oie*, the French for
'goose'.

97 **sold him a bargain, a goose** i.e. made a
complete fool of him. 'To sell one a goose
for a bargain', a saying that appears to
have originated in this passage, became
proverbial (Dent B80). Compare the mod-

ern slang expression 'To sell someone a
pup'.

99 **fast and loose** See note to 1.2.149.

101 **argument** discussion

106 **ended the market** An allusion to the
proverb 'Three women and a goose make
a market' (Tilley W690).

107 **how** in what possible sense

109 **sensibly** (a) in a way that is easily
understandable (*OED*, *adv.* 3) (b) with
real feeling—the sense in which Costard
takes it

I, Costard, running out, that was safely within,
Fell over the threshold, and broke my shin.

ARMADO We will talk no more of this matter.

COSTARD Till there be more matter in the shin.

ARMADO Sirrah Costard, I will enfranchise thee.

COSTARD O, marry me to one Frances! I smell some *l'envoi*,
some goose in this.

ARMADO By my sweet soul, I mean setting thee at liberty,
enfreedoming thy person. Thou wert immured, re-   120
strained, captivated, bound.

COSTARD True, true, and now you will be my purgation
and let me loose.

ARMADO I give thee thy liberty, set thee from durance, and
in lieu thereof impose on thee nothing but this: (*he gives
Costard a letter*) bear this significant to the country maid
Jaquenetta. (*He gives him a coin.*) There is remuneration;
for the best ward of mine honour is rewarding my
dependants. Moth, follow.   *Exit*

MOTH

Like the sequel, I. Signor Costard, adieu.   *Exit*   130

COSTARD

My sweet ounce of man's flesh, my incony Jew!
Now will I look to his remuneration. 'Remuneration'!

125–6 he ... letter] COLLIER (subs.); *not in* QF   127 He ... coin] STEEVENS (subs.); *not in* QF
128 honour] Q; honours F   129 Exit] F2; *not in* QF   130 Signor] OXFORD; Signeur QF
131 ounce] Q (ouce), F

115 **matter** pus
116 **enfranchise** release
117 **Frances** This name appears, like Doll, to
have been used as a typical name for a
prostitute. The whore whom the poet
visits in Thomas Nashe's *The Choice of
Valentines* is called Francis (Nashe, iii.
406). Francis and Frances were indiffer-
ent spellings of the same name in
Shakespeare's England.
117–18 **I smell ... this** Costard suspects, or
pretends to suspect, that Armado is seeking to inveigle him into marrying a cast-
off mistress of Armado's.
122 **be my purgation** (a) clear me of the
imputation of guilt (b) quibbling on *bound*
(l. 121) which could mean 'constipated'
126 **significant** Literally something which
conveys a meaning, here a letter.
Shakespeare seems to have been the first

writer to use *significant* as a noun.
128 **ward** guard, protection
130 **sequel** that which follows in a story or a
book
131 **incony** The precise meaning of this
word, first found in Marlowe's *The Jew of
Malta* (1589–90), is not known. Combining admiration with affection, it has been
variously glossed as *darling, rare, fine,
delicate*, etc. It occurs again at 4.1.141.
Jew Almost as puzzling as the *incony* that
qualifies it, *Jew* is used as a term of
affection in *Dream* 3.1.89, where Flute,
playing Thisby, describes Pyramus as
'Most [brisky juvenal], and eke most
lovely Jew'. This led Wilson to hazard the
view, which may be right, that it is
intended as a diminutive of *Juvenal*.
Another suggestion is that it represents a
shortened version of *jewel*.

O, that's the Latin word for three farthings. Three farthings—remuneration. 'What's the price of this inkle?' 'One penny.' 'No, I'll give you a remuneration.' Why, it carries it! 'Remuneration'! Why, it is a fairer name than French crown. I will never buy and sell out of this word.

Enter Biron

BIRON O, my good knave Costard, exceedingly well met.

COSTARD Pray you, sir, how much carnation ribbon may a   140
man buy for a remuneration?

BIRON What is a remuneration?

COSTARD Marry, sir, halfpenny-farthing.

BIRON Why then, three-farthing-worth of silk.

COSTARD I thank your worship. God be wi' you.

BIRON Stay, slave. I must employ thee.

As thou wilt win my favour, good my knave,
Do one thing for me that I shall entreat.

COSTARD When would you have it done, sir?

BIRON This afternoon.   150

COSTARD Well, I will do it, sir. Fare you well.

BIRON Thou knowest not what it is.

COSTARD I shall know, sir, when I have done it.

BIRON Why, villain, thou must know first.

COSTARD I will come to your worship tomorrow morning.

134 remuneration] Q2; remuration QF   135 One penny] CAMBRIDGE; i.d. QF   136 Why,...
it! 'Remuneration'!] THEOBALD (*subs.*); Why? ... it remuneration QF   137 than French] Q;
then a French F   139 O, my] QF (O my); My CAMBRIDGE   142 What] F; O what Q
144, 146, 150, 152, 167 Why, | Stay, | This, | Thou, | And] CAMBRIDGE; O, why, | O stay, | O
this, | O thou, | O and QF

133 **three farthings** A coin of this value was issued at various dates between 1561 and 1581.
135 **inkle** a kind of tape made of linen. Along with ribbons, cambrics, and so forth, it is sold by Autolycus (*Winter's Tale* 4.4.208).
136 **it carries it** it's a winner, it takes the prize
137 **French crown** (a) the *écu*, a French gold coin (b) the bald head caused by the 'French disease', i.e. syphilis
137-8 **out of** without using
139, 142, 144, 148, 150, 156, 167 Q, followed by F except at 142, begins each of these lines with the word 'O'. The exclamation seems natural enough at

139, where Biron suddenly meets Costard whom he is looking for, but not in the other six cases. 'O' could, of course, be a kind of verbal tic, but it seems far more likely that the compositor misread the speech-prefix '*Bero.*' as '*Ber. O*'—speech-prefix plus text.
140 **carnation** flesh-coloured
145 **God be wi' you** good-bye (which derives from it)
146 **slave** rogue (in a jestingly familiar sense) (*OED*, *sb.* 1c). Compare *Titus* 4.2.119-20: 'Look how the black slave smiles upon the father, | As who should say "Old lad, I am thine own."'
154 **villain** (used in the same way as *slave* is at line 146)

BIRON

It must be done this afternoon.

Hark, slave, it is but this:

The Princess comes to hunt here in the park,

And in her train there is a gentle lady;

When tongues speak sweetly, then they name her
name,   160

And Rosaline they call her. Ask for her,

And to her white hand see thou do commend

This sealed-up counsel.

> *He gives Costard a letter*

                     There's thy guerdon; go.

> *He gives Costard a shilling*

COSTARD Gardon, O sweet gardon! Better than remuneration, eleven-pence-farthing better. Most sweet gardon! I will do it, sir, in print. Gardon! Remuneration!   *Exit*

BIRON

And I, forsooth, in love! I, that have been love's whip,

A very beadle to a humorous sigh,

A critic, nay, a night-watch constable,

A domineering pedant o'er the boy,   170

Than whom no mortal so magnificent!

This wimpled, whining, purblind, wayward boy,

This Signor Junior, giant dwarf, Dan Cupid,

163.1 *He ... letter*] *not in* QF   163.2 *He ... shilling*] JOHNSON; *not in* QF   164–6 Gardon] QF; Guerdon F2   169 critic] Q (Crietick), F   173 Signor] OXFORD; signior QF; Senior HANMER Junior] HART; *lunios* QF   Dan] Q (dan); don F

163 **counsel** private communication (*OED*, *sb.* 5b)
  guerdon reward (pronounced by Biron, Kerrigan suggests, as in French)
164 **Gardon** Another spelling of *guerdon* showing the way the word was pronounced in England.
166 **in print** perfectly, exactly to the letter. 'A man (thing, action) in print' was proverbial (Tilley M239). Compare *Two Gentlemen* 2.1.159: 'All this I speak in print, for in print I found it.'
168 **beadle** parish officer who whipped offenders, especially whores
  humorous melancholy, love-lorn
169 **critic** censurer, adverse critic (earliest *OED* example of *critic* as a noun)
170 **pedant** schoolmaster, tutor
  boy Cupid
171 **Than** as, compared with (*OED*, 5)

magnificent proud (*OED*, *adj.* 1c)
172 **wimpled** blindfolded (not used elsewhere in Shakespeare)
  purblind completely blind
173 **Signor Junior** i.e. senior junior—alluding to the idea that Eros (Cupid) was the oldest of the classical deities, since it was love that brought order out of chaos, and simultaneously the youngest of them, a mere boy
  Dan lord, sir. A variant form of *don*, which is a contracted version of the Latin *dominus*, meaning 'master', *dan* was used as a title for Cupid by Chaucer, who calls him 'daun Cupido' in *The Hous of Fame* (l. 137). Spenser refers to 'Dan *Cupid*' in *The Faerie Queene* III. xi. 46 in the course of a very full account of his power over the other gods.

Regent of love-rhymes, lord of folded arms,
Th'anointed sovereign of sighs and groans,
Liege of all loiterers and malcontents,
Dread prince of plackets, king of codpieces,
Sole imperator and great general
Of trotting paritors—O my little heart!—
And I to be a corporal of his field,   180
And wear his colours like a tumbler's hoop!
What? I love, I sue, I seek a wife?—
A woman that is like a German clock,
Still a-repairing, ever out of frame,
And never going aright, being a watch,
But being watched that it may still go right!
Nay, to be perjured, which is worst of all;
And among three to love the worst of all,
A whitely wanton with a velvet brow,

182 What? I] QF; What I? I MALONE   183 clock] F2 (Clocke); Cloake QF   189 whitely] F3;
whitly QF

174 **Regent** ruler, governor (*OED*, *sb.* 1b).
Nashe in his *Pierce Penniless* (1592) addresses Satan as 'Lord high Regent of Lymbo' in a list of mock titles which could well have been in Shakespeare's mind when he wrote lines 172 to 179 (Nashe i. 165).

177 **plackets** A *placket* could be a petticoat, a slit in a petticoat, the pocket to which that slit gave access, and so by extension a woman or the female genitalia. Compare *Tragedy of Lear* 3.4.90: 'Keep thy foot out of brothels, thy hand out of plackets'. *OED* does not cite this example from *LLL* which is, in fact, earlier than any of those it does cite.
codpieces bagged appendages to the front of the close-fitting hose or breeches worn by men from the 15th to the 17th century; often conspicuous and ornamented (*OED*). Concealing and, at the same time, displaying the male sexual organs, the *codpiece* came to be identified with them and was used as slang for 'penis'. Compare *Measure* 3.1.378–9: 'Why, what a ruthless thing is this in him, for the rebellion of a codpiece to take away the life of a man!'

178 **imperator** emperor, absolute ruler

179 **paritors** A shortened form of *apparitors*, officers who served writs summoning men to appear before the ecclesiastical courts which tried sexual offenders.

180 **corporal of his field** i.e. field officer to Cupid the *general*. *OED* defines *corporal of the field* as 'a superior officer of the army in the 16th and 17th centuries, who acted as an assistant or a kind of aide-de-camp to the sergeant-major' (*sb.* 2).

181 **his colours** i.e. the colours denoting his regiment (*OED*, *sb.* 7b).
like a tumbler's hoop flauntingly (Wilson). A *tumbler's hoop* was a hoop decorated with ribbons with which the tumbler did his tricks and which he wore across his body like a corporal's scarf (Wilson).

183–4 **A woman . . . a-repairing** Originating in this passage, this simile was taken up by one dramatist after another (Tilley W658).

183 **German clock** A German clock in Shakespeare's day was elaborately constructed, often containing automatic figures of persons or animals (*OED*, *German*, *a.*² 4), and therefore very liable to go wrong.

184 **frame** order

185 **watch** time-piece

186 **being** i.e. needing to be

189 **whitely** pale, whitish
velvet brow forehead as smooth and soft as velvet

With two pitch-balls stuck in her face for eyes;   190
Ay, and, by heaven, one that will do the deed
Though Argus were her eunuch and her guard.
And I to sigh for her, to watch for her,
To pray for her! Go to! It is a plague
That Cupid will impose for my neglect
Of his almighty dreadful little might.
Well, I will love, write, sigh, pray, sue, and groan.
Some men must love my lady, and some Joan.   *Exit*

4.1   *Enter the Princess, Maria, Katherine, Rosaline, Boyet,*
       two more Lords, and a Forester

PRINCESS

Was that the King that spurred his horse so hard
Against the steep-up rising of the hill?

⌈BOYET⌉

I know not, but I think it was not he.

PRINCESS

Whoe'er a was, a showed a mounting mind.
Well, lords, today we shall have our dispatch.
On Saturday we will return to France.
Then, forester, my friend, where is the bush
That we must stand and play the murderer in?

FORESTER

Hereby, upon the edge of yonder coppice,
A stand where you may make the fairest shoot.   10

197 sue, and groan] F2; shue, grone QF   198 *Exit*] ROWE; *not in* QF
4.1.0.1–2 *Enter . . . Forester*] ROWE (*subs.*); *Enter the Princesse, a Forrester, her Ladyes, and her*
Lordes. QF   1 (*and throughout the scene*) PRINCESS] F2; *Quee⟨n⟩.* QF   2 steep-up rising]
HART; steepe vp rising Q; steepe vprising F   3 BOYET] F (*Boy.*); *Forr⟨ester⟩.* Q   6 On] F;
Ore Q; Ere OXFORD

190 **pitch-balls** 'As black as pitch' was and is
     proverbial (Tilley P357).
191 **do the deed** engage in sexual inter-
     course
192 **Argus** A monster with a hundred eyes,
     all of which he never closed at the same
     time, Argus was set by Juno to keep
     watch over Io and ensure that Jupiter did
     not make love to her. Jupiter, however,
     employed Mercury to kill Argus, who
     was then transformed into a peacock.
     eunuch bedchamber attendant in a
     harem, who, to be 'safe', had to be
     castrated (Partridge).
193 **watch** stay awake all night

198 **Joan** 'Joan is as good as my lady in the
     dark' was proverbial (Tilley J57). In
     Shakespeare's day *Joan* was regarded as a
     lower-class name.
4.1.2 **steep-up** abrupt, precipitous. Compare
     Sonnets 7.5: 'And having climbed the
     steep-up heavenly hill'.
  4 **mounting mind** (a) readiness to climb (b)
     aspiring mind
  5 **dispatch** i.e. official dismissal or leave to
     go, given to an ambassador after comple-
     tion of his errand (*OED*, *sb*. 2)
 10 **stand** standing place or station from
     which the archer could shoot deer
     fairest most favourable, best. The Prin-

PRINCESS

I thank my beauty, I am fair that shoot,

And thereupon thou speak'st 'the fairest shoot'.

FORESTER

Pardon me, madam, for I meant not so.

PRINCESS

What, what? First praise me, and again say no?

O short-lived pride! Not fair? Alack for woe!

FORESTER

Yes, madam, fair.

PRINCESS   Nay, never paint me now.

Where fair is not, praise cannot mend the brow.

Here, good my glass, take this for telling true;

She gives him some money

Fair payment for foul words is more than due.

FORESTER

Nothing but fair is that which you inherit.   20

PRINCESS

See, see, my beauty will be saved by merit!

O heresy in fair, fit for these days!

A giving hand, though foul, shall have fair praise.

But come, the bow. Now mercy goes to kill,

And shooting well is then accounted ill.

Thus will I save my credit in the shoot:

Not wounding, pity would not let me do't;

If wounding, then it was to show my skill,

That more for praise than purpose meant to kill.

And out of question so it is sometimes,   30

Glory grows guilty of detested crimes,

14 and again] Q; & then again F   18.1 *She ... money*] JOHNSON; *not in* QF   27 do't] Q
(doote), F

cess deliberately takes it in the sense of
'most beautiful'.

16 **paint** flatter (*OED, v.*¹ 6b)

17 **fair** beauty. Compare *Errors* 2.1.97–8:
'My decayèd fair | A sunny look of his
would soon repair.'

18 **good my glass** my reliable mirror

20 **you inherit** you own, is naturally yours

21 **by merit** (a) by its own intrinsic worth (b)
because I give rewards (c) by good works,
the way to salvation for Roman Catholics
but not for Protestants, who held that

only faith could save the soul and that
justification by works was *heresy*

22 **in fair** i.e. where beauty is concerned

23 **A giving ... praise** Referring perhaps to
the proverb 'The giving hand is fair'
(Dent H68.1).

31 **Glory** the disposition to gain honour for
oneself (*OED, sb.* 1)
detested detestable, abominable. On
Shakespeare's tendency to use the ending
-ed where modern English would use *-able*
see Abbott 375.

When, for fame's sake, for praise, an outward part,
We bend to that the working of the heart;
As I for praise alone now seek to spill
The poor deer's blood, that my heart means no ill.

BOYET

Do not curst wives hold that self sovereignty
Only for praise' sake when they strive to be
Lords o'er their lords?

PRINCESS

Only for praise—and praise we may afford
To any lady that subdues a lord.   40

        Enter Costard

BOYET Here comes a member of the commonwealth.

COSTARD God dig-you-den all! Pray you, which is the head
lady?

PRINCESS Thou shalt know her, fellow, by the rest that
have no heads.

COSTARD Which is the greatest lady, the highest?

PRINCESS The thickest and the tallest.

COSTARD

The thickest and the tallest. It is so; truth is truth.
An your waist, mistress, were as slender as my wit,
One o' these maids' girdles for your waist should be fit.   50
Are not you the chief woman? You are the thickest
        here.

PRINCESS What's your will, sir? What's your will?

COSTARD

I have a letter from Monsieur Biron to one Lady
        Rosaline.

40.1 *Enter Costard*] ROWE; *Enter Clowne.* QF   42 (*and throughout the scene*) COSTARD]
ROWE; *Clo⟨wne⟩.* QF   49 mistress] Q (Mistrs), F   50 fit] Q (*corr.*), F; fir Q (*uncorr.*)
51 here.] Q; ∼ ? F

---

36 **curst** shrewish
   self same
41 **member of the commonwealth** 'Here, I
   believe, is a kind of jest intended; a
   member of the *common*-wealth is put for
   one of the *common* people, one of the
   meanest' (Johnson). Shakespeare uses
   this expression again at 4.2.75 and in
   Merchant 3.5.31–4: 'he says you are no

good member of the commonwealth, for
in converting Jews to Christians you raise
the price of pork'. For other examples of
the phrase see Dent M868.1.
42 **God dig-you-den** An abbreviated colloquial form of 'God give you good even', a
   greeting used at any time of the day after
   noon.
48 **truth is truth** proverbial (Tilley T581)

PRINCESS

O, thy letter, thy letter! He's a good friend of mine.
She takes the letter
Stand aside, good bearer. Boyet, you can carve.
Break up this capon.

BOYET   I am bound to serve.
He looks at the letter
This letter is mistook; it importeth none here.
It is writ to Jaquenetta.

PRINCESS   We will read it, I swear.
Break the neck of the wax, and everyone give ear.

BOYET (*reads*) 'By heaven, that thou art fair is most   60
infallible; true that thou art beauteous; truth itself that
thou art lovely. More fairer than fair, beautiful than
beauteous, truer than truth itself, have commiseration
on thy heroical vassal. The magnanimous and most
illustrate King Cophetua set eye upon the penurious and
indubitate beggar Zenelophon, and he it was that might
rightly say, "*Veni, vidi, vici*", which to annothanize in

54.1 *She … letter*] *not in* QF   55 Boyet,] F; ∼ ∧ Q   56.1 *He … letter*] *not in* QF   60 BOYET
(*reads*) Q (*Boyet reedes.*), F (*reades*)   62 beautiful] QF; more beautiful TYRWHITT   65 set] Q
(*corr.*), F; sets Q (*uncorr.*); set's OXFORD   penurious] WILSON; pernicious QF   66 was] Q
(*corr.*), F; is was Q (*uncorr.*)   67 annothanize] QF; anatomize F2

56 **Break up** A technical term in carving
meaning 'cut open', 'cut up'.
capon (a) fowl (b) love-letter (*OED*, *sb.* 4).
Compare the French *poulet* signifying
both *fowl* and *billet-doux*.
57 **is mistook** i.e. has been delivered to the
wrong person
importeth concerns (*OED*, *v.* 7)
59 **Break … wax** 'Still alluding to the "capon"' (Johnson).
65 **illustrate** illustrious
King Cophetua … Zenelophon See
1.2.104–5 and note.
penurious The justification for this emendation is that 'pernicious', the reading of
both Q and F, makes no sense in this
context. The beggarmaid of the ballad is
neither 'wicked' nor 'destructive', nor,
for that matter, is Jaquenetta. The beggarmaid is, however, 'indubitably penurious', 'penurious and indubitate' being a
typically Shakespearian hendiadys. *Penurious*, especially if spelled *pennurious*,
could easily be read as *pernicious*.
67 *Veni, vidi, vici* The original source of

these famous words is Plutarch, who
writes (in North's translation): 'Caesar
… fought a great battle with King Phar-
naces by the city of Zela, where he slew
his army, and drove him out of all the
realm of Ponte. And because he would
advertise [inform] one of his friends of the
suddenness of this victory he only wrote
three words unto Anitius at Rome: *Veni,
Vidi, Vici*: to wit, I came, I saw, I overcame. These three words, ending all with
the like sound and letters in the Latin,
have a certain short grace, more pleasant
to the ear than can be well expressed in
any other tongue' (Bullough, v. 75).
annothanize give an analytical explanation (of those words). This gloss rests on
the assumption that 'annothanize',
found in both Q and F, is a Shakespearian
coinage combining the senses of *anatomize* (often spelled 'anathomize' in the 16th
century, and meaning 'analyse') and
annote (meaning 'provide with explanatory notes') in one word.

the vulgar—O base and obscure vulgar!—*videlicet*: he
came, see, and overcame. He came, one; see, two;
overcame, three. Who came? The King. Why did he   70
come? To see. Why did he see? To overcome. To whom
came he? To the beggar. What saw he? The beggar.
Who overcame he? The beggar. The conclusion is
victory. On whose side? The King's. The captive is
enriched. On whose side? The beggar's. The catastrophe
is a nuptial. On whose side? The King's. No, on both in
one, or one in both. I am the King, for so stands the
comparison; thou the beggar, for so witnesseth thy
lowliness. Shall I command thy love? I may. Shall I
enforce thy love? I could. Shall I entreat thy love? I will.   80
What shalt thou exchange for rags? Robes. For tittles?
Titles. For thyself? Me. Thus, expecting thy reply, I
profane my lips on thy foot, my eyes on thy picture, and
my heart on thy every part.
          Thine in the dearest design of industry,
                              Don Adriano de Armado.
Thus dost thou hear the Nemean lion roar
'Gainst thee, thou lamb, that standest as his prey.

---

69 see] QF (See); Saw F2   see, two] QF; saw, two ROWE   70 overcame] F3; couercame
QF, F2   74 King's] Q2 (Kinges); King QF   81 What ∧] F4; ~ , QF   83 picture] Q (corr.),
F; pictture Q (uncorr.)   86 Adriano] Q2; Adriana QF   Armado] F2; Armatho QF

<table>
<tr><td>

68 **vulgar** vernacular
   obscure humble, of lowly origin
69 **see ... see** saw ... saw. Armado is using
an archaic form, still acceptable in Eliza-
bethan English, of the past tense of the
verb 'to see'. Compare *2 Henry IV*
3.2.28–30, where Shallow says of Fal-
staff in his youth: 'I see him break
Scoggin's head at the court gate when a
was a crack, not thus high.' Shakespeare
employs the more familiar translation of
the Latin, 'I came, saw, and overcame',
which had become proverbial (Tilley
C540), on the other occasions when he
has recourse to it—*2 Henry IV* 4.2.41, *As
You Like It* 5.2.30–1, and *Cymbeline*
3.1.24.
75 **catastrophe** dénouement
81 **exchange** receive in exchange (*OED, v.*
1c)
   tittles the merest nothings. *Tittle* was 'a
name for the (usually) three dots follow-

</td><td>

ing the letters and contractions, in the
alphabet or horn-book' (*OED, sb.* 1c).
82 **expecting** awaiting
82–3 **I profane ... foot** These words come
close to being a parody of *Romeo* 1.5.92–
5: 'If I profane with my unworthiest hand |
This holy shrine, the gentler sin is this: |
My lips, two blushing pilgrims, ready
stand | To smooth that rough touch with
a tender kiss.'
   thy picture i.e. my mental image of you
85 **in ... industry** i.e. with the most heartfelt
determination to be a model of amorous
gallantry—Armado's version of 'most
sincerely'
87–90 **Thus ... play** A prolix and bombastic
rendering of the proverb 'The lion spares
the suppliant' (Tilley L316).
87 **the Nemean lion** The killing of the Ne-
mean lion, referred to again at *Hamlet*
1.4.60, was the first of the twelve labours
of Hercules.

</td></tr>
</table>

Submissive fall his princely feet before,
    And he from forage will incline to play.   90
But if thou strive, poor soul, what art thou then?
Food for his rage, repasture for his den.'
PRINCESS
What plume of feathers is he that indited this letter?
What vane? What weathercock? Did you ever hear
        better?
BOYET
I am much deceived but I remember the style.
PRINCESS
Else your memory is bad, going o'er it erewhile.
BOYET
This Armado is a Spaniard that keeps here in court,
A phantasime, a Monarcho, and one that makes sport
To the Prince and his book-mates.
PRINCESS *(to Costard)*   Thou, fellow, a word.
    Who gave thee this letter?
COSTARD   I told you: my lord.   100
PRINCESS
    To whom shouldst thou give it?
COSTARD   From my lord to my lady.
PRINCESS
    From which lord to which lady?
COSTARD
From my Lord Biron, a good master of mine,
To a lady of France that he called Rosaline.

100 you: my] THEOBALD (*subs.*); you, my QF

90 **from forage … play** will abandon his
   destructive raging in favour of acting
   playfully
92 **repasture** food (that which provides a
   repast). Apparently a coinage of
   Shakespeare's, this word is not found
   elsewhere in his writings.
93 **plume of feathers** ostentatious fool (*OED*,
   feather, sb. 8b)
94 **vane** constantly changing person, giddy-
   minded man (*OED*, 1b)
95 **but I** if I do not (Abbott 126)
96 **going o'er** since you read, since you
   climbed over (with the same quibble on
   stile as at 1.1.97)

96 **erewhile** recently, such a short time ago
97 **keeps** lodges, lives
98 **phantasime** fantastic being, creature full
   of fantasies. Presumably the same word
   as the *phantasimes* of 5.1.18, this coinage
   is to be found in these two places only.
   Monarcho The title assumed by an in-
   sane Italian who hung about Elizabeth's
   court and imagined himself to be emperor
   of the world; hence applied to one who is
   the object of ridicule for his absurd pretensions.
99 To for. Compare *Henry V* 4.3.35: 'he
   which hath no stomach to this fight'.

PRINCESS

Thou hast mistaken his letter. Come, lords, away.

(To Rosaline) Here, sweet, put up this; 'twill be thine
    another day.

        Exeunt all but Boyet, Rosaline, Maria, and Costard

BOYET

Who is the shooter? Who is the shooter?

ROSALINE　　　　　　　　　　Shall I teach you to know?

BOYET

Ay, my continent of beauty.

ROSALINE　　　　　　　　　　Why, she that bears the bow.

Finely put off!

BOYET

My lady goes to kill horns, but if thou marry,　　　　　　110

Hang me by the neck if horns that year miscarry.

Finely put on!

ROSALINE

Well then, I am the shooter.

BOYET　　　　　　　　　　And who is your deer?

ROSALINE

If we choose by the horns, yourself come not near.

Finely put on indeed!

MARIA

You still wrangle with her, Boyet, and she strikes at
    the brow.

BOYET

But she herself is hit lower. Have I hit her now?

---

106 *Exeunt ... Costard*] WILSON; *Exeunt* F; *not in* Q　　107 shooter] QF; suitor JOHNSON and
STEEVENS 1785 *(conj.* Farmer)

105 **mistaken his letter** taken his letter to the
    wrong person
106 **put up** put away, keep
    'twill be thine another day your turn will
    come one day. 'Let him mend his man-
    ners, it will be his own another day' was
    proverbial (Tilley M628).
107 **shooter ... shooter** It seems right to
    preserve this spelling, common to Q and
    F, because it establishes the quibble *shoot-*
    er / suitor, both pronounced *shooter,* on
    which the ensuing dialogue rests.
    Furthermore, this dialogue is a kind of
    shooting match in which the participants
    try to score points against one another.
108 **continent** container, treasury

109 **put off** evaded, turned aside (*OED, v.*[1]
    45g)
110 **horns** horned creatures, deer
111 **horns that year miscarry** there is a
    shortage of cuckolds that year
112 **put on** applied, laid on
113 **deer** punning on *dear*
114 **by the horns** according to the finest
    spread of cuckold's horns
116 **strikes at the brow** (a) takes good aim
    (b) accuses you of being a cuckold
117 **hit lower** i.e. wounded in a lower part of
    the body. Boyet is talking 'greasily'; the
    sexual innuendo is obvious.
    hit her hit upon her meaning

ROSALINE Shall I come upon thee with an old saying, that
  was a man when King Pépin of France was a little boy,
  as touching the hit it?   120

BOYET So I may answer thee with one as old, that was a
  woman when Queen Guinevere of Britain was a little
  wench, as touching the hit it.

ROSALINE (*sings*)
  Thou canst not hit it, hit it, hit it,
    Thou canst not hit it, my good man.

BOYET (*sings*)
  An I cannot, cannot, cannot,
    An I cannot, another can.   *Exit Rosaline*

COSTARD
  By my troth, most pleasant! How both did fit it!

MARIA
  A mark marvellous well shot, for they both did hit it.

BOYET
  A mark! O, mark but that mark! A mark, says my
    lady.   130
  Let the mark have a prick in't, to mete at, if it may be.

MARIA
  Wide o' the bow hand. I'faith, your hand is out.

COSTARD
  Indeed, a must shoot nearer, or he'll ne'er hit the
    clout.

119 France] Q (Frannce), F   120 touching] Q (touchiug), F   126 An I] Q (And I); I F
127 *Exit Rosaline*] ROWE; *Exit* (*after l. 125*) Q; *after l. 127* F   129 did hit it] F4; did hit Q
(*corr.*), F; hid hit Q (*uncorr.*)   132 o'] Q (*corr.*), F (a'); a Q (*uncorr.*)   133 a] Q (*corr.*), F (a');
a Q (*uncorr.*)

118 **come upon thee** advance against thee,
  i.e. retort
119 **King Pépin** The father of Charlemagne,
  he died in 768. Shakespeare seems to
  have regarded him as the emblem of
  bygone days; see *All's Well* 2.1.75 and
  All is True 1.3.10.
120 **the hit it** A popular song and dance. See
  Appendix C.
122 **Queen Guinevere** King Arthur's queen,
  supposed to have lived long before Pépin,
  was notorious for her infidelity.
126–7 **An … can** proverbial in the form 'If
  one will not another will' (Tilley O62)
128 **did fit it** were in perfect harmony. For
  the superfluous 'it' see Abbott 226.
129 **mark** target

129 **well shot** most accurately hit. Costard's
  use of this exclamation antedates *OED*,
  shoot, *v.* 22c by about forty-five years.
130 **mark but** only note
131 **mark** (a) target (b) female genitals
  prick (a) bull's eye (b) penis
  mete aim (*OED*, *v.*[1] 2b)
132 **Wide o' the bow hand** wide of the mark.
  This expression, which became proverbial (Tilley B567), seems to have originated here, or at least have been first
  recorded here.
  out (a) inaccurate (b) out of practice
133 **clout** 'The target was fixed by a pin or
  clout (French *clou*), the head of which
  was painted white and marked the
  centre' (David).

BOYET

An if my hand be out, then belike your hand is in.

COSTARD

Then will she get the upshoot by cleaving the pin.

MARIA

Come, come, you talk greasily, your lips grow foul.

COSTARD

She's too hard for you at pricks, sir. Challenge her to
    bowl.

BOYET

I fear too much rubbing. Good night, my good owl.

Exeunt Boyet and Maria

COSTARD

By my soul, a swain, a most simple clown!
Lord, Lord, how the ladies and I have put him down!   140
O' my troth, most sweet jests, most incony vulgar wit,
When it comes so smoothly off, so obscenely, as it
    were, so fit.
Armado o'th' t'other side—O a most dainty man!
To see him walk before a lady, and to bear her fan!
To see him kiss his hand, and how most sweetly a will
    swear!

---

135 pin] F2; is in QF   138 *Exeunt . . . Maria*] THEOBALD (*subs.*); *not in* QF   143 Armado o'th'
t'other] KEIGHTLEY (o'th't'other); *Armatho* ath toothen Q; *Armathor* ath to the F; to th'one
WILSON

134 **An . . . in** i.e. if I'm out of practice where
sex is concerned, then it's all too likely
you are not

135 **upshoot** (a) best shot of the match (b)
ejaculation
    cleaving the pin splitting the *pin* in the
centre of the target—proverbial (Tilley
P336). Compare *Romeo* 2.3.14–15: 'the
very pin of his heart cleft with the blind
bow-boy's butt-shaft'.

136 **greasily** smuttily, indecently. The earliest citation in *OED*, not used elsewhere in
Shakespeare.

137 **pricks** archery (with the inevitable
quibble)
    bowl play at bowls (pronounced like 'owl'
and 'foul')

138 **rubbing** In the game of bowls the bowl is
said to 'rub' when it meets some impedi-
ment which retards or diverts its course
(*OED, rub, v.*[1] 14b), in this case Maria's
sharp tongue. Partridge gives the word

the bawdy sense of 'a fricative sexual
caress'.
    owl Schmidt regards this as 'a term of
contempt', but 'term of condescending
raillery' would seem nearer the mark.

141 **incony** See note to 3.1.1.131.

142 **obscenely** It is not clear what word
Costard has in mind, any more than it is
clear what Bottom is thinking of when he
says: 'there we may rehearse most obscenely and courageously' (*Dream*
1.2.100–1); but *obscene* is certainly the
right word for the preceding passage.

143 **o'th' t'other side** on the other hand
(*OED, side, sb.*[1] 17b). Q reads 'ath toothen
side'; F 'ath to the side'. Costard is
contrasting Armado, very much to the
Spaniard's advantage, with Boyet. See
Wells, *Re-Editing*, pp. 54–5.
    dainty man man of most elegant man-
ners

And his page o' t'other side, that handful of wit!
Ah, heavens, it is a most pathetical nit!
   Shout within
Sola, sola!   *Exit*

4.2   *Enter Dull, Holofernes, and Nathaniel*

NATHANIEL Very reverend sport, truly, and done in the
   testimony of a good conscience.

HOLOFERNES The deer was, as you know, in blood, *sanguis*,
   ripe as the pomewater, who now hangeth like a jewel in
   the ear of *caelum*, the sky, the welkin, the heaven, and
   anon falleth like a crab on the face of *terra*, the soil, the
   land, the earth.

146 o' t'other] ROWE 1714; atother QF   147 a] F2; *not in* QF   147.1 *Shout within*] F2
(Showt within); Shoot within Q (*in roman and after l. 148*); Shoote within F (*in roman and on
separate line*); *arranged as here* CAPELL   148 *Exit*] CAPELL; *Exeunt* QF (*before 'Shoot within'*)

   4.2.0.1 *Enter ... Nathaniel*] ROWE; Enter *Dull, Holofernes, the Pedant and Nathaniel* Q, F
(*subs.*)   1–62 NATHANIEL] QF (*Nat⟨haniel⟩., with 'Curat. Nath.' at l. 8*)   3 HOLOFERNES]
ROWE; *Ped⟨ant⟩.* QF   in blood, *sanguis*] This edition; sanguis in blood QF; *sanguis*—in blood
OXFORD   4 the] Q; a F   5 *caelum*] DYCE; *Celo* QF

147 **pathetical nit** appealing little thing. A
  nit could be a gnat, or small fly (*OED, sb.*
  1b).

147.1 *Shout within* Q reads 'Shoot within'
  and F 'Shoote within'. Both treat the
  words as part of the text, and place them
  after the stage direction '*Exeunt.*', which
  follows Costard's 'Sola, sola!' This exclamation, found again at *Merchant* 5.1.39,
  appears to be a hunting cry; and, since it
  needs something to provoke it, it seems
  reasonable to read 'Shoot' as 'Shout' of
  which it was a variant spelling. The
  twang of a bow-string *within* would not,
  one imagines, be heard in the auditorium
  of an Elizabethan theatre.

4.2.0.1 *Holofernes* Shakespeare could have
  taken this name from Rabelais who gives
  it to Gargantua's tutor (I. xiv), but it
  seems far more likely that he was thinking of the biblical Holofernes, the tyrant
  slaughtered by Judith in the apocryphal
  Book of Judith. Interludes dealing with
  his fate were performed in 1556 and
  1564 (Schoenbaum, 34 and 38), and
  probably on many other occasions.

1 **reverend** worthy of respect (on account
  of the rank of those engaged in it)

1–2 **in the testimony** with the warrant.
  Nathaniel alludes to 2 Corinthians 1:12:
  'For our rejoicing is this, the testimony of
  our conscience'.

3 **in blood** in prime condition. Compare *1
  Henry VI* 4.2.48–50: 'If we be English
  deer, be then in blood, | Not rascal-like to
  fall down with a pinch, | But rather,
  moody-mad and desperate stags'.
  in blood, *sanguis* Q and F read 'sanguis in
  blood', which is meaningless. The emendation made here rests on the fact that
  the Q compositors were prone to transpose words as well as letters (see Introduction, pp. 74–5). Holofernes, it is true,
  usually gives the Latin first and then the
  English, but not invariably. See line 22:
  'Twice-sod simplicity, *bis coctus*!'

4 **pomewater** A large juicy kind of apple no
  longer cultivated.

4–5 **hangeth ... caelum** Compare *Romeo*
  1.5.44–5: 'It seems she hangs upon the
  cheek of night | As a rich jewel in an
  Ethiope's ear'.

5 *caelum* For Kerrigan's justification of
  caelum as the correct reading—the word
  appears as '*Celo*' in Q and F—see Introduction, p. 75. Subsequent emendations
  of errors in Holofernes' Latin are based on
  the assumption (see pp. 74–5) that those
  errors are far more likely to be compositorial than the result of ignorance on their
  speaker's part.

6 **anon** a moment later
  crab crab-apple

NATHANIEL Truly, Master Holofernes, the epithets are
sweetly varied, like a scholar at the least. But, sir, I
assure ye it was a buck of the first head.   10

HOLOFERNES Sir Nathaniel, *haud credo*.

DULL 'Twas not a 'auld grey doe', 'twas a pricket.

HOLOFERNES Most barbarous intimation! Yet a kind of
insinuation, as it were, *in via*, in way, of explication,
facere, as it were, replication, or rather *ostentare*, to
show, as it were, his inclination, after his undressed,
unpolished, uneducated, unpruned, untrained, or
rather unlettered, or ratherest unconfirmed fashion, to
insert again my *haud credo* for a deer.

DULL I said the deer was not a 'auld grey doe', 'twas a   20
pricket.

HOLOFERNES Twice-sod simplicity, *bis coctus*!
O thou monster Ignorance, how deformed dost thou
look!

NATHANIEL
Sir, he hath never fed of the dainties that are bred in a
book.

8 epithets] POPE; epythithes QF   11–54 HOLOFERNES] QF (Holo⟨fernes⟩.)   12, 20 a 'auld
grey doe'] OXFORD (*conj.* Rowse); an awd grey doe KERRIGAN; a *haud credo* QF   14 explication,
facere] THEOBALD (*subs.*); explication ∧ *facere* QF   22 *bis coctus*] F; bis coctus Q

9 **at the least** i.e. to go no further

10 **of the first head** in its fifth year (the age at
which a buck grows its first full set of
antlers)

11 **haud credo** I don't believe it, you are
quite wrong

12, 20 **'auld grey doe'** This is Oxford's and,
substantially, Kerrigan's emendation of
the '*haud credo*' found in Q and F. Originally proposed by A. L. Rowse in 1952,
and strongly supported by Stanley Wells
(*Re-Editing*, p. 53), it is adopted here
because it has the virtues of making sense
and raising a laugh. It also has to be said,
however, that it is out of line with what
appears to be Shakespeare's usual practice when making fun of misapprehen-
sions of foreign words and phrases,
which is to spell them out himself rather
than leave that task to the actor or
reader. For instance, when Titus asks the
Clown 'What says Jupiter?', the Clown
replies 'Ho, the gibbet-maker?' (*Titus
Andronicus* 4.3.79–80). Even more to the
point is Parson Evans's examination of
William in *Merry Wives* 4.1.23–6. Asked

by Evans 'What is "fair", William?', the
boy answers '*Pulcher*', whereupon Mistress Quickly interjects 'Polecats? There
are fairer things than polecats, sure.'

12 **pricket** buck in its second year

13 **intimation** intrusive suggestion—not
elsewhere in Shakespeare

14 **insinuation** subtle introduction
explication explanation—not elsewhere
in Shakespeare

15 *facere* Latin for 'to make'
replication reply

16 **after** according to, in keeping with
undressed shapeless

18 **unconfirmed** uninstructed, ignorant
(*OED*, 2b). Compare *Much Ado* 3.3.112–
13: 'I wonder at it.—That shows thou
art unconfirmed.' These are the only instances of 'unconfirmed' in this sense cited
by *OED*.

19 **insert again** intrusively substitute

22 **Twice-sod simplicity** i.e. stupidity upon
stupidity. 'Twice-sod' meant 'twice
boiled' (*bis coctus* in Latin). 'Cabbage
twice sodden' was proverbial (Tilley
C511).

He hath not eat paper, as it were, he hath not drunk
    ink.
His intellect is not replenished. He is only an animal,
    only sensible in the duller parts.
And such barren plants are set before us that we
    thankful should be—
Which we of taste and feeling are—for those parts that
    do fructify in us more than he.
For as it would ill become me to be vain, indiscreet, or
    a fool,
So were there a patch set on learning, to see him in a
    school. 30
But *omne bene*, say I, being of an old father's mind:
Many can brook the weather that love not the wind.

DULL
You two are book-men; can you tell me by your wit
What was a month old at Cain's birth that's not five
    weeks old as yet?

HOLOFERNES *Dictynna*, Goodman Dull. *Dictynna*, Goodman
  Dull.

DULL What is *Dictima*?

NATHANIEL A title to Phoebe, to *Luna*, to the moon.

28 of] TYRWHITT; *not in* QF   29 indiscreet] Q (indistreell), F   33 me] Q; *not in* F
35 *Dictynna* ... *Dictynna*] ROWE; *Dictisima* ... *dictisima* QF   37 *Dictima*] QF (*dictima*);
Dictinna F2

25 **eat** eaten
26 **replenished** i.e. properly furnished with
the things it needs to make it complete
(*OED*, *replenish*, *v.* 1b). Compare *Richard
III* 4.3.18–19, where the Princes in the
Tower are referred to as 'The most replen-
ishèd sweet work of nature, | That from
the prime creation e'er she framed.'
sensible capable of feeling, sensitive
28 **Which** as (*OED*, 10 and Abbott 272)
fructify bear fruit—not elsewhere in
Shakespeare
he him (Abbott 206)
30 **So ... learning** (a) it would be putting a
fool to his lessons (b) a disgrace to the
cause of learning. It is not clear which of
these two senses Nathaniel has in mind.
patch As well as having its normal sense,
patch could denote a fool because domestic fools wore patched or parti-coloured
clothes.

31 *omne bene* all's well
being ... mind i.e. holding the same
opinion as a wise old man long ago
32 **Many ... wind** i.e. 'What can't be cured
must be endured'. This line in *LLL* seems
to have become proverbial in the form of
'There is no weather ill when the wind is
still' (Tilley W220).
35 *Dictynna* goddess of the moon (as Nathaniel explains). This name for Diana is
not very common in Latin; but Holofernes' preference for the rare word is not
confined to the English words he uses.
Goodman title used when addressing
someone under the rank of gentleman
(*OED*, 3b). Compare *Much Ado* 3.5.9:
'Goodman Verges'.
37 *Dictima* The Q spelling is retained here
because the mistake could well be Dull's
rather than the compositor's.

HOLOFERNES

   The moon was a month old when Adam was no more,
   And raught not to five weeks when he came to
        fivescore.   40
   Th'allusion holds in the exchange.

DULL 'Tis true, indeed; the collusion holds in the exchange.

HOLOFERNES God comfort thy capacity! I say th'allusion
   holds in the exchange.

DULL And I say the pollution holds in the exchange, for
   the moon is never but a month old. And I say beside
   that 'twas a pricket that the Princess killed.

HOLOFERNES Sir Nathaniel, will you hear an extemporal
   epitaph on the death of the deer? And, to humour the   50
   ignorant, call I the deer the Princess killed a pricket.

NATHANIEL *Perge*, good Master Holofernes, *perge*, so it
   shall please you to abrogate scurrility.

HOLOFERNES I will something affect the letter, for it argues
   facility.

   The preyful Princess pierced and pricked a pretty
        pleasing pricket;
      Some say a sore, but not a sore till now made sore
        with shooting.

---

40 raught] HANMER (*after* Q; rought); wrought F   48 'twas] Q (*corr.*), F; was Q (*un-corr.*)   49 HOLOFERNES Sir] Q ('*Holo.* Sir' *text*); Sir Q (*c.w.*)   51 ignorant] Q (ignorault), F
call I] CAMBRIDGE; cald Q; call'd F; I have called ROWE   deer ∧] ROWE; ~ : Q; ~ , F
53 scurrility] F (scurilitie); squirilitie Q

40 **raught** reached
41 **Th'allusion ... exchange** i.e. 'the riddle is
   as good when I use the name of Adam, as
   when you use the name of Cain' (Warburton).
   allusion word-play, pun, jest (*OED*, 2)
42 **collusion** trick or ambiguity in words or
   reasoning. Dull has, for once, the right
   word. He recognizes that the two learned
   men are trying to make a fool of him.
44 **comfort** help (*OED*, *v.* 6)
   capacity ability to comprehend
46 **pollution** (a) mistakenly for *allusion* (b)
   your perversion of what I said
52 *Perge* carry on (disyllabic)
53 **abrogate** avoid, have nothing to do with.
   Nathaniel seems to fear that Holofernes
   may exploit the bawdy possibilities of
   pricket.

54 **something affect the letter** i.e. make some
   use of alliteration
54–5 **argues facility** shows an easy command (of the language)
56 **preyful** i.e. bent on hunting. The suffix
   -ful carries here the sense of 'apt to',
   'accustomed to' (*OED*, 1) rather than 'full
   of'. Defined by *OED* as meaning 'killing
   much prey or quarry; prone to prey',
   which does not fit this context, *preyful*
   appears to have originated here and
   never 'caught on'. *OED* has but one other
   citation, and that from George Chapman,
   writing in 1624.
57 **Some say a sore** i.e. some say the deer was
   a *sore* (namely a buck in its fourth year)
   but ... shooting but it was not a *sore* until
   being shot made it sore

The dogs did yell; put 'L' to sore, then sorel jumps
    from thicket,
  Or pricket sore, or else sorel; the people fall a-
    hooting.
If sore be sore, then 'L' to sore makes fifty sores o'
    sorel: 60

Of one sore I an hundred make by adding but one more
    'L'.

NATHANIEL A rare talent!

DULL If a talent be a claw, look how he claws him with a
talent.

HOLOFERNES This is a gift that I have, simple, simple, a
foolish extravagant spirit, full of forms, figures, shapes,
objects, ideas, apprehensions, motions, revolutions.
These are begot in the ventricle of memory, nourished
in the womb of *pia mater*, and delivered upon the
mellowing of occasion. But the gift is good in those in   70
whom it is acute, and I am thankful for it.

NATHANIEL Sir, I praise the Lord for you, and so may my
parishioners, for their sons are well tutored by you, and

65–102 HOLOFERNES] ROWE 1714; *Nath.* QF   69 *pia mater*] ROWE; primater QF   70–1 in
whom] F; whom Q   72–144 NATHANIEL] ROWE 1714; *Hol⟨ofernes⟩*. QF

58 **yell; put 'L' to sore, then sorel** The word
yell and the letter *L* are sufficiently alike
in pronunciation to allow the one to be
interpreted as the other; and the addition
of *L* to *sore* gives *sorel*, the name for a buck
in its third year.

59 **Or ... sorel** i.e. no matter whether it is a
wounded pricket or a sorel

60 **If sore be sore** if the deer is hurt
fifty sores (because *L* is the Roman
numeral for *fifty*)

61 **Of ... 'L'**. The line is a fitting ending for
Holofernes' laborious exercise in what
John Cleveland might have called 'vena-
tious arithmetic'.
more 'L' perhaps quibbling on 'moral'

63 **If a talent be a claw** In Shakespeare's day
a *talent* often was a *claw*, since *talent* was
a common spelling of *talon*. In fact, *talon*
appears as *talent* not only here but also in
the earliest quartos of the other four plays
in which it is used: *1 Henry IV* (2.5.333);
The First Part of the Contention (3.2.196);
Richard Duke of York (1.4.42); and *Pericles* (17.49).
claws him (a) scratches his back (in an

ingratiating manner) (b) flatters him,
curries favour with him

65 **HOLOFERNES** Both Q and F attribute this
speech to 'Nath.', thus beginning a confusion of names that continues to line 144.
See Introduction pp. 63–4.

65–70 **This ... occasion** This speech comes
remarkably close to being an anticipation
of Falstaff's praise of sack (*2 Henry IV*
4.2.93–121).

67 **motions** impulses (*OED*, *sb.* 9)
revolutions reflections (*OED*, *sb.* 5b)

68 **ventricle** belly (*OED*, 3c) used figura-
tively. *Ventricles* are divisions of the
brain; and the *memory* was thought to be
seated in the hindmost of them.

69 **pia mater** the membrane surrounding
the brain. *OED* quotes Thomas Vicary's
Anatomy (1548) to the following effect:
'It is called Piamater ... for because it is so
soft and tender over the brain that it
nourisheth the brain and feedeth it, as
doth a loving mother unto her tender
child.'

69–70 **delivered ... occasion** i.e. born when
the time is ripe for it

their daughters profit very greatly under you. You are a
good member of the commonwealth.

HOLOFERNES *Mehercle*, if their sons be ingenious, they shall
want no instruction; if their daughters be capable, I will
put it to them. But *vir sapit qui pauca loquitur*. A soul
feminine saluteth us.

  Enter Jaquenetta with a letter, and Costard

JAQUENETTA God give you good morrow, Master Person.   80

HOLOFERNES Master Person, *quasi* 'pierce one'? An if one
should be pierced, which is the one?

COSTARD Marry, Master Schoolmaster, he that is likeliest
to a hogshead.

HOLOFERNES 'Of piercing a hogshead'—a good lustre of
conceit in a turf of earth, fire enough for a flint, pearl
enough for a swine. 'Tis pretty, it is well.

JAQUENETTA Good Master Parson, be so good as read me

---

76 *Mehercle*] F (*Me hercle*); Me hercle (*in roman*) Q   ingenious] CAPELL; ingenous Q; ingen-
nous F   78 *sapit*] Q2; *sapis* QF   79.1 *Enter ... Costard*] ROWE (*subs.*); *Enter Iaquenetta and the
Clowne* QF   80, 83, 88 Master] QF (M.)   80, 81 Person] QF; Parson F2   81 'pierce one']
HALLIWELL (pierce-one); Person QF   82 pierced] QF (perst)   83 COSTARD] ROWE; *Clo⟨wne⟩*. QF
likeliest] WILSON; liklest Q; likest F

---

74 **profit** (a) make progress (b) increase in
size (by becoming pregnant). The innuendo, unconscious on Nathaniel's part, is
reinforced by 'under you'.
76 *Mehercle* by Hercules
   ingenious intelligent (*OED, a.* 2)
77 **want** lack, go short of
   capable capable of (a) learning (b) sexual
   intercourse
78 **put it** (a bawdy quibble). Compare *Winter's Tale* 1.2.278–80: 'My wife's a
hobby-horse, deserves a name | As rank
as any flax-wench that puts to | Before
her troth-plight.'
   vir ... loquitur he's a wise man who says
little. The saying was proverbial (Tilley
W799).
80 **Person** parson. *Person* and *parson* were
originally the same word, both coming
from the Latin *persona*, and in
Shakespeare's day each of them could
still be spelled in either way. *Person* is
preferred here because it seems to represent Jaquenetta's pronunciation to
which Holofernes objects as incorrect.

81 *quasi* as if it were
   pierce-one Halliwell's emendation of
   'Person', the reading of Q and F, has been
   adopted here, as in most modern editions,
   because it best fits the context. The
   pronunciation of 'pierce' is attested to by
   1 Henry IV 5.3.56: 'Well, if Percy be
   alive, I'll pierce him' and by the title of
   Nashe's pamphlet *Pierce Penniless his
   Supplication to the Devil* (1592) with its
   pun on *Pierce* and *Purse*. As for 'one', it
   was often written 'on' and pronounced
   'on' or 'un'.
83–4 **likeliest to** most like
84 **hogshead** large cask for wine or the like
85 **piercing** broaching. 'To pierce a hogshead' was probably proverbial (Dent
H504.1).
85–6 **lustre of conceit** spark of imagination
   (Riverside)
86 **turf** clod (Onions)
86–7 **fire ... swine** Holofernes brings two
   proverbs together: 'In the coldest flint
   there is hot fire' and 'Cast not pearls
   before swine' (Tilley F371 and P165).

this letter. It was given me by Costard, and sent me from
Don Armado. I beseech you, read it.   90

    Sir Nathaniel takes the letter and peruses it while
    Holofernes ruminates

HOLOFERNES

    Fauste, precor gelida quando pecus omne sub umbra
    Ruminat—

and so forth. Ah, good old Mantuan, I may speak of thee
as the traveller doth of Venice:

    Venetia, Venetia,

    Chi non ti vede, non ti pretia.

Old Mantuan, old Mantuan, who understandeth thee
not, loves thee not. (*He sings*) Ut, re, sol, la, mi, fa.—
Under pardon, sir, what are the contents? Or rather, as
Horace says in his—What, my soul, verses?   100

NATHANIEL Ay, sir, and very learned.

HOLOFERNES Let me hear a staff, a stanza, a verse. *Lege,*
domine.

90.1–2 *Sir . . . ruminates*] not in QF   91–2 *Fauste . . . Ruminat*] F2; *Facile precor gellida, quando*
pecas omnia sub vmbra ruminat QF   95–6 *Venetia . . . pretia*] CAMBRIDGE; *vemchie, vencha, que*
non te vnde, que non te perreche QF; *Venezia, Venezia, | Chi non ti vede, chi non ti prezia* OXFORD
98 loves thee not] Q; *not* in F   *He sings*] *not in* QF   100 his—] HANMER; ～, QF
102 stanza] Q (stauze), F

91–2 **Fauste . . . Ruminat** 'Faustus, since all
your flock are chewing the cud in the cool
shade, I pray you—.' This is the beginning of Mantuan's first eclogue in his
Eclogues of 1498, a work that rapidly
became extremely popular all over Europe. These opening words were so well
known that the errors Q and F make in
their rendering of them seem far more
likely to be the compositor's than
Shakespeare's or the Pedant's, a view
evidently shared by the compilers of the
Second Folio. Binns, who thinks, as
many have done, that the playwright
deliberately makes Holofernes blunder in
his Latin in order to hold him up to
ridicule, also points out that 'the Latinate
members of the audience would have
been able to deduce a kind of sense from
most of the line: "Easily, I pray, since you
are getting everything into a mess under
the cool shade" (the verb *pecco* is used

transitively by Cicero)' (p. 124).
93 **Mantuan** Johannes Baptista Spagnolo of
Mantua (1448–1516), known as Man-
tuanus, whose Latin eclogues, imitations
of Virgil's, were much used in the schools
of Tudor England.
95–6 **Venetia . . . pretia** An Italian proverb
that passed into English as 'Venice, he
that does not see thee does not esteem
thee' (Tilley V26).
98 **Ut . . . fa** *Ut* corresponds to the modern
'doh', and *sol* to the modern 'soh'; but it
is not clear whether Holofernes is trying
to sing a scale and getting it wrong, or
whether he is humming a bit of a tune.
Compare *Tragedy of Lear* 1.2.134–5: 'Fa,
sol, la, mi.'
102 **staff . . . stanza . . . verse** All three words
mean the same thing—a *stanza* (*OED*,
staff, sb.[1] 19c).
102–3 **Lege, domine** read, master

NATHANIEL (*reads*)

'If love make me forsworn, how shall I swear to love?
  Ah, never faith could hold, if not to beauty vowed!
Though to myself forsworn, to thee I'll faithful prove;
  Those thoughts to me were oaks, to thee like osiers
      bowed.
Study his bias leaves, and makes his book thine eyes,
  Where all those pleasures live that art would
      comprehend.
If knowledge be the mark, to know thee shall suffice;   110
  Well learnèd is that tongue that well can thee
      commend,
All ignorant that soul that sees thee without wonder;
  Which is to me some praise, that I thy parts admire.
Thy eye Jove's lightning bears, thy voice his dreadful
      thunder,
  Which, not to anger bent, is music and sweet fire.
Celestial as thou art, O, pardon love this wrong,
That sings heaven's praise with such an earthly
      tongue.'

HOLOFERNES You find not the apostrophus, and so miss the

104 NATHANIEL] ROWE 1714; *continued to Nathaniel (for Holofernes)* QF   reads] CAPELL
(*subs.*); *not in* QF   105 Ah] QF; O *Pilgrim*   107 were] QF; like *Pilgrim*   bowed.] F; ~ ∧ Q
108 eyes,] *Pilgrim*; ~. QF   109 would] QF; can *Pilgrim*   114 Thy ... bears] QF;
Thine ... seems *Pilgrim*   116 pardon love this] QF; do not loue that *Pilgrim*   wrong] Q
(*corr.*), F; woug Q (*uncorr.*)   117 That sings heaven's] QF; To sing heauens *Pilgrim*; That
singeth heauen's MARSHALL   118 HOLOFERNES] ROWE; Ped⟨ant⟩. QF   apostrophus] HART
(*conj. OED*); apostraphas QF

104–17 **If ... tongue** This sonnet, along
    with the poems of Longueville
    (4.3.58–71) and Dumaine (4.3.99–118),
    was taken over by William Jaggard, and
    printed in his collection *The Passionate
    Pilgrim* (1599). Although the title-page
    of the collection describes it as being 'By
    W. Shakespeare', the volume also has
    poems by a number of other authors,
    including Marlowe.
107 **thoughts to me were oaks** i.e. thoughts
    which were to me oaks (in their strength)
    osiers well known and valued for their
    pliability
108 **Study ... eyes** i.e. the student abandons
    the subject he preferred to all others and
    makes your eyes his book
109 **art** scholarship, learning (*OED, sb.* 3b)
113 **that** because (Abbott 284)
    parts could mean either or both physical

and or mental endowments
116 **love** i.e. my love for you
117 **That** i.e. that it
118 **apostrophus** A recognized variant spell-
    ing of *apostrophe*[2], i.e. the sign (') used to
    indicate the omission of a letter or letters
    in a word. Q and F read 'apostrophas',
    which could, Onions thinks, perhaps be
    the plural of 'apostropha', a word used by
    Florio in his *First Fruits* (1578). There is,
    however, so far as one can see, no word
    in the sonnet that needs to be elided in
    order to preserve the right emphasis
    ('accent'). David suggests—and it is an
    attractive suggestion—that Holofernes is
    trying 'to blind Nathaniel with science'
    as a means of asserting his own superior-
    ity, and so employs a bit of technical
    jargon that sounds impressive but means
    nothing.

accent. Let me supervise the canzonet. (*He takes the
letter*) Sir Nathaniel, here are only numbers ratified, but   120
for the elegancy, facility, and golden cadence of poesy,
caret. Ovidius Naso was the man. And why indeed
'Naso' but for smelling out the odoriferous flowers of
fancy, the jerks of invention? *Imitari* is nothing. So doth
the hound his master, the ape his keeper, the tired horse
his rider.—But, *domicella*—virgin—was this directed to
you?

JAQUENETTA Ay, sir.

HOLOFERNES I will overglance the superscript. (*He reads*)
'To the snow-white hand of the most beauteous Lady   130
Rosaline.' I will look again on the intellect of the letter
for the nomination of the party writing to the person

119 canzonet] cangenct Q; cangenet F   120 Sir Nathaniel, here] This edition; *Nath.* Here
QF; *continued to Holofernes* THEOBALD   124 fancy,] CAPELL; fancy? F; fancie? Q   invention?] THEOBALD; in-uention ∧ QF   *Imitari*] THEOBALD; imitarie QF   126 *domicella*—virgin]
OXFORD; *Damosella virgin* QF   128 Ay, sir.] OXFORD; I sir from one mounsier *Berowne*, one of
the strange Queenes Lordes QF   129 HOLOFERNES] THEOBALD; *Nath.* QF   *He reads*] not in QF
132 writing] ROWE; written QF

119 **supervise** look over, peruse (*OED, v.* 1;
earliest citation)
canzonet little poem
120–7 **here are … to you?** Q and F assign
these lines to '*Nath.*', which is patently
wrong, since they are a continuation of
Holofernes' speech. The likeliest explanation of the error is that Shakespeare
wrote 'Sir Nathaniel, here are' and the
compositor took 'Sir Nathaniel' for a
speech heading which he then abbreviated to '*Nath.*'
120 **numbers ratified** i.e. lines that are
metrically correct
121 **for** as for (Abbott 149)
elegancy elegance (*OED*, 2)
facility fluency (*OED*, 3b)
cadence rhythmical flow—not elsewhere
in Shakespeare
122 *caret* it is missing
Naso The cognomen (family name) of
Ovid, meaning 'big-nosed'.
124 **jerks** flashes, sallies (*OED, sb.*¹ 3; earliest *OED* citation of this sense; not elsewhere in Shakespeare)
Imitari to imitate
125 **tired** attired, decked out with trappings
(Onions)
126 *domicella* Medieval Latin for 'maiden'.
Q and F read '*Damosella*'. The emendation

brings the word into line with Holofernes'
characteristic manner—a bit of Latin
followed by its English equivalent. See
Wells, *Re-Editing*, p. 53.
128 **Ay, sir** Q and F read: 'I sir from one
mounsier *Berowne*, one of the strange
Queenes Lordes.' Only the first two words
here make sense. For the rest, Biron is not
in attendance on the Princess, and Jaquenetta has already said of the letter: 'It
was given me by Costard, and sent me
from Don Armado.' The nonsense is
therefore ignored in this edition.
129 **overglance** cast an eye over. Apparently
a Shakespearian coinage, it occurs again
at *Henry V* 5.2.78.
superscript superscription, address (*OED*,
sb. A; no other example of this sense
cited)
130 **snow-white** a time-honoured epithet
(Dent S591.1)
131 **intellect** *OED*, referring to this context,
defines *intellect* as 'meaning, significa-
tion, purport' (*sb.* 5). Schmidt, on the
other hand, following a suggestion by
Baynes quoted in Furness, thinks it could
mean 'sign, signature'. In the light of
what follows *signature* appears to be
right.
132 **nomination** name (*OED*, 4)

written unto: 'Your ladyship's in all desired employment, Biron.' Sir Nathaniel, this Biron is one of the
votaries with the King, and here he hath framed a letter
to a sequent of the stranger Queen's, which acciden-
tally, or by the way of progression, hath miscarried. (*To
Jaquenetta*) Trip and go, my sweet, deliver this paper into
the royal hand of the King. It may concern much. Stay
not thy compliment. I forgive thy duty. Adieu.   140

JAQUENETTA Good Costard, go with me. Sir, God save your
life.

COSTARD Have with thee, my girl.

Exeunt Costard and Jaquenetta

NATHANIEL Sir, you have done this in the fear of God, very
religiously; and as a certain father saith—

HOLOFERNES Sir, tell not me of the father, I do fear
colourable colours. But to return to the verses: did they
please you, Sir Nathaniel?

NATHANIEL Marvellous well for the pen.

HOLOFERNES I do dine today at the father's of a certain   150
pupil of mine, where, if before repast it shall please you
to gratify the table with a grace, I will, on my privilege I
have with the parents of the foresaid child or pupil,
undertake your *ben venuto*, where I will prove those

---

134 Sir] *continued to Holofernes* THEOBALD; *assigned to Ped⟨ant⟩.* Q, *and to Per⟨son⟩.* F
Nathaniel] CAPELL; *Holofernes* QF   139 royal] Q; *not in* F   140 forgive] Q (forgine), F
141 JAQUENETTA] ROWE; *Mayd.* Q; *Maid.* F   143 *Exeunt ... Jaquenetta*] ROWE; *Exit* QF
144 NATHANIEL] ROWE; *Holo⟨fernes⟩.* QF   145 saith—] F2; ~ ∧ QF   146, 150 HOLO-
FERNES] ROWE 1714; *Ped⟨ant⟩.* QF   151 before] Q; *being* F   154 *ben venuto*] ROWE
1714; *bien venuto* Q; *bien vonuto* F; *bien venu* too CAMBRIDGE *conj.*

133–4 **all desired employment** i.e. any use
you care to make of me

136 **sequent** follower (*OED*, *sb.* 1; the only
instance of *sequent* in this sense)

137 **by ... progression** i.e. as a consequence
of the route it has taken

138 **Trip and go** a common phrase, frequently used in the songs that accompanied morris dances. See, for instance,
Summer's Last Will and Testament
212–19 (Nashe, iii. 240).

139 **concern much** be of great importance
(*OED*, *v.* 4b)

139–40 **Stay ... compliment** i.e. don't waste
time on a polite farewell

140 **I forgive thy duty** i.e. I excuse you from
making a curtsy

143 **Have with thee** I'll go along with you

147 **colourable colours** plausible pretexts
(*OED*, *colour*, *sb.* 12). Holofernes is
quibbling on the proverbial assertion 'I
fear no colours' (Tilley C520), where
colours means 'hostile flags or standards'.
A staunch Protestant, he will have nothing to do with the sayings of the Fathers
of the Church.

149 **for the pen** as far as the calligraphy is
concerned

151 **repast** the meal

152 **gratify** (a) please (b) grace

154 **undertake your *ben venuto*** guarantee
your welcome. Compare *Shrew* 1.2.282
for a similar use of the Italian phrase.

verses to be very unlearned, neither savouring of
poetry, wit, nor invention. I beseech your society.

NATHANIEL And thank you too, for society, saith the text,
is the happiness of life.

HOLOFERNES And, certes, the text most infallibly concludes
it. (*To Dull*) Sir, I do invite you too; you shall not say me   160
nay. *Pauca verba.* Away, the gentles are at their game,
and we will to our recreation.   *Exeunt*

4.3   *Enter Biron with a paper in his hand, alone*

BIRON The King he is hunting the deer; I am coursing
myself. They have pitched a toil; I am toiling in a
pitch—pitch that defiles—defile! a foul word. Well, set
thee down, sorrow; for so they say the fool said, and so
say I, and I the fool. Well proved, wit! By the Lord, this
love is as mad as Ajax. It kills sheep, it kills me—I a
sheep. Well proved again o' my side! I will not love. If I
do, hang me. I'faith, I will not. O, but her eye! By this
light, but for her eye I would not love her. Yes, for her
two eyes. Well, I do nothing in the world but lie, and lie   10
in my throat. By heaven, I do love, and it hath taught
me to rhyme and to be melancholy; (*showing his paper*)
and here is part of my rhyme, (*pressing his hand to his
breast*) and here my melancholy. Well, she hath one o'

4.3.8 do,] F2 ; ~ ∧ QF   12, 14 melancholy] ROWE ; mallicholie QF   12 *showing his paper*]
OXFORD (*subs.*); *not in* QF   13–14 *pressing ... breast*] OXFORD (*subs.*); *not in* QF

157 **the text** The authority Nathaniel is
  thinking of has not been identified. Kerrigan suggests Ecclesiastes 4: 8–12; but
  the parallel is not convincing.

159 **certes** certainly

161 *Pauca verba* few words—referring to
  the tag 'Few words are best' (Dent W798)
  gentles gentlefolk
  game (a) sport (b) quarry

162 **recreation** (a) refreshment (*OED, sb.* 1)
  (b) amusement, pleasant diversion

4.3.1 **coursing** (a) hunting, chasing (b) beating, inflicting blows on (*OED, v.* 4),
  tormenting

  2 **pitched a toil** set up a net, enclosure, or
  snare. Compare *Hamlet* 3.2.334–5 : 'why
  do you go about to recover the wind of me
  as if you would drive me into a toil?'
  Having been driven into the *toil* (*OED,
  sb.*² 1), the deer were then killed with

  crossbows.

2–3 **toiling in a pitch** i.e. striving to escape
  from the feelings engendered by Rosaline's eyes, the 'two pitch-balls' of
  3.1.190.

  3 **pitch that defiles** 'He that touches pitch
  shall be defiled' was proverbial (Tilley
  P358).

3–4 **set thee down, sorrow** See 1.1.301–2,
  and note.

  6 **as mad as Ajax. It kills sheep** Disappointed because Agamemnon awarded
  the armour of Achilles to Odysseus rather
  than to him, Ajax went mad and attacked
  flocks of sheep thinking they were the
  enemy. 'As mad as Ajax' became
  proverbial (Dent A95).

10–11 **lie in my throat** lie outrageously—a
  very common expression (Dent T268)

my sonnets already. The clown bore it, the fool sent it,
and the lady hath it. Sweet clown, sweeter fool, sweetest
lady! By the world, I would not care a pin if the other
three were in. Here comes one with a paper. God give
him grace to groan.

> *He stands aside.*
> *Enter the King ⌈with a paper⌉*

KING Ay me!   20
BIRON (*aside*) Shot, by heaven! Proceed, sweet Cupid. Thou
hast thumped him with thy bird-bolt under the left pap.
In faith, secrets.
KING (*reads*)

'So sweet a kiss the golden sun gives not
    To those fresh morning drops upon the rose
As thy eye-beams when their fresh rays have smote
    The night of dew that on my cheeks down flows.
Nor shines the silver moon one half so bright
    Through the transparent bosom of the deep
As doth thy face through tears of mine give light.   30
    Thou shin'st in every tear that I do weep.
No drop but as a coach doth carry thee,
    So ridest thou triumphing in my woe.
Do but behold the tears that swell in me,
    And they thy glory through my grief will show.
But do not love thyself, then thou wilt keep
    My tears for glasses, and still make me weep.
O Queen of queens, how far dost thou excel,
    No thought can think nor tongue of mortal tell.'
How shall she know my griefs? I'll drop the paper.   40
Sweet leaves, shade folly. Who is he comes here?

> *Enter Longueville with papers. The King steps aside*

What, Longueville, and reading! Listen, ear!

19.2 *Enter ... King*] QF (*The King entreth*)   with a paper] *not in* QF   24 (*reads*)] *not in* QF
26 rays] QF (rayse)   smote ∧] ROWE; smot. QF   36 wilt] F; will Q   40 paper] Q (*corr.*), F;
pa d er Q (*uncorr.*)   41 leaves,] THEOBALD; ~ ∧ QF   41.1 *Enter ... aside*] Q (*Enter Longauill.
The King steps a side*), F

---

17 I ... **pin** proverbial (Tilley P333)
18 **in** (a) in the same predicament (b) in love
22 **bird-bolt** blunt-headed arrow for shoot-
    ing birds
    under the left pap i.e. in the heart.
    Compare *Dream* 5.1.293–4: 'that left

pap | Where heart doth hop.'
27 **night of dew** nightly dew (tears that flow
    every night)
37 **glasses** mirrors
41 **shade** hide (*OED v.*[1] 3)

BIRON (*aside*)

Now, in thy likeness, one more fool appear!

LONGUEVILLE

Ay me! I am forsworn.

BIRON (*aside*) Why, he comes in like a perjure, wearing papers.

KING (*aside*)

In love, I hope. Sweet fellowship in shame.

BIRON (*aside*)

One drunkard loves another of the name.

LONGUEVILLE

Am I the first that have been perjured so?

BIRON (*aside*)

I could put thee in comfort—not by two that I know.   50

Thou makest the triumviry, the corner-cap of society,

The shape of Love's Tyburn that hangs up simplicity.

LONGUEVILLE

I fear these stubborn lines lack power to move.

O sweet Maria, empress of my love,

These numbers will I tear, and write in prose.

BIRON (*aside*)

O rhymes are guards on wanton Cupid's hose;

Disfigure not his shop.

LONGUEVILLE   This same shall go.

He reads his sonnet

47 KING] ROWE 1714; *Long⟨auill⟩*. QF   51 triumviry] ROWE 1714; triumpherie Q;
triumphery F   57 shop] QF; slop POPE 1728   57.1 *his*] *the* QF

43 **in thy likeness** This is ambiguous. It can
mean either 'looking like the king' or 'in
your own shape'. Compare *Romeo*
2.1.17–21: 'I conjure thee ... That in
thy likeness thou appear to us.'

45 **perjure** perjurer

45–6 **wearing papers** Part of the punishment for perjury was to wear a placard
stating the nature of the offence. It looks
as though Longueville should come in
with a sonnet or two tucked into his
hatband.

49–50 **Am I ... know** 'I am not the first
(and shall not be the last)' was proverbial
(Dent F295).

51 **triumviry** triumvirate
  corner-cap cap with four (or three) corners, worn by divines and members of the
Universities in the 16th and 17th centu-

ries (*OED*)—much like the modern *mor-
tar-board*

52 **The shape ... Tyburn** Tyburn was the
regular place of execution for the county
of Middlesex. The gallows there, like
gallows in general, were triangular in
shape, being made of three pieces of
timber.
  simplicity folly, silliness

53 **stubborn** rough, unpolished

55 **numbers** verses

56 **guards** (a) ornamental borders or trim-
mings (b) defences

57 **his shop** i.e. the place where Cupid
houses and displays his wares. The reference is obviously to the *hose*, complete
with *codpiece*. This garment concealed
and protected the male genitals while, at
the same time, calling attention to them

'Did not the heavenly rhetoric of thine eye,
  'Gainst whom the world cannot hold argument,
Persuade my heart to this false perjury?   60
  Vows for thee broke deserve not punishment.
A woman I forswore, but I will prove,
  Thou being a goddess, I forswore not thee.
My vow was earthly, thou a heavenly love;
  Thy grace, being gained, cures all disgrace in me.
Vows are but breath, and breath a vapour is.
  Then thou, fair sun, which on my earth dost shine,
Exhal'st this vapour-vow, in thee it is.
  If broken then, it is no fault of mine:
If by me broke, what fool is not so wise   70
  To lose an oath to win a paradise?'

BIRON (*aside*)
  This is the liver vein, which makes flesh a deity,
  A green goose a goddess. Pure, pure idolatry.
  God amend us, God amend! We are much out o'th' way.

LONGUEVILLE (*aside*)
  By whom shall I send this?

          Enter Dumaine with a paper

                        Company? Stay.

          He stands aside

BIRON (*aside*)
  All hid, all hid, an old infant play.

58 heavenly] Q (heanenly), F   59 cannot] QF; could not *Pilgrim*   66 Vows are but] QF;
My vow was *Pilgrim*   67 which on my] QF; that on this *Pilgrim*   68 Exhal'st] Q (Exhalst);
Exhalest F   69 broken then,] QF; broken, then *Pilgrim*   70 wise ∧] *Pilgrim*; ~, QF
71 lose] QF (loose); breake *Pilgrim*   72 deity,] DYCE; ~. QF   73 idolatry] F; ydotarie Q
75.1 *Enter ... paper*] CAPELL; *Enter Dumaine.* QF (*after l. 74*)   75.2 *He ... aside*] JOHNSON
(*subs.*); *not in* QF

by its use of costly and elaborate materials.

58–71 **Did not ... paradise** See note at
4.2.104–17.

59 **whom** which. Compare *Tempest* 3.3.61–
2: 'The elements | Of whom your swords
are tempered'.

65 **grace** favour

66 **Vows ... vapour is** proverbial: 'Words
are but wind' (Tilley W833)

68 **Exhal'st** It was thought that the sun
exhaled (drew up) vapours from the earth,
and thus produced meteors. Compare
Romeo 3.5.12–13: 'Yon light is not day-

light; I know it, I, | It is some meteor that
the sun exhaled'.

70–1 **what ... paradise** Compare 'To bring
one into a fool's paradise' (Dent F523).

71 **To** as to

72 **liver vein** style of a man in love. The liver
was regarded as the source of sexual
desire.

73 **green goose** giddy young girl. See note to
1.1.97.

74 **are ... way** i.e. have gone badly astray
(from the purpose with which we began)

76 **All hid** A cry used by children when
playing at hide-and-seek or blindman's
buff. Biron sees himself as the supervisor

Like a demigod here sit I in the sky,
And wretched fools' secrets heedfully o'er-eye.
More sacks to the mill! O heavens, I have my wish!
Dumaine transformed! Four woodcocks in a dish!   80

DUMAINE O most divine Kate!

BIRON (*aside*) O most profane coxcomb!

DUMAINE

By heaven, the wonder in a mortal eye!

BIRON (*aside*)

By earth, she is not, corporal. There you lie.

DUMAINE

Her amber hairs for foul hath amber quoted.

BIRON (*aside*)

An amber-coloured raven was well noted.

DUMAINE

As upright as the cedar.

BIRON (*aside*)   Stoop, I say.

Her shoulder is with child.

DUMAINE   As fair as day.

---

80 transformed] F (transform'd); transformed Q   83 in] Q; of F   84 corporal] Q (*corr.*) F; croporall Q (*uncorr.*)

of the game, watching it from a superior position, since he knows more about what is going on than does anyone else. Exactly how the scene was staged is not clear. Biron, it would seem, is somewhere *above*, 'Like a demi god ... in the sky', while the King and Longueville are concealed somewhere on the main stage, probably each behind one of the two pillars that supported the 'shadow or cover over the stage'. Property trees which could be climbed were not unknown in the Elizabethan theatre. John Marston calls for one in 5.1 of his *The Fawn* (1605), where the initial stage direction includes the words: 'Tiberio climbs the tree, and is received above by Dulcimel'.

79 **More sacks to the mill** proverbial (Tilley S12)

80 **woodcocks** fools. Because of the ease with which it allowed itself to be caught, the *woodcock* was looked on as the emblem of stupidity. Compare *Shrew* 1.2.158: 'O this woodcock, what an ass

it is!'

84 **corporal** Biron sees Dumaine as an officer in Cupid's army, exactly as he saw himself in the same role at 3.1.180. But he also insists that Katherine is 'corporal', i.e. flesh and blood (*OED, a.* 2). Compare *Macbeth* 1.3.79–80: 'and what seemed corporal | Melted as breath into the wind'.

85 **Her amber ... quoted** i.e. her amber-coloured hair has made amber itself look ugly when compared with it
quoted regarded as

86 **An ... noted** Twisting Dumaine's *foul* to *fowl*, Biron ironically remarks that anyone who could describe Katherine's *raven* locks as amber-coloured must have been an accurate observer indeed.

87 **As ... cedar** a very conventional simile (Tilley C207)
Stoop (a) bent, bowed (b) come down to earth, 'come off it'. Both glosses have to be deduced from the context; support for them is lacking.

88 **with child** humped, bulging (like a pregnant woman: *OED, child, sb.* 17b)
As fair as day a stock simile (Dent D56.1)

165

BIRON (*aside*)

   Ay, as some days—but then no sun must shine.

DUMAINE

   O that I had my wish!

LONGUEVILLE (*aside*)   And I had mine!   90

KING (*aside*)

   And I mine too, good Lord!

BIRON (*aside*)

   Amen, so I had mine! Is not that a good word?

DUMAINE

   I would forget her, but a fever she

   Reigns in my blood, and will remembered be.

BIRON (*aside*)

   A fever in your blood? Why then incision

   Would let her out in saucers. Sweet misprision!

DUMAINE

   Once more I'll read the ode that I have writ.

BIRON (*aside*)

   Once more I'll mark how love can vary wit.

DUMAINE (*reads his sonnet*)

     'On a day—alack the day!—

     Love, whose month is ever May,   100

     Spied a blossom passing fair

     Playing in the wanton air.

     Through the velvet leaves the wind,

     All unseen, can passage find;

     That the lover, sick to death,

     Wished himself the heavens' breath.

     "Air", quoth he, "thy cheeks may blow;

---

91 I] JOHNSON; *not in* QF   96 misprision] Q (misprison), F   97 *reads his sonnet*] QF (*Dumaine reades his Sonnet.*)   100 is ever] Q; is euery F; was euer *Pilgrim, Helicon*   103 velvet ∧] F4; ～, QF   104 can] QF; gan *Pilgrim, Helicon*   106 Wished] *Pilgrim* (Wisht), *Helicon* (Wish'd); Wish QF

92 **Is not ... word?** (a) is not that kind of me? (b) is not *Amen* a good word?

95 **incision** cutting for the purpose of letting blood; regarded as the right treatment for a fever

96 **in saucers** (a) into the saucers used to catch the blood (b) by the saucerful
    misprision substitution of one meaning for another

98 **vary wit** i.e. make an intelligent man unlike himself (Schmidt). Compare 'It is

impossible to love and be wise' (Tilley L558).

99–118 **On a day ... thy love** As well as being printed in *The Passionate Pilgrim* (1599), this poem was also included in another anthology, *England's Helicon* (1600). Both collections omit lines 113 and 114 which link the lyric to the play.

101 **passing** exceedingly, surpassing

104 **can** did (*OED*, *v*.² 2)

105 **That** so that (Abbott 283)

Air, would I might triumph so!
But, alack, my hand is sworn
Ne'er to pluck thee from thy thorn.   110
Vow, alack, for youth unmeet,
Youth so apt to pluck a sweet.
Do not call it sin in me,
That I am forsworn for thee;
Thou for whom Jove would swear
Juno but an Ethiop were,
And deny himself for Jove,
Turning mortal for thy love.'''
This will I send, and something else more plain,
That shall express my true love's fasting pain.   120
O, would the King, Biron, and Longueville
Were lovers too! Ill, to example ill,
Would from my forehead wipe a perjured note,
For none offend where all alike do dote.

LONGUEVILLE (*coming forward*)

Dumaine, thy love is far from charity,
That in love's grief desir'st society.
You may look pale, but I should blush, I know,
To be o'erheard and taken napping so.

KING (*coming forward*)

Come, sir, you blush. As his your case is such.
You chide at him, offending twice as much.   130
You do not love Maria? Longueville
Did never sonnet for her sake compile,
Nor never lay his wreathèd arms athwart

108 Air] QF (Ayre); Ah! JOHNSON *conj.*   109 alack] QF; alas *Pilgrim, Helicon*   is] QF; hath
Pilgrim, Helicon   110 thorn] *Helicon* (thorne); throne QF, *Pilgrim*   113–14 Do ... thee] QF;
not in Pilgrim, Helicon   115 whom Jove] QF, *Pilgrim, Helicon*; whom great Jove COLLIER 1853;
whom ev'n Jove ROWE 1714   119 plain,] ROWE; ~. QF   120 true love's] ROWE;
trueloues Q; true-loues F   125 *coming forward*]ROWE; *not in* QF

116 **Ethiop** blackamoor (thought of as unat-
    tractive)
117 **deny himself for** disown the name of
120 **fasting pain** pain caused by abstinence
122 **example** provide a precedent for
123 **perjured note** See notes on *perjure* and
    wearing papers at lines 45 and 46 above.
125 **charity** Christian love (*caritas*) as op-
    posed to profane love (*amor*).
126 **That you** who

126 **in love's ... society** Probably referring
    to the saying 'It is good to have company
    in trouble' from the Latin *Solamen miseris
    socios habuisse doloris* (Tilley C571).
128 **taken napping** taken unawares, caught
    in the act
129–30 **As his ... much** Compare the much
    used saying 'He finds fault with others
    and does worse himself' (Tilley F107).
133 **wreathèd arms** See note on 3.1.16–18.

His loving bosom to keep down his heart?
I have been closely shrouded in this bush,
And marked you both, and for you both did blush.
I heard your guilty rhymes, observed your fashion,
Saw sighs reek from you, noted well your passion.
'Ay me!' says one; 'O Jove!' the other cries.
One, her hairs were gold; crystal the other's eyes.   140
(*To Longueville*) You would for paradise break faith and
    troth;
(*To Dumaine*) And Jove, for your love, would infringe
    an oath.
What will Biron say when that he shall hear
Faith so infringèd, which such zeal did swear?
How will he scorn, how will he spend his wit!
How will he triumph, leap, and laugh at it!
For all the wealth that ever I did see,
I would not have him know so much by me.
BIRON (*coming forward*)
Now step I forth to whip hypocrisy.
Ah, good my liege, I pray thee pardon me.   150
Good heart, what grace hast thou, thus to reprove
These worms for loving, that art most in love?
Your eyes do make no coaches; in your tears
There is no certain princess that appears;
You'll not be perjured, 'tis a hateful thing;
Tush, none but minstrels like of sonneting!

---

140 One] Q, F (On); One that TAYLOR *conj., in* OXFORD   141 *To Longueville*] JOHNSON ; *not in* QF
142 *To Dumaine*] JOHNSON ; *not in* QF   144 Faith so] GLOBE (*conj.* W. S. Walker); Fayth Q, F
(Faith); Our faith OXFORD *conj.*   149 *coming forward*] ROWE ; *not in* QF   153 coaches] ROWE
1714; couches QF   coaches; in your tears ∧] HANMER ; couches in your tears. QF

135 **closely shrouded** secretly hidden (*OED*,
    shroud, *v.* 4)
137 **fashion** behaviour (*OED*, *sb.* 6)
138 **reek** smoke, emanate. Compare *Romeo*
    1.1.187: 'Love is a smoke made with the
    fume of sighs'.
143 **when that** when (Abbott 287)
146 **leap, and laugh** proverbial (Dent
    L92a.1)
148 **by** about
149 **Now ... whip hypocrisy** Biron consci-
    ously adopts the role of the satirist, whose
    task was, it was thought, to *whip* the
    vices and the follies of the time.

152 **worms** wretches (*OED*, *sb.* 10)
156 **minstrels** i.e. hired entertainers, includ-
    ing jugglers and the like as well as
    singers. The word *minstrel* had none of
    the romantic overtones it was to acquire
    later. Mercutio, accused by Tybalt of
    consorting with Romeo, retorts: '"Con-
    sort"! What, dost thou make us min-
    strels? An thou make minstrels of us,
    look to hear nothing but discords' (*Romeo*
    3.1.44–7).
like of derive pleasure from (*OED*, *v.*¹ 5)
sonneting composing sonnets—earliest
    citation by *OED*

But are you not ashamed? Nay, are you not,
All three of you, to be thus much o'ershot?
You found his mote, the King your mote did see,
But I a beam do find in each of three.   160
O, what a scene of fool'ry have I seen,
Of sighs, of groans, of sorrow, and of teen!
O me, with what strict patience have I sat,
To see a king transformèd to a gnat!
To see great Hercules whipping a gig,
And profound Solomon to tune a jig,
And Nestor play at push-pin with the boys,
And critic Timon laugh at idle toys!
Where lies thy grief? O, tell me, good Dumaine.
And, gentle Longueville, where lies thy pain?   170
And where my liege's? All about the breast.
A caudle, ho!
KING   Too bitter is thy jest.
Are we betrayed thus to thy over-view?
BIRON
Not you to me, but I betrayed by you.
I that am honest, I that hold it sin
To break the vow I am engagèd in,
I am betrayed by keeping company
With men like you, men of inconstancy.

157 ashamed] Q (a shamed), F   159 mote ... mote] QF (Moth ... Moth)   166 to tune] Q;
tuning F   172 caudle] Q (Caudle); Candle F   174 to ... by] CAPELL; by ... to QF
178 men like you] DYCE (*conj.* W. S. Walker); men like Q; men, like F; moon-like MASON

158 **o'ershot** outshot. Compare *Henry V*
    3.7.121 and Dent O91.1.
159–60 **You found ... three** There is plainly
    an allusion here to the figure of the *mote*
    and the *beam* used by Christ in his attack
    on *hypocrisy* (Matthew 7: 3–5 and Luke
    6: 41–2), and referred to by writers
    innumerable (Tilley M1191).
162 **teen** grief, vexation
164 **gnat** i.e. something quite insignificant
165 **gig** top
166 **tune a jig** sing a lively popular song; or,
    possibly, play the accompaniment to a
    popular dance
167 **Nestor** The oldest and wisest of the
    Greeks who fought at Troy.
    push-pin A children's game in which each
    player pushes his pin with the object of
    crossing that of another player (Onions).

168 **critic** censorious (*OED, a.* 2)
    Timon The notorious misanthrope of
    classical antiquity whom Shakespeare
    would later make the hero of his *Timon of
    Athens.*
    idle toys empty nothings, pointless trifles
172 **caudle** A warm drink consisting of thin
    gruel, mixed with wine or ale, sweetened
    or spiced, given chiefly to sick people,
    especially women in childbed (*OED*).
173 **betrayed** given up or exposed (*OED, v.*
    1b). Compare *Errors* 5.1.91: 'She did
    betray me to my own reproof.'
    over-view overlooking, inspection—
    earliest *OED* citation
175 **honest** true in word and deed
176 **am engagèd in** i.e. have sworn to keep
178 **men like you, men** Q reads 'men like
    men' which F alters to 'men, like men'.

When shall you see me write a thing in rhyme?
Or groan for Joan? Or spend a minute's time   180
In pruning me? When shall you hear that I
Will praise a hand, a foot, a face, an eye,
A gait, a state, a brow, a breast, a waist,
A leg, a limb—

KING   Soft! Whither away so fast?
A true man, or a thief, that gallops so?

BIRON

I post from love. Good lover, let me go.
        Enter Jaquenetta with a letter, and Costard

JAQUENETTA

God bless the King!

KING   What present hast thou there?

COSTARD

Some certain treason.

KING   What makes treason here?

COSTARD

Nay, it makes nothing, sir.

KING   If it mar nothing neither,
The treason and you go in peace away together.   190

JAQUENETTA

I beseech your grace let this letter be read.
Our person misdoubts it; 'twas treason, he said.

180 Joan] Q (*corr.*: Ione), F (*Ioane*); Loue Q (*uncorr.*)   181 me?] F3; ~ ∧ Q; ~, F
184 limb—] DELIUS; limme. QF   186.1 *Enter ... Costard*] ROWE (*subs.*); *Enter Iaquenetta and
Clowne.* Q (*after 'God bless the King'*); *placed as here* F   188, 189 COSTARD] ROWE; *Clow⟨ne⟩.* QF
192 'twas] Q (twas); it was F

Neither reading makes sense, and both
are metrically defective. Various attempts
have been made to put things right,
including 'moon-like men, men', but the
emendation adopted here has the virtue
of simplicity—it assumes only that the
compositor omitted the word 'you'—and
it fits the context with its stress on the
contrast between 'I' and 'you'.

180 **Joan** See note to 3.1.198.
181 **pruning me** titivating myself, preening
myself
183 **state** posture, bearing, mode of standing
(Schmidt)
184 **Soft!** Steady! Be careful!
Whither away so fast i.e. why are you in
such a hurry—proverbial (Dent W316.1)
185 **true** honest

186 **post from** ride fast to get away from
187 **present** (a) gift (b) writing (*OED sb.*[1] 2b).
The singular in the latter sense is most
unusual, since the normal form was
presents, as in Rosalind's comment:
'With bills on their necks: "Be it known
unto all men by these presents"' (*As You
Like It* 1.2.114–15).
188 **makes treason** is treason doing
189 **Nay ... neither** An adaptation of the
common saying 'To make or mar' (Tilley
M48).
192 **person** See note to 4.2.81.
misdoubts is suspicious of, has misgivings
about. In fact, it was Holofernes, not
Nathaniel, who expressed the idea that
the letter might 'concern much'; but
neither mentioned the word *treason*.

KING

  Biron, read it over.

      He gives the letter to Biron, who peruses it

  (*To Jaquenetta*)   Where hadst thou it?

JAQUENETTA Of Costard.

KING (*to Costard*) Where hadst thou it?

COSTARD Of Dun Adramadio, Dun Adramadio.

      Biron tears the letter

KING

  How now, what is in you? Why dost thou tear it?

BIRON

  A toy, my liege, a toy. Your grace needs not fear it.

LONGUEVILLE

  It did move him to passion, and therefore let's hear it.

DUMAINE (*picking up the pieces*)

  It is Biron's writing, and here is his name.   200

BIRON (*to Costard*)

  Ah, you whoreson loggerhead, you were born to do

     me shame.

  Guilty, my lord, guilty! I confess, I confess.

KING What?

BIRON

  That you three fools lacked me fool to make up the mess.

  He, he, and you—and you, my liege—and I

  Are pick-purses in love, and we deserve to die.

  O, dismiss this audience, and I shall tell you more.

DUMAINE

  Now the number is even.

193.1 *He ... it*] CAPELL (*subs.*); *He reades the letter.* QF   193 Where] F2; *King.* Where QF
196.1 *Biron ... letter*] CAPELL (*subs.*); *not in* QF   200 *picking up the pieces*] CAPELL (*subs.*);
not in QF   205 —and you,] QF (and you ∧); even you, DYCE 1866; e'en you, OXFORD

201 **whoreson** (used as a term of abuse)
    loggerhead blockhead, thick-headed fool.
    If the play belongs to 1595, this is one of
    the two earliest citations in *OED*.
204 **mess** group of four people eating to-
    gether at the same table and from the
    same dishes, a common arrangement at
    great banquets, the universities, and the
    Inns of Court. 'Four make up a mess' was
    proverbial (Tilley F621).
205 **and you, my liege** i.e. yes, I mean you,
    my liege

206 **pick-purses** thieves (because they are
    trying to steal *love*)
    deserve to die The punishment for picking
    purses was hanging. Compare Ben Jon-
    son's *Bartholomew Fair* 3.5.79–80:
    'Youth, youth, thou hadst better been
    starved by thy nurse, | Than live to be
    hangèd for cutting a purse.'
208 **the number is even** i.e. we are revenged,
    because the score is now level (*OED, even,*
    a. 10c)

BIRON   True, true, we are four.
  Will these turtles be gone?
KING   Hence, sirs, away!
COSTARD
  Walk aside the true folk, and let the traitors stay.   210
                         Exeunt Costard and Jaquenetta
BIRON
  Sweet lords, sweet lovers, O, let us embrace!
    As true we are as flesh and blood can be.
  The sea will ebb and flow, heaven show his face;
    Young blood doth not obey an old decree.
  We cannot cross the cause why we were born,
  Therefore of all hands must we be forsworn.
KING
  What, did these rent lines show some love of thine?
BIRON
  'Did they?' quoth you. Who sees the heavenly Rosaline,
  That, like a rude and savage man of Ind
    At the first op'ning of the gorgeous east,   220
  Bows not his vassal head, and strucken blind,
    Kisses the base ground with obedient breast?
  What peremptory eagle-sighted eye
    Dares look upon the heaven of her brow
  That is not blinded by her majesty?
KING
  What zeal, what fury, hath inspired thee now?

---

210 COSTARD] ROWE; Clo⟨wne⟩. QF   210.1 *Exeunt ... Jaquenetta*] THEOBALD; *not in* QF
213 show] Q (shew); will shew F   215 were] Q; are F   220 op'ning] Q (opning);
opening F   223 peremptory] Q (peromptorie), F

---

209 **turtles** turtledoves, i.e. lovers
  sirs *Sir* as a polite form of address could be used when speaking to a woman. Compare *Antony* 4.16.86–7: 'Ah, women, women! Look, | Our lamp is spent, it's out. Good sirs, take heart'.
212 **as flesh ... be** 'To be flesh and blood as other men are' is proverbial (Dent F367).
213 **The sea ... flow** proverbial (Dent S182.1)
214 **Young ... decree** proverbial (Dent Y44.1)
215 **cross** thwart, oppose
216 **of all hands** in any case (*OED*, *hand, sb.* 30b)

218 **Who** is there any man who (Abbott 257)
219 **rude** ignorant
  savage uncivilized
  Ind India. Compare *Tempest* 2.2.58: 'savages and men of Ind'.
223 **peremptory** overbearing (Onions)
  eagle-sighted The eagle was credited with the unique capacity of being able to stare at the sun with no impairment of its vision (Dent E7.1). Compare *Richard Duke of York* 2.1.91–2: 'Nay, if thou be that princely eagle's bird, | Show thy descent by gazing 'gainst the sun'.
226 **fury** frenzy of poetic inspiration (*OED*, 4)

My love, her mistress, is a gracious moon,
　She, an attending star, scarce seen a light.
BIRON
My eyes are then no eyes, nor I Biron.
　O, but for my love, day would turn to night.   230
Of all complexions the culled sovereignty
　Do meet as at a fair in her fair cheek,
Where several worthies make one dignity,
　Where nothing wants that want itself doth seek.
Lend me the flourish of all gentle tongues—
　Fie, painted rhetoric! O, she needs it not.
To things of sale a seller's praise belongs.
　She passes praise, then praise too short doth blot.
A withered hermit, fivescore winters worn,
　Might shake off fifty, looking in her eye.   240
Beauty doth varnish age, as if new-born,
　And gives the crutch the cradle's infancy.
O, 'tis the sun that maketh all things shine.
KING
By heaven, thy love is black as ebony.
BIRON
Is ebony like her? O word divine!
　A wife of such wood were felicity.
O, who can give an oath? Where is a book,
　That I may swear beauty doth beauty lack,

245 word] QF; wood THEOBALD

227–8 **a gracious … star** 'To be like the moon to the stars' was proverbial (Dent S826.2).
　scarce seen a light i.e. only with great difficulty to be perceived as a light
231 **the culled sovereignty** those picked out as supreme
233 **several worthies** i.e. several different kinds of excellence
　dignity i.e. perfect beauty
234 **wants** is missing
　want the desire for perfection
235 **Lend me** endow me with
　flourish embellishment (*OED*, *sb.* 3)
　gentle noble
236 **painted rhetoric** i.e. rhetoric with its artificial colours. Compare 'Truth has no

need of rhetoric' (Dent T575).
237 **To … belongs** proverbial in the form 'He praises who wishes to sell' (Tilley P546)
　of sale for sale
238 **She … blot** i.e. she is beyond all praise, and, consequently, any attempt to praise her is bound to be inadequate and harmful
　blot stain, sully
241 **Beauty … age** i.e. the sight of a beautiful woman makes an old man feel young
242 **gives … infancy** i.e. endows old age with the youth of a child in the cradle
244 **black as ebony** proverbial (Dent E56a)
245 **word** See Wells, *Re-Editing*, p. 44.
247 **book** Bible

If that she learn not of her eye to look?
  No face is fair that is not full so black.   250

KING

O paradox! Black is the badge of hell,
  The hue of dungeons, and the school of night;
And beauty's crest becomes the heavens well.

BIRON

Devils soonest tempt, resembling spirits of light.
O, if in black my lady's brows be decked,
  It mourns that painting and usurping hair
Should ravish doters with a false aspect;
  And therefore is she born to make black fair.
Her favour turns the fashion of the days,
  For native blood is counted painting now;   260
And therefore red, that would avoid dispraise,
  Paints itself black to imitate her brow.

DUMAINE

To look like her are chimney-sweepers black.

LONGUEVILLE

And since her time are colliers counted bright.

---

252 school] QF (Schoole); scowl THEOBALD; stole HANMER; style OXFORD (*conj.* Shapiro)
253 And] QF; A WILSON 1962   256 and] F4; *not in* QF   257 doters] F; dooters Q

249 **If ... look** if she (beauty) does not learn
how to look from studying her (Rosaline's) eye
250 **fair** beautiful
251 **badge** symbol, token. 'As black as hell'
was, and remains, proverbial (Tilley
H397).
251–2 **Black is ... the school of night** The
simplest and most satisfactory way of
dealing with this much debated, much
emended, and much exploited passage is
that proposed by Sisson (*New Readings*, i.
115–16): to let the words stand as they
are in the control text and gloss them as
'night is the scholar or pupil of blackness', or, to put it another way, 'black is
the school where night learns to be really
black'. A striking parallel with *Lucrece*
endorses this explanation. Pleading with
Tarquin before the rape takes place,
Lucrece tells him: 'princes are the glass,
the school, the book | Where subjects'
eyes do learn, do read, do look. | And wilt
thou be the school where lust shall
learn?' (615–17). Just as Tarquin's lust-
fulness outdoes lust itself and so has

something to teach it, so black, the
quintessence of blackness, outdoes the
darkness of night and so has something
to teach night. Compare also 4.3.298,
where Biron calls the ladies 'beauty's
tutors'.
253 **beauty's crest** i.e. brightness which is
the badge of beauty (Schmidt)
254 **Devils ... light** proverbial (Tilley D231).
Compare *Hamlet* 2.2.600–1: 'the devil
hath power | T'assume a pleasing shape',
and 2 Corinthians 11 : 14: 'Satan himself
is transformed into an angel of light'.
resembling when they resemble
256 **usurping hair** wigs, hair that has no
right to be where it is
257 **aspect** appearance
259 **favour** countenance
turns ... days i.e. completely changes the
idea of what is fashionable
260 **native blood** a complexion that is naturally pink
counted regarded as, taken to be
261 **red** a healthy red
264 **colliers** traders in charcoal or pit-coal

KING

And Ethiops of their sweet complexion crack.

DUMAINE

Dark needs no candles now, for dark is light.

BIRON

Your mistresses dare never come in rain,

For fear their colours should be washed away.

KING

'Twere good yours did; for, sir, to tell you plain,

I'll find a fairer face not washed today.   270

BIRON

I'll prove her fair, or talk till doomsday here.

KING

No devil will fright thee then so much as she.

DUMAINE

I never knew man hold vile stuff so dear.

LONGUEVILLE (*showing his shoe*)

Look, here's thy love; my foot and her face see.

BIRON

O, if the streets were pavèd with thine eyes,

Her feet were much too dainty for such tread.

DUMAINE

O, vile! Then, as she goes, what upward lies

The street should see as she walked overhead.

KING

But what of this? Are we not all in love?

BIRON

Nothing so sure, and thereby all forsworn.   280

KING

Then leave this chat; and, good Biron, now prove

Our loving lawful and our faith not torn.

DUMAINE

Ay marry, there; some flattery for this evil.

---

274 *showing his shoe*] JOHNSON; *not in* QF   277 lies ∧] ROWE 1714; lyes? QF   280 Nothing]
F2; O nothing QF

---

265 **crack** boast (*OED*, *v.* 6)
267 **in** into contact with (Abbott 159)
272 **then** i.e. on doomsday
273 **vile** cheap, wretched
276 **tread** a path (*OED*, *sb.* 3), a surface

277 **goes** walks
280 **so** as (Abbott 275)
283 **there** that's the point, that's it
flattery ... evil i.e. nice verbal trickery to make our wickedness look better

LONGUEVILLE

O, some authority how to proceed—
Some tricks, some quillets, how to cheat the devil.

DUMAINE

Some salve for perjury.

BIRON   O, 'tis more than need.

Have at you then, affection's men-at-arms.
Consider what you first did swear unto:
To fast, to study, and to see no woman—
Flat treason 'gainst the kingly state of youth.   290
Say, can you fast? Your stomachs are too young,
And abstinence engenders maladies.
O, we have made a vow to study, lords,
And in that vow we have forsworn our books.
For when would you, my liege, or you, or you,
In leaden contemplation have found out
Such fiery numbers as the prompting eyes
Of beauty's tutors have enriched you with?
Other slow arts entirely keep the brain,
And therefore, finding barren practisers,   300
Scarce show a harvest of their heavy toil;
But love, first learnèd in a lady's eyes,
Lives not alone immurèd in the brain,
But with the motion of all elements
Courses as swift as thought in every power,

---

286 O] QF; *omitted* CAMBRIDGE   290 'gainst] Q (gainst); against F   293] *At this point* Q, *followed by* F, *prints the lines given in Appendix A (i).*

285 **quillets** verbal niceties, subtle distinctions. *OED* cites this as its first instance of the word; but Shakespeare had already used it in *1 Henry VI* 2.4.17–18: 'in these nice sharp quillets of the law, | Good faith, I am no wiser than a daw.'
   how to cheat the devil proverbial in the form 'This is the way to catch the old one' (Dent W149)

287 **Have at you** here goes
   affection's men-at-arms love's soldiers (a reversal of 1.1.8–10)

290 **state** status, rank (*OED, sb.* 15)

291 **young** unpractised, immature

292 After this line Q and F print what is obviously, and generally recognized to be, a first draft of lines 293–340. The original lines are to be found in Appendix A, and are of peculiar interest, since they

offer the most extended evidence we have of what the poet came to regard as unsatisfactory, and, when they are compared with the final version, of how he went about the task of revision.

296 **leaden** dull, heavy

297 **fiery numbers** Biron now praises his fellows' poems which earlier he held up to ridicule.

299 **Other … brain** i.e. other kinds of learning, being lethargic (by comparison with the art of love), occupy, confine themselves to, the brain alone

301 **of their** i.e. from those practisers'

303 **immurèd** walled up

304 **motion of all elements** i.e. celerity of winds and storms (*OED, element, sb.* 11)

305 **as swift as thought** proverbial (Dent T240)

And gives to every power a double power,
Above their functions and their offices.
It adds a precious seeing to the eye:
A lover's eye will gaze an eagle blind.
A lover's ear will hear the lowest sound,   310
When the suspicious head of theft is stopped.
Love's feeling is more soft and sensible
Than are the tender horns of cockled snails.
Love's tongue proves dainty Bacchus gross in taste.
For valour, is not Love a Hercules,
Still climbing trees in the Hesperides?
Subtle as Sphinx, as sweet and musical
As bright Apollo's lute, strung with his hair,
And when Love speaks, the voice of all the gods
Make heaven drowsy with the harmony.   320
Never durst poet touch a pen to write
Until his ink were tempered with Love's sighs.
O then his lines would ravish savage ears
And plant in tyrants mild humility.
From women's eyes this doctrine I derive.
They sparkle still the right Promethean fire;

310 sound,] ROWE; ~. QF   311 head] QF; heed WILSON   314 dainty ∧] F2; ~, QF
315–16 Hercules, ... Hesperides?] THEOBALD 1740; *Hercules? ... Hesperides.* QF   317 Subtle]
Q (Subtit), F   320 Make] QF; Makes HANMER

306 **every power a double power** a double
strength to every faculty
307 **Above ... offices** over and above their
allotted functions (a sort of hendiadys)
309 **gaze an eagle blind** blind an eagle that
gazes at it (thus showing itself stronger
than the sun). See note to line 223.
311 **the suspicious ... stopped** i.e. the ears of
the thief, apprehensive of the slightest
noise, can hear nothing. Shakespeare
frequently uses the abstract for the concrete. Schmidt (pages 1421–3) provides
a list of examples.
312–13 **more soft ... snails** Compare *Venus*
1033–4: 'Or as the snail, whose tender
horns being hit | Shrinks backward in his
shelly cave with pain'.
312 **sensible** sensitive
313 **cockled** equipped with a shell. *OED* cites
no other example of this sense.
316 **the Hesperides** The last of the twelve
labours of Hercules was to obtain the
golden apples from a tree growing in a

garden that was watched over by the
Hesperides, the daughters of Hesperus,
and guarded by a dragon. Shakespeare,
however, like many other writers of the
time, thought of the *Hesperides* as the
name of the garden itself.
317 **Sphinx** The monster, supposed to have
the head of a woman and the body of a
lion, that proposed the riddle which was
eventually solved by Oedipus.
319 **voice** voices (responding to, or joining
in with, Love's voice). For Shakespeare's
tendency to drop the final *s* in the plural
of words ending in *ce* and the like, see
Abbott 471.
324 **humility** 'a gentleness of the mind, or a
gentle patience without all anger or
wrath' (Richard Huloet, *Abcedarium*,
1552, as quoted by Furness).
326 **Promethean fire** i.e. the fire Prometheus
stole from heaven and gave to men. See
note to Appendix A(i).9.

They are the books, the arts, the academes,
That show, contain, and nourish all the world,
Else none at all in aught proves excellent.
Then fools you were these women to forswear,   330
Or, keeping what is sworn, you will prove fools.
For wisdom's sake, a word that all men love,
Or for love's sake, a word that loves all men,
Or for men's sake, the authors of these women,
Or women's sake, by whom we men are men,
Let us once lose our oaths to find ourselves,
Or else we lose ourselves to keep our oaths.
It is religion to be thus forsworn,
For charity itself fulfils the law,
And who can sever love from charity?   340

KING

Saint Cupid, then! And, soldiers, to the field!

BIRON

Advance your standards, and upon them, lords!
Pell-mell, down with them! But be first advised
In conflict that you get the sun of them.

LONGUEVILLE

Now to plain dealing. Lay these glozes by.
Shall we resolve to woo these girls of France?

KING

And win them too! Therefore let us devise
Some entertainment for them in their tents.

BIRON

First, from the park let us conduct them thither.
Then homeward every man attach the hand   350
Of his fair mistress. In the afternoon

---

334 authors] CAPELL; authour Q; author F   336 Let us] F2; Lets vs Q; Let's F
342 standards] F; standars Q

329 **Else ... excellent** without their help, no man can become excellent at anything
333 **loves** makes love to, woos
339 **charity ... law** Alluding to Romans 13: 8: 'he that loveth another hath fulfilled the law'.
342–3 **Advance ... with them** Biron is indulging in bawdy quibbles.
343 **be first advised** i.e. take the initial precaution

344 **get the sun of them** ensure that they have the sun in their eyes (*OED*, *sun*, *sb.* 1e(c))—possibly proverbial (Dent S987)
345 **glozes** clever comments, specious bits of word-play
346–7 **woo ... too** Compare the saying 'Woo, wed (win), and bed (wear) her' (Tilley W731).
350 **attach** seize, grasp (*OED*, *v.* 3b). The word was originally a legal one.

We will with some strange pastime solace them,
Such as the shortness of the time can shape;
For revels, dances, masques, and merry hours
Forerun fair Love, strewing her way with flowers.

KING

Away, away! No time shall be omitted
That will be time, and may by us be fitted.

BIRON

Allons, allons!

⌈*Exeunt the King, Longueville, and Dumaine*⌉
Sowed cockle reaped no corn,
And justice always whirls in equal measure:
Light wenches may prove plagues to men forsworn;   360
If so, our copper buys no better treasure.   *Exit*

5.1   *Enter Holofernes, Nathaniel, and Dull*
HOLOFERNES *Satis quod sufficit.*
NATHANIEL I praise God for you, sir. Your reasons at

356 omitted ∧] CAMBRIDGE; ~, QF   357 be time] QF; betime ROWE 1714   be fitted]
F; befitted Q   358 *Allons, allons*] THEOBALD; Alone alone Q; Alone, alone F   *Exeunt ...
Dumaine*] KERRIGAN (*subs.*); *not in* QF   360 forsworn] Q (forsorne), F   361 *Exit*] KERRIGAN;
Exeunt F; *not in* Q
5.1.0.1 *Enter ... Dull*] ROWE; *Enter the Pedant, the Curat, and Dull* Q, F (*subs.*)   1 (*and
throughout the scene*) HOLOFERNES] ROWE; *Pedant. (variously abbreviated)* QF   *quod*] ROWE; *quid* QF
2 (*and throughout the scene*) NATHANIEL] ROWE; *Curat.* QF

352 **strange** novel, highly original
357 **time** time enough (for our purpose)
(*OED*, *sb.* 8)
   fitted used in a fitting manner
358 *Allons, allons!* Q reads 'Alone alone'; F
   'Alone, alone'. There can be little doubt,
   however, that the French for 'let us go' is
   what the author intended. Exactly the
   same mistake, presumably compositorial, occurs at 5.1.139, and also in the
   1602 Quarto of *Merry Wives*, where the
   final words in Act 2 are: '*Host*. Let us wag
   then. *Doc*. Alon, alon, alon' (sig. D2).
   Compare 'Alloune, alloune, *let us march*'
   (Nashe, iii. 110. 12) and John Marston's
   'aloune' and 'aloun, aloun' in his *What
   You Will* (1601) (Harvey Wood, ii. 252
   and 266).
358.1 *Exeunt ... Dumaine* Q has no direction for getting the men off the stage,
   while F has merely '*Exeunt*' at the end of
   the scene. Biron's ominous and accurate
   forecast of what is about to happen
   appears, however, to be meant for the

audience in the theatre, rather than for
his fellow-students now turned ardent
lovers. Hence the present arrangement.
358 **Sowed ... corn** i.e. the man who sowed
   weed-seed reaped no grain. There may be
   an allusion here to the parable of the
   tares and the wheat (Matthew 13:
   24–30).
359 **whirls ... measure** i.e. is even-handed.
   Compare *Richard III* 4.4.105: 'This hath
   the course of justice whirled about' and
   the proverbial 'As they sow so let them
   reap' (Tilley S687).
360 **Light** frivolous, wanton
361 **copper** coins of small value
5.1.1 *Satis quod sufficit* This should be '*Satis
   est quod sufficit*', the Latin for 'Enough is
   enough' (Dent E159), with a glance at
   'Enough is as good as a feast' (Tilley
   E158). They have just come from dinner,
   which in Shakespeare's day was eaten
   about 11 a.m. or shortly thereafter.
2 **reasons** disquisitions (*OED*, *sb.* 3)

dinner have been sharp and sententious, pleasant without scurrility, witty without affection, audacious without impudency, learned without opinion, and strange
without heresy. I did converse this *quondam* day with a
companion of the King's, who is intituled, nominated,
or called Don Adriano de Armado.

HOLOFERNES *Novi hominem tanquam te.* His humour is lofty,
his discourse peremptory, his tongue filed, his eye   10
ambitious, his gait majestical, and his general behaviour vain, ridiculous, and thrasonical. He is too picked,
too spruce, too affected, too odd, as it were, too peregrinate, as I may call it.

NATHANIEL A most singular and choice epithet.
        He draws out his table-book

HOLOFERNES He draweth out the thread of his verbosity
finer than the staple of his argument. I abhor such
fanatical phantasimes, such insociable and point-device
companions, such rackers of orthography, as to speak

---

4 affection] QF; affectation F2   9 hominem] F3; hominum QF   15.1 *He ... table-book*] Q
(*Draw-out his Table-booke.*), F (*subs.*)

3 **sharp** pointed, acute
  sententious pithy, full of meaning (*OED*,
  1)
  pleasant amusing
4 **affection** affectation (*OED, sb.* 13)
  audacious spirited, confident
5 **impudency** immodesty, indelicacy
  opinion arrogance, dogmatism (*OED, sb.*
  5c). Compare *1 Henry IV* 3.1.181: 'Pride,
  haughtiness, opinion, and disdain'.
  strange fresh, original
6 **this** *quondam* **day** the other day
9 *Novi ... te* I know him as well as I know
  you—a phrase culled from William Lily's
  Brevissima Institutio (1549), the Latin
  Grammar used in English schools. The
  mistake of *hominum* for *hominem* in Q and
  F is almost certainly compositorial.
  humour disposition
10 **peremptory** dogmatic, overbearing
   filed smooth. Compare Sonnets 85.4:
   'precious phrase by all the muses filed',
   and Dent T400.2.
12 **thrasonical** boastful, bragging. *Thraso* is
   the name of the braggart soldier in Ter-
   ence's *Eunuchus*.
   picked finical, fastidious (*OED, ppl. a.* 2).
   Compare *K. John* 1.1.193.
13 **spruce** over-elegant
   odd eccentric, peculiar in behaviour

(*OED, a.* 9b; earliest citation of the word
in this sense)
13–14 **peregrinate** outlandish, having the
   air of one who has travelled abroad—a
   Shakespearian coinage
15 **singular** unparalleled, excellent (*OED, a.*
   11)
15.1 *table-book* notebook, memorandum
   book
16–17 **He ... argument** The figure is from
   spinning, the *staple* being the fibre of
   which a thread is composed. Holofernes
   of all people accuses Armado of 'spinning
   out' his discourse by using more words
   than his subject-matter warrants. *OED*
   cites no earlier example of *staple* in this
   figurative sense.
18 **fanatical** extravagant (*OED, a.* 2b; no
   other example cited)
   phantasimes See note to 4.1.98.
   insociable unfit for social intercourse.
   OED (*a.* 2) has no earlier instance.
   point-device pedantically precise
19 **companions** fellows (used as a term of
   contempt).   Compare   *Coriolanus*
   4.5.11–13: 'Has the porter his eyes in his
   head, that he gives entrance to such
   companions?'
   rackers of orthography torturers of spelling

'dout', *sine* 'b', when he should say 'doubt'; 'det', when   20
he should pronounce 'debt'—'d, e, b, t', not 'd, e, t'. He
clepeth a calf 'cauf'; half 'hauf'; neighbour *vocatur*
'nebour', 'neigh' abbreviated 'ne'. This is abhominable,
which he would call 'abominable'. It insinuateth me of
insanire. Ne intelligis, domine? To make frantic, lunatic.

NATHANIEL *Laus Deo, bone intelligo.*

HOLOFERNES *Bone?* 'Bone' for '*bene*'! Priscian a little
scratched; 'twill serve.

    Enter Armado, Moth, and Costard

NATHANIEL *Videsne quis venit?*

HOLOFERNES *Video et gaudeo.*   30

20 *sine* 'b'] RIDLEY; fine QF   21 'd, e, t'] POPE; det QF   24 'abominable'] Q (abbominable);
abhominable F   25 *insanire*] SINGER; infamie QF; insanie THEOBALD (*conj.* Warburton);
insania COLLIER 1858   26 *bone*] THEOBALD; bene QF   27 *Bone?* ... Priscian] THEOBALD;
Bome boon for boon prescian QF; *Bon, bon, fort bon*, Priscian CAMBRIDGE   28.1 *Enter ... Costard*]
ROWE; *Enter Bragart, Boy* QF   29 *Videsne*] POPE 1728; *Vides ne* QF   30 *gaudeo*] F2; *gaudio* QF

20 *sine* '**b**' without pronouncing the letter
'b', omitting the letter 'b'. Q and F both
read 'fine', which can be defended if
glossed as 'mincingly', but the Latin '*sine*'
is in the true Holofernes vein.

22 **clepeth** calls (archaic)
  vocatur is called

23–4 **abhominable** ... '**abominable**' As the
result of a mistaken etymology deriving
abominable from *ab homine*, i.e. 'away
from man', 'inhuman', the word was
written 'abhominable' from the 14th to
the 17th century and invariably takes
this form in the First Folio, where it
occurs some eighteen times. The correct
spelling, arising from a recognition that
abominable comes from the Latin *abomina-
bilis*, meaning 'deserving imprecation or
abhorrence', began to prevail around the
middle of the 17th century. In the light of
other Shakespearian uses of the word,
and especially of *Measure* 3.1.292, where
the Duke accuses Pompey the bawd of
making his living 'From their abominable
and beastly touches', it looks as though
the poet accepted the false etymology,
together with the spelling to which it
gave rise; but the present passage also
makes it clear that he knew the *h* was
dropped in normal speech.

24–5 **It ...** *insanire* It (this way of speaking)
seems to me to be subtly designed to drive
one mad. Q, followed by F, reads 'infamie', which makes no sense in this
context. Most editors have followed Theo-

bald in emending 'infamie' to read 'insanie', a very rare word, but *insanire* fits
better with Holofernes' own gloss 'To
make frantic, lunatic'.

25 *Ne intelligis, domine?* Do you understand, sir?

26–8 *Laus* ... **serve** This passage (see Introduction, p. 75) is hopelessly corrupt. For
some alternative emendations and comments see Binns, p. 126.

26 *Laus Deo, bone intelligo* Praise be to God,
I understand perfectly. Q and F read '*bene*'
for '*bone*', giving a sentence that is impec-
cable Latin. The ingenious Theobald
changed '*bene*', which is correct, into
'*bone*', which is a solecism, in order to
provide a justification for Holofernes'
reproof.

27 *Bone?* '*Bone*' **for** '*bene*'! Theobald's
emendation of the totally unintelligible
'*Bome boon for boon*' of Q and F.

27–8 **Priscian a little scratched** i.e. Latin
that is not quite what it ought to be—
alluding to the expression 'To break
Priscian's head' (Tilley P595), meaning
'To speak bad Latin'. Priscian's works on
Latin grammar, written in the early part
of the 6th century AD, were regarded as
standard by the scholars of the Renaissance.

29 *Videsne quis venit?* Do you see who is
coming?

30 *Video et gaudeo* I do see and I'm delighted. Q and F read '*Video, et gaudio*';
and '*gaudio*', meaning 'with joy', makes

ARMADO Chirrah!

HOLOFERNES *Quare* 'chirrah', not 'sirrah'?

ARMADO Men of peace, well encountered.

HOLOFERNES Most military sir, salutation.

MOTH (*to Costard*) They have been at a great feast of
languages and stolen the scraps.

COSTARD (*to Moth*) O, they have lived long on the alms-
basket of words. I marvel thy master hath not eaten
thee for a word, for thou art not so long by the head as
honorificabilitudinitatibus. Thou art easier swallowed   40
than a flap-dragon.

MOTH Peace, the peal begins.

ARMADO (*to Holofernes*) Monsieur, are you not lettered?

MOTH Yes, yes. He teaches boys the hornbook. What is 'a,
b' spelt backward with the horn on his head?

HOLOFERNES Ba, *pueritia*, with a horn added.

MOTH Ba, most silly sheep with a horn.—You hear his
learning.

HOLOFERNES *Quis, quis*, thou consonant?

MOTH The last of the five vowels, if you repeat them, or   50
the fifth, if I.

31 (*and for the rest of the scene*) ARMADO] ROWE; *Brag⟨gart⟩*. QF   32 *Quare*] F2; *Quari* QF
35 MOTH] ROWE; *Boy.* QF   37 (*and for the rest of the scene*) COSTARD] ROWE; *Clow⟨ne⟩*. QF
38 master] QF (M.)   40 *honorificabilitudinitatibus*] QF (*in roman*)   42 (*and for the rest of the
scene*) MOTH] ROWE; *Page.* QF   46 *pueritia*] QF (*puericia*)

quite good sense, but it does not accord,
as '*gaudeo*' does, with the Curate's love of
parallelism.

31 **Chirrah!** Hail! This explanation is J. A. K.
Thomson's. He takes 'Chirrah' to be
Armado's attempt at '*chaere*' (Greek
χαῖρε), one of the forms of salutation
listed by Erasmus in the first and most elementary part of his *Familiaria Colloquia*, a
work much used in Elizabethan schools
(*Shakespeare and the Classics*, p. 71).

32 *Quare* why

37–8 **alms-basket of words** i.e. words rejected by others. Each parish had an
alms-basket to contain scraps for distribution to the poor.

40 *honorificabilitudinitatibus* Reputed to
be the longest of words, this is the
dative/ablative plural of a medieval Latin
word meaning 'the state of being loaded
with honours'.

41 **flap-dragon** raisin, plum, or the like,

floating in burning brandy. Used in the
game of snap-dragon, it had to be caught
with the mouth and eaten.

42 **peal** peal of bells, i.e. tintinnabulation of
verbiage

43 **lettered** (a) learned (Armado's meaning)
(b) literate (Moth's meaning)

44 **hornbook** 'A leaf of paper containing the
alphabet (often with the addition of the
ten digits, some elements of spelling, and
the Lord's Prayer) protected by a thin
plate of translucent horn, and mounted
on a tablet of wood with a projecting
piece for a handle' (*OED*).

46 *pueritia* child (literally 'childishness')

49 *Quis* who
consonant nothing, nonentity—because
a consonant can only be sounded when
accompanied by a vowel. *OED* does not
record this sense.

50–3 **The last . . . o, u** Moth lures Holofernes
into repeating the five vowels, interrupts
him at *i*, thus making him a sheep, and

HOLOFERNES I will repeat them: a, e, i—

MOTH The sheep. The other two concludes it—o, u.

ARMADO Now by the salt wave of the *Mediterraneum*, a
sweet touch, a quick venue of wit, snip, snap, quick and
home! It rejoiceth my intellect. True wit!

MOTH Offered by a child to an old man—which is wit-old.

HOLOFERNES What is the figure? What is the figure?

MOTH Horns.

HOLOFERNES Thou disputes like an infant. Go whip thy gig.   60

MOTH Lend me your horn to make one, and I will whip
about your infamy *manu cita*. A gig of a cuckold's horn!

COSTARD An I had but one penny in the world, thou
shouldst have it to buy gingerbread. Hold, there is the
very remuneration I had of thy master, thou halfpenny
purse of wit, thou pigeon-egg of discretion. O, an the
heavens were so pleased that thou wert but my bastard,

---

54 salt wave] F (salt waue); sault wane Q   *Mediterraneum*] ROWE; mediteranium QF
55 venue] DYCE; vene we QF   60 disputes] QF; disputes't F2   62 *manu cita*] DAVID; *vnù
cita* Q; *vnum cita* F; *circum circa* THEOBALD   67 wert] F; wart Q

then concludes the performance and
wins the game by adding 'o, u (i.e.
ewe / you)' himself.

54 **salt** This word could have the secondary
sense of 'pungent', 'witty'. Compare *Troilus* 1.3.364: 'the pride and salt scorn of
his eyes'.
Mediterraneum Mediterranean. Armado's preference for the Latin (*mare Mediterraneum*) may not be so affected as it
looks. To judge from the examples cited
by *OED*, *Mediterranean* was just coming
into use about the time when *LLL* was
written.

55 **touch** a hit scored on an opponent in a
fencing-match. Compare *Hamlet* 5.2.239:
'A touch, a touch, I do confess.'
venue thrusting attack (*OED*, 2b)

56 **home** i.e. hitting the target

57 **wit-old** Moth quibbles on *wittol*, often
written *wittold*, a contented cuckold.

58 **figure** (a) figure of speech (the sense
Holofernes intends) (b) emblem (the
sense Moth gives it)

60 **disputes** Shakespeare often employs this
form of the second person singular, especially for verbs ending in *t* or *te* (Abbott

340). Compare 5.2.208: 'Thou now requests'.

60-1 **gig ... one** According to Halliwell,
quoted by Furness at 4.3.165, there is
some evidence that whipping-tops were
'made of the tip of a horn, hollow, but
with a small ballast at the bottom of the
inside'.

62 **manu cita** with a lively hand. Binns
(p. 125) would accept the QF reading
'*unum cita*' as it stands, taking it to mean
'cite one [example]', and explain the
entire speech thus: 'I will whip about
your Infamy—give me an instance (or
example)—a top made out of a cuckold's
horn.' This, however, sounds rather laboured for Moth, whereas '*manu cita*'
looks forward to the comic threat Falstaff's page utters to Mistress Quickly
when he tells her 'I'll tickle your catastrophe' (*2 Henry IV* 2.1.62).

65-6 **halfpenny purse** tiny purse (probably
for holding silver halfpence). Compare
Merry Wives 3.5.134-5, referring to Falstaff: 'He cannot creep into a halfpenny
purse, nor into a pepperbox'.

66 **pigeon-egg** apparently as an instance of
something small

what a joyful father wouldst thou make me! Go to, thou
hast it *ad dunghill*, at the fingers' ends, as they say.

HOLOFERNES O, I smell false Latin, 'dunghill' for '*unguem*'.   70

ARMADO Arts-man, preambulate. We will be singuled
from the barbarous. Do you not educate youth at the
charge-house on the top of the mountain?

HOLOFERNES Or *mons*, the hill.

ARMADO At your sweet pleasure, for the mountain.

HOLOFERNES I do, *sans question*.

ARMADO Sir, it is the King's most sweet pleasure and
affection to congratulate the Princess at her pavilion in
the posteriors of this day, which the rude multitude call
the afternoon.   80

HOLOFERNES The posterior of the day, most generous sir, is
liable, congruent, and measurable for the afternoon.
The word is well culled, choice, sweet, and apt, I do
assure you, sir, I do assure.

ARMADO Sir, the King is a noble gentleman, and my
familiar, I do assure ye, very good friend. For what is

---

69 dunghill] THEOBALD; *dungil* QF   70 dunghill] THEOBALD; *dunghel* QF   71 Arts-man,]
THEOBALD; *Arts-man* ∧] QF   preambulate] CAMBRIDGE; *preambulat* QF; *preambulate* OXFORD
singuled] Q; singled F   83 choice] F2 (choise); chose QF   86 ye,] ROWE; ~ ∧ QF

69–70 **ad dunghill ... unguem** 'To have
something at one's fingers' ends' was a
familiar saying (Tilley F245) stemming
from the Latin *ad unguem* meaning 'down
to the fingernail', 'exact in every detail',
originally used of a piece of sculpture.

71 **Arts-man** i.e. learned sir, man skilled in
the liberal arts (*OED*, 2). This instance
antedates *OED*'s earliest example by
about ten years.
preambulate walk forward (with me).
OED cites no instance of this rare word
prior to 1607 (Schoenbaum's date for
Every Woman in Her Humour). It is to be
found, however, in George Chapman's
An Humorous Day's Mirth (3.53), where
it has precisely the sense it has here. First
played in May 1597, Chapman's comedy
was published in 1599.
singuled singled out, separated. 'Singled'
has not the 'singularity' Armado requires, so he coins his own version of it.

72–6 **Do you ... sans question** J. A. K.
Thomson (pp. 72–3) has provided a most
attractive solution to this passage which
baffled earlier commentators. He shows

that it is based on a dialogue between
Georgius and Livinus near the beginning
of Erasmus' *Colloquies*. Georgius asks:
'*Unde prodis?* (Where do you come
from?)' Livinus replies: '*E collegio Montis
Acuti* (From the college of the pointed
Mountain).' Georgius then remarks:
'*Ergo ades nobis onustus literis* (So you
must come to us loaded with learning).'
'*Immo pediculis* (No, with lice),' answers
Livinus. The college in question is the
Collège de Montaigu in Paris where Eras-
mus had been a student in his youth, and
had suffered.

73 **charge-house** house for the charge of
youth, boarding-school (*OED*, 1; no
other instance cited)

78 **congratulate** salute (*OED*, *v*. 5)

79 **posteriors** buttocks, backside—not the
happiest of synonyms for 'later part'

81 **generous** nobly born

82 **liable** suitable, apt (*OED*, *a*. 6)
measurable fit (*OED*, *a*. 4)

86 **familiar** intimate. It is not clear whether
familiar is used as an adjective or as a
noun.

inward between us, let it pass—I do beseech thee,
remember thy courtesy; I beseech thee apparel thy
head. And among other important and most serious
designs, and of great import indeed, too—but let that   90
pass; for I must tell thee it will please his grace, by the
world, sometime to lean upon my poor shoulder, and,
with his royal finger, thus dally with my excrement,
with my mustachio—but, sweetheart, let that pass. By
the world, I recount no fable! Some certain special
honours it pleaseth his greatness to impart to Armado, a
soldier, a man of travel, that hath seen the world—but
let that pass. The very all of all is—but, sweetheart, I do
implore secrecy—that the King would have me present
the Princess—sweet chuck—with some delightful osten-   100
tation, or show, or pageant, or antic, or firework. Now,
understanding that the curate and your sweet self are
good at such eruptions and sudden breaking-out of
mirth, as it were, I have acquainted you withal, to the
end to crave your assistance.

HOLOFERNES Sir, you shall present before her the Nine
Worthies. Sir Nathaniel, as concerning some entertainment of time, some show in the posterior of this day to
be rendered by our assistance, the King's command,
and this most gallant, illustrate, and learned gentleman   110
before the Princess, I say none so fit as to present the
Nine Worthies.

---

89 important] COLLIER (*conj.* Capell); importunt Q; importunate F   94 mustachio] F;
mustachie Q   99 secrecy] F (secrecie); secretie Q   107 Nathaniel] CAPELL; *Holofernes* QF
109 rendered] F (rendred); rended Q   assistance] HANMER (*conj.* Theobald); assistants QF
111 as to present] QF; to present as HUDSON (*conj.* Dyce)

---

87 **inward** confidential, private
88 **remember thy courtesy** be covered, put
your hat on again (*OED, v.* 1d). Compare
Hamlet 5.2.105: 'I beseech you, remember'.
93 **excrement** i.e. that which grows out of
the body, such as the hair and the nails
(*OED, excrement²*, 1). Compare *Errors*
2.2.78–9: 'Why is Time such a niggard
of hair, being, as it is, so plentiful an
excrement?' There is probably a quibble,
not intentional on Armado's part, on the
modern sense of the word.
98 **all of all** sum of it all
100 **chuck** chick (used as a term of endear-

ment or familiarity; earliest citation in
OED)
100–1 **ostentation** spectacular show or ex-
hibition (*OED*, 2c). *OED* offers no other
example of this sense.
101 **antic** grotesque pageant (*OED, sb.* 3;
earliest example of this sense)
103 **eruptions** *OED*'s first example of the
word in a figurative sense.
104 **withal** with it
111–18 **the Nine Worthies ... Hercules**
Traditionally the Nine Worthies (men of
great renown) were three Gentiles (Hector of Troy, Alexander the Great, and
Julius Caesar), three Jews (Joshua, David,

NATHANIEL Where will you find men worthy enough to
present them?

HOLOFERNES Joshua, yourself; myself, Judas Maccabeus;
and this gallant gentleman, Hector. This swain, because
of his great limb or joint, shall pass Pompey the Great;
the page, Hercules.

ARMADO Pardon, sir, error! He is not quantity enough for
that Worthy's thumb. He is not so big as the end of his   120
club.

HOLOFERNES Shall I have audience? He shall present Hercules in minority. His enter and exit shall be strangling a
snake; and I will have an apology for that purpose.

MOTH An excellent device! So, if any of the audience hiss,
you may cry 'Well done, Hercules, now thou crushest
the snake!' That is the way to make an offence gracious,
though few have the grace to do it.

ARMADO For the rest of the Worthies?

HOLOFERNES I will play three myself.   130

MOTH Thrice-worthy gentleman!

ARMADO Shall I tell you a thing?

HOLOFERNES We attend.

ARMADO We will have, if this fadge not, an antic. I
beseech you, follow.

115–16 myself ... Hector] OXFORD (*conj.* Proudfoot); my selfe, and this gallant Gentleman
Iudas Machabeus QF

and Judas Maccabeus), and three Christians (King Arthur, Charlemagne, and
Godfrey of Bouillon). They were the subject of pageants from at least the latter
part of the 15th century onwards; but
there is no record of Hercules and Pompey the Great being included among
them prior to their appearance here.

114 **present** represent (*OED, v.* 7b; earliest
instance of this sense). Compare *Merry
Wives* 4.6.19–20: 'Tonight at Herne's
Oak, just 'twixt twelve and one, | Must
my sweet Nan present the Fairy Queen'.

115–16 **Joshua ... Hector** This is the reading of the Oxford Shakespeare suggested
by Richard Proudfoot. Q, followed substantially by F, runs thus: '*Iosua*, your
selfe, my selfe, and this gallant Gentleman *Iudas Machabeus*', which makes no
sense. Proudfoot thinks that either 'and
this gallant Gentleman' or '*Iudas Macha-*

beus' was misplaced by the compositor
and led to the omission of '*Hector*', and he
points out that such misplacement would
be all the more likely if either of these
phrases was interlined or written in the
margin.

117 **pass** pass for, serve to enact the role of (a
sense not recognized by *OED* but tentatively accepted by Onions)

122 **have audience** be given a hearing

123 **in minority** when a child
enter entrance. This is the most recent
example of *enter* as a noun cited by *OED*.

123–4 **strangling a snake** Hercules wasted
no time in showing his strength. When
Juno sent two large snakes to attack him
in his cradle, he took one in each hand
and strangled them.

124 **apology** explanatory justification

134 **fadge not** does not turn out well, is a
flop (*OED, v.* 4). Compare *Twelfth Night*
2.2.33: 'How will this fadge?'

HOLOFERNES *Via*, Goodman Dull! Thou hast spoken no
  word all this while.

DULL Nor understood none neither, sir.

HOLOFERNES *Allons!* We will employ thee.

DULL I'll make one in a dance, or so; or I will play on the   140
  tabor to the Worthies, and let them dance the hay.

HOLOFERNES Most dull Dull, honest Dull! To our sport,
  away!   *Exeunt*

5.2   *Enter the Princess, Maria, Katherine, and Rosaline*
PRINCESS

  Sweethearts, we shall be rich ere we depart,

  If fairings come thus plentifully in.

  A lady walled about with diamonds!

  Look you what I have from the loving King.

ROSALINE

  Madam, came nothing else along with that?

PRINCESS

  Nothing but this? Yes, as much love in rhyme

  As would be crammed up in a sheet of paper,

  Writ o' both sides the leaf, margin and all,

  That he was fain to seal on Cupid's name.

139 *Allons!*] ROWE; *Alone* QF   142 dull Dull] This edition; *Dull* QF   143 *Exeunt*] Q; *Exit* F
  5.2.0.1 *Enter ... Rosaline*] CAPELL (subs.); *Enter the Ladyes.* Q; *Enter Ladies.* F   1–709
  PRINCESS] ROWE; *Quee⟨n⟩.* QF   6 this?] ROWE; ~ : QF   8 o'] Q (a); on F

136 *Via* come on, show a bit of life
140 **make one** join, take part
141 **tabor** small drum used by clowns and
    jesters, and much in demand on festive
    occasions
    the hay a country dance having a wind-
    ing or serpentine movement (*OED, sb.*⁴)
142 **Most dull Dull** Q and F both read 'Most
    Dull', showing that the personal name is
    intended. It seems likely, therefore, that
    the word 'dull' was either deliberately,
    since the line is a very tight one, or
    accidentally omitted.
5.2.2 **fairings** gifts (originally 'a present
    given or bought from a fair')
3 **A lady ... diamonds** During Elizabeth's
    reign English taste and fashion came
    under the influence of France and Italy

and, as a result, 'the earlier geometrical
arrangements of stones in heavy gothic
settings gradually gave way to the use of
minute nude figures, realistically
modelled with exquisite taste and precision and set amongst enamelled
strapwork or arabesques, accentuated at
important points with precious stones;
this flat treatment was particularly suitable for the pendants so much sought
after and worn by both men and women'
(*Shakespeare's England*, ii. 114). Compare
Contention 3.2.106–7: 'I took a costly
jewel from my neck— | A heart it was,
bound in with diamonds'.

9 **That ... name** so that he was compelled
  to put his seal on the name of Cupid

ROSALINE

> That was the way to make his godhead wax,   10
> For he hath been five thousand year a boy.

KATHERINE

> Ay, and a shrewd unhappy gallows too.

ROSALINE

> You'll ne'er be friends with him; a killed your sister.

KATHERINE

> He made her melancholy, sad, and heavy,
> And so she died. Had she been light, like you,
> Of such a merry, nimble, stirring spirit,
> She might ha' been a grandam ere she died.
> And so may you, for a light heart lives long.

ROSALINE

> What's your dark meaning, mouse, of this light word?

KATHERINE

> A light condition in a beauty dark.   20

ROSALINE

> We need more light to find your meaning out.

KATHERINE

> You'll mar the light by taking it in snuff,
> Therefore I'll darkly end the argument.

ROSALINE

> Look what you do, you do it still i'th' dark.

KATHERINE

> So do not you, for you are a light wench.

ROSALINE

> Indeed I weigh not you, and therefore light.

---

11 year] Q (yeere); yeeres F   17 been a] F (bin a); bin Q   22 You'll] F; Yole Q

10 **wax** (a) grow up, spread (b) sealing-wax
11 **five thousand year** The world was thought to be five thousand years old.
12 **shrewd** ill-disposed, wicked
   unhappy trouble-making (*OED, a.* 5)
   gallows gallows-bird, one deserving to be hanged (*OED,* 3; earliest example)
15 **light** lively, cheerful
18 **a light heart lives long** proverbial (Tilley H320a)
19 **dark** hidden
   mouse a term of endearment. Compare *Hamlet* 3.4.166–7: 'Let the bloat King ... call you his mouse'.

19 **light** frivolous
20 **light condition** wanton nature
22 **taking it in snuff** taking offence at it—proverbial (Tilley S598). The *snuff* is that portion of a candle-wick which is only partly burnt and, if not removed, gives off an unpleasant smell, as well as spoiling the *light.*
24 **Look what** whatever
   do it (almost certainly bawdy)
26 **weigh not** am not as heavy as. Katherine, however, takes *weigh* to mean 'value', 'think much of' (*OED, v.*¹ 13).

KATHERINE

You weigh me not? O, that's you care not for me.

ROSALINE

Great reason, for past cure is still past care.

PRINCESS

Well bandied both, a set of wit well played.

But, Rosaline, you have a favour too.   30

Who sent it, and what is it?

ROSALINE   I would you knew.

An if my face were but as fair as yours,

My favour were as great: be witness this.

Nay, I have verses too, I thank Biron;

The numbers true, and, were the numb'ring too,

I were the fairest goddess on the ground.

I am compared to twenty thousand fairs.

O, he hath drawn my picture in his letter!

PRINCESS Anything like?

ROSALINE

Much in the letters, nothing in the praise.   40

PRINCESS

Beauteous as ink—a good conclusion.

KATHERINE

Fair as a text B in a copy-book.

ROSALINE

'Ware pencils, ho! Let me not die your debtor,

My red dominical, my golden letter.

O that your face were not so full of O's!

28 cure ... care] THEOBALD *(conj.* Thirlby); care ... cure QF   43 ho!] HANMER ; How? QF
45 not so] Q; *not in* F

28 **past cure is still past care** proverbial
(Tilley C921)

29 **Well ... played** The Princess sees the
stichomythic exchanges between the two
girls as a game of tennis or 'bandy'.

30 **favour** love-token (*OED, sb.* 7), twisted by
Rosaline at line 33 to mean 'looks',
'appearance' (*OED,* 9)

35 **numbers true** metre sound
numb'ring reckoning of, value set on (my
beauty) (*OED, v.* 1c)

37 **fairs** beautiful women (*OED, sb.² 2).
Compare *Dream* 1.1.182: 'O happy fair!'

40 **Much ... praise** i.e. Biron's black letters
on the white page correspond to Rosaline's black hair and eyebrows set against
her pale cheeks, but there is no such

correspondence between the praise he
gives her and what she is.

42 **text B** capital B (Onions), possibly meant
to suggest *black*

43 **'Ware** beware
pencils paint-brushes, especially of a fine
pointed kind, used by artists, and also by
ladies when applying cosmetics
Let ... debtor i.e. I mean to get my own
back—proverbial (Tilley D165)

44 **red dominical** Almanacs used a red *S* for
Sundays. Rosaline refers to Katherine's
ruddy complexion.
golden letter Used, like the *red dominical*,
to mark Sundays, this term glances at
Katherine's 'amber hairs' (4.3.85).

45 **O's** i.e. small round scars caused by

PRINCESS

A pox of that jest; I beshrew all shrews.

But, Katherine, what was sent to you from fair
    Dumaine?

KATHERINE

Madam, this glove.

PRINCESS   Did he not send you twain?

KATHERINE Yes, madam, and moreover

Some thousand verses of a faithful lover: 50

A huge translation of hypocrisy,

Vilely compiled, profound simplicity.

MARIA

This and these pearls to me sent Longueville.

The letter is too long by half a mile.

PRINCESS

I think no less. Dost thou not wish in heart

The chain were longer and the letter short?

MARIA

Ay, or I would these hands might never part.

PRINCESS

We are wise girls to mock our lovers so.

ROSALINE

They are worse fools to purchase mocking so.

That same Biron I'll torture ere I go.   60

O that I knew he were but in by th' week!

How I would make him fawn, and beg, and seek,

And wait the season, and observe the times,

46 jest; 1] OXFORD; iest, and I QF; jest, and CAPELL   47 Katherine] QF; *omitted* THEOBALD
53, 57 MARIA] F (*Mar.*); *Marg.* Q   53 pearls] F; Pearle Q   55 not] Q; *not in* F

smallpox and requiring the use of the
cosmetic *pencil*

46 **A pox ... jest** By using this strong imprecation the Princess makes it clear not only
that she sees what Rosaline is getting at
but also that she strongly disapproves.
I ... shrews I say the devil take all shrews
(pronounced to rhyme with *shows*)
51 **huge translation of hypocrisy** monstrous
transformation of hypocrisy into words,
i.e. great pack of lies (*OED, translation*,
2b; earliest example of this sense)
52 **compiled** thrown together (*OED*, 5)
profound simplicity (a) learned silliness
(b) extreme folly

54 **too long by half a mile** possibly proverbial
(Dent M924.1)
57 **Ay ... part** Capell's note seems worth
printing for its period flavour: 'Maria's
words spring from having her "chain" in
both hands, or twisted (perhaps) about
them in a womanish wantonness'.
59 **purchase mocking so** i.e. pay such a high
price for the privilege of being mocked
61 **in by th' week** caught for good and all—a
well-used phrase (Tilley W244), especially with reference to being in love
63 **wait the season** wait expectantly for the
right time
observe the times keep to the recognized
rules

And spend his prodigal wits in bootless rhymes,
And shape his service wholly to my hests,
And make him proud to make me proud that jests!
So fortune-like would I o'ersway his state
That he should be my fool, and I his fate.

PRINCESS

None are so surely caught, when they are catched,
As wit turned fool. Folly, in wisdom hatched,   70
Hath wisdom's warrant and the help of school,
And wit's own grace to grace a learnèd fool.

ROSALINE

The blood of youth burns not with such excess
As gravity's revolt to wantonness.

MARIA

Folly in fools bears not so strong a note
As fool'ry in the wise when wit doth dote,
Since all the power thereof it doth apply
To prove, by wit, worth in simplicity.

Enter Boyet

PRINCESS

Here comes Boyet, and mirth is in his face.

BOYET

O, I am stabbed with laughter! Where's her grace?   80

65 hests] DYCE *(conj.* Knight); deuice QF   67 fortune-like] This edition; perttaunt like Q;
pertaunt like F; Pair-Taunt like DAVID *(conj.* Simpson); planet-like WILSON *(conj.* Moore Smith);
pursuivant-like OXFORD   70 fool.] F2 (~ :); ~ , QF   hatched,] F2; ~ · QF   74 wanton-
ness] F2 (wantonesse); wantons be QF   79 is] Q; *not in* F   80 stabbed] F (stab'd); stable Q

64 **bootless** ineffectual
65 **hests** orders. Q and F read 'deuice' to the
    detriment of both metre and rhyme.
    Knight's happy conjecture satisfies the
    demands of both.
66 **And ... jests** i.e. Rosaline would like to
    bring Biron into such a state of subjection
    that he would take pride in being the
    object of her proud mockeries
    jests jest. For examples of Shakespeare's
    use of a verb in the third person after a
    relative that now requires the first, see
    Abbott 247.
67 **fortune-like** Q reads 'perttaunt like'; F
    'pertaunt like'. The crux that results,
    together with the more important solu-
    tions proposed, is discussed in detail by
    Stanley Wells (*Re-Editing*, pp. 34–5). I
    share his misgivings about them, but I

am not convinced by his own solution—
'pursuivant-like'. It sounds 'too peregrinate', whereas 'fortune-like' has the support of *Romeo* 3.1.136: 'O, I am fortune's
fool!' and of *Tragedy of Lear* 4.5.186–7: 'I
am even | The natural fool of fortune.'
'Fortune' is, of course, capricious, and
that is exactly what Rosaline wants to be.
69 **catched** captivated, charmed (*OED*, v.
    37)
74 **revolt to** falling into, going over to
75 **note** stigma
77–8 **Since ... simplicity** i.e. since the wise
    man turned fool will avail himself of all
    the intelligence he has to show that folly
    is true wisdom
80 **I ... laughter** I have laughed so much
    that I have the stitch

PRINCESS

Thy news, Boyet?

BOYET   Prepare, madam, prepare!
Arm, wenches, arm! Encounters mounted are
Against your peace. Love doth approach disguised,
Armèd in arguments. You'll be surprised.
Muster your wits, stand in your own defence,
Or hide your heads like cowards and fly hence.

PRINCESS

Saint Denis to Saint Cupid! What are they
That charge their breath against us? Say, scout, say.

BOYET

Under the cool shade of a sycamore
I thought to close mine eyes some half an hour,   90
When, lo, to interrupt my purposed rest,
Toward that shade I might behold addressed
The King and his companions. Warily
I stole into a neighbour thicket by,
And overheard what you shall overhear:
That, by and by, disguised they will be here.
Their herald is a pretty knavish page,
That well by heart hath conned his embassage.
Action and accent did they teach him there:
'Thus must thou speak', and 'thus thy body bear'.   100
And ever and anon they made a doubt
Presence majestical would put him out;
'For', quoth the King, 'an angel shalt thou see;
Yet fear not thou, but speak audaciously.'
The boy replied, 'An angel is not evil;

83 peace.] THEOBALD (*subs.*); Peace ∧ Q; ~, F   89 sycamore] Q (Siccamone), F   93 companions. Warily ∧] F (*subs.*); companions warely, Q   96 they] F; thy Q   97 page,] Page: QF   101 doubt ∧] COLLIER; ~, QF

82 **Encounters mounted are** an attack has
   been organized
84 **surprised** (a) taken unawares (b) taken
   prisoners (*OED*, *v*. 2b)
87 **Saint Denis** patron saint of France
88 **charge** Two different senses of *charge* are
   equally appropriate: (a) load (as with a
   gun: *OED*, *v*. 5) (b) level (as with a lance:
   OED, *v*. 21). Compare *K. John* 2.1.382:
   'Their battering cannon, chargèd to the
   mouths', and *Much Ado* 5.1.135–6: 'I
   shall meet your wit in the career an you

   charge it against me.'
88 **scout** spy, reconnoitrer
92 **might behold** beheld
   addressed making their way (*OED*, *v*. 5)
95 **overhear** hear told over again, hear at
   second hand (*OED*, *v*. 4; nonce-use)
96 **by and by** very soon
98 **conned his embassage** learned his message
101 **made a doubt** voiced their apprehension
102 **put him out** make him forget his part

192

I should have feared her had she been a devil.'
With that all laughed and clapped him on the
    shoulder,
Making the bold wag by their praises bolder.
One rubbed his elbow thus, and fleered, and swore
A better speech was never spoke before.   110
Another, with his finger and his thumb,
Cried '*Via*, we will do't, come what will come!'
The third he capered and cried 'All goes well.'
The fourth turned on the toe, and down he fell.
With that they all did tumble on the ground,
With such a zealous laughter, so profound,
That in this spleen ridiculous appears,
To check their folly, passion's solemn tears.

PRINCESS

But what, but what? Come they to visit us?

BOYET

They do, they do, and are apparelled thus,   120
Like Muscovites or Russians, as I guess.
Their purpose is to parley, court, and dance,
And every one his love-suit will advance
Unto his several mistress, which they'll know
By favours several which they did bestow.

---

111 thumb] Q (thume), F   118 folly,] THEOBALD; ~ ∧ QF   solemn] Q (solembe), F
120] *Omission marked after this line* OXFORD   122 parley, court] POPE; parlee, to court QF;
parle, to court CAPELL   123 love-suit] DYCE (*conj.* Collier); Loue-feat QF

109 **rubbed his elbow** a sign of satisfaction.
    Compare *1 Henry IV* 5.1.76–8: 'fickle
    changelings and poor discontents, |
    Which gape and rub the elbow at the
    news | Of hurly-burly innovation'. The
    phrase, first recorded here, seems to have
    caught on (Tilley E100).
    fleered grinned (*OED, v.* 1)
111 **with … thumb** i.e. snapping finger and
    thumb together
112 **come … come** proverbial (Tilley C529)
114 **turned on the toe** made a pirouette
117–18 **That … tears** i.e. they laughed until
    they cried. It is no wonder that the
    Princess becomes impatient with such
    circumlocution as this.
120 Oxford, following Keightley's example,
    marks an omission after this line because

there is no rhyme word to correspond
with 'guess' (l. 121), and nothing to
correspond with 'thus'.
121 **Like … Russians** It seems highly likely
    (see Introduction, pp. 45–7) that Shake-
    speare in devising this disguise was
    thinking of the elaborate shows staged at
    Gray's Inn to celebrate Twelfth Night in
    1595. An account of these revels, in
    which an Ambassador 'from the mighty
    Emperor of Russia and Muscovy', to-
    gether with two companions, took part,
    was published in 1688 under the title
    Gesta Grayorum. The relevant passages
    from it are most easily accessible in
    Bullough i. 438–41.
124 **several** respective
    mistress lady-love, sweetheart

PRINCESS

And will they so? The gallants shall be tasked;
For, ladies, we will every one be masked,
And not a man of them shall have the grace,
Despite of suit, to see a lady's face.
Hold, Rosaline, this favour thou shalt wear,   130
And then the King will court thee for his dear.
Hold, take thou this, my sweet, and give me thine,
So shall Biron take me for Rosaline.

She changes favours with Rosaline

(*To Maria and Katherine*) And change you favours too.
            So shall your loves
Woo contrary, deceived by these removes.

Maria and Katherine change favours

ROSALINE

Come on, then, wear the favours most in sight.

KATHERINE

But in this changing what is your intent?

PRINCESS

The effect of my intent is to cross theirs.
They do it but in mockery merriment,
And mock for mock is only my intent.   140
Their several counsels they unbosom shall
To loves mistook, and so be mocked withal
Upon the next occasion that we meet,
With visages displayed, to talk and greet.

ROSALINE

But shall we dance if they desire us to't?

---

127 ladies,] F4 ; ~ ; QF   130–1 Hold ... dear.] QF ; *relegated to 'Additional Passages'* OXFORD
(*conj.* Riverside)   133.1 *She ... Rosaline*] *not in* QF   134 you] Q; your F   too] F; two Q
135.1 *Maria ... favours*] *not in* QF   139 mockery] Q (mockerie); mocking F   141 Their] Q
(*text*), F; The Q (*c.w.*)   142 withal ∧] DYCE; ~ . QF

---

126 **tasked** put to the proof, tested
128 **grace** privilege
129 **suit** his pleading
130–1 **Hold ... dear** Oxford (following Riverside's suggestion) omits these lines on the assumption that they are a 'first shot' at 132–3. They are retained in this edition because, taken in conjunction with 132–3, they make it crystal clear what the Princess's plan is.

134 **change** exchange
135 **removes** exchanges
136 **most in sight** very conspicuously
139 **mockery** Shakespeare also uses this word as an adjective at *Richard II* 4.1.250: 'a mockery king of snow'.
140 **mock ... intent** Compare 'He who mocks shall be mocked' (Tilley M1031).
141 **counsels** secret purposes, confidences (*OED*, *sb.* 5)

PRINCESS

No, to the death we will not move a foot,

Nor to their penned speech render we no grace,

But while 'tis spoke each turn away her face.

BOYET

Why, that contempt will kill the speaker's heart,

And quite divorce his memory from his part.   150

PRINCESS

Therefore I do it, and I make no doubt

The rest will ne'er come in, if he be out.

There's no such sport as sport by sport o'erthrown,

To make theirs ours, and ours none but our own.

So shall we stay, mocking intended game,

And they, well mocked, depart away with shame.

    A trumpet sounds

BOYET

The trumpet sounds. Be masked; the masquers come.

    The ladies mask.

    Enter blackamoors with music, Moth with a speech,

    and the King and his lords disguised as Russians

MOTH

'All hail, the richest beauties on the earth!'

⌈BOYET⌉

Beauties no richer than rich taffeta.

MOTH

'A holy parcel of the fairest dames   160

    The ladies turn their backs to him

That ever turned their—backs—to mortal views.'

148 her] F2; his QF   149 speaker's] Q (speakers); keepers F   151 doubt ∧] ROWE
1714; ~, QF   152 ne'er] F2; ere QF   155 stay,] THEOBALD; ~ ∧ QF   156.1 *A trumpet
sounds*] Q (*Sound Trom.*); *Sound.* F   157.1–2 *Enter ... Russians*] Q (*Enter Black-moores with
musicke, the Boy with a speach, and the rest of the Lordes disguysed.*), F (*subs.*)   158–73 MOTH]
ROWE; *Page.* QF   159 BOYET] THEOBALD; *Berow⟨ne⟩.* QF   160.1 *The ... him*] Q (*in roman and
after l. 161*), F   161 their—backs—to] CAPELL; *their backes to* QF

146 **to the death** i.e. though we should die
for it

147 **penned speech** speech specially composed and written out for the occasion

149 **kill ... heart** completely dishearten the
speaker. Compare *Winter's Tale*
4.3.82–3: 'Offer me no money, I pray
you. That kills my heart.'

152 **out** i.e. put out of his part (so that he
'dries up')

157.2 **blackamoors** i.e. attendants got up as

African negroes

159 **BOYET** Theobald's emendation of Q's
'*Berow.*' is adopted here because the King
says explicitly and angrily that it was
Boyet who 'put Armado's page out of his
part' (5.2.336).

    taffeta i.e. the material of which the
ladies' masks are made

160 **parcel** group, company (*OED*, *sb.* 6).
Compare *All's Well* 2.3.53–4: 'This
youthful parcel | Of noble bachelors'.

195

BIRON

'Their eyes', villain, 'their eyes!'

MOTH

'That ever turned their eyes to mortal views!
Out'—

BOYET   True, out indeed!

MOTH

'Out of your favours, heavenly spirits, vouchsafe
Not to behold'—

BIRON

'Once to behold', rogue.

MOTH

'Once to behold with your sun-beamèd eyes—
With your sun-beamèd eyes'—   170

BOYET

They will not answer to that epithet.
You were best call it 'daughter-beamèd eyes'.

MOTH

They do not mark me, and that brings me out.

BIRON

Is this your perfectness? Be gone, you rogue!   *Exit Moth*

ROSALINE (*as the Princess*)

What would these strangers? Know their minds, Boyet.
If they do speak our language, 'tis our will
That some plain man recount their purposes.
Know what they would.

BOYET   What would you with the Princess?

BIRON

Nothing but peace and gentle visitation.

ROSALINE   What would they, say they?   180

BOYET

Nothing but peace and gentle visitation.

ROSALINE

Why, that they have; and bid them so be gone.

163 ever] F (*euer*); *euen* Q   174 *Exit Moth*] CAPELL (*subs.*); *not in* QF   175 strangers] Q
(stranges), F   178 Princess] F4; *Princes* QF

172 **daughter-beamèd** Boyet quibbles, not
    very happily, on *sun* | *son*.
173 **brings** puts
174 **perfectness** being word-perfect
175 **strangers** foreigners

177 **plain** plain-spoken
179, 181 **gentle visitation** a courtesy call.
    OED cites no instance of *visit* as a noun
    prior to 1621.

BOYET

  She says you have it, and you may be gone.

KING

  Say to her we have measured many miles

  To tread a measure with her on this grass.

BOYET

  They say that they have measured many a mile

  To tread a measure with you on this grass.

ROSALINE

  It is not so. Ask them how many inches

  Is in one mile. If they have measured many,

  The measure then of one is easily told.   190

BOYET

  If to come hither you have measured miles,

  And many miles, the Princess bids you tell

  How many inches doth fill up one mile.

BIRON

  Tell her we measure them by weary steps.

BOYET

  She hears herself.

ROSALINE   How many weary steps,

  Of many weary miles you have o'ergone,

  Are numbered in the travel of one mile?

BIRON

  We number nothing that we spend for you.

  Our duty is so rich, so infinite,

  That we may do it still without account.   200

  Vouchsafe to show the sunshine of your face,

  That we, like savages, may worship it.

ROSALINE

  My face is but a moon, and clouded too.

KING

  Blessèd are clouds, to do as such clouds do.

---

185 her on this] Q; you on the F

184 **measured** traversed
185 **tread a measure** dance a courtly dance
203 **but a moon** Rosaline gives the men a hint, which they fail to notice, that she is not the sun and that her light is merely borrowed.
203 **clouded** i.e. masked

Vouchsafe, bright moon, and these thy stars, to
    shine—
Those clouds removed—upon our watery eyne.

ROSALINE

O vain petitioner, beg a greater matter!
Thou now requests but moonshine in the water.

KING

Then in our measure do but vouchsafe one change.
Thou bid'st me beg; this begging is not strange.   210

ROSALINE

Play, music, then! ⌈*Music plays*⌉ Nay, you must do it
    soon.
Not yet? No dance. Thus change I like the moon.

KING

Will you not dance? How come you thus estranged?

ROSALINE

You took the moon at full, but now she's changed.

KING

Yet still she is the moon, and I the man.
The music plays, vouchsafe some motion to it.

ROSALINE

Our ears vouchsafe it.

KING   But your legs should do it.

ROSALINE

Since you are strangers, and come here by chance,
We'll not be nice. Take hands. We will not dance.

---

209 do but vouchsafe] Q; vouchsafe but F   212 yet?] HANMER; ∼ ∧ QF   214 changed.] F4;
∼ ? QF   215] *Omission marked after this line* OXFORD   217 ROSALINE] THEOBALD; *before
previous line* QF   219 nice.] COLLIER 1858; ∼ , QF

---

205 **moon ... stars** 'To be like stars to the
moon' was proverbial (Dent S826.2).

208 **requests** For verbs ending in *t* Shakespeare often uses *ts* in the second person
singular (Abbott 340).
moonshine in the water nothing at all,
the essence of insubstantiality—proverbial (Tilley M1128).

209 **change** (a) round (of a dance) (b)
change of the moon

210 **strange** outlandish, odd

211 *Music plays* Some such direction seems
to be called for by Rosaline's 'Not yet?' in
the following line, suggesting that the

men are slow to start dancing.

212 **Thus ... moon** proverbial (Tilley
M1111)

215 **she ... man** i.e. we belong together like
the moon and the man in the moon

216 **motion** (a) movement (the King's
meaning) (b) sympathetic response (Rosaline's perversion of the King's meaning). Compare Sonnets 128.1–3: 'How
oft, when thou, my music, music
play'st | Upon that blessèd wood whose
motion sounds | With thy sweet fingers'.

219 **nice** pernickety, punctilious

198

KING

Why take we hands then?

ROSALINE   Only to part friends.   220

Curtsy, sweethearts—and so the measure ends.

⌈*Music stops*⌉

KING

More measure of this measure. Be not nice.

ROSALINE

We can afford no more at such a price.

KING

Price you yourselves. What buys your company?

ROSALINE

Your absence only.

KING   That can never be.

ROSALINE

Then cannot we be bought. And so adieu—

Twice to your visor, and half once to you.

KING

If you deny to dance, let's hold more chat.

ROSALINE

In private then.

KING   I am best pleased with that.

They converse apart

BIRON (*to the Princess, taking her for Rosaline*)

White-handed mistress, one sweet word with thee.   230

PRINCESS

Honey, and milk, and sugar: there is three.

BIRON

Nay then, two treys, an if you grow so nice,

---

220 we] Q; you F   222 this measure] Q (this measue), F   224 you] Q; *not in* F   226 cannot] Q (cennot), F   229.1, 237.1, 241.1 *They converse apart*] CAPELL (*subs.*); *not in* QF

220–1 **Why ... ends** The form a courtly
  dance should take is set out in *Tempest*
  1.2.378–82: 'Come unto these yellow
  sands, | And then take hands; | Curtsied
  when you have and kissed— | The wild
  waves whist— | Foot it featly here and
  there'. Rosaline refuses to let the formal-
  ities go beyond the *curtsy*.
222 **More measure** i.e. a fuller amount
224 **Price you** set your own price on
227 **Twice ... you** 'Unless this means that
  she bids his visor a double adieu, as

wishing never to see it again, and only
  half an adieu to himself in the hope that it
  is not a full complete farewell, I do not
  understand it' (Furness).
228 **deny** refuse. Compare *Shrew* 2.1.179:
  'If she deny to wed'.
231 **Honey, and milk, and sugar** All three
  were proverbially sweet (Dent H544,
  M930.1, S957.1).
232 **treys** threes—a *trey* being a throw of
  three with the dice

Metheglin, wort, and malmsey. Well run, dice!
There's half a dozen sweets.

PRINCESS   Seventh sweet, adieu.
Since you can cog, I'll play no more with you.

BIRON
One word in secret.

PRINCESS   Let it not be sweet.

BIRON
Thou griev'st my gall.

PRINCESS   Gall—bitter!

BIRON   Therefore meet.

　　　They converse apart

DUMAINE (*to Maria, taking her for Katherine*)
Will you vouchsafe with me to change a word?

MARIA
Name it.

DUMAINE   Fair lady—

MARIA   Say you so? Fair lord!
Take that for your 'fair lady'.

DUMAINE   Please it you,   240
As much in private, and I'll bid adieu.

　　　They converse apart

KATHERINE
What, was your visor made without a tongue?

LONGUEVILLE (*taking Katherine for Maria*)
I know the reason, lady, why you ask.

---

237 griev'st] F (greeu'st); greeuest Q   240 Take that] Q; Take you that F   242–55
KATHERINE] ROWE; *Mar⟨ia⟩*. QF

233 **Metheglin, wort, and malmsey** All three
were strong sweet drinks but not
proverbially so. *Metheglin*, Welsh in origin, was made from honey and spices;
wort was sweet unfermented beer; and
malmsey a potent sweet wine.
235 **cog** cheat
237 **Thou … bitter** Biron accuses the Princess of causing him pain by rubbing on
his *gall*, i.e. sore place. She retorts by
giving *gall* its other meaning *bile*,
proverbial for its bitterness (Tilley G11).
meet fitting, appropriate
238 **change** interchange. Compare *Tempest*
1.2.444–5: 'At the first sight | They have
changed eyes.'

239 **Fair lord** The term is evidently used in
mockery.
242–6 **What … half** 'The old vizard was
what the youngster of today calls "a false
face". Made of black velvet on a leather
base, it covered the entire features and
was kept in place by a *tongue*, or interior
projection, held in the mouth' (W. J.
Lawrence, *TLS*, 7 June 1923). Longueville's point is that Katherine has two
tongues, and so is being deceptive and
ambiguous. She would do well to give
him one of them, that which holds the
mask in place, thus revealing the truth
about herself.

KATHERINE

O, for your reason! Quickly, sir; I long.

LONGUEVILLE

You have a double tongue within your mask,

And would afford my speechless visor half.

KATHERINE

'Veal', quoth the Dutchman. Is not 'veal' a calf?

LONGUEVILLE

A calf, fair lady?

KATHERINE   No, a fair lord calf.

LONGUEVILLE

Let's part the word.

KATHERINE   No, I'll not be your half.

Take all, and wean it, it may prove an ox.   250

LONGUEVILLE

Look how you butt yourself in these sharp mocks.

Will you give horns, chaste lady? Do not so.

KATHERINE

Then die a calf, before your horns do grow.

LONGUEVILLE

One word in private with you ere I die.

KATHERINE

Bleat softly then; the butcher hears you cry.

They converse apart

BOYET

The tongues of mocking wenches are as keen

As is the razor's edge invisible,

247 **'Veal', quoth the Dutchman** 'The Dutchman is trying to say "well", which represents Katherine's sarcastic judgement on Longaville's *reason*. At the same time, *Veal* puns on | "veil" (often spelled "veal"), this being Katherine's substitution for the *speechless visor* of the preceding line. Further, *Veal*, when tacked on to Katherine's last spoken word, *long* (line 244), makes up her wooer's name. By adopting Longaville's *half* (uttering *half* his name to make up the whole), Katherine demonstrates her ability to see through the *Veal* on her suitor's face' (Kerrigan).

Is not 'veal' a calf? In French *le veau* is both 'veal' and 'calf'; and in Shake-speare's time a *calf* was the emblem of physical and mental imbecility. Compare Hamlet's calling Polonius 'so capital a calf' (*Hamlet* 3.2.101).

249 **part** share, divide. Longueville means 'let us both admit we are *calves*, and have done with it', but Katherine takes him literally and refuses to be his 'better half' i.e. wife. Compare *Caesar* 2.1.273, where Portia, speaking to Brutus, calls herself 'your self, your half', and also Dent H49.

250 **prove an ox** grow up to be a numskull (*OED, ox,* 4)

251 **butt** strike (as an ox does with its horns)

252 **give horns** (a) equip with horns (b) cuckold your husband

Cutting a smaller hair than may be seen:
  Above the sense of sense, so sensible
Seemeth their conference; their conceits have wings   260
Fleeter than arrows, bullets, wind, thought, swifter
    things.

ROSALINE

Not one word more, my maids. Break off, break off!

BIRON

By heaven, all dry-beaten with pure scoff!

KING

Farewell, mad wenches, you have simple wits.

        Exeunt the King, his lords, and the blackamoors
    ⌈*The ladies unmask*⌉

PRINCESS

Twenty adieus, my frozen Muscovites.
Are these the breed of wits so wondered at?

BOYET

  Tapers they are, with your sweet breaths puffed out.

ROSALINE

Well-liking wits they have; gross, gross; fat, fat.

PRINCESS

  O poverty in wit, kingly-poor flout!
Will they not, think you, hang themselves tonight?   270
  Or ever but in visors show their faces?
This pert Biron was out of count'nance quite.

---

259 sense, so sensible] POPE; sence so sensible QF
(subs.); *Exe.* Q; *Exeunt.* F; *after l. 265* CAPELL
266 wondered] F (wondred); wondered Q

264.1 *Exeunt ... blackamoors*] THEOBALD
264.2 *The ladies unmask*] *not in* QF

259–60 **Above ... conference** i.e. their con-
    versation is so pointed and piercing that it
    outgoes the power of the senses to per-
    ceive it
259 **sensible** acutely felt by the hearer (*OED*,
    a. 6)
260 **conceits** witty sallies (*OED, sb.* 8)
261 **arrows, bullets, wind, thought** four
    time-honoured examples of speed (Dent
    A322, B719.1, W411, T240)
263 **dry-beaten** thoroughly beaten without
    blood being drawn
    scoff contemptuous ridicule
264 **mad wenches** a common saying (Dent

W274.1)
266 **breed** species, kind (*OED, sb.* 2c; earliest
    example of this sense)
268 **Well-liking** plump, obese—*OED*'s first
    citation of the word in a figurative sense
269 **O ... flout** The Princess refers to the
    King's supercilious dismissal of her and
    her ladies as 'mad wenches' who have
    but 'simple wits' at line 264, characteriz-
    ing it as a poverty-stricken jeer for a king
    to indulge in.
272 **out of count'nance quite** completely
    disconcerted

ROSALINE

Ah, they were all in lamentable cases.

The King was weeping-ripe for a good word.

PRINCESS

Biron did swear himself out of all suit.

MARIA

Dumaine was at my service, and his sword.

'*Non point*,' quoth I. My servant straight was mute.

KATHERINE

Lord Longueville said I came o'er his heart,

And trow you what he called me?

PRINCESS   'Qualm', perhaps.

KATHERINE

Yes, in good faith.

PRINCESS   Go, sickness as thou art.   280

ROSALINE

Well, better wits have worn plain statute-caps.

But will you hear? The King is my love sworn.

PRINCESS

And quick Biron hath plighted faith to me.

KATHERINE

And Longueville was for my service born.

MARIA

Dumaine is mine as sure as bark on tree.

BOYET

Madam, and pretty mistresses, give ear:

Immediately they will again be here

273 Ah, they] OXFORD; They QF; O they F2
F; ∼, Q   279 perhaps] Q (perhapt), F

277 *Non point*] QF (No poynt)   servant ∧]

273 **cases** (a) states (b) outfits, costumes (including their masks)

274 **weeping-ripe** ready to weep. According to *OED* the word first appears in 1548 as the English equivalent of the Latin *Lachrymabundus*.

275 **out of all suit** i.e. in an utterly incongruous manner, entirely out of keeping with his *love-suit*

277 *Non point* not at all (with a quibble on the *point* of Dumaine's sword). See 2.1.188 and note.

278 **came o'er** took possession of (*OED*, *v.* 43c). This instance antedates *OED*'s earliest.

279 **trow you** do you know

279 **Qualm** sudden feeling of illness that 'comes over' one unexpectedly

281 **plain statute-caps** caps of the simple kind required by the law. Attempts to regulate dress were so common in the latter half of the 16th century that it is not clear as to precisely which statute Rosaline is thinking of. The likeliest would seem to be a regulation passed by the Common Council of the City of London in 1582 ordering that apprentices should wear one sort of headgear only: 'a woollen cap, without any silk in or about the same'.

285 **as sure as bark on tree** proverbial simile for close union (Dent B83 and H88)

In their own shapes, for it can never be
They will digest this harsh indignity.

PRINCESS

Will they return?

BOYET   They will, they will, God knows,   290
And leap for joy, though they are lame with blows.
Therefore change favours, and when they repair,
Blow like sweet roses in this summer air.

PRINCESS

How 'blow'? How 'blow'? Speak to be understood.

BOYET

Fair ladies masked are roses in their bud;
Dismasked, their damask sweet commixture shown,
Are angels vailing clouds, or roses blown.

PRINCESS

Avaunt, perplexity! What shall we do,
If they return in their own shapes to woo?

ROSALINE

Good madam, if by me you'll be advised,   300
Let's mock them still, as well known as disguised.
Let us complain to them what fools were here,
Disguised like Muscovites in shapeless gear;
And wonder what they were, and to what end
Their shallow shows, and prologue vilely penned,
And their rough carriage so ridiculous,
Should be presented at our tent to us.

BOYET

Ladies, withdraw. The gallants are at hand.

297 vailing] F; varling Q

288 **In their own shapes** i.e. without their disguises
289 **digest** swallow, put up with
292 **repair** return (*OED*, *v.* 2)
293 **Blow** bloom. There may be a punning reference back to 'blows' (line 291). If so, we have the reason for the Princess's demand for clarification in the next line.
296 **Dismasked** unmasked—earliest citation in *OED*
     damask red and white, blush-coloured— earliest citation of this sense in *OED*
     commixture 'complexion', bodily habit or constitution (a sense peculiar to Shakespeare—*OED*, 3)

297 **vailing clouds** i.e. letting fall the clouds that have hidden them. Compare *1 Henry VI* 5.3.24–6: 'Now the time is come | That France must vail her lofty-plumèd crest | And let her head fall into England's lap.'
     blown in full bloom
298 **Avaunt, perplexity** i.e. away, you speaker of riddles
301 **as well ... disguised** i.e. as much when they appear as themselves as when they were disguised
303 **shapeless gear** uncouth dress, badly cut clothes
306 **carriage** behaviour

PRINCESS

Whip to our tents as roes runs o'er land!

Exeunt the Princess and her ladies

Enter the King and his lords in their proper habits

KING

Fair sir, God save you! Where's the Princess? 310

BOYET

Gone to her tent. Please it your majesty

Command me any service to her thither?

KING

That she vouchsafe me audience for one word.

BOYET

I will, and so will she, I know, my lord. *Exit*

BIRON

This fellow pecks up wit as pigeons peas,

And utters it again when God doth please.

He is wit's pedlar, and retails his wares

At wakes and wassails, meetings, markets, fairs;

And we that sell by gross, the Lord doth know,

Have not the grace to grace it with such show. 320

This gallant pins the wenches on his sleeve.

Had he been Adam, he had tempted Eve.

A can carve too, and lisp. Why, this is he

That kissed his hand away in courtesy.

---

309 runs] Q, F (runnes); run F4   o'er] QF (ore); over STEEVENS; o're the F3   309.1 *Exeunt ... ladies*] CAPELL (*subs.*); *Exeunt.* QF   309.2 *Enter ... habits*] ROWE (*subs.*); *Enter the King and the rest* QF   312 thither?] Q (~,); *not in* F   315 pecks] Q (peckes); pickes F   316 God] Q; loue F   323 A] Q; He F   324 his hand away] Q (his hand, a way); away his hand F

309 **Whip** move quickly, dash
   as ... land proverbial (Tilley R158)
   runs run. The third person plural in -s is quite common in Shakespeare (Abbott 333).
309.2 **proper** own, usual
315–16 **This ... please** This simile appears to have become proverbial (Dent C333).
316 **utters** (a) speaks (b) puts up for sale
318 **wakes** festivals (held in each parish annually to celebrate the patron saint of the church)
   wassails revels, carousals. Compare *Hamlet* 1.4.9–10: 'The King doth wake tonight and takes his rouse, | Keeps wassail ...', cited by *OED* as its earliest example of this sense.

319 **by gross** wholesale
321 **pins ... sleeve** i.e. flaunts his power over the girls, makes a show of their complete dependence on him (*OED, pin, v.*[1] 4)—proverbial (Dent S534).
322 **had** would have
323 **carve** The precise meaning of this word, which Shakespeare uses again in *Merry Wives* 1.3.39–40, where Falstaff says of Mistress Ford: 'I spy entertainment in her. She discourses, she carves, she gives the leer of invitation', is not known. It appears to have something to do with table manners of a rather affected kind, but whether it refers to 'come hither' looks or mincing speech is by no means clear.

This is the ape of form, Monsieur the Nice,
That when he plays at tables chides the dice
In honourable terms. Nay, he can sing
A mean most meanly; and in ushering
Mend him who can. The ladies call him sweet.
The stairs, as he treads on them, kiss his feet.   330
This is the flower that smiles on everyone,
To show his teeth as white as whale's bone;
And consciences that will not die in debt
Pay him the due of 'honey-tongued Boyet'.

KING

A blister on his sweet tongue, with my heart,
That put Armado's page out of his part!

     Enter the Princess, Maria, Katherine, and Rosaline,
     ushered by Boyet

BIRON

See where it comes! Behaviour, what wert thou
Till this map o' man showed thee, and what art thou
     now?

---

328 ushering ∧] F; hushering. Q   331 everyone,] F (euerie one,); euery one. Q   332
whale's] QF (Whales); whalës SINGER   334 due] Q; dutie F   336.1–2 *Enter . . . Boyet*] ROWE
(*subs.*); *Enter the Ladies.* QF   338 map o' man] This edition; mad man Q; madman F; man
THEOBALD

325 **ape of form** i.e. slave of what he regards
     as 'good form'
     Nice punctilious
326 **tables** backgammon
327 **honourable** polite (dice games were
     accompanied by strong language)
328 **mean** the middle part (tenor or alto)
     between bass and treble
     most meanly i.e. quite respectably
     ushering carrying out the duties of a
     gentleman-usher
329 **Mend him who can** let anyone who
     thinks he can improve on his perfor-
     mance try, i.e. no one can touch him
331–3 **This . . . debt** This passage is a string
     of commonplaces (Dent T430.1, W279,
     D165).
332 **whale's bone** ivory from the walrus
     (*OED, whalebone,* 1). The word *whale's* is
     disyllabic in pronunciation to emphasize,
     perhaps, the antiquity of the simile.
333 **consciences** conscientious people (ab-
     stract for concrete)
334 **honey-tongued** 'It is interesting to note
     here that Meres, who gives us the earliest

reference to *Love's Labour's Lost* by name,
and also the earliest tribute of praise to
Shakespeare by name, applies this term
to Shakespeare himself' (David). See Introduction, p. 81. *OED* cites no other use
of this typically Shakespearian compound until 1861.
337 **Behaviour** good manners, politeness
338 **map o' man** Q reads 'mad man' and F
     'madman'. The result is a metrically
     irregular line that also lacks bite and
     cogency. The reading of this edition dis-
     poses of both difficulties, and can be
     justified on three grounds. Shakespeare
     probably wrote 'map a man'; but the Q
     compositor dropped the 'a' just as he had
     done at 4.1.147. He also used a turned
     letter in setting 'map' (compare 'pader'
     for 'paper' at 4.3.40). Finally, Shake-
     speare often uses 'map' as a synonym for
     'model' or 'ideal form'. Particularly rele-
     vant in this case is the conclusion of
     Sonnets 68: 'And him as for a map doth
     nature store, | To show false art what
     beauty was of yore.'

KING

All hail, sweet madam, and fair time of day.

PRINCESS

'Fair' in 'all hail' is foul, as I conceive.   340

KING

Construe my speeches better, if you may.

PRINCESS

Then wish me better; I will give you leave.

KING

We came to visit you, and purpose now

To lead you to our court; vouchsafe it then.

PRINCESS

This field shall hold me, and so hold your vow.

Nor God nor I delights in perjured men.

KING

Rebuke me not for that which you provoke.

The virtue of your eye must break my oath.

PRINCESS

You nickname virtue; 'vice' you should have spoke;

For virtue's office never breaks men's troth.   350

Now, by my maiden honour, yet as pure

As the unsullied lily, I protest,

A world of torments though I should endure,

I would not yield to be your house's guest.

So much I hate a breaking cause to be

Of heavenly oaths, vowed with integrity.

KING

O, you have lived in desolation here,

Unseen, unvisited, much to our shame.

---

341 Construe] Q (Consture), F   speeches] Q (spaches), F   350 men's] Q (mens); men F
352 unsullied] F2; vnsallied QF   356 vowed] F (vow'd); vowed Q

340 **'Fair' ... foul** The Princess deliberately
    misinterprets the King's greeting, *hail*, as
    'hailstorm'.
346 **Nor** neither
348 **virtue** power. In the next line the Prin-
    cess gives the word its alternative sense
    'goodness'.
349 **nickname** miscall, misname (*OED, v.*
    1). Compare *Hamlet* 3.1.147–8: 'You jig,

you amble, and you lisp, and nickname
God's creatures'.
350 **office** operation, proper functioning
351–2 **pure ... lily** proverbial (Dent L295.3)
355 **breaking cause** reason for breaking. See
    Abbott 419a.
357 **in desolation** i.e. forsaken, without
    companions (*OED*, 3)

PRINCESS

Not so, my lord. It is not so, I swear.

We have had pastimes here and pleasant game.   360

A mess of Russians left us but of late.

KING

How, madam? Russians?

PRINCESS   Ay, in truth, my lord;

Trim gallants, full of courtship and of state.

ROSALINE

Madam, speak true.—It is not so, my lord.

My lady, to the manner of the days,

In courtesy gives undeserving praise.

We four indeed confronted were with four

In Russian habit. Here they stayed an hour,

And talked apace; and in that hour, my lord,

They did not bless us with one happy word.   370

I dare not call them fools, but this I think,

When they are thirsty, fools would fain have drink.

BIRON

This jest is dry to me. My gentle sweet,

Your wits makes wise things foolish. When we greet,

With eyes' best seeing, heaven's fiery eye,

By light we lose light. Your capacity

Is of that nature that to your huge store

Wise things seem foolish, and rich things but poor.

ROSALINE

This proves you wise and rich, for in my eye—

BIRON

I am a fool, and full of poverty.   380

ROSALINE

But that you take what doth to you belong,

It were a fault to snatch words from my tongue.

---

368 Russian] Q (*Russian*); Russia F   373 My] MALONE; *not in* QF   374 foolish.] ROWE
(*subs.*); ~ ∧ QF   375 With] Q (Wtih), F   379 eye—] F (eie ∧); ~ . Q

361 **mess** group of four. See 4.3.204 and
   note.
363 **courtship** courtliness of manners (*OED*,
   1)
365 **to ... days** in keeping with the present
   fashion. For this use of 'to', see Abbott
   187.
369 **talked apace** rattled on, chattered

370 **happy** felicitous
371 **dare not** hesitate to, would not go so far
   as to
373 **dry** stale, dull (quibbling on 'thirsty')
374–6 **When ... lose light** i.e. when we look
   directly at the sun, we become blind.
   Compare Dent S971.1.
377 **to** compared to

208

BIRON

O, I am yours, and all that I possess.

ROSALINE

All the fool mine?

BIRON   I cannot give you less.

ROSALINE

Which of the visors was it that you wore?

BIRON

Where? When? What visor? Why demand you this?

ROSALINE

There, then, that visor, that superfluous case,
That hid the worse, and showed the better face.

KING *(aside to his lords)*

We were descried. They'll mock us now downright.

DUMAINE *(aside to the King)*

Let us confess, and turn it to a jest.   390

PRINCESS

Amazed, my lord? Why looks your highness sad?

ROSALINE

Help! Hold his brows! He'll swoon. Why look you
    pale?
Seasick, I think, coming from Muscovy.

BIRON

Thus pour the stars down plagues for perjury.
  Can any face of brass hold longer out?
Here stand I, lady, dart thy skill at me,
  Bruise me with scorn, confound me with a flout,
Thrust thy sharp wit quite through my ignorance,
  Cut me to pieces with thy keen conceit;
And I will wish thee never more to dance,   400
  Nor never more in Russian habit wait.
O, never will I trust to speeches penned,
  Nor to the motion of a schoolboy's tongue,

384 mine?] POPE; ~. QF   389 were] Q; are F

387–8 **that visor ... face** Proverbial in the
  form 'A well-favoured visor will hide her
  ill-favoured face' (Dent V92).
387 **case** covering, mask. Compare *Romeo*
  1.4.29: 'Give me a case to put my visage
  in'.
391 **Amazed** bewildered, confounded

395 **face of brass** brazen-faced effrontery—
  proverbial (Dent F8)
397 **confound** destroy
399 **keen conceit** capacity for bitter repartee
400 **wish** invite, entreat (*OED*, v. 5)
401 **wait** attend upon you

Nor never come in visor to my friend,
   Nor woo in rhyme, like a blind harper's song.
Taffeta phrases, silken terms precise,
   Three-piled hyperboles, spruce affectation,
Figures pedantical—these summer flies
   Have blown me full of maggot ostentation.
I do forswear them, and I here protest   410
   By this white glove—how white the hand, God
     knows—
Henceforth my wooing mind shall be expressed
   In russet yeas and honest kersey noes.
And to begin, wench, so God help me, law!
My love to thee is sound, sans crack or flaw.

ROSALINE

Sans 'sans', I pray you.

---

407 hyperboles] Q (Hiberboles), F   affectation] ROWE; affection QF   414 begin,] THEOBALD;
~ ∧ QF; ~ : DAVID

404 **friend** sweetheart, mistress. Compare *Measure* 1.4.29: 'He hath got his friend with child.'

405 **a blind harper's song** Harpers were proverbially blind (Dent H175 and 176), and made their living by singing traditional ballads.

407 **Three-piled hyperboles** i.e. hyperboles that are splendidly excessive. *Three-piled* (*OED*, *a.*[1] 2) is a term, first used in writing, if not invented, by Shakespeare here, to describe the richest and finest kind of velvet. Compare *Measure* 1.2.31–2: 'Thou art good velvet, thou'rt a three-piled piece, I warrant thee.'
   affectation Q and F read 'affection', which could mean (*OED*, *sb.* 13) 'affectation', as it does at 5.1.4 in the speech of Nathaniel and in *Hamlet* 2.2.445 in Q2 only. F significantly reads 'affectation'. With these two exceptions, of which the second has only a doubtful validity, Shakespeare distinguishes between the words, as we do today. It is true that the rhyme 'affection' | 'ostentation' would have presented no difficulty for an Elizabethan, since -ion at the end of a word was disyllabic, but the triple rhyme offered by -ation is both more pronounced and funnier.

408 **Figures** rhetorical figures
   pedantical *OED* cites this as its first exam-

ple of the word, but, as David points out, Shakespeare had been anticipated by Gabriel Harvey in 1589.

408–9 **these ... ostentation** Through an associative process that leads from textile materials to the source of one of them, Shakespeare is now thinking of *sheep*, whose wool and flesh can become the breeding ground for 'summer flies', which lay their eggs, that soon turn to *maggots*, in them.

409 **blown me** deposited their eggs on me (*OED*, *v.*[1] 28c). Compare *Othello* 4.2.68–9: 'as summer flies ... | That quicken even with blowing'.
   ostentation pretentious showing off (*OED*, 3)

411 **By ... knows** probably ironical

413 **russet** homely, simple. 'Russet' was 'a coarse homespun woollen cloth' worn by countryfolk, and also the name of the colour of that cloth, a reddish-brown.
   kersey plain, unpretentious. 'Kersey', like 'russet', was a rough woollen cloth. This is the only example (4b) that *OED* offers of the word in a figurative sense.

414 **law** An interjection of an asseverative kind equivalent to 'Yes, indeed'.

416 **Sans 'sans'** without 'sans', i.e. drop this affectation of using French words instead of plain English

BIRON   Yet I have a trick
  Of the old rage. Bear with me, I am sick.
  I'll leave it by degrees. Soft, let us see:
  Write 'Lord have mercy on us' on those three.
  They are infected, in their hearts it lies,   420
  They have the plague, and caught it of your eyes.
  These lords are visited; you are not free,
  For the Lord's tokens on you do I see.
PRINCESS
  No, they are free that gave these tokens to us.
BIRON
  Our states are forfeit. Seek not to undo us.
ROSALINE
  It is not so; for how can this be true,
  That you stand forfeit, being those that sue?
BIRON
  Peace, for I will not have to do with you.
ROSALINE
  Nor shall not, if I do as I intend.
BIRON (*to the lords*)
  Speak for yourselves. My wit is at an end.   430
KING
  Teach us, sweet madam, for our rude transgression
  Some fair excuse.
PRINCESS   The fairest is confession.
  Were not you here but even now disguised?
KING
  Madam, I was.

433 not you] Q; you not F

416–17 **Yet ... rage** I still have a touch
  (Onions) of my former madness (*OED*,
  rage, sb. 1)
419 **Lord have mercy on us** These words had
  to be written on the door of every house
  affected by the plague to serve as a
  warning to all who might wish to enter.
  They were also, of course, a genuine
  prayer, since an outbreak of plague was
  regarded as God's punishment of the
  wicked.
420 **it** i.e. the plague (of love)
422 **visited** afflicted (by the plague)
423 **the Lord's tokens** (a) plague-spots

which appeared on the patient's body in
the final stages of the disease (b) the lords'
tokens i.e. the favours they gave to their
ladies
424 **free** unfettered by love, fancy-free
425 **Our states are forfeit** i.e. we have for-
  feited our status (as honourable men)
  (*OED*, *state*, sb. 15)
  undo us bring us to utter ruin
426–7 **how ... sue** Rosaline plays on two
  senses of *sue*: (a) prosecute a law suit (b)
  prosecute a love suit.
428 **have to do with** (a) have dealings with
  (b) have sexual intercourse with

PRINCESS   And were you well advised?

KING
  I was, fair madam.

PRINCESS   When you then were here,
  What did you whisper in your lady's ear?

KING
  That more than all the world I did respect her.

PRINCESS
  When she shall challenge this, you will reject her.

KING
  Upon mine honour, no.

PRINCESS   Peace, peace, forbear!
  Your oath once broke, you force not to forswear.   440

KING
  Despise me when I break this oath of mine.

PRINCESS
  I will, and therefore keep it. Rosaline,
  What did the Russian whisper in your ear?

ROSALINE
  Madam, he swore that he did hold me dear
  As precious eyesight, and did value me
  Above this world: adding thereto, moreover,
  That he would wed me, or else die my lover.

PRINCESS
  God give thee joy of him! The noble lord
  Most honourably doth uphold his word.

KING
  What mean you, madam? By my life, my troth,   450
  I never swore this lady such an oath.

ROSALINE
  By heaven, you did! And to confirm it plain,
  You gave me this; but take it, sir, again.

KING
  My faith and this the Princess I did give.
  I knew her by this jewel on her sleeve.

---

434 **well advised** in your right senses. Compare *Errors* 2.2.215–16: 'Am I . . . | Sleeping or waking? Mad or well advised?'

437 **respect** value, esteem (*OED*, *v.* 4b)

438 **challenge this** i.e. demand that you keep your word (*OED*, *challenge*, *v.* 5)

440 **Your ... forswear** i.e. now you have broken your oath once, you will make no bones about breaking your word again (*OED*, *force*, *v.* 14). Compare *Lucrece* 1021: 'I force not argument a straw'.

444–5 **dear | As precious eyesight** proverbial (Dent E249.1)

453 **again** back again

PRINCESS

Pardon me, sir, this jewel did she wear,
And Lord Biron, I thank him, is my dear.
What, will you have me, or your pearl again?

BIRON

Neither of either; I remit both twain.
I see the trick on't. Here was a consent,   460
Knowing aforehand of our merriment,
To dash it like a Christmas comedy.
Some carry-tale, some please-man, some slight zany,
Some mumble-news, some trencher-knight, some Dick
That smiles his cheek in years, and knows the trick
To make my lady laugh when she's disposed,
Told our intents before; which once disclosed,
The ladies did change favours; and then we,
Following the signs, wooed but the sign of she.
Now, to our perjury to add more terror,   470
We are again forsworn, in will and error.
Much upon this 'tis. (*To Boyet*) And might not you
Forestall our sport, to make us thus untrue?
Do not you know my lady's foot by th' squier,

---

463 zany] F (Zanie); saine Q   465 smiles ∧] F; ~ , Q   472 'tis] QF (tis); it is F2

---

459 **Neither of either** neither of the two (*OED*, *neither*, B 2b)
remit give up, surrender (*OED*, *v.* 2)
both twain both the one and the other
460 **consent** agreement, compact, plot
461 **Knowing** i.e. since they knew (Abbott 378)
462 **dash** wreck, spoil (*OED*, *v.* 6)
like a Christmas comedy 'it would seem that the "dashing" (by the spectators) was a recognized part of the fun at impromptu festival plays and masques; compare the treatment of Quince's company in *Dream*, of Holofernes' company in this play, and the story of the "Night of Errors" at Gray's Inn, Dec. 28, 1594' (Wilson).
463 **carry-tale** tale-bearer. Compare *Venus* 655–7: 'This sour informer, this bate-breeding spy . . . | This carry-tale, dissentious jealousy'.
please-man toady, sycophant. *OED* can cite no other example.
zany the rustic servant of the pantaloon in the *commedia dell' arte*, buffoon, clown. The word seems to have been introduced

into English, as David says, by Nashe in his *Pierce Penniless* of 1592 (Nashe i. 215. 10).
464 **mumble-news** gossip, prattler. *OED* cites no other example.
trencher-knight parasite with a noble appetite—*OED*'s only example
Dick common fellow, base companion
465 **in years** i.e. into wrinkles (like those on an old man's face)
466 **my lady** i.e. the lady he serves or addresses
469 **she** i.e. each respective mistress. Compare *As You Like It* 3.2.10: 'The fair, the chaste, and unexpressive she'.
472 **Much . . . 'tis** this is pretty much what has happened
474 **know . . . squier** i.e. know exactly how to flatter the Princess. A *squier* is a carpenter's set-square (*OED*, *square*, *sb.* 1b), and is indeed the older but now obsolete form of *square*. It is preserved here for the sake of the rhyme. The phrase 'To know the length of one's foot' (Tilley L202) was a proverbial synonym for 'to measure with great accuracy'.

And laugh upon the apple of her eye?
And stand between her back, sir, and the fire,
    Holding a trencher, jesting merrily?
You put our page out. Go, you are allowed;
Die when you will, a smock shall be your shroud.
You leer upon me, do you? There's an eye   480
Wounds like a leaden sword.

BOYET   Full merrily
Hath this brave manège, this career, been run.

BIRON
Lo, he is tilting straight. Peace, I have done.
        Enter Costard
Welcome, pure wit. Thou partest a fair fray.

COSTARD
O Lord, sir, they would know
Whether the three Worthies shall come in or no.

BIRON
What, are there but three?

COSTARD   No, sir, but it is vara fine,
For every one pursents three.

BIRON   And three times thrice is nine.

COSTARD
Not so, sir—under correction, sir—I hope it is not so.
You cannot beg us, sir, I can assure you, sir, we know
        what we know.   490
I hope, sir, three times thrice, sir—

---

482 manège] THEOBALD (manage); nuage Q; manager F   483.1 *Enter Costard*] ROWE; *Enter Clowne.* QF   484 partest] POPE; partst Q; part'st F   485 (*and for the rest of the scene*) COSTARD] ROWE; *Clo⟨wne⟩.* QF   491 sir—] ROWE; ~. QF

475 **laugh ... eye** i.e. jest with her in a very intimate way. 'As dear as the apple (pupil) of my eye' was proverbial (Tilley A290).

476 **stand ... fire** i.e. act as a fire-screen for her

477 **Holding a trencher** i.e. obsequiously ready to perform any service

478 **allowed** licensed. Compare *Twelfth Night* 1.5.89–91: 'There is no slander in an allowed fool, though he do nothing but rail'.

479 **a smock ... shroud** you'll die like the woman you are, covered by a smock (Kerrigan)

481 **Wounds like a leaden sword** proverbial (Tilley S1054). Leaden or wooden swords were, of course, common stage properties.

482 **this brave manège, this career** this fine gallop at full speed (*OED, manage, sb.* 2), this charge (*OED, career, sb.* 2). Boyet is using the language of the riding school and the tournament.

483 **is tilting straight** has gone straight back to his verbal jousting

485 **would** want to

487 **vara** very (of which it is a dialectal pronunciation)

488 **pursents** Costard's version of *presents* i.e. represents, personates

490 **You cannot beg us** i.e. we are not fools.

BIRON   Is not nine?

COSTARD Under correction, sir, we know whereuntil it
doth amount.

BIRON

By Jove, I always took three threes for nine.

COSTARD O Lord, sir, it were pity you should get your
living by reckoning, sir.

BIRON How much is it?

COSTARD O Lord, sir, the parties themselves, the actors, sir,
will show whereuntil it doth amount. For mine own
part, I am, as they say, but to parfect one man in one   500
poor man, Pompion the Great, sir.

BIRON Art thou one of the Worthies?

COSTARD It pleased them to think me worthy of Pompey
the Great. For mine own part, I know not the degree of
the Worthy, but I am to stand for him.

BIRON Go, bid them prepare.

COSTARD

We will turn it finely off, sir; we will take some care.

                                                    Exit

KING

Biron, they will shame us. Let them not approach.

BIRON

We are shame-proof, my lord; and 'tis some policy
To have one show worse than the King's and his
company.   510

KING I say they shall not come.

---

500 they] F; thy Q   parfect] Q; perfect F   507 *Exit*] QF (*after l. 506*)

'Let him be begged for a fool' (Dent F.496)
was a well known saying alluding to a
form of abuse practised by the Crown
through its Court of Wards. If the heir to
an estate was mentally deficient, the
Court took over the guardianship of his
property, and then transferred it to a
petitioner, either as a reward for services
rendered to the Crown or for a monetary
consideration. The successful petitioner
then enjoyed the full use of the estate he
had *begged*. See Joel Hurstfield, *The
Queen's Wards* (1958), *passim*.

492 **whereuntil** (dialectal) to what, to how

much

495 **were ... get** would be a sad thing for you
if you had to earn

500 **parfect** Costard's old-fashioned pronunciation of *perfect* which, in his mouth,
seems to be a constructive muddle of his
pursent and of a verb of his own meaning
'to be word-perfect in the role of'. See
l. 553.

501 **Pompion** pumpkin (a nice bit of folk-
etymology)

504 **degree** rank

509 **some policy** i.e. a wise move, a sound
stratagem

PRINCESS

  Nay, my good lord, let me o'errule you now.

  That sport best pleases that doth least know how:

  Where zeal strives to content, and the contents

  Dies in the zeal of that which it presents,

  There form confounded makes most form in mirth,

  When great things labouring perish in their birth.

BIRON

  A right description of our sport, my lord.

       Enter Armado

ARMADO Anointed, I implore so much expense of thy royal

  sweet breath as will utter a brace of words.   520

       He converses apart with the King, to whom he gives a
       paper

PRINCESS Doth this man serve God?

BIRON Why ask you?

PRINCESS

  A speaks not like a man of God his making.

ARMADO That is all one, my fair, sweet, honey monarch;

  for, I protest, the schoolmaster is exceeding fantastical,

  too too vain, too too vain. But we will put it, as they say,

  to *fortuna de la guerra*. I wish you the peace of mind,

  most royal couplement.   *Exit*

KING (*studying the paper*) Here is like to be a good presence

  of Worthies. He presents Hector of Troy; the swain,   530

513 least] F; best Q   516 There] CAPELL; Their QF   518.1 *Enter Armado*] ROWE; *Enter
Bragart.* QF   519 (*and for the rest of the scene*) ARMADO] ROWE; *Brag⟨gart⟩.* QF   520.1–2 *He
… paper*] CAPELL (*subs.*); *not in* QF   523 A] Q; He F   God his] Q; God's F   524 That is] Q;
That's F   527 *fortuna de la guerra*] THEOBALD; *Fortuna delaguar* QF   528 *Exit*] Q; *not in* F
529 *studying … paper*] *not in* QF

514 **zeal** i.e. eager performers
  content give pleasure
514–15 **the contents … presents** i.e. the
  substance of the show is murdered by the
  excessive enthusiasm and earnestness of
  the company that puts it on
516 **There … mirth** i.e. the collapse of
  ambitious enterprises is a prime source of
  mirth
517 **When … birth** Probably an allusion to
  Horace's '*Parturiunt montes, nascetur ridi-
  culus mus*' (*Ars Poetica*, 139), proverbial
  in English as 'The mountain was in
  labour and brought forth a mouse' (Tilley
  M1215).
518 **right** accurate

518 **our sport** i.e. the masque of Muscovites
  (in which the King and his companions
  'laboured' to little effect)
519 **Anointed** i.e. your majesty (a king being
  'the Lord's anointed')
523 **A … making** proverbial (Dent M162)
  God his God's
524 **That is all one** it is all the same to me.
  Compare *Twelfth Night* 5.1.403: 'But
  that's all one, our play is done'.
  honey (a term of endearment)
527 **fortuna de la guerra** the chance of
  war—proverbial (Dent C223)
528 **couplement** couple, pair
529 **presence** company, assembly (*OED*, 3)

Pompey the Great; the parish curate, Alexander; Arma-
do's page, Hercules; the pedant, Judas Maccabeus.
And if these four Worthies in their first show thrive,
These four will change habits, and present the other
    five.

BIRON

There is five in the first show.

KING

You are deceived, 'tis not so.

BIRON

The pedant, the braggart, the hedge-priest, the fool,
    and the boy.

Abate throw at novum, and the whole world again
Cannot pick out five such, take each one in his vein.

KING

The ship is under sail, and here she comes amain.   540

    Enter Costard as Pompey

COSTARD

'I Pompey am'—

BIRON   You lie, you are not he.

COSTARD

'I Pompey am'—

BOYET   With leopard's head on knee.

BIRON

Well said, old mocker. I must needs be friends with
    thee.

---

539 pick] Q (picke); pricke F   in his] Q; in's F   540.1 *Enter ... Pompey*] ROWE (*subs.*);
Enter Pompey. QF   541, 542 am—] THEOBALD; ∼. QF

537 **hedge-priest** illiterate or uneducated priest of inferior status, priest like Sir Oliver Martext in 3.3 of *As You Like It*

538–9 **Abate ... vein** *Novum* was a dice-game also known as *novem quinque*, in which the winning throws appear to have been nine and five. Beyond that nothing is now known about it. Kerrigan glosses the passage thus: 'set aside a throw of five or nine ... and there is nothing in the whole world good enough to be compared with these splendid characters, taken for what they are'. Biron's arithmetic tells him 'five into nine won't go'.

540 **amain** at full speed ahead

541 **You lie** There may well be a quibble here pointing to some stage business which has Costard running in 'amain', stopping suddenly to bow to the stage audience, and falling flat on his face.

542 **With ... knee** As David points out, Pompey's arms were traditionally supposed to have been a leopard or a lion 'with a sword clasped in his claw'. Painted on Pompey's shield, these arms would, if he has fallen down, be covering his *knee* rather than the main part of his body as he scrambles clumsily to his feet. Alternatively, the words may allude to what the French called *masquine*, the representation of a leopard's or a lion's head on the knees or elbows of some old-fashioned garments.

COSTARD

'I Pompey am, Pompey surnamed the Big'—

DUMAINE 'The Great'.

COSTARD

It is 'Great', sir. 'Pompey surnamed the Great,

That oft in field, with targe and shield, did make my
foe to sweat,

And travelling along this coast, I here am come by
chance,

And lay my arms before the legs of this sweet lass of
France.'

If your ladyship would say, 'Thanks, Pompey', I had   550
done.

⌈PRINCESS⌉ Great thanks, great Pompey.

COSTARD 'Tis not so much worth, but I hope I was perfect.
I made a little fault in 'Great'.

BIRON My hat to a halfpenny, Pompey proves the best
Worthy.

> *Costard stands aside.*
>
> *Enter Nathaniel as Alexander*

NATHANIEL

'When in the world I lived, I was the world's
commander.

By east, west, north, and south, I spread my
conquering might.

My scutcheon plain declares that I am Alisander'—

BOYET

Your nose says no, you are not, for it stands too right.   560

BIRON (*to Boyet*)

Your nose smells 'no' in this, most tender-smelling
knight.

---

552 PRINCESS] F2; *Lady.* QF   556.1 *Costard ... aside*] CAPELL (*subs.*); *not in* QF   556.2 *Enter
... Alexander*] ROWE (*subs.*); *Enter Curate for Alexander.* QF   557–63 NATHANIEL] ROWE;
Cura⟨te⟩. QF   561 this] F; his Q

547 **targe** (pronounced like 'large') buckler,
light shield
552 PRINCESS Q reads '*Lady.*' and F '*La.*'; but
both the tone and the content of the line
point to the Princess as its speaker.
553 **perfect** word-perfect
555 **My hat to a halfpenny** i.e. I'll bet
anything—proverbial (Dent C63.1)

559 **scutcheon** coat of arms
560 **Your nose ... right** According to some
authorities, including Plutarch,
Alexander had a wry neck.
561 **Your nose ... knight** Alexander was
supposed, according to Plutarch, to have
had a sweet-smelling skin, something,
says Biron, that Nathaniel certainly has

PRINCESS

The conqueror is dismayed. Proceed, good Alexander.

NATHANIEL

'When in the world I lived, I was the world's
     commander'—

BOYET

Most true, 'tis right. You were so, Alisander.

BIRON (*to Costard*) Pompey the Great—

COSTARD Your servant, and Costard.

BIRON Take away the conqueror, take away Alisander.

COSTARD (*to Nathaniel*) O, sir, you have overthrown Alisan-
     der the conqueror. You will be scraped out of the
     painted cloth for this. Your lion, that holds his pole-axe   570
     sitting on a close-stool, will be given to Ajax. He will be
     the ninth Worthy. A conqueror, and afeard to speak?
     Run away for shame, Alisander.

          ⌈*Nathaniel retires*⌉

     There, an't shall please you, a foolish mild man, an
     honest man, look you, and soon dashed. He is a
     marvellous good neighbour, faith, and a very good
     bowler. But for Alisander, alas, you see how 'tis, a little
     o'erparted. But there are Worthies a-coming will speak
     their mind in some other sort.

PRINCESS Stand aside, good Pompey.   580

          *Enter Holofernes as Judas Maccabeus, and Moth as
          Hercules*

562–80 PRINCESS] ROWE; *Qu*⟨*een*⟩. QF   567 conqueror] Q (Conqueronr), F   572 afeard] Q
(a feard); affraid F   573.1 *Nathaniel retires*] CAPELL; *Exit Cu*⟨*rate*⟩. QF (*after l. 579*)
574 you,] F (∼:); ∼ ∧ Q   576 faith] Q (fayth); insooth F   580.1–2 *Enter ... Hercules*]
ROWE (*subs.*); *Enter Pedant for Iudas, and the Boy for Hercules*. QF

not, as Boyet's sensitive nose must have
informed him. Compare Andrew Mar-
vell's 'Upon Appleton House', ll. 427–8.

569–70 **the painted cloth** The Nine Worthies were one of the subjects painted in oil
on the cloth or canvas hangings that
were draped over the walls of rooms in an
Elizabethan house.

570–1 **Your lion ... Ajax** The coat of arms
the Middle Ages gave Alexander was a
lion sitting on a chair or throne and
holding a battle-axe. Costard turns the

chair into a 'close-stool' (a chamber-pot
enclosed in a stool or box) and awards
this coat of arms to Ajax whose name was
jestingly transformed into 'a jakes', i.e. 'a
privy'.

574–7 **an honest man ... and a very good
bowler** Shakespeare takes an old saying
'To lack but a bowl and a besom of being
an honest man' (Dent B568.1), and
makes a new saying, which in its turn
became proverbial (Dent M183), out of it.

577–8 **a little o'erparted** i.e. not quite up to
the part—earliest instance cited by *OED*

219

HOLOFERNES

'Great Hercules is presented by this imp,
  Whose club killed Cerberus, that three-headed *canus*,
And when he was a babe, a child, a shrimp,
  Thus did he strangle serpents in his *manus*.
Quoniam he seemeth in minority,
Ergo I come with this apology.'
(To Moth) Keep some state in thy exit, and vanish.
    Moth retires
'Judas I am'—

DUMAINE A Judas!

HOLOFERNES Not Iscariot, sir.   590

'Judas I am, yclipèd Maccabeus'—

DUMAINE Judas Maccabeus clipped is plain Judas.

BIRON A kissing traitor. How art thou proved Judas?

HOLOFERNES

'Judas I am'—

DUMAINE The more shame for you, Judas.

HOLOFERNES What mean you, sir?

BOYET To make Judas hang himself.

HOLOFERNES Begin, sir, you are my elder.

BIRON Well followed: Judas was hanged on an elder.

HOLOFERNES I will not be put out of countenance.   600

BIRON Because thou hast no face.

587.1 *Moth retires*] CAPELL (*subs.*); *Exit Boy.* QF   588 'Judas] MALONE; *Peda.* Iudas QF
590 Not Iscariot, sir] QF (*in italics*)   591 yclipèd] Q (*ecliped*), F   593 proved] F (prou'd);
proud Q   599 elder] Q (Flder), F

581 **imp** child
582 **Cerberus** The three-headed dog that
guarded the entrance to Hades.
canus This should be *canis*, but Holofernes makes grammar and orthography
subservient to rhyme.
584 *manus* hands
585 *Quoniam* since
586 *Ergo* therefore
587 **state** dignity
589–622 **A Judas ... stumble** What Shakespeare gives us here is something that
John Webster would have called 'the
well with four buckets' as the three
courtiers and Boyet vie with one another
in pouring insult after insult on the head
of the wretched Holofernes. See *The White
Devil* 1.1.9–30.
592 **clipped** cut short, abbreviated (*OED, v.*²

5) with a quibble on *yclipèd*. The word
can, however, also mean 'embraced'
(*OED, v.*¹ 1), the sense Biron has given it
when he speaks the next line.
593 **A kissing traitor** Alluding, of course, to
the kiss with which Judas betrayed
Christ.
How ... Judas doesn't this prove you are
Judas
596 **mean you** (a) is your meaning (b) is
your purpose (the sense in which Boyet
takes it)
598 **Begin ... elder** i.e. hang yourself first,
since you are older than I am (and so
entitled to take precedence of me)
599 **Judas ... elder** Alluding to the medieval
legend that Judas hanged himself on a
branch of an elder tree.

HOLOFERNES What is this?

BOYET A cittern-head.

DUMAINE The head of a bodkin.

BIRON A death's face in a ring.

LONGUEVILLE The face of an old Roman coin, scarce seen.

BOYET The pommel of Caesar's falchion.

DUMAINE The carved-bone face on a flask.

BIRON Saint George's half-cheek in a brooch.

DUMAINE Ay, and in a brooch of lead.   610

BIRON Ay, and worn in the cap of a tooth-drawer. And
  now, forward, for we have put thee in countenance.

HOLOFERNES You have put me out of countenance.

BIRON False! We have given thee faces.

HOLOFERNES But you have outfaced them all.

BIRON

An thou wert a lion, we would do so.

BOYET

Therefore, as he is an ass, let him go.

And so adieu, sweet Jude. Nay, why dost thou stay?

DUMAINE For the latter end of his name.

BIRON

For the ass to the Jude? Give it him. Jud-as, away!   620

HOLOFERNES

This is not generous, not gentle, not humble.

617 is ∧ an ass,] Q2; is, an Asse, QF   620 Jud-as] F; *Judas* Q

602 **this** Holofernes points to his face and
thus unwittingly opens the way for
the barrage of insults that follows,
all of them referring to grotesquely
carved heads and faces on various objects.

603 **cittern-head** The *cittern* or *cithern* was a
musical instrument of the same family as
the guitar, and often had a carved head.
OED cites this as its earliest example of
cittern-head.

604 **bodkin** large pin used to keep ladies'
hair in place. The more expensive ones,
made of gold or silver, had elaborately
decorated heads.

605 **death's face in a ring** Rings engraved
with a death's head and the words
memento mori were common in
Shakespeare's time.

606 **scarce seen** i.e. almost obliterated

607 **pommel** 'knob terminating the hilt of a
sword' (*OED*, *sb.* 3)

607 **falchion** Originally and properly 'a broad
sword more or less curved with the edge
on the convex side' (*OED*, *sb.* 1), *falchion*
in Shakespeare is simply a convenient
synonym for *sword.*

608 **flask** gunpowder flask (made of horn or
bone)

609 **half-cheek** profile—only instance of this
sense given by *OED*

610–11 **brooch ... tooth-drawer** Trades-
men appear to have worn leaden
brooches in their caps to show the nature
of their business.

612 **put ... countenance** utterly discon-
certed me

615 **outfaced them all** put them all to shame
(with your mockery)

616–17 **lion ... ass** Referring to Aesop's
fable of the ass in the lion's skin, where
the ass succeeded in his imposture until
his ears betrayed him.

621 **generous** noble-minded, magnanimous

BOYET

A light for Monsieur Judas! It grows dark, he may
    stumble.
    Holofernes retires

PRINCESS

Alas, poor Maccabeus, how hath he been baited!
    Enter Armado as Hector

BIRON

Hide thy head, Achilles, here comes Hector in arms.

DUMAINE Though my mocks come home by me, I will now
be merry.

KING Hector was but a Trojan in respect of this.

BOYET But is this Hector?

KING I think Hector was not so clean-timbered.

LONGUEVILLE His leg is too big for Hector's.   630

DUMAINE More calf, certain.

BOYET No, he is best endowed in the small.

BIRON This cannot be Hector.

DUMAINE He's a god or a painter, for he makes faces.

ARMADO

'The armipotent Mars, of lances the almighty,
    Gave Hector a gift'—

DUMAINE A gilt nutmeg.

BIRON A lemon.

622.1 *Holofernes retires*] CAPELL; *not in* QF   623.1 *Enter ... Hector*] ROWE; *Eeter Braggart.* Q;
Enter Braggart. F   630 Hector's] Q (*Hectors*); *Hector* F   637 gilt] F; gift Q

621 **gentle** courteous, befitting well-born
    people (*OED, a.* 3c)
    humble kind

622 **A light ... stumble** Boyet probably refers
    to the *Judas candlestick* once used in parish
    churches at Easter. Made of brass, this
    candlestick had seven branches, from the
    seventh or middle one of which a tall
    thick piece of wood, painted like a candle,
    and called *the Judas of the Paschal*, rose
    nearly to the roof, and on the top of this
    was placed at Eastertide the paschal
    candle of wax (*OED, Judas,* 2). Boyet thus
    completes the list of carved or painted
    objects with which the courtiers identify
    Holofernes.

625 **come home by me** may recoil on my
    own head (the Princess has already ex-
    pressed her disapproval of the baiting)

626 **merry** facetious (*OED, a.* 3c)

627 **Trojan** (a) inhabitant of Troy (b) an
    ordinary bloke (*OED, sb.* 2; earliest cita-
    tion in this sense)

629 **clean-timbered** well-built—only cita-
    tion in *OED*

631 **calf** (a) part of the leg (b) naïve fool

632 **small** part of the leg below the calf

634 **makes** (a) creates (b) pulls

635 **armipotent** mighty in arms. Chaucer
    uses this word of Mars in *The Knight's
    Tale*, l. 1982: 'Ther stood the temple of
    Mars armypotente'.

637 **A gilt nutmeg** a nutmeg glazed with the
    yolk of an egg. Used for spicing wine or
    ale, gilt nutmegs were a common lover's
    gift.

638–40 **A lemon ... cloven** Lemons and
    oranges 'stuck with cloves' were em-
    ployed, like nutmegs, to flavour and

LONGUEVILLE Stuck with cloves.

DUMAINE No, cloven.   640

ARMADO Peace!

'The armipotent Mars, of lances the almighty,
      Gave Hector a gift, the heir of Ilion;
A man so breathed that certain he would fight, yea,
      From morn till night, out of his pavilion.
I am that flower'—

DUMAINE   That mint.

LONGUEVILLE   That columbine.

ARMADO Sweet Lord Longueville, rein thy tongue.

LONGUEVILLE I must rather give it the rein, for it runs
      against Hector.

DUMAINE Ay, and Hector's a greyhound.   650

ARMADO The sweet war-man is dead and rotten. Sweet
      chucks, beat not the bones of the buried. When he
      breathed, he was a man. But I will forward with my
      device. (*To the Princess*) Sweet royalty, bestow on me the
      sense of hearing.

            Biron steps forth ⌈and whispers to Costard⌉

PRINCESS Speak, brave Hector, we are much delighted.

ARMADO I do adore thy sweet grace's slipper.

BOYET Loves her by the foot.

DUMAINE He may not by the yard.

---

640 No,] ROWE; ~ ∧ QF   641 Peace!] Q (*Peace.*); *not in* F   646 I ... flower] QF (*in roman*)
flower—] CAPELL; ~ . QF   652–3 When ... man] Q; *not in* F   655.1 *Biron ... forth*] QF
and whispers to Costard] CAPELL (*subs.*); *not in* QF   657 I ... slipper] F; Q (*in italics*)

---

preserve drinks. Dumaine, however, determined to be 'merry', i.e. 'bawdy', takes
'lemon' as 'leman' ('sweetheart'), and,
referring to the female genitals, replaces
'cloves' with 'cloven'.

643 **Ilion** Troy
644 **breathed** fit, in training
645 **pavilion** ceremonial tent for the use of
      combatants in a medieval tournament
648 **give it the rein** proverbial (Dent B671)
650 **Hector's a greyhound** Hector was
      famous as a runner.
651 **dead and rotten** proverbial (Dent
      D126.1)
652 **beat not ... buried** A characteristically

Shakespearian variant on the very old
saying 'Speak well of the dead' (Dent
D124).
654 **device** dramatic representation (*OED,*
      11; earliest example of this meaning)
655.1 *Biron ... Costard* Both Q and F say
      only that Biron *steps forth*; but he must
      step forth, i.e. leave the stage audience, for
      some reason, and his likeliest motive
      would seem to be to put Costard up to
      making the spectacular intervention that
      he does at 662. TC suggests that Biron
      may be trying to prevent Armado from
      continuing.
659 **yard** (a) measurement of three feet (b)
      penis (*OED, sb.²* 11)

ARMADO

   'This Hector far surmounted Hannibal.   660

      The party is gone'—

COSTARD Fellow Hector, she is gone. She is two months on
her way.

ARMADO What meanest thou?

COSTARD Faith, unless you play the honest Trojan, the
poor wench is cast away. She's quick; the child brags in
her belly already. 'Tis yours.

ARMADO Dost thou infamonize me among potentates?
Thou shalt die.

COSTARD Then shall Hector be whipped for Jaquenetta that   670
is quick by him, and hanged for Pompey that is dead by
him.

DUMAINE Most rare Pompey!

BOYET Renowned Pompey!

BIRON Greater than 'Great'! Great, great, great Pompey!
Pompey the Huge!

DUMAINE Hector trembles.

BIRON Pompey is moved. More Ates, more Ates! Stir them
on, stir them on!

DUMAINE Hector will challenge him.   680

BIRON Ay, if a have no more man's blood in his belly than
will sup a flea.

ARMADO By the North Pole, I do challenge thee.

660] *Omission marked after this line* OXFORD   661 The party is gone.] *spoken by Armado,*
POPE; *centred and italicized* QF; *given to Costard* THEOBALD   678–9 them on, stir] ROWE; them,
or stir Q; them, or stirre F   681 in his] Q; in's F

661 **The party is gone** Centred and printed in
italics in both Q and F, these words
appear at first sight to be a stage direction. As such, however, they make no
sense, and since the line preceding them
is also in italics, apart from the two
personal names 'Hector' and 'Hanniball',
it seems reasonable to take them as a
continuation of Armado's speech, meaning much the same thing as 'The sweet
warman is dead and rotten'.

662 **gone** pregnant, gone with child

666 **quick** pregnant
    brags swaggers, shows off (*OED*, *v.* 2b)
(thus proving itself Armado's). Compare
Nashe i. 176. 12–14: 'properly Pride is
the disease of the Spaniard, who is borne
a Bragart in his mothers wombe' (*Pierce*

Penniless).

668 **infamonize** defame, infamize (of which
it is a perverted form peculiar to Armado)

670 **whipped** Whipping was the punishment for fornication. Compare *Measure*
5.1.506, where the Duke tells Lucio he is
to be 'Whipped first, sir, and hanged
after.'

671 **quick** (a) pregnant (b) living

671–2 **Pompey ... him** i.e. killing Pompey

678 **Ates** i.e. provocative remarks. Ate (disyllabic) was the Greek goddess of strife.
Compare *K. John* 2.1.63, where John's
mother is described as 'An Ate stirring
him to blood and strife.'

682 **sup** make a supper for (*OED*, *v.²* 3b)

683 **By the North Pole** The fashionable
practice of coining 'strange oaths', which

COSTARD I will not fight with a pole like a northern man.
I'll slash, I'll do it by the sword. I bepray you, let me
borrow my arms again.

DUMAINE Room for the incensed Worthies.

COSTARD I'll do it in my shirt.

DUMAINE Most resolute Pompey!

MOTH Master, let me take you a buttonhole lower. Do you   690
not see Pompey is uncasing for the combat? What mean
you? You will lose your reputation.

ARMADO Gentlemen and soldiers, pardon me, I will not
combat in my shirt.

DUMAINE You may not deny it. Pompey hath made the
challenge.

ARMADO Sweet bloods, I both may and will.

BIRON What reason have you for't?

ARMADO The naked truth of it is I have no shirt. I go
woolward for penance.   700

⌈MOTH⌉ True, and it was enjoined him in Rome for want
of linen. Since when, I'll be sworn, he wore none but a
dishclout of Jaquenetta's, and that a wears next his
heart for a favour.

    Enter a Messenger, Monsieur Marcadé

685 bepray] Q; pray F   699 have] Q (hane), F   701 MOTH] CAPELL; *Boy.* QF   703 a
wears] Q; hee wears F

Shakespeare tilts at here, is ridiculed at
length by Ben Jonson through the
speeches of Bobadill in *Every Man in his
Humour* (1598).

684–5 I ... sword Costard, the party challenged, asserts his rights to the choice of
weapons.

684 with ... man Hart is probably right in
his suggestion that Costard has in mind
the cattle-thieves, or reavers, as they
were called, of the northern borders who
fought with very long poles tipped with
steel.

685 bepray pray. Appearing in F as 'pray'
and not to be found anywhere else, this
word is of doubtful authenticity. It is
retained in this edition because it could
well be a 'Costardism', combining 'beseech' and 'pray' in a single word.

686 my arms i.e. the arms and armour I
wore as Pompey

690 take ... lower (a) help you off with your
doublet (b) take you down a peg or two—

proverbial (Tilley P181)

691 uncasing undressing, taking off his
outer garments

695 deny it refuse to

697 bloods men of mettle, fiery spirits

699 The naked truth proverbial (Dent
T589)

700 woolward i.e. with no linen between my
skin and my outer wear—proverbial
(Dent W757.1); not elsewhere in
Shakespeare

701 MOTH The two substantive texts head
this speech '*Boy.*' which could signify
either '*Boyet*' or '*Moth*'. Moth seems the
likelier candidate, since he can be expected to know something about the state
of Armado's wardrobe.

701–2 for want of linen Moth's point is that
Armado's shirtless state is a consequence
of penury not penance.

703 dishclout dishcloth

704.1 *Enter ... Marcadé* See Introduction
p. 10. He could leave after 709.

MARCADÉ

God save you, madam.

PRINCESS   Welcome, Marcadé,

But that thou interrupt'st our merriment.

MARCADÉ

I am sorry, madam, for the news I bring

Is heavy in my tongue. The King your father—

PRINCESS

Dead, for my life!

MARCADÉ   Even so. My tale is told.

BIRON

Worthies, away! The scene begins to cloud.   710

ARMADO For mine own part, I breathe free breath. I have
seen the day of wrong through the little hole of discretion, and I will right myself like a soldier.

Exeunt Worthies

KING How fares your majesty?

QUEEN

Boyet, prepare. I will away tonight.

KING

Madam, not so. I do beseech you, stay.

QUEEN

Prepare, I say. I thank you, gracious lords,

For all your fair endeavours, and entreat,

Out of a new-sad soul, that you vouchsafe

In your rich wisdom to excuse, or hide,   720

The liberal opposition of our spirits.

If over-boldly we have borne ourselves

In the converse of breath, your gentleness

Was guilty of it. Farewell, worthy lord!

706 interrupt'st] CAPELL; interrnpptest Q; interruptest F   708 father—] QF (~ ∧)
709 Dead,] THEOBALD; ~ ∧ QF   718 entreat,] ROWE 1714; intreat: Q; entreats: F
719 new-sad soul] THEOBALD; new sad-soule QF   721-4 spirits. | If ... ourselves | In ...
breath, your ... it.] ROWE; spirites, | If ... our selues, | In ... breath (your ... it.) QF

711-13 **I breathe ... soldier** i.e. I have a
wonderful sense of relief (at having escaped from a tight corner). I have realized
and avoided, through the little loophole
discretion gave me, the full nature of the
disgrace I was in danger of incurring, and
I will now vindicate myself as a soldier
should. Armado brings two common
sayings together: 'One may see day at a

little hole' and 'Discretion is the better
part of valour' (Dent D99 and D354).
720 **hide** disregard, overlook
721 **liberal** unrestrained
723 **the converse of breath** i.e. our conversations with you
gentleness courtesy, gentlemanly for-
bearance
724 **guilty of** to blame for, responsible for

A heavy heart bears not a nimble tongue.
Excuse me so, coming too short of thanks
For my great suit so easily obtained.

KING

The extreme parts of time extremely forms
All causes to the purpose of his speed,
And often at his very loose decides   730
That which long process could not arbitrate.
And though the mourning brow of progeny
Forbid the smiling courtesy of love
The holy suit which fain it would convince,
Yet, since love's argument was first on foot,
Let not the cloud of sorrow jostle it
From what it purposed; since to wail friends lost
Is not by much so wholesome-profitable
As to rejoice at friends but newly found.

QUEEN

I understand you not: my griefs are double.   740

BIRON

Honest plain words best pierce the ear of grief,
And by these badges understand the King.
For your fair sakes have we neglected time,
Played foul play with our oaths. Your beauty, ladies,
Hath much deformed us, fashioning our humours

725 nimble] THEOBALD; humble QF   726 too] Q; so F   733 love ∧] HANMER; ~ , Q; ~ : F
738 wholesome-profitable] WALKER; holdsome profitable Q; wholsome profitable F   740
double] QF; dull COLLIER 1858   743 time,] F; ~ . Q

725 **nimble** Theobald's emendation of
'humble', found in Q and F, is adopted
here for two reasons. First, 'nimble
tongue' provides the right antithesis to
'heavy heart'; and, secondly, as Oxford
points out, 'in all nine cases where
Shakespeare uses "humble" preceded by
the indefinite article, the form is "an",
not—as here—"a"' (*TC*, p. 275).

727 **my ... obtained** The dispute over Aquitaine has evidently been settled in a way
favourable to the Princess. Shakespeare
characteristically does not—supposing
he ever knew—tell us how, since the
matter is no longer of any consequence.

728–31 **The extreme ... arbitrate** i.e. when
the time for making important decisions
is extremely short, its extreme pressure
subjects all issues to its demand for speed,

and often at the critical moment settles
matters that could never be decided by
protracted negotiation

730 **loose** the decisive moment in which an
arrow is loosed from the bow

734 **convince** give proof of (*OED, v.* 8).

735 **on foot** in action, begun. Shakespeare's—or is it the King's?—awareness
of the literal meaning of the phrase leads
him on to the rather ludicrous image
of love's cause being 'jostled' by a 'cloud
of sorrow'.

738 **wholesome-profitable** good for the spirits

740 **double** (because I'm sorry for my inability to understand you as well as for my
father's death)

742 **badges** signs, tokens; i.e. the words I am
about to speak (*OED, sb.* 2b)

745 **deformed us** made us look ugly

Even to the opposèd end of our intents;
And what in us hath seemed ridiculous—
As love is full of unbefitting strains,
All wanton as a child, skipping and vain,
Formed by the eye and therefore like the eye,   750
Full of strange shapes, of habits, and of forms,
Varying in subjects as the eye doth roll
To every varied object in his glance;
Which parti-coated presence of loose love
Put on by us, if, in your heavenly eyes,
Have misbecomed our oaths and gravities,
Those heavenly eyes, that look into these faults,
Suggested us to make. Therefore, ladies,
Our love being yours, the error that love makes
Is likewise yours. We to ourselves prove false   760
By being once false for ever to be true
To those that make us both—fair ladies, you.
And even that falsehood, in itself a sin,
Thus purifies itself and turns to grace.

QUEEN
We have received your letters, full of love;
Your favours, the ambassadors of love;

751 strange] CAPELL; straying QF   756 misbecomed] Q (misbecombd), misbecom'd F
gravities,] CAPELL; ~ . QF   758 make] QF; make them POPE   762 both—] F (~ ,); ~ ∧ Q
766 the] F; *not in* Q

746 **Even ... intents** into the exact opposite
of what we intended
748 **strains** impulses, tendencies (including,
perhaps, a tendency to break into song)
751 **strange** The 'straying' of Q and F is
probably due to the Q compositor's misin-
terpreting the 'straing' or 'straynge' of
the manuscript, both being recognized
spellings of *strange* at the time the play
was written. In *Sir Thomas More* D, at line
11, Lincoln speaks of 'straing rootes',
meaning 'parsnips'.
habits (a) modes of behaviour (b) clothes
forms ideal forms, figures created by the
imagination
752 **the eye doth roll** Compare *Dream*
5.1.12: 'The poet's eye, in a fine frenzy
rolling'.
754–8 **Which ... make** i.e. and if the
motley appearance and behaviour of
casual lovers that we adopted have accorded ill (*misbecomed*), in your heavenly

eyes, with the grave oaths we took, don't
forget that it was those same heavenly
eyes of yours, which now see our faults
with such clarity, that tempted us into
committing those faults in the first place
754 **Which** and this (see Abbott 418)
parti-coated parti-coloured, part of one
colour and part of another like the garb of
a licensed fool—only instance cited by
OED
presence appearance (Schmidt)
758 **Suggested** tempted (*OED, v.* 2). Compare *Henry V* 2.2.111: 'other devils that
suggest by treasons', and *LLL* 1.1.157.
759 **Our love being yours** i.e. since you are
the cause of our being in love
761 **once** (when we broke our academic
oaths)
763 **falsehood** i.e. failure to keep the initial
oath
764 **grace** virtue (*OED, sb.* 13b)

And in our maiden counsel rated them
At courtship, pleasant jest, and courtesy,
As bombast and as lining to the time.
But more devout than this in our respects   770
Have we not been, and therefore met your loves
In their own fashion, like a merriment.
DUMAINE
Our letters, madam, showed much more than jest.
LONGUEVILLE
So did our looks.
ROSALINE   We did not quote them so.
KING
Now, at the latest minute of the hour,
Grant us your loves.
QUEEN   A time, methinks, too short
To make a world-without-end bargain in.
No, no, my lord, your grace is perjured much,
Full of dear guiltiness, and therefore this:
If for my love—as there is no such cause—   780
You will do aught, this shall you do for me:
Your oath I will not trust; but go with speed
To some forlorn and naked hermitage,
Remote from all the pleasures of the world.
There stay until the twelve celestial signs
Have brought about the annual reckoning.
If this austere insociable life
Change not your offer made in heat of blood;

770 this in] HANMER; this Q; these are F   779 therefore] Q (rherefore), F   786 the] Q, their F
788 blood;] F (∼ :); ∼ . Q

767 **rated** assessed, estimated their value
768 **At** i.e. as amounting to no more than
   courtship an exercise in courtly manners
769 **As ... time** i.e. as a way of filling in the
   time. *Bombast* was cotton wool used for
   stuffing and *lining* garments, and so became a synonym for words employed as
   mere 'padding'.
770–1 **more devout ... been** i.e. we have
   paid no more serious attention to the
   matter than this
772 **merriment** bit of fun
774 **quote** regard, think (*OED, v.* 6a)
777 **world-without-end** everlasting. Taken
   from *The Book of Common Prayer*, where it

appears as a phrase at the end of Matins,
this evocative compound adjective recurs
at Sonnets 57.5.
779 **dear** grievous, dire (*OED, a.*² 2). Compare Sonnets 37.3: 'I, made lame by
   fortune's dearest spite'. The Princess also
   has in mind, however, the normal sense
   of *dear*, since the King's *guiltiness* has
   made him *dear* to her.
780 **as ... cause** i.e. I can't see that as a good
   reason for your doing anything
783 **forlorn** desolate
   naked unfurnished (*OED, a.* 10b)
785 **signs** signs of the zodiac (each account-
   ing for a month)

If frosts and fasts, hard lodging and thin weeds
Nip not the gaudy blossoms of your love,   790
But that it bear this trial, and last love;
Then, at the expiration of the year,
Come challenge me, challenge me by these deserts,
And, by this virgin palm now kissing thine,
I will be thine; and till that instance shut
My woeful self up in a mourning house,
Raining the tears of lamentation
For the remembrance of my father's death.
If this thou do deny, let our hands part,
Neither entitled in the other's heart.   800

KING
If this, or more than this, I would deny,
    To flatter up these powers of mine with rest,
The sudden hand of death close up mine eye!
    Hence, hermit, then—my heart is in thy breast.
        The King and the Queen converse apart

DUMAINE (*to Katherine*)
But what to me, my love? But what to me?
A wife?

KATHERINE A beard, fair health, and honesty;
With threefold love I wish you all these three.

DUMAINE
O, shall I say, 'I thank you, gentle wife'?

KATHERINE
Not so, my lord. A twelvemonth and a day
I'll mark no words that smooth-faced wooers say.   810

793 challenge me, challenge me] QF; challenge me, challenge HANMER; challenge, challenge
me MALONE   795 instance] Q; instant F   800 entitled] F (intitled); intiled Q   804
hermit] WILSON (*conj.* Pollard); herrite Q; euer F   then—my heart ∧] F (then, my heart);
then my hart, Q   804.1 *The . . . apart*] *not in* QF.   *At this point* Q, *followed by* F, *prints the lines
given in Appendix A (ii).*   806 A wife?] *continued to Dumaine,* DYCE; *part of Katherine's next
line,* QF

789 **weeds,** clothes
790 **Nip . . . blossoms** proverbial (Dent B702)
791 **last love** endure as love
793 **challenge** lay claim to (*OED, v.* 5)
     deserts deservings, fulfilment of my re-
     quirements
795 **instance** instant (*OED, sb.* 4)
800 **entitled in** having a claim to
802 **flatter up** indulge, pamper (*OED, v.*¹ 10)
804 **my heart is in thy breast** A version of the

common saying 'The lover is not where
he lives but where he loves' (Dent L565).
After this line Q and F print six lines of
dialogue between Biron and Rosaline
which are evidently the first draft of lines
819 to 853. They are to be found in
Appendix A.
810 **smooth-faced** plausibly seductive. Compare *K. John* 2.1.574: 'That smooth-
faced gentleman, tickling commodity'.

Come when the King doth to my lady come;
Then, if I have much love, I'll give you some.
DUMAINE
I'll serve thee true and faithfully till then.
KATHERINE
Yet swear not, lest ye be forsworn again.
 They converse apart
LONGUEVILLE
What says Maria?
MARIA   At the twelvemonth's end
I'll change my black gown for a faithful friend.
LONGUEVILLE
I'll stay with patience; but the time is long.
MARIA
The liker you; few taller are so young.
 They converse apart
BIRON (*to Rosaline*)
Studies my lady? Mistress, look on me,
Behold the window of my heart, mine eye,   820
What humble suit attends thy answer there.
Impose some service on me for thy love.
ROSALINE
Oft have I heard of you, my lord Biron,
Before I saw you; and the world's large tongue
Proclaims you for a man replete with mocks,
Full of comparisons and wounding flouts,
Which you on all estates will execute
That lie within the mercy of your wit.
To weed this wormwood from your fruitful brain,
And therewithal to win me, if you please,   830
Without the which I am not to be won,
You shall this twelvemonth term from day to day

814.1 *They ... apart*] not in QF 818.1 *They ... apart*] not in QF 822 thy] Q; my F
827 estates] Q (estetes), F 828 wit.] F; wi: Q

816 **change** exchange
 friend lover (*OED, sb.* 4)
817 **stay** wait
819 **Studies my lady?** Is my lady lost in
 thought?
820 **Behold ... eye** proverbial (Dent E231)
821 **attends** waits for
826 **comparisons** scoffing similes (*OED, sb.*

 3b; earliest example of this sense)
826 **flouts** jeers
827 **estates** 'sorts and conditions of men'
 execute inflict. Compare *Richard III* Add.
 Pass. C.3 (1.4.68 + 3): 'execute thy
 wrath in me alone'.
829 **wormwood** (the emblem of bitterness)

Visit the speechless sick, and still converse
With groaning wretches; and your task shall be
With all the fierce endeavour of your wit
To enforce the painèd impotent to smile.

BIRON

To move wild laughter in the throat of death?
It cannot be, it is impossible.
Mirth cannot move a soul in agony.

ROSALINE

Why, that's the way to choke a gibing spirit,   840
Whose influence is begot of that loose grace
Which shallow laughing hearers give to fools.
A jest's prosperity lies in the ear
Of him that hears it, never in the tongue
Of him that makes it. Then if sickly ears,
Deafed with the clamours of their own dear groans,
Will hear your idle scorns, continue then,
And I will have you and that fault withal.
But if they will not, throw away that spirit,
And I shall find you empty of that fault,   850
Right joyful of your reformation.

BIRON

A twelvemonth? Well, befall what will befall,
I'll jest a twelvemonth in an hospital.

QUEEN (*to the King*)

Ay, sweet my lord, and so I take my leave.

KING

No, madam, we will bring you on your way.

BIRON

Our wooing doth not end like an old play:
Jack hath not Jill. These ladies' courtesy
Might well have made our sport a comedy.

---

833 **still converse** i.e. spend all your time
associating
835 **fierce** ardent, strenuous. Compare *Tragedy of Lear* 2.1.33–4: 'Some blood drawn
on me would beget opinion | Of my more
fierce endeavour.'
836 **the painèd impotent** those who are in
pain and incapable of helping themselves
839 **agony** the throes of death (*OED*, 3)
841 **Whose ... grace** i.e. which draws its inspiration from that easy-going indulgence

846 **dear** heartfelt, grievous. See line 779.
852 **befall what will befall** proverbial (Dent
C529)
855 **bring** accompany, escort
857 **Jack hath not Jill** (contrary to the
proverb Tilley A164). Contrast *Dream*
3.3.45–8: 'Jack shall have Jill, | Naught
shall go ill, | the man shall have his mare
again, and all shall be well.'
These ladies' courtesy i.e. a kind reception (of our efforts) by these ladies

KING

  Come, sir, it wants a twelvemonth an' a day,
  And then 'twill end.

BIRON   That's too long for a play.   860

      Enter Armado

ARMADO (*to the King*) Sweet majesty, vouchsafe me—

QUEEN Was not that Hector?

DUMAINE The worthy knight of Troy.

ARMADO I will kiss thy royal finger, and take leave. I am a
  votary, I have vowed to Jaquenetta to hold the plough
  for her sweet love three year. But, most esteemed
  greatness, will you hear the dialogue that the two
  learned men have compiled in praise of the owl and the
  cuckoo? It should have followed in the end of our show.

KING Call them forth quickly, we will do so.   870

ARMADO Holla! Approach.

      Enter all ⌈those not yet on stage⌉

  This side is Hiems, Winter; this Ver, the Spring: the
  one maintained by the owl, th'other by the cuckoo.
  Ver, begin.

                    THE SONG

SPRING (*sings*)

          When daisies pied, and violets blue,
            And lady-smocks all silver-white,
          And cuckoo-buds of yellow hue
            Do paint the meadows with delight,
          The cuckoo then, on every tree,
          Mocks married men, for thus sings he: 880
            'Cuckoo!

859 an' a day] Q (an'aday); and a day F   860.1 *Enter Armado*] ROWE; *Enter Braggart.* QF
861 me—] THEOBALD; ~. QF   866 year] Q (yeere); yeares F   871.1 *Enter ... stage*] QF
(*Enter all.*)   872 This] F; *Brag.* This Q   873 th'other] Q; Th'other F; The other ROWE
874 Ver, begin] *as part of Armado's speech*, F; *separated from the previous words by a space, and
preceded by 'B.'*, Q   874.1 SPRING (*sings*)] *not in* QF   876, 877] *as here*, THEOBALD;
in reverse order, QF

867 **dialogue** disputation, debate
872 Since no entry is provided for either
    Spring or Winter, these parts may have
    been represented by Sir Nathaniel and
    Holofernes.
873 **maintained** supported, upheld (*OED, v.*
    14). The tentative suggestion that *main-*

tained here means *represented* (*OED, v.* 16)
    seems unnecessary.
876 **lady-smocks** cuckoo flowers
877 **cuckoo-buds** *OED* circumspectly glosses
    cuckoo-bud as 'a name of some plant'.
880 **Mocks married men** (since its cry is so
    reminiscent of *cuckold*, and its habit of

Cuckoo, cuckoo!' O word of fear,
Unpleasing to a married ear.

When shepherds pipe on oaten straws,
   And merry larks are ploughmen's clocks,
When turtles tread, and rooks, and daws,
   And maidens bleach their summer smocks,
The cuckoo then, on every tree,
Mocks married men, for thus sings he:
      'Cuckoo!   890
Cuckoo, cuckoo!' O word of fear,
Unpleasing to a married ear.

WINTER (*sings*)
      When icicles hang by the wall,
         And Dick the shepherd blows his nail,
      And Tom bears logs into the hall,
         And milk comes frozen home in pail,
      When blood is nipped, and ways be foul,
      Then nightly sings the staring owl:
      'Tu-whit, Tu-whoo!'—
      A merry note,   900
      While greasy Joan doth keel the pot.

      When all aloud the wind doth blow,
         And coughing drowns the parson's saw,
      And birds sit brooding in the snow,
         And Marian's nose looks red and raw,
      When roasted crabs hiss in the bowl,
      Then nightly sings the staring owl:
      'Tu-whit, tu-whoo!'—
      A merry note,
      While greasy Joan doth keel the pot.   910

---

893 *(sings)*] *not in* QF   897 foul] F (fowle); full Q

laying its eggs in another bird's nest
resembles the behaviour of a man who
seduces another man's wife or of a married woman who couples with a man
other than her husband)

886 **turtles tread** turtle-doves mate
   daws jackdaws
894 **blows his nail** blows on his finger-nails

(to warm his hands)
901 **keel** 'cool (a hot or boiling liquid) by
   stirring, skimming, or pouring in something cold, in order to prevent it from
   boiling over' (*OED*, *v.*¹ 1b)
902 **all aloud** extremely loudly
903 **saw** sermon, discourse
906 **crabs** crab-apples
   bowl i.e. bowl filled with ale

⌈ARMADO⌉ The words of Mercury are harsh after the
    songs of Apollo. You that way. We this way.   *Exeunt*

911 ARMADO] F (*Brag.*); *not in* Q   912 You that way. We this way.] F; *not in* Q   *Exeunt*] F
(*Exeunt omnes.*); *not in* Q

911–12 **The . . . Apollo** In Q these words, not
assigned to any character, conclude the
play. 'The words' in question are almost
certainly those of Marcadé, the messenger of death, and therefore the play's
Mercury, while 'the songs of Apollo' are
probably the courtiers' sonnets and Biron's praise of love in 4.3.

912 **You . . . this way** Found only in F, where
it is given, as is the previous speech, to
Armado, this line could be addressed to
the audience about to leave the theatre,
or to the Princess and her entourage
about to return to France. In either case it
marks the end of the revels.

TWO 'FALSE STARTS'

(i) After 4.3.292, the following lines appear in Q and F:

And where that you have vowed to study, lords,
In that each of you have forsworn his book,
Can you still dream and pore and thereon look?
For when would you, my lord, or you, or you,
Have found the ground of study's excellence
Without the beauty of a woman's face?
From women's eyes this doctrine I derive:
They are the ground, the books, the academes,
From whence doth spring the true Promethean fire.
Why, universal plodding poisons up   10
The nimble spirits in the arteries,
As motion and long-during action tires
The sinewy vigour of the traveller.
Now, for not looking on a woman's face,
You have in that forsworn the use of eyes,
And study too, the causer of your vow;
For where is any author in the world
Teaches such beauty as a woman's eye?
Learning is but an adjunct to ourself,
And where we are our learning likewise is.   20
Then when ourselves we see in ladies' eyes,
With ourselves,
Do we not likewise see our learning there?

(ii) After 5.2.804, the two substantive texts read:

BIRON

And what to me, my love? And what to me?

10 poisons] QF (poysons); prisons THEOBALD   18 woman's] Q (womas), F

i.1 **where that** whereas (Abbott 134)
 2 **In that** i.e. seeing that
   have has (Abbott 412)
 5 **ground** basis, foundation
 9 **Promethean fire** i.e. divine inspiration.
   Prometheus stole fire from heaven and
   brought it to men. Shakespeare probably
   took the word, as David suggests, from
   George Chapman's *The Shadow of Night*

(1594), where Chapman writes: 'There-
fore Promethean poets with the coals | Of
their most genial, more than human
souls, | In living verse created men like
these' (lines 131–3).
10 **up** totally, absolutely
11 **The ... arteries** It was thought that the
   arteries contained an etherial fluid, called
   'spiritual blood' or 'vital spirits'. Quite

ROSALINE

You must be purgèd till your sins are racked.
You are attaint with faults and perjury.
Therefore, if you my favour mean to get,
A twelvemonth shall you spend and never rest
But seek the weary beds of people sick.

2 till] This edition (*conj.* Wilson); to Q; too F   racked] Q (rackt), F; rank ROWE

distinct from the blood in the veins, it was regarded as the source of motion and sensation.

ii.2 **till** Q reads 'to,' and F 'too,', a mere difference in spelling. But 'too, your sins are racked' yields no ready sense. The emendation adopted here rests on Wilson's suggestion 'that the compositor printed "to" for "till" (a common type of error) ... The word "attaint" in the next line seems to make the connexion between "rack" and torture certain. Rosaline has "purgatory" in mind.' She is also, it may be added, carrying out her vindictive threat at 5.2.60 to 'torture' Biron.
racked tormented (as though on the rack)

3 **attaint with** (a) disgraced by (Onions) (b) found guilty of (*OED*, *v.* 3)

APPENDIX B

ALTERATIONS TO LINEATION

THE principles governing what follows have been set out by Gary Taylor in his edition of *Henry V*. He writes:

> Since this list records only changes of verse to prose, of prose to verse, or of line-arrangement within verse, it differs from the textual collations in a few details of presentation. Both within the lemma and in the quotation of a rejected line-arrangement, punctuation at the end of the line is ignored, and spelling modernized. Attribution of an emendation or variant reading indicates only that the text or editor cited *arranges* the lines in a certain way; sometimes ... not all the words of the text are identical with those printed in this edition. (p. 303)

In what follows the word *line* means 'line of verse'.

1.1.140   What ... forgot] Q; *as two lines divided after* 'lords' F
2.1.37–8   Who ... Duke] ROWE 1714; *as prose* QF
    105–6   And ... bold] F; *as one line* Q
    115–16   How ... question] CAPELL; *as one line* QF
    179–80   Pray ... it] Q; *as two lines divided after* 'commendations' F
    198   She ... shame] Q; *as two lines divided after* 'self' F
    202–5   Good ... lady] F; *as two lines divided after* 'Falconbridge' Q
3.1.30   But ... love] Q; *as separate line* F
    55–6   Thy ... slow] POPE; *as prose* QF
    101–6   Come ... market] Q; *as eight lines divided after* 'hither', 'begin', 'shin', 'l'envoi', 'plantain', 'in', *and* 'bought' F
    110–11   Thou ... l'envoi] Q; *as two lines divided after* 'Moth' F
    130   Like ... adieu] Q; *as two lines divided after* 'I' F
    131   My ... Jew] Q; *as prose* F
    156–7   It ... this] QF; *as one line* CAPELL; *as two lines divided after* 'slave' OXFORD
    167   And ... whip] Q; *as two lines divided after* 'love' F
    168–71   A ... magnificent] POPE; *as two lines divided after* 'constable' Q; *as four lines divided after* 'critic', 'constable', *and* 'boy' F
4.1.53   I ... Rosaline] Q; *as two lines divided after* 'Biron' F
    56   Stand ... carve] Q; *as two lines divided after* 'bearer' F
    93–4   What ... better] Q; *as prose* F
    108–9   Why ... off] CAPELL; *as one line* QF
    114–15   If ... indeed] F3; *as prose* QF
    117   But ... now] Q; *as two lines divided after* 'lower' F

126–7 An ... can] F; *as one line* Q
4.2.22–3 Twice-sod ... look] DYCE; *as prose* QF
25 He ... ink] Q; *as two lines divided after* 'were' F
27–8 And ... he] HANMER; *as prose* QF
33–4 You ... yet] Q; *as prose* F
56–61 The ... more 'L'] CAPELL; *as twelve lines divided after* 'pricked', 'pricket', 'not a sore', 'shooting', 'sore', 'thicket', 'sorel', 'a-hooting', 'to sore', 'sore "L"', *and* 'make' QF
95–6 Venetia ... pretia] CAPELL; *as prose* QF
141–2 Good ... life] Q; *as two lines divided after* 'me' F
160–2 Sir ... recreation] POPE; *as two lines divided after* 'verba' QF
4.3.1–2 The ... myself] POPE; *as two lines divided after* 'deer' QF
87–8 As ... child] THEOBALD; *as two lines divided after* 'cedar' QF
181–4 In ... limb] ROWE; *as prose* QF
208–9 True ... gone] ROWE 1714; *as one line* QF
5.2.3–4 A ... King] POPE; *as prose* QF
14 He ... heavy] Q; *as prose* F
15–18 And ... long] F2; *as prose* QF
47 But ... Dumaine] THEOBALD; *as two lines divided after* 'you' QF
160–1 A ... views] THEOBALD; *as prose* QF
175 What ... Boyet] POPE; *as two lines divided after* 'strangers' QF
216–17 The ... it] Q; *as prose* F
234–5 Seventh ... you] ROWE 1714; *as two lines divided after* 'cog' QF
239–40 Say ... lady] F; *as one line* Q
240–1 Please ... adieu] F; *as one line* Q
311–2 Gone ... thither] CAPELL; *as prose* Q; *as two lines divided after* 'tent' F
386 Where ... this] Q; *as two lines divided after* 'visor' F
389 We ... downright] Q; *as two lines divided after* 'descried' F
431–2 Teach ... excuse] Q; *as prose* F
439–40 Peace ... forswear] F; *as prose* Q
450 What ... troth] *as two lines divided after* 'madam' F
481–2 Full ... run] ROWE 1714; *as prose* QF
508 Biron ... approach] Q; *as two lines divided after* 'us' F
509–10 We ... company] Q; *as prose* F
533–4 And ... five] ROWE 1714; *as prose* QF
543 Well ... thee] Q; *as two lines divided after* 'mocker' F
550–1 If ... done] *as one line* QF
560 Your ... right] Q; *as two lines divided after* 'not' F
562 The ... Alexander] Q; *as two lines divided after* 'dismayed' F
611–12 Ay ... countenance] CAPELL; *as two lines divided after* 'tooth-drawer' QF

635–6   The ... gift] *as prose* QF
651–3   The ... man] CAPELL; *as three lines divided after* 'rotten' *and*
            'buried', Q; F *omits* 'When ... man' *and divides after* 'rotten'
653–5   But ... hearing] Q; *as two lines divided after* 'device' F
668–9   Dost ... die] POPE; *as two lines divided after* 'potentates' QF
699–700 The ... penance] POPE; *as two lines divided after* 'shirt' QF
705–6   Welcome ... merriment] CAPELL; *as prose* QF
707–8   I ... father] ROWE 1714; *as prose* QF
864–6   I ... year] F; *as three lines divided after* 'leave' *and* 'Jaquen-
            etta' Q
876–7   And ... hue] THEOBALD; *lines in reversed order* QF
911–12 The ... Apollo] Q; *as two lines divided after* 'Mercury' F

A NOTE ON THE MUSIC

By John Caldwell

THE original production of *Love's Labour's Lost* would have included a considerable amount of incidental music. Apart from the usual introductory music while the audience was arriving and getting settled, the two masques in Act 5 both call for it. The first of these is announced with the sound of a trumpet (5.2.156.1); the instrumentalists enter in the guise of blackamoors (5.2.157.2); and their playing of dance-music is stated or implied by the text from 5.2.211. The punning on the word 'measure' begins at 5.2.184; the dance music that begins at 5.2.211 ends at line 221, but possibly begins again; some may well have ensued before the various tête-à-têtes are roughly broken off at line 264.[1]

The Masque of the Worthies does not specifically require music, though the individual masquers could well have been introduced by a trumpet call; but its delayed conclusion, the Dialogue between Spring and Winter, certainly does. The context implies a degree of formality—the actors concerned were probably accomplished musicians—but unfortunately no contemporary setting of the two poems survives. One possibility would be to sing the verses to a popular tune of the day, 'The leaves be green' (known as *Browning*: see Ex. 1). In itself this would be wearisomely repetitive, but the tune was often used as the basis of

Ex. 1

[1] On the 'measure' as a term of dance-music see J. M. Ward, 'The English Measure', *Early Music*, xiv (1986), 15–21. Suitable music for dancing and for incidental purposes may be found in *Elizabethan Consort Music*, ed. Paul Doe, 2 vols. (London: Stainer and Bell, 1979–88, = *Musica Britannica*, xliv–xlv) and in Anthony Holborne's *Pavans, Galliards, Almains*, 1599, ed. B. Thomas (London, 1980; score and five parts).

instrumental compositions, the melody being transferred from one part to another at each variation. Not all settings would be suitable, but there are two quite straightforward Elizabethan five-part versions, by Stoning and Woodcock respectively,[1] either of which could easily be adapted for the purpose. Ideally, each actor would play an instrumental part, singing the tune with its pre-arranged pair of lines whenever appropriate. But if this is impracticable, the actors can simply join in with the tune in turn while the piece is played independently. If the 'Cuckoo' and 'Tu-who' refrains are each extended to make a complete pair of lines the five variations of Stoning's piece and the ten of Woodcock's will be exactly the right length for the performance of one and two stanzas respectively.

Of the other musical references, the song given as 'Concolinel' (3.1.3) cannot be identified; any straightforward lute-song of the period may be used.[2] The·musical notes 'Ut re sol la mi fa' (4.2.98), whatever their significance in the context, would presumably have been sung as shown (Ex. 2, at any pitch). The only song for which a contemporary musical setting appears to have existed is 'Thou canst not hit it' (4.1.124–7). A tune labelled simply 'hit' is found in the so-called Ballet Lute-Book, Dublin, Trinity College, MS D.1.21, p. 84.[3] Another version, labelled 'Altra canson englesa', is to be found in Emanuel Adriaenssen's *Pratum musicum* (Antwerp, 1584; second edn. 1600); and this was copied, with Adriaenssen's title, into the 'Dallis' Lute Book (Dublin, Trinity College, MS D.3.30/I) on p. 171. Adriaenssen's version suits the words of the play less well, though its regular structure offers some encouragement to

Ex. 2

Ut re sol la mi fa

---

[1] *Musica Britannica*, xliv, nos. 40, 41. The settings by Baldwin (ibid., xlv, no. 124) and Byrd are unduly complex for the purpose. William Cobbold's consort song *New Fashions* (*Musica Britannica*, xxii, no. 71), though not itself suitable, offers a parallel to the suggested method of performance and to the adaptation of new text to the 'Browning' tune.

[2] Volumes of songs by Dowland, Morley, Campion, and others are included in the series *The English Lute-Songs*, published by Stainer and Bell.

[3] See J. M. Ward in *The Lute Society Journal*, x (1968), 15–32. The Alman 'Hit it and take it', by Robert Johnson, is unconnected and cannot be fitted to Shakespeare's words. A manuscript dated 1620, supposedly given to the Oxford Music School by Dr Fell, Bishop of Oxford (W. Chappell, *Popular Music of the Olden Time* (London, 1855–9, vol. i, p. 239)‡) cannot now be traced. In Wooldridge's revision of Chappell (London and New York, 1893, vol. i, p. 249), the 'Ballet' version is adapted and re-harmonized.

adapt the clearly corrupt Ballet copy to the rhythm of the words. We give both the Ballet version and an adaptation of the tune for use in the play (Ex. 3).

Ex. 3
(a)

(b)

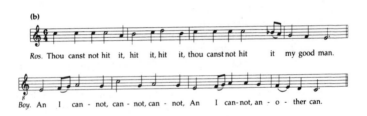

Ros. Thou canst not hit it, hit   it, hit   it, thou canst not hit   it   my good man.

Boy. An   I   can - not, can - not, can - not, An   I   can - not, an - o - ther can.

THE NAME OF ARMADO'S PAGE

It is not easy to be sure what the name of Armado's page should be in a modernized edition. John Kerrigan, in his New Penguin *Love's Labour's Lost* (1982), calls him 'Mote', a procedure which he justifies thus:

The argument for modernizing the Q and F 'Moth' (which other editors have preserved) to *Mote* goes as follows. As a result of changes in pronunciation, that form of the word 'moth' which derived from Old English *mohðe* developed a hard final 't' and became indistinguishable in Elizabethan and Jacobean English from the word 'mote', derived from Old English *mot*. This led to the spellings 'moth' and 'mote' where we should have 'mote' and 'moth'. Setting aside references to Armado's page and Titania's fairy (with whom similar difficulties arise), of the sixteen appearances of 'mo(a)th(e)(s)' in the Quartos and F, five mean 'insect(s)' and eleven (including four at IV.3.159 of Q and F *Love's Labour's Lost*) 'particle(s)'. 'Moats' occurs once, in the Shakespearian part of *Pericles* (1609 Q). In view of the ambiguity of 'moth' in these texts (including several set from Shakespeare's manuscripts and therefore likely to reflect his own spelling), the modernizing editor must decide which sense is dominant in the case of Armado's page. Since there are no references to his being insect-like but several to his being tiny ... and like a word (V.1.39–40)—a joke which relies on a pun with the French word for 'word', *mot*, which had a sounded final 't' in the sixteenth century—the primary sense is undoubtedly 'particle'. So, despite the spelling of Q and F, *Mote* must be the page's name in a modern-spelling text. (pp. 160–1)

This notion is strongly endorsed by Stanley Wells (*Re-Editing*, pp. 23–4), and adopted by him and Gary Taylor in their edition of *The Complete Works*, where the name of the page is *Mote*. Yet there are several objections to it. In the first place it is not true to say, as Kerrigan does, that 'there are no references to his being insect-like'. There is one such reference, and it is a significant one. At 4.1.147 Costard, who is much taken with the boy, his polar opposite in so many respects, describes him admiringly as a 'most pathetical nit'; and a 'nit', says *OED*, is 'an insect parasitic on man or animals ... in a young state.' It then goes on to list two obsolete uses of the word, 'gnat, or small fly' (1b), and its figurative application 'to persons in contempt or jest' (2). Its first two examples of this last meaning are both from Shakespeare: the eulogistic phrase under discussion and Petruchio's railing assault on the Tailor, whom he addresses as 'Thou flea, thou nit, thou winter-cricket, thou' (*The Taming of the Shrew*, 4.3.109). As for 'pathetical', it obviously means 'appealing', as it does again at 1.2.93, where Armado uses it in his praise of the page's 'invocation'—'My father's wit and my mother's tongue assist me!' In fact, Shakespeare employs the adjective on one other occasion only, when Rosalind tells Orlando 'if you break one jot of your promise ... I will think you the most pathetical break-promise ... that may be chosen out of the gross band of the unfaithful' (*As You Like It* 4.1.180–5). There the meaning is, of course, different, though Rosalind's mockingly ambiguous idiom leaves room for just a touch of the sense the word has when applied to Armado's page and to that page's felicity of phrasing.

A 'most pathetical nit' sums up the essence of the boy. Praised and admired by Costard, praised and loved by Armado to whom he is 'dear', he is attractive, as many an insect can be. But he also has an insect-like capacity for making a nuisance of himself by pricking and deflating the pretentious, especially in his exchanges with the pompous schoolmaster Holofernes. Moreover, it is not true to say with Kerrigan that because there are several references 'to his being tiny ... the primary sense [of his name] is undoubtedly "particle"'. What the play insists on most is not his diminutive stature but his youth. And youth is a quality of living, growing things not of inanimate objects such as specks of dust in a sunbeam. *Moth*, therefore, seems a far more appropriate name for this very lively boy than does *Mote*.

INDEX

THIS is a guide to points made and names mentioned in the Introduction and Commentary. Citations from other texts are not listed. An asterisk signifies that the note supplements information given in *OED*. A = Appendix A.

on foot, 5.2.735
once, 5.2.761
One who the music ... harmony,
  1.1.165–6
opinion, 5.1.5
O's, 5.2.45
osiers, 4.2.107
ostentation, 5.1.100–1; 5.2.409
Other slow arts entirely keep the
  brain, 4.3.299
o'th' t'other side, 4.1.143
Our love being yours, 5.2.759
our sport, 5.2.518
Our states are forfeit, 5.2.425
out, 4.1.132; 5.2.152
out of, 3.1.137–8
out of all suit, 5.2.275
out of count'nance quite, 5.2.272
outfaced them all, 5.2.615
outswear, 1.2.62
outwear, 2.1.23
overglance, 4.2.129
overhear, 5.2.95
overshot, 1.1.141
over-view, 4.3.173
Ovid (Publius Ovidius Naso), pp. 33,
  35; 4.2.122
owe, 2.1.6
owl, 4.1.138

pain, 1.1.73
painèd impotent, 5.2.836
painfully, 1.1.74
paint, *v.* 4.1.16
painted cloth, 5.2.570
painted flourish, 2.1.14
painted rhetoric, 4.3.236
parcel, 5.2.160
parfect, 5.2.500
paritors, 3.1.179
Parnassus Plays, The, pp. 54–5
Parsons, Robert, p. 56
part, *v.* 1.2.7; 5.2.249
parti-coated, 5.2.754
parts, *sb.* 4.2.113
party is gone, the, 5.2.661
pass (=pass for), 5.1.117
pass away from, 1.1.49
passado, 1.2.170
passed, 1.1.19
passion, *v.* 1.1.252
Passionate Pilgrim, The, p. 22
passing, 4.3.101

past cure is still past care, 5.2.28
pasture, 2.1.219
patch, 4.2.30
Pater, Walter, p. 5
pathetical, 1.2.93
pathetical nit, 4.1.146
pauca verba, 4.2.161
pavilion, 5.2.645
peal, 5.1.42
pedant, 3.1.170
pedantical, 5.2.408
Peele, George, p. 68
Pembroke, William Herbert, Earl of,
  p. 51
penance, 1.2.123
pencils, 5.2.43
penned speech, 5.2.147
penny, 3.1.24
penthouse-like o'er the shop, 3.1.16
pent up, 1.2.148
penurious, 4.1.65
peregrinate, 5.1.13–14
peremptory, 4.3.223; 5.1.10
perfect (=word-perfect), 5.2.553
perfectness, 5.2.174
Perge, 4.2.52
perjure, *sb.* 4.3.45
perjured note, 4.3.123
Person, 4.2.80; 4.3.192
phantasime, 4.1.98; (plural) 5.1.18
physic, 1.1.229
pia mater, 4.2.69
picked, 5.1.12
pick-purses, 4.3.206
piece (=masterpiece), 1.2.50
pierce-one, 4.2.81
Piercing, 4.2.85
pigeon-egg, 5.1.66
pins the wenches on his sleeve,
  5.2.321
pitch that defiles, 4.3.3
pitch-balls, 3.1.190
pitched a toil, 4.3.2
plackets, 3.1.177
plain, 5.2.177
plain statute-caps, 5.2.281
plantain, 3.1.70
planted, 1.1.163
play truant at, 2.1.74
plea, 2.1.7
pleasant, 5.1.3
please-man, 5.2.463
plodders, 1.1.86